# 3

**IMPRINT**

**PROJECT MANAGEMENT**
Sonja Altmeppen, Cologne

**COLLABORATION**
Florian Kobler, Cologne

**PRODUCTION**
Ute Wachendorf, Cologne

**DESIGN**
Sense/Net, Andy Disl and
Birgit Reber, Cologne

**GERMAN TRANSLATION**
Karin Haag, Vienna

**FRENCH TRANSLATION**
Jacques Bosser, Paris

**PRINTED IN ITALY**
ISBN 3–8228–2935–8

© 2004 TASCHEN GMBH
Hohenzollernring 53
D – 50672 Cologne
**www.taschen.com**

# ARCHITECTURE NOW!

*Architektur heute / L'architecture d'aujourd'hui*
Philip Jodidio

**TASCHEN**

KÖLN  LONDON  LOS ANGELES  MADRID  PARIS  TOKYO

# CONTENTS

# CONTENTS

# INTRODUCTION

## A DEATH OF THE MODERN

What is the direction of contemporary architecture? Are there discernible trends that allow the future to be predicted with any degree of certainty? Who are the form givers and the creators who are leaving their mark on our time or, more important still, showing the way to the future? Creativity is known to be difficult to judge in its own time. The art most widely admired today is likely to be the product of an earlier era. Looking forward, almost like looking into a crystal ball, is a question of extrapolating, or of being sensitive to what moves and shapes the art of designing and building architecture. Thus, the computer has opened new horizons, but perhaps not those originally imagined. Used at the outset by some as a way to visualize ever more extravagant structures, digital technology is today rapidly approaching a kind of maturity that is having a much deeper and long-lasting effect on architecture than any "crazy little buildings" as Arata Isozaki once labeled the experimental designs in Japan. The new freedom that suggested the computer could morph architecture out of its Euclidean, modernist box has surely not run its course, as many of the projects published in this book attest. Yet at the same time, computers are in the process of transforming not only the design process, but also production. And this is where the keyboard and the screen become really interesting. An exhibition organized at the end of 2003 at the Centre Pompidou by the talented curator Frédéric Migayrou under the title "Non-Standard Architecture," highlighted some of these deeper changes. What if the standardization born of nothing less than the Industrial Revolution were to come to an end? What if it became just as cheap to manufacture thousands of unique components for a building as it long has been to churn out identical boxes? Under the catchall description of "revolutionary" change, a brave band of architects set out from New York and Italy to declare the end of modernism sometime in the early 1970s. Theirs was the "post-modern" world. Architecture would be free to make reference to the past and to set aside the tabula rasa decreed by Walter Gropius and others in the heady days of the Bauhaus. A few years passed and the new king was quite naked. Philip Johnson's ATT Headquarters in New York (1979), hailed at the time as a symbol of the new, on closer inspection revealed itself as no more than an aging modernist tower in drag.

And what if today's revolution was not at all in the proliferation of exotic blobs seen from Paris to Beijing, but rather inside sometimes very "normal" looking buildings? Progressing toward a seamless process connecting the architect's design computer to digitally controlled production, new technology is making possible the end of the modern. For the modern was a dream of standardization, of assembly-line perfection like that imagined by Henry Ford when he declared that his Model-T would be available "in any color as long as it is black." Nor does this mean that stylistic trends such as the already well-worn neo-modernism of recent years are forcibly relegated to the past. This revolution is not one of appearances; it is not a question of the length of this season's skirt. It happens inside, where an architect can make a thousand different pieces of wood for a low-cost Paris fashion showroom, where a door handle can be a unique piece, where even a stone can be as unlike its neighbor as the hand-carved blocks of the past. Before the Industrial Revolution, architecture was inevitably hand-made, each piece a unique testimony to its maker. The cost-driven logic of machines made it necessary to abandon the unique in favor of the identical, of the standardized unit of production. Today and tomorrow, the machine will not be set aside rather it is the machine itself that has changed. Robotics allow lasers or other precision-guided tools to carve out a block of stone for Renzo Piano's Padre Pio Pilgrimage Church (San Giovanni Rotondo, Foggia, Italy, 1995–2003) unlike any other in the building for the same price as identical cubes. The full significance of this

* Neil M. Denari, *Gyroscopic Horizons*, Thames & Hudson, London, 1999

deep change will be brought home less by the current generation of established architects than by their younger, more computer-literate successors. Thus, Frank Gehry has indeed used sophisticated computer-assisted modeling and production to produce such sculptural buildings as his Guggenheim Bilbao (1991–1997), but the original conceptual work is more a question of traditional sketches and models than it is truly one of digital design. Younger architects, like Mark Goulthorpe (dECOi) are beginning fully to exploit the potential of new design and production technology to generate unique structures that meet the cost requirements of an industry formed out of standardization. This is a real revolution and one that is not a matter of fashion or cosmetics. This is the end of the "modernist" logic that hid cookie-cutter blocks under the occasional curve or fillip, but which offered no real conceptual alternatives. An office or apartment in any shape as long as it was square might have been the rallying call of the true modernist. That day is already finished. Euclidean shapes will surely continue to exist in architecture, but the mold has been broken.

### SYMBOLS FOR A DIGITAL WORLD

A town of 9 000 inhabitants on the southern Japanese island of Kyushu is hardly the place where one might look for significant expressions of public architecture, and yet the Reihoku Community Hall by Hitoshi Abe is proof that such designs have their place in today's world. At the origin of this commission, a project called Artpolis, initiated in 1988 under the authority of the governor of Kumamoto Prefecture by the architect Arata Isozaki, had already shown that major architects could be brought to work in almost rural Kyushu areas. Now under the control of Toyo Ito and Teiichi Takahashi, Artpolis chose Hitoshi Abe for Reihoku and he promptly engaged in long consultations with the local population. The result of these discussions was that nobody could agree on the precise function of a community facility. The architect designed a flexible space appropriate to this indecision, but what is important is that he nonetheless succeeded in making an accepted symbol for the town, a place that really has become the center of Reihoku. The billowing dark folds of the building are not what anyone might expect and yet the structure, with its woodwork, surely recalls Japanese temple architecture. It also brings to mind a great tent, erected just to draw in the townsfolk, and come they do.

Also in Japan, but on quite a different scale, the new Yokohama International Port Terminal designed by Foreign Office Architects (FOA) has gotten a large share of recent architectural publications, if only because of its unexpected appearance and heady reliance on advanced techniques of computer-assisted design. Located so close to Tokyo that it is almost part of the same urban mass, Yokohama is officially the second largest city in Japan, and the place, incidentally, where Admiral Perry landed in 1853, opening the modern era for Japan. Seen from certain angles the facility, which draws large numbers of the curious, looks almost like a kind of natural formation. It might be noted in passing that several contemporary Japanese architects, like Itsuko Hasegawa, have imagined that the role of architecture should be to create a kind of artificial nature. Here, where urban development has run rampant, the curiously tranquil jetty conceived by FOA goes a step in the direction of imagining architecture as a surrogate "Mother Nature," while not reaching at all into the imagery of "organic" design. Completed in two years just two percent above the original budget despite a five-year delay between the competition and the construction, the Terminal is a feat of engineering as well as fulfilling a purely architectural role. Like many recent buildings in Japan, the Yokohama Terminal is a kind of investment in civic pride, much as Reihoku indulged, albeit on a smaller scale, in the same reasoning. Young architects FOA won a competition and were given the keys to the city as it were. They fared well with this responsibility and further underlined the "usefulness" of quality architectural design in today's difficult economic circumstances; where a more ordinary structure would have brought no special attention to Yokohama, FOA placed this urban port at the center of attention not only of specialists, but also of the local population, proud to walk up and down the artificial jetty.

Few tasks could be more daunting for an English architect than to create the very symbol of London's municipal authority. Further, set on the South Bank of the Thames, the new Headquarters for the Greater London Authority or City Hall was to be the centerpiece of an ambitious redevelopment scheme, within view of the Tower of London and close to the new Tate Modern. Lord Norman Foster, now one of the most visible of London architects, took on this challenge with typical bravado, imagining a deformed sphere covered with no less than 3 844 unique glass panels. Foster's long interest in ecological design is here brought to a new high point, with an energy consumption less than a quarter that of a traditional office building. One key to this success is the very shape of the building, with one-quarter less surface area than a cube of the same volume, for example, reducing heat gain and loss. Ground water drawn up from a depth of 125 meters below the building is fed through ceiling beams to cool the offices naturally. As open to the general public as security restrictions allow, the GLA is a study in transparency and responsibility, two highly symbolic values for a municipal authority. Always technologically minded, Norman Foster here approaches a design whose form is almost dictated by its ambitious "green" agenda. Working with the engineers Arup, Foster obviously relies heavily on computer-assisted design and production in such a case, even though he is a hard and fast member of the "old school," pointing out how much faster he can draw with a pencil than a mouse. Working with a very large staff, approaching 600 persons, in his spacious Riverside offices Norman Foster may be more an impresario than an architect in the traditional sense. He gives an impetus to projects and surely outlines their form, while assistants exploit the most recent technological advances.

No visitor to New York since the early 1970s could avoid the monumental presence of the famous "Twin Towers" – the World Trade Center located near lower Manhattan's financial district. It is not so much that these towers, designed amongst others by Minoru Yamasaki, were so architecturally distinguished that they marked the mind, it is rather that their sheer size and double nature made them unique. Though under the control of various public agencies such as the New York Port Authority, the World Trade Center was mostly private office space. As such it was a symbol of the city but also of the economy and the country. This reasoning led quite literally it seems to the downfall of the sky-scrapers. Once the difficult task of cleaning the massive site had advanced sufficiently, the question of reconstruction was raised. Given New York politics and economic considerations, it was fully to be expected that such a prestigious site would again be turned over to office space of the most profitable configuration possible. And yet the depth of the wound to America inflicted on September 11, 2001 was such that public opinion demanded something more durable, a monument to the 3 000 dead, a remembrance of where these massive rectangular towers had stood. In December 2002, seven teams of architects were selected to submit designs for the new World Trade Center. To the credit of the authorities, who had already attempted a consultation of less prestigious architects only to endure public scorn, this second selection brought out some of the best-known architects in the world. The "Think" collaboration teamed Rafael Viñoly and Shigeru Ban, while United Architects became the temporary group name of Greg Lynn, Ben van Berkel and Kevin Kennen. Skidmore Owings & Merrill, no stranger to big-time American architecture, brought in Michael Maltzan and others to strengthen their bid, while Richard Meier, Peter Eisenman, Charles Gwathmey and Steven Holl cast their lot together. Norman Foster and Daniel Libeskind each submitted their own proposals and, after much debate and discussion, it was the latter architect who was selected. Born in Lodz, Poland, in 1946, Libeskind is the author of Berlin's Jewish Museum or the more recent Imperial War Museum North (Manchester, United Kingdom, 2000–2002). With its faceted shapes and soaring tower, Libeskind's proposal made the right concessions to local and American sensitivities by leaving a memorial space in the crater of the towers, while sufficiently reassuring promoters, developers and the money crowd so important to New York. It of course remains very much to be seen if these powerful forces will not get the better of the architect, forcing him to realign his project so much that it will lose its powerful spirit, but beyond this issue, Libeskind's victory is the victory of architecture. No matter what the final shape of the new World Trade Center, in this place, so important to contemporary America, it has been decided to entrust the future to a man with a proven sense of design. That he has spent a good part of his life and career thinking of the disastrous effects of war and destruction is surely an element in his victory, but in the World Trade Center, the United States has formally and finally recognized that an architecture of quality is the only way to pay homage to the dead and to make this space and this city rise again. Some have said that monuments are a thing of the past. Modernism was not particularly fond of them. And yet, what other way to remember and learn from the past could be more convincing than to build a lasting monument? This is a sign of a path that leads back to the future, and a confirmation of architecture's newly-found importance.

## WANT TO SEE MY LABEL?

One of the most exciting trends in recent architecture has been the increasing tendency of major companies to call on well-known or inventive architects for their headquarters or showrooms. Nowhere has this development been more visible than in the Omotesando shopping district of Tokyo. Already the location of a number of distinguished buildings such as Tadao Ando's Collezione (1987–1989) or the more recent refitting of the Comme des Garçons shop by Rei Kawakubo working with Future Systems, Omotesando has become an essential stop for anyone interested in contemporary architecture. In the same part of the street as the earlier boutiques, the Prada building by Herzog & de Meuron that opened to the public in June 2003 has already gotten a good deal of attention. The six-story structure, whose cost is variously estimated between $80 million and $140 million, features surprising windows that either bubble out or appear to be sucked in. Perforated metal ceilings or a skin of living green moss for part of the exterior are amongst the other surprises. Raw oak, like that used in the Tate Modern by Herzog & de Meuron, covers the basement floor while lacquered steel stairs and ivory-colored carpet offer themselves up to the impatient heels of frenzied buyers on other levels. A mixture of organic and decidedly manufactured surfaces (display racks in either pony skin or silicon) underlines the continual surprises willfully chosen by the architects in conjunction with a client who is obviously interested in contemporary architecture.

Two or three hundred meters down the road, still in the Minami Aoyama area, the architect Jun Aoki has designed an enormous boutique for Louis Vuitton. While Vuitton's own staff handled interior design, this structure, imagined like a stack of the trunks that made the French manufacturer famous, is most astonishing because of its metal mesh, stainless steel and glass façade. The alternation of opacity and transparency, with the changing effects of light seen in this large screen, surely makes it one of the most successful modern interpretations of Japanese tradition. Here, as in the case of the Prada building, it may be asked what the relationship of the actual products is to the architecture. These are showcases intended to convey a sense of modernity to clothing or bag design that may not always be as thoroughly modern as its promoters would like to have the public believe. An LVMH building almost across the street from Louis Vuitton (same owner) has recently been completed by Kengo Kuma. A very different design certainly seeks to establish no links between the firm's labels. Whatever the quality of the architecture, it might be fair to ask if customers will not one day be saturated by an excessive marketing strategy. In the meantime, architecture fans can thank their lucky stars that fashion is trying to make itself more permanent than it really is.

Banking is a far cry from the world of Gucci and Prada, but the profession of money also seeks, in its own way, to affirm an already obvious presence. Banks have often opted for neoclassical elegance, a bit like temples. They also curiously favor rather funereal imagery, as though death and interest rates have some unseen ties (inevitability?). Be that as it may, Alberto Campo Baeza's Caja General building in Granada blends a minimal elegance with a decidedly mortuary solidity. With its "impluvium of light" and walls of translucent Zaragoza alabaster, this bank is replete with references to Imperial Rome. Its very monumentality may be a surprise to those used to a modernist abnegation, but Spain, the land of the Escurial, is used to a mixture of stone and death in its designs. While obviously espousing a very current minimalism, the Caja General also embraces Roman grandeur, a curious mixture and yet one that speaks clearly to our time. Reference to the past, not in façade only, is now with us again. Art or architecture have always found their inspiration in the past, and few times have seen the determined rejection of tradition embodied in early modernism. If practitioners like Michael Graves and Robert A.M. Stern had not misappropriated the term in the 1970s, one could say with assurance that the early twentieth century is surely a time of post-modernism, as attested to in Granada by Alberto Campo Baeza.

The most common pattern for large corporations in the past has been to select nameless architectural offices able to capitalize on recent trends in design while doing nothing too unusual or surprising. More recently the risk involved in selecting young architects has been assumed and even sought out by companies interested in associating themselves with the culture of their times. Thus, the huge ING group selected the firm Meyer en Van Schooten to build their new Amsterdam headquarters. Visually very much akin to images like those seen in the "Star Wars" films, the ING building is set up on V-shaped stilts and looks quite ready to gallop off, firing its lasers at any threatening debtors. Any impression of extravagance is quickly set aside by a glance at the building's real design. Ecologically responsible, this is a structure intended to last "50 to 100 years," quite a tall order for any of today's new facilities. Of course it remains to be seen if this longevity is a reasonable plan, but by investing in younger designers (both architects were under 45 when they designed this headquarters), ING correctly assumed that their esthetics might not be as quickly outmoded as those of older, more "confirmed" figures. Thanks in part to the presence of such major international figures as Rotterdam's Rem Koolhaas, The Netherlands have long since accepted the idea of contemporary architecture, whereas countries that were less destroyed in World War II, such as France, have yet to be so open-minded on the whole.

Also in The Netherlands, Kas Oosterhuis indulges in more avant-garde computer driven work, yet he too has found corporate clients. His "Cockpit" project consists of a 1.5-kilometer-long acoustic barrier on the A2 highway and a 5 000-square-meter industrial building. The barrier is intended as a structure to be seen and understood from cars moving at an average of 120 kilometers per hour along the motorway. The showroom located behind the barrier is in fact integrated into its structure. Kas Oosterhuis describes the commercial building as a "cathedral for cars." The firm sells Rolls Royce, Bentley, Lamborghini and Maserati vehicles. A workshop and garage are set under the showroom. Obviously not of the scale or corporate significance of a group like ING, the Cockpit project demonstrates that, at least in The Netherlands, an awareness of the value of "quality" architecture has reached through the layers of business to become a factor in everyday life.

Nor is this phenomenon restricted to esthetically and environmentally conscious northern Europe. Working in Malaysia, the architect Ken Yeang has succeeded in convincing such corporate clients as IBM that it is possible to build attractive "green" buildings that give their sponsors a boost in public opinion and thus potentially in sales. Yeang is completing a headquarters building for a Singapore-based company that produces palm oil products and specialty fats. The program is for a four-story office (overall height 34 meters) with a four-story packing plant, and a 32-meter-high single-volume space to house an automated warehouse. As Yeang underlines, "what could have been a regular industrial plant and office is transformed into an ecological 'green-lung' that enhances the well-being of the building's users and the biomass of the site."

## BLINK AND IT'S GONE

While corporate clients, in particular those involved in the ephemeral fashion industry, have sought out the more "permanent" values of quality architecture, there are also excellent reasons to bring good design and avowedly temporary events together. Much like previous corporate attitudes, the organizers of fairs or national exhibitions have often looked to "practical" solutions in designing temporary pavilions. Undistinguished architecture does not necessarily draw in the crowds. Though they have been roundly criticized for the apparent profligacy, the organizers of Switzerland's Expo.02 made no secret of their desire to attract some of the best architects in the world for the structures erected on temporary jetties in the lakes around Neuchâtel. Thus Jean Nouvel was called on to occupy the attractive community of Morat. He did this with a highly visible monolithic block of rusting steel, sitting offshore in the lake. Another unexpected structure was an exhibition area, occupied by the Fondation Cartier and made of stacks of logs. Actually, with its reference to logging, this structure may have had more to do with Switzerland than some of the other elements of the exhibitions. Using tents, containers and military camouflage, Nouvel occupied Morat with his temporary designs, in a manner and style that in some cases approached installation art more than architecture. A second remarkable intervention for Expo.02 was that of COOP HIMMELB(L)AU in Biel. Their artificial platform covering approximately 16 000 square meters, was set four meters above the Lake of Biel. The theoretically reusable structures were made of steel covered with layers of zinc dust clad in "a kind of grid foil stretched over a frame and inserted like a panel." As the architects said, "the site of the great exhibition has been conceived as a roofed platform jutting out over the lake, ending in a space with three towers. Its resemblance to an aircraft carrier is not a matter of coincidence, but fully intended. Underneath the roof the platform is available to all kinds of utilization and gives room to the exhibition pavilions – just like the buildings of a town." Apparently quite substantial when seen from a distance, the structures, reached from a 413-meter-long pedestrian bridge, were in fact very light and airy. This was an interesting combination of apparent monumentality with extreme lightness and, obviously, the towers, ranging between 35 and 39 meters in height, had little real purpose, but to mark the moment and the location. Another perhaps even more unusual participation in Expo.02 was that of the New York architects Diller + Scofidio. Their Blur Building was intended to resemble nothing so much as a cloud hovering over Lake Neuchâtel. 100 m wide by 60 m deep and 25 m high, the "cloud" effect rising above the water was obtained through the use of filtered lake water "shot as a fine mist through a dense array of 31 500 high-pressure water nozzles integrated into a large cantilevered tensegrity structure." When wind and weather conditions permitted, the effect achieved by the Blur Building was exactly that imagined by the architects. Theirs was an effort to actually make architecture disappear, to be as light as a cloud, yet to be an environment where a kind of sensory deprivation would make visitors lose all notion of "real" space or time. If Nouvel was "artistic" in his approach to Expo.02 and COOP HIMMELB(L)AU challenged the solidity of the monumental, then Diller + Scofidio were by far the most radical participants, daring to question the very nature of the built form. Many agreed that they solved the riddle of inherently ephemeral fair architecture. What could be more ephemeral than a cloud?

London, best known for its Imperial 19th-century monumentality, has in fact been the site of a number of interesting experiments in temporary architecture. The Serpentine Pavilion in Kensington Gardens has now sponsored for the fourth time ephemeral summer pavilions designed by none other than Zaha Hadid (2000), Daniel Libeskind (2001), Toyo Ito (2002), and the venerable Oscar Niemeyer (2003). While Niemeyer sought in a way to sum up his ideas about the lyricism of concrete architecture, Ito branched out into more unexpected territory generating a seemingly random structure that was in fact determined by an algorithm derived from the rotation of a single square. Though costly ventures for a small museum, these pavilions have again demonstrated the considerable drawing power of "name" architects and shown too that, when working on a small scale with temporary structures, architects are capable of approaching a type of truly artistic expression.

The link between art and architecture was also blurred by the stunning installation of the sculptor Anish Kapoor in London's Tate Modern. His Marsyas was comprised of three steel rings joined by a single span of red PVC membrane stretched along the length of the 155-meter-long Turbine Hall. Visible in its entirety from no one vantage point, Marsyas clearly challenged conventional perceptions of space and architecture. Emptiness and fullness, standard features of any architecture, here flowed from one into the other without any discernible boundary. Actually, this enigmatic play on space was not at all contradictory with the work of Herzog & de Meuron on Tate Modern itself. Their own approach often consists in blurring the limits between reflection and unobstructed vision, for example, or more frequently lightness and heaviness. The American sculptor Richard Serra has said very pointedly that the "difference between art and architecture is that architecture serves a purpose." It may not be appropriate to call Kapoor's Marsyas a work of architecture, and yet it dealt most adroitly with perceptions of space, light and color, reconfiguring the massive Turbine Hall in a way that no other artwork has before. Perhaps it was not architecture, but it did serve to look at space and volume in a new way.

Vito Acconci has long dwelt on the border between art and architecture, working on such remarkable designs as Steven Holl's Storefront for Art and Architecture in New York. In the case of his Mur Island project in Graz, Austria, the result is surely more in the domain of architecture than of art, and yet form and space are reconfigured here as surely as they were by Anish Kapoor in the Tate Modern. Local newspapers found Acconci's "futuristic town square" anchored in the River Mur to be "totally in contradiction with the medieval and baroque architecture" of a city named Europe's "Cultural Capital" for 2003. And yet the city has also built a new and equally futuristic Kunsthaus designed by Peter Cook and Colin Fournier and baptized "the friendly alien." Surely less ephemeral than Acconci's artificial island, the Kunsthaus indeed seems to have arrived in a foreign land where a toehold was first achieved by the Mur Island project. Even in the heart of medieval Europe, contemporary architecture is making its way.

Making use of a genre whose roots go back at least into the eighteenth century, I.M. Pei, author of the Louvre Pyramid and the National Gallery's East Building in Washington, has recently completed a tea pavilion in an English garden. Calling on forms he also employed in the Miho Museum (Shigaraki, Shiga, Japan), Pei created a decidedly modern pavilion for the Oare House, the Wiltshire estate of the Keswick family. Pei is certainly not an architect known for ephemeral designs, and it may just be that this pavilion will outlast many more grandiose buildings, but the very building type implies a lightness confirmed by this particular design. With its elevated pyramidal form, the Oare Pavilion introduces the architecture of today into one of the more traditional environments in Europe. Pei has long espoused a respect for tradition, be it his own Chinese origins or the rich history of the Louvre. He has succeeded again, with the Oare Pavilion, in bringing together the past and the present in a harmonious way. The old battle between modernism and tradition is over. Especially in Europe, along the banks of the River Mur or in an English garden, the architecture of today can be integrated without disrespect or denial of what went before.

## BIG TIME FOR THE CULTURE VULTURES

As has been the case for many years, one of the privileged fields of intervention of quality architecture is that of culture. Although it is true that in the United States and elsewhere grandiose plans for new museums have been abandoned, other facilities such as concert halls have flourished. Even as the Los Angeles County Museum abandoned its ambitious reconstruction plans scheduled with Rem Koolhaas, the city completed the new Disney Concert Hall, Frank Gehry's first major public building in his hometown. And while Gehry's much publicized plans for a downtown Guggenheim in New York sank, he completed the very successful Center for the Performing Arts at Bard College in New York State. Although both of these facilities (Disney and Bard) rely on the same undulating sheets of metal that made Gehry world famous in Bilbao, they do represent a new degree of success for him: Disney because it is in the heart of downtown Los Angeles and Bard because it is a poetic, sculptural masterpiece. Although it is not certain that any architect will precisely follow in his footsteps, Frank Gehry has done more than almost any other living architect to liberate his profession. With his billowing clouds of titanium he has confirmed the artistic liberty and status of the architect. This makes it easier for younger designers to seek new forms, even if they do not adhere to the esthetic choices of Gehry.

Might it be that the choice of Zaha Hadid to build the Lois & Richard Rosenthal Center for Contemporary Art in Cincinnati has some relation to the acclaim given Gehry? A place like Cincinnati could use some of the good publicity earned by Bilbao after all. Well-known in architectural circles for her drawings and radical schemes, it seems that Zaha Hadid has now entered a new phase in her career where major projects are coming her way. It is indeed astonishing that she is the first woman architect to build a museum in America, but in this too she is a pioneer. In Cincinnati, she shows that her exuberant drawings can indeed take built form and that contemporary art and architecture can mix in the very city that saw the painful efforts to censor the work of Robert Mapplethorpe a few years ago.

Perhaps less radical in its choice of architecture, the city of Fort Worth has inaugurated its new Museum of Modern Art designed by Japanese architect Tadao Ando. Located on a very challenging site because of its proximity to Louis Kahn's legendary Kimbell Museum, Ando's Fort Worth is as rigorously geometric as could be expected. Far from the small chapels or houses that made his reputation in Japan, this is more the Ando of the massive Hyogo Prefecture Museum that he completed recently on the Kobe waterfront devastated by the 1995 earthquake. Fort Worth has long been a city that devotes means to its cultural life and Ando's contribution is yet another affirmation of the wealth and power of the city, especially vis-à-vis rival Dallas. Ando, who has had great influence on architecture students around the world, has breathed life into what would appear at first glance to be an architecture of geometric rigidity. Light, space and water flow around and through his buildings, making them an almost timeless ode to the built form rather than a retrograde manifestation of unreconstructed modernism.

Economic constraints have shifted the emphasis from the construction of ambitious new arts facilities to the kind of extensive renovation carried out by Ellis Williams in the Baltic Centre for Contemporary Arts (Newcastle, United Kingdom, 1999–2002). Architect Dominic Williams converted these former flour mills into an 8 537-meter exhibition space for the most recent art. Through its very dimensions, such disused industrial architecture offers unexpected opportunities for art. As Dominic Williams has stated, "the main aim is to allow contemporary art to happen in whatever form it takes. Often 'art' installations take on, or pervert, the nature of the space they occupy. The original function of the building was to collect, contain and distribute flour through the unseen workings of the silos. In many ways these activities would be unchanged, with the building now refocused to a new use. Works will come, be created, and travel on from the place, the function less secret though still housed between its sheer walls. Components such as the gallery floors, café and library are inserted between these two walls to create a new living body within the building."

Two New York-area projects also make use of former industrial buildings for art. The first of these in fact is directly related to another major architectural project – the reconstruction of the Museum of Modern Art by Tokyo architect Yoshio Taniguchi. While work goes on in Manhattan, it was decided to give MoMA a temporary home in Long Island City (Queens), across the river. A former factory was converted by the Californian architect Michael Maltzan, who explains that it was "of critical significance to re-imagine an established institution 'moving' to a satellite site, the former Swingline Staples factory building. Believing that the temporary facility should not forecast the soon-to-be-remade Manhattan MoMA, we looked, instead, to the complex context of the project, as well as to the experience of movement in creating an identity for MoMAQNS. This is manifest as the visitor experiences a progressive sequence of elements beginning with fleetingly legible roofscape signage and extending, through a series of expanding and contracting spaces, the processional trajectory culminating in the galleries."

On an even more ambitious scale, the creation of Dia:Beacon, in a former paper mill in upstate New York, was the ground for a unique collaboration between a major artist, Robert Irwin, a young design firm, OpenOffice, and the Dia Foundation itself, represented by its president Michael Govan. With 24 000 square meters of gallery space and the possibility to devote a gallery to each artist exhibited, this renovation amply demonstrates the possibilities offered by the conjunction of old buildings and new art, but also by the meeting of minds between artists, architects and institutional representatives with an open mind. The requirement of "quality" in architecture has come to be an accepted part of the art world, whether it be in renovation work such as that of the Baltic Centre, MoMAQNS, or Dia:Beacon, or in new construction such as the Fort Worth or Cincinnati facilities.

The need for a fruitful conjunction between architects, artists and culture is felt across the world and is expressed even in cases where budgetary constraints are a determining factor. In 1997 Herzog & de Meuron won an international design competition to build the new Laban Dance Centre on a limited budget of £14.4 million. Set on a site almost a hectare in area beside Deptford Creek in South East London, the building creates a "highly visible focus for the ongoing physical and social regeneration of Deptford and the surrounding area." The artist Michael Craig-Martin collaborated with the architects on the decorative scheme for Laban's exterior and on part of the interior design. The use of colored polycarbonate for a part of the exterior corresponds simultaneously to budgetary constraints and to the search for a way to give the building a joyful presence in a rather difficult neighborhood.

Though not tied to any such rigorous economic constraints, Renzo Piano did face the daunting task of adding an art gallery to the famous Lingotto automobile factory in Turin. His Giovanni and Marella Agnelli Art Gallery has been likened to a "flying safe" and indeed it does carry a precious cargo of 25 carefully selected artworks above the rooftop test track of Lingotto. Like the architect's previous addition to the building, a bubble-shaped conference room and helipad, the Agnelli is an odd presence, a sort of flying saucer-type addition. Judging from the 100 000 visitors counted in the first year of operation, this architectural curiosity must pay the rent quite nicely. It also serves the on-going project that Piano undertook to bring the massive factory back to life. With the Olympic Games coming up in Turin, and an expansion of the existing Meridien Hotel designed by Piano inside Lingotto underway, the wager made by Giovanni Agnelli when he first called on the architect appears to have been won.

The affirmation of the role of architecture in a cultural context is having repercussions beyond Western Europe and North America, as the recent competition for the New Holland and Mariinsky area in Saint Petersburg demonstrates. Here, in a competition at first apparently won by the Californian architect Eric Owen Moss and his promoter Samitaur Constructs, it transpired that the Frenchman Dominique Perrault was finally selected to build a new Mariinsky Theater in the Russian city. Moss remains in the area since his original victory was confirmed for the so-called New Holland district with its own theater. Ample controversy surrounded these projects in a city that is not in principle used to very contemporary architecture, but as Moss said in the course of the discussions, "with New Holland and the Mariinsky, St. Petersburg, a unique world city with an unmatched cultural pedigree, will launch a new tradition of opera, ballet, music and architecture far into the next century." With architects as innovative as Dominique Perrault and Eric Owen Moss working in a traditional city like Saint Petersburg, there can be little doubt that the marriage of different forms of artistic expression evoked by Moss does have new substance.

## ENGINEERED FOR LIVING

Housing is among the most clear and present needs met by architecture. When an enlightened client meets a talented architect, the result can be a real step ahead for architecture that may influence esthetics and more practical matters for years to come. The residences published in this book are selected precisely for their innovative qualities and for the advances they represent. Architect David Adjaye has gained quite a reputation in London, perhaps because he has had the good fortune to have a number of clients who became famous after he worked for them. He converted a 1930s East London warehouse into a home for artists Tim Noble and Sue Webster in a most surprising way.

Although the name "Dirty House" is not explained, the artists are known amongst other things for literally making works out of trash. East London is not best known for its luxurious residences, a fact that neither Adjaye nor the clients objected to. In its radical use of space, light and surfaces, the Dirty House reacts to its location in a way appropriate to a city that is used to seeing the beauty in an industrial environment. Just as New York progressively conquered former downtown warehouse areas like Soho and then Tribeca, London has made its East End more fashionable than it ever was. In a sense this is an extension of the way art has made use of everyday materials and even trash as in the Adjaye's clients. Rough and "with-it," Adjaye may be fashionable, but he is also very much in tune with the times.

Shigeru Ban's Glass Shutter House in Tokyo is another matter altogether. Located in a relatively fashionable area of Tokyo, it is a combined house and restaurant designed for the specific needs of a well-known Japanese chef. Ban is of course known for his research into flexibility in architecture, both in his choice of materials like paper and in his desire to question such fundamental elements as walls. In the Glass Shutter House, Ban has made it possible for the owner to open two walls entirely, rolling them into the roof. This is particularly useful for the chef in the summer months when he can open his restaurant directly out onto his terrace. Above all, it is an inventive solution to the very solidity of architecture. What if a building could just dissolve when we want it to? "Oh that this too too solid flesh would melt." Ban seeks practical solutions to truly radical ideas and in that he is one of the foremost architects active in the world today.

An open attitude toward recent architecture (i.e., no rejection on stylistic grounds) has contributed to the rediscovery of a certain number of early modernist buildings. An unusual example of a restoration carried out in this spirit is the Charles Deaton Sculpture House (Genesee Mountain, Golden, Colorado, 1963–1965/2000). Deaton, a self-taught architect, designed this house in 1963 as a "sculpture you could live in." As he described the original house, "I felt, first of all, the shape should be strong and simple enough to stand in a gallery as a work of art. On being enlarged to the size of the dwelling, it could be subdivided into living quarters. I knew, of course, when I started the sculpture that it would develop into a house. There was, however, no attempt to simply wrap a shell around a floor plan. In fact, no scale was set until the sculpture was done. The floor plan followed the modeling and contouring at a respectable distance." Aside from the undeniable presence of the house and its spectacular location, the ideas of Deaton do not seem terribly far from the sculptural approach of a Frank Gehry, for example. Radical in many of its ideas, modernism can surely continue to be a source of inspiration for an architecture of today that has opened its attitude toward the past in general.

The so-called Glaphyros House, a 320-square-meter apartment located near the Luxembourg Gardens in Paris, is remarkable because of the extent to which the custom fittings are almost all the product of computer assisted design. Designed by Mark Goulthorpe of dECOi, a ground floor flat in a 1960s building, the residence is designed for a client who requested "a minimal yet sensual architecture…" Employing what he calls a "non-standard logic," Mark Goulthorpe devised almost every detail specifically for the project. A concrete stairway leading to downstairs bedrooms was created using a parametric model inflected in plan and section. "The resultant heave," he states, "imparts a sense of movement to the constrained space, as if another energy were at work disturbing the simple repose of a modernist heritage; the niche under the stair deforms as if a geological force were at work, creating a curious animism." Such deformations of surface and volume are found throughout the apartment. "As a sustained exercise in non-standard production, the project tears open the repetitive and prefabricated logic inherent in industrial production, suggesting a greatly enriched formal vocabulary released in the digital wake," concludes Mark Goulthorpe. In fact, the computer work done on this apartment by Mark Goulthorpe might hardly be visible to the untrained eye. In a sense that is precisely what makes it remarkable. Digital design, based on parametric modeling, has begun to have an impact on architecture and the shapes that result from this trend need not be the kind of extravagant blob that some have already gotten us used to. The computer has entered the everyday logic of architecture and it can be present from design to completion. The Glaphyros House benefited from a relatively high budget, but the production logic employed by Goulthorpe can already be used at much lower cost.

Though not as thoroughly radical in its design-to-production approach, the Natural Ellipse house designed by Masaki Endoh in Tokyo is exemplary of the kind of inventiveness that the Japanese are prepared to accept. Set in the very densely urbanized Shibuya area of the capital, the house sits on a 53-square-meter lot. Made up of 24 elliptical steel rings, it is coated in FRP (Fiber-Reinforced-Polymer) allowing for a seamless exterior. Modern materials and an unprejudiced approach to design will surely continue to make possible such unusual departures from the shape of the traditional building. By obviating the need to structure this house in a conventional three-dimensional mode, he has seriously thought about the problems posed by a tiny lot and the attendant sensation of claustrophobia that might result from the circumstances. This is more than an architectural "joke."

Another Japanese architect has been as inventive as Shigeru Ban or Masaki Endoh, albeit in a different mode: Kengo Kuma's "Great Bamboo Wall" residence built near Beijing. Set on a 1930 square-meter-site with a total floor area of 528 square meters, this structure is intended as a small hotel unit. An extensive use of glass and bamboo walls with fairly large openings between each pole and bamboo cladding on pillars gives an impression of lightness and a relationship to the traditional architecture of Asia. Kuma however attains a simplicity and a modernity that have more to do with the most recent trends in architecture than with the ancient past. As he says about bamboo, "skin and outer surface are different. Concrete has an outer surface, but not skin. On top of that, I don't find concrete to be particularly attractive. That's because, without skin, the soul within never appears. Bamboo has particularly beautiful skin. And, bamboo has a soul residing within. In Japan there is a famous children's tale about how 'Princess Kakuyahime,' the Moon Goddess, was born inside a stalk of bamboo. People believed the story that she was born inside a stalk of bamboo because bamboo has a peculiar type of skin and possesses a soul."

Of course not every architect has significant means at his or her disposal. Inventiveness is clearly not just a question of sophisticated equipment and materials. The very young Norwegian firm Saunders & Wilhelmsen confirms this obvious fact with their Summer House (Hardanger Fjord, Norway). Built in two sections (respectively 20 m² and 30 m² in area), this very small structure is insulated with recycled newspaper and built with local woods. A convenient outdoor floor/terrace links the two volumes. Of course this kind of project is made more attractive by the location near one of the largest and most beautiful fjords of Norway, but the combativeness of the architects who needed to show clients that they could do interesting things is proof of a vitality that is the real source of the architecture of tomorrow. Of course local styles and materials influence them, but they are also ready to challenge assumptions.

Nor are architects the only players in the field of construction capable of making forms and designs evolve. The engineer Werner Sobek imagined his own energy efficient "glass house" on a Stuttgart hillside and built it in an amazing eleven weeks. A system of prefabricated plastic-covered wood panels measuring 3.75 x 2.8 meters simply placed between the floor beams without the use of screws, and aluminum ceiling panels also clipped in place, assured ease of construction and maintenance. Devices such a heat exchanger set below the foundation to take advantage of the natural earth temperature and the impressive triple-glazed panels filled with inert gas to reduce heat gain or loss contribute to the "green" solutions adapted by Sobek. Though severe in appearance this glass house has none of the odd appearance sometimes associated with ecologically responsible architecture. Technically minded by profession, Sobek has grouped many of the lessons he has learned through his profession into his own residence, called Haus R-128.

## TO SLEEP, PERCHANCE TO DREAM

Perhaps the most interesting area of architecture is its capacity to dream, to imagine solutions that have never existed before. This may be a matter of new technologies, or simply of thinking differently. Michael Sorkin, a New York teacher and designer, has made a profession of imagining communities that would solve many of the problems that afflict the modern world. His attractive drawings and descriptions based on a serious knowledge of architecture and urbanism are the kind of almost utopian thought that architecture needs to survive and advance. At the opposite end of the spectrum from Sorkin's musings, Michael Jantzen is deeply involved in the possibilities offered by new technologies. His VRI (Virtual Reality Interface) is an effort to imagine just how far computer generated images might be able to take a future homeowner. Imagine walls that project any image the owner desires – in other words, an infinitely variable personal environment. Though it might be difficult to go beyond the image to the reality of an imagined environment, Jantzen will surely continue to push this reasoning forward. His Malibu Video Beach House (also published in this volume) comes closer to an actual residence that would make extensive use of video screens to project pictures of the outside world, for example. In furnishing and decoration, his house would intentionally create a confusion between the inside and the outside of the beach environment. Perhaps, one day, a homeowner will be able to walk through the "looking glass" of a plasma screen and enter its virtual reality.

The Son-O-House imagined by the Rotterdam architect Lars Spuybroek (NOX) is "a house where sounds live, not being a 'real' house, but a structure that refers to living and the bodily movements that accompany habit and habitation. In the Son-O-House a sound work is continuously generating new sound patterns activated by sensors picking up actual movements of visitors." In a sense Spuybroek's project is a natural compliment to the VRI of Michael Jantzen's dreams. In California the environment inside an imagined house is purely visual. In Son en Breugel, The Netherlands, the house of NOX is one where "the score is an evolutionary memoryscape that develops with the traced behavior of the actual bodies in the space." In their purest states, neither the Son-O-House nor the VRI seem entirely practical, but they are indicative of directions of thought and the potential for radical evolution in home design being advanced by new technologies.

The dream of living underwater has long haunted novelists and architects. Jacques Rougerie in France consistently attempted to solve the problems involved in living in the sea. Today, the Los Angeles-based Office of Mobile Design is taking a more high-technology approach. Their Hydra House is a proposal for a series of inflated neoprene residences that would be completely energy self-sufficient and able to desalinate seawater, for example. Once the stuff of science fiction, such a seaborne home may today in fact be possible. Like Arverne, a recent urban design by Michael Sorkin, the Hydra House may not be quite the solution to the immediate housing problems of cities like New York or Los Angeles, but Sorkin and the Office of Mobile Design are different faces of the architectural profession's attempt to devise ways to move forward.

Much less utopian, the "Houses at Sagaponac" project is a residential development of 34 houses on wooded sites in Southampton, Long Island, New York. The initiator of the project, Coco Brown, working with the architect Richard Meier, has selected a kind of "Who's Who" of contemporary architecture to participate in the project, giving each one a house to design. Participating in the scheme, Philip Johnson, Michael Graves, James Freed, Zaha Hadid, Richard Rogers, Shigeru Ban, and Jean-Michel Wilmotte have been called on to imagine single-family residences ranging in size from about 200 to 440 square meters. The use of "traditional materials from the region, but in a modern way, which is visually entertaining and dynamic," characterizes the whole project.

Intended as a survey of architecture since 2000, this book gives an overview of the extraordinary wealth of creativity that has been unleashed by a combination of technological advances and conceptual openness. There is no one style today, nor should there be. Architecture has always been influenced first and foremost by practical considerations. Architecture, unlike art, as Richard Serra says, serves a purpose. The most significant development that has begun to reshape architecture is the real possibility of design-to-production integration using computers and robotics. This has already made the production of unique components possible, overturning the esthetics and deeper logic of nearly a century of "modern" architecture. The Modern that demanded that every Model-T should be black or every window the same size and shape is dead. Esthetics may still lead architects to indulge in neo-modernism or neo-minimalism, but they no longer see their real choices fundamentally limited by the economics of the standardized production line. Computer-assisted design is quickly changing from a kind of circus act trained to produce irregular blobs into a real tool of the future, driving cutting-edge processes that will produce a new freedom in architecture.

# EINLEITUNG

## DAS ENDE DES MODERNISMUS

Welche Richtung nimmt die zeitgenössische Architektur? Lassen sich Trends ausmachen, die es ermöglichen, die Zukunft der Architektur vorauszusagen? Wer sind die Formgebenden und Kreativen, die unserer Zeit ihren Stempel aufdrücken, oder – was noch wichtiger ist – die den Weg in die Zukunft weisen? Dies lässt sich bekanntermaßen schwer in der eigenen Zeit beurteilen. Kunstformen, die heute allgemein anerkannt und geschätzt werden, sind in der Regel in einer früheren Ära entstanden. Um in die Zukunft der Architektur zu blicken, muss man das, was heute die Kunst des Gestaltens und Bauens bewegt und formt, weiterdenken oder auch nur dafür empfänglich sein. In dieser Hinsicht haben sich durch den Computer neue Horizonte aufgetan, wenn es auch nicht jene sein mögen, die man sich ursprünglich vorgestellt hatte. Während die digitale Technologie von einigen Planern anfänglich eingesetzt wurde, um immer extravagantere Formen und Strukturen zu visualisieren, nähert sie sich heute einem Grad der Ausgereiftheit, der wesentlich tiefer gehende und anhaltendere Auswirkungen auf die Architektur hat als alle „verrückten kleinen Gebäude", wie Arata Isozaki einmal die in Japan entstandenen experimentellen Bauformen genannt hat. Die neue Freiheit, die suggeriert hatte, der Computer könne die Architektur aus ihrer euklidischen, modernistischen Beengtheit befreien, hat sich mit Sicherheit noch nicht verbraucht, wie viele der in diesem Buch vorgestellten Projekte beweisen. Gleichzeitig jedoch verändern Computer nicht nur den Gestaltungsprozess selbst, sondern auch die Produktionsabläufe. Das ist auch der Punkt, an dem Tastatur und Bildschirm wirklich interessant werden. Eine Ende 2003 vom talentierten Frédéric Migayrou am Centre Pompidou geleitete Ausstellung mit dem Titel „Architectures non standard" lenkte die Aufmerksamkeit auf einige dieser tiefgreifenden Veränderungen. Was, wenn die Standardisierung, deren Ursprung in der industriellen Revolution liegt, an ihrem Ende angelangt wäre? Was, wenn sich Tausende individuell gestalteter Einzelteile für ein Gebäude ebenso billig produzieren ließen wie die massenhafte Herstellung identischer Boxen? Unter der alle in einen Topf werfenden Bezeichnung der „revolutionären" Veränderung machte sich in den frühen 1970er Jahren eine mutige Schar von Architekten in New York und Italien daran, das Ende der Moderne zu verkünden. Sie propagierten die Postmoderne, in der die Architektur die Freiheit haben sollte, auf die Vergangenheit Bezug zu nehmen und damit die von Walter Gropius und anderen in der Blütezeit des Bauhaus geforderte *tabula rasa* zu verwerfen. Nach ein paar Jahren stand der Kaiser jedoch ziemlich nackt da. Philip Johnsons ATT Zentrale in New York von 1979, zu ihrer Zeit als ein Symbol des Neuen bejubelt, entpuppte sich bei genauerer Betrachtung lediglich als modernistisch aufgemotzter Turm.

Was, wenn auch die Revolution unserer Tage sich nicht in den exotischen Spielereien abspielte, wie sie sich von Paris bis Peking ausbreiten, sondern vielmehr in zuweilen ganz „normal" aussehenden Gebäuden? Weil die neue Technologie auf einen Prozess zusteuert, in dem sich das computergenerierte Gestalten nahtlos mit einer digital gesteuerten Produktionsweise verbindet, macht sie das Ende der Moderne möglich. Schließlich hatte die Moderne den Traum von einer allgemeinen Standardisierung, von einer fließbandmäßigen Perfektion, wie sie Henry Ford im Sinn hatte, als er erklärte, sein Model-T sei „in jeder Farbe erhältlich, solange sie schwarz sei". Bei der neuen Form von Revolution handelt es sich nicht um eine äußere Erscheinung. Sie findet vielmehr im Innenraum statt, wo ein Architekt 1 000 unterschiedliche Holzteilchen für eine gar nicht so teure Pariser Modeboutique einsetzen, wo ein Türgriff ein Unikat sein kann und wo sich sogar ein Stein vom andern so stark unterscheiden kann wie die handgemeißelten Quadersteine der Vergangenheit. Vor der industriellen Revolution war jede Architektur zwangsläufig handgemacht und jedes Bestandteil war ein einzigartiges Zeugnis für die Fertigkeit seines Erzeugers. Die kosten-

---

* Neil M. Denari, *Gyroscopic Horizons*, Thames & Hudson, London, 1999

orientierte Logik der Maschinen dagegen machte eine Vereinheitlichung der Produktion notwendig, womit das Individuelle zugunsten des Identischen aufgegeben wurde. Weder heute noch morgen wird man die Maschinen abschaffen. Es ist vielmehr so, dass sich die Maschinen selbst gewandelt haben. So macht es zum Beispiel die Robotertechnik möglich, dass alle Steinquader für Renzo Pianos Wallfahrtskirche Padre Pio (San Giovanni Rotondo, Foggia, Italien, 1995–2003) mit Laser und anderen Präzisionsgeräten ohne Mehrkosten vollkommen unterschiedlich gemeißelt werden. Die volle Bedeutung dieser Veränderung zeigt sich jedoch weniger bei der heutigen Generation der etablierten Architekten als bei den jüngeren, noch computer-versierteren Nachfolgern. So hat Frank O. Gehry zwar ausgeklügelte computergestützte Gestaltungs- und Produktionsverfahren eingesetzt, um skulpturale Bauten wie sein Guggenheim Bilbao zu entwerfen (1991–1997). Aber gerade hier besteht die zugrundeliegende konzeptionelle Arbeit mehr in traditionellen Zeichnungen als in der digitalen Gestaltung im eigentlichen Sinne. Es sind jüngere Architekten, wie Mark Goulthorpe von dECOi, die gerade damit beginnen, das Potential neuer Gestaltungs- und Herstellungstechniken voll auszuschöpfen und einzigartige Strukturen zu schaffen. Darin besteht die eigentliche Revolution. Sie bedeutet das Ende der „modernistischen" Logik, mit der zwar funktionale Merkmale unter einer Bogenlinie oder anderen Spielereien versteckt wurden, die aber keine reale konzeptionelle Alternative zu bieten hatte. Ein Büro oder eine Wohnung „in jeder beliebigen Form, so lange sie quadratisch ist", mag der Schlachtruf der eingefleischten Modernisten gewesen sein. Diese Zeiten sind vorbei. Zwar werden die euklidischen Formen mit Sicherheit auch in der Architektur der Zukunft fortbestehen, die Gussform aber ist zerbrochen.

## SYMBOLE FÜR EINE DIGITALE WELT

Eine kleine Stadt mit 9 000 Einwohnern auf der südjapanischen Insel Kyushu ist nicht gerade der Ort, an dem man bedeutende Bauten erwarten würde. Und doch ist das von Hitoshi Abe gestaltete Gemeindezentrum in Reihoku ein Beweis dafür, dass Bauten dieser Art auch in der Welt von heute ihren Platz haben. Der Bauauftrag ergab sich aus einem Projekt namens Artpolis, das 1988 von dem Architekten Arata Isozaki im Auftrag des Gouverneurs der Präfektur Kumamoto begonnen wurde und bereits einige namhafte Architekten in die ländlichen Gegenden von Kyushu gebracht hat. Toyo Ito und Teiichi Takahashi, die jetzigen Leiter von Artpolis, wählten Hitoshi Abe für das Reihoku Projekt, woraufhin sich dieser eingehend mit der lokalen Bevölkerung beriet. Am Ende der Diskussionen stand fest, dass sich die Bewohner nicht auf eine genaue Funktion des Gemeindezentrums einigen konnten, und so entwarf der Architekt einen flexiblen Raum, der dieser Unentschiedenheit Rechnung trägt. Die dunklen, sich türmenden Falten des Gebäudes mögen Verblüffung hervorrufen und doch bezieht sich das Haus mit seinem Gebälk eindeutig auf die traditionelle japanische Tempelarchitektur. Außerdem erinnert es an ein großes Zelt, in das die Stadtbewohner strömen sollen, und genau das tun sie auch.

Das ebenfalls in Japan, jedoch in einer ganz anderen Größenordnung angesiedelte, neue Gebäude für den internationalen Hafen von Yokohama erhielt viel Aufmerksamkeit in den Medien. Vermutlich in erster Linie wegen seines verblüffenden Äußeren und der Tatsache, dass sein Design von der Gruppe Foreign Office Architects (FOA) in hohem Maß auf den neuesten Techniken des computergestützten Gestaltens beruht. Yokohama, das so nahe bei Tokio liegt, dass es schon fast zu seinem Stadtgefüge gehört, ist die zweitgrößte Stadt Japans. Hier legte Admiral Perry im Jahr 1853 an und leitete damit den Eintritt Japans in das moderne Zeitalter ein. Das Gebäude, das viele Neugierige anzieht, sieht aus bestimmten Blickwinkeln wie ein Naturgebilde aus. In diesem Zusammenhang sei erwähnt, dass nach Ansicht einiger zeitgenössischer japanischer Architekten, wie Itsuko Hasegawa, die Rolle der Architektur darin besteht, eine Art künstliche Natur zu schaffen. Und gerade an diesem Ort, wo eine rückhaltlose Verstädterung betrieben wird, geht FOA mit ihrer seltsam unbewegt gestalteten Hafenmole einen Schritt in Richtung einer Architektur, die als ein Ersatz für „Mutter Natur" imaginiert wird, ohne sich allerdings der Bildsprache des „organischen" Designs zu bedienen. Der Terminal, der nach fünfjähriger Verzögerung zwischen Wettbewerb und Baubeginn in nur zwei Jahren fertig gestellt wurde und das ursprüngliche Budget um lediglich zwei Prozent überstieg, ist eine ingenieurstechnische Meisterleistung und erfüllt gleichzeitig eine rein architektonische Funktion. Die jungen Architekten von FOA haben ihre verantwortungsvolle Aufgabe erfolgreich gemeistert und damit die „Nützlichkeit" hochwertiger Architektur unter den schwierigen wirtschaftlichen Bedingungen unserer Zeit unterstrichen. Während eine weniger ausgefallene bauliche Gestaltung Yokohama keine besondere Beachtung eingebracht hätte, rückt FOA diese städtische Hafenanlage in den Mittelpunkt der Aufmerksamkeit nicht nur der Architekturexperten, sondern ebenso der lokalen Bevölkerung, die stolz auf der künstlichen Hafenmole entlangspaziert.

Es gibt wohl nur wenige Aufgaben, die mehr Wagemut von einem englischen Architekten verlangen, als die, das Symbol der Londoner Stadtverwaltung zu gestalten. Zumal der am Südufer der Themse mit Blick auf den Tower und in unmittelbarer Nähe der neuen Tate Modern gelegene Hauptsitz der Greater London Authority das Herzstück eines ehrgeizigen Stadterneuerungsprogramms werden soll. Lord Norman Foster, inzwischen einer der herausragendsten Londoner Architekten, nahm diese Herausforderung mit typischer Bravour in Angriff und entwarf eine aus der Form geratene Kugel, die mit exakt 3 844 einzeln zugeschnittenen Glasplatten verkleidet ist. Fosters Engagement für ökologisches Bauen beweist sich hier am Energieverbrauch, der weniger als ein Viertel eines konventionellen Bürogebäudes beträgt. Damit erreicht er einen neuen Höhepunkt. Eine der wichtigsten Voraussetzungen dafür ist die Form des Gebäudes. Es weist eine um ein Viertel geringere Oberfläche auf, als ein Kubus des gleichen Volumens, was Wärmeverbrauch und Wärmeverlust reduziert. Aus einer Tiefe von 125 m unterhalb des Gebäudes wird Grundwasser an die Oberfläche und durch die Deckenträger geleitet, um die Büroräume auf natürliche Weise zu kühlen. So zugänglich für die Allgemeinheit wie es die Sicherheitsvorschriften erlauben, steht das neue GLA für Transparenz und Verantwortlichkeit und verkörpert damit zwei für eine Stadtverwaltung sehr wichtige Werte. Der grundsätzlich technologisch orientierte Norman Foster entschied sich hier für ein Gestaltungskonzept, dessen äußere Form fast vollständig von seinem „grünen" Anspruch bestimmt wird. In der Zusammenarbeit mit der Ingenieurfirma Arup stützte sich Foster in diesem Fall ganz offensichtlich stark auf computergestütztes Design, obwohl er persönlich ein eingefleischter Vertreter der „alten Schule" ist und stets betont, wie viel schneller er mit dem Bleistift zeichnen könne.

Kein Besucher, der seit den frühen 1970er Jahren nach New York kam, konnte die monumentale Präsenz der berühmten Twin Towers übersehen, die das World Trade Center bildeten. Dabei waren diese von Minoru Yamasaki und anderen geplanten Türme architektonisch nicht einmal so bemerkenswert. Die eindrucksvolle Wirkung lag vielmehr in ihrer Größe und ihrer Doppelnatur. Obwohl das World Trade Center der Kontrolle verschiedener öffentlicher Stellen wie der New York Port Authority unterlag, gehörten die Büros zum größten Teil Privatfirmen. Das Gebäude war nicht nur ein Symbol für die Stadt New York, sondern auch für das ganze Land und dessen Wirtschaftssystem. Dieser gedankliche Hintergrund dürfte auch im wahrsten Sinne des Wortes zum Sturz der beiden Wolkenkratzer geführt haben. Kaum war die schwierige Aufgabe, das riesige Gelände von den Trümmern zu räumen, ein gutes Stück voran gekommen, wurde bereits die Frage nach einem Wiederaufbau laut. Angesichts der politischen und ökonomischen Konstellationen in New York konnte man davon ausgehen, dass ein so prestigeträchtiges Objekt wieder auf möglichst Gewinn bringende Art für Büroflächen genutzt würde. Aber die Wunde, die Amerika am 11. September 2001 zugefügt wurde, war so tief, dass die Öffentlichkeit etwas Dauerhafteres einforderte, ein Monument zum Gedenken an die 3 000 Toten und zur Erinnerung an die beiden wuchtigen, rechteckigen Türme. Und so wurden im Dezember 2002 sieben ausgewählte Architektenteams aufgefordert, ihre Entwürfe für ein neues World Trade Center einzureichen. Nachdem die Behörden zuvor eine Reihe weniger bekannte Architekten kontaktiert und sich damit den Unmut der Öffentlichkeit zugezogen hatten, präsentierten sie mit dieser zweiten Auswahl einige der namhaftesten Architekten der Welt. Im Think Team schlossen sich Rafael Viñoly und Shigeru Ban zusammen, während United Architects der Name des Teams von Greg Lynn, Ben van Berkel und Kevin Kennen wurde. Skidmore Owings & Merrill, wahrlich keine Unbekannten im Bereich der amerikanischen Hochhausarchitektur, holten Michael Maltzan und andere zur Verstärkung in ihr Team, während sich in einer weiteren Gruppe Richard Meier, Peter Eisenmann, Charles Gwathmey und Steven Holl zusammentaten. Norman Foster und Daniel Libeskind brachten jeweils ihre eigenen Entwürfe ein. Nach vielen Debatten und Diskussionen fiel die Wahl auf Letzteren. Mit seinen facettierten Formen und dem hoch aufstrebenden Turm kam Libeskinds Entwurf sowohl den lokalen und landesweiten Empfindlichkeiten in Form eines Gedenkraums im Krater des Turms als auch den Vorstellungen der für New York so wichtigen Promoter, Stadtplaner und Finanzleute entgegen. Natürlich bleibt abzuwarten, ob diese starken Kräfte nicht die Oberhand über den Architekten gewinnen und ihn zu Kompromissen zwingen werden, was dazu führen könnte, dass der Entwurf seine kraftvolle Aura verliert. Davon abgesehen aber ist Libeskinds Sieg gleichzeitig ein Sieg für die Architektur. Wie auch immer das neue World Trade Center letztlich aussehen wird: An jenem für das Amerika von heute so wichtigen Ort wurde ein Mann mit dieser zukunftsweisenden Aufgabe betraut, der sein Gespür für die Bedeutung von Design vielfach unter Beweis gestellt hat.

### DIE LABEL ZEIGEN FLAGGE

Einer der spannendsten Trends in der neueren Architektur ist die wachsende Tendenz großer Unternehmen, besonders bekannte oder originelle Architekten mit der Planung ihrer Firmensitze oder Schauräume zu beauftragen. Nirgendwo zeigt sich diese Entwicklung deutlicher als im Tokioter Geschäftsviertel Omotesando. Dieser Stadtteil ist mit seinen architektonisch hervorragenden Bauten wie Tadao Andos Collezione Building (1987–1989) oder dem in jüngerer Zeit durch Rei Kawakubo in Zusammenarbeit mit Future Systems gestalteten Flagship Store von Comme des Garçons zu einem wichtigen Ort für all jene geworden, die sich für zeitgenössische Architektur interessieren. Das im Juni 2003 eröffnete Prada-Gebäude von Herzog & de Meuron hat bereits für einiges Aufsehen gesorgt. Das sechsstöckige Gebäude, dessen Baukosten je nach Quelle auf 80 bzw. 140 Millionen Dollar geschätzt werden, ist mit ungewöhnlichen Fenstern ausgestattet, die sich entweder blasenartig nach außen stülpen oder aussehen, als würden sie nach innen gesaugt. Weitere verblüffende Gestaltungsmerkmale sind perforierte Metalldecken und eine Haut aus echtem Moos, mit der Teile der Außenseite verkleidet sind. Für die Böden im Erdgeschoss verwendeten Herzog & de Meuron, ebenso wie in ihrer Tate Modern, grob bearbeitetes Eichenholz, während die Kunden auf anderen Stockwerken über Treppen aus lackiertem Stahl und elfenbeinfarbene Läufer schreiten.

Etwa 300 m entfernt liegt die großzügige Boutique, die der Architekt Jun Aoki für Louis Vuitton gestaltet hat. Während für das Interieur die hauseigenen Innenarchitekten zuständig waren, fällt die Form dieses Gebäudes auf, das einem Stapel von Reisekoffern, mit denen das französische Unternehmen berühmt wurde, ähnelt. Auch seine Fassade aus Metallgitter, Edelstahl und Glas hebt es besonders hervor. Die alternierend opaken und transparenten Elemente mit ihren auf der großflächigen Verkleidung changierenden Lichteffekten machen das Gebäude zu einer der gelungensten modernen Interpretationen japanischer Tradition. Hier, ebenso wie im Fall des Prada-Gebäudes, lässt sich die Frage nach der Beziehung zwischen Verkaufsartikel und Architektur stellen: Beide Bauten sind so konzipiert, dass sie den präsentierten Kleidungsstücken oder Taschen ein moderneres Image verleihen, wie sie es nach Meinung der Auftraggeber in der Öffentlichkeit haben. Kengo Kuma hat kürzlich – auch für Vuitton – das in unmittelbarer Nähe zur Vuitton Boutique gelegene LVMH-Gebäude realisiert. Letzteres unterscheidet sich im Design sehr von der Boutique – anscheinend war nicht beabsichtigt, eine Verbindung zwischen den verschiedenen Labels des Unternehmens herzustellen.

Die Welt der Finanz hat nicht viel mit der von Gucci und Prada gemeinsam. Aber auch diese Branche sucht – auf ihre Weise – eine augenfällige Präsenz zu schaffen. Bankgebäude strahlen häufig eine neoklassische, ein wenig tempelartige Eleganz aus. Merkwürdigerweise bevorzugen sie außerdem eine Atmosphäre, die an ein Bestattungsinstitut erinnert, so als gäbe es eine geheime Verbindung zwischen Tod und Zinsen. Jedenfalls verbindet sich auch in Alberto Campo Baezas Gebäude der Caja General in Granada eine minimalistische Eleganz mit einer entschieden friedhofsartigen Solidität. Mit dem „Impluvium des Lichts" und Wänden aus Zaragoza-Alabaster steckt dieses Geldinstitut zudem voller Anspielungen auf die Bauten des kaiserlichen Roms. Seine schiere Monumentalität mag jene überraschen, die an die modernistische Form der Selbstverleugnung gewöhnt sind, doch steht die Baukunst in Spanien, dem Land des Escorial, immer noch auf vertrautem Fuß mit der Kombination von Stein und Tod. Das Design der Caja General propagiert deutlich einen sehr gegenwärtigen Minimalismus und macht sich gleichzeitig eine klassisch römische Erhabenheit zu Eigen, was eine seltsame, aber dennoch eindeutig zeitnahe Mischung ergibt. Bezüge zur Vergangenheit, und zwar nicht nur in der Fassadengestaltung, sind wieder angesagt. Dabei war die Vergangenheit immer schon eine Quelle der Inspiration für Kunst und Architektur und nur selten wurde die Beeinflussung durch Traditionen so entschieden abgelehnt wie zur Zeit der frühen Moderne.

In der Vergangenheit gingen große Unternehmen meist so vor, dass sie anonyme Architektengruppen auswählten, die sich der neuesten Trends zu bedienen wussten, ohne allzu ungewöhnlich oder originell zu sein. Dagegen wird seit einiger Zeit das mit dem Engagement junger, eigenwilliger Architekten verbundene Risiko eingegangen oder sogar gesucht, und zwar von Firmen, die sich bewusst mit der Kultur ihrer Zeit identifizieren wollen. So beauftragte beispielsweise der Großkonzern ING das Büro Meyer en Van Schooten mit der Planung seines neuen Hauptsitzes in Amsterdam. Rein optisch gleicht das fertige ING-Gebäude einer Architektur, wie man sie aus Star Wars Filmen kennt. Mit seinen V-förmigen Stelzen sieht es aus, als könne es jederzeit davon galoppieren und dabei mit Laserkanonen um sich schießen. Dieser Eindruck von Extravaganz verfliegt jedoch rasch, wenn man sich das eigentliche Design des Gebäudes ansieht. Dieser mit ökologischem Verantwortungsbewusstsein konzipierte Bau soll nämlich „50 bis 100 Jahre" halten, was für ein Firmengebäude von heute ziemlich viel verlangt ist. Natürlich bleibt abzuwarten, wie vernünftig und realistisch diese langfristige Planung ist. Mit der Auftragsvergabe an jüngere Designer (beide Architekten waren zum Zeitpunkt der Realisierung unter 45) ging das Unternehmen jedoch von der richtigen Annahme aus, dass deren Ästhetik nicht so schnell überholt sein würde wie die älterer und etablierterer Architekten.

Gleichfalls in den Niederlanden hat auch Kas Oosterhuis mit seiner Leidenschaft für noch avantgardistischere, computergesteuerte Formen Auftraggeber aus der Wirtschaft für sich gewonnen. Sein Projekt Cockpit besteht aus einer 1,5 km langen Schallschutzmauer an der

Autobahn A2 und einem dahinter liegenden, 5 000 m² umfassenden Gewerbebau. Die Barriere soll die mit durchschnittlich 120 km/h vorbeifahrenden Autofahrer auf das Gebäude aufmerksam machen, das Kas Oosterhuis als eine „Kathedrale für Autos" bezeichnet. Im Showroom, der in die Konstruktion der Schutzmauer integriert ist, stehen Autos der Marken Rolls Royce, Bentley, Lamborghini und Maserati zum Verkauf, im Stockwerk darunter befinden sich eine Werkstatt und Garagen. Wenngleich in Größe oder Bedeutung nicht mit einem Konzern wie ING zu vergleichen, demonstriert das Cockpit-Projekt, dass – zumindest in den Niederlanden – der Wert von „Qualitätsarchitektur" nicht nur in der Geschäftswelt, sondern auch im Alltagsleben zu einem wesentlichen Faktor geworden ist.

Dieses Phänomen ist jedoch keineswegs auf das ästhetisch und ökologisch bewusstere Nordeuropa beschränkt. So konnte in Malaysia der Architekt Ken Yeang seinen Auftraggeber IBM davon überzeugen, dass ein attraktives „grünes" Gebäude das öffentliche Ansehen des Unternehmens und damit potentiell auch seine Verkaufszahlen fördert. Derzeit vollendet Yeang in Singapur die Firmenzentrale eines Herstellers von Palmölprodukten und Spezialfetten. Das Projekt umfasst ein vierstöckiges Bürogebäude mit einer Gesamthöhe von 34 m, mit einer ebenfalls vierstöckigen Verpackungshalle und einen 32 m hohen, separaten Bau für das automatisierte Warenlager. Yeang erläutert: „Anstelle eines normalen Fabrikgebäudes haben wir eine umweltfreundliche ‚grüne Lunge' gestaltet, die sich positiv auf das Wohlbefinden der Nutzer und die Biomasse des Standorts auswirkt."

### FLÜCHTIGE AUGENBLICKE

Auch wenn bei den Bauherren aus der Wirtschaft, besonders solchen aus der kurzlebigen Modeindustrie, zur Zeit eher die „dauerhaften" Qualitäten hochwertiger Architektur gefragt sind, gibt es triftige Gründe, gutes Design auch auf Ereignisse oder Veranstaltungen anzuwenden, die erklärtermaßen temporärer Natur sind. Ebenso wie es früher bei den Firmen üblich war, haben sich auch die Organisatoren von Messen oder Landesausstellungen häufig auf „praktische" Lösungen für das Design ihrer Präsentationen verlassen. Allerdings zieht eine solche Architektur nicht gerade die Massen an. Obwohl sie für ihre angebliche Verschwendung gehörig kritisiert wurden, bestanden die Veranstalter der Schweizer Expo.02 auf ihrer Absicht, einige der besten Architekten der Welt für die Entwürfe zu gewinnen, die für die Dauer der Ausstellung in den Seen und dem Gebiet um Neuenburg (Neuchâtel) realisiert werden sollten. Folglich wurde auch Jean Nouvel eingeladen, der einen spektakulären monolithischen Block aus rostigem Stahl in einiger Entfernung vom Ufer auf die Wasseroberfläche des reizvollen Murtensees setzte. Weitere Beiträge von Nouvel, die über die ganze Gemeinde Murten verteilt waren, hatten mit Bestandteilen wie Zelten, Containern und Tarnnetzen mehr Ähnlichkeit mit Installationskunst als mit Architektur. Eine andere, ebenfalls sehr ungewöhnliche Arbeit, war die Ausstellungsplattform der Fondation Cartier, die aus übereinander gestapelten Holzstämmen bestand. Mit ihrem Bezug auf die Holzindustrie hatte diese Arbeit wohl mehr mit der Schweiz zu tun als viele andere Ausstellungsobjekte. Ein ebenfalls bemerkenswerter Beitrag zur Expo.02 stammte von COOP HIMMELB(L)AU, deren 16 000 m² umfassende Plattform 4 m über dem Bieler See schwebte. Der im Prinzip wieder verwendbare Baukörper war aus Stahl, hatte eine Umhüllung aus Zinkofenstaub und war von einer Art Gitterfolie umgeben, die über einen Rahmen gespannt war. Auch wenn sie aus einiger Entfernung betrachtet ziemlich robust zu sein schien, war die über eine 413 m lange Fußgängerbrücke erreichbare Konstruktion überaus leicht und luftig, was eine interessante Kombination aus scheinbarer Massivität und tatsächlicher Leichtigkeit ergab. Ein weiterer, vielleicht sogar noch ungewöhnlicherer Beitrag zur Expo.02 stammte von den New Yorker Architekten

Diller + Scofidio. Ihr Blur Building, das aussah aus wie eine über dem Neuenburger See schwebende Wolke, war eine 100 m lange und 60 m breite Konstruktion, die sich 25 m über den Wasserspiegel erhob. Der Wolken-Effekt wurde durch den Einsatz gefilterten Seewassers erzielt, das als feiner Nebel aus 31 500 in dichter Folge angeordneten Hochdruck-Wasserdüsen versprüht wurde, die in eine große, freitragende Seilnetz-Konstruktion eingebaut waren. Bei günstigen Wind- und Wetterverhältnissen war die Wirkung des Blur Building genauso, wie es sich die Architekten vorgestellt hatten. Deren Bestreben war hier, die Architektur im eigentlichen Sinne zum Verschwinden zu bringen, und so leicht werden zu lassen wie eine Wolke. Gleichzeitig sollte dadurch eine Umgebung entstehen, in der eine Art sinnliche Deprivation die Besucher jedes Gefühl für den „realen" Raum und die Zeit verlieren ließ. Hatte Nouvel einen „künstlerischen" Zugang zur Expo.02 gewählt und COOP HIMMELB(L)AU die Solidität des Monumentalen unterlaufen, so lieferten Diller + Scofidio den weitaus radikalsten Beitrag, indem sie es wagten, das eigentliche Wesen der gebauten Form in Frage zu stellen.

London, bekannt für seine Monumentalbauten aus dem britischen Empire des 19. Jahrhunderts, wurde in jüngster Zeit zum Standort einer Reihe äußerst interessanter Experimente auf dem Gebiet temporärer Architektur. Zum vierten Mal fungierte dieses Jahr die Serpentine Gallery in Kensington Gardens als Auftraggeber für Arbeiten, die jeweils einen Sommer lang präsentiert und von so namhaften Architekten gestaltet wurden wie Zaha Hadid (2000), Daniel Libeskind (2002), Toyo Ito (2002) und dem verehrungswürdigen Oscar Niemeyer (2003). Letzterer unternahm mit seinem Entwurf den Versuch, alle seine Ideen über den lyrischen Charakter von Betonarchitektur zusammenzufassen. Dagegen drang Ito in eher unbekanntes Terrain vor, indem er eine scheinbar willkürliche Form entwarf, die in Wahrheit durch einen von der Rotation eines einzelnen Quadrats abgeleiteten Algorithmus definiert war. Obgleich sehr kostspielig für ein kleines Museum, haben diese Projekte wieder einmal die enorme Anziehungskraft von „Star-Architekten" demonstriert und darüber hinaus gezeigt, dass es möglich ist, auch mit kleinformatigen und temporären Bauten einen wahrhaft künstlerischen Ausdruck zu erzielen.

Die Grenze zwischen Kunst und Architektur wurde auch durch eine beeindruckende Installation des Bildhauers Anish Kapoor in der Londoner Tate Modern verwischt. Sie trug den Titel „Marsyas" und bestand aus drei Stahlringen, die durch eine rote, sich durch die gesamte, 155 m lange Turbinenhalle spannende PVC-Folie verbunden waren. Diese von keinem einzigen Punkt in ihrer Gänze überschaubare Installation stellte überzeugend die konventionellen Wahrnehmungen von Raum und Architektur in Frage. Leere und Fülle, zwei maßgebende Elemente jeder architektonischen Gestaltung, gingen hier vollkommen nahtlos ineinander über. Tatsächlich befand sich dieses enigmatische Spiel mit dem Raum durchaus im Einklang mit der Arbeit von Herzog & de Meuron an der Tate Modern selbst. Schließlich besteht auch deren Zugang häufig darin, die Grenzen zwischen Reflektion und ungehinderter Sicht oder die zwischen Leichtigkeit und Schwere zu verwischen. Der Unterschied zwischen Kunst und Architektur liegt darin, wie der amerikanische Bildhauer Richard Serra einmal pointiert sagte, dass die Architektur immer einem Zweck dient. Auch wenn man Kapoors „Marsyas" nicht als Architektur bezeichnen kann, so setzte sich dieses Werk doch auf raffinierte Weise mit der Wahrnehmung von Raum, Licht und Farbe auseinander und gab der riesigen Turbinenhalle eine räumliche Struktur wie noch kein anderes Kunstwerk zuvor. Es war keine Architektur, aber es brachte einen dazu, Raum und Volumen mit neuen Augen zu sehen.

Auch Vito Acconci bewegt sich seit langem an der Grenze zwischen Kunst und Architektur, was sich an seinen bemerkenswerten Arbeiten wie etwa Steven Holls Storefront for Art and Architecture in New York erkennen lässt. Im Fall seines Mur-Insel Projekts in Graz gehört das

Resultat eindeutig mehr in die Domäne der Architektur als in die der Kunst und doch sind hier ebenso wie in der Installation von Anish Kapoor die Elemente Form und Raum auf ganz neue Art und Weise konfiguriert. Die lokale Presse empfand den in der Mur verankerten „futuristischen Stadtplatz" als „völlig unvereinbar mit der mittelalterlichen und barocken Architektur" dieser Stadt, die zur Kulturhauptstadt Europas 2003 ernannt worden war. Doch eben diese Stadt hat sich auch ein neues, gleichermaßen futuristisches Kunsthaus von Peter Cook und Colin Fournier bauen lassen und sie „friendly alien" getauft. Von zweifellos dauerhafterer Natur als Acconcis künstliche Insel scheint das Kunsthaus tatsächlich auf einem fremden Planeten gelandet zu sein, wobei der erste Schritt zu dieser Landung vom Mur-Insel Projekt gemacht worden war.

In einem Architekturgenre arbeitend, dessen Wurzeln bis ins 18. Jahrhundert zurückreichen, hat I. M. Pei, der Gestalter der Louvre-Pyramide und des Ostflügels der National Gallery in Washington, kürzlich ein Lusthaus in einem englischen Park realisiert. Indem er auf Formen zurückgriff, die er auch in seinem Museum Miho (Shigaraki, Shiga, Japan) verwendet hatte, schuf Pei eine entschieden moderne Version eines Pavillons für Oare House, den in Wiltshire liegenden Landsitz der Familie Keswick. Pei ist mit Sicherheit kein für schnelllebiges Design bekannter Architekt, und möglicherweise überdauert diese Konstruktion etliche Bauten, die prächtiger sind. Aber gerade diese Art von Gebäuden impliziert eine Leichtigkeit, die von Peis Entwurf bestätigt wird. Pei plädiert seit langem für einen respektvollen Umgang mit der Tradition, sei es im Kontext seiner eigenen chinesischen Herkunft oder der reichen Geschichte des Louvre. Mit seinem Oare Pavilion ist es ihm abermals gelungen, Vergangenheit und Gegenwart auf harmonische Weise miteinander zu verbinden. Der alte Kampf zwischen Modernismus und Tradition ist vorüber. Besonders in Europa, etwa am Ufer der Mur oder in einem englischen Park, ist es möglich geworden, eine zeitgemäße Architektur zu verwirklichen, ohne das, was ihr voraus gegangen ist, zu missachten oder zu verleugnen.

## DIE GROSSE ZEIT DER KULTURGEIER

Seit vielen Jahren ist der Kulturbereich eines der bevorzugten Aufgabengebiete für hochwertige Architektur. Zwar wurden nicht nur in den Vereinigten Staaten großartige Pläne für neue Museen wieder verworfen. Andere Kultureinrichtungen, wie etwa Konzerthallen, gedeihen dafür umso prächtiger. Während zum Beispiel das Los Angeles County Museum seine ehrgeizigen Modernisierungspläne aufgab, für deren Ausführung Rem Koolhaas vorgesehen war, ist im Zentrum von Los Angeles die neue Disney Concert Hall von Frank O. Gehry fertig gestellt worden, das erste große, öffentliche Gebäude in seiner Heimatstadt. Auch wenn Gehrys vielbeachtete Pläne für eine Guggenheim Niederlassung in Downtown New York im Sande verliefen, so realisierte er gleichzeitig das äußerst erfolgreiche Center for the Performing Arts für das Bard College in Upstate New York. Obgleich beide Bauwerke, Disney wie Bard, auf die geschwungenen Metallformen zurückgreifen, die Gehry in Bilbao weltberühmt gemacht haben, setzen sie neue Maßstäbe für den Erfolg dieses Architekten. Mit seinen aufgetürmten Wolken aus Titan hat er für sich und alle anderen Architekten die Freiheit und den Status als Künstler beansprucht. Das macht die Suche nach neuen Formen für die jüngeren Gestalter einfacher, auch wenn sie den ästhetischen Vorlieben von Gehry folgen.

Könnte es sein, dass ein Zusammenhang zwischen der Wahl von Zaha Hadid zur Planerin des Lois & Richard Rosenthal Center for Contemporary Art in Cincinnati und der öffentlichen Begeisterung für Gehrys Bauten besteht? Die in Architekturkreisen seit langem für ihre radikalen Konzepte berühmte Zaha Hadid scheint in eine neue Phase ihrer Karriere eingetreten zu sein, in der sie mit bedeutenden Aufträgen bedacht wird – und ist die erste Frau, die ein Museum in den Vereinigten Staaten baut. In Cincinnati demonstriert sie, dass sich ihre dynamischen Zeichnungen tatsächlich materialisieren lassen, und dass zeitgenössische Kunst und Architektur selbst in jener Stadt eine Verbindung eingehen können, in der vor einigen Jahren der peinliche Versuch unternommen wurde, das Werk von Robert Mapplethorpe zu zensieren.

Die in der Wahl des Architekten vielleicht weniger radikale Stadt Fort Worth hat kürzlich ihr neues, von dem Japaner Tadao Ando gestaltetes Museum of Modern Art eröffnet. Andos Bauwerk ist wie zu erwarten streng geometrisch. Ganz anders als die kleinformatigen Kapellen oder Wohnhäuser, mit denen er sich in Japan einen Namen machte, entspricht dieses Projekt mehr dem wuchtigen Museum der Präfektur Hyogo, das er vor kurzem an der durch das Erdbeben 1995 zerstörten Uferpromenade in Kobe fertig stellte. Ando, der mit seinen Arbeiten Architekturstudenten in der ganzen Welt beeinflusst, hat in Fort Worth ein Bauwerk mit Leben erfüllt, von dem sich nur auf den ersten Blick sagen ließe, dass es sich in geometrischer Strenge erschöpft. Indem Ando Licht und Wasser um und durch seine Gebäude fließen lässt, macht er diese zu einer beinahe zeitlosen Ode an die gebaute Form, statt sie in einer rückwärtsgewandten Manifestation eines überkommenen Modernismus erstarren zu lassen.

Ökonomische Zwänge haben den Schwerpunkt von der Realisierung ambitiöser neuer Bauprojekte für die Kunst zu einer umfassenden Renovierung bereits bestehender Gebäude verlagert, wie sie etwa von Ellis Williams für das Baltic Centre for Contemporary Arts im schottischen Newcastle durchgeführt wurde. Architekt Dominic Williams baute die Gebäude einer ehemaligen Mühle zu einer 8 537 m² messenden Ausstellungsfläche für die jüngsten Beispiele zeitgenössischer Kunst um. Allein durch ihre Dimensionen bieten stillgelegte Industriebauten ganz neue Möglichkeiten für die Kunst. Wie Dominic Williams betont: „Das Hauptziel ist, zeitgenössische Kunst einfach geschehen zu lassen, in welcher Form auch immer."

Zwei weitere im Gebiet von New York angesiedelte Projekte machen ebenfalls frühere Industriebauten für die Kunst nutzbar. Das Erste steht in direktem Zusammenhang mit einem anderen wichtigen Architekturprojekt – dem Umbau des Museum of Modern Art durch den Tokioter Architekten Yoshio Taniguchi. Für die Zeit der Bauarbeiten soll das in Manhatten beheimatete Museum of Modern Art (MoMA) auf die andere Seite des Flusses, nach Long Island (Queens), verlegt werden. Hierfür wurde eine ehemalige Fabrik vom kalifornischen Architekten Michael Maltzan adaptiert, der erklärt, wie wichtig es sei, eine neues Image für eine etablierte Institution zu kreieren, die an einen Nebenschauplatz umzieht, das ehemalige Swingline Staples Fabrikgebäude. „In der Überzeugung, dass die vorübergehende Einrichtung nicht das bald fertig gestellte MoMA in Manhattan vorwegnehmen sollte, setzten wir uns bei der Schaffung einer Identität für das MoMAQNS (Museum of Modern Art Queens) stattdessen mit der komplexen Umgebung des Projekts und der Erfahrung von Bewegung auseinander."

Auf einem noch ehrgeizigeren Niveau war die Ansiedlung des Dia:Beacon in einer ehemaligen Papiermühle im nördlichen Teil von Upstate New York Anlass für eine einzigartige Zusammenarbeit zwischen dem bekannten Künstler Robert Irwin, der jungen Designergruppe OpenOffice und der durch ihren Präsidenten Michael Govan vertretenen Dia Foundation selbst. Mit 24 000 m² Ausstellungsfläche und der Möglichkeit, jedem der präsentierten Künstler einen eigenen Raum zu widmen, demonstriert dieses Renovierungsprojekt überzeugend die neuen Möglichkeiten, die sich durch eine Verbindung von alten Gebäuden und neuer Kunst, aber auch durch die Gesinnungsgemeinschaft zwischen Künstlern, Architekten und aufgeschlossenen Vertretern einer Institution eröffnen. Grundsätzlich ist festzustellen, dass die Qualität von Architektur zu einem allgemein anerkannten Aspekt des Kunstbetriebs geworden ist, sei es im Zusammenhang mit Umbauten wie denen des Baltic Centre, MoMAQNS oder Dia:Beacon auf der einen oder mit Neubauten wie denen in Fort Worth oder Cincinnati auf der anderen Seite.

Auf der ganzen Welt macht sich das Bedürfnis nach einer fruchtbaren Zusammenarbeit von Architekten, Künstlern und Kulturinstitutionen bemerkbar, was sogar in Projekten zum Ausdruck kommt, in denen finanzielle Zwänge ein bestimmender Faktor sind. 1997 gewannen Herzog & de Meuron einen internationalen Wettbewerb zum Bau des neuen Laban Dance Centre, für das ein auf 14,4 Millionen Pfund begrenztes Budget zur Verfügung stand. Das auf einem fast 1 ha großen Grundstück nahe Deptford Creek im südöstlichen London gelegene Gebäude bildet „einen spektakulären Markierungspunkt für die fortschreitende materielle und soziale Regenerierung von Deptford und Umgebung." In diesem Fall arbeitete der Künstler Michael Craig-Martin gemeinsam mit den Architekten an der Gestaltung der Außenfassaden und der Inneneinrichtung. Die Verkleidung eines Teils der Außenwände mit farbigem Polycarbonat entspricht dabei den budgetären Vorgaben und verleiht dem in einer eher problematischen Gegend liegenden Gebäude gleichzeitig eine fröhliche Ausstrahlung.

Auch ohne derart strenge finanzielle Vorgaben war die Aufgabe, eine Kunstgalerie für die berühmte Turiner Autofabrik Lingotto zu entwerfen, eine schwierige Herausforderung für Renzo Piano. Seine Giovanni und Marella Agnelli Galerie, die über der Autoteststrecke von Lingotto liegt, wurde mit einem „fliegenden Safe" verglichen. Tatsächlich birgt sie einen kostbaren Inhalt von 25 hochkarätigen Kunstwerken. Ebenso wie Pianos frühere Erweiterungen des Gebäudes, ein blasenförmiger Konferenzsaal und ein Hubschrauberlandeplatz, wirkt die Kunstgalerie mit ihrem Ufo-artigen Aussehen eher seltsam. Nach den 100 000 gezählten Besuchern im ersten Jahr zu urteilen, scheint sich diese architektonische Kuriosität jedoch durchaus bezahlt zu machen. Außerdem stellt sie einen Beitrag zu dem fortlaufenden Projekt dar, das Piano zur Revitalisierung des riesigen Fabrikkomplexes in Angriff genommen hat.

Die wachsende Bedeutung der Rolle von Architektur im kulturellen Kontext macht sich auch über Westeuropa und die Vereinigten Staaten hinaus bemerkbar, wie der kürzlich stattgefundene Wettbewerb für das Viertel Neu-Holland und das Mariinsky Theater in Petersburg demonstriert hat. Hierbei schien es zunächst, als ob der kalifornische Architekt Eric Owen Moss und dessen Promoter Samitaur Constructs als Sieger hervorgegangen seien. Dann jedoch wurde bekannt, dass der Franzose Dominique Perrault den Auftrag erhalten hatte, ein neues Gebäude für das Mariinsky Theater in der Innenstadt von St. Petersburg zu planen. Aber auch Moss bleibt in der Gegend tätig, da sein ursprünglicher Wettbewerbsbeitrag für das Viertel Neu-Holland und dessen eigenes Theater ausgewählt wurde. In der Folge entbrannte in dieser Stadt, die mit zeitgenössischer Architektur nicht sehr vertraut ist, eine heftige Kontroverse um die beiden Projekte. Aber wie Moss im Verlauf der Debatte sagte: „Mit Neu-Holland und dem Mariinsky wird die Weltstadt St. Petersburg mit ihrer einzigartigen kulturellen Geschichte eine neue Tradition von Oper, Ballett, Musik und Architektur bis weit ins nächste Jahrhundert einleiten." Wenn so innovative Architekten wie Dominique Perrault und Eric Owen Moss in einer so traditionsreichen Stadt wie St. Petersburg tätig werden, lässt sich kaum noch bezweifeln, dass es für die von Moss heraufbeschworene Vereinigung verschiedener künstlerischer Ausdrucksformen tatsächlich eine neue Grundlage gibt.

**KONSTRUIERT ZUM LEBEN UND WOHNEN**

Der Wohnungsbau gehört zu den eindeutigsten und aktuellsten Aufgaben der Architektur. Trifft ein aufgeklärter Bauherr auf einen talentierten Architekten, so kann das Resultat einen Fortschritt für die Architektur bedeuten, der die ästhetischen und auch die praktischen Seiten des Bauens auf Jahre hinaus beeinflusst. Die in diesem Buch präsentierten Wohnhäuser wurden aufgrund ihrer innovativen Merkmale und der sich in ihnen manifestierenden fortschrittlichen Aspekte ausgewählt. Der Architekt David Adjaye hat sich in London einen klangvollen Namen gemacht, vielleicht auch deswegen, weil er das Glück hatte, dass eine Reihe von Auftraggebern berühmt wurde, nachdem er für sie gearbeitet hatte. So baute er beispielsweise ein im Londoner East End gelegenes Lagerhaus aus den 1930er Jahren zu einem höchst ungewöhnlichen Wohnhaus für das Künstlerpaar Tim Noble und Sue Webster um. Die Tatsache, dass das East End nicht gerade als luxuriöse Wohngegend gilt, schreckte weder Adjaye noch seine Auftraggeber ab. In seiner radikalen Behandlung von Raum, Licht und Oberflächen geht das Dirty House in einer Weise auf seinen Standort ein, wie es einer Stadt entspricht, in der man imstande ist, das Schöne auch in einer industriellen Umgebung zu erkennen. Ähnlich wie New York, das sukzessive ehemalige Gewerbegebiete wie Soho und Tribeca für sich erobert hat, ist London dabei, das East End zu einem seiner begehrtesten Wohnviertel zu machen. Dieser Vorgang ist gewissermaßen eine Fortsetzung der Methode wie die Kunst Alltagsmaterialien und, wie im Fall von Adjayes Auftraggeber, sogar Müll für sich nutzbar gemacht hat. Mit seinem robusten und dynamischen Stil liegt Adjaye nicht nur im Trend, sondern trifft auch genau den Zeitgeist.

Ganz anders dagegen Shigeru Bans Glass Shutter House in Tokio. In einer relativ schicken Gegend von Tokio gelegen, handelt es sich hierbei um eine Kombination von Wohnhaus und Restaurant, speziell zugeschnitten auf die Bedürfnisse eines japanischen Starkochs. Ban ist bekannt für seine beständige Auseinandersetzung mit dem Thema Flexibilität in der Architektur, was sich sowohl in der Wahl seiner Baumaterialien wie Papier, als auch in seinem Drang niederschlägt, so fundamentale Elemente wie Wände in Frage zu stellen. So ermöglicht Ban nun in seinem Glass Shutter House dem Hausherrn, zwei Wände, die in das Dach hinein eingerollt werden können, komplett zu öffnen. Das ist besonders praktisch während der Sommermonate, weil das Restaurant dadurch nahtlos in die Terrasse übergehen kann. Vor allem ist es jedoch eine ausgesprochen originale Alternative zu der herkömmlichen Solidität von Architektur.

Eine aufgeschlossene Haltung gegenüber neuer Architektur (d. h. ohne stilistische Bedenken) hat auch zur Wiederentdeckung einer Reihe von Gebäuden der frühen Moderne beigetragen. Als außergewöhnliches Beispiel einer in diesem Geist durchgeführten Rekonstruktion kann das Charles Deaton Sculpture House in Golden, Colorado, gelten. Deaton, als Architekt Autodidakt, gestaltete 1963 dieses Wohnhaus als eine „Skulptur, in der man leben kann". Er beschrieb das ursprüngliche Haus so: „Ich hatte das Gefühl, in erster Linie sollte die Form stark und einfach genug sein, um in einer Galerie als Kunstwerk zu bestehen. Wenn man dieses zu einem Haus vergrößerte, sollte es in einzelne Wohnbereiche unterteilt werden. Ich wusste natürlich von Anfang an, dass sich diese Skulptur zu einem Haus entwickeln würde, es war aber nie beabsichtigt, daraus einfach eine Hülle für einen Grundriss zu machen. Tatsächlich wurde kein Maßstab festgesetzt, bis die Skulptur fertig war. Der Grundriss folgte der Formgebung in respektvollem Abstand." Abgesehen von der unanfechtbaren Präsenz des Hauses und seiner spektakulären Lage scheinen sich Deatons Ideen nicht allzu sehr von dem bildhauerisch orientierten Zugang eines Frank O. Gehry zu unterscheiden. Der in vielen seiner Ideen durchaus radikale Modernismus kann also mit Sicherheit weiterhin Inspirationsquelle für eine zeitgenössische Architektur sein, die eine aufgeschlossene Haltung gegenüber der Vergangenheit einnimmt.

Das Glaphyros House, ein 320 m² großer Wohnsitz unweit des Jardin du Luxembourg in Paris, ist insofern bemerkenswert, als seine Ausstattung fast ausschließlich mit dem Computer gestaltet wurde. Die Erdgeschosswohnung in einem Gebäude aus den 1960er Jahren wurde von Mark Goulthorpe von dECOi für einen Kunden entworfen, der sich „eine minimalistische und doch sinnliche Architektur" wünschte. Unter Anwendung eines von Goulthorpe „nicht-normierte Logik" genannten Verfahrens wurde fast jedes Einzelteil speziell für dieses Projekt maßgeschneidert. Eine Betontreppe, die zu den tiefer gelegenen Schlafzimmern führt, wurde nach einem vergrößerten Parametermodell entworfen. „Die daraus resultierende Verschiebung", so der Architekt, „verleiht dem eng begrenzten Raum ein Gefühl von Bewegung, als wäre hier eine andere Form von Energie am Werk, welche die schlichte Ausgewogenheit einer modernistischen Ästhetik stört. Auch die Nische unter der Treppe ist wie unter Einwirkung einer geologischen Kraft deformiert, was einen merkwürdigen Animismus erzeugt." Derartige Verzerrungen von Oberfläche und Volumen sind in der gesamten Wohnung zu finden. Dazu Mark Goulthorpe zusammenfassend: „Als eine kontinuierliche Übung in nicht-standardisierter Produktion bricht das Projekt die sich ständig wiederholende und vorgefertigte Logik auf, die der industriellen Produktion eigen ist und bringt damit eine durch die Digitalisierung in hohem Maß bereicherte Formensprache hervor." Für das ungeschulte Auge wird die von Goulthorpe für diese Wohnung durchgeführte Computerarbeit jedoch kaum erkennbar sein, und in gewissem Sinne ist es genau das, was dieses Projekt bemerkenswert macht. Denn die digitale und parametrische Formgebung hat zwar begonnen, die Architektur zu verändern. Aber die aus diesem Trend resultierenden Gestaltungen müssen sich nicht in extravaganten, blasenartigen Gebilden erschöpfen, wie uns manche schon fast eingeredet haben. Der Computer hat in die Alltagslogik der Architektur Einzug gehalten und ist teilweise bereits im gesamten Prozess des Planens und Bauens vorherrschend.

Wenngleich in seiner Gesamtkonzeption nicht ganz so kompromisslos angelegt, ist das von Masaki Endoh geplante Haus Natural Ellipse in Tokio beispielhaft für die Art von architektonischer Originalität, welche die Japaner zu akzeptieren bereit sind. Das Haus liegt auf einem nur 53 m² großen Grundstück im sehr dicht besiedelten Stadtviertel Shibuya. Es wurde aus 24 elliptischen Stahlringen konstruiert und ist mit faserverstärktem Polymer (FRP) beschichtet, was eine fugenlose Außenfassade ermöglicht. Neue Materialien und ein vorurteilsfreier Zugang zum Design werden mit Sicherheit auch in Zukunft derart ungewöhnliche Alternativen zu traditionellen Gebäudeformen ermöglichen. Indem der Architekt vermied, das Haus in einem konventionellen Modus zu strukturieren, hat er sich mit der Problematik, die ein winziges Grundstück und das damit möglicherweise einhergehende Gefühl der Beklemmung bedeutet, ernsthaft auseinandergesetzt.

Ein weiterer japanischer Architekt bewies ebenso viel Einfallsreichtum wie Shigeru Ban oder Masaki Endoh, wenn auch im Rahmen einer ganz anderen Bauaufgabe. Kengo Kumas Great-Bamboo-Wall-Haus steht in der Nähe von Peking auf einem 1 930 m² großen Grundstück, hat eine Gesamtnutzfläche von 528 m² und ist als kleines Hotel konzipiert. Durch die großzügige Ausstattung mit Glas und Bambus für die Wände und Säulen entsteht der Eindruck von Leichtigkeit und Nähe zur traditionellen Architektur Asiens. Allerdings ist Kuma hier eine Schlichtheit und Modernität gelungen, die mehr mit den neuesten Architekturtrends als mit der Vergangenheit zu tun hat.

Natürlich haben nicht alle Architekten entsprechend umfangreiche Mittel zur Verfügung. Aber Einfallsreichtum ist nicht nur eine Frage großzügiger und ausgeklügelter Ausstattung. Die junge norwegische Firma Saunders & Wilhelmsen bestätigt diese Tatsache mit ihrem Sommerhaus am Hardanger Fjord in Norwegen. Das aus zwei Baukörpern mit einer Nutzfläche von 20 bzw. 30 m² bestehende, kleinformatige

Haus wurde mit recyceltem Zeitungspapier isoliert und aus lokalem Holz gebaut. Ein praktischer Außengang, der auch als Terrasse dient, verbindet die beiden Trakte. Natürlich trägt die Lage an einem der größten und schönsten Fjorde Norwegens zu dessen Attraktivität bei. Die Risikobereitschaft der Architekten, die den Kunden beweisen wollten, dass sie auch mit einem begrenzten Budget Interessantes zu leisten verstehen, beweist jedoch auch eine Vitalität, welche die wichtigste Quelle für die Architektur von morgen darstellt.

Architekten sind nicht die Einzigen, denen es gelungen ist, die Entwicklung des Gestaltens und Bauens voranzutreiben. So hat beispielsweise der Ingenieur Werner Sobek sein eigenes energiesparendes „Glashaus" entworfen und in der erstaunlichen Zeit von nur elf Wochen auf einem Stuttgarter Hanggrundstück errichtet. Ein System aus vorgefertigten, 3,75 x 2,80 m großen Holzpaneelen mit Kunststoffüberzug oder Deckenplatten aus Aluminium, die ohne Einsatz von Schrauben einfach zwischen die Fußboden- bzw. Deckenbalken eingesetzt werden, erlaubt eine unkomplizierte Konstruktion und Instandhaltung. Vorrichtungen wie der Wärmeaustauscher, der unter das Fundament verlegt wurde, um die natürliche Erdwärme zu nutzen, und die mit Schutzgas gefüllten, dreifach verglasten Paneele, die den Wärmeverlust reduzieren, gehören zu den von Sobek gefundenen „grünen" Lösungen. Trotz seines schmucklosen Äußeren hat dieses Glashaus nichts von der manchmal etwas seltsam anmutenden Optik ökologisch korrekter Architektur. Von Berufs wegen technisch orientiert, hat Sobek vieles von dem, was er in seinem Arbeitsfeld gelernt hat, in die Gestaltung seines eigenen, Haus R-128 genannten Zuhauses eingebracht.

### SCHLAFEN, VIELLEICHT SOGAR TRÄUMEN

Die vielleicht interessanteste Eigenschaft der Architektur ist ihre Fähigkeit, zu träumen und noch nie da gewesene Lösungen zu ersinnen. Das mag mit neuen Technologien zusammenhängen oder einfach damit, dass anders gedacht wird. Michael Sorkin, ein New Yorker Lehrer und Designer, widmet sich beruflich dem Entwerfen von Formen menschlichen Zusammenlebens, mit denen viele der Probleme der modernen Welt gelöst wären. Seine ansprechenden Zeichnungen und Texte basieren auf einem fundierten Wissen über Architektur und Stadtplanung und verkörpern die Art von utopischem Denken, das die Architektur braucht, um zu überleben und voranzukommen. An dem Sorkins nachdenklichen Betrachtungen entgegengesetzten Ende des Spektrums ist Michael Jantzen anzusiedeln, der sich intensiv mit den Möglichkeiten beschäftigt, die sich durch die neuen Technologien eröffnet haben. Mit seinem VRI (Virtual Reality Interface) lotet er aus, wie weit computergenerierte Bilder zukünftige Hausbesitzer überzeugen können. Zum Beispiel mit Wänden, die jedes Bild projizieren, das die Bewohner wünschen und damit ein praktisch endlos variables persönliches Wohnumfeld schaffen. Obwohl es schwierig sein dürfte, das Bild in die Realität eines Wohnumfelds umzusetzen, wird Jantzen mit Sicherheit seinen Weg weiterverfolgen. Sein in diesem Band präsentiertes Malibu Video Beach House ist bereits ein richtiges Wohnhaus, in dem Bilder von der Außenwelt auf großzügig in den Räumen verteilte Videoeinwände projiziert werden. Ganz bewusst soll mit der Einrichtung und Ausstattung eine Vermischung von Innen und Außen hergestellt werden.

Das von dem Rotterdamer Architekten Lars Spuybroek (NOX) entworfene Son-O-House ist „ein Haus, in dem Geräusche leben." „Es ist kein ‚reales' Haus, sondern eine Konstruktion, die sich an den Lebensäußerungen und Bewegungen der Bewohner orientiert, die sich darin bewegen oder wohnen. Im Son-O-House erzeugt eine Soundanlage ständig neue Geräuschmuster, die von den durch Sensoren übertragenen Bewegungen der Besucher ausgelöst werden." Spuybroeks Projekt ist also gewissermaßen eine natürliche Ergänzung zu Michael Jantzens

VRI. Während in Kalifornien das häusliche Environment rein visuell ist, zeigt sich im niederländischen Son en Breugel das Haus von NOX als „eine evolutionäre Erinnerungslandschaft mit dem aufgezeichneten Verhalten realer Körper im Raum". In ihrer reinsten Form sind weder das Son-O-House noch das VRI wirklich praktikabel. Sie zeigen jedoch Richtungen des Denkens und ein Potential für radikale Veränderungen im Wohnungsdesign auf, die mit Hilfe neuer Technologien möglich wurden.

Der Traum von menschlichen Lebensräumen unter Wasser beschäftigt seit langem sowohl Literaten als auch Architekten. So hat sich etwa in Frankreich Jacques Rougerie konsequent der Suche nach Lösungen für das Wohnen im Meer verschrieben. Gegenwärtig verfolgt das in Los Angeles beheimatete Architekturbüro Office of Mobile Design einen mehr an der Hochtechnologie ausgerichteten Zugang. Hydra House nennt sich ihr Konzept für eine Serie von Wohnbauten aus Neopren, die über eine vollkommen autarke Energieversorgung verfügen, und selbst Meerwasser aufbereiten könnten. Einst Gegenstand von Science Fiction Romanen, liegt ein solches Unterwasserzuhause heute tatsächlich im Bereich des Möglichen. Hydra House mag ebenso wenig wie Arverne, Michael Sorkins Entwurf für den zukünftigen Städtebau, nicht gerade die nahe liegendste Lösung für die drängenden Wohnungsprobleme von Städten wie New York oder Los Angeles bieten. Aber Sorkin und das Office of Mobile Design stehen für die verschiedenen Versuche der Architektenzunft, neue Wege in die Zukunft zu ersinnen.

Bei einem wesentlich weniger utopischen, Houses at Sagaponac genannten Projekt handelt es sich um eine aus 34 Einheiten bestehende Wohnanlage auf einem bewaldeten Gelände in Southampton, Long Island, New York. Coco Brown, die Initiatorin des Projekts hat in Zusammenarbeit mit dem Architekten Richard Meier eine Liste von Teilnehmern zusammengestellt, die man als eine Art „Who's Who" der zeitgenössischen Architektur bezeichnen könnte. So gehören zu den Planern, die beauftragt wurden, jeweils eines der ca. 200 bis 440 m² großen Wohnhäuser zu entwerfen, Philip Johnson, Michael Graves, James Freed, Zaha Hadid, Richard Rogers, Shigeru Ban und Jean-Michel Wilmotte. Charakteristisch für das gesamte Projekt ist der Einsatz traditioneller Materialien aus der Region, jedoch in einem modernen, optisch ansprechenden und dynamischen Stil.

Dieses Buch vermittelt im Rahmen eines Überblicks über die seit 2000 entstandene Architektur einen plastischen Eindruck von dem enormen Kreativitätsschub, der durch eine Kombination aus technologischem Fortschritt und inhaltlicher Unvoreingenommenheit ausgelöst wurde. Es gibt heutzutage nicht mehr den einen Stil und das soll es auch gar nicht. Die Architektur ist immer schon in erster Linie von praktischen Erwägungen bestimmt worden. Im Gegensatz zur Kunst dient die Architektur, wie Richard Serra sagt, einem Zweck. Die bedeutendste Veränderung, die sich in der Architektur derzeit bemerkbar macht, ist die reale Möglichkeit einer Integration sämtlicher Prozesse von Entwurf bis Produktion durch Computer und Robotertechnik. Dies hat bereits die Herstellung individueller Einzelteile ermöglicht, was eine Überwindung der Ästhetik und wirtschaftlichen Logik eines knappen Jahrhunderts „moderner" Architektur bedeutet. Jene Moderne, die verlangte, dass jedes Model-T Auto schwarz sein und jedes Fenster die gleiche Größe und Farbe haben müsse, ist tot. Zwar mögen Architekten aus ästhetischen Gründen nach wie vor auf die Formensprache eines „Neo-Modernismus" oder „Neo-Minimalismus" zurückgreifen, ihre Umsetzungen sind jedoch nicht länger durch die ökonomischen Grenzen einer standardisierten Produktionsweise limitiert. Computergestütztes Design wandelt sich derzeit von einer Art Zirkusnummer, mit der seltsame Gebilde produziert werden, zu einem praktikablen Instrumentarium der Zukunft, das eine neue Freiheit für die Gestaltungsmöglichkeiten der Architektur mit sich bringen wird.

# INTRODUCTION

## LA MORT DU MODERNISME

Dans quelle direction s'oriente aujourd'hui l'architecture contemporaine ? Peut-on repérer des tendances claires qui permettent d'entrevoir le futur avec quelque degré de certitude ? Qui sont les créateurs de formes ? Qui va laisser sa marque sur notre temps ou, plus important encore, qui nous montre la voie de l'avenir ? On sait que toute époque éprouve des difficultés à juger de sa propre créativité. L'art le plus admiré aujourd'hui est vraisemblablement le produit de périodes antérieures. Regarder vers l'avant – un peu comme dans une boule de cristal – est un problème d'extrapolation, de sensibilité à ce qui mobilise et formalise l'art de la conception et de la construction architecturales. L'ordinateur nous a ouvert de nouveaux horizons, qui ne sont pas forcément ceux auxquels on avait pensé à l'origine. Utilisée au départ par certains comme un mode de visualisation de structures de plus en plus extravagantes, la technologie numérique approche rapidement d'une relative maturité qui exercera un effet beaucoup plus profond et durable sur l'architecture que toutes ces « petites constructions folles », comme Arata Isozaki qualifiait certains projets japonais expérimentaux. La nouvelle liberté que suggère un ordinateur capable de faire sortir l'architecture de sa boîte euclidienne et moderniste n'a certainement pas encore atteint son but, comme beaucoup de projets publiés dans cet ouvrage en attestent. Cependant les ordinateurs sont en passe de transformer non seulement le processus de conception, mais aussi de production. C'est justement à ce niveau que le clavier et l'écran commencent à devenir vraiment intéressants. Une exposition organisée au Centre Pompidou à Paris, fin 2003, par le talentueux commissaire Frédéric Migayrou, intitulée « Une architecture non standard » a identifié quelques-uns de ces changements importants. Que va-t-il se passer si la standardisation, née de la Révolution industrielle, disparaît ? Qu'arrivera-t-il s'il est aussi économique de fabriquer des milliers de composants uniques que des pièces identiques ? Sous l'appellation attrape-tout de changement « révolutionnaire », un groupe d'architectes new-yorkais et italiens avait annoncé la fin du modernisme vers le début des années 1970. Leur monde était celui du postmodernisme. Pour eux, l'architecture devait être libre de faire référence au passé et de laisser de côté la *tabula rasa* décrétée par Walter Gropius et autres à la grande époque du Bauhaus. Quelques années se sont écoulées et le nouveau roi s'est révélé un peu nu. Vu de plus près, le siège d'ATT par Philip Johnson à New York (1979), salué en son temps comme le symbole de la nouveauté, est-il autre chose qu'une tour moderniste déguisée ?

Et si la révolution que nous connaissons s'observait plus dans certaines constructions à l'air tout à fait « normal » que dans la prolifération de *blobs* exotiques de Paris à Pékin ? En favorisant la progression d'un processus apparemment lisse, qui va du logiciel de conception architecturale à une production contrôlée par informatique, la nouvelle technologie rend possible la fin du modernisme. Car celui-ci était aussi un rêve de standardisation, celui de la perfection de la ligne de montage imaginée par Henry Ford qui déclarait que son modèle T était disponible « dans toutes les couleurs à condition que ce soit le noir ». La révolution actuelle n'est pas une révolution d'apparence. Il ne s'agit pas de la longueur de jupe à la mode cette saison. Elle est intériorisée, intégrée. C'est le cas lorsqu'un architecte peut faire fabriquer un millier de pièces de bois différentes pour un show-room parisien de vêtements bon marché, lorsqu'une poignée de porte peut être une pièce unique, lorsque même une pierre peut être aussi différente de sa voisine que les blocs taillés jadis à la main. Avant la Révolution industrielle, l'architecture était inévitablement quelque chose de manuel. Chaque pièce était un témoignage de la main de son créateur. La logique économique des machines pousse à l'abandon de l'unique au profit de l'identique et de l'unité standardisée de production. Aujourd'hui et demain, la

* Neil M. Denari, *Gyroscopic Horizons*, Thames & Hudson, Londres, 1999

machine ne sera certes pas écartée, mais elle aura évolué. La robotique permet aux lasers et autres outils guidés avec précision, un découpage spécifique de chaque bloc de pierre, différent de tous les autres, pour un prix semblable à celui de blocs identiques (église du pèlerinage de Padre Pio, San Giovanni Rotondo, Foggia, Italie, 1995–2003). La pleine signification de ce profond changement profitera moins à la génération actuelle des architectes établis qu'à leurs successeurs plus jeunes et plus familiarisés avec l'informatique. Si Frank Gehry a bien sûr fait appel à des logiciels de modélisation et de production sophistiqués pour réaliser des bâtiments aussi sculpturaux que le Musée Guggenheim à Bilbao (1991–1997), son travail de conception relève davantage du croquis et de la maquette que de la CAO. Des architectes plus jeunes, comme Mark Goulthorpe (dECOi), commencent à exploiter pleinement le potentiel des nouvelles technologies de conception et de production pour produire des structures de caractère unique qui répondent aux exigences de coût d'une industrie vouée à la standardisation. Il s'agit bien d'une vraie révolution, qui n'a rien à voir avec la mode ou les solutions cosmétiques. C'est la fin de la logique « moderniste » qui cachait les parpaings de béton dans une courbe ou sous un remplissage, mais n'offrait aucune alternative conceptuelle réelle. Un bureau ou un appartement de n'importe quelle forme, pourvu qu'elle soit orthogonale, a pu être le cri de ralliement des modernistes purs et durs. Cette époque est terminée. Les formes euclidiennes perdureront certainement, mais leur moule a été brisé.

## SYMBOLES POUR UN MONDE NUMÉRIQUE

Une ville de 9 000 habitants sur une île du sud du Japon, Kyushu, n'est sans doute guère le lieu où l'on pourrait s'attendre à trouver des expressions significatives d'une grande architecture publique. Néanmoins, le Hall communautaire de Reihoku, par Hitoshi Abe, prouve que ce type de projet a toute sa place dans le monde actuel. À l'origine de cette commande, un programme intitulé Artpolis, initié par l'architecte Arata Isozaki en 1988 sous l'autorité du gouverneur de la préfecture de Kumamoto, avait montré que de grands architectes pouvaient avoir envie de travailler dans ces contrées quasi rurales de Kyushu. Aujourd'hui sous le contrôle de Toyo Ito et de Teiichi Takahashi, Artpolis a sélectionné Hitoshi Abe pour le projet de Reihoku. L'architecte a rapidement lancé de longues consultations avec la population locale, mais personne n'était d'accord sur la fonction précise de ce type d'équipement communautaire. Abe a conçu un espace flexible adapté à cette indécision, mais réussit néanmoins à en faire un symbole bien accepté par Reihoku, un lieu devenu réellement le centre de la cité. Les sombres plis en forme de vague du bâtiment ne ressemblent à rien de connu, et cependant cette structure et son travail du bois évoquent l'architecture des temples japonais, un peu comme une grande tente dressée pour attirer le public. Et celui-ci vient.

Au Japon également, mais à une échelle assez différente, le nouveau terminal international du port de Yokohama conçu par Foreign Office Architects (FOA) a été abondamment reproduit dans de multiples publications architecturales récentes, ne serait-ce que pour son aspect inattendu et son recours aux techniques de CAO les plus avancées. Située si près de Tokyo qu'elle fait presque partie de la même mégalopole, Yokohama est officiellement la seconde ville du Japon, et pour mémoire le lieu du débarquement de l'amiral Perry en 1853, qui allait ouvrir les portes de la modernisation au Japon. Vu sous certains angles, cet équipement qui attire de nombreux curieux, fait presque penser à une formation naturelle. On peut noter, au passage, que plusieurs architectes japonais contemporains, comme Itsuko Hasegawa, pensent que le rôle de l'architecture devrait être de créer une sorte de nature artificielle. Ici, dans le cadre d'un développement urbain inexorable, la simple et curieuse jetée conçue par FOA va dans le sens de cette architecture qui serait une « Mère-Nature » subrogée, sans pour autant faire appel à une imagerie «organique». Achevée en deux ans, pour un prix d'à peine 2 % supérieur aux devis initiaux malgré un délai de cinq ans entre le concours et la réalisation, ce terminal est un véritable festival d'ingénierie qui remplit néanmoins son rôle architectural. Comme de nombreuses constructions récentes au Japon, il représente aussi à sa façon une affirmation de la fierté d'appartenance locale, un peu comme Reihoku. Les jeunes associés de FOA ont remporté le concours et se sont vu remettre les clés de la ville sans plus de manières. Ils ont bien supporté cette responsabilité et ont montré à quel point la qualité architecturale peut se révéler «utile» dans les circonstances économiques difficiles du moment. Alors qu'une construction plus banale n'aurait pas attiré l'attention sur Yokohama, FOA a propulsé ce port au centre de l'attention des spécialistes, mais aussi de celle de la population locale, fière d'arpenter cette nouvelle jetée.

Pour un architecte britannique, peu de défis étaient aussi tentants que de créer l'immeuble-symbole de la municipalité londonienne. De plus, situé sur la rive sud de la Tamise, le nouveau siège de la Greater London Authority (GLA), le «City Hall», était l'élément central d'un ambitieux projet de rénovation urbaine, dans les perspectives de la tour de Londres et de la nouvelle Tate Modern. Lord Norman Foster, aujourd'hui l'un des architectes londoniens les plus célèbres, a relevé le gant avec son panache habituel. Il a imaginé une sphère déformée recouverte de pas moins de 3 844 panneaux de verre de formes différentes. L'intérêt ancien de Foster pour la conception environnementale atteint ici de nouveaux sommets, l'immeuble consommant moins d'un quart de l'énergie de ce qu'une solution conventionnelle aurait entraîné. L'une des explications de cette réussite est la forme du bâtiment, qui représente une surface de 25% inférieure à ce qu'aurait représenté un cube de même volume, par exemple, ce qui permet de réduire les pertes et les gains de chaleur. L'eau phréatique, tirée d'un puits de 125 mètres de profondeur creusé sous l'immeuble, circule dans les poutres des plafonds pour rafraîchir naturellement les bureaux. Aussi ouvert au public quand les consignes de sécurité le permettent, le GLA est un véritable exercice de transparence et de responsabilité, deux valeurs hautement symboliques pour l'administration municipale. Toujours aussi inspiré par la technologie, Norman Foster a ainsi proposé un projet dont la forme est presque entièrement dictée par des objectifs écologiques ambitieux. En collaboration avec les ingénieurs d'Arup, il s'est appuyé sur des outils de conception et de production assistées par ordinateur, même s'il fait remarquer qu'il reste un membre convaincu de la «vieille école» et montre qu'il peut dessiner bien plus vite avec un crayon qu'avec une souris. Animant une énorme équipe de près de 600 personnes dans sa spacieuse agence au bord de la Tamise, Foster est peut-être davantage devenu un imprésario qu'un architecte au sens traditionnel du terme. Il donne une impulsion aux projets et détermine leur forme avec assurance, tandis que ses assistants développent et intègrent les plus récentes avancées technologiques.

Depuis le début des années 1970, aucun visiteur de New York ne pouvait ignorer la présence monumentale des fameuses Twin Towers du World Trade Center dans le quartier financier du bas de Manhattan, conçues, entre autres, par Minoru Yamasaki. Elles ne marquaient pas tant les esprits par leur originalité architecturale que par leur gigantisme et leur gémellité. Sous le contrôle de diverses agences publiques comme la New York Port Authority, le World Trade Center contenait essentiellement des bureaux privés. Il représentait un symbole de la grande métropole mais aussi de l'économie américaine et des États-Unis dans leur ensemble. C'est probablement la même analyse qui a conduit à sa destruction. Le problème de la reconstruction fut soulevé, une fois le difficile nettoyage du site suffisamment avancé. Le contexte politique et économique de New York ne permettait sans doute pas d'éviter qu'un site aussi prestigieux ne soit de nouveau rendu à une configuration de bureaux, aussi rentable que possible. Cependant, la blessure infligée à l'Amérique le 11 septembre 2001 était si profonde que l'opinion publique demandait quelque chose de plus durable. Elle souhaitait un monument aux 3 000 morts et un rappel de ces deux massives tours rectangulaires. Après une première consultation d'architectes dont les projets furent rejetés par le public, il faut féliciter les autorités publiques d'avoir convié à un second concours quelques-uns des architectes les plus célèbres du monde. Certains se regroupèrent en partenariat, comme « Think » (Rafael Viñoly et Shigeru Ban), ou « United Architects » (Greg Lynn, Ben van Berkel et Kevin Kennen). L'agence Skidmore Owings & Merrill, symbole de l'architecture de la grande époque américaine, fit appel à Michael Maltzan et d'autres pour renforcer ses équipes, tandis que Richard Meier, Peter Eisenman, Charles Gwathmey et Steven Holl présentèrent un projet commun. Norman Foster et Daniel Libeskind soumirent chacun leurs propres propositions, et après de nombreux débats et discussions, c'est ce dernier qui fut retenu. Né à Lodz, en Pologne, en 1946, Libeskind est l'auteur du Musée juif de Berlin et, plus récemment, de l'Imperial War Museum North (Manchester, Angleterre, 2000–2002). Au moyen de formes à facettes et d'une tour vertigineuse, sa proposition a su faire les concessions nécessaires aux sensibilités new-yorkaises et américaines, tout en laissant la place à un lieu de mémoire au centre du cratère et en rassurant les promoteurs et les financiers dont le rôle est si important à New York. Il reste à voir si ces puissants groupes de pression ne viendront pas à bout de l'architecte et ne le forceront pas à rentrer dans le rang et à édulcorer la créativité de son projet. La victoire de Libeskind reste néanmoins celle de l'architecture. Quelle que soit la forme finale du nouveau World Trade Center, sur cet emplacement si important pour l'Amérique contemporaine, on a décidé de confier le futur à un homme d'une vitalité conceptuelle évidente. Qu'il ait passé une bonne partie de sa vie professionnelle à réfléchir aux effets désastreux de la guerre et de la destruction a certainement joué un rôle dans sa victoire, mais dans ce cas précis, les États-Unis ont formellement et finalement reconnu qu'une architecture de qualité était la seule voie possible pour rendre hommage aux disparus et redonner confiance à ce lieu et à cette ville. Certains ont déclaré que les monuments relevaient de l'histoire, et le modernisme lui-même ne s'y est jamais vraiment intéressé. Mais de quelle autre façon pourrions-nous nous souvenir du passé et apprendre de lui qu'en édifiant des monuments destinés à durer ? Ce sont des signes sur le chemin de l'avenir, et une confirmation de la redécouverte de l'importance de l'architecture.

## VOUS VOULEZ VOIR MON LABEL ?

Les grandes entreprises font de plus en plus souvent appel à des architectes créatifs, ou du moins célèbres, pour concevoir leur siège ou leur showroom. C'est l'une des tendances les plus stimulantes de l'architecture récente. Nulle part ce phénomène n'est plus marqué que dans le quartier commercial d'Omotesando à Tokyo. Déjà terre d'élection d'un certain nombre de réalisations éminentes comme le Collezione de Tadao Ando (1987–1989), ou la rénovation plus récente du magasin Comme des garçons par Rei Kawakubo en collaboration avec Future Systems, Omotesando est devenu une étape essentielle pour tous les amateurs d'architecture contemporaine. Dans la même section de la rue que les boutiques déjà citées, l'immeuble Prada par Herzog & de Meuron, ouvert au public en juin 2003, a déjà attiré sur lui l'attention des médias. Cette construction de six niveaux, dont le coût annoncé varie entre 80 et 140 millions de dollars, se caractérise par d'étranges fenêtres qui semblent tantôt soufflées de l'intérieur tantôt aspirées. Les plafonds en métal perforé ou la peau en vraie mousse verte sur une partie de la façade surprennent. Un plancher de chêne brut, comme à la Tate Modern, constitue le sol du rez-de-chaussée tandis que des escaliers en acier laqué et des moquettes ivoire accueillent la foule des acheteuses impatientes aux autres étages. Un mélange de surfaces de traitement organique ou d'esprit volontairement industriel (présentoirs en peau de poney ou en silicone) met en scène ces surprises imaginées par les architectes en accord avec un client qui s'intéresse à l'évidence à l'architecture contemporaine.

Deux ou trois cent mètres plus bas, toujours dans le quartier de Minamio Aoyama, l'architecte Jun Aoki a conçu un énorme magasin pour Louis Vuitton. Cette structure en forme de pile de bagages qui ont rendu la maison française si célèbre, est particulièrement étonnante pour ses façades en métal tissé, acier inox et verre. L'alternance d'opacité et de transparence, et les effets changeants de la lumière à travers ces écrans immenses, en font certainement l'une des interprétations modernes les plus réussies de la tradition japonaise. Les aménagements intérieurs sont signés de l'équipe interne de Vuitton. Ici, comme pour Prada, on peut se poser la question de la relation entre les produits vendus et l'architecture, mais il s'agit en réalité de vitrines qui veulent donner un sens de modernité à des vêtements et des accessoires qui ne sont pas toujours aussi modernes que l'on voudrait le faire croire au public. Presque en face de celui de Louis Vuitton, un immeuble LVMH vient d'être récemment achevé par Kengo Kuma. Sa conception très différente ne cherche pas à établir de liens avec les marques du groupe. Quelle que soit la qualité de l'architecture, on peut d'ailleurs se demander si un jour les clients ne seront pas saturés par ces stratégies d'omniprésence de la marque. Dans le même temps, les amateurs d'architecture peuvent se féliciter que le secteur de la mode essaye de se conférer une permanence qui dépasse celle qui est concrètement la sienne

Le secteur bancaire n'a pas grand chose à voir avec Gucci et Prada, mais les professions financières cherchent également à affirmer leur présence, pourtant déjà très évidente. Les banques ont généralement opté pour une élégance classique, souvent inspirée des modèles des temples. Curieusement, elles manifestent aussi un certain goût pour l'imagerie funéraire, comme si la mort et les taux d'intérêt entretenaient quelques liens invisibles (l'inévitabilité ?). Quoi qu'il en soit, dans l'immeuble de la Caja General à Grenade, Alberto Campo Baeza marie une élégance minimaliste à une massivité résolument mortuaire. Avec son « impluvium de lumière » et ses murs translucides en albâtre de Saragosse, cet immeuble déborde de références à la Rome impériale. Sa monumentalité même peut surprendre les habitués de la réserve moderniste, mais l'Espagne, pays de l'Escurial, pratique souvent ce mariage de la pierre et de la mort. Tout en se ralliant au courant minimaliste, la Caja General évoque la grandeur romaine dans un mélange étrange mais qui nous parle. La référence au passé – et pas seulement en façade – refait surface. L'art ou l'architecture ont toujours trouvé leur inspiration dans le passé, et peu d'époques ont vécu un rejet aussi déterminé de la tradition que celui du modernisme à ses débuts. Si des architectes comme Michael Graves ou Robert A. M. Stern ne s'étaient pas malheureusement approprié le terme dans les années 1970, on pourrait affirmer que le début du XXIe siècle est décidément postmoderne, comme en témoigne la banque de Grenade.

Jadis, les grandes entreprises étaient attachées à un modèle anonyme d'immeuble de bureaux inspiré des tendances récentes de l'architecture mais qui évitait soigneusement tout effet de surprise ou de curiosité. Plus récemment, certaines ont décidé de prendre le risque de faire confiance à des architectes plus jeunes, recherchés aujourd'hui par les firmes soucieuses de manifester leur attachement à la culture de notre temps. Ainsi le puissant groupe ING a choisi l'agence Meyer en Van Schooten pour édifier son nouveau siège amstellodamois. Visuellement, très proche de l'imagerie de films comme *La Guerre des étoiles*, cet immeuble dressé sur ses pilotis en V donne l'impression d'être prêt à partir au galop, en tirant de tous ses canons laser sur ses débiteurs impécunieux. Toute impression d'extravagance disparaît cependant dans les plans de l'immeuble. D'esprit environnemental, cette structure veut durer « 50 ou 100 ans », ce qui est pratiquement un défi pour beaucoup de réalisations actuelles. Il reste bien sûr à vérifier si cette longévité est une espérance raisonnable, mais en investissant dans de jeunes praticiens (les deux architectes n'avaient pas encore atteint 45 ans au moment des plans), ING parie sans doute que leur esthétique ne se démodera pas aussi rapidement que celle de confrères plus confirmés et plus âgés. Grâce en partie à la présence de personnalités inter-nationales, dont Rem Koolhaas, les Pays-Bas ont depuis longtemps intégré l'idée de l'architecture contemporaine, alors que des pays moins touchés par les destructions de la Seconde Guerre mondiale, comme la France, éprouvent encore des difficultés à s'y ouvrir autant.

Aux Pays-Bas également, Kas Oosterhuis, adepte d'un travail de conception par ordinateur encore plus avant-gardiste, a cependant trouvé des clients parmi de grandes entreprises. Son projet « Cockpit » consiste en une barrière acoustique de 1,5 kilomètre de long sur l'au-toroute A2 et en un bâtiment industriel de 5 000 m². La barrière est une structure conçue pour être vue et décryptée par des automobilistes se déplaçant à 120 Km/h sur l'autoroute. Le showroom, situé derrière elle, lui est en fait intégré. Oosterhuis présente cette réalisation comme une « cathédrale pour voitures ». L'entreprise vend des Rolls-Royce, des Bentley, des Lamborghini et des Maserati. Un atelier et un garage sont insérés sous le hall d'exposition. Sans être à l'échelle d'ING ni au même niveau d'image institutionnelle, ce projet montre qu'au moins aux Pays-Bas, la conscience de la valeur d'une architecture « de qualité » a réussi, via les entreprises, à s'intégrer à la vie quotidienne.

Ce phénomène ne se réduit pas à une Europe du Nord particulièrement sensible à l'esthétique et à l'environnement. En Malaisie, l'ar-chitecte Ken Yeang a réussi à convaincre des clients comme IBM que l'on peut construire des immeubles « verts » qui améliorent l'image de leurs commanditaires auprès de l'opinion publique et peuvent même favoriser les ventes. Il achève actuellement le siège social d'une société de Singapour spécialisée dans l'huile de palme et les produits gras. Pour une hauteur totale de 34 mètres, le programme comprend quatre niveaux de bureaux, quatre autres pour le conditionnement et un volume de 32 mètres de haut réservé à un entrepôt automatisé. Comme le souligne Yeang : « Ce qui aurait pu n'être qu'un banal immeuble d'activités industrielles est devenu un ‹ poumon vert › écologique qui améliore les conditions de vie de ses utilisateurs et la biomasse du site. »

### DISPARU EN UN CLIN D'ŒIL

Si les grandes entreprises, en particulier celles du domaine éphémère de la mode, sont à la recherche des valeurs plus « permanentes » d'une architecture de qualité, de bonnes raisons militent également en faveur de l'application du *Good Design* à des événements temporaires par nature. Un peu comme les grandes institutions, les organisateurs d'expositions universelles ou nationales ont souvent recherché des solu-tions « pratiques » pour leurs pavillons éphémères. Mais une architecture banale n'attire pas les foules. Bien qu'ils aient été globalement criti-qués pour l'ampleur de leurs dépenses, les organisateurs de l'Expo nationale suisse 02 n'ont pas caché leur souhait d'attirer les meilleurs architectes du monde pour concrétiser des projets prévus sur des jetées provisoires en bordure des lacs de Neuchâtel et de Morat. Jean Nou-vel a été chargé de Morat. Il a imaginé un monolithe en acier rouillé amarré à quelques encablures de la rive et que l'on ne pouvait manquer de voir. À l'aide de tentes, de conteneurs et d'éléments de camouflage militaire, il a « occupé » la petite ville de Morat d'une façon et d'un sty-le plus proches de l'art de l'installation que de l'architecture. Une autre construction étonnante, occupée par la Fondation Cartier, se compo-sait d'un empilement de rondins. Par sa référence à un mode de construction traditionnel, elle était peut être plus en rapport avec le contexte suisse que certains autres éléments de l'Expo.02. Une autre intervention remarquable était celle de COOP HIMMELB(L)AU à Biel. Leur plate-forme artificielle de 16 000 m² environ était suspendue à quatre mètres au-dessus de la surface du lac. Les structures théoriquement réutilisables étaient recouvertes de plusieurs couches de projections de zinc comme « une sorte de trame mince étirée sur un cadre et glissé comme un panneau ». Les architectes présentaient ainsi leur projet : « Le site de la grande exposition est conçu comme une plate-forme couverte jetée audessus du lac, et s'achevant par un volume doté de trois tours. Sa ressemblance avec un avion de transport n'est pas une coïncidence mais un effet voulu. Sous le toit de la plate-forme, toutes sortes d'utilisations sont possibles y compris l'installation de pavillons d'exposition, exactement comme des immeubles dans une ville. » Apparemment assez massives vues de loin, ces constructions accessibles grâce à une passerelle de 413 mètres de long étaient en fait légères et aériennes. Dans cette combinaison intéressante de monumentalité apparente et d'extrême légèreté, les tours de 35 et 39 mètres de haut n'avaient pas de fonction précise en dehors de celle de signal. Une autre participation très remarquée était signée des New-yorkais Diller + Scofidio. Leur Blur Building se proposait tout simplement de ressembler à un nuage en arrêt au-dessus du lac de Neuchâtel. De 100 m de large, 60 de profondeur et 25 de haut, cet effet de « nuage » était obtenu par la production d'une « fine brume générée par un réseau de 31 500 buses haute-pression intégrées à une grande ossature en porte-à-faux et tenségrité ». L'eau était celle du lac, filtrée bien sûr. Lorsque les conditions météorologiques le permettaient, l'effet obtenu était exactement celui imaginé. Leur propos était de faire disparaître leur architecture, aussi légère qu'un cumulus, et de susciter une sorte de privation sensorielle pour que les visiteurs perdent toute notion d'espace ou de temps « réels ». Si Nouvel a été « artistique » dans son approche d'Expo.02 et si COOP HIMMELB(L)AU a remis en cause la solidité du monumental, la proposition de Diller + Scofidio fut de loin la plus radicale, car elle osait remettre en question la nature même de la forme construite. Beaucoup de visiteurs ont pensé qu'ils avaient résolu la quadrature d'une architecture de foire par nature éphémère. Quoi de plus éphémère en effet qu'un nuage ?

Londres, surtout connu pour sa monumentalité impériale qui date du XIXe siècle, a été le site d'un certain nombre d'expériences intéressantes dans le domaine de l'architecture temporaire. Le Serpentine Pavilion, dans les jardins de Kensington, a financé pour la quatrième fois des pavillons d'été éphémères conçus par quelques grands noms comme Zaha Hadid (2000), Daniel Libeskind (2001), Toyo Ito (2002) et le vénérable Oscar Niemeyer (2003). Alors que Niemeyer a cherché à résumer ses idées sur le lyrisme de l'architecture en béton, Ito s'est aventuré dans un territoire plus inattendu avec une structure apparemment aléatoire déterminée par un algorithme dérivé de la rotation d'un carré. Ces expérimentations coûteuses pour un petit musée, ont néanmoins démontré le considérable pouvoir d'attraction de grands architectes et montré que même lorsqu'ils travaillent à petite échelle sur des structures temporaires, ceux-ci peuvent s'approcher d'une forme d'expression authentiquement artistique.

Les rapports entre l'art et l'architecture ont été brouillés une fois de plus par l'étonnante installation du sculpteur Anish Kapoor à la Tate Modern de Londres. Son *Marsyas* composé de trois anneaux d'acier réunis par une membrane de PVC rouge s'étirait sur les 155 mètres du Hall de la turbine. Cette pièce – visible dans son intégralité d'un point unique –, remettait en cause les perceptions conventionnelles de l'espace et de l'architecture. Le plein et le vide, éléments standard de toute architecture, alternaient dans un flux continu, sans frontière visible. En fait, ce jeu énigmatique sur l'espace n'était en rien contradictoire avec le travail de Herzog & de Meuron sur la Tate Modern elle-même. Leur approche consiste en effet souvent à brouiller les limites entre le reflet et la vision directe, par exemple, ou plus fréquemment encore le poids et la légèreté. Le sculpteur américain Richard Serra a noté avec pertinence que « la différence entre l'art et l'architecture est que l'architecture répond à un objectif ». S'il ne convient peut-être pas de qualifier *Marsyas* d'œuvre d'architecture, elle traite néanmoins avec beaucoup d'habileté les perceptions de l'espace, de la lumière et de la couleur, et reconfigure le hall de la turbine d'une façon qu'aucune œuvre d'art n'avait approché jusqu'alors. Ce n'est peut-être pas de l'architecture, mais cette sculpture contribue à faire regarder l'espace et le volume d'un œil nouveau.

Vito Acconci a longtemps œuvré à la frontière de l'art et de l'architecture, et a collaboré à des projets remarquables comme le Storefront for Art and Architecture de Steven Holl à New York. Son projet d'île sur la Mur à Graz, en Autriche, relève certainement davantage de l'architecture que de l'art, et pourtant la forme et l'espace s'y trouvent reconfigurés avec autant de maîtrise que Kapoor à la Tate Modern. Les journaux locaux ont jugé cette « place de ville future » au bord de la rivière de la Mur « en contradiction totale avec l'architecture baroque et médiévale » de cette ville, « capitale culturelle de l'Europe » en 2003. Graz a également édifié une nouvelle Kunsthaus tout aussi futuriste conçue par Peter Cook et Colin Fournier, et qualifiée « d'aimable extra-terrestre ». Moins éphémère sans doute que l'île artificielle d'Acconci, cette Kunsthaus semble venue d'une autre planète.

Faisant appel à un genre dont les racines remontent au moins au XVIIIe siècle, I. M. Pei, auteur de la Pyramide du Louvre et de l'East Building de la National Gallery de Washington, vient d'achever un pavillon de thé dans un jardin anglais. Faisant appel à des formes qu'il avait déjà employées pour le musée de Miho (Shigaraki, Shiga, Japon), il a créé un pavillon résolument moderne pour Oare House, résidence de la famille Keswick dans le Wiltshire. Pei n'est certainement pas connu pour ses projets éphémères, et il se peut que ce petit pavillon dure plus longtemps que certains immeubles grandioses, mais ce type même de construction implique par sa nature même une légèreté confirmée par sa conception particulière. Attaché à ses origines chinoises comme à la richesse historique du Louvre, Pei a longtemps manifesté son respect pour la tradition. Pour Oare House, il a réussi une fois de plus à réunir harmonieusement le passé et le présent. Le très ancien combat entre le modernisme et la tradition est dépassé. En Europe en particulier, que ce soit sur les rives de la Mur ou dans un parc anglais, l'architecture d'aujourd'hui s'intègre, sans manque de respect ni rejet des précédents.

## LA CONSOMMATION DE LA CULTURE

Comme c'est le cas depuis de nombreuses années, un des champs d'intervention privilégiés de l'architecture de qualité reste le domaine de la culture. Bien qu'aux États-Unis comme ailleurs de grandioses projets de nouveaux musées aient été abandonnés, d'autres types d'équipements culturels comme les salles de concerts se sont multipliés. Si le Los Angeles County Museum a abandonné ses ambitieux plans de reconstruction sous la houlette de Rem Koolhaas, la ville a enfin achevé le Disney Concert Hall, première commande publique d'importance de Frank Gehry dans sa ville de résidence. Les plans très publicisés pour le Guggenheim de Downtown à New York ont sombré, mais l'architecte a terminé le très réussi Center for the Performing Arts de Bard College dans l'État de New York. Disney et Bard ont recours aux mêmes ondulantes métalliques qui ont assuré la célébrité du Guggenheim de Bilbao, mais représentent cependant une nouvelle étape de sa réussite. S'il n'est pas certain que beaucoup d'architectes soient prêts à suivre ses traces, Gehry a fait plus que n'importe qui pour libérer sa profession. Ses vagues de titane ont affirmé la liberté artistique et le statut de l'architecte. Ceci aide des praticiens plus jeunes à rechercher des formes nouvelles, même s'ils n'adhèrent pas aux choix esthétiques du maître.

Le choix de Zaha Hadid pour le Lois & Richard Rosenthal Center for Contemporary Art à Cincinnati a-t-il quelque rapport avec les triomphes de Gehry ? Une ville comme Cincinnati aurait sans doute bien besoin de la publicité dont a bénéficié Bilbao. Très connue des cercles architecturaux pour ses dessins et ses projets radicaux, Zaha Hadid semble entrer aujourd'hui dans une phase nouvelle de sa carrière qui voit affluer les projets majeurs. Première femme à édifier un musée en Amérique – elle est donc aussi une pionnière à cet égard –, elle montre à Cincinnati que son mode de dessin exubérant est concrètement réalisable et que l'art et l'architecture d'aujourd'hui peuvent fusionner, y compris dans la ville qui voulait censurer l'œuvre de Robert Mapplethorpe il y a quelques années.

Peut-être moins radicale dans ses choix architecturaux, la ville de Fort Worth a récemment inauguré son nouveau Museum of Modern Art, œuvre de l'architecte japonais Tadao Ando. Situé sur un site rendu sensible par sa proximité avec le légendaire Kimbell Museum de Louis Kahn, le musée d'Ando est aussi rigoureusement géométrique que l'on pouvait s'y attendre. Très éloigné des petites chapelles ou maisons qui ont fait la réputation de l'architecte au Japon, il est plus proche du Ando massif du musée de la préfecture de Hyogo récemment achevé sur le front de mer de Kobe, la ville ravagée par un tremblement de terre en 1995. Ando, qui exerce une importante influence sur les étudiants en architecture du monde entier, a insufflé la vie dans ce qui peut sembler à première vue une architecture rigide. En fait, la lumière, l'eau et l'espace qui se déploient dans et autour des bâtiments en font une sorte d'ode intemporelle au construit plus qu'une manifestation rétrograde de modernisme classique.

Les contraintes économiques expliquent que d'ambitieux projets d'équipements culturels cèdent parfois le pas à des restructurations approfondies, comme celle menée par l'agence Ellis Williams pour le Baltic Centre for Contemporary Arts (Newcastle, Écosse, 1999–2002). L'architecte Dominic Williams a converti une ancienne minoterie en un espace d'exposition de 8 537 m² consacré aux formes artistiques les plus actuelles. Par ses dimensions, ce type de bâtiment abandonné offre des opportunités exceptionnelles à l'art actuel. Comme Williams l'écrit : « L'objectif principal est de permettre à l'art contemporain de se produire, sous quelque forme que ce soit. Souvent, les installations artistiques prennent le dessus ou pervertissent la nature de l'espace qu'elles occupent. La fonction originale de ce bâtiment était la collecte, la conservation et la distribution de la farine par des processus invisibles de l'extérieur. À de nombreux égards ces activités seront identiques, le bâtiment étant réorienté sur une autre fonction. Les œuvres arriveront, seront créées et voyageront d'un lieu à l'autre, la fonction, moins secrète, restant toujours abritée derrière ces murs aveugles. Des éléments comme les sols des galeries, le café et la bibliothèque sont insérés entre les deux murs pour créer un organisme vivant et nouveau à l'intérieur du bâtiment. »

Dans le même but, deux projets de l'agglomération new-yorkaise réutilisent d'anciens bâtiments industriels. Le premier est en fait directement lié à une autre transformation architecturale majeure – la reconstruction du Museum of Modern Art par l'architecte tokyoïte Yoshio Taniguchi. Pendant les travaux en cours à Manhattan, il a été décidé de trouver un abri temporaire pour le MoMA à Long Island City (Queens) de l'autre côté du fleuve. Une ancienne usine a été transformée par l'architecte californien Michael Maltzan: « Re-imaginer une installation établie ‹déménageant› vers un site satellite, l'ancienne usine d'agrafes Seringline, revêtait une signification critique. Convaincu que cette installation temporaire ne devait pas faire ombrage au MoMA de Manhattan, en cours de réflexion, nous avons plutôt regardé du côté du contexte compliqué du project ainsi que l'expérience du mouvement dans la création d'une identité pour ce MoMAQNS. C'est manifeste lorsque le visiteur découvre la séquence pogressive d'éléments qui débute par la signalétique très ostensible du toit et se poursuit par une succession d'espaces en expansion ou en contraction, et un parcours qui culmine dans les galeries. »

À une échelle encore plus ambitieuse, la création de Dia : Beacon, dans une ancienne papeterie du nord de l'État de New York, a été l'occasion d'une collaboration exceptionnelle entre un artiste majeur, Robert Irwin, une jeune agence, OpenOffice, et la Dia Foundation elle-même, représentée par son président Michael Govan. Avec ses 24 000 m² de galeries d'exposition et la possibilité de consacrer une galerie à chaque artiste exposé, cette rénovation qui illustre une rencontre entre des artistes, des architectes et des représentants d'institutions d'esprit ouvert, illustre les possibilités offertes par la conjonction de bâtiments anciens et de l'art contemporain. La demande de « qualité » en architecture a fini par être acceptée par le monde de l'art, que ce soit en rénovation, comme dans les exemples précédents, ou à l'occasion de constructions nouvelles comme à Fort Worth ou Cincinnati.

Le besoin d'un rapprochement fructueux entre architecture, artistes et culture se ressent dans le monde entier et s'exprime même dans des cas où les contraintes budgétaires sont déterminantes. En 1997, Herzog & de Meuron ont remporté le concours international pour la construction du nouveau Laban Dance Centre, pour un budget réduit de 14,4 millions de livres sterling. Sur un terrain de près d'un hectare près de Deptford Creek dans le sud-est de Londres, le bâtiment a créé « concentration d'attention spectaculaire sur la rénovation physique et sociale en cours de Deptford et dans ses envirous ». L'artiste Michael Craig-Martin a collaboré avec les architectes sur le projet décoratif extérieur et une partie des aménagements intérieurs. Le recours à du polycarbonate de couleur pour une partie des façades répond à la fois à des contraintes budgétaires et à la volonté de donner au bâtiment une présence animée et même joyeuse dans un environnement assez difficile.

Bien qu'il n'ait pas été soumis à des contraintes économiques aussi rigoureuses, le défi lancé à Renzo Piano par sa dernière adjonction à la célèbre usine FIAT du Lingotto n'était pas mince. Sa Galerie d'art Giovanni et Marella Agnelli, comparée à un « coffre-fort volant » posé sur la fameuse piste d'essai en toiture, recèle 25 œuvres précieuses choisies avec soin. De même que les précédentes additions antérieures de l'architecte à ce complexe – une salle de conférence en forme de bulle et une plate-forme pour hélicoptère – le musée des Agnelli impose sa présence curieuse qui fait penser à une soucoupe volante. À en juger par les 100 000 visiteurs qui s'y sont rendus au cours de la première année d'exploitation, cette curiosité architecturale semble remplir son rôle. Elle participe également à cet énorme chantier ouvert que constitue le retour à la vie de cette immense usine.

L'affirmation du rôle de l'architecture dans le contexte de la culture se poursuit au-delà de l'Europe de l'Ouest et de l'Amérique du Nord, comme le montre le récent concours pour le quartier de la Nouvelle-Hollande et du Mariinsky à Saint-Pétersbourg. Si cette compétition avait été remportée au départ par l'architecte californien Eric Owen Moss et le promoteur Samitaur Constructs, c'est finalement le Français Dominique Perrault qui a été sélectionné pour le nouveau théâtre Mariinsky. Moss est cependant resté en jeu, puisque sa victoire a été confirmée pour les projets de la Nouvelle-Hollande qui incluent également un théâtre. De grandes controverses ont entouré ces projets dans une ville qui n'est pas habituée à l'architecture vraiment contemporaine, mais comme Moss l'a déclaré au cours des discussions : « Avec la Nouvelle-Hollande et le Mariinsky, Saint-Pétersbourg, une des grandes villes du monde au caractère et au passé culturel uniques, inaugure une nouvelle tradition de l'opéra, du ballet, de la musique et de l'architecture qui transcendera le XXIe siècle. » Avec le concours d'architectes aussi créatifs que Dominique Perrault et Eric Owen Moss dans une ville marquée par la tradition, il est certain que le mariage des différentes formes d'expression artistique évoquées par Moss prendra une nouvelle réalité.

## L'INGÉNIERIE DE LA VIE QUOTIDIENNE

L'habitat fait partie des besoins actuels les plus pressants auxquels doit répondre l'architecture. De la rencontre entre un client éclairé et un architecte de talent, peut naître une avancée architecturale qui influencera l'esthétique et la vie quotidienne pendant des années. Les résidences publiées ici sont précisément choisies pour les innovations et les progrès qu'elles représentent. L'architecte David Adjaye s'est acquis une certaine réputation à Londres, peut-être parce qu'il a eu la chance de voir un certain nombre de ses clients devenir célèbres après qu'il ait travaillé pour eux. Dans l'est de Londres, il a converti un entrepôt des années 1930 en maison pour les artistes Tim Noble et Sue Webster. L'East London n'est pas réputé pour le luxe de son habitat, ce qui ne gênait ni l'architecte ni ses clients. Dans son utilisation radicale de l'espace, de la lumière et des surfaces, la Dirty House répond au site d'une façon adaptée à une ville qui sait apprécier la beauté dans les environnements industriels. De même que New York a progressivement reconquis les anciens quartiers d'entrepôts de Downtown, comme Soho puis Tribeca, l'East End londonien est plus à la mode qu'il ne l'a jamais été. C'est en un sens une application de la façon dont l'art se sert des matériaux quotidiens et même des déchets comme les clients d'Adjaye. Brut et concret, le style Adjaye est à la mode, tout à fait dans l'esprit de l'époque.

La Glass Shutter House (maison à volet de verre) de Shigeru Ban à Tokyo est tout autre. Située dans un quartier relativement élégant de la capitale japonaise, c'est une combinaison de maison et de restaurant conçue pour un chef japonais très connu. Ban est de son côté réputé pour ses recherches sur la flexibilité en architecture, à la fois dans ses choix de matériaux, dont le papier, et dans son désir de remettre en question des éléments fondamentaux comme le mur. Dans cette maison, le propriétaire peut entièrement faire disparaître deux des murs, qui s'enroulent dans le toit. C'est particulièrement pratique en été pour ouvrir le restaurant sur la terrasse, mais c'est surtout une solution inventive en termes de matérialité même de l'architecture.

C'est une attitude ouverte envers l'architecture récente (c'est-à-dire qui exclut tout rejet pour des raisons stylistiques) qui a contribué à la redécouverte d'un certain nombre de réalisations des débuts du modernisme. Un exemple inhabituel de restauration menée dans cet esprit est la Charles Deaton Sculpture House (Genesee Mountain, Golden, Colorado, 1963–1965/2000). Deaton, architecte autodidacte, a conçu cette maison en 1963 en pensant à une « sculpture à vivre ». Il décrivait ainsi son projet : « Au départ, j'ai senti que la forme devait être suffisamment puissante et simple pour être installée dans un musée, comme une œuvre d'art. Agrandie à la taille d'une maison, elle pouvait se subdiviser en zones à vivre. Je savais, bien sûr, en commençant qu'elle serait par la suite développée en maison. Ce n'était cependant pas une simple tentative d'envelopper un plan au sol dans une coquille. En fait, son échelle n'a pas été déterminée avant que la sculpture ne soit achevée. Le plan suit le modelé et les contours à distance respectable. » Présence indéniable et implantation spectaculaire mises à part, les idées qui président à cette maison ne semblent pas très éloignées de l'approche sculpturale d'un Frank Gehry, par exemple. Radical à de multiples égards, le modernisme peut certainement demeurer une source d'inspiration pour une architecture contemporaine qui s'est ouverte au passé en général.

La Glaphyros House, un appartement de 320 m² près des jardins du Luxembourg à Paris, est remarquable pour la façon dont ses aménagements sur mesure ont massivement fait appel à la CAO. Conçue par Mark Goulthorpe de dECOi, cet appartement en rez-de-chaussée dans un immeuble des années 1960, a été réalisé pour un client qui souhaitait «une architecture à la fois minimaliste et sensuelle…» recourant à ce qu'il appelle une «logique non standard». L'architecte a pratiquement conçu tous les détails spécifiques du projet. Un escalier de béton qui conduit aux chambres du bas a été créé grâce à un modèle paramétrique renversé en plan et en coupe. «L'effet de soulèvement qui en résulte», fait remarquer Goulthorpe, «anime ce volume réduit, comme si une source d'énergie autre venait troubler la simplicité de l'héritage moderniste. La niche sous l'escalier semble déformée par une mystérieuse force tellurique, suggérant des évocations animistes.» Ce type de déformation des surfaces et des volumes se retrouve dans tout l'appartement. «En tant qu'exercice approfondi de production non standardisée, le projet remet en cause la logique du préfabriqué inhérente à la production industrielle, et suggère un vocabulaire formel beaucoup plus riche libéré par la numérisation», conclut Mark Goulthorpe. En fait le travail sur ordinateur réalisé ici peut sembler à peine visible à un regard non formé, et, en un sens, c'est précisément ce qui le rend remarquable. La conception numérique, appuyée sur une modélisation paramétrique, a commencé à exercer un réel impact sur l'architecture, et les formes issues de cette tendance ne sont pas nécessairement ces *blobs* extravagants auxquels certains nous ont déjà habitués. L'ordinateur a pénétré la logique quotidienne de l'architecture et peut intervenir de la conception à la réalisation finale.

Bien qu'elle ne soit pas aussi radicale dans son approche de conception/réalisation, la maison Natural Ellipse conçue par Masaki Endoh à Tokyo est exemplaire du type d'inventivité que les Japonais sont prêts à accepter. Implantée à Shibuya, un quartier très densément urbanisé de la capitale, elle occupe un terrain de 53 m². Construite à partir de 24 anneaux d'acier de forme elliptique, elle est revêtue de FRP (polymère renforcé de fibres) qui lui donne un aspect lisse. Des matériaux modernes et une approche conceptuelle libérée peuvent permettre ces ruptures par rapport aux formes traditionnelles de la construction. En contournant le besoin de structurer sa maison sur un mode tridimensionnel classique, l'architecte a réfléchi aux problèmes posés par un terrain minuscule et la sensation de claustrophobie qui pouvait en résulter.

Un autre architecte japonais s'est montré tout aussi inventif que Shigeru Ban ou Masaki Endoh, mais sur un mode différent. Il s'agit de Kengo Kuma pour le petit hôtel de la «Grande muraille de bambou», édifié près de Pékin sur un terrain de 1930 m² et pour une surface totale de 528 m². L'usage extensif de verre et de murs de bambou, de grandes ouvertures protégées par des écrans en perches de bambou espacées, et un habillage de piliers, toujours en bambou, crée une impression de légèreté et un sentiment de parenté avec l'architecture traditionnelle asiatique. Kuma atteint ici une simplicité et une modernité plus en rapport cependant avec les tendances les plus récentes de l'architecture qu'avec celles d'un passé ancien. Il précise au sujet du bambou : «Peau et surface extérieures sont différentes. Le béton possède une surface, pas une peau. De plus, je ne trouve pas le béton particulièrement séduisant. Quand il n'y a pas de peau, l'âme est absente. Le bambou possède précisément une peau magnifique. Et il a une âme en lui. Un célèbre conte japonais pour enfants parle de la Princesse Kakuyahime, déesse de la lune, née dans une âme de bambou.»

Tous les architectes ne disposent pas de matériaux aussi chargés de sens. L'inventivité n'est pas seulement une question d'équipement et de matériaux sophistiqués. La très jeune agence norvégienne Saunders & Wilhelmsen confirme cette évidence dans sa maison d'été (fjord d'Hardanger, Norvège). Construite en deux parties (respectivement de 20 et 30 m² de surface), cette très petite construction en bois locaux est isolée par du papier journal recyclé. Une terrasse extérieure habilement dessinée relie les deux volumes. Il est certain que la séduction de ce projet tient aussi beaucoup à sa proximité de l'un des plus grands et plus beaux fjords norvégiens, mais la combativité des architectes qui voulaient montrer à des clients potentiels ce qu'ils pouvaient faire est la preuve d'une vitalité qui est la vraie source de l'architecture de demain.

Les architectes ne sont pas les seuls capables de faire évoluer les formes et les conceptions. L'ingénieur Werner Sobek a imaginé sa propre « maison de verre » écologique sur une colline de Stuttgart, la Haus R-128, construite en onze semaines seulement. Des panneaux de bois préfabriqués enduits de plastique de 3,75 x 2,8 mètres simplement déposés entre les poutres du sol sans même un boulonnage et des panneaux de plafond en aluminium clipsés, permettent une grande facilité de construction et de maintenance. Des procédés techniques comme l'échangeur de chaleur posé sous les fondations pour bénéficier de la chaleur naturelle du sol et d'impressionnants panneaux à triple vitrage emplis d'un gaz inerte pour réduire les gains ou les pertes de chaleur relèvent des solutions « vertes » adoptées par Sobek. Bien que d'apparence sévère, cette maison de verre n'a pas pour autant l'aspect parfois bizarre associé à l'architecture environnementale. Sensible aux techniques, par profession d'origine, Sobek a concentré dans sa propre maison un grand nombre des leçons apprises grâce à son métier.

### RÊVER LE RÉEL

L'un des aspects sans doute les plus fascinants de l'architecture est sa capacité à rêver, et à imaginer des solutions totalement neuves, que ce soit à travers de nouvelles technologies ou une manière de pensée différente. Michael Sorkin, designer et enseignant new-yorkais, a pour métier de réfléchir à des formes communautaires qui puissent résoudre un certain nombre de problèmes dont souffre le monde moderne. Ses dessins et ses descriptifs séduisants qui reposent sur une connaissance approfondie de l'architecture et de l'urbanisme illustrent une pensée presque utopiste dont l'architecture a besoin pour survivre et avancer. À l'opposé des rêveries de Sorkin, Michael Jantzen s'est plongé dans les possibilités offertes par les nouvelles technologies. Son VRI (Interface de réalité virtuelle) est une tentative pour voir jusqu'à quel point les images de synthèse peuvent convaincre un futur propriétaire de logement. On peut imaginer, par exemple, des murs qui projettent n'importe quelle image souhaitée, en d'autres termes un environnement personnalisé variable à l'infini. S'il est difficile d'aller au-delà de l'image d'un environnement imaginaire, Jantzen poursuit néanmoins sur cette voie. Sa Video Beach House de Malibu (présentée ici) est plus proche d'une maison bien réelle qui utiliserait les écrans vidéo à foison pour projeter, par exemple, des images du monde extérieur. Dans son mobilier et sa décoration, elle générerait intentionnellement une confusion entre l'intérieur et l'extérieur, c'est-à-dire la plage.

La Son-O-House imaginée par l'architecte de Rotterdam Lars Spuybroek (NOX) est « pas une ‹ vraie › maison, mais une structure qui se réfère à la vie et aux mouvements corporels qui accompagnent les habitudes et le fait d'habiter. Dans cette maison une centrale sonore génère en continu de nouveaux motifs sonores activés par des capteurs qui enregistrent les mouvements réels des visiteurs. » En un sens, ce projet est un hommage aux rêves de Michael Jantzen. En Californie, l'environnement de la maison imaginée est purement visuel. Aux Pays-Bas, l'objectif de maison de NOX « est un paysage de mémoire évolutif qui se développe à travers le traçage des corps réel dans l'espace ». Si la Son-O-House ou la VRI ne paraissent pas vraiment « pratiques », elles indiquent néanmoins les orientations de la réflexion et le potentiel d'évolution radical que peuvent apporter les technologies nouvelles dans la conception de l'habitat.

Le rêve de vivre sous l'eau a longtemps hanté les romanciers et les architectes. En France, Jacques Rougerie cherche depuis long-temps à résoudre les problèmes d'une vie sous-marine. Aujourd'hui, l'agence de Los Angeles Office of Mobile Design a opté pour une approche plus technologique. Son Hydra-House propose des résidences en néoprène gonflables qui bénéficieraient d'une autonomie énergé-tique totale et pourraient, par exemple, dessaler elles-mêmes l'eau de mer. Relevant jadis de la science-fiction, une telle maison marine est en fait aujourd'hui possible. Comme Arverne, un récent projet urbain de Michael Sorkin, Hydra House n'est peut-être pas une solution immé-diate aux problèmes de logement de villes comme New York ou Los Angeles, mais Sorkin, et Office of Mobile Design sont les faces différentes d'une tentative de la profession architecturale pour trouver de nouvelles voies de progrès.

Beaucoup moins utopiste, le projet des « Houses at Sagaponac » est une opération immobilière de 34 maisons édifiées sur un site boi-sé de Southampton, Long Island, près de New York. L'initiateur de ce projet, Coco Brown, en collaboration avec l'architecte Richard Meier, a sélectionné une sorte de *Who's Who* de l'architecture contemporaine, confiant à chacun une maison à concevoir. Les participants – Philip Johnson, Michael Graves, James Freed, Zaha Hadid, Richard Rogers, Shigeru Nan ou Jean-Michel Wilmotte – ont été conviés à imaginer des résidences familiales de 200 à 440 m$^2$. Une utilisation de « matériaux traditionnels de la région, mais de façon actuelle, visuellement intéres-sante et dynamique » caractérise l'ensemble du projet.

Survol de l'architecture depuis 2000, cet ouvrage offre une vision globale de l'extraordinaire richesse d'une créativité libérée par une combinaison de progrès technologiques et d'ouverture conceptuelle. Nous ne sommes plus confrontés à un seul style, et là n'est plus le pro-blème. L'architecture a toujours été influencée d'abord et avant tout par des considérations pratiques. À la différence de l'art, comme le disait Richard Serra, elle est au service d'un but. Les développements les plus significatifs qui commencent à donner une forme nouvelle tiennent à la possibilité concrète d'une intégration conception-production via les ordinateurs et la robotique. Ce phénomène a déjà permis la production de composants uniques, qui bouleversent l'esthétique et la logique profonde de près d'un siècle d'architecture « moderne ». Le modernisme qui voulait que chaque Ford Model-T soit noire et chaque fenêtre de la même taille est mort. Des raisons esthétiques peuvent encore pousser certains architectes à se complaire dans le néo-modernisme ou le néo-minimalisme, mais leurs choix concrets ne sont plus fondamentale-ment limités par l'économie de chaînes de production standardisées. La conception assistée par ordinateur va rapidement passer de la per-formance de cirque consistant à produire des *blobs* plein de fantaisie à un outil concret, qui pilotera dans le futur des outils aptes à offrir à l'architecture une nouvelle liberté.

# HITOSHI ABE

*Atelier Hitoshi Abe*
*3-3-16 Oroshimachi,*
*Wakabayashi-ku, Sendai*
*Miyagi, 984-0015*
*Japan*

*Tel: +81 22 784 3411*
*Fax: +81 22 782 1233*
*e-mail: house@a-slash.jp*
*Web: http://www.a-slash.jp/*

*Reihoku Community Hall* ▶

Hitoshi Abe was born in 1962 in Sendai. He worked from 1988 to 1992 in the office of COOP HIMMELB(L)AU and obtained his Master of Architecture degree from the Southern California Institute of Architecture (SCI-Arc) in 1989. He created his own firm, Atelier Hitoshi Abe, in 1992. From 1994 he directed the Hitoshi Abe Architectural Design Laboratory at the Tohoku Institute of Technology. He has been a Professor in the same Institute since 2002. His work includes the Miyagi Water Tower (Rifu, Miyagi, Japan, 1994), the Gravel-2 House (Sendai, Miyagi, Japan, 1998), the Neige, Lune, Fleur Restaurant (Sendai, Miyagi, Japan, 1999), the Miyagi Stadium (Rifu, Miyagi, Japan, 2000), the Michinoku Folklore Museum (Kurikoma, Miyagi, Japan, 2000) and the A-House (Sendai, Miyagi, Japan, 2000). More recently, he has been working on the JB House, the S-Orthopedics Factory and Office Building, all located in Sendai. He won the 2003 Architectural Institute of Japan Award, for the Reihoku Community Hall, published here.

Hitoshi Abe, 1962 im japanischen Sendai geboren, arbeitete von 1988 bis 1992 im Büro von COOP HIMMELB(L)AU und erwarb 1989 seinen Master of Architecture am Southern California Institute of Architecture (SCI-Arc). 1992 gründete er seine eigene Firma, das Atelier Hitoshi Abe. Seit 1994 leitet er die Hitoshi Abe Werkstätte für Architekturdesign am Institut für Technologie in Tohoku und ist seit 2002 Professor an diesem Institut. Zu seinen Bauwerken, die alle in der japanischen Präfektur Miyagi entstanden sind, gehören: der Miyagi Water Tower in Rifu (1994), das Haus Gravel-2 in Sendai (1998), das Restaurant Neige-Lune-Fleur in Sendai (1999), das Miyagi-Stadium in Rifu (2000), das Volkskundemuseum Michinoku in Kurikoma (2000) und das A-House in Sendai (2000). In jüngster Zeit plante er das Haus JB und die Fabrik und Bürogebäude für die orthopädische Klinik Sasaki, alle in Sendai. 2003 wurde er für das hier vorgestellte Gemeindezentrum in Reihoku mit dem Preis des japanischen Architekturinstituts ausgezeichnet.

Hitoshi Abe est né en 1962 à Sendai. Obtient son Master of Architecture au South California Institute of Architecture (SCI-Arc) en 1989, il travaille de 1988 à 1992 chez COOP HIMMELB(L)AU. Il crée sa propre agence, Atelier Hitoshi Abe, en 1992. Depuis 1994, il dirige le Hitoshi Abe Architectural Design Laboratory à l'Institut de technologie Tohoku, où il enseigne également depuis 2002. Parmi ses réalisations, toutes au Japon : le château d'eau de Miyagi (Rifu, Miyagi, 1994) ; la maison Gravel-2 (Sendai, Miyagi, 1998) ; le restaurant Neige-Lune-Fleur (Sendai, Miyagi, 1999) ; le stade de Miyagi (2000) ; le Musée du folklore Michinoku (Kurikoma, Miyagi, 2000) et la Maison A (Sendai, Miyagi, 2000). Plus récemment, il a travaillé sur la Maison JB et les bâtiments d'orthopédie Sasaki, tous à Sendai. Il a remporté le Prix 2003 de l'Institut d'architecture du Japon, pour le Centre communautaire de Reihoku, publié ici.

# REIHOKU COMMUNITY HALL

*Reihoku, Kumamoto, Japan, 2001–02*

*Client: Town of Reihoku, Kumamoto. Ground area: 993 m². Costs: not specified.*

This community hall and 207-seat theater for a town of 9 000 persons is a 993-square-meter laminated lumber structure built on a reinforced concrete base. The two-story building is 9.95 meters high. The site area is 3 830 square meters. As part of the Kumamoto Artpolis originated in 1988 under the authority of Kumamoto Governor Morihiro Hosokawa and the architect Arata Isozaki, the project is the result of three years of close consultations between the architect and the local population. Set apart from the town by a green area, the structure has an unusual billowing exterior appearance. Though it appears rather closed, in part because of its dark local cedar cladding, it is quite open to outside light. Despite the complex exterior curves, the structure was designed so that local craftsmen could place the glazing and its horizontal wooden supports. Inside corridors are limited to a strict minimum and an intentional ambiguity is maintained in the division between one space and another. In a sense, this ambiguity, a frequent feature of Japanese architecture, also corresponds to the case of the Reihoku Community Hall in a more specific way – despite the lengthy consultations, townspeople could not agree on a precise use for the building and the architect opted for giving them the most flexible space possible.

Das Gemeindezentrum und Theater mit 207 Sitzen wurde für eine Kleinstadt mit 9 000 Einwohnern entworfen. Es besteht aus einer 993 m² messenden Schichtholzkonstruktion, die auf einem Fundament aus Stahlbeton ruht. Das Grundstück, auf dem der zweigeschossige, knapp 10 m hohe Bau errichtet wurde, umfasst 3 830 m². Das Gebäude ist Teil des Artpolis-Projekts, das 1988 vom Gouverneur der Präfektur Kumamoto, Morihiro Hosokawa, und dem Architekten Arata Isozaki ins Leben gerufen wurde. Der Entwurf ist das Ergebnis eingehender Befragungen, die der Planer Hitoshi Abe über einen Zeitraum von drei Jahren mit der lokalen Bevölkerung durchführte. Von außen fällt das durch eine Grünfläche von der Stadt abgesetzte Bauwerk durch seine wellenartig geschwungenen Formen auf. Und obwohl der Bau recht geschlossen wirkt, was teilweise auf seine Fassadenverkleidung aus dunklem Zedernholz zurückzuführen ist, lässt er viel Tageslicht ein. Trotz der komplexen Bogenlinien der Fassaden wurde der Entwurf so konzipiert, dass lokale Handwerker die Verglasungen und horizontalen Holzstützen ohne Schwierigkeiten anbringen konnten. Im Innern wurde die Zahl der Flure auf ein absolutes Minimum begrenzt und die Trennlinien zwischen den einzelnen Räumen blieben bewusst unklar. Diese Ambivalenz, ein häufiges Merkmal in der japanischen Architektur, hat im Fall des Gemeindezentrums von Reihoku noch einen besonderen Grund: Auch nach den ausführlichen Diskussionen konnten sich die Bewohner nicht auf einen genauen Zweck des Gebäudes einigen, so dass sich der Architekt für eine Raumgestaltung entschied, die eine möglichst flexible Nutzung zulässt.

Édifié pour une ville de 9 000 habitants, ce bâtiment municipal de 993 m² sur un terrain de 3 830 m² regroupe une salle de réunion et un théâtre de 207 places. Il fait appel à une structure en bois lamellé-collé sur soubassement en béton armé, et compte deux niveaux pour une hauteur totale de 9,95 m. Réalisé dans le cadre du projet Kumamoto Artpolis lancé en 1988 sous l'autorité du gouverneur de Kumamoto, Morihiro Hosokawa, et de Arata Isozaki, il est l'aboutissement de trois années de consultations approfondies entre l'architecte et la population locale. Le bâtiment qui est séparé de la ville par un espace vert présente un curieux aspect sinusoïdal. Bien qu'il semble assez fermé, en partie parce qu'il est habillé de cèdre local foncé, il reste ouvert à la lumière naturelle. Malgré ses courbes extérieures complexes, la précision de sa conception a permis aux artisans locaux de poser facilement les vitrages. À l'intérieur, les corridors sont limités à un strict minimum et l'ambiguïté entretenue entre les volumes est voulue. Fréquente dans l'architecture japonaise, elle correspond également à la situation locale puisque, malgré les longues consultations, les habitants n'ont pu se mettre d'accord sur l'utilisation précise du bâtiment. L'architecte s'est donc efforcé de leur offrir un espace qui permette l'utilisation la plus souple possible.

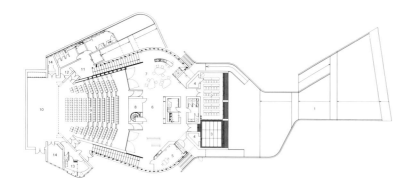
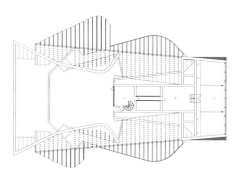

Plans show the relatively simple disposition of the interior spaces with the unexpected billowing volumes flanking each side of the structure.

Die Grundrisse zeigen die relativ einfache Anordnung der Innenräume mit den Ausbuchtungen, die das Gebäude zu beiden Seiten flankieren.

Les plans montrent la disposition relativement simple des espaces intérieurs et les volumes gonflés qui flanquent chaque côté du bâtiment.

Mixing the concrete base with wood and glazing, the architect animates the exterior surfaces without sacrificing an intentional austerity.

In der Kombination aus Betonsockel mit Holz und Glas lockert der Architekt die Außenfassaden auf, ohne die gewollte Strenge aufzuheben.

L'architecte a animé les façades au moyen du soubassement en ciment, du bardage en bois et du vitrage, sans rien perdre de l'austérité voulue.

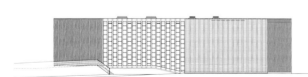
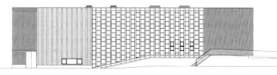

Aus bestimmten Blickwinkeln wirkt
das Gemeindezentrum von Reihoku
nahezu undurchbrochen und fenster-
los. Darin und in seinem schwarzen
Äußeren erinnert es an einige japanische Tempelbauten.

Sous certains angles, cette salle
polyvalente semble presque aveugle
et dénuée de fenêtres. Elle rappelle
à cet égard, et par sa couleur noire,
certains temples japonais.

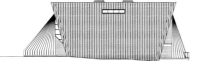

# VITO ACCONCI

*Acconci Studio*
*70 Washington Street, #501, Brooklyn, NY 11201, USA*
*Tel: +1 718 852 6591, Fax: +1 718 624 3178*
*e-mail: studio@acconci.com, Web: www.acconci.com*

*Idea developed by: Robert Punkenhofer*
*ART & IDEA, Morizgasse 8/12, 1060 Vienna, Austria*
*Tel: +43 1 596 4736, Fax: +43 1 596 4738*
*e-mail: punkenhofer@art-idea.com, Web: www.art-idea.com*

Born in the Bronx in 1940, Vito Acconci lives and works in Brooklyn. Vito Acconci's early work was in the area of fiction and poetry. In the late 1960s and early 1970s, his first artworks used performance, photos, film and video as instruments of self-analysis. His audio and video installations of the mid-70s turned exhibition spaces into community meeting places. His "architectural games" of the early 80s made performance spaces for viewers, whose activity resulted in the construction and deconstruction of house prototypes. In the mid-80s his work crossed over into architecture, landscape and industrial design. In 1988 he created the Acconci Studio, a theoretical-design and building workshop. The Studio treats architecture as an "occasion to make spaces fluid, changeable, portable." The Studio has recently completed an artificial island in Graz, published here; a plaza for a Performing Arts Center in Memphis; an art gallery (Kenny Schachter's contTEMPorary Adjustable gallery in New York); and a clothing store for United Bamboo in Tokyo. The Acconci Studio is working on a skate park in San Juan, a park on a street median in Vienna, and a spiraling-ramped house in Kalamata, Greece. Their past projects include a screened walkway for a station in Tokyo, 2000; a movable landscape in Munich, 2000; and the Renovation of the Storefront for Art & Architecture (New York, in collaboration with Steven Holl, 1994).

Vito Acconci, geboren 1940 in der Bronx, lebt und arbeitet heute in Brooklyn. Seine ersten Arbeiten stammten aus den Bereichen Literatur und Poesie. In den späten 1960er und frühen 1970er Jahren widmete er sich den Kunstformen Performance, Fotografie, Film und Video, die er als Instrumente der Selbstanalyse einsetzte. Mitte der 1970er Jahre verwandelten seine Audio- und Videoinstallationen die Galerien in Versammlungsräume. Seine „architektonischen Spiele" aus den frühen 1980er Jahren schufen Präsentationsräume für Besucher, deren Aktivitäten in der Konstruktion und Dekonstruktion von Prototypen für Häuser bestanden. Mitte der 1980er Jahre wechselten seine Arbeiten in die Bereiche Architektur, Landschafts- und Industriedesign. 1988 gründete er das Acconci Studio, eine Denkwerkstatt für Design und Bauen. Die Mitarbeiter des Studios behandeln Architektur als eine „Gelegenheit, Räume fließend, veränderbar, tragbar zu machen". Zu ihren früheren Projekten gehören ein Gehweg mit Schutzblende für einen Bahnhof in Tokio (2000), eine bewegliche Landschaft in München (2000) und die gemeinsam mit Steven Holl durchgeführte Renovierung der Geschäftsfassade für Art & Architecture in New York (1994). In jüngster Zeit hat das Studio die hier vorgestellte künstliche Mur-Insel in Graz, einen öffentlichen Platz für das Performing Arts Center in Memphis, die Kunstgalerie Kenny Schachter's contTEMPorary Adjustable gallery in New York und eine Modeboutique für United Bamboo in Tokio fertig gestellt. Zur Zeit arbeitet das Acconci Studio Team an einem Park für Skater in San Juan, einem Park auf einer Allee in Wien sowie einem mit einer Spiralrampe ausgestatteten Haus in Kalamata, Griechenland.

Né dans le Bronx en 1940, Vito Acconci vit et travaille à Brooklyn. Ses premiers essais créatifs portent sur la fiction et la poésie. À la fin des années 1960 et au début des années 1970, ses premières interventions artisytiques utilisent la performance, la photographie, le film et la vidéo comme instruments d'auto-analyse. Ses installations audio et vidéo du milieu des années 1970 transforment les espaces d'exposition en lieux communautaires. Ses « jeux architecturaux » du début des années 1980 proposent des espaces de performance aux spectateurs, autour de la construction et de la déconstruction de prototypes de maisons. À cette époque, son travail aborde l'architecture, le paysage et le design industriel. En 1988, il crée le Acconci Studio, atelier de conception théorique et de construction qui traite l'architecture comme une « occasion de rendre l'espace fluide, modifiable, portatif. » Le Studio a récemment achevé une île artificielle à Graz, publiée ici, une place pour le Performing Arts Center de Memphis, une galerie d'art à New York (conTEMPorary Adjustable gallery de Kenny Schachter) et un magasin de vêtement pour United Bamboo à Tokyo. Il travaille également sur un parc pour la pratique du skate board à San Juan, un parc au milieu d'une rue à Vienne et une maison en rampe spiralée à Kalamata (Grèce). Parmi ses projets passés : une passerelle à écrans pour une gare à Tokyo (2000), un paysage déplaçable à Munich (2000) et la rénovation. En dehors du projet sur la Mur, Vito Acconci est intervenu sur des « Écrans pour une passerelle entre bâtiments, bus et voitures » (Passage d'entrée, gare de Shibuya, Tokyo, Japon, 2000) ; la rénovation du Storefront for Art & Architecture (en collaboration avec Steven Holl, New York, 1994).

# MUR ISLAND PROJECT

*Mur Island, Graz, Austria, 2003*

*Client: Graz 2003 – Cultural Capital of Europe GmbH. Length: 46.6 m, width 16.6 m. Costs: € 5 000 000.*

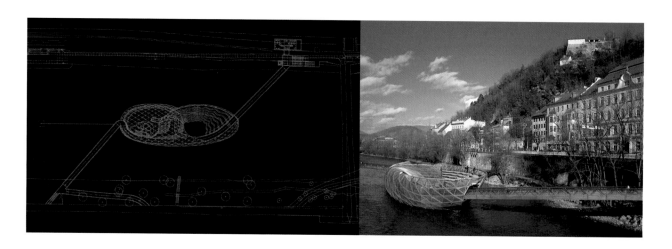

"Project: A twist in the river, a node in the river, a circulation-route in the middle of the river. The circulation-route is an island; the island is a dome that morphs into a bowl that morphs into a dome." This is the way that Vito Acconci describes the floating island he built near the Mariahilferplatz and the old city of Graz. Built in the Mur River to celebrate Graz's selection as European Capital of Culture in 2003, the 7 x 17 x 47 m structure was made of "steel, glass, rubber, asphalt, water, and light" as Acconci put it. The bowl-like space was intended for meetings or to serve as a theater, while the dome was a café/restaurant. "Where dome and bowl intersect," says Acconci, "and where the dome is transformed into a bowl and vice versa, a playground is formed by the collision and by the melting. This in-between space is a three-dimensional grid, like a space frame; the grid functions as monkey bars, a field to climb up and crawl through and hang onto; slides are cut through the grid." The project was originally an idea of Robert Punkenhofer. Born 1965 in Austria, Punkenhofer founded Art & Idea, "a not for profit institution devoted to promoting and facilitating a cultural dialogue by organizing contemporary arts programs of international scope." As he states, "my aim was to break the prevailing isolation between the river and the city by establishing a multifunctional, futuristic platform that offers a new public space for communication, adventure and artistic creation. Housing an open-air theater, a children's playground and a café, the island should take the city into the river and the river into the city."

„Das Projekt: eine Biegung im Fluss, ein Knoten im Fluss, eine Umlaufroute in der Mitte des Flusses. Die Umlaufroute ist eine Insel; die Insel ist eine Kuppel, die zu einer Schale wird, welche sich wiederum zu einer Kuppel formt." So beschreibt Vito Acconci die schwimmende Insel, die er nahe dem in der Altstadt von Graz gelegenen Mariahilferplatz in die Mur gesetzt hat. Die 7 x 17 x 47 m messende Konstruktion, die anlässlich der Ernennung von Graz zur Europäischen Kulturhauptstadt 2003 errichtet wurde, bestand – so Acconci – aus „Stahl, Glas, Gummi, Asphalt, Wasser und Licht". Der schalenartige Raum war für Zusammenkünfte oder als Theater gedacht, während die Kuppel als Café und Restaurant diente. Dazu Acconci: „Wo sich Kuppel und Schale überschneiden, entsteht durch die Kollision und die Verschmelzung ein Spielplatz. Dieser Zwischen-Raum bildet ein dreidimensionales Gitter, das wie ein Klettergerüst funktioniert: man kann daran hochklettern, hindurch kriechen oder sich dranhängen. Auch Rutschen wurden durch das Gitter gelegt." Das Projekt geht auf eine Idee des 1965 geborenen Österreichers Robert Punkenhofer zurück, dem Begründer von Art & Idea, „einer Non-Profit-Institution, die einen kulturellen Dialog ermöglichen und fördern will, indem sie aktuelle Kunstprogramme von internationaler Reichweite organisiert." Wie Punkenhofer erklärt, war es sein Ziel, die bestehende Isolierung zwischen Fluss und Stadt durch eine multifunktionale, futuristische Plattform aufzubrechen, die einen neuen öffentlichen Raum für Kommunikation, Abenteuer und künstlerische Kreativität bietet.

« Projet : un toron dans la rivière, un nœud dans la rivière, une voie de circulation au milieu de la rivière. La voie de circulation est une île ; l'île est un dôme qui se transforme en vasque qui se transforme en dôme. » Telle est la manière dont Vito Acconci décrit l'île flottante ancrée dans la Mur près de la Mariahilferplatz dans la vieille ville de Graz. Cette structure de 7 x 17 x 47 m en « acier, verre, caoutchouc, asphalte, eau et lumière », selon Acconci, célébrait la désignation de Graz comme « Capitale européenne de la culture 2003 ». Le volume en forme de vasque était prévu pour accueillir des manifestations publiques ou servir de théâtre, le dôme étant un café-restaurant. « Là où le dôme et la vasque se coupent », explique Acconci, « là où le dôme se transforme en vasque et vice-versa, un terrain de jeu se dessine en profitant de cette collision et de cette fusion. Cet espace ‹ entre-deux › est une trame tridimensionnelle, une structure spatiale ; la trame sert d'espalier de gymnastique, de terrain d'escalade que l'on traverse en rampant et auquel on peut s'accrocher ; des fentes sont découpées dans sa grille. » Le projet vient d'une idée de Robert Punkenhofer. Né en Autriche en 1965, Punkenhofer a fondé Art & Idea, « organisme sans but lucratif qui se consacre à la promotion et à la facilitation du dialogue culturel par l'organisation de manifestations artistiques contemporaines, de niveau international ». Il précise : « Mon objectif était de rompre la coupure entre la rivière et la ville en établissant une plate-forme futuriste multifonctions qui offre un nouveau lieu de communication, d'aventure et de création artistique. »

To say that the Mur Island project is unexpected in the traditionally minded city of Graz would be an understatement.

Ohne Untertreibung war das Mur-Insel-Projekt für eine traditionell eingestellte Stadt wie Graz eine ganz unerwartete Architektur.

Dire que le « Mur Island Project » a surpris dans une ville aussi traditionnelle que Graz est une litote.

Lighting makes the project an integral part of the city, even at night. Although intended to float on the river, it also seems to emerge from the waters.

Das Lichtdesign macht das Projekt zu einem integralen Bestandteil der Stadt, sogar bei Nacht. Auch wenn die Konstruktion auf dem Fluss schwebt, scheint sie gleichzeitig aus dem Wasser aufzutauchen.

L'éclairage intègre totalement le projet à la ville, même la nuit. L'île flotte à la surface de la rivière, tout en semblant en émerger.

The intersecting ovals are turned up in one instance and down in the other, creating covered and open spaces.

Die ineinander greifenden Ovale sind einmal nach oben und einmal nach unten gekehrt, was eine Abfolge bedeckter und offener Räume ergibt.

Les ovales qui s'entrecoupent sont l'un tourné vers le haut, l'autre vers le bas, pour créer des volumes couverts et découverts.

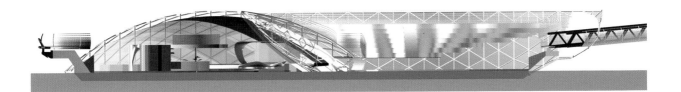

The hilly landscape around Graz is reflected in the stainless steel design, and through Nirosta steel lattices and glass windows the surroundings can even be seen from within the artificial island.

Die hügelige Umgebung von Graz spiegelt sich im Design aus rostfreiem Stahl. Durch die Nirostastahlgitter und Glasfenster kann sie sogar vom Innern der künstlichen Insel aus betrachtet werden.

L'environnement montagneux de Graz se reflète dans l'acier inoxydable, les lattis en acier Nirosta et les vitrages. Il se perçoit aussi de l'intérieur de cette île artificielle.

The shell contains an open-air theater, and the whole of the island can hold about 300 persons at any one time.

Die muschelförmige Schale umschließt ein Freilufttheater. Die gesamte Inselkonstruktion bietet circa 300 Personen Platz.

La vasque contient un théâtre en plein air et l'ensemble de l'île peut accueillir simultanément 300 personnes environ.

Underneath the dome, the "Insel Café," run by the traditional Graz bakery Sorger, was designed by the Acconci Studio and the Graz-based architecture studio purpur.

Das von der Grazer Traditionskonditorei Sorger betriebene „Insel Café" wurde vom Acconci Studio in Zusammenarbeit mit dem Grazer Architekturbüro studio purpur gestaltet.

Sous le dôme, le « Insel Café », géré par une célèbre pâtisserie de Graz, Sorger, a été conçu par le Acconci Studio et l'agence d'architecture locale, purpur.

Set between the historic city center
and Mariahilferplatz the "Island in the
Mur" has been described as "a small
concentration of urban life in a place
that has never been part of the city."

Zwischen historischem Stadtkern
und Mariahilferplatz gelegen, ist die
„Insel in der Mur" als eine „kleine
Ansammlung urbanen Lebens an
einem Ort, der nie ein Teil der Stadt
gewesen war", beschrieben worden.

Entre le centre historique de la ville
et la Mariahilferplatz, « L'île sur la
Mur » a pu être décrite comme « un
petit concentré de vie urbaine en un
lieu qui n'avait jamais fait partie de
la cité. »

*Dirty House* ▶

# DAVID ADJAYE

*Adjaye Associates*
*23-28 Penn Street*
*London N1 5DL*
*UK*

*Tel: +44 20 7739 4969*
*Fax: +44 20 7739 3484*
*e-mail: info@adjaye.com*
*Web: www.adjaye.com*

David Adjaye was born in 1966 in Dar-Es-Salaam, Tanzania. He studied at the Royal College of Art (Masters in Architecture 1993), and worked in the offices of David Chipperfield and Eduardo Souto de Moura before creating his own firm in London in 2000 (Chassay Architects, 1988–1990; David Chipperfield Architects, 1991; Eduardo Souto de Moura Architects, 1991; Adjaye & Russell, 1994–2000). He has been widely recognized as one of the leading architects of his generation in the UK, in part because of the talks he has given in various locations such as the Architectural Association, the Royal College of Art and Cambridge University, as well as Harvard, Cornell, and the Universidad de Luisdad in Lisbon. He was also the co-presenter of the BBC's six part series on modern architecture "Dreamspaces." His Idea Store library in East London was selected by Deyan Sudjic for the exhibition highlighting 100 projects that are changing the world at the 8th Venice Biennale of Architecture in 2002. His offices currently employ a staff of 35, and some of his key works are: Studio/home for Chris Ofili (London, 1999); Extension to house (St. John's Wood, 1998); Siefert Penthouse (London, 2001); Elektra House (London, 2001); Studio/gallery/home for Tim Noble and Sue Webster (London, 2003); and the SHADA Pavillon (London, 2000, with artist Henna Nadeem). Current work includes: The Nobel Peace Center, Oslo (2002–2005); Bernie Grant Centre, Tottenham, London (2001–2006); Stephen Lawrence Centre, Deptford, London (2004–2006); and the Museum of Contemporary Art/Denver, Denver, Colorado, USA (2004–2006).

David Adjaye, geboren 1966 in Daressalam, Tansania, studierte am Londoner Royal College of Art, wo er 1993 seinen Master of Architecture erwarb. Von 1988 bis 1990 arbeitete er im Architekturbüro Chassay Architects, 1991 bei David Chipperfield und bei Eduardo Souto de Moura und von 1994 bis 2000 bei Adjaye & Russell, bevor er noch im selben Jahr seine eigene Firma in London gründete. Er ist weithin anerkannt als einer der führenden britischen Architekten seiner Generation. Dies ist zum Teil auf die Vorträge zurückzuführen, die er an so renommierten Institutionen wie der Architectural Association, dem Royal College of Art sowie den Universitäten Cambridge, Harvard, Cornell und Lissabon gehalten hat. Außerdem war er Co-Moderator der sechsteiligen BBC-Serie „Dreamspaces" über moderne Architektur. Seine „Idea Store"-Bibliothek in East London wurde von Deyan Sudjic in die Ausstellung der 100 Projekte, die die Welt verändert haben, aufgenommen, die 2002 im Rahmen der 8. Architekturbiennale in Venedig gezeigt wurde. Zu den wichtigsten Arbeiten seines Büros, das derzeit 35 Mitarbeiter beschäftigt, gehören: ein Hausanbau in St. John's Wood (1998), ein Studio mit Wohnung für Chris Ofili in London (1999), der SHADA Pavillon (2000) – in Zusammenarbeit mit der Künstlerin Henna Nadeem, das Elektra House (2001), das Penthouse Siefert (2001) sowie eine Kombination aus Studio, Galerie und Wohnung für Tim Noble und Sue Webster (2003), alle in London. Zu den aktuellen Arbeiten zählen: Das Nobel Friedenszentrum in Oslo (2002–2005), das Bernie Grant Centre in Tottenham, London (2001–2006), das Stephen Lawrence Centre in Deptford, London (2004–2006) und das Museum of Contemporary Art in Denver, Colorado (2004–2006).

David Adjaye, né en 1966 à Dar-Es-Salam (Tanzanie), étudie au Royal College of Art (Master of Architecture, 1993), puis travaille dans les agences de David Chipperfield et d'Eduardo Souto de Moura avant de créer sa propre structure à Londres en 2000 (Chassay Architects, 1988–1990 ; David Chipperfield Architects, 1991 ; Eduardo Souto de Moura Architects, 1991 ; Adjaye & Russell, 1994–2000). Il est généralement reconnu comme un des plus brillants architectes de sa génération au Royaume-Uni, en partie pour ses conférences données devant divers publics dont l'Architectural Association, le Royal College of Art et la Cambridge University, ainsi qu'Harvard, Cornell ou l'Universidad de Luisdad à Lisbonne. Il a été coprésentateur d'une série de la BBC sur l'architecture. Sa bibliothèque Idea Store dans l'East Londres a été sélectionnée par Deyan Sudjic pour la grande exposition « 100 projets qui ont changé le monde » présentée à la 8ème Biennale d'architecture de Venise en 2002. Son agence emploie actuellement 35 collaborateurs. Parmi ses principales réalisations : maison-atelier pour Chris Ofili (Londres, 1999) ; extension d'une maison (St. John's Wood, 1998) ; Siefert Penthouse (Londres, 2001) ; Maison Elektra (Londres, 2001) ; l'atelier-galerie-maison de Tim Noble et Sue Webster (Londres, 2003) et le SHADA Pavilion (Londres, 2000 avec l'artiste Henna Nadeem). Ses chantiers actuels comprennent le Centre Nobel de la paix (Oslo, 2002–2005) ; le Bernie Grant Centre (Tottenham, Londres, 2001–2006) ; le Stephen Lawrence Centre (Deptford, Londres, 2004–2006) et le Museum of Contemporary Art (Denver, Colorado, 2004–2006).

# DIRTY HOUSE

*East London, UK, 2003*

*Client: Tim Noble and Sue Webster. Building area: 350 m². Costs: £ 300 000.*

David Adjaye converted a 1930s East London warehouse into a home for artists Tim Noble and Sue Webster in a most surprising way. Ground-floor windows surfaced in mirrored glass lie flush with the façade, while the upper story windows are deeply recessed. A high glass wall to the rear of the building brings daylight into the upper-floor bedrooms, but again offers no possible view into the house. The lightness of this glass wall is in sharp contrast to the voluntary heaviness of the lower part of the house. As Sue Webster has said, "we love the contradictions the glass wall creates, the feeling of an inside-outside space. We feel very exposed yet there's a sense of being protected." Removing interior columns and the first floor of the warehouse to create double-height space for the artists, the architect intentionally used industrial and inexpensive off-the-shelf products for the finishing. White concrete was chosen for the kitchen work surfaces for example, and standard strip lights were used for much of the interior lighting. Although the name "Dirty House" is not explained, the artists are known amongst other things for literally making works out of trash.

David Adjaye gelang es, ein im Londoner East End gelegenes, ehemaliges Lagergebäude aus den 1930er Jahren auf sehr originelle Weise in ein Zuhause für die beiden Künstler Tim Noble und Sue Webster zu verwandeln. Während die mit Spiegelglas ausgestatteten Fenster im Erdgeschoss eine Ebene mit der Fassade bilden, sind die Fenster im oberen Stockwerk stark zurückversetzt. Die hohe Glaswand an der Hinterseite des Gebäudes lässt Tageslicht in die Räume im Obergeschoss, ohne jedoch Einblicke von außen zuzulassen. Die Leichtigkeit, die diese Glaswand ausstrahlt, steht in scharfem Kontrast zu dem bewusst massiv gestalteten unteren Teil des Hauses. Dazu Sue Webster: „Wir lieben die Widersprüchlichkeit, die durch die Glaswand entsteht, dieses Gefühl, gleichzeitig drinnen und draußen zu sein. Wir fühlen uns sehr exponiert und dennoch geschützt." David Adjaye ließ im Inneren Säulen und eine Zwischendecke entfernen, um Räume zu schaffen, die sich über zwei Stockwerke erstrecken. Für die Ausstattung wurden kostengünstige und gebrauchsfertige Industrieerzeugnisse verwendet. So wurden beispielsweise weißer Beton für die Arbeitsflächen in der Küche und Standardneonlampen für den Großteil der Beleuchtung gewählt. Wenn auch der Name „Dirty House" vom Architekten nicht erklärt wird, sind die beiden Künstler dafür bekannt, dass sie im wahrsten Sinne des Wortes aus Müll Kunst machen.

Pour les artistes Tim Noble et Sue Webster, David Adjaye a transformé en maison cet entrepôt de l'East End londonien, datant des années 1930, d'une manière qui ne manque pas de surprendre. Les fenêtres du rez-de-chaussée en verre argenté sont montées à fleur de façade, tandis que celles de l'étage sont en retrait marqué. À l'arrière, un haut mur de verre éclaire les chambres de l'étage, sans laisser pour autant le regard pénétrer dans la maison. La légèreté de ce mur contraste nettement avec la lourdeur voulue de la partie inférieure. Comme l'explique Sue Webster : « Nous aimons les contradictions que crée le mur de verre, le sentiment d'un espace dedans-dehors. Nous nous sentons très exposés et très protégés à la fois. » L'architecte a supprimé des colonnes intérieures et le premier niveau de l'entrepôt afin de créer un volume double hauteur pour les artistes, et a volontairement choisi des matériaux et des équipements industriels et bon marché pour les finitions. Par exemple, il a retenu le béton pour les plans de travail de la cuisine, et des bandeaux de néon standard pour la plupart des éclairages intérieurs. Bien que le nom de « Dirty House » (maison sale) ne soit pas explicité, les artistes sont connus, entre autres, pour utiliser des déchets dans leurs œuvres.

*In its rather harsh East London surroundings, the Dirty House stands out because of its austerity and lighting that appears to make the roof float over the dark cubic shape of the structure.*

*Das Dirty House fällt aus seiner ziemlich rauen Ostlondoner Umgebung heraus, aufgrund seiner Strenge und einer Beleuchtung, die das Dach scheinbar über der dunklen, kubischen Form des Gebäudes schweben lässt.*

*Dans le contexte assez brutal de l'East London, la Dirty House se remarque par son austérité et son éclairage, qui donnent l'impression que le toit flotte au dessus de la forme cubique et sombre de la maison.*

The austerity visible from the outside of the house is reflected in these interior views where light and volume play as much of a role as the stark furniture and kitchen installation (above).

Die äußere Strenge des Hauses spiegelt sich in den Innenansichten wider, in denen Licht und Rauminhalt eine ebenso große Rolle spielen wie die sachlich funktionalen Möbel und die Kücheneinrichtung (oben).

L'austérité extérieure affichée se retrouve dans ces vues de l'intérieur, où la lumière et les volumes jouent un rôle aussi important que le mobilier et l'équipement de cuisine dépouillés (ci-dessus).

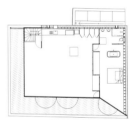

David Adjaye plays on unexpected
openings and sources of light, just as
he masterfully modulates the contrast
between a weighty opacity and an
almost ethereal lightness.

David Adjaye setzt spielerisch unerwartete Öffnungen und Lichtquellen
ein und moduliert meisterhaft den
Kontrast zwischen massiger Opazität
und einer fast ätherischen Helligkeit.

David Adjaye joue de sources de
lumière et d'ouvertures inattendues,
de même qu'il module magistrale-
ment le contraste entre une opacité
pesante et une légèreté presque
éthérée.

# WERNER AISSLINGER

Studio Aisslinger
Oranienplatz 4
10999 Berlin
Germany

Tel: +49 30 315 05 400
Fax: +49 30 315 05 401
e-mail: studio@aisslinger.de
Web: www.aisslinger.de

*Loftcube* ▶

Werner Aisslinger was born in Nördlingen, Germany in 1964. He studied design at the University of Arts (Hochschule der Künste,1987–1991), Berlin. From 1989 to 1992, he freelanced with the offices of Jasper Morrison and Ron Arad in London, and at the Studio de Lucchi in Milan. He founded Studio Aisslinger in Berlin, focusing on product design, design concepts and brand architecture, in 1993. Since 1998, he has been a Design Professor at Design College (Hochschule für Gestaltung), Karlsruhe (Department of Product Design). He created the "Juli Chair" in 1996 for Cappellini, a soft seat shell made of polyurethane integral foam – a material more frequently used in the automobile industry – which was selected as the first German chair-design since 1964 for the permanent collection of the Museum of Modern Art in New York; the "Endless Shelf" (Porro 1994/1998, Italy), a modular shelf with aluminum joints and boards made of wood or translucent plastic that won the German Design Prize in 1997 and was selected for the Museum Pinakothek der Moderne in Munich; a "Case" (Interlübke, 2002, Germany) which is a 100% modular container-trolley system in an aluminum structure with matt plastic walls; and the "soft Gel chaise longue" (Zanotta, Italy), using gel-upholstery produced with the latest technologies.

Werner Aisslinger, 1964 in Nördlingen geboren, studierte von 1987 bis 1991 Design an der Hochschule der Künste in Berlin. Daneben war er von 1989 bis 1992 freiberuflich für die Büros von Jasper Morrison und Ron Arad in London und das Studio de Lucchi in Mailand tätig. Im Jahr 1993 gründete er in Berlin das Studio Aisslinger, das sich auf Produktdesign, Designkonzepte und Markenarchitektur spezialisierte. Seit 1998 ist er Professor an der Fakultät für Produktdesign der Hochschule für Gestaltung in Karlsruhe. 1996 entwarf er den „Juli Stuhl" für Cappellini, eine weiche Sitzschale aus Polyurethan-Integralschaum – einem Material, das in der Automobilindustrie verwendet wird. Dieses Sitzmöbel war das erste, das das New Yorker Museum of Modern Art seit 1964 für seine permanente Sammlung angekauft hat. Zu seinen weiteren Projekten zählen: „The Endless Shelf" für die italienische Firma Porro (1994/1998), ein bausteinartig erweiterbares Regalsystem mit Einlegeböden aus Holz oder durchscheinendem Kunststoff und Verbindungsteilen aus Aluminium, das 1997 mit dem Deutschen Designpreis ausgezeichnet und für die Einrichtung der Münchner Pinakothek der Moderne ausgewählt wurde; ferner „Case" für Interlübke (2002), eine modulare Kombination aus Behälter und Rollkarren aus Aluminium mit Seitenwänden aus mattiertem Kunststoff sowie die „Soft Gel Chaiselongue" für das italienische Unternehmen Zanotta, bei der eine mit neuester Technologien produzierte Gelpolsterung eingesetzt wurde.

Werner Aisslinger, né en 1964 à Nördlingen, en Allemagne, étudie le design à la Hochschule der Künste à Berlin (1987–1991). De 1989 à 1992, il travaille en indépendant pour les agences de Jasper Morrison et de Ron Arad à Londres et le Studio de Lucchi, à Milan. Il fonde en 1993 le Studio Aisslinger à Berlin, spécialisé dans le design produit, le design-concept et l'architecture commerciale. Depuis 1998, il est professeur de design à la Hochschule für Gestaltung de Karlsruhe (Département du design produit). Il crée le siège « Juli » en 1996 pour Cappellini, coque de siège molle en mousse intégrale de polyuréthane, matériau plus fréquemment utilisé dans l'industrie automobile, premier siège allemand sélectionné depuis 1964 par le Museum of Modern Art de New York; la « Endless Shelf » (Porro, 1994–1998, Italie), étagère modulaire à portants d'aluminium, rayonnages en bois ou pastique translucide qui a remporté le Prix allemand du design en 1997 et a été sélectionnée par le Museum Pinakothek der Moderne à Munich ; « Case » (Interlübke, 2002, Allemagne), conteneur roulant 100% modulaire à structure d'aluminium, parois de plastic mat, et la « Soft Gel chaise longue » (Zanotta, Italie), à rembourrage en gel, technique issue de technologies de pointe.

# LOFTCUBE

*Berlin, Germany, 2003*

*Prototype Studio Aisslinger. Floor area: 36 m². Costs: € 55 000.*

Although the idea of mobile homes, even structures that can be carried and placed by helicopter, is far from new, Werner Aisslinger has taken the concept one step further by imagining his "Loftcubes" being located in large numbers on urban rooftops. Describing these locations as "a treasure of sunny sites in prime urban spaces," "what could a minimal home unit look like," he asks, "a temporary retreat, where urban nomads in big cities and dense urban zones could find privacy?" A first experiment with these units was carried out at Berlin's first design festival, "DesignMai" Berlin (May 3 to 18, 2003), where two "Loftcube" prototypes (a "living" version and a "home office" version, featuring real-life equipment, without connections to utilities) were put in place. These prototypes were designed with honeycomb wooden modules with plastic laminate suitable for dismantling. 6.6 meters in width and length, the cubes are three meters high, and include 36 square meters of interior space. Made largely with material provided by DuPont, the Loftcubes in Berlin included furniture designed by Aisslinger.

Auch wenn die Idee mobiler Wohnformen, sogar Bauten, die mit dem Hubschrauber transportiert und aufgestellt werden können, alles andere als neu ist, hat Werner Aisslinger dieses Konzept einen Schritt weiter geführt, indem er „Loftcubes" in großer Zahl auf die Dächer von Stadthäusern setzten will. Aisslinger beschreibt diese Standorte als „einen Schatz sonniger Plätze" im urbanen Raum und fragt: „Wie könnte die Minimalform einer solchen Wohneinheit aussehen, als temporärer Zufluchtsort, in dem urbane Nomaden in großen und dicht besiedelten Städten Abgeschiedenheit finden können?" Ein erstes Experiment mit den Loftcubes wurde vom 3. bis 18. Mai 2003 auf dem Designfestival in Berlin, dem DesignMai durchgeführt, wo zwei Prototypen – eine Wohn- und eine Home-Office-Version mit authentischer Ausstattung, aber ohne Anschluss ans öffentliche Netz – präsentiert wurden. Diese Prototypen waren in Wabenbauweise aus Holzmodulen mit Kunststoffbeschichtung gefertigt, eine Konstruktion, die sich leicht auf- und abbauen lässt. Die Einheiten sind jeweils 6,6 m lang und breit, 3 m hoch und enthalten einen Innenraum von 36 m². Während das Baumaterial hauptsächlich von DuPont stammte, waren die Loftcubes in Berlin mit Möbeln ausgestattet, die Aisslinger selbst entworfen hatte.

Si l'idée de maisons mobiles, ou même de constructions importantes, transportées et mises en place par hélicoptère n'est pas nouvelle, Werner Aisslinger lui a fait franchir une nouvelle étape en imaginant ces «Loftcubes» que l'on pourrait imaginer déposés en grand nombre sur des toits d'immeubles urbains. Il parle de ces sites comme d'« un trésor méconnu de sites ensoleillés au cœur d'espaces urbains de qualité… une retraite temporaire où les nomades urbains des grandes cités et des zones urbaines denses pourraient retrouver l'intimité. » Une première expérimentation a été présentée au premier festival de design de Berlin «DesignMai» Berlin (3–18 mai 2003), où deux prototypes de Loftcube (une version « à vivre » et une autre de « bureau à la maison » équipée d'appareils réels mais sans connexion aux réseaux) ont été installés. Ces prototypes utilisaient des modules de bois en nid d'abeille à plastique lamifié permettant un démontage aisé. De 6,6 m de côté, ces «cubes» mesurent 3 m de haut et offrent 36 m² de surface utile. Réalisés en grande partie à partir de matériaux fournis par DuPont, le mobilier a été dessiné par Aisslinger.

*Though he is much more a designer than an architect, Werner Aisslinger seems to have imagined a new way of living – in a bright open space sitting on just about any urban rooftop.*

*Auch wenn er viel mehr Designer als Architekt ist, scheint Werner Aisslinger eine neue Form des Wohnens erfunden zu haben – in einem hellen, offenen Baukörper, der sich auf jedes Dach eines Stadthauses setzen lässt.*

*Bien qu'il soit davantage un designer qu'un architecte, Aisslinger semble avoir imaginé un nouveau style de vie dans ce volume largement ouvert qui pourrait être posé sur n'importe quelle toiture d'immeuble urbain.*

Despite its restricted dimensions, the Loftcube appears to be very spacious. This is also due to its open volumes.

Trotz seiner geringen Ausmaße wirkt der Loftcube sehr geräumig, was nicht zuletzt an seiner offenen Bauform liegt.

Malgré ses dimensions réduites, le Loftcube paraît très spacieux, ce qui est également dû à l'ouverture de ses volumes.

A bathroom or bedroom or kitchen blend into each other almost seamlessly, setting aside the traditional hierarchical division of home spaces.

Badezimmer, Schlafzimmer oder Küche gehen fast nahtlos ineinander über und lassen die traditionell hierarchische Aufteilung von Wohnräumen hinter sich.

Salle-de-bains, chambre ou cuisine se fondent l'une dans l'autre presque sans barrière, rejetant la division hiérarchique traditionnelle de l'espace domestique.

# JUN AOKI

*Jun Aoki & Associates*
*#701, Harajuku New Royal Building*
*3-38-11, Jingumae,*
*Shibuya-ku, Tokyo, 150-0001*
*Japan*

*Tel: +81 3 54 14 34 71*
*Fax: +81 3 34 78 05 08*
*e-mail: juna@pop11.odn.ne.jp*
*web: www.aokijun.com*

*Louis Vuitton, Omotesando* ▶

Born in1956 in Yokohama, Jun Aoki graduated from the University of Tokyo in 1980, completed the Master Course in Architecture two years later, and became a registered architect in 1983. He worked in the office of Arata Isozaki (1981–1990) and created his own firm, Jun Aoki & Associates, in 1991. He has lectured at Tokyo University (1995–1998), the Tokyo Institute of Technology (1998–2000) and the Tokyo National University of Fine Arts and Music (1999–2001). His work includes: H House (Katsuura, Chiba 1994); O House (Setagaya, Tokyo, 1996); Yusuikan (swimming pool, Toyosaka, Niigata 1997); Fukushima Lagoon Museum (Toyosaka, Niigata, 1997); Louis Vuitton Nagoya (Nagoya, Aichi 1999); Louis Vuitton Ginza (exterior design, Ginza, Tokyo 2000); Aomori Museum of Art (Aomori, Aomori 2000–); Louis Vuitton New York (exterior design, New York, 2001–); and the Bird Feather Building (shopping complex, Ginza, Tokyo, 2003–). He won the Tokyo House Prize in 1994 for the H House, and the 1999 Architectural Institute of Japan Annual Award for the Fukushima Lagoon Museum.

Jun Aoki, geboren 1956 in Yokohama, schloss 1980 sein Studium an der Universität Tokio ab, machte zwei Jahre später seinen Master of Architecture und wurde 1983 amtlich zugelassener Architekt. Von 1981 bis 1990 arbeitete er im Büro von Arata Isozaki und gründete 1991 seine eigene Firma, Jun Aoki & Associates. Er lehrte an der Universität Tokio (1995–1998), dem Institut für Technologie in Tokio (1998–2000) und an der Tokioter Nationaluniversität für Schöne Künste und Musik (1999–2001). Zu seinen Arbeiten zählen: das H House in Katsuura, Chiba (1994), das O House in Setagaya, Tokio (1996) sowie das Schwimmbad Yusuikan und das Fukushima Lagoon Museum, beide 1997 in Toyosaka, Niigata, fertig gestellt. In neuerer Zeit folgten das Gebäude für Louis Vuitton in Nagoya, Aichi (1999), die Fassade für Louis Vuitton in Ginza, Tokio (2000), das Aomori Museum in Aomori (seit 2000), die Fassade für Louis Vuitton in New York (seit 2001) und das Bird Feather Gebäude im Einkaufszentrum Ginza, Tokio (seit 2003). 1994 wurde Aoki mit dem Tokyo House Prize für das H House und 1999 mit dem Jahrespreis des japanischen Architekturinstituts für das Fukushima Lagoon Museum ausgezeichnet.

Né en 1956 à Yokohama, Jun Aoki est diplômé de l'Université de Tokyo en 1980, obtient son Master of Architecture deux ans plus tard et prend le titre d'architecte en 1983. Il travaille chez Arata Isozaki (1981–1990) et crée sa propre agence, Jun Aoki & Associates en 1991. Il a donné des cours à l'Université de Tokyo (1995–1998), à l'Institut de technologie de Tokyo (1998–2000) et à l'Université nationale des Beaux-Arts et de la Musique de Tokyo (1999–2001). Parmi ses réalisations : H House (Katsuura, Chiba, 1994) ; O House (Setagaya, Tokyo, 1996) ; piscine de Yusuikan (Toyosaka, Niigata, 1997) ; Musée du lagon de Fukushima (Toyosaka, Niigata, 1997) ; Louis Vuitton Nagoya (Nagoya, Aichi, 1999) ; Louis Vuitton Ginza (façades, Ginza, Tokyo, 2000) ; Musée d'art de Aomori (Aomori, 2000–) ; Louis Vuitton New York (façades, New York, 2001–) et l'Immeuble Plume d'oiseau (complexe commercial, Ginza, Tokyo, 2003–). Il a remporté le Prix de la maison de Tokyo en 1994 pour sa H House, et en 1999, le Prix annuel de l'Institut d'architecture du Japon pour le Musée du lagon de Fukushima.

# LOUIS VUITTON, OMOTESANDO

*Tokyo, Japan, 1999–2002*

*Client: Louis Vuitton Malletier SA. Total floor area: 3327 m². Costs: not specified.*

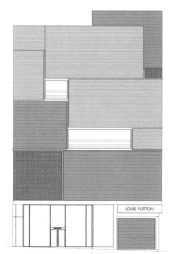  

This 3327-square-meter facility with 1000 square meters of retail sales space is located in the heart of the Omotesando shopping district, where such architects as Tadao Ando, Herzog & de Meuron, Kengo Kuma and Kazuyo Sejima are making fashion and art go well together. The ten-story structure devotes its four lower floors to a generous sales area and the rest of its space to offices, an event hall, VIP Lounge and penthouse. Jun Aoki's building for Vuitton was conceived as a "pile of trunks" for this maker of suitcases and handbags. The structural system for these volumes, apparently stacked at random, is a 30-meter-high, three-dimensional frame containing six boxes that are shaped by a composition of floor and wall plates. The structural system allows the building, which seems very open and light, to meet stringent Japanese earthquake construction standards. The most remarkable aspect of the building is its main façade, which is draped in a double layer with three different kinds of metal mesh fabric and two kinds of polished stainless steel panels laid 50cm over glass panels with a striped pattern. As the architect says, "the idea of using metal fabric was initially derived from the idea of 'piling up trunks.' I thought the surface should be covered in fabric like trunks. At the same time, because I did not want to realize them literally as enlarged trunks but as mirages, the double skin was proposed." The interior of the building was realized by the Architecture Department of Louis Vuitton, Paris.

Der insgesamt 3327 m² umfassende Bau hat eine Verkaufsfläche von insgesamt 1000 m² und liegt im Herzen des Tokioter Geschäftsviertels Omotesando, wo Architekten wie Tadao Ando, Herzog & de Meuron, Kengo Kuma und Kazuyo Sejima Mode und Kunst auf gelungene Weise miteinander in Einklang bringen. Die unteren vier Stockwerke des zehngeschossigen Komplexes werden von großzügig angelegten Einzelhandelsgeschäften eingenommen, während die restliche Nutzfläche auf Büros, einen Veranstaltungssaal, eine VIP-Lounge und ein Penthouse entfällt. Die Gestaltung von Jun Aokis Vuitton-Gebäude erinnert, in Anspielung auf den berühmten Hersteller von Reiseutensilien und Handtaschen, an einen "Kofferstapel". Dabei besteht das Konstruktionsprinzip dieser scheinbar willkürlich aufgeschichteten Baukörper aus einem 30 m hohen, dreidimensionalen Rahmen, der sechs Boxen enthält, deren Formen sich aus der Zusammensetzung von Boden- und Wandplatten ergeben. Dieses Prinzip lässt das sehr offen und hell wirkende Gebäude den strengen japanischen Bauvorschriften in punkto Erdbebensicherheit entsprechen. Das auffallendste Merkmal des Gebäudes ist jedoch seine Vorderfront, die wie von einem Faltenwurf eingehüllt ist. Diese doppellagige Drapierung besteht aus drei unterschiedlich strukturierten Metallgeflechten und Paneelen aus poliertem Edelstahl. Dazu der Architekt: "Die Idee, ein Metallgewebe zu verwenden, entwickelte sich aus dem Einfall mit den aufeinander gestapelten Koffern. Ich fand, die Oberfläche sollte ebenso wie bei Koffern mit Stoff überzogen sein."

Cet immeuble commercial de 10 niveaux et 3327 m², dont 1000 pour un magasin Vuitton, se dresse au cœur du célèbre quartier de shopping d'Omotesando, où Tadao Ando, Herzog & de Meuron, Kengo Kuma et Kazuyo Sejima ont déjà montré que l'art et la mode pouvaient parfaitement coexister. Les quatre premiers niveaux sont consacrés à de généreux espaces de vente, et les autres à un hall de réception, des bureaux, un salon VIP et une penthouse. Jun Aoki a conçu son projet comme une « pile de valises » pour évoquer le fabricant de malles et de sacs. Le système structurel de l'échafaudage apparemment aléatoire de ces volumes consiste en une ossature tridimensionnelle de 30 m de haut qui contient six boîtes issues d'une manipulation complexe de plateaux de sols et de murs. Il permet à cette construction apparemment légère et ouverte de se conformer à la rigoureuse réglementation antisismique japonaise. L'aspect le plus remarquable est la façade principale, drapée dans une double peau composée de trois différentes sortes de toile métallique et de deux types de plaques d'acier inoxydable. Pour Jun Aoki, « l'idée d'utiliser cette toile métallique vient de celle de ‹ l'empilement de malles ›. J'ai pensé que la surface devait être tendue de toile, comme pour des malles. »

*As the elevation above shows, the building is designed like a stack of suitcases. In the middle, above, the interior that was designed by Vuitton's internal staff. Metal mesh gives the exterior surfaces a distinctive appearance (right).*

*Wie der obige Aufriss zeigt, ist das Gebäude wie ein Stapel aus Koffern geformt. Oben Mitte: Das von den Innenarchitekten von Louis Vuitton gestaltete Interieur. Rechts: Das Metallgeflecht verleiht der Außenfassade eine auffallende Note.*

*Comme le montre l'élévation, l'immeuble est composé à la manière d'un empilement de malles. Au milieu, l'intérieur a été conçu par les équipes Vuitton. Le treillis de métal confère aux surfaces extérieures un aspect remarqué (à droite).*

# ASYMPTOTE

*Asymptote Architecture*
*561 Broadway, #5A*
*New York, NY 10012*
*USA*

*Tel: +1 212 343 7333*
*Fax: +1 212 343 7099*
*e-mail: info@asymptote.net*
*Web: www.asymptote.net*

Lise Ann Couture was born in Montreal in 1959. She received her Bachelor of Architecture degree from Carlton University, Canada, and her Master of Architecture degree from Yale. Couture currently holds the Davenport Chair at Yale University School of Architecture. Hani Rashid received his degree as Master of Architecture from the Cranbrook Academy of Art, Bloomfield Hills, Michigan. He is presently a Professor of Architecture at Columbia University in New York and at the Swiss Federal Institute of Technology (ETH) in Zurich. They created Asymptote in 1987. Projects include their 1988 prize-winning commission for the Los Angeles West Coast Gateway, 1989; a commissioned housing project for Brig, Switzerland; and their participation in the 1993 competition for an Art Center in Tours, France (1993). Other work by Asymptote includes a theater festival structure built in Denmark in 1997, a virtual trading floor for the New York Stock Exchange, and the Guggenheim Virtual Museum, an ongoing multimedia project aiming to create an on-line museum. In 2001, Asymptote participated in competitions for the Daimler Chrysler and Mercedes-Benz Museums in Stuttgart, an expansion of the Queen's Museum, and the Eyebeam Center in New York. Most recently Asymptote completed the construction of HydraPier in the Netherlands, a public building housing technology and art located near Schipol Airport. Asymptote was involved in the design of the 2004 Venice Biennale of Architecture, Metamorph and a new theater for the Hans Christian Andersen festival in Odense, Denmark. Asymptote is also completing a Crematorium and Memorial Chapel in Rotterdam.

Lise Ann Couture, geboren 1959 in Montreal, erwarb ihren Bachelor of Architecture an der Carlton University in Kanada und ihren Master of Architecture an der Yale University. Derzeit hat sie den Davenport Lehrstuhl an der Yale University School of Architecture inne. Hani Rashid machte seinen Master of Architecture an der Cranbrook Academy of Art in Bloomfield Hills, Michigan. Gegenwärtig ist er als Professor für Architektur an der Columbia University in New York und der Eidgenössischen Technischen Hochschule (ETH) in Zürich tätig. Zusammen gründeten sie 1987 das Architekturbüro Asymptote. Zu ihren Projekten gehören der preisgekrönte Entwurf für den Los Angeles West Coast Gateway (1989), ein Wohnhausprojekt in Brig in der Schweiz und ihr Wettbewerbsbeitrag für ein Kunstzentrum im französischen Tours (1993). Außerdem: ein Bau für ein Theaterfestival in Dänemark (1997), ein virtuelles Börsenparkett für die New Yorker Börse sowie das Guggenheim Virtual Museum, ein fortlaufendes Multimediaprojekt, das ein Online-Museum präsentiert. 2001 beteiligte sich Asymptote an den Wettbewerben für das Mercedes-Benz-Museum in Stuttgart, den Erweiterungsbau des Queen's Museum of Art und das Eyebeam Center, beide in New York. In jüngster Zeit realisierte Asymptote in den Niederlanden, nahe dem Flughafen Schiphol, das Projekt HydraPier. Außerdem ist Asymptote am Design der Architekturbiennale von 2004 in Venedig, Metamorph und eines neuen Theaters für das Hans Christian Andersen Festival im dänischen Odense beteiligt und plant ein Krematorium mit Friedhofskapelle in Rotterdam.

Lise Anne Couture, née à Montréal en 1959, est Bachelor of Architecture de la Carlton University, Canada, et Master of Architecture de Yale. Elle a été « Design Critic » du programme de maîtrise d'architecture de la Parsons School of Design, New York, et est titulaire actuellement de la chaire Davenport de la Yale University School of Architecture. Hani Rashid est Master of Architecture de Cranbrook Academy of Art, Bloomfield Hills, Michigan. Il est actuellement professeur d'architecture à Columbia University (New York) et à l'Institut fédéral suisse de technologie (ETH, Zurich). Ils créent Asymptote en 1987. Parmi leurs projets : celui primé pour la West Coast Gateway (Los Angeles, 1989), un immeuble de logements (Brig, Suisse, 1991), leur participation au concours de 1993 pour un Centre d'art à Tours, en France (1993). Parmi leurs autres réalisations : une structure pour un festival de théâtre (Århus, Danemark, 1997), une salle des marchés virtuelle pour le New York Stock Exchange et le Guggenheim Virtual Museum, projet multimédia de musée en-ligne. En 2001, Asymptote a participé aux concours pour le musée Daimler-Chrysler et Mercedes Benz à Stuttgart, l'extension du Queen's Museum et le Eyebeam Center à New York. Plus récemment, Asymptote a achevé la construction de HydraPier (Pays-Bas), situé près de l'aéroport de School, et a participé à la conception de la Biennale d'architecture de Venise 2004, de Metamorph et d'une nouvelle salle pour le festival Hans Christian Andersen à Odense (Danemark). L'équipe achève actuellement un crématorium et une chapelle du souvenir à Rotterdam.

# CARLOS MIELE FLAGSHIP STORE

*New York, New York, USA, 2002–03*

*Client: Carlos Miele, São Paulo, Brazil. Floor area: 300 m². Costs: not specified.*

Opened to the public on June 5, 2003, this fashion boutique with about 300 square meters of floor space is located on West 14th Street in Manhattan. Intended for a Brazilian clothing designer, the boutique is conceived as an open space with pale coloring meant to highlight the items that are for sale. As Asymptote's description has it, "the architectural environment is a spatial narrative, centered primarily on an abstracted reading of what constitutes Brazilian culture, landscape and architecture, while also being a contemporary Manhattan experience situated in what is now the quickly transforming meat market district of West 14th Street... The environment is a deliberate insertion and provocation of not only the worlds of fashion, art and architecture but also a trans-urban meditation that merges the cultures of New York and Sao Paulo." There is high gloss epoxy floor with embedded neon and halogen lights, while the ceiling is made of glossy stretched PVC rubber. A floor to ceiling "sculpture form," made of plywood that was cut with lasers guided by the original CAD drawings crosses through the interior space. Computer-generated drawings and digital manufacturing were used on all of the curved forms and surfaces of the shop. Finally, two Asymptote video installations developed for Dokumenta XI in Kassel and the last Venice architecture Biennale are integrated into the architecture.

Der am 5. Juni 2003 eröffnete Flagship Store hat eine Nutzfläche von circa 300 m² und liegt an der West 14th Street in Manhattan. Die für den brasilianischen Modedesigner Carlos Miele entworfene Boutique ist als offener Raum konzipiert, dessen helle Farbe die Verkaufsartikel optimal zur Geltung bringen soll. „Die Architektur", so die Beschreibung der Architektengruppe Asymptote, „stellt in räumlich narrativer Form eine Zusammenfassung dessen dar, was die brasilianische Kultur, Landschaft und Architektur ausmacht und vermittelt gleichzeitig durch ihren Standort in dem sich rasant entwickelnden Viertel um den Fleischmarkt in der West 14th Street ein authentisches Gefühl vom heutigen Manhattan. Ganz bewusst integriert und provoziert die Architektur nicht nur die Welten der Mode, der Kunst und Architektur, sondern ist auch eine trans-urbane Meditation, in der sich die Kulturen von New York und Sao Paulo vermischen." Während der Fußboden der Boutique mit hochglänzendem Epoxydharz belegt ist, in den Neon- und Halogenlampen eingelassen sind, besteht die Decke aus einer glänzenden PVC-Bespannung. Quer durch den Innenraum erstreckt sich eine vom Boden bis zur Decke reichende „sculpture form" aus Sperrholz, die durch Lasergeräte nach den CAD-Originalzeichnungen zugeschnitten wurde. Außerdem hat Asymptote Video-Installationen, die sie für die Documenta 11 in Kassel sowie die letzte Architekturbiennale in Venedig entwickelten, in ihre Gestaltung integriert.

Ouverte au public le 5 juin 2003, cette boutique de mode de 300 m² est située sur West 14th Street à Manhattan. Conçue pour un styliste brésilien, elle a été traitée en espace ouvert peint de couleurs pâles qui mettent en valeur les vêtements. Asymptote décrit ainsi son projet : « L'environnement architectural est une narration spatiale, centrée sur une lecture abstraite de ce qui constitue la culture, le paysage et l'architecture du Brésil, tout en étant implantée dans le Manhattan actuel et le quartier des bouchers de West 14th Street qui connaît une transformation rapide. L'environnement est une insertion et provocation délibérées des mondes de la mode, de l'art et de l'architecture, mais aussi une méditation transurbaine qui fusionne les cultures de New York et de Sao Paulo. » On trouve un sol verni époxy très brillant, incrusté de néons et d'halogènes et un plafond en PVS tendu tout aussi luisant. Une « forme-sculpture » en contreplaqué découpé par des lasers pilotés par commande numérique traverse l'espace. De même, ce sont des dessins et des plans techniques réalisés par ordinateur qui ont permis de tracer toutes les formes et les surfaces courbes. Deux installations vidéo d'Asymptote présentées à Documenta XI à Kassel et à la dernière Biennale d'architecture de Venise sont aussi intégrées.

*With its floating white mannequins and its continuous complex curves, the Carlos Miele Store almost seems to be carved out of a single block.*

*Mit seinen im Raum schwebenden weißen Kleiderpuppen und komplexen Kurvenlinien wirkt der Carlos Miele Store wie aus einem Guss geformt.*

*Avec ses mannequins suspendus et le flux de ses courbes complexes, la Carlos Miele Store semble avoir été sculptée dans un bloc de matière.*

Despite the overall whiteness of the shop, variations in light levels serve to define the space and to highlight its multiple curves. The white walls and floors serve to accentuate the dresses.

Trotz der durchgehend weißen Farbgebung des Interieurs gibt es Abstufungen in den Helligkeitsgraden, die den Raum definieren und seine geschwungenen Linien akzentuieren. Die weißen Wände und Böden wiederum heben die Kleidungsstücke hervor.

Si la boutique est entièrement blanche, les variations de niveau de l'éclairage définissent l'espace et font ressortir ses multiples courbes. Les murs et les sols blancs mettent en valeur les vêtements.

# SHIGERU BAN

*Shigeru Ban Architects*
*5-2-4 Matubara Ban Bldg. 1Fl*
*Setagaya-ku, Tokyo 156-0043*
*Japan*

*Tel: +81 3 3324 6760*
*Fax: +81 3 3324 6789*
*e-mail: SBA@tokyo.email.ne.jp*
*Web: www.shigeruban.com*

Born in 1957 in Tokyo, Shigeru Ban studied at the Southern California Institute of Architecture (SCI-Arc) from 1977 to 1980. He attended the Cooper Union School of Architecture, where he studied under John Hejduk (1980–1982). He worked in the office of Arata Isozaki (1982–83) before founding his own firm in Tokyo in 1985. His work includes numerous exhibition designs (Alvar Aalto show at the Axis Gallery, Tokyo, 1986). His buildings include the Paper Church (Takatori, Hyogo, 1995), the Naked House (Kawagoe, Saitama, 2000), the Paper Art Museum (Mishima, Shizuoka, 2002), and the Picture Window House (Izu, Shizuoka, 2002). He has also designed ephemeral structures such as his Paper Refugee Shelter made with plastic sheets and paper tubes for the United Nations High Commissioner for Refugees (UNHCR). He designed the Japanese Pavilion at Expo 2000 in Hanover. Current work includes a small museum of Canal History in Pouilly-en-Auxois, France; Forest Park Pavilion – Bamboo Gridshell-02 (St. Louis, Missouri); Mul(ti)houses (Mulhouse, France); Sagaponac House/Furniture House-05 (Long Island, New York); Seikei University Library (Kichijoji, Tokyo); and the Centre Pompidou in Metz, France.

Shigeru Ban, 1957 in Tokio geboren, studierte von 1977 bis 1980 am Southern California Institute of Architecture (SCI-Arc) und von 1980 bis 1982 bei John Hejduk an der Cooper Union School of Architecture in New York. Von 1982 bis 1983 arbeitete er im Büro von Arata Isozaki und gründete 1985 seine eigene Firma in Tokio. Shigeru Ban gestaltete zahlreiche Ausstellungen, so die 1986 in der Galerie Axis in Tokio gezeigte Alvar-Aalto-Schau. Zu seinen Bauten gehören die Paper Church in Takatori, Hyogo (1995), das Naked House in Kawagoe, Saitama (2000), das Paper Art Museum in Mishima, Shizuoka (2002) sowie das Picture Window House in Izu, Shizuoka (2002). Ban hat auch Behelfsbauten entworfen wie sein für den Hohen Flüchtlingskommissar der Vereinten Nationen (UNHCR) aus Plastikfolie und Papprören gebauter Paper Refugee Shelter. Für die Expo 2000 in Hannover plante er den Japanischen Pavillon. Zu seinen jüngsten Projekten zählen ein kleines Museum für die Geschichte des Kanalbaus im französischen Pouilly-en-Auxois, der Forest Park Pavilion – Bamboo Gridshell-02 in St. Louis, Missouri, die Mul(ti)houses im französischen Mulhouse, das Haus Sagaponac/Furniture House-05 in Long Island, New York, sowie die Bibliothek der Seikei Universität in Kichijoji, Tokio, und das Centre Pompidou in Metz, Frankreich.

Né en 1957 à Tokyo, Shigeru Ban étudie au Southern California Institute of Architecture (SCI-Arc) de 1977 à 1980, puis à la Cooper Union School of Architecture, où il suit l'enseignement de John Hejduk (1980–1982). Il travaille pour Arata Isozaki (1982–83), avant de fonder son agence à Tokyo en 1985. Il a conçu de nombreuses expositions (dont celle d'Alvar Aalto, Axis Gallery, Tokyo, 1986). Ses réalisations comprennent l'Église de papier (Takatori, Hyogo, 1995), la maison nue (Kawagoe, Saitama, 2000), le Musée de l'art du papier (Mishima, Shizuoka, 2002) et le Maison-cadre (Izu, Shizuoka, 2002). Il conçoit également des structures éphémères comme un abri pour réfugiés en feuilles de plastique et tubes de papier, pour le Haut Commissariat aux Réfugiés (HCRNU). Il a signé le pavillon japonais à Expo 2000 de Hanovre. Parmi ses réalisations en cours figurent un petit musée sur l'Histoire du canal (Pouilly-en-Auxois, France) ; le Forest Park Pavilion – Bamboo Gridshell –02 (St Louis, Missouri) ; Mul(ti)houses (Mulhouse, France) ; Sagaponac House, Furniture House-05 (Long Island, New York) et la bibliothèque de l'Université Seikei (Kichijoji, Tokyo) et le centre Pompidou (Metz, France).

# GLASS SHUTTER HOUSE

*Meguro-ku, Tokyo, Japan, 2001–2003*

Client: Yashiharu Doi. Building area: 73.67 m², total floor area: 151.79 m². Costs: not specified.

An exploded axonometric drawing shows the very simple volume and the shutters. The living spaces are above the restaurant, seen with its shutters closed to the right.

Die in Einzelteile aufgelöste axonometrische Darstellung zeigt den äußerst schlichten Baukörper mit den Jalousiewänden. Die Wohnräume liegen über dem Restaurant (rechts).

Une vue axonométrique éclatée montre le volume très simple et les volets roulants géants. Les espaces de vie se trouvent au-dessus du restaurant, ici volets fermés (à droite).

Located in the Meguro area of Tokyo, this combined residence and restaurant is located on a small, 139-square-meter site. It was built for a chef well known for his television appearances and his cooking school, also located in the new structure. The building area is just 73 square meters and total floor area is 151 square meters. The three-story 4 x 16 meter steel-frame house is remarkable because two of its façades open entirely from street level to roof. Rolling glass shutters disappear into the roof allowing an outside patio with a bamboo wall to become an integral part of the restaurant in warm weather. Local regulations normally permitted only two stories on this site, but as Shigeru Ban says, "the three-story volume which has only two floors is legally considered to be two-storied. The stairs connecting to the second level legally mean a floor dividing the first and the second floor. The whole volume is equivalent to three ordinary stories. The completed building has a restaurant on the ground floor, a kitchen studio on the second and housing on the third floor. Each area vertically conveys a sense of unity and the borderline, workplace or housing, is intentionally unclear." Ban concludes, "I have tried to connect inner space to the outside by using consecutive outward-opening doors in a series of housing projects. The shutters can be fully opened or be set at the height of each floor, which enables inner space to connect to outside in various ways and to be barrier free. Also, the fence made of bamboo defines the border to the neighboring site and secures its privacy." Because of its refined support design, the Glass Shutter House is extremely light and airy, giving new meaning to the typically Japanese idea of "in-between space."

Das im Tokioter Wohnviertel Meguro auf einem nur 139 m² großen Grundstück gelegene Gebäude ist eine Kombination aus Wohnhaus und Restaurant. Es wurde für einen Koch entworfen, der für seine Kochsendung im Fernsehen und seine – ebenfalls im Haus untergebrachte – Kochschule bekannt ist. Als besonderes Merkmal der dreigeschossigen, 4 x 16 m messenden Stahlrahmenkonstruktion lassen sich zwei seiner Fassaden vom Erdgeschoss bis zum Dach vollkommen öffnen, indem man die Glasjalousien ins Dach hochziehen kann, wodurch der offene Hof zu einem Teil des Restaurants wird. Zwar erlauben die lokalen Bauvorschriften an diesem Standort nur zwei Stockwerke, doch gilt das eigentlich dreigeschossige Haus durch die Treppe, die den ersten mit dem zweiten Stock verbindet, rechtlich als zweistöckig. Im Erdgeschoss befindet sich das Restaurant, während im ersten Stock eine Studioküche und auf den oberen Ebenen die Wohnräume liegen. Die vertikale Anordnung dieser Bereiche vermittelt einen zusammenhängenden Eindruck, wobei zwischen Arbeiten und Wohnen bewusst nicht klar getrennt wurde. Auch in anderer Hinsicht wurden Grenzen offen gelassen, wie Shigeru Ban erläutert: „Ich habe bereits zuvor bei einer Reihe von Wohnhäusern versucht, Innen und Außen durch Türen zu verbinden. Hier sind es die Jalousien, die ganz oder einzeln geöffnet werden können, wodurch sich die Innenräume auf verschiedene Weise und nahtlos mit der äußeren Umgebung verbinden lassen. Ansonsten wird durch den Bambuszaun die Grenze zum Nachbargrundstück definiert und damit die Privatsphäre gewahrt." Aufgrund seines ausgeklügelten Tragwerks ist das Glas Shutter House äußerst leicht und luftig gebaut, was dem typisch japanischen Gedanken vom „Zwischen-Raum" eine neue Bedeutung gibt.

Située à Tokyo, dans le quartier de Meguro, cette maison qui associe un restaurant et un logement, occupe un petit terrain de 139 m². Elle a été construite à l'intention d'un cuisinier connu pour ses émissions de télévision et son école de cuisine, installée à la même adresse. L'emprise au sol n'est que de 73 m² et la surface utile de 151 m². Cette construction de trois niveaux, à ossature d'acier et mesurant 4 x 16 m, étonne par ses deux façades qui s'ouvrent entièrement, du niveau de la rue jusqu'au toit. D'énormes volets roulants de verre disparaissent dans la couverture ce qui permet à un patio extérieur à clôture de bambou de venir agrandir le restaurant à la belle saison. La réglementation locale n'autorisait que deux niveaux, mais comme l'explique Shigeru Ban : «Le volume sur trois niveaux mais avec deux planchers intérieurs est légalement considéré comme une maison à un seul étage. Il équivaut à deux étages ordinaires. La structure comprend le restaurant au rez-de-chaussée, l'école au premier et le logement au deuxième étage. Verticalement chaque zone exprime une impression d'unité et la limite entre logement et travail reste volontairement floue. » Il conclut : « J'avais déjà essayé de relier l'espace intérieur et extérieur par différents types de portes ouvrant sur l'extérieur dans de précédents projets. Les volets roulants peuvent s'ouvrir en grand ou seulement à la hauteur de chaque niveau, ce qui offre au volume intérieur des connexion variées avec l'extérieur, sans barrière. La clôture de bambou définit la frontière avec le terrain voisin et assure l'intimité. » Grâce à son dessin raffiné, cette maison extrêmement légère et aérée donne un sens nouveau au concept japonais traditionnel d'espace « entre-deux ».

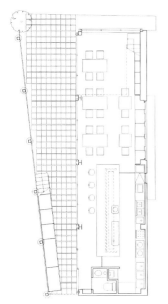 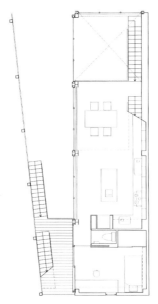 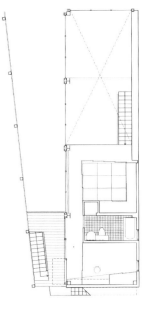

The restaurant/home is flanked by a small terrace, used to serve outdoors in the warmer months. Above right, the shutters in their open and closed positions. Below right, the closed structure.

Das Restaurant wird von einer kleinen Terrasse flankiert, auf der im Sommer im Freien serviert wird. Oben rechts: die Jalousien im geöffneten und geschlossen Zustand. Unten rechts: das komplett geschlossene Gebäude.

Le restaurant-appartement est flanqué d'une petite terrasse utilisée pour le service pendant les mois d'été. En haut à droite: les volets fermés et ouverts. En bas à droite: la structure entièrement fermée.

On a small site and with limited floor space, this Glass Shutter House is a very unusual mixture of restaurant and living area.

Das auf einem kleinen Grundstück errichtete Glass Shutter House bildet eine sehr ungewöhnliche Mischung aus Restaurant und Wohnhaus.

Sur un petit terrain et pour une surface réduite, la Glass Shutter House est une association assez rare de restaurant et de logement.

# ATSUSHI IMAI MEMORIAL GYMNASIUM

*Odate, Akita, Japan, 2001–02*

Client: Imai Hospital, Odate. Building area: 940 m². Costs: not specified.

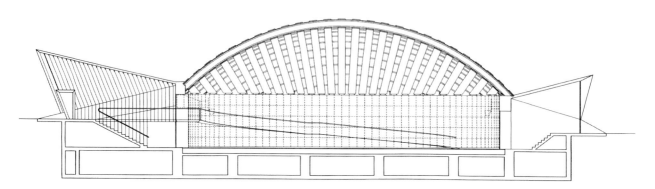

This section of the Gymnasium shows the relative simplicity of the design. Shigeru Ban has a talent for creating striking buildings using very pared-down forms.

Der Aufriss zeigt die relative Schlichtheit des Designs. Shigeru Ban demonstriert hier sein Talent, unter Einsatz reduzierter Formen auffallende Gebäude zu schaffen.

Cette élévation du gymnase montre la simplicité relative de son plan. Shigeru Ban possède le talent de créer des bâtiments étonnants à partir de formes très dépouillées.

Located in the far north of the Island of Honshu, this one-story timber and reinforced concrete structure is in the same town as Toyo Ito's Odate Jukai Dome Park (1995–1997). The total floor area of the building is 940 square meters, and the site measures 2 042 square meters. Intended as a gymnasium and swimming pool, the building uses a laminated strand lumber (LSL) structural system. Creating a 28 m x 20 m oval dome with the capacity to resist heavy snow loads in the winter was a challenge for Shigeru Ban. He chose to create an LSL space frame with successive trussed wooden arches, proving that thin wood can be used effectively on larger spans than might be expected. In much the same way, Shigeru Ban has shown that paper tubes can be employed as structural elements. An added advantage of the system is that it uses much less wood than other systems of lamination. Shigeru Ban has not feared to take on some of the most firmly rooted beliefs of the architectural profession, in particular its reliance on tried and tested but often expensive construction methods. In this he is almost unique, going far beyond the traditional issues of design, dealing too with fundamental questions of the use of space. He succeeds in mastering form even as he innovates in other areas.

Der einstöckige Bau aus Holz und Stahlbeton liegt im äußersten Norden der Insel Honshu, im selben Ort wie der zwischen 1995 und 1997 erbaute Odate Jukai Dome Park von Toyo Ito. Das Grundstück ist 2 042 m² groß, und die Nutzfläche umfasst 940 m². Das wichtigste Bauelement des als Sporthalle und Schwimmbad konzipierten Gebäudes ist Schichtholz. Die Konstruktion einer 28 x 20 m messenden ovalen Kuppel, die den in dieser Region üblichen schweren Schneemassen im Winter standhalten muss, war eine Herausforderung für Shigeru Ban. Er löste sie, indem er sich für ein Rahmenwerk aus Furnierholz entschied, das zu einer Abfolge aus hölzernen Wölbungen geformt wurde, und bewies damit, dass sich dünnes Sperrholz in größeren Spannbreiten überraschend effizient nutzen lässt. Auf ebenso unkonventionelle Weise hat Shigeru Ban mit seinen früheren Arbeiten den Beweis angetreten, dass Pappröhren ein geeignetes Konstruktionsmaterial sein können. Ein zusätzlicher Vorteil der hier verwendeten Methode besteht darin, dass sie mit wesentlich weniger Holz auskommt als andere Arten der Furnierung. Shigeru Ban fürchtet sich nicht, fest verwurzelte Überzeugungen der Architektenzunft in Frage zu stellen, besonders deren Pochen auf bewährte, aber häufig kostspielige Konstruktionsmethoden. In dieser Auseinandersetzung mit den Grundfragen des räumlichen Gestaltens ist Ban beinahe einzigartig und geht weit über die traditionellen Aspekte der Architektur hinaus. Immer gelingt ihm dabei die meisterhafte Beherrschung der Form.

À l'extrême nord de l'île de Honshu, cette construction d'un seul niveau en bois et béton armé se trouve dans la même ville que le Parc du dôme Jukai d'Odate de Toyo Ito (1995–1997). La surface utile totale est de 940 m² pour un terrain de 2 042 m². Gymnase et piscine, le bâtiment fait appel à un système structurel à base de bois lamifié verni (LVL). Son dôme ovale de 28 x 20 m capable de résister aux abondantes chutes de neige de la région a relevé un défi technique. Son ossature en LVL composée d'une succession d'arches de bois, montre que le contre-plaqué peut être utilisé sur des portées plus longues que l'on ne croyait. De la même façon, Ban avait montré que des tubes de papier pouvaient servir de supports structurels. L'avantage supplémentaire de ce système est d'utiliser beaucoup moins de bois que les autres techniques de lamellé. L'architecte n'a pas craint de remettre en cause certaines certitudes bien ancrées de la profession architecturale, en particulier sur la préférence donnée à ce qui est testé et essayé, qui aboutit souvent à des procédés coûteux. Sa personnalité unique va au-delà des acquis traditionnels de la conception et s'attache à trouver des solutions nouvelles aux questions fondamentales sur l'utilisation de l'espace. Il n'en maîtrise pas moins la forme, même dans ses innovations techniques.

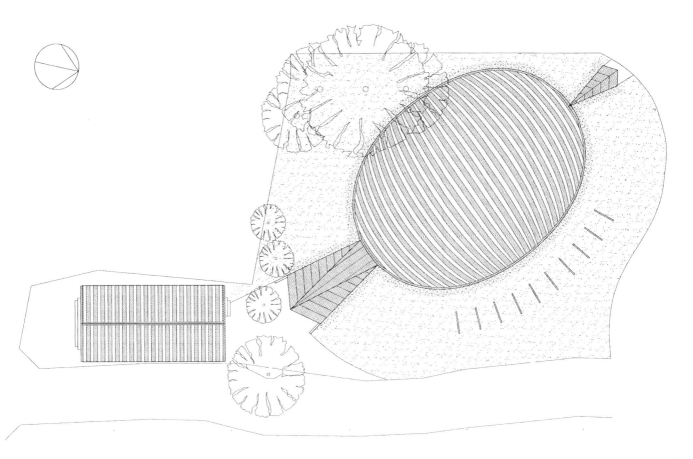

Seen from the exterior, the dome is even more unobtrusive than the section on the left page might imply. Though the term "minimalism" might not be applied here, the architect is clearly interested in the economy of design, but in terms of his materials and esthetically speaking.

Von außen betrachtet wirkt die Kuppel noch unaufdringlicher als im Querschnitt auf der linken Seite. Obwohl der Begriff „Minimalismus" in diesem Fall nicht zutreffend scheint, neigt der Architekt zu einer ökonomischen Gestaltung, zumindest im Hinblick auf Materialwahl und Ästhetik.

Vu de l'extérieur, le dôme est encore plus discret que la coupe ne l'implique (page de gauche). Bien que le terme de minimalisme ne s'applique pas ici, l'architecte s'intéresse à l'évidence à l'économie de conception, mais en termes de matériaux et d'esthétique.

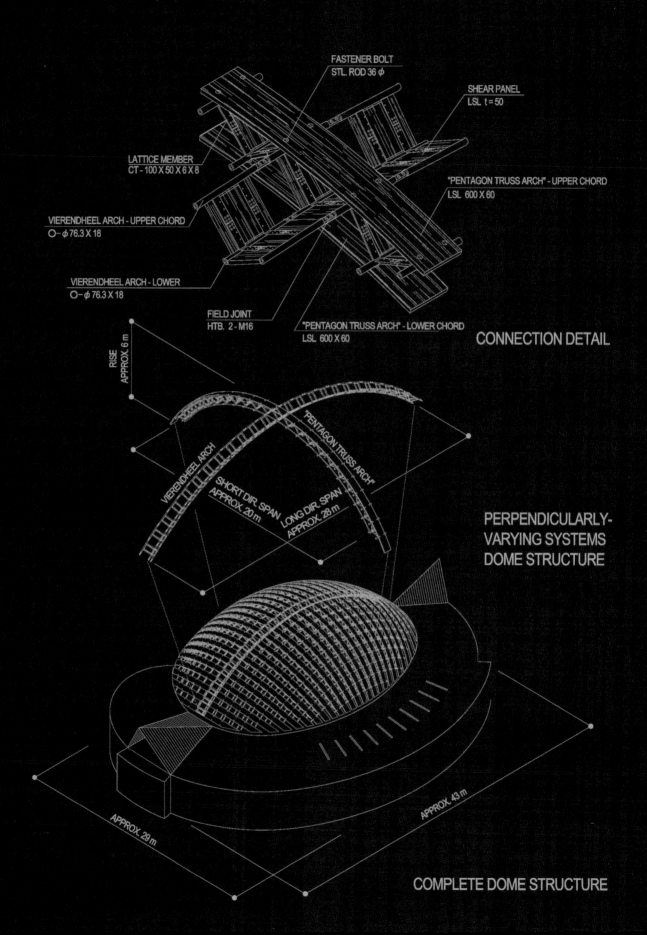

FASTENER BOLT
STL. ROD 36 φ

SHEAR PANEL
LSL t = 50

LATTICE MEMBER
CT - 100 X 50 X 6 X 8

"PENTAGON TRUSS ARCH" - UPPER CHORD
LSL 600 X 60

VIERENDHEEL ARCH - UPPER CHORD
O- φ 76.3 X 18

VIERENDHEEL ARCH - LOWER
O- φ 76.3 X 18

FIELD JOINT
HTB. 2 - M16

"PENTAGON TRUSS ARCH" - LOWER CHORD
LSL 600 X 60

CONNECTION DETAIL

RISE
APPROX. 6 m

VIERENDHEEL ARCH

"PENTAGON TRUSS ARCH"

SHORT DIR. SPAN
APPROX. 20 m

LONG DIR. SPAN
APPROX. 28 m

PERPENDICULARLY-
VARYING SYSTEMS
DOME STRUCTURE

APPROX. 29 m

APPROX. 43 m

COMPLETE DOME STRUCTURE

The 940-square-meter structure includes a swimming pool as well as the main gymnasium.

Das 940 m² umfassende Gebäude enthält sowohl ein Schwimmbad als auch eine Sporthalle.

Le bâtiment de 940 m² comprend le gymnase principal et une piscine.

As Ban describes the structure, "in the short direction a pair of arches are set parallel to each other and placed to form the oval dome. In the longer direction, another set of arches are sandwiched in between the paired arches along the short side. The arches along the long side are set at such an angle that they work as lattice members."

Bans Beschreibung der Konstruktion: „Nach der kürzeren Richtung bilden zwei parallel zueinander stehende Bögen die ovale Kuppel, während in der längeren Richtung eine weitere Bogenreihe schichtweise zwischen den beiden ersten angeordnet wurde, und zwar in einem solchen Winkel, dass sie als Gitterstäbe fungieren."

Pour Ban : « Dans l'axe court, des couples d'arcs parallèles forment l'ovale du dôme. Dans l'axe long, d'autres arcs sont pris en sandwich entre ceux de l'axe court. Les arches de l'axe long sont posés à un angle qui leur permet de fonctionner comme des poutres de treillis. »

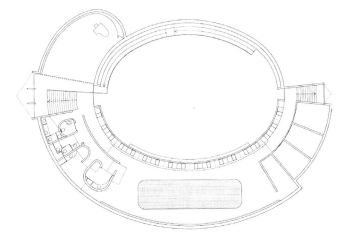

# BEHNISCH, BEHNISCH & PARTNER

*Behnisch, Behnisch & Partner*
*Günter Behnisch, Stefan Behnisch, Günther Schaller*
*Rotebühlstr. 163a*
*70197 Stuttgart*
*Germany*

*Tel: +49 711 607 720*
*Fax: +49 711 607 7299*
*e-mail: buero@behnisch.com*
*Web: www.behnisch.com*

Born in 1922 in Dresden, Gunter Behnisch grew up in Dresden and in Chemnitz. He studied architecture from 1947 to 1951 at the Technical University of Stuttgart (Dipl. Ing.) before setting up his own office in 1952. In 1966 he founded the firm of Behnisch & Partner, and from 1967 to 1987 he was a Professor of Design, Industrial Buildings and Planning, and Director of the Institute for Building Standardization at the Technical University, Darmstadt. In 1989, he established a city-office in Stuttgart, which has today become Behnisch, Behnisch & Partner. Stefan Behnisch was born in 1957 in Stuttgart. He studied philosophy at the Philosophische Hochschule der Jesuiten, Munich (1976–1979), economics at the Ludwig Maximilians University, Munich, and architecture at the University of Karlsruhe (1979–1987). He worked at Stephen Woolley & Associates (Venice, CA, 1984–85), and has been a Principal Partner at Behnisch, Behnisch & Partner since 1989. He has been involved in numerous workshops and conferences on sustainable and green buildings since 1997. Born 1959 in Neuhausen, Günther Schaller studied architecture at the Technical College of Stuttgart (Dipl. Ing. FH) and the University of Stuttgart (Dipl. Ing.) from 1982 to 1991, when he joined the offices of Behnisch & Partner. Project architect and project partner for the New Administration Building of the Landesgirokasse in Stuttgart, he has been a Partner in Behnisch, Behnisch & Partner since 1997.

Günter Behnisch, geboren 1922 in Dresden, wuchs in Dresden und Chemnitz auf. Von 1947 bis 1951 studierte er Architektur an der Technischen Universität in Stuttgart, wo er sein Ingenieurdiplom erwarb, und machte sich 1952 mit einem eigenen Architekturbüro selbstständig. 1966 gründete er die Firma Behnisch & Partner. Von 1967 bis 1987 war er Professor für Entwerfen, Industriebauten und Baugestaltung sowie Direktor des Instituts für Baunormung an der TH Darmstadt. 1989 eröffnete Günter Behnisch ein Büro in der Stuttgarter Innenstadt, das heutige Behnisch, Behnisch & Partner. Stefan Behnisch wurde 1957 in Stuttgart geboren. Er studierte Philosophie an der Philosophischen Hochschule der Jesuiten in München (1976–1979), Wirtschaftswissenschaft an der Ludwig Maximilians Universität in München und Architektur an der Universität Karlsruhe (1979–1987). Von 1984 bis 1985 arbeitete er bei Stephen Woolley & Associates in Venice, Kalifornien, und ist seit 1989 in leitender Funktion bei Behnisch, Behnisch & Partner. Seit 1997 führte er durch zahlreiche Workshops und Konferenzen zum Thema nachhaltiges und ökologisches Bauen. Günther Schaller, 1959 in Neuhausen geboren, studierte von 1982 bis 1991 Architektur an der Fachhochschule für Technik (Diplom 1987) und an der Technischen Universität in Stuttgart (Diplom 1991). Anschließend trat er in das Büro Behnisch & Partner ein. Er war Projektarchitekt und Projektpartner für das neue Verwaltungsgebäude der Landesgirokasse in Stuttgart und ist seit 1997 Partner im Büro Behnisch, Behnisch & Partner.

Né en 1922 à Dresde, Gunter Behnish a grandi dans cette ville et à Chemnitz. Il étudie l'architecture de 1947 à 1951 à l'Université technique de Stuttgart (Dipl. Ing.), et crée son agence en 1952. En 1966, il fonde Behnisch & Partner et, de 1967 à 1987, est professeur de design de bâtiments industriels et de programmation ainsi que directeur de l'Institut de standardisation de la construction à l'Université technique de Darmstadt. En 1989, il ouvre une agence à Stuttgart, devenue Behnisch, Behnisch & Partner. Stefan Behnisch est né en 1957 à Stuttgart. Il étudie la philosophie à l'École supérieure de philosophie des Jésuites (Munich, 1976–1979), l'économie à l'Université Ludwig Maximilian (Munich) et l'architecture à l'Université de Karlsruhe (1979–1987). Il a travaillé chez Stephen Woolley & Associates (Venice, Californie, 1984–85) et dirige depuis 1989 l'agence créée par son père. Il a participé à de nombreux colloques et conférences sur les immeubles écologiques durables depuis 1997. Né en 1959 à Neuhausen, Günther Schaller a étudié l'architecture au Collège Technique de Stuttgart (Dipl. Ing. FH) et à l'Unversité de Stuttgart (Dipl. Ing.) de 1982 à 1991, date de son arrivée chez Behnisch & Partner. Architecte de projet et responsable de celui du nouvel immeuble administratif de la Landesgirokasse à Stuttgart, il est associé de l'agence depuis 1997.

# NORDDEUTSCHE LANDESBANK

*Friedrichswall, Hanover, Germany 2000–2002*

*Client: Norddeutsche Landesbank Hannover. Building area: 14 000 m², gross floor area: 75 000 m². Costs: not specified.*

This large structure (40 000 square meters of floor area; space for 1 500 workers) is located at the intersection of the city itself to the north and the residential districts of southern Hanover. With the varying heights of its different components, the building is intended to integrate itself gently into the existing town pattern. An open and easily accessible ground-floor area, which remains a part of the town, serves to underline the pivotal role of the complex in the urban pattern. The offices do not have any air conditioning. During the day, concrete ceilings serve as storage mass, while a soil heat exchanger provides cooling. Air conditioning is limited to the kitchen and restaurant. The actual bank facilities begin one level above the ground floor. They are reached via a generous freestanding stairway. Transparent tubular passageways that can be opened during the summer link the different building parts. The high-rise part of the complex detaches itself from the formal order of the blocks addressing the street, rising to 70 meters and making connections with the wider context of the city. The high-rise area accommodates special elements such as a lounge and executive rooms. The office façades respond to the different requirements of the surroundings. The sides where there is heavier traffic (Friedrichswall, Willy-Brandt-Allee) have noise- and heat-absorbing double façades. The sides of the building exposed to the sun have external shading devices, while less exposed sides have high-quality sun protection glazing. Due to the optimisation of daylight in the offices the use of artificial lighting can be considerably reduced. The performance of the shading installations and glazing have been determined on the basis of computer-assisted studies. All rooms can be ventilated naturally by opening the windows, a means of exploiting the outdoor air which exceeds 22°C during less than five per cent of the year. Although the Chief Executive Officer of the Bank, Manfred Bodin, has admitted that "for us as bankers, it was not always easy to follow the highly creative approach of the architects," the result is a spectacular, ecologically and economically responsible building.

Das Großprojekt mit 40 000 m² Nutzfläche und Raum für 1 500 Angestellte grenzt im Norden an die Innenstadt und im Süden an die Wohnbezirke von Hannover. Mit der unterschiedlichen Höhe seiner einzelnen Bauteile soll sich das Gebäude natürlich in seine Umgebung einfügen. Durch den offenen, leicht zugänglichen Bereich im Erdgeschoss, der Teil des urbanen Raums bleibt, wird die zentrale Rolle, die der Bau innerhalb des Stadtgefüges einnimmt, noch unterstrichen. Da nur die Küche und das Restaurant mit Klimaanlage ausgestattet sind, dienen die Betondecken in den Büros als Wärmespeicher, während eine Wärmeaustauschanlage für Kühlung sorgt. Die eigentlichen Bankräume beginnen im ersten Stock, in den man über einen breiten, freistehenden Treppenaufgang gelangt. Die einzelnen Bauteile des Komplexes sind durch transparente, röhrenförmige Gänge, die im Sommer geöffnet werden können, miteinander verbunden. Der mit 70 m höchste der Baukörper, der unter anderem eine Lounge und Sitzungsräume beherbergt, ist durch seine Ausrichtung zur Straße aus der Anordnung der anderen Blocks herausgelöst und stellt die Verbindung zum städtischen Umfeld her. Ansonsten entsprechen die Fassaden des Bürogebäudes den unterschiedlichen Erfordernissen des jeweiligen Umfelds. So sind die zu den verkehrsreicheren Straßen wie Friedrichswall oder Willy-Brandt-Allee gehenden Seiten mit lärm- und hitzeabsorbierenden Doppelwänden ausgestattet. Die am stärksten dem Sonnenlicht ausgesetzten Fassaden verfügen über externe Sonnenschutzvorrichtungen, während die weniger sonnenbeschienenen Wände mit einer hochwertigen Sonnenschutzverglasung versehen sind. Dabei wurden sowohl Sonnenblenden als auch Verglasungen auf der Basis von computergenerierten Raumstudien konzipiert. Aufgrund der optimalen Nutzung des Tageslichts konnte der Einsatz von künstlichem Licht auf ein Minimum reduziert werden. Sämtliche Räume lassen sich durch Öffnen der Fenster natürlich belüften. Obwohl Manfred Bodin, CEO der Norddeutschen Landesbank, zugibt, dass es „für uns als Banker nicht immer leicht war, den äußerst kreativen Zugang der Architekten nachzuvollziehen", ist das Resultat ein großartiges, ökologisch und ökonomisch verantwortungsvolles Gebäude.

Cette importante construction (40 000 m² de surface utile, prévue pour 1 500 employés), se trouve à la limite de la ville et des quartiers résidentiels du sud de Hanovre. Par la variété de ses hauteurs, l'ensemble cherche à s'intégrer à la trame urbaine existante. Le rez-de-chaussée, ouvert et aisément accessible, fait encore partie de la ville et souligne le rôle charnière du complexe dans son contexte urbain. Les bureaux ne sont pas climatisés. De jour, les plafonds en béton servent de masse de stockage, tandis qu'un échangeur de chaleur au sol rafraîchit l'atmosphère. La climatisation est limitée à la cuisine et au restaurant. Les bureaux de la banque commencent au premier étage et sont accessibles par un escalier autoporteur de généreuses dimensions. Des passages tubulaires transparents, ouvrables en été, relient les différentes parties du bâtiment. La tour de 70 m de haut se détache de la composition des blocs longeant la rue et crée une connexion avec le contexte plus vaste de la ville. Elle accueille des installations particulières comme un salon et les bureaux de la direction. Les façades des bureaux répondent aux différentes exigences de l'environnement. Les façades latérales, devant lesquelles la circulation est plus dense (Friedrichswall, Willy-Brandt-Allee), possèdent une double peau absorbant le bruit et la chaleur. Celles orientées au soleil sont équipées de screens externes, tandis que les autres, moins exposées, sont équipées de verre de protection solaire de haute qualité. L'optimisation de la lumière du jour dans les bureaux permet de réduire considérablement le recours à l'éclairage artificiel. Les performances en matière de protection solaire ont été déterminées par des études informatiques. Toutes les pièces peuvent être naturellement ventilées par l'ouverture des fenêtres, ce qui permet de bénéficier d'un air frais extérieur dont la température ne dépasse 22° C que cinq pourcent du temps chaque année. Bien que le président de la banque, Manfred Bodin, ait déclaré que « pour nous, en tant que banquiers, il n'est pas toujours facile de suivre l'approche hautement créative des architectes », le résultat est un immeuble de haute qualité écologique et de maintenance économique.

*The rotated volumes of the main tower sit atop a base that recalls the scale of an older building seen to the right (above).*

*Die ausschwenkenden Baukörper des Hauptturms ruhen auf einem Unterbau, der die Struktur eines älteren, im Bild rechts sichtbaren Gebäudes aufnimmt (oben).*

*Les volumes pivotés de la tour principale sont posés sur une base qui rappelle l'échelle de l'ancien immeuble que l'on aperçoit à droite (en haut).*

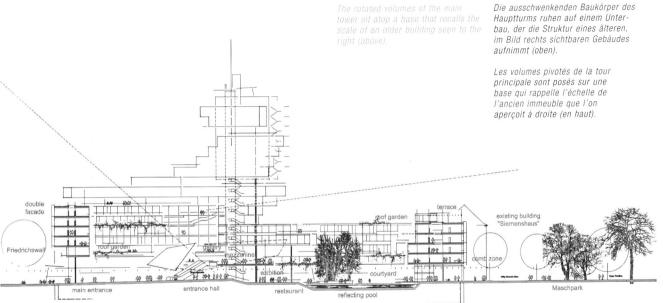

double facade

Friedrichswall

roof garden

gallery

mezzanine

main entrance

entrance hall

exhibition

restaurant

reflecting pool

roof garden

terrace

courtyard

existing building "Siemenshaus"

comb zone

Maschpark

Glass tube walkways link elements of
the complex structure and allow
users to view the rest of the building
as they move through it.

Gläserne Röhrengänge verbinden die
einzelnen Bauteile miteinander und
gewähren ihren Benutzern Ausblicke
auf den übrigen Gebäudekomplex.

Des passerelles tubulaires en verre
relient les éléments du complexe et
permettent à ceux qui les empruntent
de voir le reste de l'immeuble en se
déplaçant.

*Transparency and a technologically oriented lightness make the building agreeable to be in, even as it responds to high standards of ecological awareness and office efficiency.*

*Transparenz und eine gewisse technologisch geprägte Helligkeit sorgen für ein angenehmes Raumgefühl, wobei das Gebäude hohen ökologischen und bürotechnischen Standards entspricht.*

*La transparence et une certaine légèreté d'esprit technologique rendent agréable à vivre cet immeuble qui obéit à des standards élevés de respect de l'environnement et d'efficacité fonctionnelle.*

*Gardens and reflecting pools to some extent obviate or counteract the harshness of some surfaces of this rather complicated series of volumes.*

*Wintergärten und Wasserbecken bilden ein Gegengewicht zur kantigen Strenge, die einige der komplexen Baukörper ausstrahlen.*

*Les jardins et les bassins adoucissent la rudesse de certaines surfaces de cet ensemble de volumes assez complexe.*

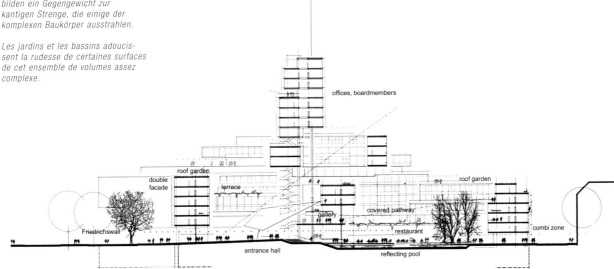

section b-b

Rather than the closed facades that many modern office buildings present in urban areas, the Norddeutsche Landesbank appears to move and breathe with its surroundings.

Im Unterschied zu den geschlossenen Fassaden, die viele moderne Bürogebäude in urbanen Zonen präsentieren, scheint die Norddeutsche Landesbank mit ihrer Umgebung mitzuschwingen.

À la différence des façades fermées de nombreux immeubles de bureaux en ville, la Norddeutsche Landesbank semble bouger et respirer avec son environnement.

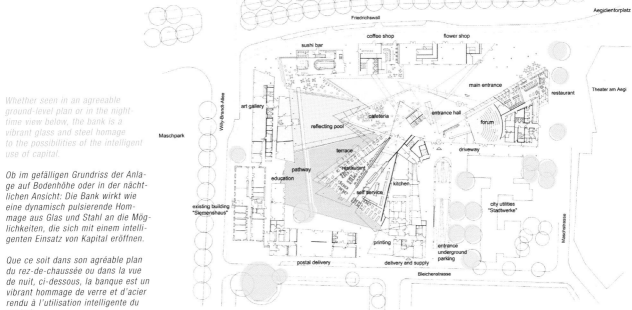

Whether seen in an agreeable ground-level plan or in the night-time view below, the bank is a vibrant glass and steel homage to the possibilities of the intelligent use of capital.

Ob im gefälligen Grundriss der Anlage auf Bodenhöhe oder in der nächtlichen Ansicht: Die Bank wirkt wie eine dynamisch pulsierende Hommage aus Glas und Stahl an die Möglichkeiten, die sich mit einem intelligenten Einsatz von Kapital eröffnen.

Que ce soit dans son agréable plan du rez-de-chaussée ou dans la vue de nuit, ci-dessous, la banque est un vibrant hommage de verre et d'acier rendu à l'utilisation intelligente du capital.

# SANTIAGO CALATRAVA

*Santiago Calatrava SA*
*Parkring 11*
*8002 Zürich*
*Switzerland*

*Tel: +41 1 204 50 00*
*Fax: +41 1 204 50 01*
*e-mail: zurich-admin@scsa-mail.com*
*Web: www.calatrava.com*

Born in Valencia in 1951, Santiago Calatrava studied art and architecture at the Escuela Técnica Superior de Arquitectura in Valencia (1968–1973) and engineering at the ETH in Zurich (doctorate in Technical Science, 1981). He opened his own architecture and civil engineering office the same year. His built work includes: Gallery and Heritage Square, BCE Place (Toronto, 1987), the Bach de Roda Bridge (Barcelona, 1985–1987), the Torre de Montjuic (Barcelona, 1989–1992), the Kuwait Pavilion at Expo '92 in Seville, and the Alamillo Bridge for the same exhibition, as well as the TGV Station Lyon-Saint-Exupéry (1989–1994). He completed the Oriente Station in Lisbon in 1998. He was a finalist in the competition for the Reichstag in Berlin, and he recently completed the Valencia City of Science and Planetarium, (Valencia, Spain, 1996–2000); the Sondica Airport (Bilbao, Spain, 1990–2000); and a bridge in Orléans (1996–2000). Other current work includes: Blackhall Place Bridge (Dublin, Ireland, 2003); Tenerife Auditorium (Santa Cruz, Canary Islands, 2003); Petach Tikvah Bridge, (Tel Aviv, Israel, 2003); Quatro Ponte sul Canal Grande (Venice, 2004); Turtle Bay Bridge (Redding, California, 2004); the Athens Olympic Sports Complex (summer 2004); and the Valencia Opera House (2004), the last major building in his City of Arts and Sciences. Calatrava has also been selected to design Christ the Light Cathedral for the Roman Catholic Diocese of Oakland, California; the expansion of the Museo dell'Opera del Duomo in Florence, Italy; and the Symphony Center for the Atlanta Symphony Orchestra in Atlanta, Georgia.

Santiago Calatrava, geboren 1951 in Valencia, studierte von 1968 bis 1973 an der dortigen Escuela Técnica Superior de Arquitectura Kunst und Architektur sowie Ingenieurbau an der Eidgenössischen Technischen Hochschule (ETH) in Zürich, wo er 1981 promovierte. Im selben Jahr gründete er sein eigenes Architektur- und Ingenieurbüro. Zu Calatravas Bauten gehören der Gallery and Heritage Square, BCE Place, in Toronto (1987), die Bach-de-Roda-Brücke (1985–1987) und die Torre de Montjuic (1989–1992), beide in Barcelona, der Kuwait-Pavillon und die Alamillo-Brücke für die Expo '92 in Sevilla sowie der TGV-Bahnhof Lyon-Saint-Exupéry (1989–1994). 1998 realisierte er den Bahnhof Oriente in Lissabon. Calatravas Entwurf für den Reichstag in Berlin kam in die Endauswahl. Zwischen 1996 und 2000 wurden das Wissenschaftsmuseum und Planetarium in Valencia, der Flughafen Sondica in Bilbao und eine Brücke in Orléans fertig gestellt. Zu seinen jüngsten Arbeiten gehören: die Blackhall-Place-Brücke in Dublin (2003), das Tenerife Auditorium in Santa Cruz auf den Kanarischen Inseln (2003), die Petach-Tikvah-Brücke in Tel Aviv (2003), die Quatro Ponte sul Canal Grande in Venedig (2004), die Turtle-Bay-Brücke im kalifornischen Redding (2004), eine Sportanlage für die Olympischen Spiele in Athen (2004) sowie, als letztes Hauptgebäude seiner Stadt der Künste und Wissenschaften, die Oper in Valencia (2004). Außerdem erhielt Calatrava die Aufträge für die Kathedrale Christ the Light für die römisch-katholische Diözese im kalifornischen Oakland, den Erweiterungsbau des Museo dell'Opera del Duomo in Florenz und das Symphony Center for the Atlanta Symphony Orchestra in Atlanta, Georgia.

Né à Valence en 1951, Santiago Calatrava étudie l'art et l'architecture à la Escuela Técnica Superior de Arquitectura de Valence (1968–1973) et l'ingénierie à l'ETH de Zurich. Docteur en science des téchniques en 1981, il ouvre sa propre agence d'architecture et d'ingénierie civile la même année. Parmi ses réalisations : Gallery and Heritage Square, BCE Place, (Toronto, Canada, 1987) ; le pont Bach de Roda (Barcelone, 1985–1987) ; la Torre de Montjuic (Barcelone, 1989–1992) ; le Pavillon du Koweït à l'Expo '92 et le pont de l'Alamillo (Séville) ; la gare de TGV de l'aéroport Lyon-Saint-Exupéry (1989–1994) ; la gare de l'Orient (Lisbonne, 1998). Il a été finaliste du concours du Reichstag à Berlin, et a récemment achevé la Cité des Sciences et le Planetarium de Valence (Valence, Espagne, 1996–2000) ; l'aéroport de Sondica (Bilbao, Espagne, 1990–2000) ; le pont de l'Europe à Orléans (1996–2000). Parmi ses chantiers actuels : pont de Blackhall Place (Dublin, Irlande, 2003) ; auditorium de Ténérife (Santa Cruz, Îles Canaries, 2003) ; pont Petach Tikvah (Tel Aviv, Israël, 2003) ; Quatro Ponte sur le Grand Canal (Venise, Italie, 2004) ; pont de Turtle Bay (Redding, Californie, 2004) ; complexe pour les Jeux Olympiques d'Athènes (été 2004), et l'opéra de Valence, dernier grand élément de sa Cité des arts et des sciences. Calatrava a également été sélectionné pour concevoir la Cathédrale de lumière pour le diocèse catholique d'Oakland (Californie) ; l'extension du Museo dell'Opera del Duomo (Florence, Italie) et le Symphony Center pour l'Atlanta Symphony Orchestra d'Atlanta (Géorgie, USA).

# YSIOS WINERY

*Laguardia, Álava, Spain, 1998–2001*

*Client: Bodegas & Bebidas SA. Building area: 8 000 m². Costs: not specified.*

The Bodegas & Bebidas group wanted a building that would be an icon for its prestigious new Rioja Alavesa wine. They called on architect Santiago Calatrava to design an 8 000-square-meter winery complex, a building that had to be designed to make, store and sell wine. Half of the uneven, rectangular site is occupied by vineyards. The linear program for the wine-making process dictated that the structure should be rectangular and it was set along an east-west axis. Two longitudinal concrete load-bearing walls, separated from each other by 26 meters, trace a 196-meter-long sinusoidal shape in plan and elevation. These walls are covered with wooden planks, which are mirrored in a reflecting pool and "evoke the image of a row of wine barrels." The roof, composed of a series of laminated wood beams, is designed as a continuation of the façades. The result is a "ruled surface wave," which combines concave and convex surfaces as it evolves along the longitudinal axis. The roof is clad in aluminum, creating a contrast with the warmth of the wooden façades.

Die Bodegas & Bebidas Gruppe wollte ein Gebäude, das ihren berühmten Rioja Alavesa Wein symbolisieren soll, und beauftragte Santiago Calatrava, eine 8 000 m² große Weinkellerei zu gestalten. Die Anlage sollte so konzipiert sein, dass dort Wein hergestellt, gelagert und verkauft werden kann. Das dafür vorgesehene Grundstück wird zur Hälfte von Weingärten eingenommen. Der linear verlaufende Herstellungsprozess schrieb eine rechteckige Anlage vor, deren Mittelachse in ost-westlicher Richtung verläuft. Die zwei längs gerichteten, im Abstand von 26 m aufgestellten tragenden Außenwände des Gebäudes beschreiben in Grundriss und Erhebung eine 196 m lange Sinuslinie. Sie sind mit Holzplanken verkleidet, die sich in einem Teich spiegeln, und evozieren das Bild aneinander gereihter Weinfässer. Die Fassadengestaltung setzt sich in dem aus Schichtholzbalken konstruierten Dach fort. Hierdurch ergibt sich eine „linierte Oberflächenwelle", die in ihrem längs gerichteten Verlauf konkave und konvexe Elemente kombiniert. Das Dach ist zudem mit Aluminium verkleidet, was einen reizvollen Kontrast zum warmen Charakter der Holzwände ergibt.

Le groupe Bodegas & Bebidas souhaitait édifier un immeuble symbolique pour son prestigieux vin de Rioja, Alavesa. C'est la raison du choix de Santiago Calatrava pour ce nouveau chais de 8 000 m², destiné à l'élaboration, la conservation et la vente du vin. La moitié du terrain rectangulaire de niveau irrégulier est occupée par la vigne. Le déroulement linéaire du processus vinicole impliquait une construction rectangulaire, orientée selon un axe est-ouest. Deux murs porteurs en béton, séparés de 26 m l'un de l'autre, déterminent un volume de 196 m de long, sinusoïdal en plan comme en élévation. Ces deux parois sont bardées de planches qui se reflètent dans un bassin et « évoquent l'image d'un alignement de tonneaux ». Le toit, soutenu par des poutres en bois lamellé-collé, vient dans la continuation des façades, d'où un effet de « vague de surface régulière » qui combine des plans concaves et convexes le long de l'axe longitudinal. La toiture est en aluminium, matériau qui contraste avec la chaleur des façades de bois.

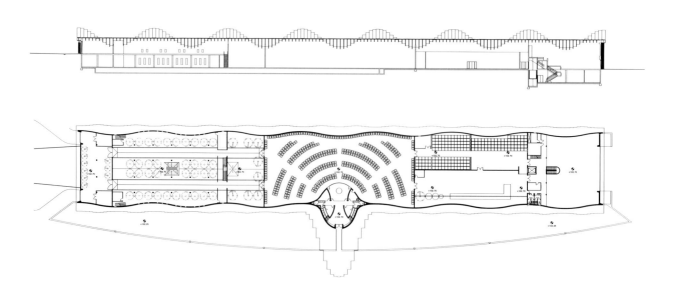

*Laid out as a long rectangle for functional reasons, the winery's most distinctive feature is its undulating roof.*

*Auffallendstes Merkmal der aus funktionalen Gründen als langgestrecktes Rechteck angelegten Weinkellerei ist ihr wellenförmig gestaltetes Dach.*

*Le composant le plus caractéristique de ce chais en forme de rectangle allongé, pour des raisons fonctionnelles, est la vigoureuse ondulation de son toit.*

The stepped, undulating roof culminates in a surprising canopy over the main entrance that juts forward.

Das Dach schwingt sich in Stufen bis zu einem über den Haupteingang herausragenden Vordach auf.

Le point culminant de la toiture en vague est l'étonnant auvent qui se projette au-dessus de l'entrée principale.

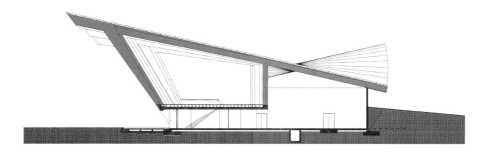

The entrance canopy covers the space visible to the left, with a broad view onto the surrounding landscape.

Das Vordach überdeckt den links abgebildeten Raum mit einem weiten Ausblick auf die Landschaft.

L'auvent de l'entrée abrite le volume visible à gauche, d'où l'on bénéficie d'une ample vue sur le paysage.

# TENERIFE AUDITORIUM SANTA CRUZ

*Canary Islands, Spain, 1997–2003*

*Client: City of Santa Cruz, Tenerife. Building area: 17 270 m². Costs: € 65 787 000.*

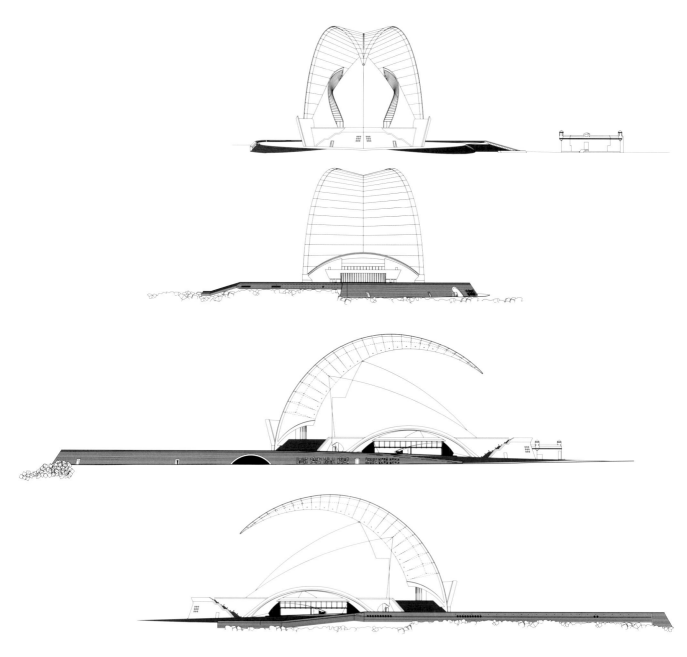

The essential shapes of the Tenerife Auditorium can be traced to other Calatrava structures featuring eye-like or bird-like shapes, as in the railway station Lyon-Saint-Exupéry.

Die grundlegenden Formen des Tenerife Auditoriums lassen sich auch in früheren Calatrava Bauten mit ihren augen- oder vogelförmigen Gestaltungsmerkmalen wiederfinden, so im Bahnhof Lyon-Saint-Exupéry.

La forme de l'auditorium peut être rapprochée d'autres réalisations de Calatrava en forme d'œil ou d'oiseau, comme, par exemple, la gare de l'aéroport de Lyon-Saint-Exupéry.

King Juan Carlos of Spain inaugurated the Tenerife Auditorium on September 26, 2003. The auditorium is located on the waterfront in the Los Llanos area of Santa Cruz, the capital of Tenerife and the second most populous city in the Canary Islands. Situated between the Marine Park and the edge of the port, the Auditorium connects the city to the ocean and creates a significant urban landmark. The Auditorium is the new home of the Orquesta Sintónica de Tenerife (Tenerife Symphony Orchestra). Its principal components are a 1 660-seat concert hall, which can be adapted to accommodate opera performances, and a 428-seat hall for chamber music. The program also provides for public amenities (café, cloakrooms, etc.), back-stage facilities (dressing rooms, rehearsal rooms, etc.) and separate structures for parking and offices. In addition to its primary function, the Auditorium will also serve as a conference center and exhibition hall. The 2.1-hectare site houses the 17 270-square-meter facility in an area measuring 126 by 60 meters. The cost of the structure was 65 787 000 Euros. The most expressive element of the design is the roof: a free-standing concrete structure known as the "Wing". Rising from a base 60 meters wide at the side of the building that faces the city, the Wing sweeps upward in a curve to a height of 60 meters. As it rises, pointing northeast toward the Auditorium's public plaza and the ocean, the Wing narrows and thins, terminating in a spear-shaped tip located 98 meters from the base of its arc. Though described as a wing, this arc and the auditorium itself recall Calatrava's frequent fascination with the form of the eye and eyelid. The curved geometry of the concert hall is the generating element of both the form and structure of the building. The 1 660-seat hall, with an area of 1 311 square meters, is equipped for opera and stage productions. The 428-seat hall for chamber music measures 411 square meters and has an almost triangular plan. Tenerife Auditorium is acoustically unique, since it is conical. Reflection of sound from the ceiling is provided by a series of convex reflectors.

Das Tenerife Auditorium wurde am 26. September 2003 vom spanischen König Juan Carlos eingeweiht. Es wurde im Uferbezirk Los Llanos von Santa Cruz, der Hauptstadt von Teneriffa und zweitgrößten Stadt der Kanarischen Inseln, erbaut. Zwischen Marine Park und Hafen gelegen, verbindet das Gebäude die Stadt mit dem Meer und bildet damit einen wichtigen städtebaulichen Markierungspunkt. Das Auditorium, die neue Heimat des Symphonieorchesters von Teneriffa, besteht in der Hauptsache aus einem Konzertsaal mit 1 660 Sitzen, der für Opern- und Bühnenproduktionen adaptiert werden kann, und einem Saal mit 428 Sitzen für Kammermusikaufführungen. Außerdem gehören zu dem Komplex öffentliche Räume wie ein Café sowie Künstler- und Proberäume und eigene Gebäudeteile für Büros. Neben seiner eigentlichen Funktion bietet das Auditorium auch Räume für Konferenzen und Ausstellungen. Der auf einem 2,1 ha großen Grundstück errichte Bau mit den Maßen 126 x 60 m bietet eine Nutzfläche von 17 270 m²; seine Baukosten beliefen sich auf 65 787 000 Euro. Das auffallendste Gestaltungsmerkmal ist das Dach: Ausgehend von einem 60 m breiten Sockel an der zur Stadt hin gelegenen Gebäudeseite schwingt sich diese „Flügel" genannte Betonkonstruktion bogenförmig zu einer Höhe von 60 m hinauf. Dieser nach Nordosten auf den öffentlichen Platz des Auditoriums und den dahinter liegenden Atlantik ausgerichtete Flügel läuft, immer schmaler und dünner werdend, 98 m über dem Sockel in einer lanzenförmigen Spitze aus. Auch wenn er als Flügel bezeichnet wird, erinnert dieser Bauteil wie auch das Auditorium selbst an die bei Calatravas Arbeiten häufig zum Ausdruck kommende Faszination des Architekten für die Form des Auges und des Augenlids. Zugrunde liegendes Gestaltungselement des Gebäudes ist die geschwungene Geometrie des großen Konzertsaals. Während dieser eine Fläche von 1 311 m² einnimmt, misst der fast rechteckig angelegte Saal für Kammermusikaufführungen 411 m². Das Tenerife Auditorium bietet dank seiner konischen Form eine einmalige Akustik, wobei die Klangreflexion von der Decke durch eine Reihe konvexer Rückstrahler erfolgt.

C'est le 26 septembre 2003 que le roi Juan Carlos a inauguré cet auditorium sur le front de mer du quartier de Los Llanos à Santa Cruz, capitale de Ténériffe et deuxième ville des Canaries. Entre le Parc marin et l'extrémité du port, l'Auditorium, qui abrite l'Orchestre symphonique de Ténériffe, est un monument urbain faisant le lien entre la ville et l'océan. Il se compose pour l'essentiel d'une salle de concert de 1 600 places, adaptable à des représentations d'opéra et de théâtre, d'une salle quasi triangulaire de 428 places pour la musique de chambre, d'un café, de vestiaires, d'installations en coulisses (loges, salles de répétition, etc.) et d'un bâtiment indépendant pour les bureaux et les parkings. L'ensemble devrait également servir de centre de conférence et de hall d'expositions. Sa surface totale utile est de 17 270 m² sur un terrain de 2,1 hectares et occupe une emprise au sol de 126 x 60 m. Son coût s'est élevé à 65 787 000 euros. L'élément le plus expressif est le toit, structure autoporteuse en béton appelée «L'Aile», qui s'élève d'une base de 60 m de large, face à la ville selon une courbe qui monte jusqu'à 60 m de haut. Orientée vers le nord-est et la place de l'Auditorium au-dessus de l'océan, l'Aile se termine à son apogée par un éperon qui s'élève à 98 m de la base de l'arc. Même si l'architecte parle d'aile, cet arc et l'auditorium lui-même rappellent sa fascination pour la forme de l'œil et de la paupière. La géométrie des courbes de la salle de concert génère à la fois la forme et la structure. L'acoustique de la salle conique, dans laquelle le son est réfléchi par le plafond et est renvoyé par une succession de réflecteurs convexes, est exceptionnelle.

  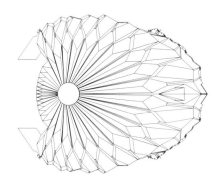

Calatrava's mastery of engineering allows him to go further than some architects in creating shapes that have an unexpected equilibrium, such as that of the point of the roof visible to the right.

Calatravas meisterhafte Beherrschung der Ingenieurstechnik erlaubt ihm, weiter als andere Architekten in der Gestaltung von Formen zu gehen, die eine spannungsvolle Balance halten, wie die rechts abgebildete Spitze der Dachkonstruktion.

La maîtrise de l'ingénierie dont fait preuve Calatrava lui permet d'aller plus loin que certains de ses confrères dans la création de formes et d'équilibres inattendus, comme le voile de béton de la toiture qui se termine en pointe (à droite).

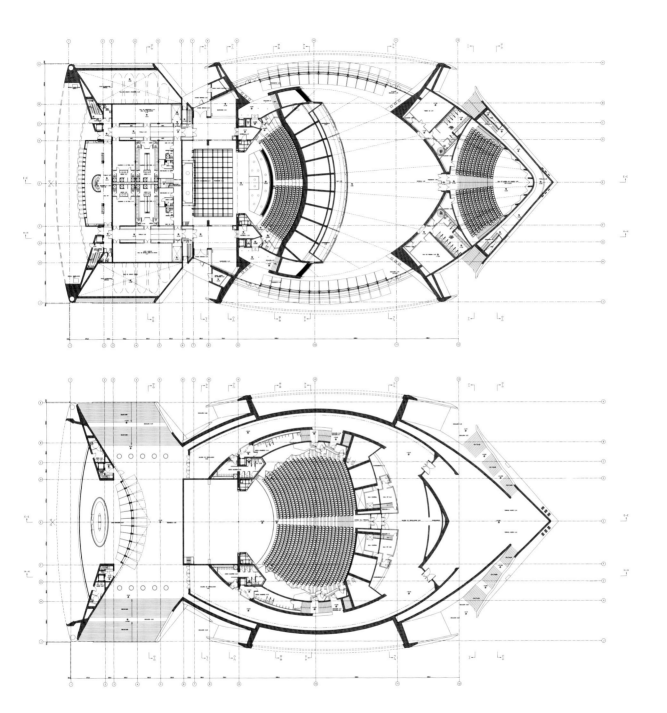

There is an undeniable continuity
between the white and spectacular
forms of the exterior of the Tenerife
Auditorium visible on the preceding
double page as well as to the left.
Even the overall plans on this page
retain a sense of the drama of the
outside shapes.

Die Kontinuität zwischen den weißen,
spektakulären Außenformen des Auditoriums wird auf den Abbildungen
der vorherigen Doppelseite und links
evident. Selbst die Grundrisse auf
dieser Seite vermitteln noch ein Gefühl von der dramatischen äußeren
Gestaltung.

La continuité est indéniable entre les
formes blanches spectaculaires de
l'auditorium de Ténériffe (double-
page précédente et à gauche). Même
les plans intérieurs, ci-dessus,
conservent le souffle de l'aspect
extérieur.

# COOK/FOURNIER

*Peter Cook, Colin Fournier*
*The Bartlett School of Architecture, UCL University College London*
*22 Gordon Street, London WC1H 0QB, UK*

*Tel: +44 20 7679 -4830 / -4861,*
*Fax: +44 20 7679 4831*
*e-mail: peter.cook@ucl.ac.uk, c.fournier@ucl.ac.uk*

*Kunsthaus Graz*

Peter Cook was born in 1936 in Southend-on-Sea, England. He studied architecture at the Bournemouth College of Art (1953–1958) and then at the Architectural Association in London. He created the magazine *Architecture + Gram* in 1961, and with Warren Chalk, Dennis Crompton, David Green, Ron Herron and Michael Webb the Archigram group set out to do nothing less than "revolutionize" architecture beginning in 1963. This group of young London-based architects began and sustained a campaign of "environmental revolution." They created images based on mechanical invention and pop culture. Archigram explored the continuities of change and choice using the opportunities offered by new technologies. "Plug-in City," "Living Pod," "Instant City" and "Ad Hoc" design were Archigram inventions that became part of the vocabulary of modern art and architecture. More recently, together with Christine Hawley, Peter Cook has built the social housing scheme of Lützowplatz in Berlin and the cantine of the Staedelschule in Frankfurt. He is currently Chairman of the Bartlett School of Architecture, University College, London (UCL). Together with the other founding members of Archigram, he won the RIBA Gold Medal in 2002. Colin Fournier was born in 1944 in London and is a Professor of Architecture and Urbanism at the Bartlett School (UCL). He was the partner of Bernard Tschumi for the overall planning and design of the Parc de la Villette in Paris, and developed the Master Plan for the city of Yanbu, Saudi Arabia. He is a joint founding partner with Peter Cook of the firm SpaceLab Cook-Fournier GmbH which was created in Graz for the Kunsthaus project.

Peter Cook, 1936 im englischen Southend-on-Sea geboren, studierte von 1953 bis 1958 am Bournemouth College of Art und anschließend an der Architectural Association in London. 1961 gründete er die Zeitschrift *Architecture + Gram*. Zusammen mit Warren Chalk, Dennis Crompton, David Green, Ron Herron und Michael Webb bildete er die Gruppe Archigram, die kein geringeres Ziel hatte, als die Architektur zu „revolutionieren". Ab 1963 führte diese Gruppe junger Londoner Architekten eine Kampagne durch, die sich „Umwelt-Revolution" nannte. Dabei schufen sie Bilder, die auf mechanischen Erfindungen und Popkultur basierten, und erforschten die Kontinuität von Veränderung und Wahl unter Einsatz neuer Technologien. „Plug-in City", „Living Pod", „Instant City" und „Ad Hoc Design" waren Erfindungen von Archigram, die in den Sprachschatz moderner Kunst und Architektur eingingen. In jüngerer Zeit hat Peter Cook zusammen mit Christine Hawley den Sozialwohnungsbau am Lützow-platz in Berlin und die Kantine der Städelschule in Frankfurt am Main realisiert. Derzeit ist Cook Präsident der Bartlett School of Architecture am University College London (UCL). Im Jahr 2002 gewann er zusammen mit den anderen Gründungsmitgliedern von Archigram die RIBA Goldmedaille. Colin Fournier, 1944 in London geboren, ist Professor für Architektur und Stadtplanung an der Bartlett School of Architecture. Als Partner von Bernard Tschumi erarbeitete er den Generalplan und das Gestaltungskonzept des Parc de la Villette in Paris und entwickelte den Masterplan für die Stadt Yanbu in Saudi-Arabien. Im Rahmen des Kunsthaus-Projekts gründete er zusammen mit Peter Cook die Firma SpaceLab Cook-Fournier GmbH in Graz.

Peter Cook est né en 1936 à Southend-on-Sea, en Grande-Bretagne. Il étudie l'architecture au Bournemouth College of Art (1953–1958) et à l'Architectural Association de Londres. Il crée le magazine *Architecture + Gram* en 1961 et fonde en 1963, avec Warren Chalk, Dennis Crompton, David Green, Ron Herron et Michael Webb, le groupe Archigram qui ne propose rien de moins que de « révolutionner » l'architecture. Ce groupe de jeunes architectes londoniens lance une campagne de « révolution environnementale », crée des images inspirées de la culture pop et de la mécanique, explore les problématiques du changement et du choix à travers les opportunités offertes par les technologies nouvelles. « Plug in City », « Living Pod », « Instant City » et « Ad hoc » sont des inventions d'Archigram qui finissent par faire partie du vocabulaire de l'architecture et de l'art modernes. Plus récemment, avec Christine Hawley, Peter Cook a réalisé un projet de logements sociaux à Lützowplatz à Berlin et la cantine de la Staedelschule à Francfort. Il est actuellement président de la Bartlett School of Architecture, University College, à Londres. Avec les autres membres fondateurs d'Archigram, il a remporté la médaille d'or du RIBA en 2002. Colin Fournier, né en 1944 à Londres, est professeur d'architecture et d'urbanisme à la Bartlett School (UCL). Il a été associé à Bernard Tschumi pour le plan d'ensemble et la conception du Parc de la Villette à Paris et a développé le plan directeur de la ville de Yanbu en Arabie saoudite. Avec Peter Cook, il est cofondateur et associé de SpaceLab Cook-Fournier GmbH créer à Graz pour le projet de la Kunsthaus.

# KUNSTHAUS GRAZ

*Graz, Austria, 2002–03*

*Client: Town of Graz, Kunsthaus Graz AG. Gross floor area: 13 100 m². Costs: € 40 000 000.*

Described as a "friendly alien" by its creators, the Kunsthaus Graz is located on the bank of the Mur river, at the corner of Südtiroler Platz and Lendkai. The bluish skin of the structure appears to float above the glass-walled ground floor. The biomorphic upper section of the building contains two large exhibition decks. Sixteen nozzle-like north oriented openings project upward from the skin of the building to admit daylight. In the upper levels, bridges link the 23-meter-high new structure with the "Eisernes Haus" whose cast-iron construction – which is the oldest of its kind in Europe and listed as an historical monument – was renovated as part of the construction work on the Kunsthaus. As Fournier has written, "the genealogy of the project's biomorphic form lies in its designers' fascination with the animal presence of architecture and in the checkered history of the competition for the Kunsthaus, which was originally intended to inhabit a large cavity within the Schlossberg, the hill standing in the center of the city. The part adopted by the authors at the time was to line this rocky cavity with an organically shaped membrane filling its complex and rough internal contours and to allow this membrane to protrude out of the mountain and into the city, like the tail or tongue of a dragon. When the location of the museum was changed to its current site, the dragon skin found its way across the river, flowed into the irregular geometric boundary of the new site and wrapped itself around the two elevated decks of the museum, forming an environmental enclosure that resembles neither roofs nor walls nor floors but a seamless morphing of the three."

Das von seinen Gestaltern als „friendly alien" bezeichnete Kunsthaus Graz liegt am Ufer der Mur, an der Ecke von Südtiroler Platz und Lendkai. Die bläuliche Ummantelung des biomorphen Baukörpers, der zwei große Ausstellungsplattformen beherbergt, scheint über den Glaswänden des Unterbaus zu schweben. Das Tageslicht kommt über 16 tentakelartige Öffnungen, die über die Außenhaut verteilt sind. In den oberen Etagen ist das 23 m hohe Gebäude durch Brücken mit dem „Eisernen Haus" verbunden. Dessen Gusseisenkonstruktion ist die älteste ihrer Art in Europa und wurde im Zuge der Arbeiten am Kunsthaus renoviert. Wie Fournier schreibt: „Die Genealogie der biomorphen Form dieses Entwurfs liegt in der Faszination seiner Gestalter für die animalische Seite der Architektur und in der wechselvollen Geschichte des Wettbewerbs um das Kunsthaus, das ursprünglich in einer großen Höhle im Schlossberg untergebracht werden sollte. Die Planer hatten die Absicht, diese Felsenhöhle mit einer organisch geformten Membran auszukleiden, deren Spitze sich wie der Schweif oder die Zunge eines Drachens aus dem im Stadtzentrum liegenden Berg herausstrecken sollte. Als dann der Standort des Museums verlegt wurde, fand die Drachenhaut ihren Weg über den Fluss, glitt in das geometrisch unregelmäßig eingehegte neue Grundstück und legte sich schließlich um die beiden erhöhten Plattformen des Museums, was ein Gebilde ergab, das weder Dach noch Wand oder Boden ist, sondern ein nahtloses Ineinanderverschmelzen aller drei Elemente."

Décrite comme « un aimable extra-terrestre » par ses créateurs, la Kunsthaus de Graz est située sur la rive de la Mur, à l'angle de la Südtiroler Platz et du Lendkai. Sa peau bleuâtre semble flotter au-dessus de son rez-de-chaussée paré de verre. Sa partie supérieure biomorphique contient deux grands plateaux d'exposition. Seize ouvertures en forme de lances d'arrosage, orientées vers le nord, se projettent vers le ciel pour attirer la lumière. Aux niveaux supérieurs, des passerelles relient le nouveau bâtiment de 23 m de haut à l'Eisernes Haus dont le bâtiment en fonte – le plus ancien de ce type en Europe, classé monument historique – a été rénové à l'occasion du chantier de la Kunsthaus. Comme l'a écrit Fournier : « La généalogie de la forme biomorphique du projet tient à la fascination de ses concepteurs pour la présence animale de l'architecture et pour l'histoire même du concours de la Kunsthaus, qui devait au départ occuper une énorme cavité dans le Schlossberg, la colline qui se dresse au milieu de la ville. Le parti adopté à l'époque était de doubler cette cavité rocheuse par une membrane organique remplissant ses contours complexes et laissés bruts et de permettre à celle-ci de se projeter de la montagne vers la ville, comme la queue ou la langue d'un dragon. Lorsque la localisation du musée a été modifiée au profit du site actuel, la peau de dragon a suivi, s'est infiltrée dans les limites géométriques irrégulières du nouveau terrain et s'est enveloppée autour des deux plates-formes du musée pour former un enclos environnemental qui ne ressemble ni à un toit, ni à des murs, ni à des sols, mais est une mise en forme (morphing) lissée de ces trois éléments. »

Overhanging a pre-existing building and imposing its very surprising shape on the otherwise quite traditional city, the Kunsthaus is a new focal point for Graz.

Ein älteres Gebäude überragend und das eher traditionelle Stadtbild mit seiner ungewöhnlichen Form prägend, ist das Kunsthaus zu einem neuen Brennpunkt für Graz geworden.

Superposée à un bâtiment ancien et imposant sa forme étonnante dans une cité assez traditionnelle, la Kunsthaus est le nouveau centre d'attraction de Graz.

In the section below and the image above, the bulbous upper volume stands out in contrast to the base and neighboring structures.

Dans la coupe ci-dessous et l'image ci-dessus, le volume bulbeux contraste fortement avec son soubassement et les constructions voisines.

Wie in unterem Querschnitt und der Abbildung oben sichtbar, steht der kugelige Baukörper in starkem Kontrast zu seinem Unterbau und den Nachbargebäuden.

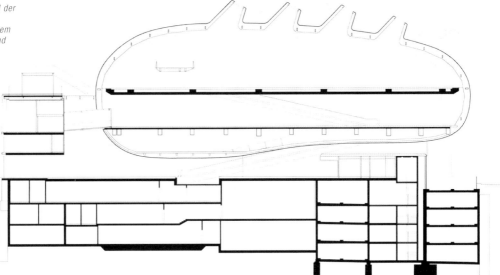

Im Innern stehen niedrige Ausstellungswände unter der dunklen Decke mit ihren Halogenlampen. Unten: Der Grundriss demonstriert die Übereinstimmung zwischen dem kugelförmigen Äußeren und den Innenräumen.

Vu de l'intérieur, les murs de cimaises blancs et bas sous un plafond sombre et haut équipé de luminaires circulaires. Ci-dessous, plan montrant l'implantation des volumes intérieurs par rapport à la façade bulbeuse.

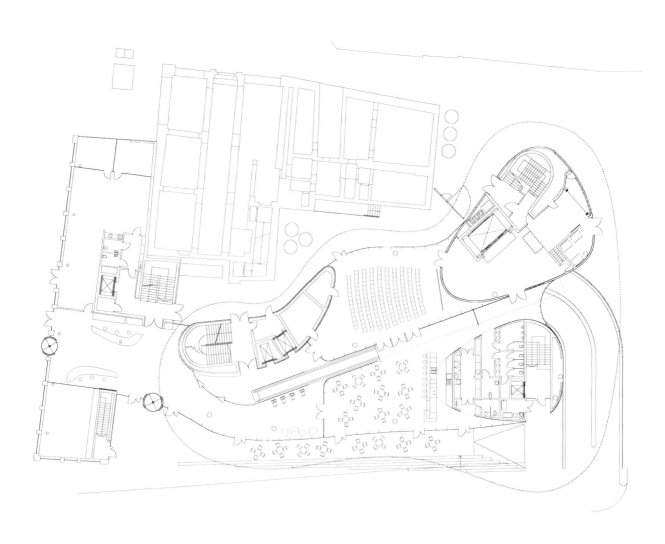

*Glowing like a space-ship that has landed in the midst of the city, the building's skylights jut out in a tentacle arrangement (right).*

*Wie bei einem gleißenden Raumschiff, das mitten in der Stadt gelandet ist, stehen die Skylights des Gebäudes in einer tentakelartigen Anordnung hervor (rechts).*

*La Kunsthaus irradie de lumière, telle un vaisseau spatial qui aurait atterri au milieu de la ville. Sur le toit, les lanterneaux évoquent des départs de tentacules (à droite).*

# COOP HIMMELB(L)AU

*COOP HIMMELB(L)AU*
*Prix & Swiczinsky & Dreibholz ZT GmbH*
*Spengergasse 37*
*1050 Vienna*
*Austria*

*Tel: +43 1 546 60 0*
*Fax: +43 1 546 60 600*
*e-mail: office@coop-himmelblau.at*
*Web: www.coop-himmelblau.at*

Wolf D. Prix and Helmut Swiczinsky founded COOP HIMMELB(L)AU in 1968 in Vienna, Austria. In 1988, they opened a second office in Los Angeles. Wolf D. Prix was born in 1942 in Vienna, and educated at the Technische Universität, Vienna, the Southern California Institute of Architecture (SCI-Arc), and the Architectural Association (AA), London. Since 1993 he has been Professor of Architectural Design, since October 2003 he has held the position of Vice-Rector for Space and Quality as well as the position of Head of the Institute of Architecture. From 1999 to 2003 he was Dean of Architecture, Industrial Design, Product Design, Fashion Design and Stage Design at the University of Applied Arts in Vienna, Austria. Helmut Swiczinsky, born in 1944 in Poznań, Poland, was raised in Vienna, and educated at the Technische Universität, Vienna and at the AA, London. Recent work includes the Academy of Fine Arts, Munich; the UFA Cinema Center (Dresden, Germany, 1997–98), the SEG Apartment Tower (Vienna, 1998) and the Apartment Building Gasometer B (Vienna, 1999–2001). Aside from BMW Welt (Munich, Germany, 2001–2006), current work includes: Akron Art Museum (Akron, Ohio, USA, 2001–2006); Musée des Confluences (Lyon, France, 2001–2007); and the North Jutland House of Music (Aalborg, Denmark, 2004–2006). In February 2004, COOP HIMMELB(L)AU won the competition for the new headquarters of the European Central Bank in Frankfurt.

Wolf D. Prix und Helmut Swiczinsky gründeten COOP HIMMELB(L)AU 1968 in Wien. 1988 eröffneten sie ein zweites Büro in Los Angeles. Der 1942 in Wien geborene Wolf D. Prix studierte an der Technischen Universität Wien, am Southern California Institute of Architecture (SCI-Arc) und an der Architectural Association (AA) in London. Er ist seit 1993 Professor für Architekturentwurf, seit Oktober 2003 Vizerektor für Raum und Qualität und Vorstand des Instituts für Architektur. Er war von 1999 bis 2003 Studiendekan für die Studienrichtungen Architektur, Industrial Design, Produktgestaltung, Mode und Bühnengestaltung der Universität für Angewandte Kunst Wien. Helmut Swiczinsky wurde 1944 in Posen (heute Poznań, Polen) geboren, wuchs in Wien auf und studierte an der Technischen Universität Wien sowie an der Architectural Association in London. Zu ihren neueren Arbeiten zählen das UFA-Multiplexkino in Dresden (1997–98), die Akademie der Bildenden Künste in München, der „SEG Wohnturm" in Wien 1998 sowie die „Wohnbebauung Gasometer B" in Wien (1999–2001). Neben der BMW Welt in München (2001–2006) gehören zu den aktuellen Projekten des Duos: das Akron Art Museum in Akron, Ohio (2001–2006), das Musée des Confluences im französischen Lyon (2001–2007) sowie das „House of Music" im dänischen Aalborg, Nordjütland (2004–2006). Im Februar 2004 gewann COOP HIMMELB(L)AU den Wettbewerb für den neuen Hauptsitz der Europäischen Zentralbank in Frankfurt/Main.

Wolf D. Prix et Helmut Swiczinsky fondent COOP HIMMELB(L)AU à Vienne (Autriche) en 1968, et ouvrent une seconde agence à Los Angeles en 1988. Wolf D. Prix est né à Vienne en 1942 et a étudié à la Technische Universität de Vienne, au Southern Califonia Institute of Architecture (SCI-Arc) et à l'Architectural Association de Londres (AA). Depuis 1993, il est professeur de design architectural et depuis octobre 2003, vice-recteur pour l'Espace et la qualité ainsi que président de l'Institut d'architecture de l'Université des arts appliqués de Vienne (Autriche). De 1999 à 2003, il a été doyen d'architecture, design industriel, design produit, design de mode et scénographie. Helmut Swiczinski est né en 1944 à Poznań, Pologne, mais élevé à Vienne, a étudié à la Technische Unversität de cette ville ainsi qu'à l'AA de Londres. Récemment, ils ont réalisé l'Académie des Beaux-Arts de Munich, le complexe de salles de cinéma UFA (Dresde, Allemagne, 1997–98), la tour d'appartements SEG (Vienne, 1998) et le bâtiment d'appartements Gasometer B (Vienne, 1999–2001). En dehors du BMW Welt (Munich, Allemagne, 2001–2006), ils réalisent actuellement l'Akron Art Museum (Akron, Ohio, USA, 2001–2006) ; le Musée des Confluences (Lyon, France, 2001–2007) et la Maison de la musique du Jutland du Nord (Aalborg, Danemark, 2004–2006). En février 2004, COOP HIMMELB(L)AU a remporté le concours pour le siège de la banque centrale européenne à Francfort.

# FORUM ARTEPLAGE BIEL, EXPO.02

*Biel, Switzerland, 1999–2002*

*Client: Swiss Expo.02. Site area: 14 200 m². Total costs: CHF 75 000 000.*

Built according to the rules set out by the organizers of Switzerland's Expo.02, the Biel structure was an artificial platform covering approximately 16 000 square meters, and set four meters above the Lake of Biel. The theoretically reusable structures were made of steel covered with layers of zinc dust clad in "a kind of grid foil stretched over a frame and inserted like a panel." As the architects said, "the site of the great exhibition has been conceived as a roofed platform jutting out over the lake, ending in a space with three towers. Its resemblance to an aircraft carrier is not a matter of coincidence but fully intended. Underneath the roof the platform is available to all kinds of utilization and gives room to the exhibition pavilions – just like the buildings of a town." Apparently quite substantial when seen from a distance, the structures, reached from a 413-meter-long pedestrian bridge, were in fact very light and airy. They were intended to house four exhibitions, two flexible activity spaces, as well as restaurants and bars. Varying between 33 and 39 meters in height, the towers and exhibition structures cost 33 million Swiss francs to build, while the platform itself cost 38 million Swiss francs.

Der Beitrag von COOP HIMMELB(L)AU war nach den von den Organisatoren der Schweizer Expo.02 aufgestellten Regeln konstruiert und bestand aus einer 16 000 m² umfassenden Plattform, die 4 m über der Wasseroberfläche des Bieler Sees lag. Die theoretisch wieder verwendbaren Bauteile aus Stahl mit Zinkofenstaubbeschichtung waren von einer Art Gitterfolie umgeben, die über einen Rahmen gespannt war. Die Architekten über ihr Projekt: „Die große Ausstellungsfläche ist als überdachte Plattform konzipiert, die über den See ragt und in eine Fläche mündet, auf der drei Türme stehen. Ihre Ähnlichkeit mit einem Flugzeugträger ist kein Zufall, sondern vollkommen beabsichtigt. Unter der Überdachung lässt sich die Plattform für alle möglichen Zwecke nutzen und es stehen auch Ausstellungspavillons zur Verfügung – wie die Häuser einer Stadt." Auch wenn sie aus einiger Entfernung betrachtet eher massig wirkte, war die über eine 413 m lange Fußgängerbrücke erreichbare Konstruktion sehr leicht und luftig. Während der Expo bot sie Raum für vier Ausstellungen, zwei Mehrzweckbereiche sowie Restaurants und Bars. Die Konstruktionskosten für die zwischen 33 und 39 m hohen Türme und die Ausstellungsflächen betrugen 33 Millionen Schweizer Franken, während die Plattform selbst 38 Millionen Franken kostete.

Réalisé dans le cadre du programme établi par les organisateurs de l'Exposition nationale suisse, Expo.02, ce « Forum » est une plate-forme artificielle d'environ 16 000 m², élevée à quatre mètres au-dessus du niveau du lac de Biel. Théoriquement réutilisable, elle était en acier zingué habillé « d'une sorte de trame mince étirée sur un cadre et glissée comme un panneau ». Les architectes expliquent que « le site de la grande exposition est conçu comme une plate-forme couverte jetée au-dessus du lac, et s'achevant par un volume doté de trois tours. Sa ressemblance avec un avion de transport n'est pas une coïncidence mais un effet voulu. Sous le toit de la plate-forme, toutes sortes d'utilisations sont possibles y compris l'installation de pavillons d'exposition, exactement comme des immeubles dans une ville. » Apparemment très volumineuse, vue de loin, la structure, accessible par une passerelle de 413 m de long, était en fait légère et aérienne. Elle contenait quatre expositions permanentes, deux zones d'activités variées, des restaurants et des bars. De 33 à 39 m de haut, les tours et les structures d'exposition ont coûté 33 millions de francs suisses, la plate-forme elle-même 38 millions.

Built out onto the water near the marina of Biel, the spectacular zig-zagging forms of the towers designed by Coop Himmelb(l)au are a counter-point to the essentially long and low shape of the pavilion.

Die spektakulären, auf dem Wasser nahe dem Jachthafen von Biel in Zickzackform errichteten Türme bilden einen Kontrapunkt zu der langgestreckten und niedrigen Aus-stellungsplattform.

Édifiées sur l'eau près de la marina de Biel, les spectaculaires tours en zigzag dessinées par Coop Himmel-b(l)au viennent en contrepoint de la forme longue et basse du pavillon.

The towers are essentially empty,
providing a soaring backdrop for the
temporary shows designed for the
Swiss national exhibition. Apparently
solid, the high-rise volumes are in
fact light-weight and empty.

Die Türme bilden einen steil aufragenden Hintergrund für die Präsentationen der Schweizer Landesausstellung.
Obgleich sie massiv wirken, sind die
Baukörper in Wirklichkeit größtenteils
hohl und deshalb leichtgewichtig.

Les tours sont vides pour l'essentiel.
Elles servent de signal aux manifestations temporaires organisées
pour l'Exposition nationale suisse.
Apparemment massifs, leurs volumes
sont en fait d'une grande légèreté.

The architects play on a contrast between apparent weight and lightness as can be seen in the juxtaposition of the solid looking slab on very light pilotis above.

Die Architekten spielen mit dem Kontrast zwischen Schwere und Leichtigkeit, wie man an der massiv wirkenden Platte, die auf sehr leichten Stützen ruht, sehen kann (oben).

Les architectes ont joué sur le contraste entre le poids apparent et la légèreté, comme on le voit dans la pose de cette dalle apparemment massive sur de légers piliers.

The covered walkway encourages visitors not only to see the lake from a different angle, but also the neighboring city.

Der überdachte Gang gibt den Besuchern die Gelegenheit, nicht nur den See, sondern auch die benachbarte Stadt aus einer neuen Perspektive zu betrachten.

Un passage couvert permet aux visiteurs de regarder le lac et la ville sous des angles différents.

# CHARLES DEATON

*Praxis Design LLC, Nicholas Antonopoulos*
*Mariko Arts, Charlee Deaton*
*1035 South Gaylord Street*
*Denver, CO 80209*
*USA*

*Tel: +1 303 282 1100*
*Fax: +1 303 733 1688*
*e-mail: praxarc@yahoo.com*

Born in Clayton, New Mexico in 1921, Charles Deaton and his family lived in a tent on the Oklahoma plains for two years until they were able to afford building a one-room house. By the age of 16, he was supporting himself as a commercial artist. He studied structural engineering, industrial design and architecture on his own, and earned certification. Deaton eventually became the designer of several buildings, including a two-stadium sports complex in Kansas City, Missouri known as the Truman Sports Complex or Arrowhead Stadium. An inventor and holder of over thirty US Patents, industrial designer, and creator of some 100 products in manufacture, Deaton died in 1996. Born in Centralia, Illinois in 1950, Charlee Deaton grew up in Colorado. She studied fine art, interior design, and graphic design at the Kansas City Art Institute, the Maryland Art Institute, and the Art Institute of Colorado. Her formal training was complemented by an apprenticeship with her father, Charles Deaton. In addition to her interior design practice, Charlee has worked as an artist, art educator and gallery owner and curator. She is principal and head designer of Mariko Arts. Nicholas Antonopoulos was born in Athens, Greece in 1955. He emigrated to the United States at an early age. As Principal and head designer of Praxis Design LLC, Nicholas Antonopoulos' professional background spans back to the offices of I. M. Pei and Partners in New York, where he received his architectural training. He apprenticed with architect Charles Deaton after receiving his Masters in architecture at the University of Colorado at Denver.

Charles Deaton, geboren 1921 in Clayton, New Mexico, lebte mit seiner Familie zwei Jahre lang in einem Zelt in der Prärie von Oklahoma, bevor sie es sich leisten konnte, ein Haus zu bauen, das aus einem Raum bestand. Im Alter von 16 Jahren verdiente er sich seinen Lebensunterhalt als Werbegrafiker. Nach einem Selbststudium in Bauingenieurwesen, Industriedesign und Architektur erwarb er eine amtliche Beglaubigung und plante im Anschluss mehrere Gebäude, darunter eine Sportanlage mit zwei Stadien in Kansas City, Missouri, die als Truman Sports Complex oder Arrowhead Stadium bekannt wurde. Deaton, der außerdem als Erfinder tätig war, über 30 US-Patente besaß und etwa 100 Industrieerzeugnisse gestaltet hatte, starb 1996. Seine Tochter, Charlee Deaton, wurde 1950 in Centralia, Illinois, geboren und wuchs in Colorado auf. Sie studierte Kunst, Innenarchitektur und Grafikdesign am Kansas City Art Institute, am Maryland Art Institute und am Art Institute of Colorado. Ihre akademische Ausbildung ergänzte sie durch eine Lehre bei ihrem Vater, Charles Deaton. Zusätzlich zu ihrer Arbeit als Innenarchitektin war Charlee Deaton als freie Künstlerin, Kunsterzieherin, Galeriebesitzerin und Kuratorin tätig. Heute ist sie Direktorin und leitende Designerin von Mariko Arts. Nicholas Antonopoulos, 1955 in Athen geboren, wanderte in jungen Jahren in die Vereinigten Staaten aus. Nicholas Antonopoulos, heute als Direktor und leitender Designer von Praxis Design LLC tätig, begann seine Laufbahn in den Büros von I. M. Pei and Partners in New York, wo er seine Ausbildung als Architekt erhielt. Nachdem er seinen Master of Architecture an der University of Colorado in Denver erworben hatte, absolvierte er eine Lehre bei Charles Deaton.

Charles Deaton, né à Clayton (Nouveau-Mexique) en 1921, et sa famille vivent sous une tente dans les plaines de l'Oklahoma pendant deux ans avant de pouvoir se construire une maison d'une pièce. À l'âge de 16 ans, il gagne déjà sa vie comme illustrateur. Il étudie l'ingénierie structurelle, le design industriel et l'architecture de lui-même et obtient les diplômes d'exercice de sa profession. Il conçoit plusieurs réalisations dont un complexe sportif de deux stades à Kansas City, Missouri, le Truman Sports Complex ou Arrowhead Stadium. Inventeur et dépositaire de plus de trente brevets, designer industriel et créateur de quelques 100 produits fabriqués, il disparaît en 1996. Née à Centralia, dans l'Illinois, en 1950, Charlee Deaton a grandi au Colorado. Elle étudie les beaux-arts, l'architecture intérieure et le graphisme au Kansas City Art Institute, au Maryland Art Institute et à l'Art Institute du Colorado. Sa formation est complétée par un apprentissage chez son père, Charles Deaton. En dehors de ses interventions d'architecte d'intérieur, elle exerce des activités d'artiste, d'enseignante, de galeriste et de conservatrice de musée. Elle dirige Mariko Arts. Nicholas Antonopoulos est né à Athènes, en Grèce, en 1955. Il émigre très tôt aux USA. Directeur et principal designer de Paxis Design LLC, son curriculum comprend un long passage dans l'agence de I. M. Pei and Partners à New York, où il se forme à l'architecture. Il fait son apprentissage auprès de Charles Deaton après avoir obtenu son Master of Architecture de l'Université du Colorado à Denver.

# CHARLES DEATON SCULPTURE HOUSE

*Genesee Mountain, Golden, Colorado, USA 1963–1965/2000*

*Client: Charles Deaton/John Huggins. Floor area: 250/500 m². Costs: $ 2 000 000 (year 2000 addition).*

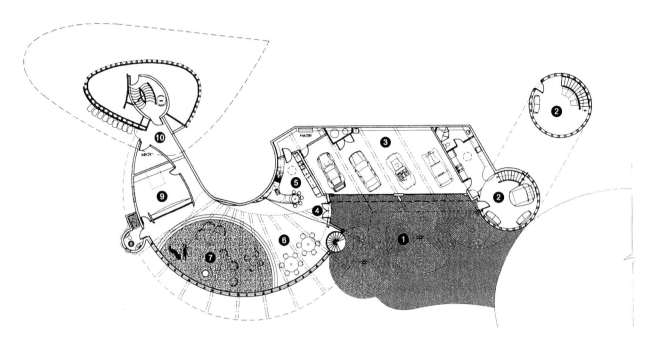

*Conceived as a sculpture, the Deaton House was carefully restored and extended by the architect's daughter Charlee and Nicholas Antonopuolos.*

*Das als Skulptur entworfene Haus wurde von der Tochter des Architekten Charlee und von Nicholas Antonopuolos restauriert und erweitert.*

*Conçue comme une sculpture, la maison a été restaurée et agrandie par la fille de l'architecte, Charlee Deaton, et Nicholas Antonopoulos.*

Charles Deaton, a self-taught architect, designed this house in 1963 as a "sculpture you could live in." Set on the north slope of Genesee Ridge outside of Denver at an altitude of over 2 000 meters, the house was built between 1963 and 1965, but its interior was not completed when the architect died in 1996. The house, described as a "clamshell" or "flying saucer," was a 250-square-meter shell. Praxis Design completed a new 500-square-meter addition in 2000. Charlee Deaton of Mariko Arts, the architect's daughter, designed the interior of the original house and the addition. As Charles Deaton described the original house, "I felt, first of all, the shape should be strong and simple enough to stand in a gallery as a work of art. On being enlarged to the size of the dwelling, it could be subdivided into living quarters. I knew, of course, when I started the sculpture that it would develop into a house. There was, however, no attempt to simply wrap a shell around a floor plan. In fact, no scale was set until the sculpture was done. The floor plan followed the modeling and contouring at a respectable distance."

Der Autodidakt Charles Deaton entwarf das Haus 1963 als eine „Skulptur, in der man leben kann". Es wurde zwischen 1963 und 1965 in der Nähe von Denver in einer Höhe von über 2 000 m errichtet, doch die Innenausstattung war noch nicht fertig, als der Architekt 1996 starb. Der als „Muschelschale" und „fliegende Untertasse" bezeichnete Bau hatte ursprünglich eine Nutzfläche von 250 m². Im Jahr 2000 realisierten die Planer von Praxis Design einen 500 m² umfassenden Anbau. Charlee Deaton von Mariko Arts, die Tochter des Architekten, gestaltete die Innenräume sowohl des ursprünglichen Hauses als auch des Erweiterungsbaus. Ihr Vater über seinen Entwurf: „Ich hatte das Gefühl, in erster Linie sollte die Form stark und einfach genug sein, um in einer Galerie als Kunstwerk zu bestehen. Wenn man dieses zu einem Haus vergrößerte, sollte es in einzelne Wohnbereiche unterteilt werden. Ich wusste natürlich von Anfang an, dass sich diese Skulptur zu einem Haus entwickeln würde, es war aber nie beabsichtigt, daraus einfach eine Hülle für einen Grundriss zu machen. Tatsächlich wurde kein Maßstab festgesetzt, bis die Skulptur fertig war."

C'est en 1963 que Charles Deaton, architecte autodidacte a conçu cette maison, qui est une « sculpture à vivre ». Édifiée entre 1963 et 1965 à 2 000 m d'altitude sur le flanc nord de la Genesee Ridge, près de Denver, son aménagement intérieur n'était pas encore achevé à la mort de l'architecte en 1996. Coque de 250 m², la maison est tantôt décrite comme une « palourde » tantôt comme une « soucoupe volante ». Praxis Design lui a ajouté une extension de 500 m² en 2000. Charlee Deaton, de Mariko Arts, fille de l'architecte, a conçu l'intérieur de la maison et son extension. Charles Deaton a décrit ainsi son projet : « Au départ, j'ai senti que la forme devait être suffisamment puissante et simple pour être installée dans un musée, comme une œuvre d'art. Agrandie à la taille d'une maison, elle pouvait se subdiviser en zones à vivre. Je savais, bien sûr, en commençant qu'elle serait par la suite développée en maison. Ce n'était cependant pas une simple tentative d'envelopper un plan au sol dans une coquille. En fait, son échelle n'a pas été déterminée avant que la sculpture ne soit achevée. Le plan suit le modelé et les contours à distance respectable. »

Looking like a self-contained viewing deck, the house boasts a view over more than 180° of the neighboring mountain landscape.

Das wie eine Aussichtsplattform wirkende Bauwerk bietet einen Rundblick von mehr als 180° auf die umliegende Berglandschaft.

Telle un belvédère, la maison bénéficie d'une vue à 180° sur le paysage et les montagnes.

Despite its essentially abstract form, and its artistic origins, the house shows a modernist propensity for functional efficiency, even where the viewing platform (above) is concerned.

Trotz seiner im Wesentlichen abstrakten Form und seines künstlerischen Ursprungs zeigt das Haus einen modernistisch anmutenden Hang zu funktionaler Effizienz, was auch für die Aussichtsterrasse gilt (oben).

Bien qu'elle soit de forme essentiellement abstraite et issue d'une réflexion artistique, la maison n'en a pas moins opté pour l'efficacité fonctionnelle, y compris dans ses aspects de plate-forme d'observation.

The curved, sleek forms of the house do recall its origins in the early 1960's, but the renovation allows the viewer to appreciate how little many shapes of modernity have evolved despite the rise of computer-driven technologies, for example.

Wenn auch die geschwungenen, glatten Linien des Gebäudes an seine Entstehungszeit in den frühen 1960er Jahren erinnern, lässt die Renovierung den Betrachter dankbar erkennen, dass sich viele Formen der Moderne trotz des Aufkommens computergesteuerter Gestaltungs-techniken seither kaum verändert haben.

Les formes lisse et incurvées de la maison rappellent ses origines du début des années 1960, mais sa rénovation permet au visiteur d'apprécier à quel point de nombreux aspects formels de la modernité ont faiblement évolué, malgré l'arrivée, par exemple, des technologies de CAO.

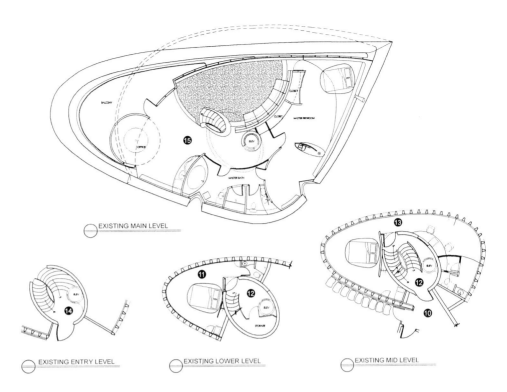

EXISTING MAIN LEVEL

EXISTING ENTRY LEVEL

EXISTING LOWER LEVEL

EXISTING MID LEVEL

This spiraling staircase is in perfect harmony with the curving exterior shapes of the house. An emphasis on sculptural shapes pervades the entire design.

Die Wendeltreppe befindet sich in vollkommener Harmonie mit den gewölbten Außenwänden des Hauses. Diese Vorliebe für skulpturale Formen durchzieht die gesamte Gestaltung.

L'escalier en spirale est en parfaite harmonie avec les formes extérieures de la maison. L'accent mis sur la qualité sculpturale des formes est omniprésent.

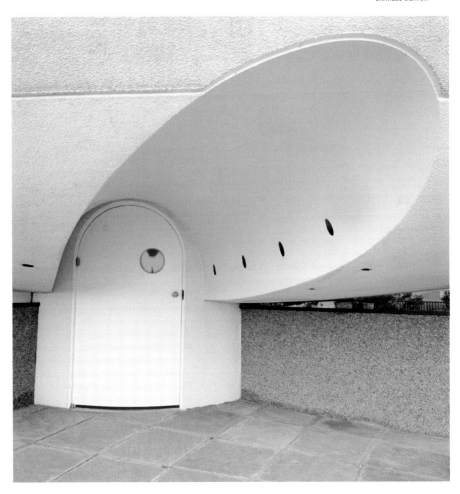

*The entrance door to the rear of the house expresses its "flying-saucer" esthetic, and is surprisingly closed vis-à-vis the openness of the interior.*

*Die Hinterseite des Hauses mit der Eingangstür hat etwas von der Ästhetik einer fliegenden Untertasse. Im Gegensatz zur Offenheit des Interieurs überwiegt hier eine geschlossene Gestaltung.*

*La porte d'entrée, à l'arrière de la maison exprime une esthétique de « soucoupe volante. » Elle s'oppose à l'impression d'ouverture donnée par l'intérieur.*

*Whiteness, rounded shapes and an alternation of opaque and translucent surfaces characterize the interior of the restored house.*

*Weiße Wände, gerundete Formen und der Wechsel von opaken und transluzenten Oberflächen kennzeichnen das Innere des restaurierten Hauses.*

*La maison restaurée se caractérise par des formes blanches et arrondies et l'alternance de surfaces opaques et transparentes.*

Finishes, bathroom design and windows confirm the concept of the house where every aspect seems conceived to emphasize continuity and modernity.

Oberflächen, Badezimmerdesign und Fenster folgen einem Gestaltungskonzept, in dem jedes Element Kontinuität und Modernität ausdrückt.

Les finitions comme la conception de la salle-de-bains et des fenêtres confirment le concept de la maison : tout semble conçu pour mettre en valeur la continuité et la modernité.

A couch offers a rare touch of bright color to the otherwise almost entirely white and beige interior.

Die Couch bringt einen fröhlichen Farbtupfer in das ansonsten fast ausschließlich weiße und beige Interieur.

Un canapé apporte une des rares touches de couleur dans un intérieur par ailleurs presque entièrement blanc et beige.

A flat-screen computer monitor seems very much in tune with the furniture and with the structural simplicity of the house at the level of the viewing platform.

Der Computer-Flachbildschirm auf der Ebene der Aussichtsplattform passt sehr gut zu den Möbeln und der strukturellen Schlichtheit des Hauses.

L'écran plat de l'ordinateur est en accord avec le mobilier et la simplicité de structure de la maison au niveau de la plate-forme d'observation.

# DECOI ARCHITECTS

*Mark Goulthorpe*
*Room 10-461*
*Massachusetts Institute of Technology*
*77 Massachusetts Avenue*
*Cambridge, MA 02139*
*USA*

*Tel: +1 617 452 3061*
*e-mail: mg_decoi@mit.edu*

dECOi is a small architectural/design practice that seeks to open the boundaries of conventional practice by a fresh and exploratory approach to design. In 1991 Mark Goulthorpe established dECOi to undertake a series of architectural competitions, often with a theoretical base. dECOi's work ranges from pure design and artwork through interior design to architecture and urbanism. Projects include: Bankside Paramorph (addition of a penthouse to the top of a tower, South Bank, London, 2004); Glaphyros House (Paris, France, 2002); Dietrich House (London, 2000); Swiss Re Headquarters (technical/design studies for Foster & Partners, London, 1998); Missoni Showroom (Paris, France, 1996); and the Chan (Origin) House (Kuala Lumpur, 1995). Art and research works include: Excideuil Folly (parametric 3D glyphting, Excideuil, France, 2001); Aegis Hyposurface (dynamically reconfigurable interactive architectural surface, Birmingham, 2000); and in 1993, "In the Shadow of Ledoux" (an "application/implication" exhibition, Le Magasin, Grenoble). Born in Kent, educated in Liverpool and Oregon, Mark Goulthorpe established dECOi in 1991 after having worked for four years in the office of Richard Meier in New York. He was a Unit Master Intermediate, Unit 2 at the Architectural Association (London, 1995–96); and is currently teaching Advanced Digital Design at MIT in Cambridge, Massachusetts.

dECOi ist ein kleines Architektur- und Designbüro, das sich zum Ziel gesetzt hat, die Grenzen der konventionellen Gestaltungspraxis durch einen frischen und experimentellen Zugang aufzubrechen. 1991 gründete Mark Goulthorpe das dECOi Atelier, um seine Beiträge für eine Reihe von Architekturwettbewerben einreichen zu können. dECOi's Arbeiten schließen Design und Grafik, Innenraumgestaltung sowie Architektur und Stadtentwicklung ein. Zu ihren Projekten zählen: das Haus Chan (Origin) in Kuala Lumpur (1995), der Missoni Showroom in Paris (1996), die Zentrale von Swiss Re – Technik- und Designstudien für Foster & Partners, London (1998), das Haus Dietrich in London (2000), das Haus Glaphyros in Paris (2002) und das Wohnprojekt Bankside Paramorph – die Erweiterung eines Penthouses auf einem Hochhausturm an der South Bank in London (2004). Zu seinen Kunst- und Forschungsprojekten gehören: 1993 eine „Applikation/Implikation"-Ausstellung im Le Magasin, Grenoble, mit dem Titel „In the Shadow of Ledoux", Aegis Hyposurface, eine dynamisch konfigurierbare und interaktive Architekturoberfläche in Birmingham (2000) und Excideuil Folly, eine parametrische 3D-Glyphographie im französischen Excideuil (2001). Bevor der in Kent geborene, in Liverpool und Oregon ausgebildete Mark Goulthorpe dECOi gründete, hatte er vier Jahre im Büro von Richard Meier in New York gearbeitet. Von 1995 bis 1996 war er Unit Master Intermediate der Unit 2 an der Architectural Association in London und lehrt gegenwärtig das Fach Advanced Digital Design am MIT in Cambridge, Massachusetts.

dECOi est une petite agence d'architecture et de design qui se propose de bousculer les frontières conventionnelles par une approche exploratoire nouvelle de la conception. En 1991, Mark Goulthorpe fonde dECOi-atelier pour participer à une série de concours d'architecture, souvent à partir d'une réflexion théorique. Les interventions de dECOi vont du design et de la création artistique purs à l'architecture et l'urbanisme en passant par l'architecture intérieure. Parmi ses réalisations : Bankside Paramorph (extension d'une penthouse au sommet d'une tour, South Bank, Londres, 2004) ; Glaphyros House (Paris, France, 2002) ; Dietrich House (Londres, 2000) ; siège de Swiss Re (études de design et techniques pour Foster & Partners, Londres, 1998) ; showroom Missoni (Paris, France, 1996) et Chan House (Kuala Lumpur, Malaisie, 1995). Parmi les travaux artistiques et de recherche : Excideuil Folly (glyphage paramétrique en 3D, Excideuil, France, 2001) ; Hyposurface Aegis (surface architecturale interactive à reconfiguration dynamique, Birmingham, 2000) ; « À l'ombre de Ledoux » (exposition « d'application/implication », Le Magasin, Grenoble, France, 1993). Né dans le Kent, après des études à Liverpool et en Oregon, Mark Goulthorpe fonde dECOi en 1991 après avoir travaillé quatre ans chez Richard Meier à New York. Il a été Unit Master Intermediate, Unit 2, de l'Architectural Association de Londres (1995–96) et enseigne actuellement la conception avancée par ordinateur au MIT.

# GLAPHYROS HOUSE

*Paris, France, 2000–2002*

*Client: private. Floor area: 320 m². Costs: not specified.*

A 320-square-meter apartment located near the Luxembourg Gardens in Paris is remarkable because of the extent to which the custom fittings are almost all the product of computer-assisted design. A ground-floor flat in a 1960s building, the residence is designed for a client who requested "a minimal yet sensual architecture, austere yet rich in its material and mass, no 'design,' no 'decoration…'" Employing what he calls a "non-standard logic," Mark Goulthorpe created almost every detail specifically for the project. A concrete stairway leading to downstairs bedrooms was created using a parametric model inflected in plan and section. "The resultant heave," he states, "imparts a sense of movement to the constrained space, as if another energy were at work disturbing the simple repose of a modernist heritage; the niche under the stair deforms as if a geological force were at work, creating a curious animism." Such deformations of surface and volume are found throughout the apartment. The fireplace, basins or bathtub were computer-modeled, milled as positives in polyurethane by CNC machine prior to being cast in bronze or aluminum. Using unusual materials such as 2000-year-old Chêne de Marais (marsh oak) stained charcoal-black by natural tanins in water, and finishes such as Teflon to preserve the texture of the wood, the architect develops an esthetic of restraint whose flights of fancy are really visible only to the trained eye. "As a sustained exercise in non-standard production, the project tears open the repetitive and prefabricated logic inherent in industrial production, suggesting a greatly enriched formal vocabulary released in the digital wake," concludes Mark Goulthorpe.

Das Bemerkenswerte an der in der Nähe des Jardin du Luxembourg in Paris gelegenen Wohnung ist ihre maßgeschneiderte Innenausstattung, die fast vollständig mit CAD entworfen wurde. Die Erdgeschosswohnung in einem Gebäude aus den 1960er Jahren wurde für einen Kunden gestaltet, der sich „eine minimalistische und doch sinnliche Architektur" wünschte, „streng und dennoch reich an Materialien und Masse, kein ‚Design', kein ‚Dekor'". Unter Anwendung eines von Goulthorpe „nicht-normierte Logik" genannten Verfahrens wurde von ihm beinahe jedes Detail speziell für dieses Projekt ausgeführt. Eine Betontreppe, die zu den tiefer gelegenen Schlafzimmern führt, ist nach einem vergrößerten Parametermodell geplant. „Die daraus resultierende Verschiebung", so der Architekt, „verleiht dem eng begrenzten Raum ein Gefühl von Bewegung, als wäre hier eine andere Form von Energie am Werk, welche die schlichte Ausgewogenheit einer modernistischen Ästhetik stört. Auch die Nische unter der Treppe ist wie unter Einwirkung einer geologischen Kraft deformiert, was einen merkwürdigen Animismus erzeugt." Derartige Verzerrungen von Oberfläche und Volumen sind in der gesamten Wohnung zu finden. Kamin, Bade- und Duschwannen wurden mit dem Computer modelliert, dann als Positive mittels CNC-Maschine in Polyurethan gegossen und schließlich in Bronze oder Aluminium ausgeformt. Mit seinem Einsatz ungewöhnlicher Materialien, wie etwa 2000 Jahre altem Chêne-de-Marais-Eichenholz, das mit natürlichem Tannin schwarz gefärbt wurde, und Teflon als Oberflächenbehandlung, um die Holztextur zu bewahren, entwickelte der Architekt eine Ästhetik der Zurückhaltung, deren gelegentliche exzentrische Anwandlungen nur dem geschulten Auge auffallen. Dazu noch einmal Mark Goulthorpe: „Als eine kontinuierliche Übung in nicht-standardisierter Produktion bricht das Projekt die sich ständig wiederholende und vorgefertigte Logik auf, die der industriellen Produktion eigen ist und bringt damit eine durch die Digitalisierung in hohem Maß bereicherte Formensprache hervor."

C'est le recours à la CAO pour une grande partie des aménagements de cet appartement de 320 m², qui le rend particulièrement remarquable. En rez-de-chaussée d'un immeuble des années 1960 près des Jardins du Luxembourg à Paris, il a été conçu pour un client qui souhaitait « une architecture à la fois minimaliste et sensuelle, austère mais riche dans ses matériaux et ses masses, sans ‹ design ›, ni ‹ décoration ›… » Faisant appel à ce qu'il appelle une « logique non standard », Mark Goulthorpe a étudié spécifiquement chaque détail du projet. Un escalier en béton qui mène aux chambres au niveau inférieur a été dessiné à l'aide d'un modèle paramétrique inversé, en plan comme en coupe. « L'effet de soulèvement qui en résulte », fait remarquer Goulthorpe, « anime ce volume réduit, comme si une source d'énergie autre venait troubler la simplicité de l'héritage moderniste. La niche sous l'escalier semble déformée par une mystérieuse force tellurique, suggérant des évocations animistes. » Ce type de déformation des surfaces et des volumes se retrouve dans tout l'appartement. La cheminée, les lavabos ou la baignoire ont été dessinés par ordinateur, et réalisés en polyuréthane par une machine de modélisation en volume avant d'être fondus en bronze ou aluminium. En faisant appel à des matériaux rares comme du chêne des marais vieux de 2 000 ans, teint en noir aux tanins naturels, et à des finitions comme le Téflon qui préserve la texture du bois, l'architecte a développé une esthétique toute de réserve, dont la créativité n'est repérable que pour un œil entraîné. « En tant qu'exercice approfondi de production non standardisée, le projet remet en cause la logique du préfabriqué inhérente à la production industrielle, et suggère un vocabulaire formel beaucoup plus riche libéré par la numérisation », conclut Mark Goulthorpe.

*Kitchen and living spaces communicate freely and seem to express a simplicity that in fact reveals a complex and very carefully thought out use of materials and forms.*

*Küche und Wohnraum stehen in offenem Dialog miteinander. Sie bringen eine Schlichtheit zum Ausdruck, hinter der in Wahrheit eine komplexe und äußerst durchdachte Verwendung von Material und Form steckt.*

*La cuisine et les espaces de séjour qui communiquent librement semblent exprimer une simplicité qui cache en fait une réflexion complexe et approfondie sur les matériaux et les formes.*

Living and dining areas are open and place an emphasis on such unique features as the computer designed fireplace seen in the image above.

In den offen angelegten Wohn- und Essbereichen kommen so ungewöhnliche Ausstattungsmerkmale wie der mittels CAD gestaltete Kamin (oben) besonders gut zur Geltung.

Les zones de repas et de séjour ouvertes mettent en valeur des équipements originaux comme la cheminée conçue par ordinateur (ci-dessus).

*Seltene Hölzer und Details wie die
unterschiedliche Breite der
Bodenbretter (oben) ergeben zusammen eine Form von Modernität, die
keiner Uniformität mehr bedarf.*

*Des bois rares et des éléments
visibles comme la largeur variable
des lattes de parquet – ci-dessus –
se fondent dans un style d'une
modernité qui n'a plus besoin de
l'uniformité pour s'exprimer.*

Even such features as the wash basins are unique and designed on computers for manufacture by digitally controlled tools.

Selbst die Waschbecken wurden auf dem Computer gestaltet und mittels digitalgesteuerter Werkzeuge einzeln angefertigt.

Certains équipements comme les lavabos sont des pièces uniques dessinées sur ordinateur et réalisés par des outils à commande numérique.

A computer-crafted, hanging solid aluminum screen is one of the most unusual features of the interior décor. Its liquid surface seems to move according to the lighting conditions.

Eine gleichfalls computergefertigte, hängende Wand aus massivem Aluminium ist eins der auffallendsten Merkmale der Innenraumgestaltung. Ihre Oberfläche verändert sich mit dem Lichteinfall.

Un écran en aluminium massif, dessiné par ordinateur, est l'un des éléments les plus frappants du décor intérieur. Sa surface, qui évoque un liquide, semble bouger en fonction de l'éclairage.

# BANKSIDE PARAMORPH

*London, UK, 2003–04*

*Client: private. Floor area: 320 m². Costs: not specified.*

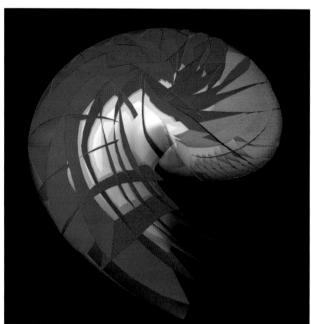

*Despite its apparent complexity, the Bankside Paramorph is designed to be manufactured and assembled within the budgets of "normal" construction methods.*

*Trotz seiner offensichtlichen Komplexität ist das Bankside Paramorph so konzipiert, dass es im Rahmen des Budgets „normaler" Konstruktionsmethoden umgesetzt werden kann.*

*Malgré sa complexité apparente, le Bankside Paramorph est conçu pour être fabriqué et assemblé pour le coût de méthodes de construction « normales. »*

This project includes the remodeling of an existing 320-square-meter flat and, above all, the rooftop addition of a 130-square-meter aluminum honeycomb structure. Taken from airline or space technology, the aluminum honeycomb skin has sufficient strength to replace traditional structural elements and the addition is to cost no more than an ordinary space (about £500 000 in this instance). With half the weight of "normal" construction, the new elements are to be delivered in six sections and bolted together on top of this apartment building located near the Tate Modern in the Southwark area of London. Working with the engineers Arup, dECOi feels that their method of parametric modeling and their ability, with the use of new materials, to "make the skin the structure" is nothing short of revolutionary. Shaped something like a seashell, the addition is described by architect Mark Goulthorpe as an "accelerating curve," and he says he is not surprised that the mathematically derived shape approaches some of those found in nature.

Das Projekt beinhaltet den Umbau einer 320 m² großen Wohnung und einen 130 m² umfassenden Dachausbau in aluminiumverkleideter Wabenbauweise. Die aus der Raumfahrt entlehnte Aluminiumaußenhaut verfügt über genügend Formfestigkeit, um traditionelle Konstruktionsmaterialien zu ersetzen, und die Kosten für den Dachausbau liegen mit 500 000 Pfund auch nicht höher als bei weniger ausgefallenen Methoden. Der halb so viel wie „normale" Konstruktionen wiegende Aluminiumkörper wurde in sechs Abschnitten geliefert und auf dem Dach des nahe der Tate Modern liegenden Wohnblocks zusammengeschraubt. Die Architekten von dECOi, die bei diesem Projekt mit der Ingenieurfirma Arup zusammengearbeitet haben, sind davon überzeugt, dass ihre Methode des parametrischen Modellierens zusammen mit dem Einsatz neuer Materialien durchaus revolutionär ist. Der wie eine Muschel geformte Aufbau wird von dem Planer Mark Goulthorpe als eine „sich beschleunigende Kurve" beschrieben. Es habe ihn zudem nicht überrascht, dass die mathematisch entwickelte Form Ähnlichkeit mit Gebilden hat, die man in der Natur findet.

Ce projet porte sur le réaménagement d'un appartement de 320 m² non loin de la Tate Modern (Southwark, Londres) et surtout sur l'addition en toiture d'une structure en nid d'abeille d'aluminium de 130 m². Empruntée à la technologie spatiale ou aéronautique, la peau d'aluminium en nid d'abeille offre une résistance suffisante pour remplacer les éléments structurels traditionnels et cette extension ne devrait pas coûter au total plus cher qu'une construction classique (environ 500 000 de livres sterling). Pesant moitié moins qu'une solution « normale », ces nouveaux éléments ont été livrés en six parties et boulonnés ensemble sur place. Collaborant ici avec les ingénieurs d'Arup, dECOi pense que cette méthode de modélisation paramétrique et le recours à des matériaux nouveaux pour « faire de la peau la structure » est quasiment révolutionnaire. Pour Mark Goulthorpe, il n'est pas étonnant que cette forme issue de calculs mathématiques se rapproche de celles de la nature. Pour lui, ce volume qui évoque un coquillage fait penser à « une courbe en accélération ».

The Bankside Paramorph is conceptually related to an earlier dECOi design, the Excideuil Folly (parametric 3D glyphting, Excideuil, France, 2001).

Das Bankside Paramorph ist konzeptionell mit einem früheren dECOi Entwurf verwandt, dem 2001 entstandenen Projekt Excideuil Folly, einer parametrischen 3D-Glyphograpie in Excideuil, Frankreich.

Conceptuellement, le Bankside Paramorph est voisin d'un précédant projet de dECOi, l'Excideuil Folly (Paramétric 3D Glyphting, Excideuil, France, 2001).

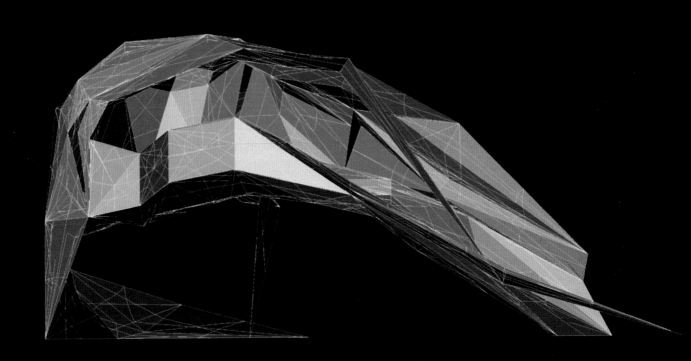

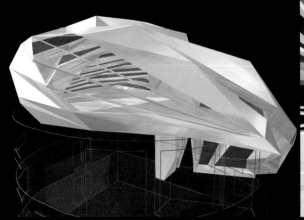

Intended for computer-driven manufacture, the addition to the roof of a building located just next to the Tate Modern is seen in the photo-montage below.

Die Fotomontage (unten) zeigt den für eine computergesteuerte Produktion entworfenen Dachausbau auf einem Gebäude direkt neben der Tate Modern.

Dans le photomontage ci-dessus, une extension en toiture d'un immeuble tout proche de la Tate Moderne, prévue pour être réalisée selon des processus de production pilotés par informatique.

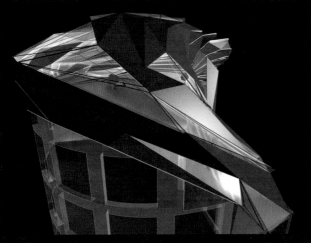

In the picture below, the edge of Tate Modern can be seen on the left. The Thames is just to the right of the field of this image.

Am linken Rand der unteren Abbildung ist eine Außenwand der Tate Modern zu erkennen. Die Themse befindet sich rechts von dem im Bild dargestellten Ausschnitt.

Dans l'image ci-dessous, un angle de la Tate Modern, à gauche. La Tamise est à droite, hors champ.

# NEIL M. DENARI

*Neil M. Denari Architects Inc.*
*12615 Washington Boulevard*
*Los Angeles, CA 90066*
*USA*

*Tel: +1 310 390 3033*
*Fax: +1 310 390 9810*
*e-mail: info@nmda-inc.com*
*Web: www.nmda-inc.com*

Neil M. Denari received a Bachelor of Architecture in 1980 from the University of Houston, and a Master of Architecture degree from Harvard in 1982, where he also studied art theory and the philosophy of science. He then spent six months working as an intern for Aerospatiale, the French aviation and space company. Neil Denari worked in New York from 1983 to 1988 as a senior designer at James Stewart Polshek & Partners before teaching at Columbia's Graduate School of Architecture and Planning. Denari moved to Los Angeles in 1988 and taught at the Southern California Institute of Architecture (SCI-Arc). In 1997, he was named the third Director of SCI-Arc. In 1996, he completed the construction of a small, experimental space at Gallery Ma in Tokyo. His other work, though highly influential, has often remained in its rather seductive virtual form. Recent projects and proposals include: L. A. Eyeworks, Showroom/Store (Los Angeles, 2001–02); Concept Design for SUN Microsystems Trade Show Structure and Office/Work Environment; Concept Design for QWEST Communications Broadband Kiosk; Concept design for SONY Qualia brand hotel and retail store; 15-story Loft Building, Union Square (New York), Feasibility study/envelope design; Water Center (Nashville, TN); D/J House, house renovation and addition (Mt. Washington, LA); NCAP Master Plan, a 16.5-acre plan for housing, park space, lease space, commissioned by the Nashville Cultural Arts Project; and Endeavor Talent and Literary Agency Offices and Theater (Beverly Hills, CA).

Neil M. Denari erwarb 1980 den Bachelor of Architecture an der University of Houston und 1982 den Master of Architecture in Harvard, wo er außerdem Kunsttheorie und Wissenschaftsphilosophie studierte. Anschließend arbeitete er ein halbes Jahr als Praktikant bei dem französischen Flugzeug- und Raumfahrtunternehmen Aerospatiale. Von 1983 bis 1988 war Denari als Planungsleiter bei James Stewart Polshek & Partners in New York tätig und lehrte an der Graduate School of Architecture and Planning der Columbia University. 1988 zog er nach Los Angeles und lehrte am Southern California Institute of Architecture (SCI-Arc). 1996 führte er die Konstruktion eines kleinen, experimentellen Raums in der Galerie Ma in Tokio aus. Obgleich sehr einflussreich, blieben viele seiner Arbeiten virtuelle Konstrukte. Zu seinen jüngsten Projekten und Entwürfen gehören: der Laden/Showroom von L. A. Eyeworks in Los Angeles (2001–02), die Designkonzepte für Messestand und Büro/Workstation von SUN Microsystems, für den Verkaufspavillon von QWEST Communications Broadband und für das Qualia Hotel mit Ladenlokal von SONY, die Machbarkeitsstudie und das Umhüllungsdesign für ein 15-stöckiges Loftgebäude am Union Square in New York, das Water Center in Nashville, Tennessee, Renovierung und Anbau für das D/J House in Mt. Washington, Los Angeles, der Masterplan für NCAP, der vom Nashville Cultural Arts Project in Auftrag gegebene Bebauungsplan für ein 16,5 ha großes Gelände mit Wohnanlage, Geschäften und Parkplatz sowie Büro und Theater für die Endeavor Talent and Literary Agency im kalifornischen Beverly Hills.

Neil M. Denari est Bachelor of Architecture de l'Université de Houston (1980) et Master of Architecture de Harvard (1982), où il a également étudié la théorie de l'art et la philosophie des sciences. Il travaille ensuite pendant six mois chez le constructeur aéronautique Aérospatiale, en France. Il est senior designer chez James Stewart Polshek & Partners à New York (1983–1988) avant d'enseigner à la Graduate School of Architecture and Planning de la Columbia University. Il s'installe à Los Angeles en 1988 et enseigne au Southern California Institute of Architecture (SCI-Arc) dont il sera le troisième directeur en 1997. En 1996, il achève la construction d'un petit espace expérimental pour la Galerie Ma à Tokyo. Ses autres travaux, bien que très influents, restent souvent sous une forme virtuelle séduisante. Parmi ses projets et propositions récents : le showroom-magasin d'Eyeworks (Los Angeles, 2001–02) ; le concept structurel de salle des marchés et d'environnement de bureaux de SUN Microsystems ; le concept de kiosque de communications ADSL de QWEST ; le concept d'hôtel et de magasin SONY Qualia ; l'immeuble de lofts de 15 niveaux, Union Square (New York, étude de faisabilité/conception de l'enveloppe) ; Water Center (Nashville, Tennessee) ; D/J House, rénovation et extension d'une maison (Mount Washington, Los Angeles) ; le plan directeur de la NCAP, plan pour logements, parc, locaux à louer, commande du Nashville Cultural Arts Project ; les bureaux et théâtre de l'agence littéraire Endeavor (Beverly Hills, Californie).

# TOMIHIRO HOSHINO MUSEUM

*Azuma-Mura, Gunma, Japan, 2001*

*Client: Tomihiro Museum of Shi-Ga, Azuma-Mura. Floor area: 3 000 m². Costs: not specified.*

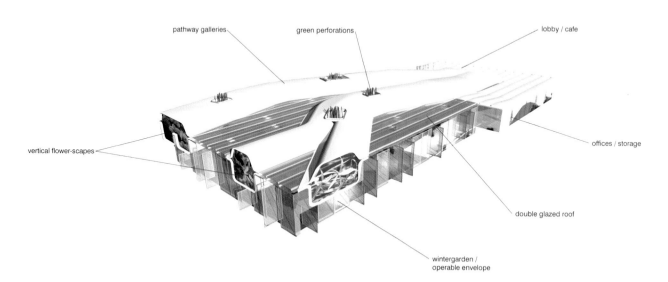

Like many small, isolated Japanese villages, the community of Azuma-Mura in the mountains of Gunma prefecture decided that certain government credits would be well spent on a new museum. They organized a competition for a 3 000-square-meter facility to be dedicated to the work of a locally famous painter, Tomihiro Hoshino. Severely injured in a 1972 gymnastics accident, the artist began painting with pencil or brush held in his mouth. He calls his work "shi-ga" – watercolors of flowers and poetry. As the architect puts it, "his poetic images are an expression of his search for the essence of life, its simplicity and gentleness as reflected in the form of flowers." Of some 300 works painted by Tomihiro Hoshino in the past 30 years, 120 are to be exhibited in this museum at any one time. Offices, a gift shop, café, temporary exhibition space and a learning center were also part of the program requirements. As Neil Denari has written, "the scheme has a formal relation to the artist's brush and to the flower itself, but more importantly it articulates the Tomihiro galleries as pathways intended to generate a feeling of movement, of a search for essences; the entrance area is located 1.5 meters below grade with a winter garden level at 3.0 meters below grade. The galleries float above this level." There were 1 250 entries in this open international competition for which Toyo Ito chaired a jury that included Kengo Kuma, Rikken Yamamoto and Wiel Arets. Neil Denari was in the final 60, but did not win the competition.

Wie viele kleine und abgelegene Gemeinden Japans entschied sich auch die Verwaltung des in den Bergen der Präfektur Gunma gelegenen Dorfes Azuma-Mura, die von der Landesregierung bereitgestellten Gelder für ein neues Museum auszugeben. Der Wettbewerb zur Gestaltung der 3 000 m² umfassenden Anlage war dem regional berühmten Maler Tomihiro Hoshino gewidmet. Nach einer schweren Verletzung, die sich der Künstler 1972 bei einem Sportunfall zugezogen hatte, begann er zu malen, indem er Bleistift oder Pinsel mit dem Mund führt. Er nennt seine Bilder „shi-ga" – Aquarelle der Blumen und Poesie. „Hoshinos poetische Bilder", so Neil Denari, der Planer des hier vorgestellten Entwurfs, „sind Ausdruck seiner Suche nach der Essenz des Lebens, seiner Schlichtheit und Sanftheit, wie sie sich in der Gestalt der Blumen spiegelt." Von den 300 Bildern, die der Künstler im Lauf der letzten 30 Jahre gemalt hat, sollen 120 in einer Dauerausstellung zu sehen sein. Darüber hinaus sollte das Projekt Büros, einen Museumsshop, ein Café sowie Räume für Sonderausstellungen und für ein Lernzentrum umfassen. Sein Entwurf, so Denari, stellt einen formalen Bezug zu dem Pinsel des Künstlers und zu einer Blume her. In erster Linie wird hier jedoch die Anordnung der Ausstellungsräume als Weg inszeniert, der im Besucher ein Gefühl von Bewegung und der Suche nach dem Wesentlichen hervorruft. Der Eingangsbereich wurde 1,5 m und der Wintergarten 3 m unter die Grasnarbe versenkt, während sich die Ausstellungsräume auf der darüber liegenden Ebene befinden. Für den offenen, internationalen Wettbewerb, bei dem Toyo Ito einer Jury vorsaß, zu der unter anderem Kengo Kuma, Rikken Yamamoto und Wiel Arets gehörten, wurden 1 250 Beiträge eingereicht. Neil Denaris Vorschlag kam zwar in die aus 60 Entwürfen bestehende Endauswahl, ging aber nicht als Sieger aus dem Wettbewerb hervor.

Comme plusieurs petits bourgs japonais isolés, la commune d'Azuma-Mura dans les montagnes de la préfecture de Gunma a décidé de consacrer certains crédits publics à un nouveau musée. Elle a donc lancé un concours pour un bâtiment de 3 000 m² consacré à l'œuvre d'un célèbre peintre de la région, Tomihiro Hoshino. Gravement blessé en 1972 en faisant de la gymnastique, l'artiste peint en tenant ses instruments dans sa bouche. Il qualifie ses œuvres de *shi-ga*, d'aquarelles de fleurs et de poésie. Pour Neil Denari : « Ses images poétiques sont une expression de sa quête de l'essence de la vie… sa simplicité et sa gentillesse se retrouvent dans les formes de ses fleurs. » 120 des 300 œuvres réalisées par le peintre au cours de ces 30 dernières années sont exposées en permanence. Des bureaux, une boutique, un café, un lieu d'expositions temporaires et un centre d'éducation figuraient également au programme. « Le projet évoque une relation formelle avec la brosse utilisée par l'artiste et les fleurs elles-mêmes, mais surtout articule les galeries selon des itinéraires qui génèrent un sentiment de mouvement à la recherche de l'essentiel. L'entrée est située à 1,5 m au-dessous du niveau du sol et le jardin d'hiver à 3 m. Les galeries semblent flotter au-dessus. » 1 250 participations ont été adressées au jury du concours présidé par Toyo Ito, qui comprenait Kengo Kuma, Rikken Yamamoto et Wiel Arets. Neil Denari, retenu lors de la première sélection de 60 projets, n'a pas remporté ce concours.

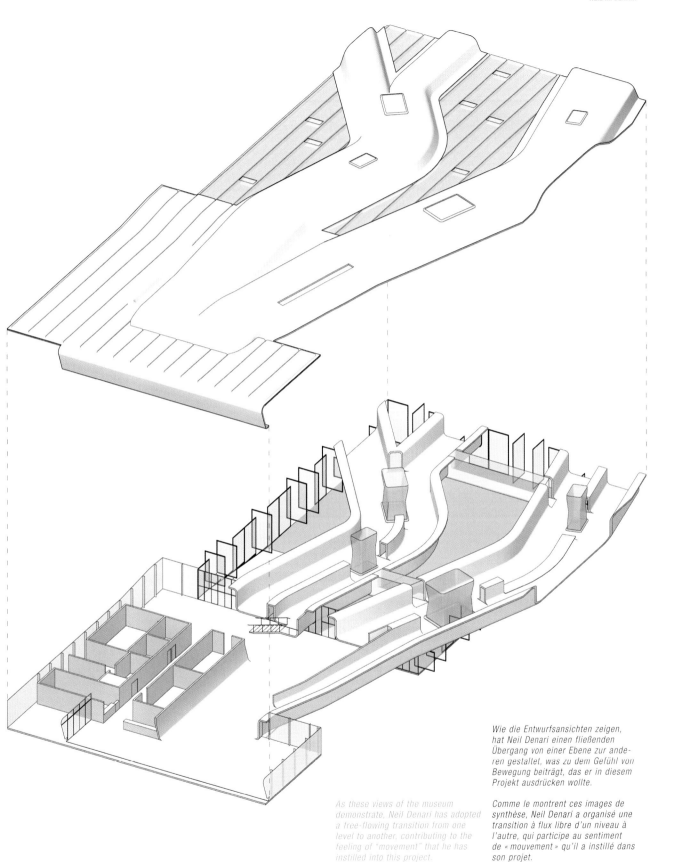

Wie die Entwurfsansichten zeigen,
hat Neil Denari einen fließenden
Übergang von einer Ebene zur ande-
ren gestaltet, was zu dem Gefühl von
Bewegung beiträgt, das er in diesem
Projekt ausdrücken wollte.

As these views of the museum
demonstrate, Neil Denari has adopted
a free-flowing transition from one
level to another, contributing to the
feeling of "movement" that he has
instilled into this project.

Comme le montrent ces images de
synthèse, Neil Denari a organisé une
transition à flux libre d'un niveau à
l'autre, qui participe au sentiment
de « mouvement » qu'il a instillé dans
son projet.

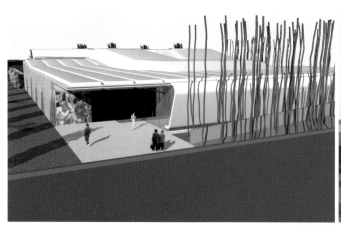

Faithful to the seamless, unified surfaces that he favors, Denari redefines such essential features as the museum entrance and its glazing.

Den von ihm bevorzugten, nahtlos ineinanderübergehenden Oberflächen treu bleibend, bietet Denari eine Neudefinition so wesentlicher Merkmale wie des Museumseingangs mit seiner Verglasung.

Fidèle aux type de surfaces fluides et unies qu'il apprécie, Denari a redéfini des éléments essentiels comme l'entrée du musée et son vitrage.

Wrap-around surfaces and a generally light-toned color scheme used for these interior views emphasize the continuity of the architecture from inside to outside.

Umlaufende Wandoberflächen und eine durchgehend helle Farbgebung für die Innenräume unterstreichen das architektonische Kontinuum von Innen und Außen.

Des surfaces enveloppantes et une palette chromatique de tons généralement légers soulignent la continuité architecturale entre extérieur et intérieur.

In Denari's hands, solid façades and glazing blend into one another giving a feeling of unity that escaped more box-like modernist designs of the past.

In Denaris Gestaltung verschmelzen solide Fassaden und Verglasungen miteinander und vermitteln so ein Gefühl von Harmonie, das den eher schachtelartigen modernistischen Designs der Vergangenheit fehlte.

Les façades pleines et les parois vitrées fusionnent pour donner un sentiment d'unité différent des précédents projets de l'architecte, davantage orientés vers des formes de boîtes modernistes.

The presence of natural forms, but also a flowing openness in the design, seem well adapted to the artist's paintings of flowers.

Die Präsenz natürlicher Formen und eine fließende Offenheit in der Gestaltung bilden einen passenden Hintergrund für die Blumenbilder des Malers Hoshino.

La présence de formes naturelles, mais aussi l'ouverture et la fluidité, semblent bien adaptée aux peintures de fleurs de l'artiste.

# DILLER + SCOFIDIO

*Diller + Scofidio*
*36 Cooper Sq 5F*
*New York, NY 10003*
*USA*

*Tel: +1 212 260 7971*
*Fax: +1 212 260 7924*
*e-mail: disco@dillerscofidio.com*
*Web: www.dillerscofidio.com*

Elizabeth Diller is Professor of Architecture at Princeton University and Ricardo Scofidio is Professor of Architecture at The Cooper Union in New York. According to their own description, "Diller + Scofidio is a collaborative, interdisciplinary studio involved in architecture, the visual arts and the performing arts. The team is primarily involved in thematically-driven experimental works that take the form of architectural commissions, temporary installations and permanent site-specific installations, multi-media theater, electronic media, and print." Their work includes "Slither," 100 units of social housing in Gifu, Japan, and "Moving Target," a collaborative dance work with Charleroi/Danse Belgium. Installations by Diller + Scofidio have been seen at the Cartier Foundation in Paris (Master/Slave, 1999); the Museum of Modern Art in New York, and the Musée de la Mode in Paris. Recently, they completed The Brasserie Restaurant (Seagram Building, New York, 1998–99) and the Blur Building, (Expo.02, Yverdon-les-Bains, Switzerland, 2000–2002). They were selected as architects for the Institute of Contemporary Art in Boston, the Eyebeam Institute in the Chelsea area of Manhattan, and Lincoln Center (New York).

Elizabeth Diller ist als Professorin für Architektur an der Princeton University und Ricardo Scofidio als Professor für Architektur an der Cooper Union School of Architecture in New York tätig. Ihrer eigenen Beschreibung zufolge ist „Diller + Scofidio ein interdisziplinäres Gemeinschaftsprojekt, das sich mit Architektur, bildender und darstellender Kunst beschäftigt. Das Team führt hauptsächlich experimentelle Arbeiten durch, die sich auf der Grundlage von Architektur, Installation, Multimediapräsentation, elektronischen Medien und Druckgrafik mit bestimmten Themen auseinandersetzen." Zu ihren Projekten zählen: „Slither", 100 Sozialwohnungen in Gifu, Japan, und „Moving Target", eine Tanztheaterproduktion in Zusammenarbeit mit der Tanzformation Charleroi/Danse Belgium. Installationen von Diller + Scofidio wurden in der Fondation Cartier in Paris (Master/Slave, 1999), im Museum of Modern Art in New York und im Musée de la Mode in Paris gezeigt. Zu ihren neueren Architekturarbeiten gehören das Restaurant The Brasserie im Seagram Building in New York (1998–99) und das Blur Building für die Expo.02 im schweizerischen Yverdon-les-Bains (2000–2002). Außerdem erhielten sie die Aufträge für das Institute of Contemporary Art in Boston, das Eyebeam Institute im Manhattener Stadtteil Chelsea sowie das Lincoln Center in New York.

Elizabeth Diller est professeur associé à Princeton et Ricardo Scofidio professeur d'architecture à The Cooper Union, New York. Selon leur présentation : « Diller + Scofidio est une agence interdisciplinaire coopérative qui se consacre à l'architecture, aux arts plastiques et aux arts du spectacle. L'équipe travaille essentiellement sur des recherches thématiques expérimentales qui prennent la forme de commandes architecturales, d'installations temporaires, d'installations permanentes adaptées au site, théâtre multimédia, médias électroniques et édition. » Parmi leurs projets récents : Slither, 100 logements sociaux (Gifu, Japon), Moving Target, œuvre chorégraphique en collaboration avec Charleroi/Danse (Belgique). Les installations de Diller + Scofidio ont été présentées à la Fondation Cartier à Paris (Master/Slave, 1999) au Museum of Modern Art de New York et au Musée de la mode à Paris. Plus récemment, ils ont achevé le Brasserie Restaurant (Seagram Building, New York, 1998–99) ; le Blur Building (Expo.02, Yverdon-les-Bains, Suisse, 2000–2002) et ont été sélectionnés pour la construction de l'Institute of Contemporary Art à Boston, l'Eyebeam Institute à Manhattan (Chelsea) et le Lincoln Center (New York).

# BLUR BUILDING, EXPO.02

*Yverdon-les-Bains, Switzerland, 2000–2002*

*Client: Swiss Expo.02. Dimensions: 100 x 60 x 12 m (fog structure). Costs: $ 7 500 000.*

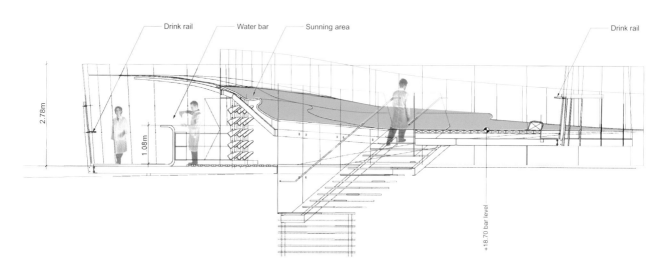

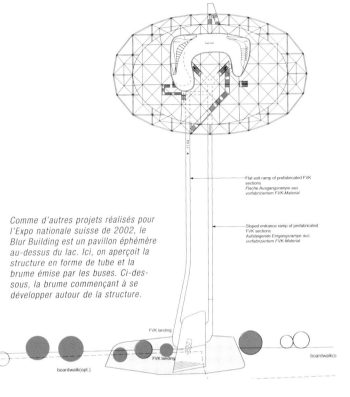

Like other structures intended for
the Swiss Expo.02, the Blur Building
was conceived as an ephemeral
building anchored in the lake. Here
the tube-like structure with the
water-mist emitting nozzles is visible.
Below, the mist begins to emerge
around the frame.

Wie andere Beiträge für die Schwei-
zer Expo.02 wurde auch das Blur
Building als eine vorübergehend im
See verankerte Architektur konzipiert.
Hier ist die röhrenförmige Anlage
mit den Nebel-Düsen sichtbar. Unten:
Der Nebel beginnt, sich um die Rah-
menkonstruktion auszubreiten.

Comme d'autres projets réalisés pour
l'Expo nationale suisse de 2002, le
Blur Building est un pavillon éphémère
au-dessus du lac. Ici, on aperçoit la
structure en forme de tube et la
brume émise par les buses. Ci-dessous, la brume commençant à se
développer autour de la structure.

Flat exit ramp of prefabricated FVK
sections
Flache Ausgangsrampe aus
vorfabriziertem FVK-Material

Sloped entrance ramp of prefabricated
FVK sections
Aufsteigende Eingangsrampe aus
vorfabriziertem FVK-Material

FVK landing

boardwalk(opt.)

FVK landing

boardwalk(o

This structure was intended to resemble nothing so much as a cloud hovering over Lake Neuchâtel. 100 m wide by 60 m deep and 25 m high, rising above the water, the "cloud" effect was obtained through the use of filtered lake water "shot as a fine mist through a dense array of 31 500 high-pressure water nozzles integrated into a large cantilevered tensegrity structure." The first fog building was made by the Japanese artist Fujiko Nakaya for the 1970 Osaka World's Fair. Hers was a fog layer surfacing a geodesic dome. Nakaya was an advisor to the architects in Yverdon on technical and esthetic matters. A ramp led visitors into the cloud where they were enveloped by a sort of sensory deprivation due to the "white-out" accompanied by "white noise" related to the mist projectors. "Unlike entering a space, entering Blur," say Diller and Scofidio, "is like stepping into a habitable medium, one that is formless, featureless, depthless, scaleless, massless, surfaceless, and dimensionless." As the architects further explained, "Blur is a reaction to the over-saturation of visual media in recent national and world expositions that, more and more, have become competition grounds for state-of-the-art immersion technologies and simulation extravaganzas. These large-scale exhibitions feed our insatiable appetite for visual stimulation with ever-greater digital virtuosity. In concert with consumer culture, satisfaction is measured in pixels per inch. High definition has become the new orthodoxy. By contrast, Blur is decidedly low-definition." In somewhat more poetic terms, the English newsweekly *The Economist* published an article on the Blur Building under the title "Heaven's Gate" (August 24, 2002). They wrote: "To enter this sublime building perched in the landscape of the Swiss Alps feels like walking into a poem – it is part of nature but removed from reality."

Das Blur Building, eine 100 m lange und 60 m breite Konstruktion, die sich 25 m über dem Wasserspiegel erhob, sollte aussehen wie eine über dem Neuburger See schwebende Wolke. Dieser Wolken-Effekt wurde durch gefiltertes Seewasser erzielt, das als feiner Nebel aus 31 500 Hochdruck-Wasserdüsen versprüht wurde, die in eine große, freitragende Seilnetz-Konstruktion eingebaut waren. Das erste „Nebelgebäude" stammte von der japanischen Künstlerin Fujiko Nakaya, das 1970 für die Weltausstellung in Osaka entworfen wurde. Nakaya fungierte bei der Realisierung des Blur Building als Beraterin für technische und ästhetische Fragen. In Yverdon gelangten die Besucher über eine Rampe ins Innere der Wolke, wo sie aufgrund eines optischen „weißen Nichts", begleitet vom „weißen Rauschen" der Nebelapparate, eine Art sensorischen Entzug erlebten. „Im Gegensatz zum Betreten eines Raums", so Diller und Scofidio, „ist das Betreten des Blur, als schritte man in ein bewohnbares Medium, aber eines ohne Form, ohne besondere Merkmale, ohne Tiefe, ohne Volumen, ohne Gewicht, ohne Oberfläche und ohne Dimension. Blur ist eine Reaktion auf die Übersättigung durch visuelle Medien, wie sie in letzter Zeit auf nationalen und internationalen Ausstellungen üblich geworden ist. Diese Großereignisse sind mehr und mehr zum Austragungsort von Wettbewerben der neuesten und ausgefallensten Technologien und Simulationen geworden und bedienen unseren unstillbaren Appetit nach visuellen Reizen mit immer größerer digitaler Virtuosität. In Übereinstimmung mit unserer Konsumkultur wird die Qualität nur mehr in Pixelauflösung gemessen, und ‚high definition' ist zur neuen Religion geworden. Blur dagegen ist entschieden ‚low-definition'." In etwas poetischeren Worten wird das Blur Building in einem Artikel der englischen Wochenzeitung *The Economist* beschrieben, der am 24. August 2002 unter der Überschrift „Heaven's Gate" erschien: „Wenn man dieses grandiose, in der Landschaft der Schweizer Alpen gelandete Bauwerk betritt, kommt es einem vor, als betrete man ein Gedicht – es ist Teil der Natur, aber weit entfernt von der Realität."

Cette réalisation avait pour ambition de créer un nuage au-dessus du lac de Neuchâtel. De 100 m de large, 60 de profondeur et 25 de haut, « flottant » au-dessus de l'eau, elle obtenait l'effet recherché grâce à la projection d'eau du lac « en une fine brume générée par un réseau de 31 500 buses haute-pression intégrées à une grande ossature en porte-à-faux et tenségrité ». La première construction de ce genre, vue à l'Exposition universelle d'Osaka en 1970, était signée de l'artiste japonais Fujiko Nakaya. Il avait recréé un brouillard à la surface d'un dôme géodésique, et a d'ailleurs conseillé les architectes d'Yverdon aussi bien sur le plan technique que l'esthétique. En Suisse, une rampe menait les visiteurs à l'intérieur du nuage, où ils se trouvaient plongés dans une atmosphère de privation sensorielle due à l'effet de trop-plein produit par la projection d'eau et le bruit écrasant. « À la différence de la sensation de pénétrer dans un volume », expliquent Diller et Scofidio, « c'était comme accéder à un médium habitable, mais sans forme, sans caractéristique quelconque, sans profondeur, sans échelle, sans masse, sans surface et sans dimension… Blur est une réaction à la sursaturation des médias visuels dans les expositions internationales récentes qui deviennent de plus en plus un lieu de compétition pour technologies d'avant-garde et jeux sur la stimulation des sens. Ces grandes expositions nourrissent notre appétit insatiable pour la stimulation visuelle et une virtuosité numérique sans cesse croissante. De concert avec la culture de consommation, la satisfaction se mesure maintenant en pixels au cm². La haute définition est devenue la nouvelle orthodoxie. Par contraste, Blur, est résolument basse-définition. » En termes presque poétiques, l'hebdomadaire britannique *The Economist* a publié un article sur ce projet sous le titre de « La Porte du ciel » (24 août 2002), écrivant : « Entrer dans ce bâtiment sublime perché dans les Alpes suisse est comme entrer dans un poème, c'est un morceau de nature mais détaché du réel. »

*In good weather and wind conditions, the Blur Building was a remarkable success, almost appearing to be a cloud floating on the lake. Visitors within the structure saw only shadow-like forms of each other.*

*Bei guten Wetter- und Windverhältnissen war das Blur Building ein großer Erfolg und sah fast aus, wie eine über dem See schwebende Wolke. Die Besucher im Innern waren nur schemenhaft zu erkennen.*

*Par beau temps et lorsque le vent était favorable, le Blur Building, nuage au-dessus du lac, s'est révélé une remarquable réussite. Les visiteurs ne voyaient d'eux-mêmes que des formes fantomatiques.*

# OLAFUR ELIASSON

*Tanya Bonakdar Gallery*
*521 West 21st Street*
*New York, NY 10011*
*USA*

*Tel: +1 212 414 4144*
*Fax: +1 212 414 1535*
*e-mail: mail@tanyabonakdargallery.com*
*Web: www.olafureliasson.net*

Olafur Eliasson was born in 1967 in Copenhagen, Denmark of Icelandic parents. He attended the Royal Academy of Arts in Copenhagen (1989-95). He has participated in numerous exhibitions and his work is included in collections ranging from the Solomon R Guggenheim Museum, New York, the Museum of Contemporary Art, Los Angeles and the Deste Foundation, Athens to the Tate Modern, London. Recently he has had solo exhibitions at Kunsthaus Bregenz, the Musée d'Art Moderne de la Ville de Paris and the ZKM in Karlsruhe and represented Denmark in the 2003 Venice Biennale. He lives and works in Berlin. His installations feature elements appropriated from nature – billowing steam evoking a water geyser, rainbows or fog-filled rooms. By introducing "natural" phenomena, such as water, mist or light, into an artificial setting, be it a city street or an art gallery, the artist encourages the viewer to reflect on their perception of the physical world. This moment of perception, when the viewer pauses to consider what they are experiencing, has been described by Eliasson as "seeing yourself sensing." For "The Mediated Motion" at the Kunsthaus Bregenz (2001), Eliasson created a sequence of spaces filled with natural materials including water, fog, earth, wood, fungus and duckweed. During their visit to the exhibition, visitors were exposed to a variety of sights, smells, and textures – which had been precisely selected by the artist. Eliasson also modified the orthogonal nature of the building by inserting a slanting floor, which made visitors more conscious of the act of movement through the gallery space.

Olafur Eliasson, 1967 als Kind isländischer Eltern in Kopenhagen geboren, studierte von 1989 bis 1995 an der Königlichen Kunstakademie in Kopenhagen. Er war bereits auf zahlreichen Ausstellungen vertreten und seine Arbeiten befinden sich in den Sammlungen von Museen wie dem Solomon R. Guggenheim Museum in New York, dem Museum of Contemporary Art in Los Angeles, der Stiftung Deste in Athen sowie der Tate Modern in London. In jüngster Zeit waren ihm Einzelausstellungen im Kunsthaus Bregenz, dem Musée d'Art Moderne de la Ville de Paris und dem Zentrum für Kunst und Medientechnologie (ZKM) in Karlsruhe gewidmet. Außerdem vertrat er Dänemark auf der Biennale 2003 in Venedig. Derzeit lebt und arbeitet er in Berlin. Seine Installationen enthalten häufig Elemente aus der Natur – wogende Dampfschwaden, die an Geysire denken lassen, Regenbogen oder nebelgefüllte Räume. Indem er „natürliche" Phänomene wie Wasser, Nebel oder Licht in ein künstliches Umfeld integriert, sei es eine Innenstadtstraße oder eine Kunstgalerie, lädt er den Betrachter dazu ein, über ihre Wahrnehmung der physischen Welt zu reflektieren. Dieser Moment der Bewusstwerdung, in dem der Betrachter innehält, um darüber nachzudenken, was er oder sie gerade erlebt, wurde von Eliasson als „seeing yourself sensing" beschrieben, als ein Sich-dabei-zusehen, wie man empfindet. Für die Ausstellung „The Mediated Motion", die 2001 im Kunsthaus Bregenz gezeigt wurde, schuf Eliasson eine Abfolge von Innenräumen, die mit natürlichen Materialien wie Wasser, Nebel, Erde, Holz, Schwämmen und Wasserpflanzen gefüllt waren. Während die Besucher durch die Ausstellung gingen, wurden sie mit einer Vielzahl von Anblicken, Gerüchen und Oberflächen konfrontiert – Sinneseindrücken, die der Künstler genau kalkuliert hatte. Darüber hinaus verlegte Eliasson in den Ausstellungsräumen einen geneigten Fußboden, durch den sich die Besucher ihrer Bewegungen bewusster wurden.

Olafur Eliasson est né à Copenhague en 1967 de parents islandais. Il étudie à l'Académie royale des arts de Copenhague (1989–1995). Il a participé à de nombreuses expositions et ses travaux sont présents dans des collections comme le Solomon R. Guggenheim Museum, New York, le Museum of Contemporary Art, Los Angeles, la Deste Foundation, Athènes ou la Tate Modern de Londres. Il a tenu des expositions personnelles à la Kunsthaus de Bregenz (Suisse), au Musée d'art moderne de la ville de Paris, au ZKM à Karlsruhe (Allemagne) et a représenté le Danemark à la Biennale de Venise (2003). Il vit et travaille à Berlin. Ses installations utilisent des éléments pris dans la nature : geyser d'eau tourbillonnante et fumante, arc-en-ciel, pièces remplies de brouillard. En introduisant des phénomènes «naturels» comme l'eau, la brume ou la lumière dans un cadre artificiel que ce soit dans une rue ou une galerie, il encourage le spectateur à réfléchir sur sa perception du monde physique. Ce moment de perception est décrit par Eliasson comme «se voir soi-même en train de ressentir». Pour «Le mouvement médiatisé» à la Kunsthaus Bregenz (2001), il a créé une séquence d'espaces remplis de matériaux naturels : eau, brouillard, terre, bois, champignons et duvet de canard. Au cours de leur visite, les spectateurs sont exposés à diverses visions, odeurs et textures, choisies par l'artiste. Il a également modifié le caractère orthogonal du bâtiment en insérant un sol incliné.

# THE WEATHER PROJECT

*Turbine Hall, Tate Modern, London, UK, October 16, 2003–March 21, 2004*

*Client: Tate Modern/Unilever. Size: 3 250 m² (mirrored surface). Costs: £ 250 000.*

In The Weather Project, the fourth in the annual Unilever Series of commissions for the Turbine Hall, Olafur Eliasson takes the ubiquitous subject of the weather as the basis for exploring ideas about experience, mediation and representation. The earlier participants in the series, Louise Bourgeois, Juan Muñoz, and Anish Kapoor saw the expanse of the Turbine Hall as a location of sculptures or environments on the scale of the space. Eliasson has occupied it just as surely, but in a much less intrusive way. Representations of the sun and sky dominate the expanse of the Hall. The entire ceiling is covered by a mirror, giving visitors the rare opportunity to see themselves "from above." At the end of the Hall a giant semi-circular form made up of hundreds of mono-frequency lamps is reflected in the mirrors, giving the impression of a full, setting sun. Often used in street lighting, mono-frequency lamps emit light at a narrow frequency making colors other than yellow and black invisible, transforming the area around the "sun" into "a vast duotone landscape." A fine mist permeates the space, as though visitors had suddenly been transported to an unnamed outdoor location. Throughout the day, the mist accumulates into faint, cloud-like formations, before dissipating across the space. Although photographs do capture something of the magic of this installation, the surprise of actually seeing it in the space is unequalled. The industrial volume of the Turbine Hall has less to do with architects Herzog & de Meuron than it does with the initial design of the Bankside Power Station. More than the architects themselves, this artist, Olafur Eliasson, has transformed the space with little more than smoke and mirrors – an act of architectural magic.

In „The Weather Project", dem vierten Teil der alljährlich von Unilever veranstalteten Auftragsserie für die Turbinenhalle in der Tate Modern, setzt sich Olafur Eliasson ausgehend vom Thema Wetter mit Ideen über Erfahrung, Vermittlung und Repräsentation auseinander. Während die früheren Teilnehmer, Louise Bourgeois, Juan Muñoz und Anish Kapoor, den ausgedehnten Raum für Skulpturen oder Environments nutzten, die in ihren Ausmaßen dem Standort entsprachen, hat Eliasson den Raum zwar ebenso selbstbewusst, aber wesentlich weniger invasiv in Besitz genommen. In seiner Installation mit Darstellungen der Sonne und des Himmels wird der gesamte Deckenbereich von einer Spiegelfläche eingenommen. Am hinteren Ende der Halle sieht man eine riesige, kreisrunde Form, die aus Hunderten Monofrequenzlampen besteht, und wie eine untergehende Sonne wirkt. Die häufig bei Straßenbeleuchtungen verwendeten Monofrequenzlampen verströmen ihr Licht als schmales Strahlenbündel, wodurch alle Farben außer Gelb und Schwarz ausgeblendet werden. In Eliassons Installation führt dieser Effekt dazu, dass sich der Bereich um die „Sonne" in eine weite Zweifarbenlandschaft verwandelt. Außerdem liegt ein feiner Nebel über der Szenerie, was das Ganze noch unwirklicher macht. Im Lauf des Tages verdichtet sich der Nebel regelmäßig in zarte, wolkenähnliche Gebilde, die sich im ganzen Raum verteilen und wieder auflösen. Obwohl sich auch auf Fotografien etwas von der Magie dieser Installation einfangen lässt, ist das Raumerlebnis in Natura unvergleichlich. Der industrielle Charakter der Turbinenhalle wurde von den Architekten Herzog & de Meuron unverändert gelassen und erinnert damit an ihren ursprünglichen Zweck im ehemaligen Kraftwerk. Und so hat Olafur Eliasson mehr als die Architekten der Tate Modern selbst den Raum mit wenig mehr als Nebel und Spiegeln transformiert – ein Akt architektonischer Magie.

Dans The Weather Project, quatrième des commandes Unilever pour le Turbine Hall de la Tate Modern, Olafur Eliasson s'est emparé du sujet du temps pour explorer l'expérimentation, la médiation et la représentation. Les précédents participants, Louise Bourgeois, Juan Muñoz et Anish Kapoor avaient créé des sculptures ou des environnements à l'échelle de ce hall gigantesque. Eliasson l'a occupé tout aussi efficacement, mais d'une façon beaucoup moins intrusive. Ses représentations du soleil et du ciel dominent le volume du hall. Le plafond tout entier est recouvert d'un miroir qui permet aux visiteurs de se voir « du dessus ». À l'extrémité du hall, une forme géante semi-circulaire composée de centaines de lampes monofréquence se reflète dans les miroirs donnant l'impression d'un soleil couchant. Souvent utilisées en éclairage public, ces ampoules émettent une lumière de fréquence réduite qui rend les couleurs autres que le noir et le jaune invisibles, et transforment la zone autour du « soleil » en un « vaste paysage en bichromie ». Une brume très fine envahit le volume comme si les spectateurs étaient subitement transportés dans un lieu extérieur et inconnu. Tout au long de la journée, la brume s'accumule en petites formations nuageuses, avant de se dissiper dans l'espace. Si les photographies captent une partie de la magie de cette installation, la surprise provoquée par la réalité reste extraordinaire. Plus encore qu'Herzog & de Meuron, Olafur Eliasson a su transformer cet immense espace avec juste un peu de fumée et quelques miroirs : un tour de magie architecturale.

*Using a simple combination of mono-frequency lamps, mirrors on the ceiling and mist, Eliasson succeeded in transforming the cavernous volume of Tate Modern's Turbine Hall into a remarkable, sun-lit, interior space.*

*Mit einer einfachen Kombination aus Monofrequenzlampen, Deckenspiegeln und Nebel gelang es Eliasson, die höhlenartige Turbinenhalle in einen ungewöhnlichen, sonnenbeleuchteten Innenraum zu verwandeln.*

*A partir d'une combinaison de lampes monofréquence, de miroirs au plafond et de projections de brume, Eliasson a réussi à transformer le caverneux volume du Hall de la turbine en un surprenant espace ensoleillé.*

Though it could be described as nothing more than "smoke and mirrors" the Olafur Eliasson installation at Tate Modern came as close to a magical effect as imaginable in the vast industrial space of the former power plant.

Obwohl sie im Grunde aus nichts weiter als „Nebel und Spiegel" bestand, kam Olafur Eliassons Installation in der Tate Modern einer magischen Raumwirkung so nahe, wie es in dem riesigen Raum des ehemaligen Kraftwerks nur denkbar ist.

Bien qu'elle ne soit rien de plus que « un peu de fumée et des miroirs » l'installation d'Olafur Eliasson a réussi à créer un effet aussi magique que possible dans le vaste volume industriel d'une ancienne centrale thermique.

# ELLIS WILLIAMS

*Ellis Williams Architects*
*Exmouth House*
*Pine Street*
*London EC1 0JH*
*UK*

*Tel: +44 20 7841 7200*
*Fax: +44 20 7833 3850*
*e-mail: info@ewa.co.uk*
*Web: www.ewa.co.uk/ewa.html*

*Baltic Centre for Contemporay Arts* ▸

Ellis Williams is an architecture practice with studios in London, Cheshire, and Berlin. There are three directors in the London studio, Dominic Williams, Tim Baker and Brian Fairbrother, all architects who have a wide range of experience in many different building typologies. The art team in London is led by Dominic Williams, who has a particular interest and experience in working on arts projects and directly with artists. Born in 1965, he worked at Skidmore, Owings & Merrill (1991–1994) before joining the Ellis Williams Partnership in 1994. Past projects have included a virtual mausoleum, an experimental technology college and an art and music urban box thesis in Manchester, his home town. He studied art at Manchester, architecture at Sheffield and "life on the road" as a guitarist with the band "Junk." He is currently involved in a performance center in Oxford and a zero IT retreat for Franciscan nuns in Derbyshire, England. The Baltic is his first major completed work, which was won in competition when he was 28 years old.

Ellis Williams ist ein Architekturbüro mit Niederlassungen in London, Cheshire und Berlin. Die drei Direktoren des Londoner Büros sind die Architekten Dominic Williams, Tim Baker und Brian Fairbrother, die alle umfassende Erfahrungen mit vielen verschiedenen Bautypen aufzuweisen haben. Das Londoner Kunstteam wird von dem 1965 geborenen Dominic Williams geleitet, dessen besonderes Interesse der Arbeit an Kunstprojekten mit Künstlern gilt. Er studierte Kunst in Manchester, Architektur in Sheffield und „das Leben auf der Straße" als Gitarrist der Band „Junk". Von 1991 bis 1994 arbeitete er bei Skidmore, Owings & Merrill, bevor er 1994 bei Ellis Williams Partnership eintrat. Zu seinen Projekten gehören ein virtuelles Mausoleum, ein experimentelles Technologiekolleg sowie ein Kunst und Musik umfassendes Projekt in seiner Heimatstadt Manchester. Derzeit arbeitet er an einem Performance Center in Oxford und einem Refugium für franziskanische Nonnen in Derbyshire, England, das auf jegliche Informationstechnologie verzichtet. Das Baltic ist sein erstes realisiertes Bauprojekt, mit dessen Entwurf er im Alter von 28 Jahren den Wettbewerb gewann.

Ellis Williams est une agence d'architecture présente à Londres, Berlin et dans le Cheshire. Son bureau londonien est animé par trois directeurs, Dominic Williams, Tim Baker et Brian Fairbrother, qui possèdent tous une large expérience de différents types de constructions. L'équipe artistique est dirigée par Dominic Williams qui s'intéresse particulièrement aux projets artistiques et travaille directement avec des artistes. Né en 1965, il a travaillé pour Skidmore, Owings & Merrill (1991–1994) avant de rejoindre Ellis Williams Partnership en 1994. Ses réalisations comprennent un mausolée virtuel, un collège expérimental de technologie et le « Urban Box Thesis », un ensemble de studios de musique et d'ateliers d'art à Manchester, sa ville natale. Il a étudié l'art à Manchester, l'architecture à Sheffield et a vécu en tournée comme guitariste du groupe « Junk ». Il travaille actuellement à un centre de spectacle vivant à Oxford et une maison de retraite « Zero IT » (Zéro technologie de l'information, pas de téléphone, pas d'Internet) pour des nonnes franciscaines dans le Derbyshire, Royaume-Uni. Le Baltic, dont il a remporté le concours à l'âge de 28 ans, est sa première œuvre importante achevée.

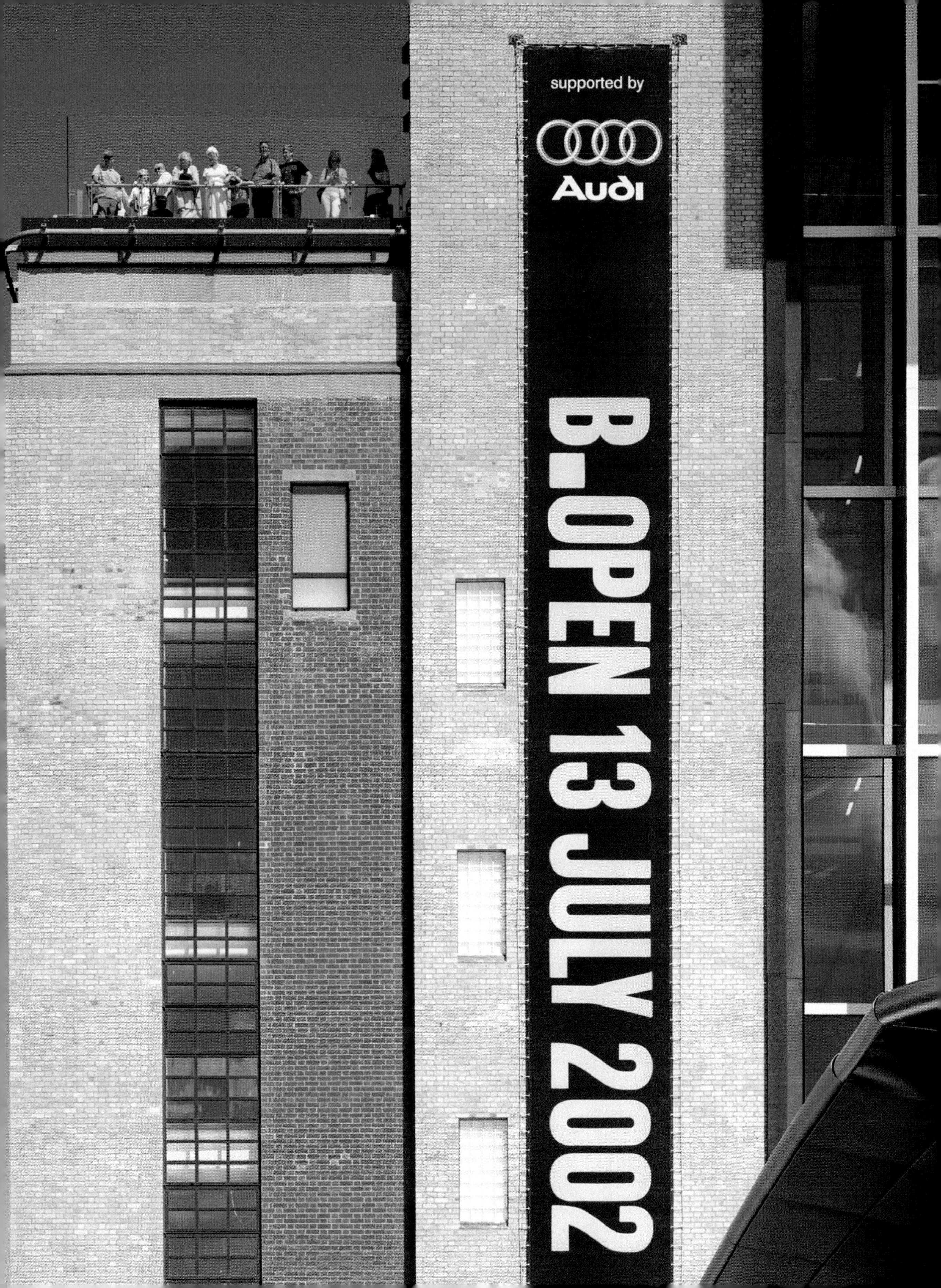
supported by
Audi
B_OPEN 13 JULY 2002

# BALTIC CENTRE FOR CONTEMPORARY ARTS

*Newcastle, UK, 1999–2002*

*Client: Gateshead Metropolitan Borough Council. Total floor area: 8 537 m². Costs: £ 27 000 000.*

In 1994, the Gateshead Metropolitan Borough Council invited architects to submit ideas for the conversion of the Baltic Flour Mills into a contemporary art gallery. The objective was to "provide a national and international Centre for Contemporary Visual Arts." The existing building was 25 meters wide, 50 meters long, 40 meters high, and originally contained 148 square concrete silos. These were removed in 1998–99 to create new space. The net internal floor area of the new gallery building is 8 537 square meters with spaces such as that on level one boasting a 7.4-meter ceiling height and a capacity to place point loads of six tons on the concrete floors – ideal conditions for often large or weighty contemporary artworks. Environmental concerns also motivated the architects, who made provision for high levels of insulation, efficient heat recovery, and air conditioning and ventilation systems. The building's thermal mass is used to limit summer temperatures and daylight is carefully controlled. As the architect Dominic Williams has stated, "the main aim is to allow contemporary art to happen in whatever form it takes. Often 'art' installations take on, or pervert, the nature of the space they occupy. The original function of the building was to collect, contain and distribute flour through the unseen workings of the silos. In many ways these activities would be unchanged, with the building now refocused to a new use. Works will come, be created, and travel on from the place, the function less secret though still housed between its sheer walls. Components such as the gallery floors, café and library are inserted between these two walls to create a new living body within the building."

Im Jahr 1994 lud der Stadtrat von Gateshead Architekten ein, an einem Ideenwettbewerb für die Umwandlung der alten Mühle Baltic Flour Mills in ein nationales und internationales Zentrum für die bildende Kunst der Gegenwart teilzunehmen. Das bestehende Gebäude war 25 m breit, 50 m lang, 40 m hoch und enthielt 148 quadratische Betonsilos. Diese wurden zwischen 1998 und 1999 entfernt, um mehr Platz zu schaffen. Die reine Nutzfläche des neuen Ausstellungsgebäudes beträgt nun 8 537 m². Darin sind Räume enthalten, die eine Höhe von 7,4 m haben, und deren Betonböden eine Einzellast von sechs Tonnen tragen können – ideale Bedingungen für die häufig besonders großformatigen oder schweren Kunstwerke. Auch ökologische Anliegen flossen in den Entwurf der Architekten mit ein und so wurde für hochwertige und effiziente Methoden der Wärmeisolierung und Wärmerückgewinnung, Klimatisierung und Lüftung gesorgt. Die Thermomasse des Gebäudes wird genutzt, um die Temperaturen im Sommer zu begrenzen, und auch das Tageslicht wird sorgfältig reguliert. Der Architekt Dominic Williams über die Gestaltung: „Das Hauptziel ist, zeitgenössische Kunst einfach geschehen zu lassen, in welcher Form auch immer. Häufig ist es jedoch so, dass ,Kunst'-Installationen das Wesen des Raums, den sie einnehmen, entweder vereinnahmen oder verzerren. Die ursprüngliche Funktion dieses Gebäudes bestand darin, Mehl zu produzieren, zu lagern und zu vertreiben. In vielerlei Hinsicht bleiben sich diese Aktivitäten auch mit der Adaptierung für eine neue Funktion gleich: Kunstwerke werden hier produziert, aufbewahrt und weitergegeben, nur dass diese Vorgänge weniger versteckt sind als früher. Andere Bestandteile, wie die Galerieräume, das Café und die Bibliothek, wurden eingefügt, um einen neuen, lebendigen Körper innerhalb des Gebäudes zu schaffen."

En 1994, le Gateshead Metropolitan Borough Council avait organisé un concours pour la reconversion des silos de farine des Baltic Flour Mills en galerie d'art contemporain. L'objectif était « de créer un Centre d'arts visuels contemporains d'intérêt national et international ». La construction existante de 25 m de large, 50 de long et 40 de haut contenait à l'origine 148 silos de béton carrés, qui furent supprimés en 1998–99 pour laisser place aux nouveaux volumes. La surface utile intérieure de la nouvelle galerie est de 8 537 m². Certaines salles mesurent plus de 7,4 m de haut et la charge possible est de 6 tonnes /m², conditions idéales pour des œuvres contemporaines souvent très lourdes. Les préoccupations environnementales ont également motivé les architectes, qui ont abondamment utilisé l'isolation, la récupération de chaleur, la climatisation et la ventilation naturelles. La masse thermique du bâtiment limite la température intérieure en été, et la lumière naturelle est soigneusement contrôlée. Comme l'a écrit Dominic Williams : « L'objectif principal est de permettre à l'art contemporain de se produire, sous quelque forme que ce soit. Souvent, les installations artistiques prennent le dessus ou pervertissent la nature de l'espace qu'elles occupent. La fonction originale de ce bâtiment était la collecte, la conservation et la distribution de la farine par des processus invisibles de l'extérieur. À de nombreux égards ces activités seront identiques, le bâtiment étant réorienté sur une autre fonction. Les œuvres arriveront, seront créées et voyageront d'un lieu à l'autre, la fonction, moins secrète, restant toujours abritée derrière ces murs aveugles. Des éléments comme les sols des galeries, le café et la bibliothèque sont insérés entre les deux murs pour créer un organisme vivant et nouveau à l'intérieur du bâtiment. »

Turning an austere flourmill into a center of art and public activity was a difficult wager for local authorities and the architects. The bridge visible here is the Gateshead Memorial Bridge (Wilkinson Eyre Architects).

Das nüchterne Gebäude einer ehemaligen Mühle in ein Zentrum für Kunst und Kultur zu verwandeln, war eine schwierige Aufgabe für die lokalen Behörden wie für die Architekten. Bei der Brücke handelt es sich um die Gateshead Memorial Bridge von Wilkinson Eyre Architects.

Transformer un austère silo à farine en centre d'art public était une gageure pour les autorités locales et l'architecte. Le pont que l'on aperçoit est le Gateshead Memorial Bridge de Wilkinson Eyre Architects.

A sketch by the architect shows the form of the restored building with its large white "wing door" visible.

Eine Entwurfszeichnung des Architekten zeigt die Form des restaurierten Gebäudes mit seiner ausladenden weißen „Flügeltür".

Un croquis de l'architecte montre la forme du bâtiment restauré et son énorme « aile-porte ».

A good part of the intelligence of the architects consisted in using the exterior of the building more or less as it was. This was also the case for Herzog & de Meuron at the Tate Modern, the former Bankside Power Plant.

Die Eingabe der Architekten bestand zum großen Teil darin, das Äußere des Gebäudes mehr oder weniger so zu belassen, wie es war. Das trifft auch auf Herzog & de Meuron und ihre Gestaltung der Tate Modern zu, eines ehemaligen Kraftwerks.

Une bonne part de l'habileté de l'architecte consiste à avoir laissé l'extérieur du bâtiment plus ou moins tel qu'il était. Ce fut également le cas de Herzog & de Meuron pour la Tate Modern, ancienne Bankside Power Plant.

A section and an image from the same angle of the side of the building show an opening that admits light into the galleries. The arch of Wilkinson Eyre's bridge can be seen above.

Ein Querschnitt und eine aus der selben Perspektive aufgenommene Außenansicht zeigen eine Öffnung, die Licht in die Ausstellungsräume einlässt. Oben: Der von Wilkinson Eyre gestaltete Brückenbogen.

Une coupe et une image, prise sous le même angle, montrent l'ouverture qui éclaire les galeries. À gauche, l'arc du pont de Wilkinson Eyre.

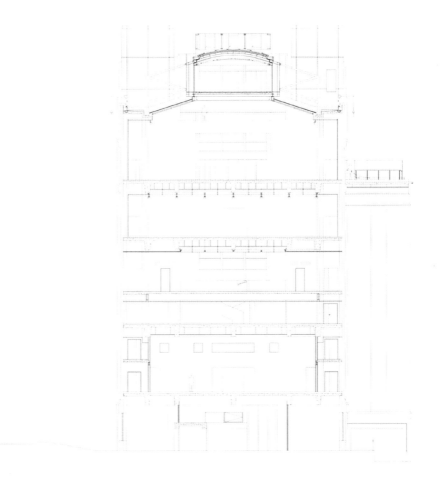

Large scale drawings by Julian
Opie animate the floors, walls, and
windows of an exhibition gallery.

Großformatige Zeichnungen von Julian Opie beleben die Böden, Wände
und Fenster eines Ausstellungssaals.

Des dessins à grande échelle de
Julian Opie animent les sols, les
murs et les fenêtres d'une des
galeries d'exposition.

Architect Dominic Williams has succeeded in creating modern open spaces well suited to the display of contemporary art within the originally confined volumes of an industrial building.

Dem Architekten Dominic Williams ist es gelungen, im Rahmen der beschränkten Möglichkeiten eines ehemaligen Industriegebäudes moderne und offene Räume für die Präsentation zeitgenössischer Kunst zu gestalten.

L'architecte Dominic Williams a réussi à créer des espaces modernes et ouverts, bien adaptés à la présentation d'œuvres d'art dans les volumes initialement confinés d'un bâtiment industriel.

Openings to the exterior, light-filled zones and an intelligent use of materials bring a modern feeling to the structure such that its original functions are all but invisible from certain points.

Öffnungen nach außen, lichtdurchflutete Raumzonen und eine intelligente Materialauswahl bringen ein modernes Raumgefühl in ein Gebäude, dessen ursprüngliche Funktion stellenweise noch gut zu erkennen ist.

Des ouvertures sur l'extérieur, des zones très lumineuses et une intelligente utilisation des matériaux introduisent un esprit moderne dans cette structure dont les fonctions originelles sont pratiquement invisibles sauf sous certains angles.

# MASAKI ENDOH
# AND MASAHIRO IKEDA

*Masaki Endoh*
*EDH Endoh Design House*
*2-13-8, Honnmachi, Shibuya-ku, Tokyo, 151-0071 Japan*
*Tel: +81 3 3377 6293, Fax: +81 3 3377 6293*
*e-mail edh-endoh@mvi.biglobe.ne.jp, Web: www.edh-web.com*

*Masahiro Ikeda*
*MIAS Masahiro Ikeda Architecture Studio*
*202 Silhouette-Ohyamacho 1-20 Ohyama-cho, Shibuya-ku, Tokyo, 151-0065 Japan*
*Tel: +81 3 5738 5564, Fax: +81 3 5738 5565*
*e-mail: info@miascoltd.net*

Masaki Endoh was born in Tokyo, Japan in 1963. He graduated from the Science University of Tokyo in 1987 and completed the Master Course of Architecture in 1989, at the same University. He worked the KAI-Workshop (1989–1994) and established his firm EDH Endoh Design House in 1994. He is currently a lecturer at the Science University of Tokyo. He was awarded the Tokyo House Prize for "Natural Shelter" in 2000, the Yoshioka Award for "Natural Shelter" in 2000, and the JIA "Rookie of the Year 2003" for "Natural Ellipse" in 2003. His works include "Natural Shelter" (Tokyo, 1999); "Natural Illuminance" (Tokyo, 2001); "Natural Slats" (Tokyo, 2002); "Natural Ellipse" (Tokyo, 2002); "Natural Wedge" (Tokyo, 2003); and "Natural Strata" (Kawasaki, 2003). Masahiro Ikeda was born in Shizuoka, Japan in 1964. He graduated from the Nagoya University in 1987 and completed the School of Engineering at Nagoya University in 1989. He worked with Kimura Structural Engineers (1989–1991) and Sasaki Structural Consultants (1991–1994) before establishing his firm MIAS (Masahiro Ikeda Architecture Studio) in 1994. Masahiro Ikeda has acted as the architect and structural designer for these houses. As Masaki Endoh says, however, Masahiro Ikeda has played such a significant role in these projects that he too should be considered as one of the architects.

Masaki Endoh, geboren 1963 in Tokio, schloss 1987 sein Studium an der Wissenschaftsuniversität in Tokio ab und erwarb 1987 dort auch seinen Master of Architecture. Von 1989 bis 1994 arbeitete er im KAI-Workshop und gründete 1994 seine eigene Firma EDH Endoh Design House. Derzeit ist er Dozent an der Tokioter Wissenschaftsuniversität. Im Jahr 2000 wurde ihm der Tokyo House Prize und der Yoshioka Award, beide für Natural Shelter verliehen, und 2003 erhielt er den vom japanischen Architekturinstitut verliehenen Preis Rookie of the Year 2003 für Natural Ellipse. Zu seinen Projekten zählen: Natural Shelter (1999), Natural Illuminance (2001), Natural Slats (2002), Natural Ellipse (2002), Natural Wedge (2003), alle in Tokio, sowie Natural Strata in Kawasaki (2003). Masahiro Ikeda, geboren 1964 in Shizuoka, Japan, schloss 1987 sein Architekturstudium und 1989 sein Ingenieurstudium an der Universität in Nagoya ab. Von 1989 bis 1991 arbeitete er bei Kimura Structural Engineers und von 1991 bis 1994 bei Sasaki Structural Consultants, bevor er 1994 seine eigene Firma MIAS (Masahiro Ikeda Architecture Studio) gründete. Masahiro Ikeda war als Architekt und Bauzeichner für Endohs Architekturprojekte tätig. Wie Masaki Endoh jedoch betont, hat Masahiro Ikeda eine so bedeutende Rolle bei diesen Projekten gespielt, dass auch er als einer der Architekten zu betrachten ist.

Masaki Endoh est né à Tokyo en 1963. Diplômé de l'Université des Sciences de Tokyo en 1987, il est Master of Architecture de la même université en 1989. Il a travaillé pour KAI-Workshop (1989–1994) et a créé son agence EDH Endoh Design House, en 1994. Il est actuellement assistant à l'Université des Sciences de Tokyo. Il a reçu le Prix de la maison de Tokyo et le Prix Yoshioka pour son « Abri naturel » (Tokyo, 1999) ; « Illumination naturelle » (Tokyo, 2001) ; « Ardoises naturelles » (Tokyo, 2002) ; « Ellipse naturelle » (Tokyo, 2002) ; « Coin naturel » (Tokyo, 2003) et « Strates naturelles » (Kawasaki, 2003). Masahiro Ikeda est né à Shizuoka, Japon, en 1964. Il est diplômé de l'Université de Nagoya en 1987 et a étudié à l'École d'ingéniérie de l'Université de Nagoya en 1989. Il a collaboré avec Kimura Structural Engineers (1989–1991) et Sasaki Structural Consultants (1991–1994), avant de créer son agence MIAS (Masahiro Ikeda Architecture Studio) en 1994. Il est l'architecte et l'ingénieur structurel des maisons présentées ici. Pour Masaki Endoh cependant : « Masahiro Ikeda a joué un tel rôle dans ces projets qu'il devrait en être considéré comme l'un des architectes. »

# NATURAL ELLIPSE

*Tokyo, Japan 2001–02*

*Client: private. Building area: 31.20 m², total floor area: 131.74 m². Costs: not specified.*

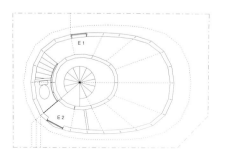
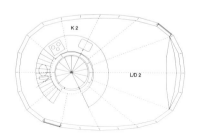
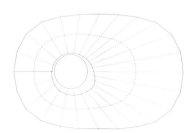

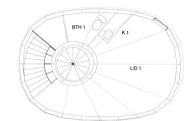
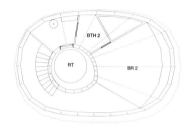

This unusual house with a floor area of 132 square meters is set on just 31 square meters of a tiny 53-square-meter site located at the edge of the Shibuya shopping and entertainment district. The architect chose to compose the house out of 24 elliptical steel rings. As Masaki Endoh says, "the ellipse makes it possible to adjust the form according to the external requirements, or to modify the allocation of space by varying the ratio between its major and minor axes. Also, its double focus deprives this figure of centrality, making it possible to erase the hierarchy of details such as the pillar or the beam, and to create a continuity from the outside toward the interior. The plan consists of a cylindrical central block composed of these rings and zones for natural lighting and longitudinal flow lines that continue from the exterior, radiating outward. FRP (Fiber-Reinforced Polymer) is employed for the external finish, as a material capable of joining the rings and expressing such continuity. It has the merit of being waterproof, and can be molded and applied at will, to realize a seamless exterior."

Das ungewöhnliche Haus mit einer Nutzfläche von 132 m² und einer Grundfläche von nur 31 m² liegt auf einem winzigen, 53 m² großen Grundstück am Rand des Tokioter Einkaufs- und Vergnügungsviertels Shibuya. Der Architekt Masaki Endoh zu seiner Konstruktion, die aus 24 elliptischen Stahlringen besteht: „Die Ellipse ermöglicht es, die Form des Hauses an die äußeren Anforderungen anzupassen oder die Raumeinteilung zu modifizieren, indem man das Verhältnis zwischen Haupt- und Nebenachse der Ellipse variiert. Außerdem wird diese Figur durch den Doppelfokus ihrer Zentralität beraubt, wodurch sich unter Umgehung der Hierarchie solcher Einzelteile wie Säule oder Balken ein Raumkontinuum von außen nach innen herstellen lässt. Der Grundriss besteht aus einem zylindrischen Kern, der sich aus Ringen und Zonen für natürliche Belichtung und aus Längslinien, die nach außen strahlen, zusammensetzt. Für die Fassaden wurde eine Beschichtung aus faserverstärktem Polymer (FRP) gewählt, da sich mit diesem Material die einzelnen Ringe fugenlos miteinander verbinden lassen. Darüber hinaus hat es den Vorteil, wasserfest zu sein und dass man es nach Belieben formen und auftragen kann."

Cette curieuse maison de 132 m² de surface totale occupe 31 m² d'une petite parcelle de 53 m² en bordure du quartier commercial et de nuit de Shibuya, à Tokyo. L'architecte a réalisé ce projet à l'aide de 24 anneaux elliptiques en acier : « Les ellipses ont permis d'ajuster la forme aux contraintes externes et de modifier l'allocation de l'espace en variant le rapport entre le grand et le petit axe. La double ellipse supprime tout point central, ce qui permet d'éliminer la hiérarchie d'éléments comme les piliers ou les poutres, et de créer une continuité de l'extérieur vers l'intérieur. Le plan consiste en un bloc central cylindrique composé des anneaux et de zones naturellement éclairées qui s'orientent vers l'extérieur à l'horizontale. La couverture est en FRP (polymère renforcé de fibres), matériau capable de maintenir ensemble les anneaux et d'exprimer la continuité recherchée. De plus, il est étanche et peut être plié ou appliqué comme on veut, afin d'obtenir une couverture lisse, sans interruption. »

The drawings for the Natural Ellipse resemble mathematical constructions almost more than they do architecture. The elliptical shape of the house makes this digital logic possible, while creating a truly unexpected residence.

Die Entwurfszeichnungen für das Natural Ellipse Haus gleichen eher mathematischen Konstruktionen als Architektur. Die elliptische Form des Gebäudes macht diese digitale Logik möglich. Daraus resultiert ein wahrhaftig ungewöhnliches Wohnhaus.

Les dessins préparatoires à la Natural Ellipse font davantage penser à des constructions mathématiques qu'à de l'architecture. La forme elliptique de la maison permet cette logique numérique, tout en créant une maison totalement inattendue.

MASAKI ENDOH
AND MASAHIRO IKEDA

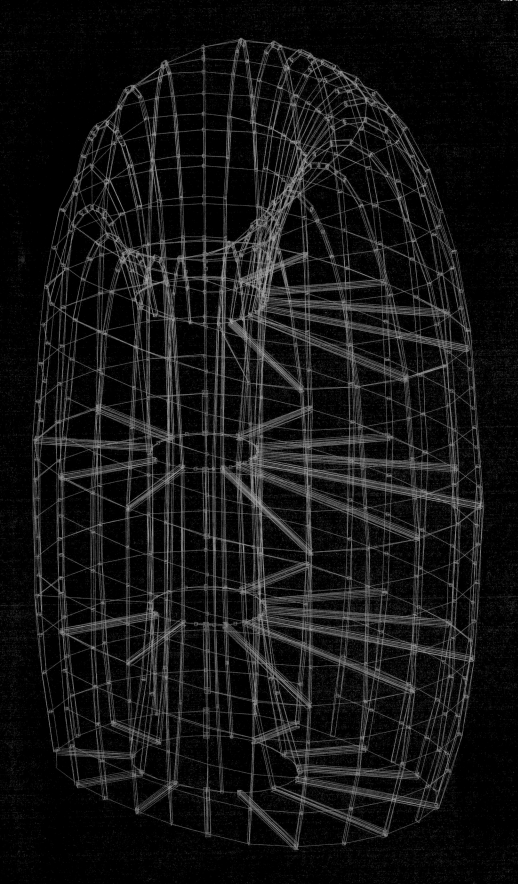

A spiral staircase links the different
levels of the house, as can be seen
in the drawing to the right and the
image to the left.

Eine Wendeltreppe bildet die Verbindung zwischen den verschiedenen
Ebenen des Hauses, wie in der Zeichnung rechts und der Abbildung links
erkennbar.

Un escalier en spirale réunit les
différents niveaux de la maison,
comme le montrent les dessins,
à droite, et l'image de gauche.

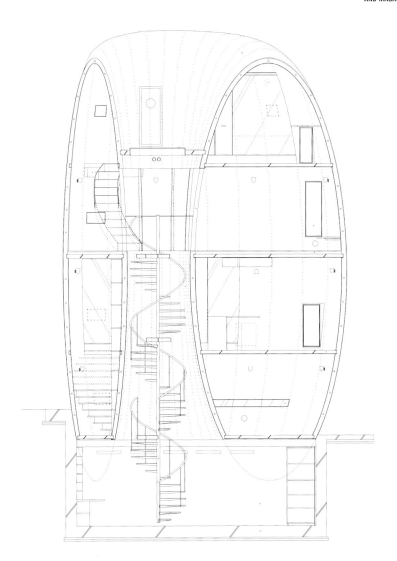

Light enters the top of the structure
and filters down the staircase.

Das von oben einfallende Licht wird
durch das Treppenhaus gefiltert.

La lumière pénètre par le haut de la
structure et suit la cage de l'escalier
en spirale.

# NATURAL ILLUMINANCE

*Tokyo, Japan, 2001*

*Client: private. Building area: 34.46 m², total floor area: 65.56 m². Costs: not specified.*

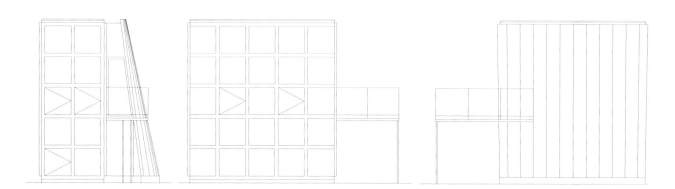

Also located in a densely populated residential area of Tokyo, Natural Illuminance is even smaller than the Natural Ellipse house. It has a total floor area of 65 square meters and a narrow site measuring just 80 square meters. The built area on this site is precisely 34.46 square meters. Preoccupied, as are many Japanese architects, with the ideas of boundaries and the presence of "nature" in a highly urbanized environment, Endoh placed the emphasis here on natural light. As he says "my proposition consists specifically of a masonry construction composed of 1200mm-square wall units made of insulated steel. Natural light is introduced through the gaps between the units along the four sides... As a result, the numerical values of illumination are uniform at every point of this space. There is a lack of hierarchy because of the absence of a feeling of being surrounded, and the fact that the edges of the materials are all imperceptible. This turns out to be effective in relieving the feeling of spatial narrowness in the house."

Das ebenfalls in einer dichtbesiedelten Wohngegend von Tokio gelegene Haus Natural Illuminance ist sogar noch kleiner als das Haus Natural Ellipse. Es hat eine Nutzfläche von 65 m² und nimmt auf dem schmalen, 80 m² großen Grundstück exakt 34,46 m² ein. Endoh, der sich wie viele japanische Architekten intensiv mit den baulichen Aspekten von Grenzen und der Präsenz von Natur in einem hoch urbanisierten Umfeld auseinandersetzt, legte den Schwerpunkt im vorliegenden Entwurf auf das natürliche Licht. „Meine Konstruktion", so Endoh, „besteht in der Hauptsache aus einem Mauerwerk, das sich aus 1,2 m² großen Platten aus Isolierstahl zusammensetzt. An den vier Außenwänden wird das natürliche Licht durch die Spalten zwischen den einzelnen Tafeln nach innen geführt. Daraus folgt, dass die numerischen Lichtwerte an jeder Stelle des Innenraums einheitlich sind. Außerdem entsteht keine Hierarchie, weil sämtliche Materialränder unsichtbar bleiben. Das hat sich als wirksam erwiesen, um in diesem kleinen Haus kein Gefühl von räumlicher Enge aufkommen zu lassen."

Également située dans un quartier résidentiel de Tokyo très peuplé, cette maison est encore plus petite que la Natural Ellipse House. Sur un étroit terrain de 80 m², elle offre 65 m² de surface utile, pour 34,46 m² d'emprise au sol. Préoccupé, comme beaucoup d'architectes japonais, par les notions de limites et la présence de la « nature » dans un environnement hautement urbanisé, Endoh a mis l'accent sur l'éclairage naturel : « Ma proposition consiste en une construction en maçonnerie habillée de plaques d'acier isolant carrées de 1 200 m² de côté. L'éclairage naturel pénètre par des fentes ménagées entre les quatre côtés de ces plaques... Les valeurs numériques d'illumination sont ainsi uniformes en chaque point du volume. L'absence de hiérarchie est due au fait que l'on ne se sent pas enfermé, et que les bords des matériaux sont tous imperceptibles. Ceci réduit efficacement la perception de l'étroitesse spatiale de la maison. »

Applying the same mathematical rigor used for the Natural Ellipse, the Natural Illuminance house is based on a subdivided cube.

Unter Anwendung mathematischer Strenge wie bei Natural Ellipse, basiert auch Natural Illuminance auf einem gegliederten Kubus.

Appliquant la même rigueur mathématique que pour la Natural Ellipse, cette maison repose sur un principe de cube subdivisé.

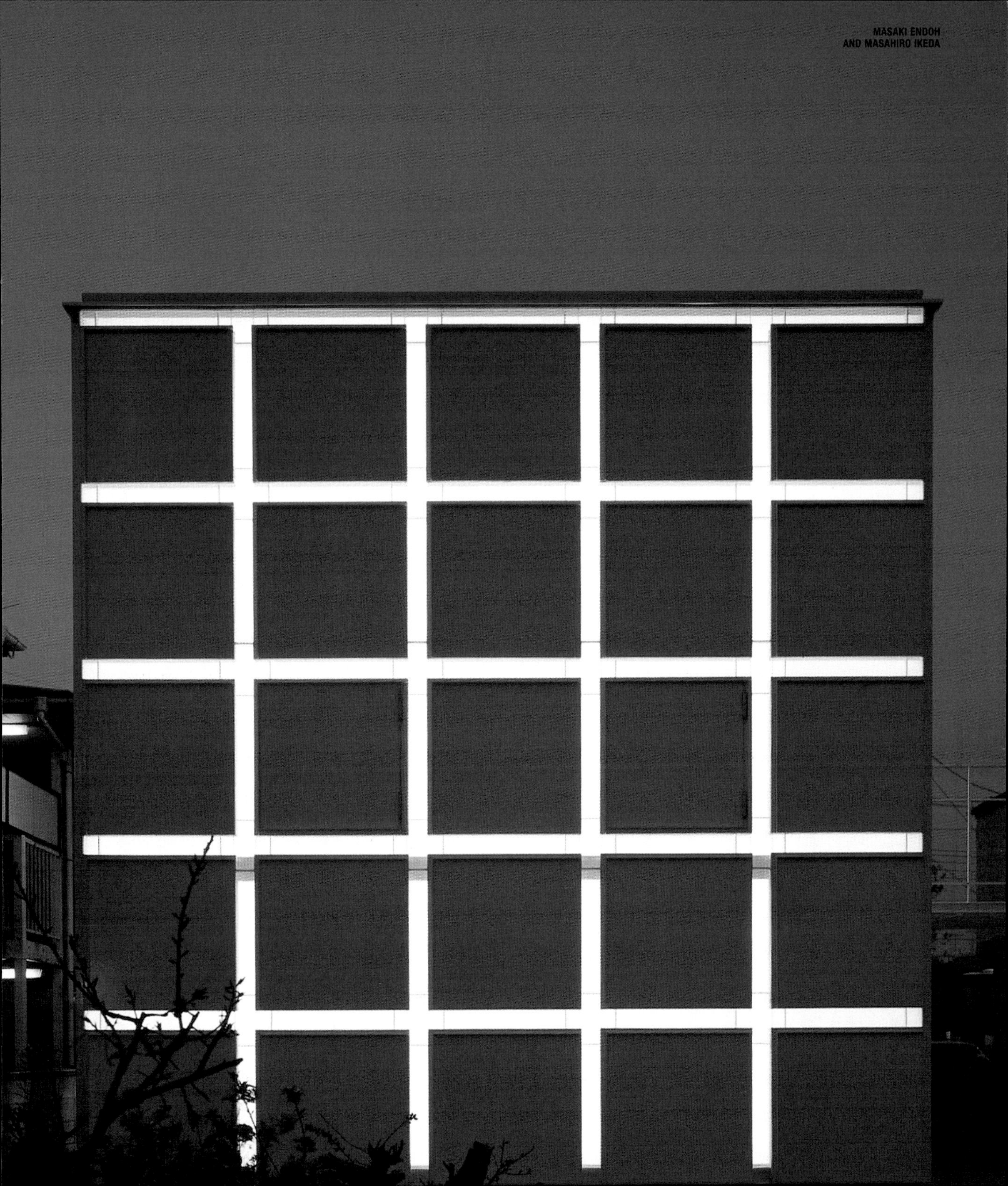

The openings visible between the grid lines of the exterior correspond to interior wall panels encircled with light during the day.

Die zwischen den Außenplatten sichtbaren Lücken korrespondieren mit den Tafeln der Innenwände, die tagsüber von Licht umrandet sind.

Les ouvertures visibles dans la trame extérieure correspondent aux panneaux muraux intérieurs, encadrés de lumière pendant la journée.

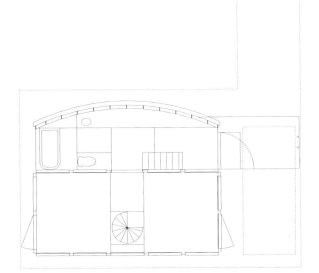

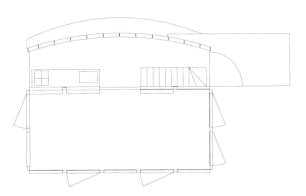

Despite its cubic appearance, plans show that the basic form of the house is rectangular with one side in the shape of an arc.

Trotz seiner kubischen Gestalt zeigen die Grundrisse, dass die Grundform des Hauses ein Rechteck mit einer bogenförmigen Seite ist.

Malgré l'apparence cubique, les plans montrent que la forme de base de la maison est un rectangle dont un côté est arqué.

# ARTHUR ERICKSON

*Arthur Erickson Architectural Corporation, 1672 West First Avenue, Vancouver, BC V6J 1G1, Canada*
*Tel: +1 604 737 9801, Fax: +1 604 737 9092*
*e-mail: info@arthurerickson.com, Web: www.arthurerickson.com*

*Nick Milkovich Architects Inc., 1672 West First Avenue, Vancouver, BC V6J 1G1, Canada*
*Tel: +1 604 737 6061, Fax: +1 604 737 6091, e-mail: nma@nmainc.ca*

*FOR THE BRIDGE*
*Andersson Wise Architects, 1801 North Lamar, Suite 100, Austin, TX 78701, USA*
*Tel: +1 512 476 5780, Fax: +1 512 476 0858, Web: www.anderssonwise.com*

*Dale Chihuly, Chihuly Studio, 1111 NW 50th Street, Seattle, WA 98107-5120, USA*
*Tel: +1 206 781 8707, Fax: +1 206 781 1906, Web: www.chihuly.com*

Born in Vancouver in 1924, Arthur Erickson attended the University of British Columbia (1942–43) before becoming a Captain in the Canadian Intelligence Corps (1945) and then returning to complete his studies at McGill University. Considered one of the greatest Canadian modern architects, his built work includes the Museum of Anthropology at the University of British Columbia and the Canadian Embassy in Washington, DC. He was also the Chief Architect of Simon Fraser University, located in Burnaby, British Columbia, and of the the Province Law Courts Complex in Vancouver, British Columbia. Recent work includes the Kuwait Oil Sector Headquarters (Kuwait City, Kuwait, 1995–2004); the Waterfall Building (Vancouver, BC, 2001); the Weihai South Haibin Road Urban Design (Weihai, China, 2002); and the Suzhou Jinji Lake North Residential Development (Suzhou, China, 2002); as well as the Museum of Glass published here. Arthur Erickson won the American Institute of Architects Gold Medal in 1986. His associate for a number of recent projects including the Tacoma Museum of Glass, Nick Milkovich received his Bachelor of Architecture degree from the University of British Columbia in 1968. He joined the firm of Erickson/Massey in 1968, and worked with the new firm Arthur Erickson Architects from the first (1972), becoming an Associate in 1979 and Director of Design in 1987.

Arthur Erickson, 1924 in Vancouver geboren, studierte von 1942 bis 1943 an der University of British Columbia und war bis 1945 Captain im kanadischen Intelligence Corps, bevor er sein Studium an der McGill University abschloss. Er gilt als einer der bedeutendsten zeitgenössischen Architekten Kanadas, zu dessen Bauten das Museum of Anthropology an der University of British Columbia und die Kanadische Botschaft in Washington, DC, gehören. Außerdem war er leitender Architekt an der Simon Fraser University in Burnaby, British Columbia, und beim Bau des Gebäudekomplexes für den Verwaltungsgerichtshof in Vancouver, British Columbia. Zu seinen neueren Projekten zählen: Zentrale für Kuwait Oil Sector in Kuwait City, Kuwait (1995–2004), das Waterfall Building in Vancouver (2001), das Stadtbauprojekt Weihai South Haibin Road in Weihai, China (2002), das Wohnbauprojekt Suzhou Jinji Lake North im chinesischen Suzhou (2002) sowie das hier vorgestellte Glasmuseum in Tacoma. 1986 erhielt Arthur Erickson die Gold Medal des American Institute of Architects. Bei etlichen seiner Projekte, einschließlich des Tacoma Museum of Glass, war sein Partner Nick Milkovich, der 1968 den Bachelor of Architecture an der University of British Columbia erwarb und im selben Jahren bei Erickson/Massey eintrat. Seit dem Gründungsjahr 1972 arbeitete er auch bei der neuen Firma, Arthur Erickson Architects, wo er 1979 Partner und 1987 Director of Design wurde.

Né à Vancouver en 1924, Arthur Erickson étudie à l'Université de Colombie britannique (1942–43) avant de devenir capitaine dans les services d'espionnage canadiens (1945). Il achève ses études à la McGill University. Considéré comme l'un des plus grands achitectes modernistes canadiens, ses réalisations comprennent entre autres le musée d'anthropologie de l'Université de Colombie britannique et l'ambassade canadienne à Washington. Il a été architecte en chef de la Simon Fraser University, (Burnaby, Colombie britannique) et du complexe judiciaire de la province de Colombie britannique à Vancouver. Parmi ses travaux récents : le siège du secteur public des pétroles (Koweït City, Koweït, 1995–2004) ; le Waterfall Building (Vancouver, Canada, 2001), un projet d'urbanisme à Weihai sud (Chine, 2002), et le musée du verre, publié ici. Il a remporté la médaille d'or de l'American Institute of Architects (1986). Son associé dans un certain nombre de projets récents, dont le musée du verre de Tacoma, Nick Milkovich est Bachelor of Architecture de l'Université de Colombie britannique (1968). Il est entré à l'agence Erickson/Massey cette même année et a travaillé dès le départ (1972) avec la nouvelle agence Arthur Erickson Architects, devenant associé en 1979 et directeur de la conception en 1987.

# TACOMA MUSEUM OF GLASS

*Tacoma, Washington, USA, 1998–2002*

*Client: Museum of Glass Board of Trustees. Area: 7 000 m². Costs: $ 24 000 000.*
*Associated firm: Thomas Cook Reed Reinvald.*

This 7 000-square-meter, $24 million project was designed by the Canadian architect Arthur Erickson in collaboration with Nick Milkovich Architects Inc., of Vancouver, British Columbia, and Thomas Cook Reed Reinvald of Tacoma. The most striking feature of the Museum of Glass is a 27-meter-high tilted cone, located at its southern end and covered in diamond-shaped stainless steel plates. The cone houses the museum's "Hot Shop Amphitheater" where glassmaking is demonstrated. According to Arthur Erickson, the conical shape is a reference to the former sawdust burners of the region's lumber mills. The stepped forms of the building are clad in colored pre-cast concrete panels. The structure is organized around a large multi-purpose public lobby that provides access to the Hot Shop, 1 200 square meters of versatile gallery space, a 180-seat theatre, an education studio, the museum store, and a café. The Museum of Glass joins the Washington State History Museum, the new Tacoma Art Museum, and a new University of Washington campus, participating in an evolving cultural and educational district to support the rejuvenation of Tacoma's urban core. The 152-meter-long Chihuly Bridge of Glass connects the Museum to these facilities. Conceived by Dale Chihuly, a glass artist and native of Tacoma, and designed in collaboration with Arthur Andersson of Andersson Wise Architects, this pedestrian bridge is a display of color and form rising twenty-one meters into the air.

Dieses 7 000 m² umfassende, 24 Millionen Dollar teure Projekt wurde von dem kanadischen Architekten Arthur Erickson in Zusammenarbeit mit den Firmen Nick Milkovich Architects Inc. in Vancouver und Thomas Cook Reed Reinvald in Tacoma, Washington, geplant. Auffälligstes Gestaltungsmerkmal des Glasmuseums ist ein 27 m hoher, schräg gestellter Kegel, der am südlichen Ende des Baus aufragt und mit rautenförmigen Platten aus Edelstahl verkleidet ist. Dieser Baukörper enthält das „Hot Shop Amphitheater", wo den Besuchern die Kunst des Glasmachens demonstriert wird. Laut Erickson ist die konische Form eine Referenz an die charakteristischen Sägemehlbrenner der früher in dieser Region zahlreich beheimateten Sägewerke. Der treppenförmig gestaltete Museumsbau ist mit Fertigteilplatten aus farbigem Beton ummantelt. Das Gebäude ist um eine große Eingangshalle angelegt, von der aus man Zugang hat zum Hot Shop, der 1 200 m² großen, vielseitig nutzbaren Ausstellungsfläche, einem Theater mit 180 Sitzen, einem Atelier, in dem Kurse stattfinden, dem Museumsshop und einem Café. Zusammen mit dem Washington State History Museum, dem Tacoma Art Museum und dem Campus gehört das Museum of Glass zu einem neu entstandenen Kultur- und Universitätsviertel und trägt damit zur Verjüngung des Stadtkerns von Tacoma bei. Die Verbindung zwischen Glasmuseum und den anderen Gebäuden wird durch die 152 m lange Chihuly Bridge of Glass hergestellt. Diese Fußgängerbrücke, die ihr gelungenes Zusammenspiel von Farbe und Form in einer Höhe von 21 m entfaltet, wurde von dem in Tacoma geborenen Glaskünstler Dale Chihuly in Zusammenarbeit mit Arthur Andersson von Andersson Wise Architects entworfen.

Ce musée du verre de 7 000 m² qui a coûté 24 millions de dollars a été conçu par l'architecte canadien Arthur Erickson en collaboration avec Nick Milkovitch Architects Inc. de Vancouver, et Thomas Cook Reed Reinvald, de Tacoma. L'élément le plus frappant de ce projet est un cône incliné de 27 m de haut, habillé de plaques d'acier inoxydable en pointes de diamant, situé à l'extrémité sud. Il abrite le « Hot Shop Amphitheater » du musée où sont organisées des démonstrations sur la fabrication du verre. Selon Erickson, il fait référence aux anciens brûloirs de sciure des scieries de la région. Les formes en escalier du bâtiment sont habillées de panneaux de béton préfabriqués. La construction s'organise autour d'un vaste hall d'entrée multifonctions qui donne accès au cône, aux 1 200 m² de galeries d'exposition polyvalentes, à un auditorium de 180 places, à un atelier éducatif, à la boutique du musée et à un café. Le bâtiment jouxte un complexe culturel et éducatif qui participe à la rénovation du cœur de la ville et contient le Musée de l'Histoire de l'État de Washington, le nouveau Musée d'art de Tacoma et un nouveau campus universitaire. Le pont de verre Chihuly (152 m de long) relie le musée aux autres bâtiments. Conçue par Dale Chihuly, artiste verrier natif de Tacoma, et dessinée en collaboration avec Arthur Andersson de Andersson Wise Architects, cette passerelle piétonnière offre à 21 m de haut un véritable spectacle de couleurs et de formes.

Seen from certain angles, Erickson's Museum of Glass has much of the rather weighty institutional character that he is known for in other circumstances.

*Aus bestimmten Blickwinkeln hat Ericksons Glasmuseum viel von dem etwas wuchtigen Charakter, der auch früheren öffentlichen Bauten des Architekten eigen ist.*

*Sous certains angles, le Musée du verre rappelle le caractère institutionnel un peu pesant de ses autres réalisations.*

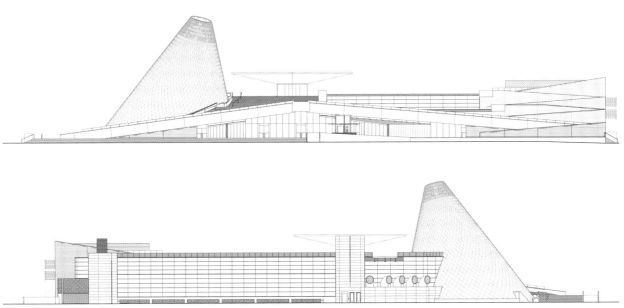

Elevations and an image above show the importance of the tilted cone that differentiates this building from more ordinary, purely rectilinear architecture.

Die Aufrisse und obige Ansicht zeigen, wie wichtig der schräggestellte Kegel ist, um das Gebäude von einer konventionellen, völlig geradlinigen Architektur zu unterscheiden.

Les élévations et l'image ci-dessus montre l'importance du cône incliné qui fait échapper le bâtiment à une architecture plus ordinaire, purement rectiligne.

The extensive use of glass, including the tilted panes seen in the image above, bring forward the central theme of the museum itself.

Die großflächige Verwendung von Glas, einschließlich der oben abgebildeten Reihe aneinander gelehnter Glasplatten, betonen das zentrale Thema des Museums.

L'utilisation extensive du verre, y compris les panneaux inclinés ci-dessus, illustrent également la thématique du musée.

The glazed, tilting cone is the most emblematic feature of the architecture; reminiscent of a furnace or even a volcano it symbolizes the fiery origin of glass.

Der verglaste, geneigte Kegel stellt das emblematischste Merkmal der Anlage dar: Indem er an einen Brennofen oder sogar Vulkan denken lässt, symbolisiert er den feurig glühenden Ursprung von Glas.

Le cône incliné et vitré est l'élément le plus emblématique du projet. Dans son évocation d'un four ou d'un volcan, il rappelle l'origine physique du verre.

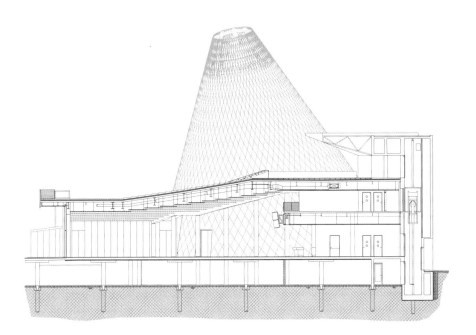

The interior of the cone is somewhat heavier and less transparent than one might expect from the outside. Housing an auditorium it seems metallic and mechanical from the inside.

Das Innere des Kegels ist massiger und weniger transparent als sein Äußeres erwarten lässt. Mit seinem Auditorium wirkt das Interieur metallisch und maschinenartig.

L'intérieur du cône semble plus lourd et moins transparent que son extérieur ne le laisse présager. Il abrite un auditorium dans une ambiance métallique et mécanique.

*Conceived by Dale Chihuly, a glass artist and native of Tacoma, and designed in collaboration with Arthur Andersson of Andersson Wise Architects, this pedestrian bridge is strict in its exterior form and brilliantly playful within.*

*Die von Dale Chihuly, einem in Tacoma beheimateten Glaskünstler, in Zusammenarbeit mit Arthur Andersson von Andersson Wise Architects entworfene Fußgängerbrücke wirkt von ihrer äußeren Form her streng, im Innern ist sie jedoch auf brillante Weise verspielt.*

*Conçu par Dale Chihuly, artiste verrier natif de Tacoma, et conçu en collaboration avec Arthur Andersson d'Andersson Wise Architects, la passerelle piétonnière d'aspect extérieur strict se révèle ludique et joyeuse à l'intérieur.*

Chihuly's mastery of glass, known well beyond his own city, is fully displayed day and night in this riot of color and form.

Chihulys meisterhafte Beherrschung der Glaskunst, für die er weit über seine Heimatstadt hinaus bekannt wurde, ist Tag und Nacht in all ihrer Farben- und Formenpracht zu sehen.

La maîtrise du verre par l'artiste, dont la réputation n'est pas seulement locale, se donne en spectacle de jour comme de nuit dans un flamboiement de couleurs et de formes.

Extravagant works by Chihuly are displayed in the bridge as though its interior were as much of a museum as the main building that it leads to.

Extravagante Glasobjekte von Chihuly sind in der Brücke ausgestellt, die damit wie das Hauptgebäude ebenfalls zum Museum wird.

D'extravagantes œuvres de Chihuly sont présentées le long de la passerelle, comme si elle faisaient déjà partie du musée dont celle-ci est un accès.

# FOA

*FOA*
*55 Curtain Road*
*London EC2A 3PT*
*UK*

*Tel: +44 20 7033 9800*
*Fax: +44 20 7033 9801*
*e-mail: mail@f-o-a.net*
*Web: www.f-o-a.net/flash/*

*Yokohama International Port Terminal* ▶

FOA is led by architects Farshid Moussavi and Alejandro Zaera Polo, and is "dedicated to the exploration of contemporary urban conditions, lifestyles and construction technologies." Aside from the Yokohama International Port Terminal published here, they have worked on: Barcelona South-East Coastal Park; Municipal Theater and Auditorium, Torrevieja, Spain; Publishing Headquarters, Paju, South Korea; Belgo restaurants in London, Bristol and New York; and Blue Moon Housing and Tent projects in Groningen, The Netherlands. They have also designed a central police station (La Vila Joyosa, Spain); harbor facilities for Amersfoort, The Netherlands; and a car park for Basel, Switzerland. Farshid Moussavi received her Masters in Architecture from the Harvard Graduate School of Design. She worked for the Renzo Piano Building Workshop in Genoa in 1988 and for the Office for Metropolitan Architecture (OMA) in Rotterdam (Rem Koolhaas, 1991–1993), while establishing Foreign Office Architects (FOA) in 1992. Also educated at Harvard, Alejandro Zaera Polo worked with OMA in Rotterdam at the same time as Farshid Moussavi.

FOA wird von den Architekten Farshid Moussavi und Alejandro Zaera Polo geleitet und widmet sich laut eigener Aussage der Erforschung zeitgenössischer urbaner Wohnverhältnisse, Lebensstile und Konstruktionstechnologien. Neben dem hier präsentierten Terminal für den internationalen Hafen in Yokohama zählen zu ihren Projekten: ein Park am Meer in Barcelona, ein Theater mit Auditorium im spanischen Torrevieja, ein Verlagsgebäude in Paju, Südkorea, Belgo Restaurants in London, Bristol und New York sowie das Wohnbauten und Zelte umfassende Projekt Blue Moon im niederländischen Groningen. Außerdem gestalteten Moussavi und Zaera Polo ein Polizeirevier in der Innenstadt von La Vila Joyosa, Spanien, Hafengebäude im niederländischen Amersfoort und einen Parkplatz in Basel. Farshid Moussavi erwarb ihren Master of Architecture an der Harvard Graduate School of Design. 1988 arbeitete sie im Baubüro von Renzo Piano in Genua und von 1991 bis 1993 im Office for Metropolitan Architecture (OMA) von Rem Koolhaas in Rotterdam. 1992 gründete sie die Firma Foreign Office Architects (FOA). Alejandro Zaera Polo studierte ebenfalls in Harvard und arbeitete zur selben Zeit wie Farshid Moussavi im OMA in Rotterdam.

FOA est animé par les architectes Farshid Moussavi et Alejandro Zaera Polo. L'agence se consacre à « l'exploration des conditions urbaines, des styles de vie et des technologies de construction contemporaines ». En dehors du terminal du port international de Yokohama publié ici, ils ont travaillé sur le parc côtier du sud-est de Barcelone ; le théâtre et l'auditorium municipaux de Torrevieja (Espagne) ; le siège d'une maison d'édition (Paju, Corée du Sud) ; les restaurants Belgo à Londres, Bristol et New York, et le programme de logements Blue Moon Housing and Tent à Groningue (Pays-Bas). Ils ont également conçu un poste de police central (La Villa Joyosa, Espagne) ; des installations portuaires (Amersfoort, Pays-Bas) et un parking à Bâle (Suisse). Farshid Moussavi est Master of Architecture de la Harvard Graduate School of Design. Elle a travaillé pour Renzo Piano à Gènes (1988) et pour OMA de Rem Koolhaas à Rotterdam (1991–1993), tout en créant Foreign Office Architects (FOA) en 1992. Après avoir également effectué ses études à Harvard, Alejandro Zaera Polo a travaillé chez OMA au même moment que Farshid Moussavi.

# YOKOHAMA INTERNATIONAL
# PORT TERMINAL
*Yokohama, Japan, 2000–2002*

*Client: The City of Yokohama Port & Harbor Bureau. Floor area: 17 000 m² (cruise terminal), 13 000 m² (citizens amenities), 18 000 m² (traffic facilities). Costs: € 220 000 000.*

*Rectangular and functional, FOA's Pier has little other resemblance to traditional facilities of its type. One layer wraps into another, like an artificial, computer generated landscape.*

*Der rechteckig funktionale Pier von FOA hat wenig Ähnlichkeit mit traditionellen Konstruktionen dieser Art. Eine Schicht legt sich hier um die andere, wie bei einer künstlichen, vom Computer erzeugten Landschaft.*

*Rectangulaire et fonctionnelle, la jetée de FOA ne ressemble cependant pas aux équipement traditionnels de ce type. Ses strates s'enroulent les unes autour des autres, tel un paysage artificiel généré par ordinateur.*

The 1995 competition organized by the Port and Harbor Authority and the City of Yokohama, Japan, marked the emergence of Foreign Office Architects as an important architectural practice. The actual construction of the project marked a significant step in the adaptation of computer-driven design techniques to the "real world" problems of a large building. In fact, the sophisticated design has a bearing on much more than esthetics, as FOA explains: "Our proposal for the Yokohama project is generated from a circulation diagram that aspires to eliminate the linear structure characteristic of piers, and the directionality of the circulation ... Rather than developing the building as an object or figure on the pier, the project is produced as an extension of the urban ground, constructed as a systematic transformation of the lines of the circulation diagram into a folded and bifurcated surface.... the folded ground distributes the loads through the surfaces themselves, moving them diagonally to the ground. This structure is also especially adequate in coping with the lateral forces generated by seismic movements that affect Japan. The result is the hybridization of given types of space and program through a distinct tectonic system, in this case, a folded surface."

Mit ihrem prämierten Beitrag zu dem 1995 von der Hafen- und Stadtverwaltung von Yokohama organisierten Wettbewerb trat das Büro Foreign Office Architects erstmals als bedeutende Architektengruppe in Erscheinung. Die Konstruktion dieser Anlage war ein wichtiger Schritt in der Anwendung computergenerierter Gestaltungstechniken auf die realen Probleme bei der Fertigstellung von Großbauten. Dabei bezieht sich das ausgeklügelte Design nicht nur auf die gestalterische Ästhetik, wie einer der FOA-Architekten erläutert: „Unser Entwurf leitet sich von einem Umlaufdiagramm ab, das die für einen Pier typische lineare Anordnung sowie die übliche Zirkulationsrichtung durchbrechen soll ... Statt das Gebäude als isoliertes Objekt oder als geometrische Form zu entwickeln, wurde das gesamte Yokohama-Projekt als eine Erweiterung des städtischen Raums angelegt. Es ist aus einer systematischen Transformation der Linien des Zirkulationsdiagramms in eine gabelförmig gefaltete Oberfläche entstanden ... welche die Lasten auf den diagonal angeordneten Bodenfläche verteilt. Diese Konstruktionsweise ist außerdem besonders geeignet, um den Lateralkräften entgegenzuwirken, die in Japan häufig durch seismische Bewegungen verursacht werden. Das Resultat ist eine Hybridisierung eines bestehenden Raumtyps und Bauprogramms durch ein spezielles tektonisches System, in diesem Fall eine gefaltete Oberfläche."

Le concours organisé en 1995 pour ce terminal par l'Autorité du port et la ville de Yokohama est à l'origine de l'émergence internationale de Foreign Office Architects parmi les agences qui comptent. La mise en œuvre du projet a marqué une nouvelle étape dans l'application des techniques de CAO aux problèmes concrets d'un vaste bâtiment. En fait, cette conception sophistiquée a porté sur beaucoup plus que l'esthétique comme l'explique FAO : « Notre proposition pour Yokohama est issue du schéma de circulation qui veut éliminer la structure linéaire caractéristique en jetée et la directionn habituelle des circulations... Au lieu d'être un bâtiment qui ne serait qu'un objet posé sur une jetée, le projet devient une extension de la ville, dans une transformation systématique des axes du plan de circulation en une surface pliée et bifurquée... le sol replié distribue les charges à travers les plans, et les reporte en diagonale vers le sol. Cette structure est particulièrement adaptée pour résister aux forces latérales générées par les mouvements sismiques qui affectent le Japon. Le résultat final est une hybridation de types d'espaces et d'éléments du programme dans un système tectonique original, en l'occurrence, une surface pliée. »

Surfaces on the Pier bend and fold together in ways that architecture could hardly have imagined, let alone executed before the full development of computer-assisted design.

Die Oberflächen des Piers biegen und falten sich in einer Weise, wie sie in der Architektur kaum vorstellbar war, geschweige denn vor der Entwicklung von CAD-Programmen.

Les surfaces de la jetée se plient et se replient d'une manière rarement vue en architecture, surtout dans les réalisations d'avant l'apparition de la CAO.

Despite their attachment to nature, the Japanese are particularly accustomed to architecture and landscape design that mimics or recreates an artificial "natural" world.

Bei all ihrer Liebe zur Natur sind die Japaner besonders vertraut mit einer Architektur und Landschaftsgestaltung, die eine künstliche Form von Natur schafft oder nachahmt.

Malgré leur attachement à la nature, les Japonais sont particulièrement ouverts à une conception de l'architecture et du paysage qui imite ou recrée un monde « naturel » artificiel.

Intended for heavy use, the Yokohama Pier succeeds in reconciling an esthetically ambitious concept with a rigorous and challenging program.

Für eine hohe Beanspruchung konzipiert, vereint das Yokohama Pier ein ästhetisch ambitiöses Konzept mit einem anspruchsvollen Bauplan.

Prévu pour un usage intensif, le terminal de Yokohama réussit à concilier un concept esthétique ambitieux et un programme rigoureux et chargé.

Interior areas continue the bending, folding rhythm of the exterior, admitting daylight into spaces where pure horizontal or vertical surfaces are relatively rare.

Die Innenräume führen den äußeren Rhythmus weiter und lassen Tageslicht in Zonen, in denen es kaum eine ungebrochen horizontale oder vertikale Oberfläche gibt.

Les espaces intérieurs reprennent le rythme de pliage de l'extérieur, et admettent l'éclairage naturel dans des volumes où les plans horizontaux ou verticaux sont relativement rares.

Again, despite the playfulness of the seemingly eccentric design, it is clear that FOA have thought out the very real demands of such a facility.

Trotz des spielerischen Charakters ihres exzentrischen Entwurfs haben die Architekten von FOA die realen Anforderungen einer solchen Anlage wohl bedacht.

L'aspect ludique et légèrement excentrique du projet, ne doit pas masquer que FOA a réfléchi à toutes les contraintes d'un tel équipement.

Mimicking the surface of the earth or natural formations, on the outside the Pier gives way to this cathedral-like space within.

Der äußerlich der Erdoberfläche oder Naturformen nachgebildete Pier öffnet sich in seinem Innern zu einem kathedralenartigen Raum.

Si, vue de l'extérieur, la jetée semble imiter une formation géologique naturelle, elle n'en laisse pas moins place à l'intérieur à un volume aux dimensions de cathédrale.

# MANUELLE GAUTRAND

*Manuelle Gautrand Architectes*
*36, Boulevard de la Bastille*
*75012 Paris*
*France*

*Tel: +33 1 56 95 06 46*
*Fax: +33 1 56 95 06 47*
*e-mail: contact@manuelle-gautrand.com*
*Web: www.manuelle-gautrand.com*

*Espace Citroën* ▶

Born in 1961, Manuelle Gautrand received her architecture degree in 1985 and created her own office in 1991. In 2001, she was selected to participate in the limited competition for the François Pinault Contemporary Art Museum to be located on the Ile Seguin near Paris. She has been the architectural consultant of the Rectory of Grenoble since 1992. Her varied design experience includes a 72-meter-long pedestrian bridge (Lyon, 1993); five highway toll booths (in the Somme region on the A16 highway, 1998); the restructuring of the administrative offices of the Pompidou Center in Paris (1996); the Theater of the National Center for Dramatic Arts (Béthune, 1998); an airport catering center in Nantes (1999) and a hospital laundry (Le Havre, 2003). Aside from the Espace Citroën published here, her current work includes the extension and restructuring of the Lille Museum of Contemporary Art (2005); a 105-unit apartment building in Rennes (2005); and the "Gaîté Lyrique" digital arts, and Music Center in Paris (2006). She works with a permanent staff of five, including four other architects.

Manuelle Gautrand, 1961 geboren, schloss 1985 ihr Architekturstudium ab und gründete 1991 ihr eigenes Büro. 2001 gehörte sie zu den ausgewählten Teilnehmern am Wettbewerb für das Museum zeitgenössischer Kunst der Stiftung François Pinault, das auf der Ile Seguin nahe Paris entstehen soll, und seit 1992 ist sie als architektonische Beraterin für den Leiter des Schulaufsichtsbezirks von Grenoble tätig. Zu ihren vielfältigen Projekten gehören eine 72 m lange Fußgängerbrücke in Lyon (1993), fünf Autobahnmautstellen entlang der A16 im französischen Somme-Gebiet (1998), die Neugestaltung der Verwaltungsbüros des Centre Pompidou in Paris (1996), das Theater des staatlichen Zentrums für darstellende Künste in Béthune (1998), ein Airport Catering-Zentrum in Nantes (1999) sowie eine Krankenhauswäscherei in Le Havre (2003). Neben dem hier vorgestellten Espace Citroën zählen zu ihren aktuellen Arbeiten die Erweiterung und Umgestaltung des Museums für zeitgenössische Kunst in Lille (2005), ein Showroom mit 105 Wohnungen in Rennes (2005) und das „Gaîté Lyrique" Zentrum für digitale Kunst und Musik in Paris (2006). Zu ihren fünf ständigen Mitarbeitern gehören vier weitere Architekten.

Née en 1961, Manuelle Gontrand a obtenu son diplôme d'architecte en 1985 et a fondé son agence en 1991. En 2001, elle a été sélectionnée pour participer au concours sur invitation de la Fondation François Pinault sur l'Île Seguin à Paris. Elle est consultante pour l'architecture du rectorat de Grenoble depuis 1992. Son expérience diversifiée comprend une passerelle piétonnière de 72 m de long (Lyon, 1993) ; cinq postes de péage d'autoroute (autoroute A6, Somme, 1998) ; la restructuration des bureaux administratifs du Centre Pompidou à Paris (1996) ; le theâtre du Centre national des arts dramatiques (Béthune, 1998) ; un centre de logistique pour traiteur à l'aéroport de Nantes (1999) et une lingerie d'hôpital (Le Havre, 2003). En dehors de l'Espace Citroën publié ici, elle travaille actuellement à l'extension-restructuration du Musée d'art contemporain de Lille (2005) ; un immeuble de 105 appartements à Rennes (2005) et le Centre des musiques et des arts numériques de la Gaîté Lyrique (Paris, 2006). Elle opère avec une équipe de cinq personnes dont quatre architectes.

# ESPACE CITROËN

*42 Champs-Elysées, Paris, France, 2003–2005*

*Client: Citroën, PSA Group. Total floor area: 1 200 m². Costs: € 11 000 000.*

The car manufacturer Citroën installed a showroom at number 42, Champs-Elysées, in 1927. In 1931, the firm called on its factory designer Ravazé and its own art director Pierre Louys to redo the building in a style judged befitting of the brand until 1984. Home to a restaurant for the next twenty years, the Citroën showroom had become outdated and the company decided in 2002 to organize an international design competition with such participants as Zaha Hadid, Daniel Libeskind and Christian de Portzamparc. The winner was the young French architect Manuelle Gautrand, who is to rebuild the 1 200-square-meter structure entirely before 2005. Using the inverted double-V symbol of the firm, Gautrand designed a complex glass façade that will reveal the successive platforms where Citroën vehicles will be exhibited. She makes subtle reference to the previous "Art Deco" façade of the showroom that was so long admired. Her intention is that the interior platforms should not only be moveable but also actually turn slowly. The platform system permits a full use of the considerable interior height while not actually breaking up the space. The architect took as her cue words of the car designer Pininfarina, who stated that "Citroën means non-aggressive performance…" Performance nonetheless.

Im Jahr 1927 bezog der Autohersteller Citroën einen Showroom in der Champs Elysées 42. Vier Jahre später beauftragte das Unternehmen seinen Industriedesigner Ravazé und seinen Artdirector Pierre Louys, das Gebäude in einem Stil umzugestalten, der bis ins Jahr 1984 als zu der Automarke passend galt. Nachdem der ehemalige Citroën-Showroom, der dann ein Restaurant beherbergte, unmodern geworden war, beschloss die Firmenleitung 2002, einen internationalen Wettbewerb zu organisieren, an dem unter anderen Zaha Hadid, Daniel Libeskind und Christian de Portzamparc teilnahmen. Siegerin wurde jedoch die junge französische Architektin Manuelle Gautrand, die nun das gesamte, 1 200 m² umfassende Gebäude bis 2005 umbauen soll. Unter Verwendung des Firmensignets – das umgekehrte Doppel-V – entwarf Gautrand eine komplex strukturierte Glasfassade, durch die man die übereinander angeordneten Plattformen, auf denen die Citroën-Modelle präsentiert werden, erkennen kann. Dabei stellt sie einen raffinierten Bezug zu der einst so bewunderten Art déco Fassade des Autogeschäfts her. Ihre Absicht ist außerdem, dass die Plattformen im Innenraum nicht nur beweglich sind, sondern sich auch noch langsam um die eigene Achse drehen. Dieses Bühnensystem erlaubt die volle Nutzung der beträchtlichen Höhe des Gebäudes, ohne den Raum selbst zu zerteilen. Die Architektin richtete sich bei ihrer Gestaltung nach den Worten des Autodesigners Pininfarina, der einmal sagte: „Citroën bedeutet unaggressive Leistung". Nichtsdestoweniger eine Leistung.

Le constructeur automobile Citroën a installé son premier magasin au 42, avenue des Champs-Élysées en 1927. En 1931, il fit appel à son designer Ravazé et à son directeur artistique Pierre Louys pour reconstruire l'immeuble dans un style qui exprima la marque avec pertinence jusqu'en 1984. Un nouveau showroom Citroën accouplé à un restaurant est alors réaménagé, mais se démode assez vite. En 2002, le constructeur a lancé un concours international qui réunit des participants comme Zaha Hadid, Daniel Libeskind et Christian de Portzamparc. Il fut remporté par la jeune architecte française Manuelle Gautrand, chargée de reconstruire entièrement cette structure de 1 200 m² avant 2005. Utilisant le double chevron symbole de la firme, elle a conçu une façade complexe en verre qui mettra en valeur diverses platesformes sur lesquelles seront exposés des véhicules, dans une référence subtile à l'ancienne façade Art Déco longtemps admirée. Les plates-formes intérieures devraient être à la fois mobiles et tourner lentement sur elles-mêmes. Ce système permettra d'utiliser pleinement la considérable hauteur du volume intérieur sans le rompre pour autant. Gautrand a pris au mot ce commentaire du designer automobile Pininfarina disant que « Citroën signifie performance non agressive… »

Located on the Champs-Elysees, the Citroen building will be entirely devoted to the exhibition of automobiles, set on rotating platforms.

Das auf den Champs-Elysées liegende Gebäude ist ganz der Präsentation von Autos gewidmet, die auf rotierenden Plattformen ausgestellt werden.

L'immeuble Citroën sera entièrement consacré à la présentation des véhicules sur des plates-formes tournantes.

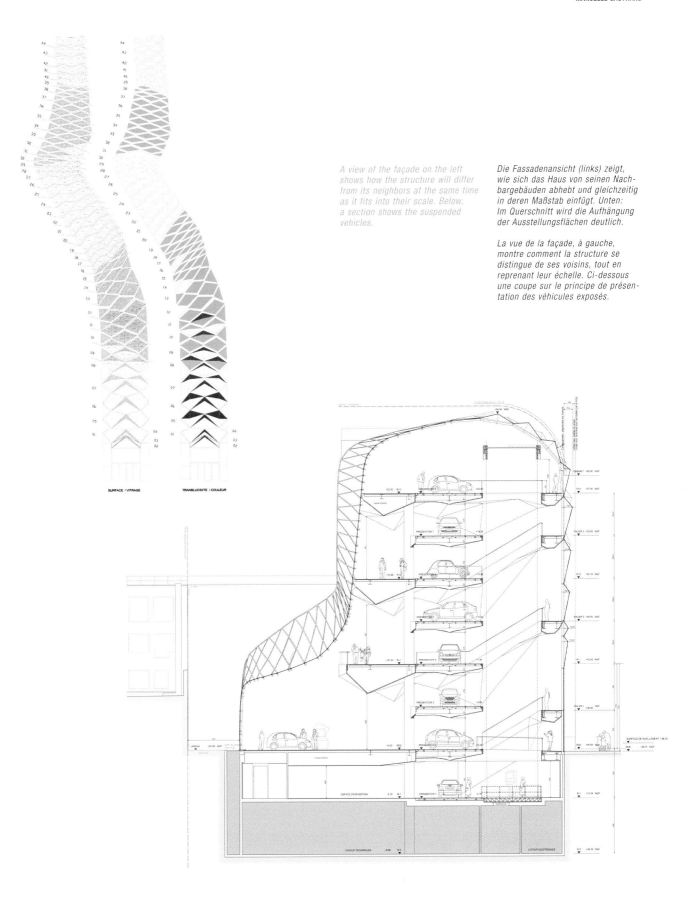

A view of the façade on the left
shows how the structure will differ
from its neighbors at the same time
as it fits into their scale. Below,
a section shows the suspended
vehicles.

*Die Fassadenansicht (links) zeigt,
wie sich das Haus von seinen Nachbargebäuden abhebt und gleichzeitig
in deren Maßstab einfügt. Unten:
Im Querschnitt wird die Aufhängung
der Ausstellungsflächen deutlich.*

*La vue de la façade, à gauche,
montre comment la structure se
distingue de ses voisins, tout en
reprenant leur échelle. Ci-dessous
une coupe sur le principe de présentation des véhicules exposés.*

SURFACE / VITRAGE          TRANSLUCIDITE / COULEUR

# FRANK O. GEHRY

*Gehry Partners LLP*
*12541 Beatrice Street*
*Los Angeles, CA 90066*
*USA*

*Tel: +1 310 482 3000*
*Fax: +1 310 482 3006*

Born in Toronto, Canada, in 1929, Frank Gehry studied at the University of Southern California, Los Angeles (1949–1951), and at Harvard (1956–57). Principal of Gehry Partners LLP., Los Angeles, since 1962, he received the 1989 Pritzker Prize. Some of his notable projects are the Loyola Law School, Los Angeles (1981–1984); the Norton Residence, Venice, California (1983); California Aerospace Museum, Los Angeles (1982–1984); Schnabel Residence, Brentwood (1989); Festival Disney, Marne-la-Vallée, France (1989–1992); Guggenheim Museum, Bilbao, Spain (1991–1997); Experience Music Project (Seattle, Washington, 1995–2000); and the unbuilt Guggenheim Museum (New York, 1998–). Recent work includes: DG Bank Headquarters (Berlin, Germany, 2000); Fisher Center for the Performing Arts at Bard College (Annandale-on-Hudson, NY, 2003, published here); Walt Disney Concert Hall (Los Angeles, 2003, also published here); and the Massachusetts Institute of Technology Stata Complex (Cambridge, MA, 2003).

Frank O. Gehry, 1929 in Toronto geboren, studierte von 1949 bis 1951 an der University of Southern California (USC) in Los Angeles und von 1956 bis 1957 in Harvard. Seit 1962 ist er Leiter der Firma Gehry Partners LLP. in Los Angeles. 1989 erhielt er den Pritzker Prize. Zu seinen bekanntesten Bauten gehören die Loyola Law School in Los Angeles (1981–1984), das California Aerospace Museum in Los Angeles (1982–1984), die Villa Norton im kalifornischen Venice (1983), die Villa Schnabel in Brentwood (1989), das Festival Disney im französischen Marne-la-Vallée (1989–1992), das Guggenheim Museum in Bilbao (1991–1997) und das Experience Music Project in Seattle, Washington (1995–2000). Sein 1998 entworfener Bau für das Guggenheim Museum in New York blieb bislang unrealisiert. Zu seinen jüngsten Projekten zählen: die Zentrale der DG Bank in Berlin (2000), das hier vorgestellte Fisher Center for the Performing Arts am Bard College in Annandale-on-Hudson, New York (2003), die ebenfalls hier gezeigte Walt Disney Concert Hall in Los Angeles (2003) sowie der Stata Complex für das Massachusetts Institute of Technology in Cambridge, Massachusetts (2003).

Né à Toronto, Canada, en 1929, Frank Gehry étudie à l'University of Southern California, Los Angeles (1949–1951), puis à Harvard (1956–57). Directeur de l'agence Gehry Partners LLP., Los Angeles, depuis 1962, il reçoit en 1989 le prix Pritzker. Parmi ses projets les plus remarqués : la Loyola Law School, Los Angeles (1981–1984) ; la Norton Residence, Venice, Californie (1983) ; le California Aerospace Museum, Los Angeles (1982–1984) ; la Schnabel Residence, Brentwood (1989) ; Festival Disney, Marne-la-Vallée, France (1989–1992) ; le Guggenheim Museum, Bilbao, Espagne (1991–1997) ; Experience Music Project, Seattle, Washington (1995–2000) et le Guggenheim Museum de New York (1998–) qui reste à construire. Parmi ses chantiers récents : siège de la DG Bank (Berlin, Allemagne, 2000) ; Fisher Center for the Performing Arts at Bard College (Annandale-on-Hudson, NY, 2003, publié ici) ; Walt Disney Concert Hall (Los Angeles, 2003, également publié ici) et le Massachusetts Institute of Technology Stata Complex (Cambridge, Massachusetts, USA, 2003).

# RICHARD B. FISHER CENTER FOR THE PERFORMING ARTS AT BARD COLLEGE

*Annandale-on-Hudson, New York, USA, 2000–2003*

*Client: Bard College. Total floor area: 10 000 m². Costs: $ 62 000 000.*

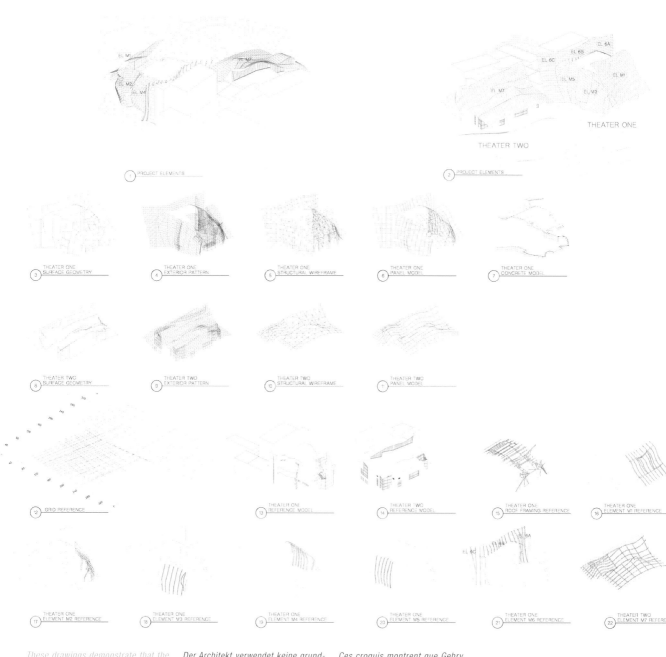

*These drawings demonstrate that the architect does not use a fundamentally computer-driven design method but rather applies CAD techniques after the original design evolves in a more traditional mode.*

*Der Architekt verwendet keine grundlegend computergenerierte Gestaltungsmethode, sondern setzt CAD-Techniken erst ein, nachdem das ursprüngliche Design auf traditionellere Weise entwickelt wurde.*

*Ces croquis montrent que Gehry n'utilise pas directement la CAO mais en utilise la technique une fois que le projet développé selon des méthodes traditionnelles est suffisamment avancé.*

An unexpected object in any context, the Fisher Center stands out of its natural setting like a gleaming jewel.

Das Fisher Center sticht wie ein funkelnder Juwel aus seiner natürlichen Umgebung hervor.

Objet inattendu dans n'importe quel contexte, le Fisher Centre se détache de son cadre naturel à la manière d'un bijou brillant de tous ses feux.

More than some other Gehry designed sculptural works, the Fisher Center lifts its veil of metal to reveal a glowing interior space.

Mehr als die anderen skulpturalen Bauten von Gehry verbirgt das Center unter seinem Metallschleier einen warm strahlenden Innenraum.

Plus que dans d'autres réalisations sculpturales de Gehry, le bâtiment soulève son voile métallique pour révéler son intérieur étincelant.

The Fisher Center at Bard College provides spaces for dance, drama, opera and music performances. The 10 000-square-meter building, which contains two multi-purpose performance theaters, is located on the Bard College campus in an area of tall trees and open lawns. A number of different exterior materials and finishes were considered for the building. After a lengthy on-site review process, a soft, brushed stainless steel was selected for the exterior cladding, "because of the material's ability to reflect the light and colors of the sky and the surrounding landscape." Despite the fact that Gehry has become well known for his billowing metal façades, the structure at Bard appears to be a particularly masterful interpretation of this theme. Inside the building, Theater 1 has 850 seats in an orchestra section and two balcony areas. As Gehry's description points out, "the highly sculptural exterior of Theater 1 responds to its internal organization. A sail-like canopy clad in stainless steel panels projects out over the box office and lobby. The stainless steel panels loosely wrap around the sides of the theater toward the proscenium, creating two tall, sky-lit gathering areas on either side of the main lobby. The stainless steel panels then flare out at the proscenium creating a sculptural collar-like shape that rests on the simple concrete and plaster form of the stage house." Theater 2 is a black box dedicated to student dance and drama productions, and can accommodate up to 300 seats. Two dance rehearsal rooms and two drama rehearsal rooms are located adjacent to Theater 2.

Das 10 000 m² umfassende Fisher Center des Bard College beherbergt zwei Mehrzwecksäle für Tanz-, Theater-, Oper- und Musikaufführungen und liegt am College Campus, inmitten hoher Bäume und offener Rasenflächen. Nachdem man verschiedene Materialien für die Fassaden erwogen und vor Ort ausprobiert hatte, wurde ein weicher, mattverchromter Edelstahl als Außenverkleidung gewählt. Auch wenn Gehry für seine geschwungenen Metallfassaden weltbekannt geworden ist, stellt das Fisher Center eine besonders meisterhafte Interpretation dieses Themas dar. Das Theater 1 ist mit 850 Sitzen im Parkett und zwei Balkonen ausgestattet und die in hohem Maße skulptural gestaltete Außenform entspricht, so Gehry, seiner internen Anordnung. Weiter heißt es in Gehrys Beschreibung: „Ein mit Edelstahlplatten ummanteltes, segelförmiges Vordach ragt über die Eingangshalle. Die Stahlplatten legen sich in einigem Abstand um die Längswände des Theaters, wodurch zu beiden Seiten der Eingangshalle zwei hohe, von oben belichtete Aufenthaltsräume entstehen. Beim Proszenium bauchen sie sich zu einem kragenartigen Gebilde aus, das auf dem schlichten, aus Beton und Gips gefertigten Bauteil ruht, in dem sich die Bühne befindet." Theater 2 ist eine Blackbox, die für studentische Tanz- und Theaterproduktionen vorgesehen ist und bis zu 300 Besucher fasst. An das Theater 2 schließen sich zwei Tanz- und zwei Theaterproberäume an.

Le Fisher Center de Bard College se consacre aux spectacles de danse, de théâtre, d'opéra et aux concerts. Bâtiment de 10 000 m², qui contient deux salles polyvalentes, il se dresse sur le campus de Bard College au milieu d'une pelouse plantée de grands arbres. Diverses alternatives de matériaux et de finitions extérieurs ont été étudiées. Après des recherches poussées, c'est un acier inoxydable brossé qui a été retenu. Si Gehry est réputé pour l'animation de ses façades métalliques, celles de Bard en sont une illustration particulièrement brillante. Le Theater 1 offre 850 places à l'orchestre et sur deux balcons. Selon le descriptif de Gehry : « L'apparence extérieure très sculpturale du Theater 1 répond à son organisation interne. Un auvent en forme de voile habillé de panneaux d'acier inox se projette au-dessus de la billetterie et du hall d'entrée. Des panneaux d'acier enveloppent de façon libre les côtés du théâtre vers le proscenium, déterminant deux zones de grande hauteur à éclairage zénithal de chaque côté du hall principal. Les panneaux s'évasent ensuite vers la scène pour créer une forme sculpturale en forme de col qui repose sur la simple structure en béton et plâtre de la cage de scène. » Le Theater 2 est une boîte noire réservée aux productions de spectacles de danse et de théâtre des étudiants. Il peut recevoir jusqu'à 300 spectateurs. Deux salles de répétitions de danse et deux pour le théâtre sont prévues à proximité immédiate.

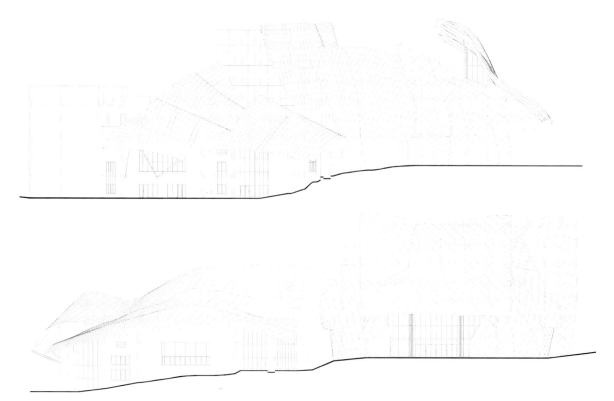

*Undulating veils of metal give a primacy to the architecture itself, perhaps at the cost of making the structure's function almost enigmatic.*

*Die geschwungenen Metallgebilde geben der Architektur selbst den Vorrang, wobei die Funktion des Gebäudes dabei fast verschleiert wird.*

*Des voiles flottants de métal donnent la primauté à l'architecture elle-même, peut-être au risque de rendre la fonction du bâtiment quasi énigmatique.*

Although apparently abstract in its undulating progression of forms, the Fisher Center does on occasion reveal the anthropomorphic proclivities of the author of "Fish Dance."

Wenngleich scheinbar abstrakt in seiner wellenartigen Formgebung, enthüllt das Fisher Center stellenweise die anthropomorphen Neigungen des Schöpfers von „Fish Dance".

Bien qu'apparemment abstrait dans la progression de l'ondulation de ses formes, le Fisher Center illustre à l'occasion les penchants anthropomorphiques de l'auteur de la « fish dance ».

P 244.245

Interior spaces soar like those of the Guggenheim Bilbao, but here assume a more mechanical or metal appearance than in other Gehry works.

Die Innenräume schwingen sich ebenso wie beim Guggenheim Bilbao hoch auf, haben hier jedoch einen mehr maschinenartigen und metallischen Charakter als andere Interieurs von Gehry.

Si les volumes intérieurs se dressent comme ceux du Guggenheim Bilbao, ils prennent ici un aspect plus métallique ou mécanique que dans d'autres œuvres de l'architecte.

The static volumes of traditional modernism here give way to a symphony of arching, rising metal shapes that give movement it not sound to architecture.

Die statischen Baukörper eines traditionellen Modernismus weichen hier einer Symphonie aus Bögen und emporstrebenden Metallformen, die der Architektur Bewegung, wenn nicht gar Klang verleihen.

Les volumes statiques du modernisme classique laissent ici place à une symphonie de formes métalliques en arc ou en projection, qui donnent à l'architecture son mouvement.

# WALT DISNEY CONCERT HALL

*Los Angeles, California, USA, 1999–2003*

Client: Walt Disney Concert Hall Committee. Total floor area: 18 600 m². Costs: $ 274 000 000.

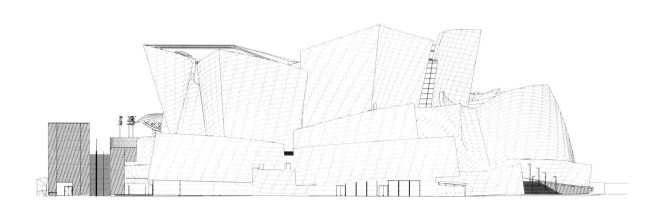

It had long been noted that, in spite of his international notoriety, Los Angeles architect Frank Gehry had not built a significant public building in his home town. With the opening of the Walt Disney Concert Hall in the fall of 2003, that failing was rectified. Located in the Bunker Hill area of downtown Los Angeles, close to Arata Isozaki's Museum of Contemporary Art, the project originated in 1987 with a $50 million gift from the late Lillian Disney. Since then, other gifts and accumulated interest bring the Disney family's total contribution to over $100 million. The County of Los Angeles agreed to provide the land and significant additional funding to finance Walt Disney Concert Hall's six-level subterranean parking garage. Total cost was $274 million for the 2 265-seat facility. Gehry was selected as the architect in 1988 and his design became public in 1991. The garage was built between 1992 and 1996 and work on the Concert Hall began in November 1999. As was the case for the Bilbao Guggenheim, Gehry used Dassault's CATIA program to design and help build the structure. Rather than titanium cladding, stainless steel was used in Los Angeles, though he did consider a combination of limestone and steel at one point. According to Terry Bell, project architect for Gehry's office, "It's an enormously complicated structure because of the curved shapes and intricate joinery. The esthetic goals with the exterior wall, all the acoustic issues, there is so much that is atypical... this is in no sense a conventional building." The architect was also closely involved in the Concert Hall interior – designing it in wood. Even the wooden pipe organ, built with Manuel Rosales, was designed by Frank Gehry.

Seit langem wurde festgestellt, dass es trotz der internationalen Berühmtheit von Frank O. Gehry kein wichtiges öffentliches Gebäude in seiner Heimatstadt gab. Mit der Eröffnung der Walt Disney Concert Hall im Herbst 2003 wurde dieser Mangel behoben. Für die Realisierung des Projekts im Bezirk Bunker Hill von Downtown Los Angeles ging man von den 50 Millionen Dollar aus, die die inzwischen verstorbene Lillian Disney 1987 gespendet hatte und die durch weitere Spenden und Zinsen auf über 100 Millionen Dollar angewachsen waren. Schließlich beschloss die Kreisverwaltung, das Grundstück und eine beträchtliche Summe öffentlicher Gelder für die Finanzierung der unterirdisch angelegten Parkgarage zur Verfügung zu stellen. Die Gesamtkosten für das mit 2 265 Sitzen ausgestattete Konzerthaus lagen letztendlich bei 274 Millionen Dollar. Gehry wurde 1988 als Architekt ernannt, 1991 wurde sein Entwurf der Öffentlichkeit präsentiert. Zwischen 1992 und 1996 entstand die Parkgarage, und im November 1999 wurde mit dem Bau des Konzerthauses begonnen. Wie beim Bilbao Guggenheim setzte Gehry für die Gestaltung das Computerprogramm CATIA der Firma Dassault ein, nur dass in Los Angeles statt Titan eine Verkleidung aus Edelstahl verwendet wurde, obwohl der Architekt ursprünglich an eine Kombination aus Kalkstein und Stahl gedacht hatte. Wie Terry Bell, Projektarchitektin in Gehrys Firma, erläutert: „Es ist eine ungeheuer komplizierte Konstruktion wegen seiner geschwungenen Formen und der ausgeklügelten Schreinerarbeiten. Der ästhetische Anspruch bei der Fassadengestaltung, all die akustischen Fragen, da ist so viel Neues und Ungewohntes dabei, dass es in keiner Hinsicht ein konventionelles Gebäude ist." Gehry war außerdem zum großen Teil verantwortlich für die Innenraumgestaltung des Konzertsaals, die er ganz in Holz ausführte. Selbst die in Zusammenarbeit mit Manuel Rosales konstruierte hölzerne Orgel ist ein Entwurf von Frank Gehry.

On savait depuis longtemps qu'en dépit de sa notoriété internationale, Frank Gehry n'avait pas construit d'édifice public important dans sa ville natale. Avec l'ouverture du Walt Disney Concert Hall à l'automne 2003, cette absence est enfin compensée. Situé en centre-ville dans le quartier de Bunker Hill, ce projet est né d'un don de 50 millions de dollars de feu Lilian Disney en 1987. Depuis, d'autres dons et le cumul des intérêts ont porté la contribution de la famille Disney à plus de 100 millions de dollars. Le comté de Los Angeles a fourni le terrain et d'importantes subventions pour financer le parking souterrain de six niveaux. Le coût total de cette salle de 2 265 places s'est élevé à 274 millions de dollars. Gehry a été choisi en 1988 et ses plans rendus publics en 1991. Le garage a été construit entre 1992 et 1996, et les travaux sur la salle ont débuté en novembre 1999. Comme pour le Guggenheim de Bilbao, Gehry a utilisé le logiciel CATIA de Dassault aussi bien en conception que pour la construction. L'acier inoxydable a été préféré à un habillage en titane, même si l'architecte a pensé à un certain moment à utiliser la pierre et l'acier. Selon Terry Bell, architecte projet pour Gehry, « c'est une structure extrêmement compliquée du fait de ses formes en courbes et de l'imbrication de ses joints. Ambitions esthétiques du mur extérieur, enjeux acoustiques : il y a tellement d'éléments atypiques que ce n'est certainement pas une construction traditionnelle. » L'architecte s'est également beaucoup impliqué dans les aménagements intérieurs, traités en bois. En collaboration avec Manuel Rosales, il a même dessiné l'orgue.

*An elevation of the building reveals something of its irregular profile.*

*Der Aufriss des Gebäudes offenbart dessen unregelmäßiges Profil.*

*L'élévation ci-dessus montre l'irrégularité marquée du profil.*

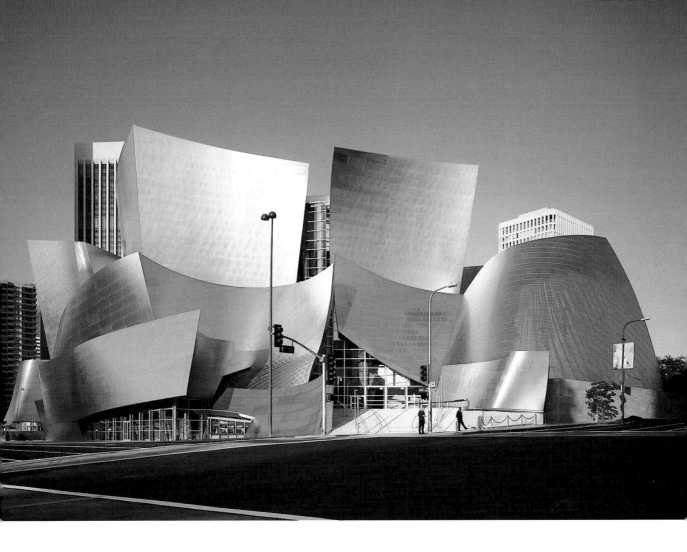

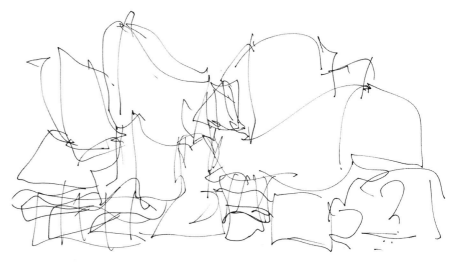

A sketch by Gehry and the nearly completed work bear an uncanny resemblance to each other, showing again that his methods are not truly those of computer-based design.

Die Skizze von Gehry und das fast vollendete Bauwerk weisen eine starke Ähnlichkeit auf, was zeigt, dass sein Vorgehen nicht wirklich dem computergenerierten Gestalten folgt.

Le croquis de Gehry et l'œuvre presque achevée se ressemblent indéniablement, ce qui montre une fois de plus que sa méthode se démarque de l'approche informatique.

Gehry's Disney Concert Hall may be
his most dramatic and complete work
to date. Far from the small houses he
designed in nearby Santa Monica or
Venice, this is a mature masterpiece.

Die Disney Concert Hall ist vielleicht
das bislang dramatischste und voll-
kommenste von Gehrys Werken. Weit
entfernt von den kleinen Häusern in
Santa Monica oder Venice handelt es
sich um ein reifes Meisterwerk.

Le Disney Concert Hall de Gehry est
peut-être son œuvre la plus spectaculaire et la plus achevée à ce jour.
Loin des petites maisons conçues
pour Santa Monica ou Venice, il s'agit
d'un chef-d'œuvre de sa maturité.

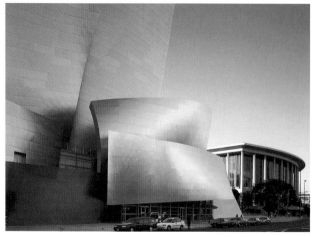

Sitting above a parking garage across the street from Arata Isozaki's MoCA, the Disney Concert Hall has something of a ship to it. The volume of the complex also brings to mind natural rock formations or a rocky island rising from the urban sea of conformity that afflicts all its neighbors aside from the MoCA.

Die auf der gegenüberliegenden Straßenseite von Arata Isozakis MoCA auf einer Parkgarage errichtete Konzerthalle hat etwas von einem Schiff an sich. Gleichzeitig lässt der Baukörper auch an Felsformationen oder eine Felseninsel denken, die sich aus dem urbanen Meer der Konformität erhebt.

Au-dessus d'un vaste parking et face au MoCA d'Arata Isozaki, le Disney Concert Hall rappelle des images nautiques. Le volume du complexe fait aussi penser à des formations rocheuses naturelles ou à une île de rocaille surgie de la mer urbaine du conformisme.

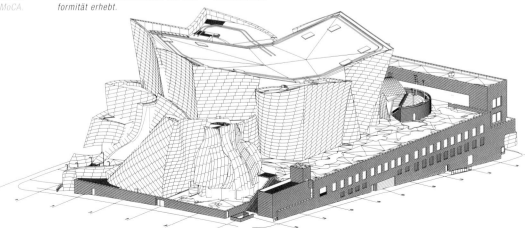

The Concert Hall itself is also very much a work of the architect, right down to the extravagantly "deconstructed" organ visible on the right page.

Auch das Innere der Konzerthalle trägt in hohem Maß die Handschrift des Architekten, bis hin zu der rechts abgebildeten, phantastisch „dekonstruktivistischen" Orgel.

La salle de concert elle-même est également typique du style de l'architecte, jusque dans son extravagant orgue « déconstruit » (page de droite).

# GIGON/GUYER

*Annette Gigon/Mike Guyer Architekten*
*Carmenstrasse 28*
*8032 Zürich*
*Switzerland*

*Tel: +41 1 257 1111*
*Fax: +41 1 257 1110*
*e-mail: info@gigon-guyer.ch*
*Web: www.gigon-guyer.ch*

*Archeological Museum and Park*

Born in 1959, Annette Gigon received her diploma from the ETH in Zurich in 1984. She worked in the office of Herzog & de Meuron in Basel (1985–1988) before setting up her own practice (1987–1989) and creating her present firm with Mike Guyer in 1989. Born in 1958, Mike Guyer also graduated from the ETH in 1984, worked with Rem Koolhaas (OMA, 1984–1987), and taught with Hans Kollhoff at the ETH (1987–88). Their built work includes the Kirchner Museum (Davos, 1990–1992); the Vinikus Restaurant (Davos, 1990–1992); and a renovation of the Oskar Reinhart Collection (Am Römerholz, Winterthur, 1997–98). Gigon/Guyer have participated in numerous international competitions such as those for the Nelson-Atkins Museum extension (Kansas, 1999), or the Santiago de Compostela "City of Culture" project (1999). Current work includes the extension of the Aviation/Space Museum in Lucerne (2000–2003); the Museum for the Albers/Honegger collection (Mouans Sartoux, France, 2003); and a housing project in Rüschlikon, Switzerland. The office currently employs a total of 18 architects.

Annette Gigon, geboren 1959, erwarb 1984 ihr Diplom an der ETH in Zürich. Von 1985 bis 1988 arbeitete sie im Büro von Herzog & de Meuron in Basel, bevor sie 1987 ein eigenes Büro und 1989 zusammen mit Mike Guyer ihre jetzige Firma gründete. Auch der 1958 geborene Mike Guyer schloss 1984 sein Studium an der ETH ab. Von 1984 bis 1987 arbeitete er im Office for Metropolitan Architecture (OMA) von Rem Koolhaas und lehrte von 1987 bis 1988 zusammen mit Hans Kollhoff an der ETH. Zu den in der Schweiz realisierten Projekten von Gigon/Guyer gehören das Kirchner-Museum in Davos (1990–1992), das Restaurant Vinikus in Davos (1990–1992) und die Renovierung der Sammlung Oskar Reinhart 'Am Römerholz' in Winterthur (1997–98). Darüber hinaus nahmen sie an zahlreichen internationalen Wettbewerben teil, so für die Erweiterung des Nelson-Atkins Museum in Kansas City (1999) oder das „City of Culture" Projekt in Santiago de Compostela (1999). Zu den jüngsten Arbeiten des Büros Gigon/Guyer, das derzeit 18 Architekten beschäftigt, zählen: der Erweiterungsbau des Museums für Flugwesen und Raumfahrt in Luzern (2000–2003), das Museumsgebäude für die Sammlung Albers/Honegger im französischen Mouans Sartoux (2003) sowie ein Wohnbauprojekt im schweizerischen Rüschlikon.

Née en 1959, Annette Gigon est diplômée de l'ETH de Zurich (1984). Elle a travaillé dans l'agence de Herzog & de Meuron à Bâle (1985–1988) avant de créer sa propre structure (1987–1989) devenue l'agence actuelle après son association avec Mike Guyer en 1989. Né en 1958, Mike Guyer, également diplômé de l'ETH en 1984, a travaillé chez Rem Koolhaas (OMA, 1984–1987) et enseigné avec Hans Kollhoff à l'ETH (1987–88). Leurs réalisations comprennent le musée Kirchner (Davos, 1990–1992) ; le restaurant Vinikus (Davos, 1990–1992) et la rénovation de la Collection Oskar Reinhart (Am Römerholz, Winterthur, 1997–98). Gigon/Guyer a participé à de nombreux concours internationaux dont ceux de l'extension du Nelson-Atkins Museum (Kansas, 1999), ou le projet de « Cité de la culture » de Saint-Jacques-de-Compostelle (1999). Ils travaillent actuellement à la présentation de la collection Albers/Honegger (Mouans-Sartoux, France, 2003) et un projet de logements à Rüschlikon (Suisse). Leur agence emploie 18 architectes.

# ARCHEOLOGICAL MUSEUM AND PARK

*Bramsche-Kalkriese, Germany, 1999–2002*

*Client: Kalkriese Archeological Museum Park GmbH, Osnabrück. Total floor area: 1 972 m² (museum).*
*Total Costs: € 14 000 000.*

This museum and its 20-hectare park are located on the site of the famous "Battle of Varus" or "Battle in the Teutoburgen Forest" fought by the Teutons against the Romans in 9 AD. Unlike more traditional archeological sites where the remains of buildings can be put into evidence, the Kalkriese project was at the outset more abstract. A flattened earthen rampart was the only tangible evidence of this ancient triumph of the Germans over Roman invaders. Large iron plates mark the probable path of the Romans, while the Teutons' positions are outlined by narrow wood chip paths. More recent agricultural paths permit visitors to move more freely between one area and the other. As the architects say, "the coexistence of the curving, so-called "Roman route," the fine branches of the so-called "Teutonic trails" and the contemporary visitor trails traced out in agrarian patterns elucidate and symbolize a superimposition of the layers of time and cultures present at this place." The location and assumed height of the former Teutonic earthen rampart is marked by a series of iron poles. Three pavilions set in the park and titled "Seeing," "Hearing," and "Questioning" "broaden and put into perspective the impressions gained outdoors." Like the pavilions, the museum is constructed with a steel skeleton and clad with large, rusting steel plates. The museum consists of a one-story volume raised up from the earth and a tower like structure on top. The landscape and battlefield can be seen from nearly 40 meters above the ground. The actual exhibition is to be found in the "torso" of the building where artifacts discovered on the site are stored and exhibited.

Das Museum und sein 20 ha großer Park befinden sich an dem Ort, den man heute für den Schauplatz der Varusschlacht oder Schlacht im Teutoburger Wald hält, die 9 n. Chr. zwischen Cheruskern und Römern stattfand. Im Gegensatz zu anderen archäologischen Stätten gab es beim Kalkriese-Projekt keinerlei Überreste von Gebäuden, sondern lediglich einen abgeflachten Erdwall. Große Eisenplatten markieren den Weg, den die römische Truppenkolonne wahrscheinlich genommen hat, während die teutonischen Positionen durch schmale, mit Holzspänen ausgelegte Pfade kenntlich gemacht sind. Die in jüngster Zeit angelegten Feldwege erlauben den Besuchern inzwischen, sich freier von einem Bereich zum anderen zu bewegen. Die beiden Architekten erklären: „Die Koexistenz der gewundenen Römerstraße mit der feinverzweigten Spur der Teutonen und den nach dem Muster von Feldwegen angelegten neuen Besucherpfaden erhellt und symbolisiert eine Überlagerung der an diesem Ort präsenten Schichten der Zeiten und Kulturen." Lage und angenommene Höhe des teutonischen Erdwalls werden durch eine Reihe von Eisenpfosten markiert. Drei im Parkgelände verteilte und mit „Sehen", „Hören" und „Fragen" betitelte Pavillons liefern Hintergrundinformationen für die draußen gesammelten Eindrücke. Ebenso wie diese Pavillons besteht das Museumsgebäude aus einem Stahlskelett, das mit großformatigen, rostigen Stahlplatten umhüllt wurde. Sein eingeschossiger, direkt auf den Erdboden aufgesetzter Bauteil trägt an einem Ende einen turmartigen Aufbau. Von dort kann man aus einer Höhe von fast 40 m die umliegende Landschaft überblicken. Die eigentliche Ausstellung befindet sich im „Torso" des Gebäudes, wo auf dem Gelände gefundene Artefakte präsentiert und gelagert werden.

Ce musée et son parc de 20 hectares sont situés sur le site de la fameuse bataille de Varus, ou bataille de la forêt de Teutobourg, qui vit s'affronter les Germains et les Romains en l'an 9. À la différence de nombreux sites archéologiques où des vestiges peuvent être mis en évidence, ce projet reposait au départ sur des bases plus abstraites. Un rempart en terre battue était la seule preuve tangible de cette ancienne victoire des Germains. De grandes plaques de fer indiquent les mouvements probables des troupes romaines, tandis que les positions germaines sont soulignées par d'étroits chemins recouverts de copeaux de bois. Des cheminements plus récents permettent aux visiteurs de se déplacer plus librement d'une zone à l'autre. Pour les architectes : « La coexistence dans les champs de la courbe de la voie romaine, des fines ramifications des ‹ pistes › germaines et des chemins pour les visiteurs actuels éclairent et symbolisent la superposition des strates du temps et des cultures en ce lieu. » La situation et la hauteur présumée de l'ancien rempart de terre germain est marquée par un alignement de poteaux de fer. Trois pavillons nommés « Voire », « Entendre » et « Questionner » mettent en perspective et précisent les impressions données par la découverte du champ de bataille. Comme les pavillons, le musée se compose d'un volume d'un seul niveau surélevé par rapport au sol, et surmonté d'une sorte de tour. Le paysage et le champ de bataille peuvent être ainsi observés de ce belvédère de 40 m de haut. Une exposition est aménagée dans le « torse » du bâtiment où des objets découverts sur place sont conservés et présentés.

*The forms can be described as minimal or harsh. Despite their modernity, they have a weathered appearance related to the age of the site.*

*Die Formen lassen sich als reduziert oder sogar abweisend beschreiben. Trotz ihrer Modernität wirken sie mit Bezug auf den Standort verwittert.*

*Les formes peuvent être décrites comme minimalistes voire même brutales. Malgré leur modernité, elles présentent un aspect patiné.*

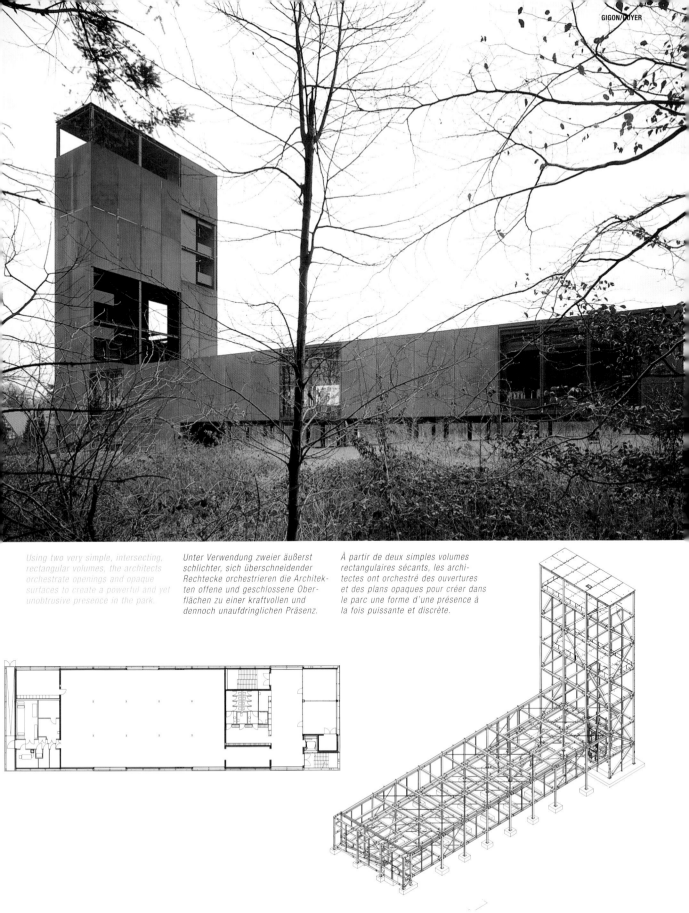

Using two very simple, intersecting, rectangular volumes, the architects orchestrate openings and opaque surfaces to create a powerful and yet unobtrusive presence in the park.

Unter Verwendung zweier äußerst schlichter, sich überschneidender Rechtecke orchestrieren die Architekten offene und geschlossene Oberflächen zu einer kraftvollen und dennoch unaufdringlichen Präsenz.

À partir de deux simples volumes rectangulaires sécants, les architectes ont orchestré des ouvertures et des plans opaques pour créer dans le parc une forme d'une présence à la fois puissante et discrète.

Set in the forest, the structures designed by Gigon/Guyer are like singularites, unexpected and largely inexplicable architectural events that guide the visitor in this strange lost world.

Die von Gigon/Guyer gestalteten, im Wald errichteten Baukörper wirken wie solitäre, unerwartete und letztlich unerklärliche Architekturereignisse, die den Besucher durch eine seltsame, vergangene Welt geleiten.

En pleine forêt, les constructions conçues par Gigon/Guyer se présentent comme des événements architecturaux singuliers, inattendus, et en grande partie inexplicables qui guident le visiteur dans cet étrange monde oublié.

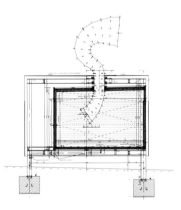
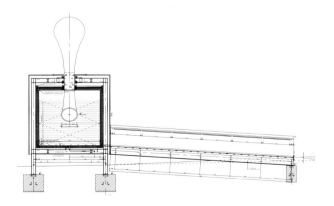

Pavilions are devoted to seeing, hearing and questioning as might almost be obvious from their external forms.

Die Pavillons sind dem Sehen, Hören und Fragen gewidmet, was man an ihren Formen erkennen kann.

Les pavillons sont consacrés à la vision, à l'écoute et aux questions, comme l'illustrent leur forme externe.

# SEAN GODSELL

*Sean Godsell Architects*
*45 Flinders Lane*
*Melbourne*
*Victoria 3000*
*Australia*

*Tel: +61 3 9654 2677*
*Fax: +61 3 9654 3877*
*e-mail: godsell@netspace.net.au*
*Web: www.seangodsell.com*

*Peninsula House* ▶

Sean Godsell was born in Melbourne, Australia in 1960. He graduated from the University of Melbourne in 1984 and worked from 1986 to 1988 in London with Sir Denys Lasdun. He created Godsell Associates Pty Ltd. Architects in 1994. After receiving a Masters of Architecture degree from RMIT University in 1999, he was a finalist in the Seppelt Contemporary Art Awards held by the Museum of Contemporary Art in Sydney for his work "FutureShack." He won the RAIA Award of Merit for new residential work for the Carter/Tucker House in 2000. He taught in the RMIT Department of Architecture from 1986 to 1997. His work has been shown at exhibitions in New York, Paris, London and Mendrisio, Switzerland. Recent work includes: Carter/Tucker House (Breamlea, Victoria, Australia, 1999–2000); Peninsula House (Victoria, Australia, 2001–02; ar+d Prizewinner 2002, RAIA Architecture Award 2003); Woodleigh School Science Faculty (Baxter, Victoria, Australia (2002; RAIA William Wardell Award 2003). Current work includes: Lewis House (Dunkeld, Victoria, Australia, 2003); Westwood House (Sydney, Australia, 2003); ACN Headquarters (Victoria, Australia, 2003); CIPEA Housing Project (Nanjing, China, 2003).

Sean Godsell, 1960 in Melbourne geboren, schloss 1984 sein Studium an der Universität von Melbourne ab und arbeitete von 1986 bis 1988 bei Sir Denys Lasdun in London. 1994 gründete er Godsell Associates Pty Ltd. Architects. Nachdem er 1999 den Masters of Architecture an der RMIT University erworben hatte, kam er mit seiner Arbeit „FutureShack" in die Endauswahl für die vom Museum of Contemporary Art in Sydney veranstaltete Verleihung der Seppelt Contemporary Art Awards. Im Jahr 2000 wurde Sean Godsell vom Royal Australian Institute of Architects für das Haus Carter/Tucker mit dem RAIA Award of Merit für neue Wohnbauarchitektur ausgezeichnet. Von 1986 bis 1997 lehrte er an der Architekturabteilung der RMIT University. Seine Arbeit wurde in Ausstellungen in New York, Paris, London und Mendrisio, Schweiz, präsentiert. Zu seinen neueren Architekturprojekten zählen: das Haus Carter/Tucker in Breamlea, Victoria (1999–2000), das Peninsula House in Victoria (2001–02), die naturwissenschaftliche Fakultät der Woodleigh School in Baxter, Victoria (2002), das Haus Lewis in Dunkeld, Victoria (2003), das Haus Westwood in Sydney (2003), die ACN-Zentrale in Victoria (2003), alle in Australien, sowie das CIPEA Wohnbauprojekt im chinesischen Nanjing (2003). Sean Godsell ist Träger des ar+d Preises (2002), des RAIA Architecture Award (2003) und des RAIA William Wardell Award (2003).

Sean Godsell est né en 1960 à Melbourne, en Australie. Diplômé de l'Université de Melbourne en 1984, il travaille à Londres de 1986 à 1988 dans l'agence de Sir Denys Lasdun. Il crée Godsell Associates Pty Ltd Architects en 1994. Master of Architecture de la RMIT University en 1999, il est finaliste des Seppelt Contemporary Arts Awards organisés par le Museum of Contemporary Art de Sydney pour son œuvre *FutureShack*. Il remporte le RAIA Award of Merit de création résidentielle pour sa Carter/Tucker House en 2000. Il enseigne au département d'architecture de la RMIT de 1986 à 1997. Son œuvre a été présentée dans des expositions à New York, Paris, Londres et Mendrisio (Suisse). Parmi ses réalisations récentes : Carter/Tucker House (Breamlea, Victoria Australie, 1999/2000) ; Peninsula House (Victoria, Australie, 2001–02, prix ar+d 2002, RAIA Architecture Award 2003) ; faculté des Sciences de Woodleigh School (Baxter, Victoria, Australie, 2002 ; RAIA William Wardell Award 2003), Lewis House (Dunkeld, Victoria, Australie, 2003) ; Westwood House (Sydney, Australie, 2003) ; le siège de CAN (Victoria, Australie, 2003) ; projet d'immeuble de logements CIPEA (Nankin, Chine, 2003).

# PENINSULA HOUSE

*Victoria, Australia, 2001–02*

*Client: private. Total floor area: 210 m². Costs: not specified.*

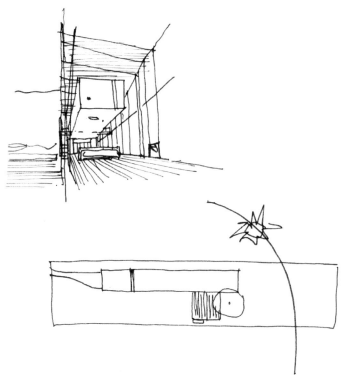

This 30-meter x 7-meter oxidized steel "portal structure" was embedded into the side of a sand dune. This element forms the "exoskeleton" of the house on which the outer skin – operable Jarrah timber shutters, glass roof and walls – are mounted. The house consists of a living/dining room, library and bedroom. The bedroom is accessed by a private stairway. As Sean Godsell says, "the house itself is the nurturing inner room, protected from the elements by a coarse outer hide." The verandah has become further abstracted in this work to become the protective outer layer of the building. The architect goes on to say, "this is a further investigation into the similarities between the enclosed verandah of the traditional Japanese house and the 'sun room' of the Australian house. My interest lies in the iconic nature of these elements to both cultures – Asian and European – and the common architectural ground which they afford to the region." Godsell had already explored the ideas of the closed verandah and inner room in his Carter/Tucker House (Breamlea, Victoria, Australia,1999-2000).

Die 30 x 7 m messende Portalrahmenkonstruktion aus oxidiertem Stahl wurde in die Seitenfläche einer Sanddüne eingebettet. Diese Konstruktion bildet das „Exoskelett" des Hauses, auf das die Außenhaut – bewegliche Jalousien aus Dscharrah-Holz, Wände und Dach aus Glas – montiert sind. Im Innern besteht das Haus aus Wohn- und Essbereich, einer Bibliothek und einem Schlafzimmer, in das man über eine Treppe gelangt. „Das Haus selbst ist der nährende Innenraum", so Jean Godsell, „der durch eine raue Schale vor den äußeren Elementen geschützt ist." Dabei wurde das Gestaltungsthema Terrasse hier so weit abstrahiert, dass diese zur schützenden Außenhaut des Gebäudes wurde. Dazu der Architekt: „Das ist eine Weiterführung meiner Beschäftigung mit den Parallelen zwischen der umschlossenen Veranda des traditionellen japanischen Hauses und dem ‚sun room' des australischen Hauses. Dabei gilt mein Interesse den zu Ikonen gewordenen Elementen der beiden unterschiedlichen Kulturen und den architektonischen Gemeinsamkeiten, die sich daraus ableiten lassen." Godsell hat diese Ideen bereits in seinem 2000 fertig gestellten Haus Carter/Tucker im australischen Breamlea, Victoria, verarbeitet.

Cette « structure en portique » de 30 x 7 m est incrustée dans le flanc d'une dune. Elle forme l'exosquelette de la maison sur lequel s'applique une peau composée de volets mobiles en bois de jarrah, d'une couverture et de murs de verre. La maison comprend un séjour/zone de repas, une bibliothèque et une chambre, accessible par un escalier direct. Pour Sean Godsell : « La maison est une pièce intérieure de ressourcement, protégée des éléments par une peau rugueuse. » La véranda traitée de manière abstraite, constitue la totalité de la protection externe. « C'est une nouvelle exploration des similarités entre la maison japonaise traditionnelle et la *sun room*, la véranda, de la maison australienne. Je m'intéresse à la nature iconique de ces éléments dans ces deux cultures – asiatique et européenne – et la richesse architecturale qu'elles apportent ensemble à la région. » Godsell avait déjà exploré l'idée de véranda fermée et de pièce intérieure dans sa Carter/Tucker House (Breamlea, Victoria, Australie, 1999–2000)

The Peninsula House benefits from a splendid, isolated natural setting, into which its forms have been set without undue destruction of the environment.

Das Peninsula House profitiert von seiner wunderbaren und abgeschiedenen Umgebung, in die seine Formen gesetzt wurden, ohne die Natur unnötig zu belasten.

La Peninsula House bénéficie d'un cadre isolé et splendide, dans lequel elle s'insère sans porter d'atteinte inutile à l'environnement.

With its light, wooden slat exterior
and relatively low profile, the house
fits into the topography and even the
coloring of the existing site.

Mit seinen Außenwänden aus hellen
Holzlatten und relativ niedrigen Konturen fügt sich das Haus in die Topo-
grafie und sogar die Farben seiner
Umgebung ein.

Par sa façade extérieure habillée de
lattes de bois et son profil relativement bas, la maison s'intègre à la
topographie et même aux couleurs
du lieu.

The fine, wooden slats visible from
the exterior of the house bring to
mind some Japanese designs.

Die schmalen Holzstreifen der Außenwände erinnern an einige japanische
Designs.

Le lattis de bois visibles de l'extérieur de la maison rappelle certaines
conceptions japonaises.

Airy and open, the Peninsula House has many adjustable surfaces, like other residences designed by Sean Godsell.

Das luftig und offen angelegte Peninsula House ist wie frühere Wohnhäuser von Sean Godsell mit verstellbaren Oberflächen ausgestattet.

Aérée et ouverte la Peninsula House s'ouvre par de nombreuses ouvertures ajustables, comme d'autres résidences conçue par Sean Godsell.

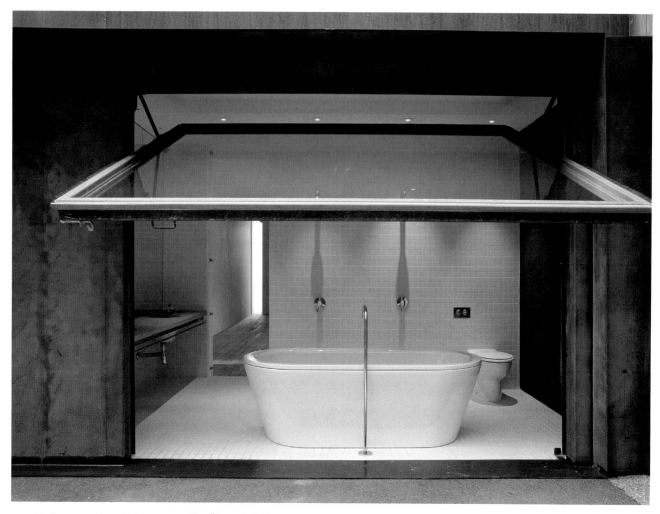

A bathroom opening out into an enclosed garden or interior light modulated by overhead slats give an unusual warmth and brightness to the house.

Eine Öffnung im Badezimmer oder das Licht, das durch ein Holzraster gefiltert wird, verleihen dem Haus Wärme und Helligkeit.

La salle-de-bains ouvre sur un jardin clos, ou l'éclairage modulé par le lattis en toiture introduit une luminosité et une chaleur inhabituelles.

# ALEXANDER GORLIN

*Alexander Gorlin Architects*
*137 Varick Street*
*New York, NY 10013*
*USA*

*Tel: +1 212 229 1199*
*Fax: +1 212 260 3590*
*e-mail: agorlin@gorlinarchitects.com*
*Web: www.gorlinarchitects.com*

*House in the Rocky Mountains* ▸

Alexander Gorlin received his Bachelor's degree from the Cooper Union School of Architecture (1978), his Masters from Yale (1980) and then worked in the offices of I. M. Pei and Partners (1981–82) and Kohn Pederson Fox (1984–85) before founding his own firm. He has designed housing in Santa Fe, Chicago, Nova Scotia and Miami; synagogues in New York and Tulsa, Oklahoma; a new boathouse at Yale (1998); the Gravesend Community Center in Brooklyn (2002); and participated in the competitions for the Berlin Spreebogen district (1993) and Madrid's Prado (1995). He has done residential work for such prestigious clients as Alexander Liberman, Grace Mirabella and S. I. Newhouse. He has been an Adjunct Professor at Yale (1982–1990) and a Visiting Professor of Architecture at the Cooper Union (1999, 2000). Current work includes the Aqua Apartment Tower in Miami, and the Liberty Harbor townhouses in Jersey City, New Jersey. His World Trade Center Memorial proposal was exhibited at the 2002 Venice Biennale and he is working presently on the apartment of Daniel Libeskind in New York.

Alexander Gorlin erwarb 1978 seinen Bachelor of Architecture an der Cooper Union School of Architecture in New York und 1980 seinen Master of Architecture an der Yale University. Von 1981 bis 1982 arbeitete er bei I. M. Pei and Partners und von 1984 bis 1985 bei Kohn Pederson Fox, bevor er seine eigene Firma gründete. Zu seinen Projekten gehören Wohnhäuser in Santa Fe, Chicago, Nova Scotia und Miami, Synagogen in New York und Tulsa, Oklahoma, ein neues Bootshaus für Yale (1998), das Gravesend Gemeindezentrum in Brooklyn (2002) sowie seine Wettbewerbsbeiträge für den Bezirk Berlin Spreebogen (1993) und den Madrider Prado (1995). Außerdem hat er Wohnungen für so namhafte Klienten wie Alexander Liberman, Grace Mirabella und S. I. Newhouse gestaltet. Daneben war er von 1982 bis 1990 als außerordentlicher Professor an der Yale University tätig und hatte 1999 und 2000 eine Gastprofessur für Architektur an der Cooper Union inne. Derzeit arbeitet er unter anderem am Aqua Apartment Tower in Miami und den Liberty Harbor Terrassenhäusern in Jersey City, New Jersey. Sein Entwurf für ein World Trade Center Mahnmal wurde 2002 auf der Biennale in Venedig ausgestellt. Zu den aktuellen Projekten gehört außerdem die Wohnung von Daniel Libeskind in New York.

Alexander Gorlin est Bachelor of Architecture de la Cooper Union School of Architecture (1978) et Master of Architecture de Yale (1980). Il a travaillé dans les agences de I. M. Pei and Partners (1981–82) et Kohn Pederson Fox (1984–85) avant de créer sa propre structure. Il a conçu des logements à Santa Fe, Chicago, en Nouvelle-Écosse et à Miami ; des synagogues à New York et Tulsa (Oklahoma) ; un nouveau garage à bateaux à Yale (1998) ; le Gravesend Community Center à Brooklyn (2002) et a participé aux concours pour le quartier du Spreebogen à Berlin (1993) et le musée du Prado à Madrid (1995). Il a conçu les résidences de clients prestigieux dont Alexander Liberman, Grace Mirabella et S. I. Newhouse. Professeur adjoint à Yale (1982–1990) et professeur d'architecture invité à la Cooper Union (1999, 2000). Il travaille actuellement à la tour d'appartements Aqua à Miami et à des maisons urbaines à Libert Harbor (Jersey City, New Jersey). Sa proposition pour le Mémorial du World Trade Center a été exposée à la Biennale de Venise 2002, et il travaille actuellement à un appartement pour Daniel Libeskind à New York.

# HOUSE IN THE ROCKY MOUNTAINS

*Genesee, Colorado, USA, 2000–01*

*Client: Stuart and Chris Allen. Floor area: 1 000 m². Costs: $ 2 500 000.*

This 1 000-square-meter house is built on a two-hectare mountainside site between two streams and within view of 4 200-meter Mount Evans. It is made of concrete block with moss rock stone veneer (a local stone that changes with the humidity, becoming greener with the morning dew) and a steel frame structure. It uses geothermal heating, and is oriented to the mountain winds, obviating the need for air conditioning. Alexander Gorlin states, "this house is conceived as both an abstraction of the rugged landscape of the Colorado Rockies and as a re-inhabited ruin, inspired but the Anasazi stone constructions of the Southwest in Chaco Canyon… There is a constant interplay between inside and outside, blurring the boundary between the two so that one feels part of the wooded site." The entry of the house is by way of a steel bridge over a ravine, sheltering an elk path that runs through the site. Terraces provide flat outside space that otherwise would be missing from the steep site. Sliding steel doors open into a curved entry hall with the dining room overlooking, the living room below and the kitchen and family room beyond. The children's area is separate from the parents' tower with the husband's office above. In a poetic vein, the architect says: "The terraced site, with its stone walls, recalls Dante's ascent in Purgatory, 'Now we were drawing closer; we had reached the part from where first I'd seen a breach, precisely like a gap that cleaves a wall. He led us to a cleft in the rock… approach, the steps are close at hand; from this point on one can climb easily.'"

Das 1 000 m² umfassende Wohnhaus liegt auf einem 2 ha großen Hanggrundstück, zwischen zwei Wasserläufen und mit Blick auf den 4 200 m hohen Mount Evans. Es besteht aus einer Stahlrahmenkonstruktion und einer Kombination aus Beton- und Moosstein (ein lokaler Stein, dessen Farbe sich je nach Feuchtigkeitsgrad ändert, und der mit dem Morgentau grün wird). Für die Klimatisierung des Gebäudes werden Erdwärme und Bergwinde genutzt, wodurch sich eine Klimaanlage erübrigt. Alexander Gorlin sagt über seinen Entwurf, er sei sowohl von der Felslandschaft der Colorado Rockies als auch von den in die Steilhänge des Chaco Canyon eingebauten Wohnanlagen der Anasazi-Indianer inspiriert: „Es herrscht ein ständiges Wechselspiel zwischen Innen und Außen, was die Grenzen zwischen beiden Elementen verwischt, so dass man sich als Teil der bewaldeten Umgebung fühlt." Der Zugang zum Haus verläuft über eine Stahlbrücke. Damit wird ein Pfad durch die darunter liegende Schlucht geschützt, der regelmäßig von Elchen genutzt wird. Terrassen sind die einzigen horizontalen Außenflächen auf diesem ansonsten steil abfallenden Grundstück. Hinter den stählernen Schiebetüren öffnet sich ein geschwungener Eingangsbereich, vom Esszimmer überblickt man den darunter liegenden Wohnraum und die angrenzende Küche. Der Bereich für die Kinder ist vom turmartigen Trakt der Eltern mit dem Büro des Hausherrn im obersten Stock abgetrennt. In der poetischen Deutung des Architekten soll die terrassenförmige Anordnung der Steinwände an Dantes Abstieg ins Fegefeuer und besonders jene Stelle erinnern, an der sich in der Felswand ein Spalt auftut, von wo aus sich leichter herabklettern lässt.

Cette maison de 1000 m² est édifiée en pleine montagne dans la perspective du Mount Evans (4 200 m d'altitude), sur un terrain de deux hectares, pris entre deux torrents. Elle fait appel à une ossature en acier et à des parpaings de béton parés de *moss rock*, une pierre locale qui change de couleur avec l'humidité et tourne au vert sous l'effet de la rosée matinale. Chauffée par géothermie, elle est orientée face aux vents venus de la montagne, ce qui évite la climatisation. Pour Alexander Gorling : « Cette maison est conçue à la fois comme une abstraction du paysage sauvage des Colorado Rockies et comme une ruine qui aurait été ré-habitée, inspirée des constructions en pierre des Ansazi du sud-ouest du Caco Canyon… Un jeu permanent intervient entre l'intérieur et l'extérieur, qui perturbe leurs relations et donne l'impression de faire partie de cet environnement boisé. » On accède par une passerelle d'acier lancée au-dessus d'un petit ravin, pour respecter un passage de rennes. Des terrasses offrent des espaces extérieurs plats dont le site escarpé était dénué. Des portes coulissantes en acier ouvrent sur un hall d'entrée arrondi. La salle à manger domine le séjour en contrebas et la cuisine et le séjour familial plus loin. La zone des enfants est séparée de la tour des parents occupée en partie supérieure par un bureau. Pour l'architecte, épris de poésie, « ce site en terrasses, avec ses murs de pierre, évoque la montée de Dante vers le Purgatoire : Maintenant, nous nous rapprochions ; nous avions atteint l'endroit d'où j'avais déjà aperçu une ouverture, exactement comme une fissure dans un mur… des marches furent bientôt à notre portée, et de là nous pouvions aisément monter. »

*The large, flat expanses of this house allow it to fit into its natural setting as does the moss rock facing.*

*Mit der Wandverkleidung aus Moosstein fügt sich das Haus harmonisch in seine natürliche Umgebung ein.*

*Les terrasses de la maison et son habillage de* moss rock *contribuent à son intégration dans le cadre naturel.*

Rather than a massive central volume, the house is laid out as "an abstraction" of the local landscape.

Statt als massiver und zentraler Baukörper ist das Haus als eine „Abstraktion" der lokalen Landschaft angelegt.

Plutôt qu'un volume massif qui s'impose, la maison est une « abstraction » du paysage dans lequel elle se trouve.

*The architect plays on a contrast between the rough stone façade and the open glazed surfaces with their metal fittings.*

*Der Architekt setzt spielerische Kontraste zwischen der rauen Steinfassade und den offenen Glasflächen mit ihren Metalleinfassungen.*

*L'architecte joue de contrastes entre la façade de pierre brute et les surfaces vitrées prises dans une menuiserie métallique.*

On a downhill slope, the house steps with the land, allowing for the creation of a double height living room that does not project above the other alignments of the structure.

Indem die Anlage dem abschüssigen Gelände folgt, wurde ein Wohnraum möglich, der sich über zwei Stockwerke erstreckt, ohne über die anderen Bauteile hinauszuragen.

Établie sur une pente, la maison se sert du profil du terrain pour créer un séjour double hauteur qui ne se projette pas pour autant au-dessus des autres alignements.

The spacious, almost fully glazed living room offers generous views over the surroundings. Rough stone, also seen as an outside cladding continues within, near the fireplace for example.

Der geräumige, fast zur Gänze verglaste Wohnraum bietet weite Ausblicke auf die Umgegend. Grob gearbeitete Steine, die auch als Außenverkleidung dienen, setzen sich im Innern fort, wie hier beim Kamin.

Le séjour spacieux, presque entièrement vitré, offre de généreuses perspectives sur l'environnement. La pierre brute, vue dans l'habillage extérieur, se retrouve dans le mur de la cheminée, par exemple.

The house is a combination of archi
tectural sophistication and a rough
natural setting. Within its walls the
resident can observe nature without being submitted to any of the
inconveniences of survival in the
wilderness.

Das Haus wirkt durch die Kombination
aus architektonischer Raffinesse und
seiner rauen natürlichen Umgebung.
Die Bewohner in seinem Innern können an der Natur teilhaben, ohne den
Unannehmlichkeiten eines Lebens in
der Wildnis ausgesetzt zu sein.

La maison est une combinaison entre
une architecture sophistiquée et la
nature intacte. De ses murs, le rési-
dant peut observer la nature sauvage
sans être soumis à ses contraintes.

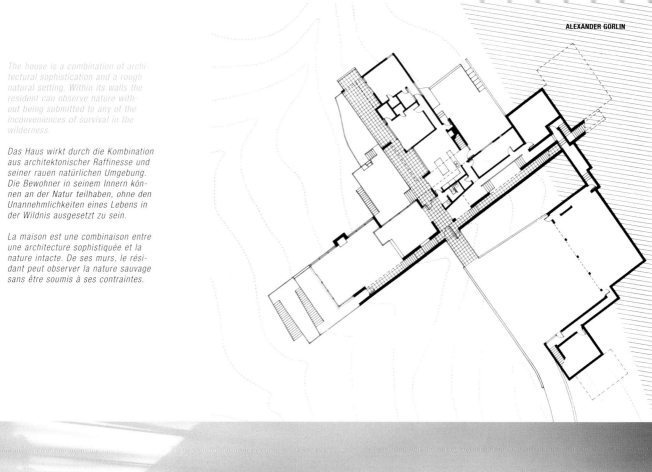

The bathrooms offer one of the most spectacular contrasts between the roughness of the natural setting and the refinement of the interior.

Einer der spektakulärsten Kontraste zwischen der urwüchsigen Umgebung und der schlichten Eleganz der Innenräume stellt das Badezimmer dar.

L'un des contrastes les plus spectaculaires entre le cadre naturel et le raffinement des intérieurs est donné par les salles-de-bains.

# GOULD EVANS

*Gould Evans Associates*
*3136 North 3rd Avenue*
*Phoenix, AR 85013*
*USA*

*Tel: +1 602 234 1140*
*Fax: +1 602 234 1156*
*e-mail: info@gouldevans.com*
*Web: www.gouldevans.com*

Gould Evans is a comprehensive design firm of 200 employees providing architecture, interior design, landscape architecture, planning, and graphic design services to public and private clients. The firm was founded in 1974 and has offices in Phoenix, Arizona; Kansas City, Missouri; Lawrence, Kansas; San Antonio, Texas; Salt Lake City, Utah; Tampa, Florida; and Sausalito, California. These offices operate as a network of affiliated organizations with strong local and regional ties yet have access to a national knowledge base and talent pool. Recent and current projects include the University of Arizona Stevie Eller Dance Theater (Tucson, Arizona, published here); Snow College Performing Arts Center (Ephraim, Utah); Cerner Corporation World Headquarters (Kansas City, Missouri); Community Health Facility (Lawrence, Kansas); and University of Florida Rinker Hall (Gainesville, Florida). Amongst those working on the Stevie Eller Theater, Trudi Hummel received her Bachelor of Architecture from the University of Texas in Austin and is one of the founding principals of the Phoenix office, while Jose D. Pombo received his Bachelor of Science degree from the Arizona State University in Tempe (1994) and his Master of Architecture from UCLA (1997). He worked in the office of Mark Mack in Los Angeles (1996–97) before joining Gould Evans. Donna Barry received her degrees from the Georgia Institute of Technology (BA, 1986; MArch, 1989). She worked with Kohn Pederson Fox (New York, 1994–95), William Bruder (Phoenix, 1996–97) and Peter Eisenman (New York, 1989–1994) before joining Gould Evans in 1998.

Gould Evans, eine Firma mit 200 Angestellten, ist für öffentliche und private Auftraggeber in den Bereichen Architektur, Innenarchitektur, Landschaftsarchitektur, Planung und Grafikdesign tätig. Das Unternehmen wurde 1974 gegründet und hat Niederlassungen in Phoenix (Arizona), Kansas City (Missouri), Lawrence (Kansas), San Antonio (Texas), Salt Lake City (Utah), Tampa (Florida) und Sausalito (Kalifornien). Diese Büros fungieren als ein Netzwerk von Einheiten, die einerseits lokal und regional stark verwurzelt sind, aber gleichzeitig jederzeit auf den landesweiten Unternehmenspool an Wissen und Talent zugreifen können. Zu ihren neueren und aktuellen Projekten zählen: das hier vorgestellte Stevie Eller Dance Theatre der University of Arizona in Tucson, Arizona, das Snow College Performing Arts Center in Ephraim, Utah, die internationale Zentrale der Cerner Corporation in Kansas City, Missouri, das Gemeindegesundheitszentrum in Lawrence, Kansas und die Rinker Hall der University of Florida in Gainesville. Am Stevie Eller Theater arbeiteten unter anderem Trudi Hummel, Jose D. Pombo und Donna Barry mit. Trudi Hummel erwarb ihren Bachelor of Architecture an der University of Texas in Austin und ist eines der leitenden Gründungsmitglieder des Büros in Phoenix. Jose D. Pombo erwarb 1994 seinen Bachelor of Science an der Arizona State University in Tempe und 1997 seinen Master of Architecture an der University of California in Los Angeles (UCLA). Bevor er bei Gould Evans eintrat, arbeitete er von 1996 bis 1997 im Büro von Mark Mack in Los Angeles. Donna Barry erwarb 1986 ihren Bachelor und 1989 den Master of Architecture am Georgia Institute of Technology. Sie arbeitete bei Kohn Pederson Fox in New York (1994–95), bei William Bruder in Phoenix (1996–97) und bei Peter Eisenman in New York (1989–1994), bevor sie 1998 bei Gould Evans eintrat.

Gould Evans est une agence de conception globale de 200 collaborateurs intervenant en architecture, architecture intérieure, architecture du paysage, urbanisme et graphisme pour des clients publics ou privés. L'agence a été fondée en 1974 et possède des bureaux à Phoenix (Arizona), Kansas City (Missouri), Lawrence (Kansas), San Antonio (Texas), Salt Lake City (Utah), Tampa (Floride) et Sausalito (Californie). Ces bureaux travaillent en réseau à implantation locale et régionale forte. Parmi ses projets récents et actuels : le Stevie Eller Dance Theater pour l'Université de l'Arizona (Tucson, Arizona, publié ici) ; le Performing Arts Center du Snow College (Ephraim, Utah) ; le siège mondial de la Cerner Corporation (Kansas City) ; un dispensaire (Lawrence) et le Rinker Hall pour l'Université de Floride (Gainesville). Parmi les concepteurs du Stevie Eller Theater figurent : Trudi Hummel, B. Arch de l'University of Texas in Austin et un des associés-fondateurs de l'agence de Phoenix ; Jose D. Pombo, Bachelor of Architecture, Arizona State University in Tempe, en 1994, Master of Architecture de UCLA, en 1997. Il a travaillé pour l'agence de Mark Mack à Los Angeles (1996–97) avant de rejoindre Gould Evans. Donna Barry est B. A. (1986) et Master of Architecture (1989) du Georgia Institute of Technology. Elle a travaillé pour Kohn Pederson Fox (New York, 1994–95), William Bruder (Phoenix, 1996–97) et Peter Eisenman (New York, 1989–1994) avant de rejoindre Gould Evans en 1998.

# STEVIE ELLER DANCE THEATER

*University of Arizona, Tucson, Arizona, USA, 2000–2003*

*Client: University of Arizona. Floor area: 2 790 m². Costs: $ 9 000 000.*

Built for the College of Fine Arts, School of Music and Dance at the University of Arizona, the Stevie Eller Dance Theater includes a 300-seat theater, dance studio and facilities for an outdoor stage, scene shop and costume shop. Proud of the collaborative process that allowed workers to contribute to the project in the construction phase, Gould Evans calls this "a built work of art that works." The building was initially conceived out of a father and daughter's quest to find a distinguished college dance program. During their search, they found the University of Arizona had the BEST dance program with the WORST facility. The father went to the University President, Peter Likins, and Dean of Fine Arts, Maurice Sevigny, with an offer of a large monetary gift, but stipulating that the University and the College of Fine Arts each match his gift. Three years later, this building was born and the man's daughter will dance Ballanchine's "Serenade" with her graduating class in the spring. The design process clearly included reference to "Serenade." As the architects say, "for the design of the Stevie Eller Dance Theater, we learned about dance, about movement, about graphically representing dance through notation formally called 'labanotation.' We immersed ourselves in the IDEA of movement. The faculty taught us about dance, and we taught them about structure and together we created 'dancing columns.' We asked the client to tell us about 'Serenade,' Ballanchine's first ballet written for the students of the American Ballet. We contacted the Dance Notation Bureau and the Ballanchine Foundation in New York and we acquired the labanotation and score for 'Serenade.' We overlaid the 'plans' of the starting positions for each movement of 'Serenade' and created a matrix from which emerged the 'grid' of tilted columns that support the glass encased dance studio on the second floor of the building."

Das Stevie Eller Dance Theater wurde für das College of Fine Arts, School of Music and Dance der University of Arizona gebaut und enthält ein Theater mit 300 Sitzen, ein Tanzstudio, eine Freilichtbühne sowie eine Kostüm- und Kulissenwerkstatt. Auf der Suche nach einem ausgezeichneten College mit Tanzausbildung für seine Tochter stellte der Vater fest, dass die University of Arizona zwar das BESTE Ausbildungsprogramm, aber die SCHLECHTESTEN Räumlichkeiten dafür hatte. Daraufhin bot er dem Universitätspräsidenten, Peter Likins, und dem Dekan der schönen Künste, Maurice Sevigny, eine große Spende an, machte jedoch zur Bedingung, dass von Seiten der Hochschule eine Gegenleistung erbracht wird. Diese erfolgte drei Jahre später in Form des Stevie Eller Dance Theater. Und inzwischen hat die Tochter dort mit ihrer Abschlussklasse Ballanchines ‚Serenade' aufgeführt. Im Gestaltungsprozess, so die beteiligten Architekten, finden sich deutliche Bezüge auf dieses Stück. Sie betonen, dass sie im Zuge der Planung des Gebäudes viel über den Tanz gelernt haben und darüber, wie man Bewegungen durch ein Bezeichnungssystem, das nach dem Tanzpädagogen Rudolf von Laban „Laban-Notation" genannt wird, grafisch darstellen kann: „Dabei beschäftigten wir uns intensivst mit der IDEE von Bewegung. Die Mitglieder der Tanzabteilung lehrten uns Tanz, wir lehrten sie Bauformen und zusammen schufen wir die ‚tanzenden Säulen'. Wir baten die Bauherren, uns von ‚Serenade' zu erzählen, dem ersten Ballett, das Ballanchine für die Studenten der School of American Ballet geschrieben hatte. Wir setzten uns mit dem Dance Notation Bureau und der Ballanchine Foundation in New York in Verbindung und erwarben die Laban-Notation und Partitur für ‚Serenade'. Dann übertrugen wir die Ausgangspositionen für jede Bewegung in diesem Stück in eine Matrix, aus der das ‚Gitterwerk' der schrägen Säulen entstand, die das mit Glas ummantelte Studio im zweiten Stock des Theaters tragen."

Construit pour le College of Fine Arts, School of Music and Dance of the University of Arizona, le Stevie Eller Dance Theater comprend un théâtre de 300 places, un studio de danse, une scène en plein air, un atelier pour les décors et un pour les costumes. Fier du processus de collaboration qui a permis aux ouvriers de contribuer au projet au cours de la phase de chantier, Gould Evans parle d'une « œuvre d'art construite et qui fonctionne ». Ce bâtiment est né de la quête d'un père et sa fille qui recherchaient une école de danse supérieure au programme élitaire. Pendant leur recherche, son père et elle découvrent que l'Université de l'Arizona possède le MEILLEUR programme, et les PIRES installations. Le père va voir le président de l'Université, Peter Likins, et le doyen des Beaux Arts, Maurice Sevigny, pour leur proposer un don important à condition que l'Université et le College of Fine Arts en fassent autant. Trois ans plus tard, le bâtiment est né et sa fille dansera le ballet *Serenade* de Ballanchine avec sa classe de diplôme au printemps. » Le processus de conception comprenait à l'évidence une référence à *Serenade*. « ... Nous avons beaucoup appris sur la danse, le mouvement, la représentation graphique de la danse sous forme d'une notation appelée labanotation. Nous nous sommes immergés dans l'idée du mouvement. L'université nous a enseigné la danse, nous lui avons appris la structure, et ensemble nous avons créé des ‹ colonnes dansantes. › Nous avons demandé au client de nous parler de *Serenade*, la première chorégraphie écrite par Ballanchine pour les élèves de l'American Ballet. Nous avons contacté le Dance Notation Bureau de la Ballanchine Foundation à New York et avons acquis la labanotation et la partition de *Serenade*. Nous avons superposé les ‹ plans › de positions de départ de chaque mouvement du ballet pour créer une matrice d'où a émergé la ‹ grille › de colonnes inclinées qui soutiennent le studio de danse en verre installé au second niveau du bâtiment. »

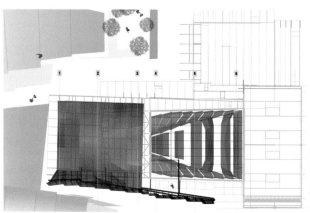
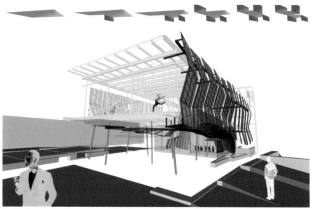

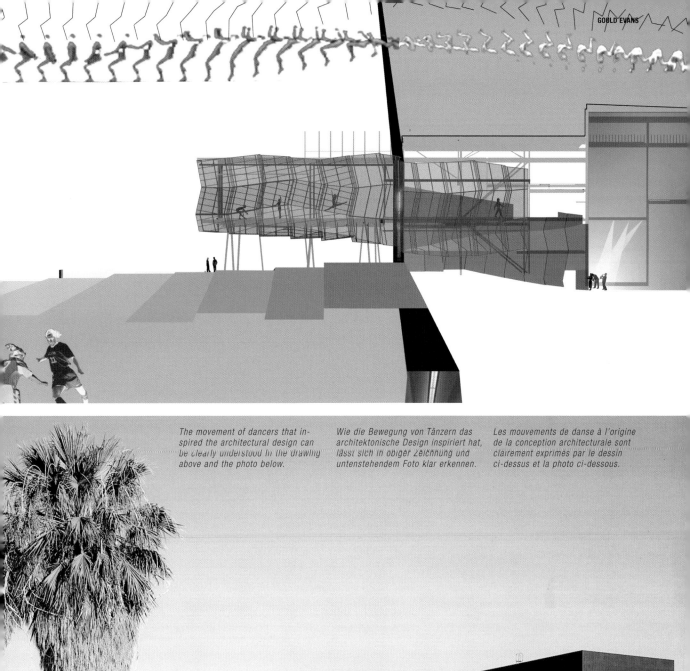

The movement of dancers that inspired the architectural design can be clearly understood in the drawing above and the photo below.

Wie die Bewegung von Tänzern das architektonische Design inspiriert hat, lässt sich in obiger Zeichnung und untenstehendem Foto klar erkennen.

Les mouvements de danse à l'origine de la conception architecturale sont clairement exprimés par le dessin ci-dessus et la photo ci-dessous.

With its successive shells and volumes raised on thin pilotis, the Stevie Eller Dance Theater is animated by its interior lighting and the dancers who are visible even from the exterior.

Mit seinen aufeinanderfolgenden Verschalungen und auf zierlichen Säulen ruhenden Baukörpern wird das Stevie Eller Dance Theater durch seine Innenbeleuchtung und die Tänzer belebt, die sogar von außen zu sehen sind.

Composé de coques et d'une succession de volumes sur pilotis, le Stevie Eller Dance Theater est animé par son éclairage intérieur et même par les danseurs que l'on aperçoit de l'extérieur.

Bright open rehearsal spaces and outside terraces sheltered by façade elements give a feeling of freedom and openness that is entirely appropriate to dance.

Helle, offene Proberäume und Außenterrassen, die durch Fassadenelemente geschützt sind, vermitteln ein Gefühl von Freiheit und Weite, das sehr gut zum Thema Tanz passt.

Les salles de répétitions largement ouvertes et les terrasses extérieures donnent un sentiment de liberté ou d'ouverture qui correspond parfaitement à l'idée même de danse.

Behind the scenes, spaces seem to be treated with the same respect for detail and spaciousness that is usually reserved for public areas.

Auch die Nebenräume wurden mit viel Respekt für Details und Raumwirkung behandelt, wie er üblicherweise öffentlichen Bereichen zukommt.

Derrières les scènes, les espaces fonctionnels semblent traités avec le même sens du détail et de l'espace que les zones publiques.

Tilted columns and irregularly aligned metal plates carry the sense of movement created by the outside into the interior of the structure.

Schräggestellte Säulen und unregelmäßig ausgerichtete Metallplatten setzen das Gefühl von Bewegung im Gebäudeinnern fort.

Des colonnes inclinées et des parois métalliques alignées irrégulièrement introduisent dans les espaces intérieurs le sentiment de mouvement.

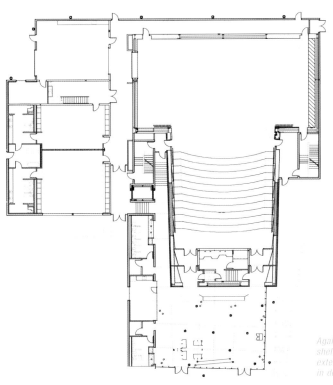

Mit seinen aufeinanderfolgenden
Schalen wiederholt der Theaterraum
sowohl farblich als auch formal die
äußere Gestaltung.

Utilisant là encore le thème de la succession de coques, la salle de spectacles rappelle l'extérieur, dans sa
conception comme dans sa coloration.

*Again using the theme of successive
shells, the theater itself echoes the
exterior, both in color schemes and
in design.*

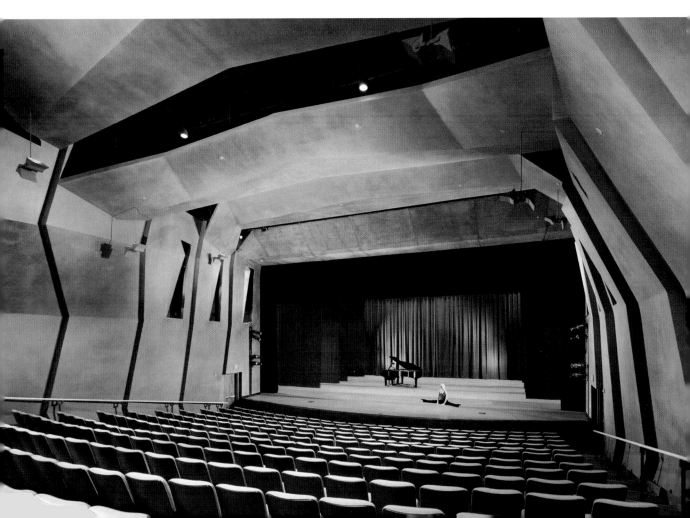

# ZAHA HADID

*Zaha Hadid Architects*
*Studio 9, 10 Bowling Green Lane*
*London EC1R OBQ*
*UK*

*Tel: +44 20 7253 5147*
*Fax: +44 20 7251 8322*
*e-mail: mail@zaha-hadid.com*
*Web: www.zaha-hadid.com*

Zaha Hadid studied architecture at the Architectural Association in London (AA) beginning in 1972 and was awarded the Diploma Prize in 1977. She then became a partner of Rem Koolhaas in the Office for Metropolitan Architecture (OMA) and taught at the AA. She has also taught at Harvard, the University of Chicago, in Hamburg and at Columbia University in New York. Well known for her paintings and drawings she has had a substantial influence, despite having built relatively few buildings. She has completed the Vitra Fire Station, Weil am Rhein, Germany, 1990–1994 and exhibition designs such as that for "The Great Utopia," Solomon R. Guggenheim Museum, New York, 1992. Significant competition entries include her design for the Cardiff Bay Opera House, 1994–1996; the Habitable Bridge, London, 1996; and the Luxembourg Philharmonic Hall, Luxembourg, 1997. More recently, Zaha Hadid has entered a phase of active construction with such projects as the Innsbruck Ski Jump and the Cincinatti Arts Center published here. In 2004, Zaha Hadid became the first woman to win the coveted Pritzker Prize.

Zaha Hadid studierte ab 1972 an der Architectural Association (AA) in London und erhielt 1977 den Diploma Prize. Danach wurde sie Partnerin von Rem Koolhaas im Office for Metropolitan Architecture (OMA). Sie lehrte an der AA in Harvard, an der University of Chicago, in Hamburg und an der Columbia University in New York. Hadid ist besonders durch ihre Gemälde und Zeichnungen bekannt geworden. Obwohl nur wenige ihrer Entwürfe realisiert wurden, so das Vitra-Feuerwehrhaus in Weil am Rhein (1990–1994), gehört sie zu den einflussreichsten Vertreterinnen ihrer Zunft. 1992 entwarf sie das Ausstellungsdesign für „The Great Utopia" im New Yorker Solomon R. Guggenheim Museum. Zu ihren bedeutendsten Wettbewerbsbeiträgen gehören Entwürfe für das Cardiff Bay Opera House (1994–1996), für die Habitable Bridge in London (1996) und die Philharmonie in Luxemburg (1997). In jüngster Zeit ist Zaha Hadid in eine Phase aktiven Bauens eingetreten, so mit den hier vorgestellten Projekten der Sprungschanze in Innsbruck und dem Cincinnati Arts Center. Anfang 2004 wurde sie als erste Frau mit dem begehrten Pritzker Prize ausgezeichnet.

Zaha M. Hadid a étudié l'architecture à l'Architectural Association (AA) de Londres de 1972 à 1977, date à laquelle elle reçoit le Prix du diplôme. Elle est ensuite associée de l'agence de Rem Koolhaas, Office for Metropolitan Architecture, et enseigne à l'AA, Harvard, University of Chicago, la Columbia University, et l'Université de Hambourg. Très connue pour ses peintures et dessins, elle exerce une réelle influence, même si elle n'a que peu construit. Parmi ses réalisations : le poste d'incendie de Vitra (Weil am Rhein, Allemagne, 1990–1994), et des projets pour expositions comme « La Grande Utopie », Solomon R. Guggenheim Museum (New York, 1992). Elle a participé à des concours dont les plus importants sont le projet de la Cardiff Bay Opera House (Pays-de-Galles, 1994–1996), un Pont habitable (Londres, 1996) et la salle de concerts philharmoniques de Luxembourg (1997). Plus récemment, elle est entrée dans une phase de chantiers concrets avec des projets comme un tremplin de ski à Innsbruck (Autriche) et le Cincinnati Arts Center, reproduit ici. En 2004, elle est la première femme à recevoir le Pritzker Prize.

# BERGISEL SKI JUMP

*Innsbruck, Austria, 2001–02*

*Client: Austrian Ski Federation, Innsbruck. Length: 90 m, height: 48 m. Costs: not specified.*

Created in 1926, the Bergisel ski jump has been well known almost since its construction, and was the site of the 1964 and 1976 Winter Olympic competitions. The schedule of international ski jumping events is such that local authorities could allow only one year from demolition to opening of the new facility. Cleverly, the Ski Jump includes a steel plate clad café situated ten meters above the jumping ramp, and it is apparent in the design that the Austrian Ski Federation wanted to create a monument as much as they sought a high-quality sports facility. Seating 150 persons, the cafe boasts a 360° view of the city and mountain scenery. In spite of local resistance to contemporary architecture of notable quality, both Hadid and Dominique Perrault (Innsbruck Town Hall) have succeeded in breaking into this Tyrolean stronghold of traditionalism. Forty-eight meters tall and seven by seven meters on the ground, the concrete structure has already permitted long flights over the snowy slopes such as the 134.5-meter jump achieved here by Sven Hannawald in January 2002. Hadid has described the structure as an "organic hybrid" – a sort of mixture of a tower and a bridge, but it succeeds in abstracting the speed of motion and flight that characterizes the most spectacular of winter sports events.

Die historische, 1926 gebaute Skisprungschanze Bergisel im Innsbrucker Stadtteil Wilten war Austragungsort der Olympischen Winterspiele 1964 und 1976. Aufgrund programmtechnischer Besonderheiten der internationalen Skisprungwettbewerbe konnten die lokalen Behörden erst ein Jahr nach Abriss der alten Konstruktion die Eröffnung der neuen Schanze genehmigen. Diese ist nun mit einem 10 m über der Absprungstelle liegenden Café ausgestattet, das mit Stahlplatten ummantelt ist. Insgesamt wird aus der Gestaltung deutlich, dass der österreichische Skiverband mit einer anspruchsvollen Sportanlage auch ein Monument schaffen wollte. Das Café mit 150 Sitzen bietet einen vollständigen Rundblick über die Stadt Innsbruck und die umliegende Berglandschaft. Trotz lokaler Vorbehalte gegenüber zeitgenössischer Architektur ist es Zaha Hadid wie schon Dominique Perrault mit seinem Innsbrucker Rathaus gelungen, diese Tiroler Hochburg des Traditionalismus einzunehmen. Ausgehend von einem 7 x 7 m messenden Sockel ragt die Betonkonstruktion 48 m hoch und hat sportliche Höchstleistungen wie den 134,5 m weiten Sprung von Sven Hannawald im Januar 2002 ermöglicht. Hadid hat sie als einen „organischen Hybriden" bezeichnet – eine Mischung aus Turm und Brücke. In jedem Fall artikuliert sich in ihrem Bauwerk auf gelungene Weise die Geschwindigkeit von Bewegung und Flug, die diesen spektakulärsten aller Wintersportwettbewerbe kennzeichnet.

Célèbre depuis sa construction en 1926, le tremplin de saut à ski de Bergisel a été le siège de compétitions olympiques en 1964 et 1976. Le calendrier des compétitions est si serré que les autorités locales ne pouvaient accorder qu'une année entre la démolition et l'inauguration d'un nouveau tremplin. La Fédération autrichienne de ski souhaitait autant un monument qu'une installation sportive. La nouvelle installation comprend un café de 150 places habillé de panneaux d'acier, suspendu à 10 m au-dessus de la rampe de départ, qui offre une vue à 360° sur la ville et la montagne. Malgré une certaine résistance locale à l'architecture contemporaine de qualité, Zaha Hadid comme Dominique Perrrault (Hôtel de ville d'Innsbruck) ont réussi à s'imposer dans ce haut lieu du traditionalisme tyrolien. De 48 m de haut pour une emprise au sol de 7 x 7 m, la structure en béton a déjà enregistré des records comme le saut de 134,5 m de Sven Hannawald en janvier 2002. Hadid décrit ce projet comme « un hybride organique », sorte de mélange de pont et de tour, mais réussit à symboliser la vitesse et le vol qui caractérisent l'une des disciplines olympiques d'hiver les plus spectaculaires.

*Jutting out of its wooded mountain setting, the Ski Jump tower appears to be poised to launch the athletes into the air.*

*Der Turm der Sprungschanze reckt sich aus dem bewaldeten Berghang in die Höhe, wie um die Skispringer in die Luft zu katapultieren.*

*Surgissant de son cadre montagneux et boisé, le tremplin de ski semble voué à la projection de skieurs dans les airs.*

Like a launch ramp, the actual ski run looks as though it winds out of the head of the tower.

*Die eigentliche Sprungschanze sieht aus wie eine spiralförmige Abschussrampe, die sich aus der Turmspitze windet*

*Comme une rampe de lancement, la piste donne l'impression de se dérouler à partir du sommet de la tour.*

Given its location and its design, the tower offers spectacular views of the mountain and woodland scenery in every direction.

*Dank seines Standorts und Designs bietet der Turm phantastische Ausblicke auf die Berge und Wälder ringsum.*

*Par sa position, la tour offre naturellement des vues panoramiques spectaculaires sur les montagnes et les forêts avoisinantes.*

A curved back makes the tower look as though the ski ramp is tightly wound around it and about to spring into action. The normally static nature of a tower is thus adapted to the sport for which it is intended.

Die geschwungene Rückseite lässt den Turm aussehen, als sei die Sprungschanze um ihn herumgewickelt und entfalte sich wie im Absprung. Die für einen Turm gegebene Statik richtet sich hier nach der Sportart, für die er konzipiert ist.

La face arrière incurvée de la tour donne l'impression que la rampe l'entoure étroitement, parée pour la compétition. La nature normalement statique d'une tour est ainsi adaptée au sport pour lequel elle a été prévue.

INNSBRUCK
*SKI AUSTRIA*

# LOIS & RICHARD ROSENTHAL CENTER FOR CONTEMPORARY ART

*Cincinnati, Ohio, USA, 1999–2003*

*Client: Contemporary Arts Center. Floor area: 7 900 m². Costs: $ 34 100 000.*

In an institution and a city that may be more famous for censorship than for an open attitude to the arts, the presence of the Rosenthal Center in downtown Cincinnati is nothing short of a triumph for Zaha Hadid.

In einer Stadt, die vielleicht eher für Zensurversuche als für Aufgeschlossenheit gegenüber der Kunst bekannt ist, stellt das Rosenthal Center in Downtown Cincinnati geradezu einen Triumph für Zaha Hadid dar.

Dans une institution et une ville qui fit parler d'elle pour son esprit de censure artistique, la présence du Rosenthal Center au centre de Cincinnati constitue presque un triomphe pour le projet de Zaha Hadid.

With the opening of the Rosenthal Center, Zaha Hadid became, surprisingly enough, the first woman to design an American art museum. Even more surprising for the usually angular and complicated Hadid, her new museum fits nicely into a city street of mixed architectural merit. Indeed the only thing that signals the presence of an architectural "star" in this unlikely location is the closed succession of cantilevered boxes that faces on 6th Street. True, Marcel Breuer's Whitney Museum on Madison Avenue presents similarly blind volumes of stone to the street. Then, too, this is the very institution that dared to defy the strictures of Puritan America by exhibiting the controversial photographs of Robert Mapplethorpe, becoming embroiled in a famous obscenity trial. Measuring about 7 900 square meters, this is not a very large building, but it does signal the arrival of Hadid as a serious builder as opposed to a largely theoretical designer. Poured-in-place concrete floors seem to curve effortlessly into walls near the entrance, and visitors see heavy painted black steel ramp-stairs that rise almost 30 meters up to skylights. Each flight of stairs weighs 15 tons, as much as the construction cranes could carry. This staircase is the central mediating feature of the Center, leading to the exhibition space and providing a continuous focal point for the movement of visitors. This is actually more of a "kunsthalle" than it is a museum because the Center has no permanent collection. Hadid's architecture relies on the art it will exhibit to bring its exhibition spaces to life, even if some artists may find her spaces challenging or difficult.

Zaha Hadid, die als erste Frau ein amerikanisches Kunstmuseum entworfen hat, übernahm für das Rosenthal Center nicht ihre meist kantige und komplizierte Formensprache, sondern fügte es in die benachbarte Stadtarchitektur ein, die von durchaus gemischter Qualität ist. Tatsächlich ist das einzige Merkmal für die Handschrift einer „Stararchitektin" an diesem Ort die geschlossene Abfolge von kastenförmigen Bauteilen, die über die 6th Street auskragen. Zugegeben, Marcel Breuers Whitney Museum auf der Madison Avenue präsentiert sich zur Straßenseite hin mit ähnlich blinden Steingebilden. Und das ist eben jene Institution, die es wagte, mit der umstrittenen Ausstellung der Fotografien von Robert Mapplethorpe der scharfen Kritik des puritanischen Amerika zu trotzen und dafür wegen Obszönität in einen berühmt gewordenen Prozess verwickelt wurde. Zurück zum Rosenthal Center: Es ist zwar mit 7 900 m² kein besonders großformatiger Bau. Aber es zeigt, dass sich Hadid von einer eher im theoretischen Bereich wichtigen Gestalterin zur ernsthaften Praktikerin entwickelt hat. Im Inneren scheinen die vor Ort gegossenen Betonböden mit sanftem Schwung mühelos in die Wände beim Eingang überzugehen, während das massive, rampenförmige Treppen aus schwarzgestrichenem Stahl fast 30 m bis zu den Oberlichtern hochziehen. Jeder dieser Treppenaufgänge wiegt 15 Tonnen, so viel wie die Baukräne maximal tragen konnten. Die Treppen sind außerdem das zentrale Bindeglied des Museumsgebäudes: Sie führen zu den Ausstellungsräumen und bündeln den Besucherstrom. Es handelt sich hier übrigens mehr um eine „Kunsthalle" als um ein Museum, da das Center über keine permanente Sammlung verfügt. Hadids Gestaltung verlässt sich daher auf die ausgestellte Kunst, um ihre Räume zum Leben zu erwecken, selbst wenn einige Künstler diese herausfordernd oder schwierig finden könnten.

L'inauguration du Rosenthal Center a fait de Zaha Hadid la première femme à avoir conçu un musée en Amérique. Son style anguleux et complexe s'est plaisamment intégré dans une rue très fréquentée mais d'intérêt architectural moyen. Le seul élément qui signale la présence d'une « star » architecturale dans ce lieu improbable est l'effet d'empilement de boîtes en porte à faux qui donne sur la 6th Street. Il est vrai que le Whitney Museum de Marcel Breuer, sur Madison Avenue, offre lui aussi des volumes aveugles similaires. Le Rosenthal Center est l'institution qui avait osé défier les blocages de l'Amérique puritaine en exposant des photographies controversées de Robert Mapplethorpe, déclenchant un célèbre procès pour obscénité. Mesurant environ 7 900 m², le bâtiment n'est pas très vaste, mais annonce l'arrivée de Hadid parmi les constructeurs après son cantonnement dans la théorie. Les sols en béton coulé in situ semblent s'incurver sans effort le long des murs de l'entrée d'où partent de lourdes rampes-escaliers en béton peint en noir qui s'élèvent jusqu'à 30 m de haut sous une verrière zénithale. Chaque volée d'escalier pèse 15 tonnes, la limite de portée des grues utilisées. Cet escalier est l'élément central du Centre et conduit aux espaces d'exposition tout en focalisant la circulation des visiteurs. Le centre est davantage une galerie qu'un musée car il ne possède pas de collection permanente. L'architecture de Hadid compte sur l'art exposé pour donner vie aux volumes, même si certains artistes les trouveront sans doute difficiles à occuper.

Although its interlocking block facade creates a surprising contrast to the heterogeneous and traditional downtown street, exterior and interior views of the Center show that it echoes the movement and even the architecture of its surroundings.

Obwohl die ineinandergreifenden Fassadenblöcke einen Kontrast zu dem heterogenen Straßenbild bilden, spiegeln die Innen- und Außenansichten des Gebäudes die Dynamik und sogar die Architektur seiner Umgebung wieder.

Bien que la façade composée de blocs imbriqués crée un contraste avec le cadre traditionnel d'une rue de centre-ville, les vues extérieures et intérieures rappellent cependant l'animation et même l'architecture de son environnement.

By alternating the opaque and seemingly more weighty blocks with glazed surfaces below them, Hadid animates the surface of the building in a surprising way.

Durch den Wechsel von opaken und scheinbar massiven Blöcken mit darunter liegenden verglasten Oberflächen, belebt Hadid die Fassade des Gebäudes auf ungewöhnliche Weise.

En positionnant des surfaces vitrées entre des blocs opaques apparemment plus lourds, Zaha Hadid anime l'enveloppe de son musée de façon surprenante.

Laban Centre London ▶

# HERZOG & DE MEURON

*Herzog & de Meuron*
*Rheinschanze 6*
*4056 Basel*
*Switzerland*

*Tel: +41 61 385 57 57*
*Fax: +41 61 385 57 58*
*e-mail: info@herzogdemeuron.com*

Jacques Herzog and Pierre de Meuron were both born in Basel in 1950. They received degrees in architecture at the Swiss Federal Institute of Technology (ETH) in Zürich in 1975 after studying with Aldo Rossi, and founded their firm Herzog & de Meuron Architecture Studio in Basel in 1978. Harry Gugger and Christine Binswanger joined the firm in 1991, while Robert Hösl and Ascan Mergenthaler became partners in 2004. Their built work includes the Antipodes I Student Housing at the Université de Bourgogne, Dijon (1991–92), the Ricola Europe Factory and Storage Building in Mulhouse (1993) and a gallery for a private collection of contemporary art in Munich (1991–92). Most notably they were chosen early in 1995 to design the new Tate Gallery extension for contemporary art in London, situated in the Bankside Power Station, on the Thames, opposite St. Paul's Cathedral that opened in May 2000. They were also shortlisted in the competition for the new design of the Museum of Modern Art in New York (1997). More recently, they have built the Forum 2004 Building and Plaza (Barcelona, 2002–2004), and plan to build the Caixa Forum-Madrid; the Davines Head Office (Parma); and the National Stadium, main stadium for the 2008 Olympic Games in Beijing.

Jacques Herzog und Pierre de Meuron wurden beide 1950 in Basel geboren. Sie studierten bei Aldo Rossi an der Eidgenössischen Technischen Hochschule (ETH) in Zürich, wo sie 1975 ihr Diplom machten. 1978 gründeten sie in Basel ihre Firma Herzog & de Meuron. 1991 traten Harry Gugger und Christine Binswanger der Firma bei, während Robert Hösl und Ascan Mergenthaler 2004 Partner wurden. Zu ihren Bauten gehören das Studentenwohnheim Antipodes I der Université de Bourgogne in Dijon (1991–92), das Ausstellungsgebäude für eine Privatsammlung moderner Kunst in München (1991–92) und das Fabrik- und Lagergebäude der Firma Ricola Europe in Mülhausen (1993). 1995 erhielten sie ihren bedeutendsten Auftrag: das Tate Modern genannte Museum für zeitgenössische Kunst, das im Mai 2000 in der umgebauten Bankside Power Station an der Themse, gegenüber St. Paul's Cathedral, eröffnet wurde. Beim Wettbewerb für die Umgestaltung des Museum of Modern Art in New York (1997) kamen Herzog & de Meuron in die engere Wahl. Zu den aktuellen Projekten zählen das Forum 2004 Building und Plaza in Barcelona (2004–2004) sowie die Entwürfe für das Caixa Forum in Madrid, das Davines Head Offices in Parma und das Hauptstadion für die Olympischen Spiele in Peking (2008).

Jacques Herzog et Pierre de Meuron sont tous deux nés à Bâle en 1950. Diplômés en architecture de l'institut fédéral suisse de technologie (ETH) de Zurich (1975), ils étudient auprès d'Aldo Rossi et fondent leur agence, Herzog & de Meuron Architecture Studio, à Bâle, en 1978. Harry Gugger et Christine Binswanger rejoignent l'agence en 1991, tandis que Robert Hösl et Ascan Mergenthaler deviennent partenaires en 2004. Parmi leurs réalisations : le foyer d'étudiants Antipodes 1 pour l'Université de Bourgogne, à Dijon (1991–1992), l'usine-entrepôt Ricola Europe, à Mulhouse (1993), et une galerie pour une collection privée d'art contemporain, à Munich (1991–92). Ils ont été sélectionnés en 1995 pour l'extension de la Tate Gallery of Modern Art de Londres, installée dans une ancienne centrale électrique, Bankside Power Station, au bord de la Tamise, face à la cathédrale Saint-Paul, et inaugurée en mai 2000. Ils ont fait partie des architectes retenus pour le concours de la transformation du Museum of Modern Art de New York (1997). Plus récemment, ils ont réalisé le bâtiment du Forum 2004 et la Plaza (Barcelone, 2002–2004) et planifié la construction du Caixa Forum-Madrid, le bureau Davines Head (Parme) et le stade national, principal stade olympique pour les Jeux à Pékin en 2008.

# LABAN CENTRE LONDON

*Creekside, Deptford, London, UK, 2000–2003*

*Client: Laban Centre London. Floor area: 8 203 m². Costs: £ 14 400 000.*

With its shimmering surface and bands of color the Laban Centre stands out from its environment and animates it in a bright, optimistic way.

*Mit seinen schimmernden Oberflächen und Farbbändern hebt sich das Laban Centre von seiner Umgebung ab und verleiht ihr gleichzeitig eine fröhliche, optimistische Note.*

*Par sa façade illuminée et ses bandeaux de couleur, le Laban Centre se distingue de son environnement qu'il anime avec optimisme.*

The cladding of the building reflects light in different ways, sometimes almost disappearing against its background.

*Die Verkleidung des Gebäudes reflektiert das Licht auf unterschiedliche Weise, wodurch es stellenweise beinahe vor seinem Hintergrund verschwindet.*

*L'habillage du bâtiment reflète la lumière de différentes façons, jusqu'à parfois disparaître dans son contexte.*

The Laban Centre is named after Rudolf Laban (1879–1958), one of the founding figures of European modern dance, choreographer responsible for the Opening Ceremonies of the 1936 Berlin Olympics. Following his escape from Germany, Rudolf Laban made his way to Britain and in 1948 founded the Art of Movement Studio in Manchester. The studio later moved to Addlestone in Surrey. In 1974, it relocated to New Cross in South London and was called the Laban Centre for Movement and Dance. In 1997, Herzog & de Meuron won an international design competition to build the new Laban building on a limited budget of £14.4 million. Set on a site almost a hectare in area beside Deptford Creek in South East London, the building creates a "highly visible focus for the ongoing physical and social regeneration of Deptford and the surrounding area." The Zurich firm Vogt Landschaftarchitekten did the landscaping. The artist Michael Craig-Martin collaborated with the architects on the decorative scheme for Laban's exterior and on part of the interior design. The 8 203-square-meter structure is covered in semi-translucent, colored polycarbonate punctuated by large clear windows. More precisely, as the architects say, "the exterior façades consist of transparent or translucent glass panels, depending on whether the space behind them requires a view. Colored, transparent polycarbonate panels are mounted in front of the glass panels and serve as a protective shield (against sun, glare, heat radiation) and contribute to the overall energy system. The shadow images of the dancers, which fall onto the matt glass surfaces of the interior walls and façades, have a magical effect and play an active part in the Laban's architectural identity. Inside, the building is structured as an urban 'streetscape,' a series of corridors, interior courtyards and meeting places, centered round the 'literal and metaphorical heart' of the building, the 300 seat theater."

Das Laban Centre ist nach Rudolf von Laban (1879–1958) benannt, einer der Gründer des modernen Tanzes in Europa und Choreograf der Eröffnungszeremonie der Olympischen Spiele 1936 in Berlin. Nach seiner Flucht aus Deutschland kam Rudolf von Laban nach England, wo er 1948 in Manchester das Tanzstudio Art of Movement gründete. Es wurde später nach Addlestone in Surrey und schließlich 1974 nach New Cross im Süden von London verlegt, wo es fortan Laban Centre for Movement and Dance hieß. Im Jahr 1997 gewannen Herzog & de Meuron den internationalen Wettbewerb zum Bau des neuen Laban-Gebäudes. Das dafür vorgesehene Budget war mit 14,4 Millionen Pfund bemessen. Das Gebäude, das auf einem fast 1 ha großen Grundstück nahe Deptford Creek im südöstlichen London liegt, bildet „einen spektakulären Markierungspunkt für die fortschreitende materielle und soziale Regenerierung von Deptford und Umgebung." Für die Landschaftsgestaltung war die Zürcher Firma Vogt zuständig, der Künstler Michael Craig-Martin war bei der Außenfassade und der Inneneinrichtung beteiligt. Das Gebäude hat eine Nutzfläche von 8 203 m² und ist mit durchscheinendem, farbigem Polycarbonat verkleidet, in das große, transparente Fensterflächen gesetzt sind. Oder, wie es die Architekten beschreiben: „Die Außenwände bestehen aus Glaspaneelen, die durchscheinend oder durchsichtig sind, je nachdem ob die dahinter liegenden Räume einen Ausblick erfordern. Auf die Glaspaneele sind Platten aus farbigem, durchsichtigem Polycarbonat montiert, die als Schutz vor grellem Sonnenlicht oder Wärmestrahlung dienen und zum Energiesystem des Gebäudes gehören. Die Schattenfiguren der Tänzer, die auf die matten Glasflächen der Innenwände und Fassaden fallen, verleihen dem Gebäude etwas Magisches und sind ein aktiver Teil der architektonischen Identität des Zentrums. Im Inneren ist das Gebäude mit seinen Korridoren, Innenhöfen und Treffpunkten als urbanes Straßengefüge um einen ebenso konkreten wie metaphorischen Kern, das Theater mit 300 Sitzen, angelegt."

Le Laban Centre porte le nom de Rudolf Laban (1879–1958), un des fondateurs de la danse européenne moderne. Chorégraphe des cérémonies d'ouverture des Jeux Olympiques de Berlin en 1936, il fuit l'Allemagne pour la Grande-Bretagne, et fonde en 1948 le Art of Movement Studio à Manchester, qui déménagera plus tard à Addlestone dans le Surrey. En 1974, le studio s'installe à New Cross dans le sud de Londres et prend le nom de Laban Centre for Movement and Dance. C'est en 1997 qu'Herzog & de Meuron ont remporté le concours international pour lui édifier un nouveau siège dans le cadre d'un budget limité à 14,4 millions de livres sterling. Sur un terrain de près d'un hectare non loin de Deptford Creek dans le sud-est de Londres, ce bâtiment crée une « concentration d'attention spectaculaire sur la rénovation physique et sociale en cours à Deptford et dans ses environs ». La firme zurichoise Vogt Landschaftarchitekten a réalisé les aménagements paysagers. L'artiste Michael Craig-Martin a collaboré avec les architectes au projet décoratif de l'extérieur du centre et à une partie de l'architecture intérieure. La construction de 8 203 m² est habillée de polycarbonate semi-translucide coloré, ponctué de grandes fenêtres de verre clair. Comme l'ont précisé les architectes : « Les façades extérieures consistent en panneaux de verre transparent ou translucide, selon les besoins de l'espace qu'ils renferment. Les panneaux de polycarbonate coloré ou transparent sont montés devant les panneaux de verre, servent de protection (contre le soleil, l'éblouissement, la chaleur) et participent au système énergétique de l'ensemble. L'ombre des danseurs, qui se détache sur les surfaces mattes des murs intérieurs et des façades exerce un effet magique qui joue un rôle actif dans l'identité architecturale du centre. » À l'intérieur, « le bâtiment est structuré comme un paysage urbain, en une série de corridors, de cours intérieurs et de lieux de réunion, centrés autour du ‹ cœur littéral et métaphorique › du bâtiment, qu'est la salle de 300 places. »

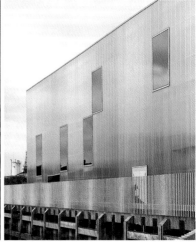

Becoming translucent or partially transparent at night, the polycarbonate facades of the center are a source of constant surprise.

Die in der Nacht durchscheinend oder teilweise transparent werdenden, aus Polycarbonat gefertigten Fassaden bieten überraschende Anblicke.

Devenant translucides ou partiellement transparentes de nuit, les façades en polycarbonate créent un élément de surprise permanente.

studio
7

*Bright colors and plays on transparency and opacity characterize the entire space of the center, filtering views of interior movement just as they color the light within.*

*Helle Farben und das Spiel von Transparenz und Opazität charakterisieren den gesamten Innenraum des Gebäudes, lassen Bewegung sichtbar werden und geben dem Licht Farbe.*

*Le Centre se caractérise par des couleurs vives et des jeux de transparence ou d'opacité qui filtrent les vues de l'extérieur ou colorent l'intérieur.*

*There is a cinematographic feeling about spaces where such unexpected details as undulating hand rails animate the architectural forms.*

*Interieurs, in denen so ungwöhnliche Details wie wellenförmige Handläufe die Bauformen beleben, schaffen ein kinematographisches Raumgefühl.*

*Le traitement des espaces crée une atmosphère cinématographique, en particulier à travers des détails inattendus comme les rampes ondulées.*

# PRADA AOYAMA TOKYO

*Minato-ku, Tokyo, Japan, 2001–2003*

Client: Prada Japan Co. Ltd. Floor area: 2 860 m². Costs: not specified.

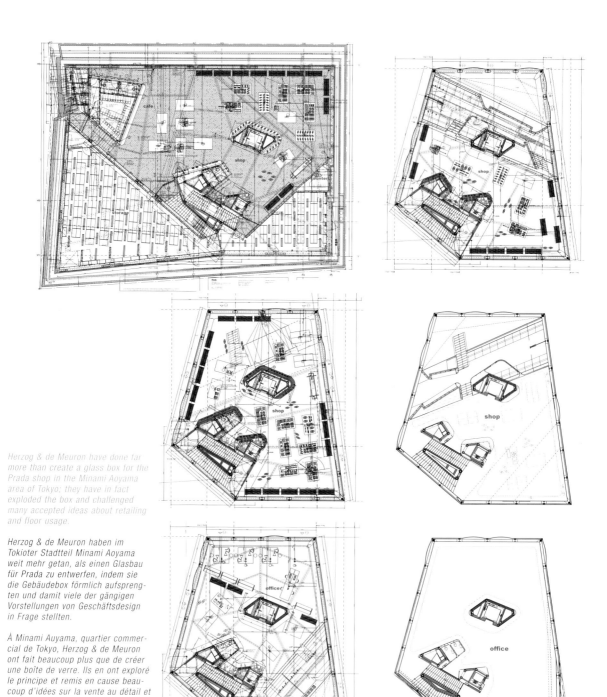

*Herzog & de Meuron have done far more than create a glass box for the Prada shop in the Minami Aoyama area of Tokyo; they have in fact exploded the box and challenged many accepted ideas about retailing and floor usage.*

Herzog & de Meuron haben im Tokioter Stadtteil Minami Aoyama weit mehr getan, als einen Glasbau für Prada zu entwerfen, indem sie die Gebäudebox förmlich aufsprengten und damit viele der gängigen Vorstellungen von Geschäftsdesign in Frage stellten.

À Minami Auyama, quartier commercial de Tokyo, Herzog & de Meuron ont fait beaucoup plus que de créer une boîte de verre. Ils en ont exploré le principe et remis en cause beaucoup d'idées sur la vente au détail et l'utilisation des niveaux.

Built on a 953-square-meter site in the heart of the Omotesando shopping district, this structure has a 369-square-meter footprint and is 32 meters high. The gross floor area is 2 860 square meters. The area contains densely packed low-rise buildings of no particular distinction, aside perhaps from the Collezione Building by Tadao Ando just down the street. This fact freed the architects of many of the usual contextual requirements, although local zoning laws distinctly limited possible forms. Within the zoning framework, Herzog & de Meuron imagined a fairly tall structure as compared to the neighborhood, and an unusual outdoor plaza. They settled on a simple, immediately recognizable shape clad in 840 glass panes, 205 of which have a spherical, convex shape and 16 (ground floor) a concave shape. Inside the structure, the architects put an emphasis on openings between floors that give an impression of continuous, flowing space. As they say, "the Prada Aoyama store is the first building by Herzog & de Meuron in which the structure, space and façade form a single unit. The vertical cores, the horizontal tubes, the floor slabs and the façade grilles define the space, but at the same time, they are the structure and the façade." This aspect of the design as well as its internal fluidity resulted, together with the stringent fire and earthquake rules, in making this one of the more complex small buildings recently erected in Japan. Within, the architects consciously referred to the famous pictures by Andreas Gursky of other Prada boutiques and decided that they wanted "to develop a slightly more 'primitive' or 'archaic' form of presentation, somewhat like a market stall." As for the interiors and material choices, the architects have said, "the fittings with lamps and furniture for the presentation of Prada products and for visitors were designed especially for this location. The materials are either hyper-artificial, like resin, silicon and fiberglass, or hyper-natural, like leather, moss or porous planks of wood. Such contrasting materials prevent fixed stylistic classifications of the site, allowing both traditional and radically contemporary aspects to appear as self-evident and equal components of today's global culture."

Das neue Prada-Gebäude steht im Herzen des Tokioter Geschäftsviertels Omotesando auf einem 953 m² großen Grundstück. Es hat eine Aufstandsfläche von 369 m², ist 32 m hoch und bietet eine Nutzfläche von 2 860 m². Abgesehen von Tadao Andos Collezione Building, das nur wenige Meter entfernt in derselben Straße liegt, besteht die dicht bebaute Umgebung aus niedrigen, unauffälligen Gebäuden. Innerhalb des vorgeschriebenen Rahmens entwarfen Herzog & de Meuron ein im Vergleich zur Nachbarschaft ziemlich hohes Gebäude und einen ungewöhnlichen Vorplatz. Sie entschieden sich für eine schlichte, dennoch charakteristische Außenform, die mit 840 Glasplatten ummantelt ist, von denen 205 nach außen und 16 im Erdgeschoss nach innen gewölbt sind. Im Inneren haben die Architekten Wert auf eine durchgehende, fließende Raumwirkung zwischen den Stockwerken gelegt. Sie erläutern: „Das Prada-Aoyama Gebäude ist der erste Entwurf von Herzog & de Meuron, in dem Baukörper, Innenraum und Fassade eine Einheit bilden. Die vertikalen Kernelemente, die horizontalen Röhren, die Bodenplatten und das Fassadengitter definieren den Raum und bilden gleichzeitig die Gesamtkonstruktion." Dieser Aspekt der Gestaltung führte zusammen mit der durchlässigen Innenraumgestaltung und den strengen Feuer- und Erdbebenschutzbestimmungen dazu, dass hier eins der komplexesten in jüngster Zeit in Japan realisierten kleineren Bauwerke entstanden ist. Sich bewusst auf die berühmten Bilder beziehend, die Andreas Gursky von anderen Prada-Boutiquen gemacht hat, beschlossen die beiden Architekten, eine etwas primitivere oder archaischere Form der Präsentation zu wählen – mehr in der Art eines Marktstands. Über die Materialauswahl für das Interieur sagen sie: „Die Ausstattungsstücke wie Lampen und Verkaufsmöbel wurden speziell für dieses Projekt entworfen. Die Materialien sind entweder hyper-künstlich so wie Kunstharz, Silikon und Glasfaser oder hyper-natürlich wie Leder, Moos oder poröse Holzplanken. Derart kontrastierende Materialien verhindern eine bestimmte stilistische Klassifizierung und lassen sowohl traditionelle wie auch radikal zeitgenössische Gestaltungsmittel als selbstverständliche und gleichwertige Elemente der globalen Kultur von heute bestehen."

Édifié sur un terrain de 953 m² au cœur du quartier commercial d'Omotesando, cet immeuble de 32 m de haut occupe une emprise au sol de 369 m², pour une surface totale de 2 860 m². Le quartier se compose de petits immeubles sans grand intérêt, en dehors peut-être du Collezione Building de Tadao Ando, un peu plus bas dans la rue. Dans le cadre du zonage existant, Herzog & de Meuron ont imaginé une structure assez haute, comparée à son voisinage, et une curieuse plazza. La forme simple mais à forte identité est habillée de 840 panneaux de verre, dont 205 sont semi-sphériques convexes et 16 (au rez-de-chaussée) concaves. À l'intérieur, les architectes ont mis l'accent sur les liaisons entre les niveaux, ce qui donne l'impression d'un espace en flux continu : « Le magasin Prada Aoyama est le premier immeuble de Herzog & de Meuron dans lequel la structure, l'espace et la façade forment un seul tout. Les noyaux verticaux, les tubes horizontaux, les dalles des planchers et les grilles de façade définissent l'espace, tout en étant à la fois structure et façade. » Cet aspect de la conception et la fluidité interne qui en résultent, associées à la stricte réglementation sur les incendies et les tremblements de terre, en fait l'un des plus complexes petits immeubles récemment érigés au Japon. Pour l'aménagement intérieur, les architectes se sont volontairement référés à de célèbres photographies prises par Andreas Gursky dans d'autres magasins Prada et décidé « qu'ils voulaient mettre au point une forme de présentation plus primitive ou archaïque, un peu comme un étal de marché… Les équipements, dont les lampes et les meubles de présentation des produits Prada, ont été spécialement dessinés pour le lieu. Les matériaux sont soit hyper artificiels, comme la résine, le silicone et la fibre de verre, soit hyper naturels, comme le cuir, la mousse ou les planches de bois brut. Le contraste entre ces matériaux fait échapper l'endroit aux classifications stylistiques rigides, et fait que des aspects à la fois traditionnels et radicalement contemporains semblent devenir des composants évidents et égaux de la culture globale d'aujourd'hui. »

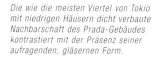

Crowded with low buildings like most of Tokyo, the neighborhood of the Prada building contrasts with its jutting glass presence.

Die wie die meisten Viertel von Tokio mit niedrigen Häusern dicht verbaute Nachbarschaft des Prada-Gebäudes kontrastiert mit der Präsenz seiner aufragenden, gläsernen Form.

Par sa présence transparente et dynamique l'immeuble Prada contraste avec son voisinage saturé de constructions basses, comme presque partout à Tokyo.

Unlike any of its neighbors, the Prada building has a small outdoor plaza.

Im Gegensatz zu seinen Nachbarn ist das Prada-Gebäude mit einem kleinen Vorplatz ausgestattet.

À la différence de ses voisins, l'immeuble Prada est précédé d'une petite place.

The web of glass blocks that characterizes the façade as seen from the outside also animates and defines the unusual interior spaces.

Das Netzwerk aus Glassegmenten, das die Außenfassade charakterisiert, belebt und definiert auch die ungewöhnlichen Innenräume.

La trame de blocs de verres si caractéristique de cette façade vue de l'extérieur, définit et anime des volumes intérieurs inhabituels.

Determined to create an architectural "event", client and designers have made the rather staid image of Prada evolve toward the cutting edge of current architecture.

Mit dem Ziel, ein architektonisches „Ereignis" zu schaffen, haben Auftraggeber und Planer das eher gesetzte Image von Prada mit der Avantgarde zeitgenössischer Architektur in Zusammenhang gebracht.

Déterminé à créer un « événement » architectural, le client et les architectes ont fait évoluer l'image assez rigide de Prada aux confins de l'architecture contemporaine.

# ARATA ISOZAKI

*Arata Isozaki & Associates*
*Nogizaka Atelier*
*9-6-17 Akasaka, Minato-ku*
*Tokyo 107-0052*
*Japan*

*Tel: +81 33 405 1526*
*Fax: +81 33 475 5265*

*Ceramics Park Mino* ▶

Born in Oita City on the Island of Kyushu in 1931, Arata Isozaki graduated from the Architectural Faculty of the University of Tokyo in 1954 and established Arata Isozaki & Associates in 1963, having worked in the office Kenzo Tange. Winner of the 1986 Royal Institute of British Architects Gold Medal, he has been a juror of major competitions such as that held in 1988 for the new Kansai International Airport. Notable buildings include: The Museum of Modern Art, Gunma (1971–1974); the Tsukuba Center Building, Tsukuba (1978–1983); The Museum of Contemporary Art, Los Angeles (1981–1986); Art Tower Mito, Mito (1986–1990); Team Disney Building, Florida (1990–1994); Center for Japanese Art and Technology, Krakow, Poland (1991–1994); B-con Plaza, Oita (1991–1995). Recent projects include Shizuoka Convention and Arts Center "Granship," Shizuoka, Japan (1995–1998); the Nara Centennial Hall, Nara, Japan (1996–1998); and Ohio's Center of Science and Industry (COSI), Columbus, Ohio.

Arata Isozaki, 1931 in Oita auf der Insel Kyushu geboren, beendete 1954 sein Architekturstudium an der Universität Tokio. Danach arbeitete er im Büro von Kenzo Tange und gründete 1963 Arata Isozaki & Associates. 1986 wurde er mit der Gold Medal des Royal Institute of British Architects ausgezeichnet. Er war Preisrichter in bedeutenden Wettbewerben, so 1988 bei der Ausschreibung für den Internationalen Flughafen Kansai. Zu Isozakis wichtigsten Bauten zählen das Museum für moderne Kunst in Gunma (1971–1974) und das Tsukuba Center Building in Tsukuba (1978–1983), beide in Japan, das Museum of Contemporary Art in Los Angeles (1981–1986), der Art Tower Mito in Mito, Japan (1986–1990), das Team Disney Building in Florida (1990–1994), das Zentrum für japanische Kunst und Technologie in Krakau, Polen (1991–1994) und B-con Plaza im japanischen Oita (1991–1995). Seine jüngsten Projekte sind das Center of Science and Industry (COSI) in Columbus, Ohio, der Konferenz- und Kunstkomplex Granship in Shizuoka (1995–1998) sowie die Nara Centennial Hall in Nara (1996–1998), beide in Japan.

Né à Oita (île de Kyushu), en 1931, Arata Isozaki est diplômé de la faculté d'architecture de l'Université de Tokyo en 1954, et fonde Arata Isozaki & Associates en 1963, après avoir travaillé dans l'agence de Kenzo Tange. Titulaire de la médaille d'or du Royal Institute of British Architects en 1986, il fait partie du jury dans de nombreux concours internationaux dont celui de l'aéroport international de Kansai (1988). Parmi ses réalisations les plus connues : Musée d'art moderne, Gunma (Takasaki, Japon, 1971–1974) ; le Centre Tsukuba (Tsukuba, Japon, 1978–1983) ; The Museum of Contemporary Art (Los Angeles, 1981–1986) ; la Tour d'art Mito (Japon, 1986–1990) ; l'immeuble Team Disney (près d'Orlando, Floride, 1990–1994) ; le Centre d'art et de technologie du Japon (Cracovie, Pologne, 1991–1994) ; B-con Plaza (Oita, Japon, 1991–1995). Projets récents : le complexe culturel Higashi Shizuoka Plaza et le Centre des Arts « Granship » (1995–1998), tous deux à Shizuoka, Japon, le Hall du Siècle de Nara (Nara, Japon, 1996–1998) et l'Ohio's Center of Science and Industry (COSI) (Columbus, Ohio).

# CERAMICS PARK MINO

*Tajimi, Gifu, Japan, 2000–2002*

*Client: Gifu Prefecture. Total floor area: 14 466 m². Costs: not specified.*

Located in the central part of Honshu, Gifu Prefecture has long been an area noted for transport and trade. The so-called Tono district where Tajimi is located is famous for its ceramics and thus the construction of a large Museum of Modern Ceramic Art there was logical. Set on a vast, wooded, 173 000-square-meter site, this steel-framed reinforced concrete structure boasts a total floor area of 14 466 square meters. Despite its large size, the project was conceived so as to have a minimal impact on the natural surroundings. The main entry to the complex is via a bridge and tunnel and the structures have been inserted as much as possible into the existing terrain. A certain irregularity in the plan is attributable to this effort to fit the contours of the hilly site. One unusual feature of the construction is the suspension of the galleries from the main beams of the roof. According to the architect, "this is an attempt to completely isolate the floor from lateral swing caused by earthquakes." Running water fills the center of the complex and the upper pond faces a seemingly incongruous traditional tea ceremony house. A path leads up the hillside from the museum to an observation tower that gives a fine view of the entire region. In the design of this museum, Isozaki remains faithful to the complex juxtaposition of materials and even styles that has been a hallmark of his work for many years.

Die im Zentralgebiet der japanischen Insel Honshu liegende Präfektur Gifu ist seit langer Zeit für ihr reges Verkehrs- und Handelswesen bekannt. Und da der zur Präfektur gehörende Tono Distrikt, in dem der Ort Tajimi liegt, berühmt für seine Töpferwaren ist, lag der Bau eines Museums für moderne künstlerische Keramik nahe. Das auf einem ausgedehnten, 173 000 m² großen Waldgrundstück errichtete Museumsgebäude besteht aus einer Stahlrahmen- und Stahlbetonkonstruktion und hat eine Gesamtnutzfläche von 14 466 m². Der Hauptzugang zur Museumsanlage erfolgt über eine Brücke und durch einen Tunnel; die einzelnen Bauteile wurden so weit wie möglich in das bestehende Terrain versetzt. Eine gewisse Unregelmäßigkeit im Grundriss ist ebenfalls auf das Bestreben zurückzuführen, sich den Konturen des hügeligen Geländes anzupassen. Ungewöhnlich an der Konstruktion ist die Aufhängung der Ausstellungsräume an den Hauptträgern des Daches. Ein Merkmal, das den Boden völlig von Seitenschwingungen abschirmen soll, die durch Erdbeben ausgelöst werden. Durch das Zentrum der Anlage fließt Wasser und ein im oberen Teil des Gebäudes angelegter Teich ist auf das Teehaus ausgerichtet. Vom Museum führt ein Pfad den Hang zu einem Observatorium hinauf, von dessen Turm aus man eine wunderbare Aussicht auf das gesamte Umland hat. Insgesamt ist Isozaki in seiner Gestaltung dieses Museums dem komplexen Nebeneinander von verschiedenen Materialien und Stilen treu geblieben, das seit vielen Jahren zu einem Markenzeichen seiner Arbeit geworden ist.

Située dans la partie centrale de Honshu, la région de la préfecture de Gifu est vouée au commerce et aux transports. Le district de Tono, où se trouve Tajimi, est célèbre pour ses fabriques de céramique, ce qui explique la construction d'un vaste musée d'art moderne consacré à ce médium. Implantée sur un vaste terrain boisé de 173 000 m², la construction en béton armé à ossature d'acier offre 14 466 m² de surface utile. Malgré ses importantes dimensions, elle a été conçue pour exercer un impact minimal sur son environnement naturel. L'entrée principale dans le complexe se fait par un pont et un tunnel et les bâtiments ont été enterrés autant que possible. Une certaine irrégularité de plan est due à l'adaptation aux contours du site vallonné. Un détail inhabituel est la suspension des galeries aux poutres principales du toit. Selon l'architecte, « c'est une tentative d'isoler totalement le sol des balancements latéraux provoqués par les tremblements de terre. » L'eau occupe le centre du complexe, tandis que le bassin supérieur s'étend devant une maison de thé. Un chemin conduit du musée vers la colline et une tour d'observation, d'où l'on bénéficie d'une belle vue sur la région. Isozaki reste ici fidèle aux juxtapositions complexes de matériaux et de styles qui sont sa marque depuis de nombreuses années.

As is often the case in his work, Isozaki has created a complex articulation of architectural volumes, set here into a verdant natural setting.

Comme souvent dans son travail, Isozaki a créé une articulation complexe de volumes architecturaux dans un cadre naturel verdoyant.

Wie häufig in seinen Projekten hat Isozaki auch in diesem Fall komplex artikulierte Bauformen geschaffen, die er hier in das Grün der natürlichen Umgebung eingebettet hat.

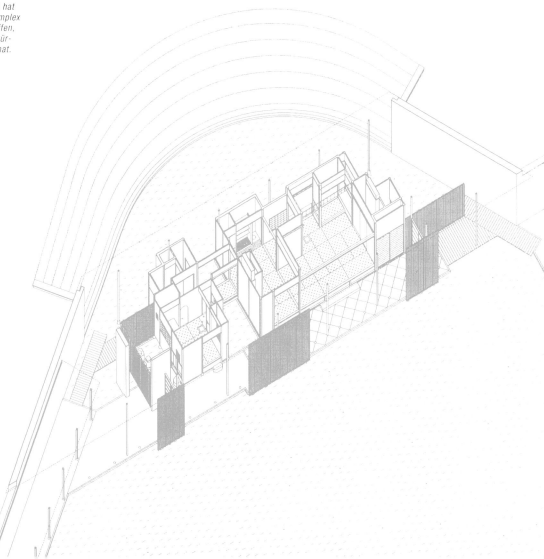

The architect has inserted the complex into the natural forms of the
land. At the back of the museum, a
basin paved with rough granite is the
site for a traditional and yet modern
style Japanese tea house.

An der Hinterseite des Museums
grenzt ein traditionelles und doch im
modernen Stil gestaltetes japanisches
Teehaus an ein Wasserbecken aus
grob gearbeiteten Granitsteinen.

L'architecte a inséré le musée dans
la forme même du terrain. À l'arrière,
un bassin pavé de granit brut est le
site d'une maison de thé japonaise
traditionnelle mais de style moderne.

This section and the photo above
show how the architecture fits into
the natural steep drop in the site,
with a waterfall leading down from
the upper basin.

Der Querschnitt und das Foto oben
veranschaulichen, wie sich die Architektur mit dem herabstürzenden
Wasserfall dem natürlichen Gefälle
des Grundstücks anpasst.

Cette coupe et la photo ci-dessus
montre comment l'architecture
s'intègre dans un creux du terrain,
une cascade tombant du bassin
supérieur.

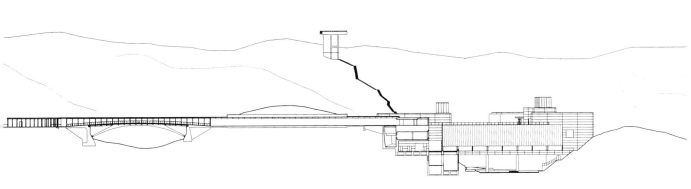

The interior of the structure includes a vast exhibition space (above) which can be rented, as well as the actual ceramics galleries that are suspended above the fair area (left page).

Das Gebäudeinnere enthält einen ausgedehnten Saal für Ausstellungen (oben) sowie die oberhalb davon sichtbare Hängekonstruktion der eigentlichen Keramikgalerien (links).

L'intérieur du bâtiment comprend les galeries consacrées à la céramique, suspendues au-dessus de vastes salles louées pour des manifestations commerciales (ci-dessus).

# TOYO ITO

*Toyo Ito & Associates, Architects*
*1-19-4 Shibuya, Shibuya-ku,*
*Tokyo 150-0002*
*Japan*

*Tel: +81 3 3409 5822*
*Fax: +81 3 3409 5969*
*e-mail: mayumi@toyo-ito.co.jp*
*Web: www.toyo-ito.co.jp*

Born in 1941 in Seoul, Korea, Toyo Ito graduated from the University of Tokyo in 1965, and worked in the office of Kiyonori Kikutake until 1969. He created his own office in 1971, assuming the name of Toyo Ito & Associates, Architects in 1979. His completed work includes the Silver Hut residence (Tokyo, 1984); Tower of the Winds (Yokohama, Kanagawa, 1986); Yatsushiro Municipal Museum (Yatsushiro, Kumamoto, 1989–1991); and the Elderly People's Home (1992–1994) and Fire Station (1992–1995) both located in the same city on the island of Kyushu. He participated in the Shanghai Luijiazui Center Area International Planning and Urban Design Consultation in 1992, and has built a Public Kindergarten (Eckenheim, Frankfurt, Germany, 1988–1991). Recent projects include his Odate Jukai Dome Park (Odate, Japan, 1995–1997); Nagaoka Lyric Hall (Nagaoka, Niigata, Japan, 1995–1997); and Ota-ku Resort Complex (Tobu-cho, Chiisagata-gun, Nagano, 1996–1998). One of his most successful and widely published projects, the Mediatheque in Sendai, was completed in 2001.

Toyo Ito, geboren 1941 in Seoul, Korea, schloss 1965 sein Studium an der Universität Tokio ab und arbeitete bis 1969 im Büro von Kiyonori Kikutake. 1971 gründete er sein eigenes Architekturbüro, das seit 1979 unter dem Namen Toyo Ito & Associates, Architects firmiert. Zu seinen Bauten gehören das Wohnhaus Silver Hut in Tokio (1984), der Turm der Winde in Yokohama, Kanagawa (1986), das städtische Museum in Yatsushiro, Kumamoto (1989–1991) sowie ein Seniorenwohnheim (1992–1994) und eine Feuerwehrstation (1992–1995) auf der Insel Kyushu. 1992 nahm Toyo Ito an der internationalen Konferenz für Planung und Entwicklung des Gebiets um das Luijiazui Center in Shanghai teil. Ferner baute er einen städtischen Kindergarten im Frankfurter Stadtteil Eckenheim (1988–1991). Zu seinen jüngsten Projekten zählen der Odate Jukai Dome Park in Odate (1995–1997), die Nagaoka Lyric Hall in Nagaoka, Niigata (1995–1997) und der Freizeitkomplex Ota-ku in Tobu-cho, Chiisagata-gun, Nagano (1996–1998), alle in Japan. Eines seiner erfolgreichsten und bekanntesten Werke, die Mediathek im nordjapanischen Sendai, wurde 2001 fertig gestellt.

Né en 1941 à Séoul, en Corée, Toyo Ito est diplômé de l'Université de Tokyo en 1965 et travaille dans l'agence de Kiyonori Kikutaké jusqu'en 1969. Il crée sa propre agence en 1971, qui prend le nom de Toyo Ito & Associates, Architects en 1979. Parmi ses réalisations : la maison Silver Hut (Tokyo, 1984) ; la Tour des vents (Yokohama, Kanagawa, 1986) ; le Musée municipal de Yatsushiro (Yatsushiro, Kumamoto, 1989–1991) ; une maison de retraite (1992–1994) et une caserne de pompiers (1992–1995) dans une ville de l'île de Kyushu. Il a participé au concours international d'urbanisme de la zone de Luijiazui à Shangaï (1992), et a dessiné un jardin d'enfants (Eckenheim, Francfort, Allemagne 1988–1991). Parmi ses récents projets : le Odate Jukai Dome Park (Odate, Japon, 1995–1997) ; la salle de concerts lyriques de Nagaoka (Nagaoka, Niigata, Japon, 1995–1997) et le complexe touristique Ota-ku (Tobu-Cho, Chiisagata-gun, Nagano, 1996–1998). L'un de ses projets les plus réussis et les plus médiatisés est la médiathèque de Sendai, achevée en 2001.

# SERPENTINE GALLERY PAVILION 2002

*Kensington Gardens, London, UK, 2002*

*Client: Serpentine Gallery, Kensington Gardens. Floor area: 310 m². Costs: £ 600 000.*

Each year, the Serpentine Gallery in London's Kensington Park commissions international architects to design a pavilion for the Gallery. Toyo Ito's 2002 participation was the third in the series, following Zaha Hadid (2000) and Daniel Libeskind with Arup (2001). His single story structure was covered in aluminum panels and glass. The 5.3-meter-high structure was formed by a steel grillage of flat bars. The concept was to create a columnless structure that was not dependent on an orthogonal grid system, making an open space to be used during the summer months as a café and event space. The seemingly random structure was determined by an algorithm derived from the rotation of a single square. Each piece of the structure functioned not only as a beam, but also to absorb vibrations so that all elements combined to form a complex, mutually interdependent whole. The point, as explained by the architect, was "to render visible again the systems that make the most basic conditions of architecture possible, but which were being obscured by a rationalism obsessed with uniformity." The £600 000 pavilion, designed with the engineering firm Arup, had painted structural plywood floors and 3mm aluminum panels for the walls and ceiling and was left in place for three months.

Jedes Jahr beauftragt die im Londoner Park Kensington Gardens gelegene Serpentine Gallery einen Architekten mit der Gestaltung eines Pavillons. Toyo Itos Beitrag aus dem Jahr 2002 war der dritte in dieser Serie, dem die Arbeiten von Zaha Hadid (2000) und Daniel Libeskind (2001) vorangegangen waren. Seine knapp 5,3 m hohe, eingeschossige Konstruktion bestand aus einem Trägerrost aus Flachstahl, umhüllt von unregelmäßig geformten Aluminiumplatten und Glas. Die Grundidee war ein Bauwerk, das ohne tragende Säulen und rechtwinkliges Rastersystem auskommen und als offener Raum gestaltet werden sollte. Dabei kam den einzelnen Elementen der Konstruktion nicht nur die Funktion eines Trägers zu, sondern auch die, Schwingungen zu absorbieren, so dass alle Teile zusammen ein komplexes und ineinandergreifendes Ganzes bildeten. Dabei ging es ihm darum, jene Systeme wieder sichtbar zu machen, auf denen die einfachsten Grundformen der Architektur aufbauen, die aber von einem Rationalismus verdeckt worden sind, der von der Idee der Uniformität besessen ist. Der zusammen mit Arup für die Summe von 600 000 Pfund gestaltete Pavillon war im Inneren mit Böden aus gestrichenem Furnierholz und 3 mm starken Aluminiumtafeln für Wände und Decken ausgestattet.

Chaque année, la Serpentine Gallery à Kensington Park à Londres commande un pavillon à un architecte connu. La participation de Toyo Ito en 2002 était la troisième de la série, après Zaha Hadid (2000) et Daniel Libeskind (2001). Ce pavillon sans étage était habillé de panneaux d'aluminium et de verre. La structure de 5,3 m de haut, était constituée d'une grille composée de barres de section plate. L'idée était de créer une structure sans colonne qui ne dépende pas d'une trame orthogonale. La forme apparemment aléatoire avait été déterminée par un algorithme issu de la rotation d'un carré. Chaque élément de la structure fonctionnait non seulement à la manière d'une poutre mais absorbait les vibrations pour que les éléments combinés constituent un tout complexe et interdépendant. Pour l'architecte, l'idée était de « rendre de nouveau visibles les systèmes qui ont rendu possibles les conditions de base de l'architecture mais qui ont été masqués par un rationalisme obsédé par l'uniformité ». Ce pavillon, qui a coûté 600 000 livres sterling, conçu en collaboration avec l'agence d'ingénierie Arup, faisait appel à des planchers de contreplaqué structurel peint, de murs et de plafonds en panneaux d'aluminium de 3 mm d'épaisseur. Il est resté trois mois en place.

*The exploded appearance of Ito's pavilion is a demonstration of his inventiveness. It is difficult to guess that he had designed this pavilion.*

*Das in Segmente aufgebrochene äußere Design des Pavillons ist eine Demonstration von Itos kaum zu erratendem Ideenreichtum.*

*L'apparence explosée du pavillon de Ito est une démonstration de son inventivité. Il serait difficile de deviner qu'il a conçu cette forme.*

Trotz seiner im Wesentlichen rechteckigen Form wirkt der Pavillon, als
würden seine massiven Baukörper in
der Luft schweben.

Bien que de forme essentiellement
rectangulaire, le pavillon donne l'impression que ses volumes aveugles
flottent dans les airs.

Despite its essentially rectangular
form, the pavilion seems to make
solid volumes float in the air.

The angular, white structural
elements give ample openings for
the interior space that is bright,
cheerful and airy.

Die winkelförmigen weißen Konstruk-
tionselemente sorgen für zahlreiche
Öffnungen im Innenraum, was diesen
hell, fröhlich und luftig wirken lässt.

Les grands éléments anguleux blancs
dégagent de vastes ouvertures qui
éclairent un volume intérieur lumineux, animé et aéré.

# MICHAEL JANTZEN

*Michael Jantzen*
*27800 N. McBean Parkway, Suite 319*
*Valencia, CA 91354*
*USA*

*Tel: +1 310 989 1897*
*Fax: +1 661 513 9901*
*e-mail: mjantzen@yahoo.com*
*Web: www.humanshelter.org*

*Malibu Video Beach House* ▶

In 1971, Michael Jantzen received a Bachelor's degree with a major in fine arts from Southern Illinois University (Edwardsville, Illinois). In 1973, he received an MFA degree with a major in Multi-media from Washington University (St. Louis, Missouri). Jantzen was then hired by Washington University's School of Fine Arts and by the School of Architecture, to teach studio courses as a visiting professor. In 1975, one of his first solar houses was featured in numerous national and international magazines. Over the next ten years, he continued to design and build energy-efficient structures with an emphasis on modular high-tech housing systems. In 1997, he was awarded a grant from the Art Center College of Design Digital Media Department to develop ideas for an interface between media and architecture. In 1998, Jantzen developed several digital media projects that were published widely. He created a conceptual house called the Malibu Video Beach House, and Elements, an interactive digital media theme park for the next millennium. Early in 1999, he began to design and build the M-house project, "a modular, relocatable, environmentally responsive, alternative housing system."

Michael Jantzen erwarb 1971 seinen Bachelor und Master of Fine Arts an der Southern Illinois University in Edwardsville, Illinois, und 1973 den Master of Fine Arts im Fach Multimedia an der Washington University in St. Louis, Missouri. Anschließend war Jantzen an der School of Fine Arts und der School of Architecture der Washington University als Gastprofessor tätig. 1975 wurde eines seiner ersten Solarhäuser in etlichen amerikanischen und internationalen Zeitschriften vorgestellt. Während der nächsten zehn Jahre entwarf und realisierte er Niedrigenergiebauten mit dem Schwerpunkt auf modulare Hightech-Wohnbausysteme. 1997 wurde er vom Art Center College of Design Digital Media Department mit einem Stipendium ausgezeichnet, um seine Ideen für ein Interface zwischen elektronischen Medien und Architektur weiterentwickeln zu können. 1998 führte Jantzen mehrere digitale Medienprojekte durch, die große Beachtung fanden. Er entwarf das Modellhaus Malibu Video Beach House sowie Elements, einen interaktiven, digitalen Medienthemenpark für das neue Jahrtausend. Anfang 1999 begann er mit der Planung und Konstruktion des Projekts M-House, „ein modulares, mobiles und ökologisch-alternatives Wohnbausystem".

Michael Jantzen est Bachelor et Major in fine arts de la Southern Illinois University (Edwardsville, Illinois) en 1971. En 1973, il est M. Fine Arts et multimédias de la Washington University (St. Louis, Missouri) dont il devient professeur d'atelier invité par l'École des beaux-arts et l'École d'architecture. En 1975, l'une de ses premières maisons solaires est publiée dans de nombreux journaux et magazines internationaux. Au cours des dix années suivantes, il continue à concevoir et réaliser des constructions axées sur les économies d'énergie et étudie particulièrement des sytèmes de logement high-tech modulaires. En 1997, il reçoit une bourse du Art Center College of Design Digital Media Department pour développer ses idées sur une interface médias – architecture. En 1998, il met au point plusieurs projets sur médias numériques, largement publiés. Il a créé une maison conceptuelle, la Malibu Video Beach House, et Elements, un parc thématique en images de synthèse. Début 1999, il entreprend la conception et la construction de la M House, « système de logement alternatif modulaire, déplaçable et écologique ».

# MALIBU VIDEO BEACH HOUSE

*Malibu, California, USA, 2002*

*Client: Michael Jantzen. Total floor area: 230 m². Costs: not specified.*

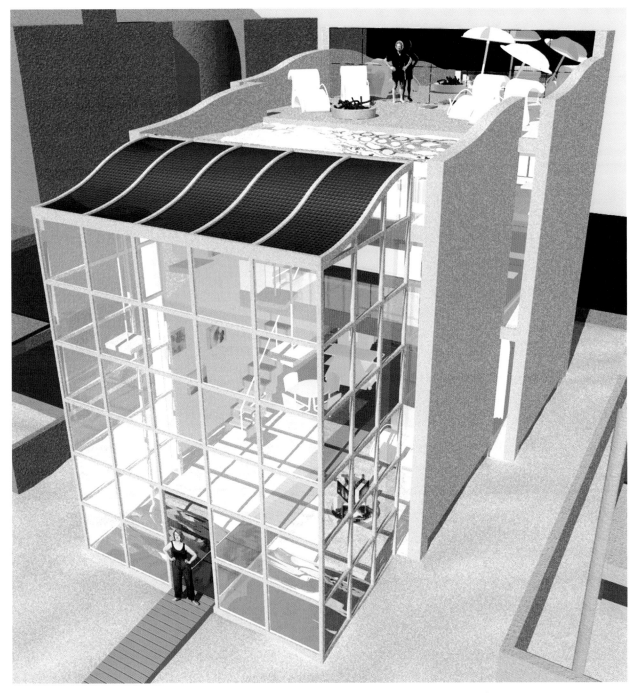

Within a generously glazed space on the beach side, the architect has imagined a house that plays on fundamental ambiguities that can be created using the latest technologies.

Im Rahmen einer großzügig verglasten Konstruktion ist ein Haus entstanden, das seinen Reiz aus einer Ambiguität bezieht, die mit Hilfe der neuesten Technologien kreiert wurde.

À partir d'un généreux volume vitré côté plage, l'architecte a imaginé une maison qui joue avec les ambiguïtés fondamentales que peuvent créer les technologies le plus récentes.

Examining the typology of the rows of houses located along the beach near Los Angeles, Jantzen has chosen not so much to change architectural form as to integrate video and other elements that accentuate questions about the solidity and space of the house.

In der Auseinandersetzung mit der Typologie von Häusern am Strand bei Los Angeles hat Jantzen nicht eine Veränderung der Bauform, sondern den Einsatz von Videoinstallationen und anderen Elementen gewählt, um Fragen über die Solidität und den Raum eines Hauses aufzuwerfen.

Dans son étude de la typologie de l'alignement des maisons le long des plages de Los Angeles, Jantzen a moins cherché à modifier la forme architecturale qu'à intégrer la vidéo et d'autres éléments qui accentuent le questionnement sur la solidité et l'espace de la maison.

The words of Michael Jantzen best describe this project, which mixes a real presence on the beach with its virtual sublimation: "This is a conceptual proposal for a weekend beach house to be built on a vacant lot sandwiched in-between two existing houses along the Pacific Coast Highway in Malibu. The façade of the house facing the busy highway is covered with thin gas-plasma television screens that create a full-size video interface with the real world. These screens would display images and sounds of the real beach that is obscured by the house itself. A board-walk leads guests up to the video beach wall where they can walk in through a mirrored doorway. The interior of the video wall is partially covered with a grid of mirrors that reflect the real beach back into the house. Some of the mirrors are actually plasma TV screens that can display real-time full sized or detailed images and sounds from the outside. Three walls of the house are made of structural concrete, surfaced with beach sand. This sand texture, inside and outside, suggests that the house may have been formed from the beach like a child's sand castle. Real beach sand also covers much of the interior floor area and all of the open deck on top of the house adjacent to a shallow wading pool. The design of all of the facilities inside the house that accommodate basic living functions like bathing, sleeping, eating, working and entertaining are symbolically based on images of objects associated with the beach environment. The food preparation module refers to food carts seen at the beach. The bath, toilet, storage and closet modules suggest the portable toilets use at the beach. The house would have its own website on the Internet and could be accessed in real time to, among other things, share the ocean view and sounds."

Die beste Beschreibung dieses Projekts, in dem sich die reale Umgebung eines Hauses mit deren virtueller Sublimation vermischt, stammt von Michael Jantzen selbst: „Es ist ein konzeptioneller Entwurf für ein Wochenendhaus, das, eingezwängt zwischen zwei bestehenden Häusern, am Strand nahe dem Pacific Coast Highway in Malibu gebaut werden soll. Die Fassade wendet sich der verkehrsreichen Fernstraße zu und ist mit flachen Plasmabildschirmen verkleidet, die als Video-Interface fungieren, indem sie die reale Welt im Maßstab 1:1 abbilden. Auf diese Weise werden auf die Bildschirme Bilder und Töne von jenem Strand übertragen, der vom Haus selbst verdeckt ist. Ein Plankenweg führt zu der in dieser Videowand eingelassenen verspiegelten Eingangstür. Die Innenseite der Videowand ist zum Teil mit einem Gitter aus Spiegeln bedeckt, welche die Bilder des realen Strands ins Hausinnere reflektieren. Bei einigen dieser Spiegel handelt es sich um Plasmabildschirme, die in Echtzeit entweder lebensgroß oder im Ausschnitt Bilder und Töne von draußen wiedergeben können. Drei der Hauswände bestehen aus Strukturbeton, der mit Sand verspachtelt wurde. Diese Sandtextur vermittelt den Eindruck, als wäre das Haus ein Produkt des Strandes selbst, wie eine von Kindern gebaute Sandburg. Auch im Hausinnern bedeckt echter Sand große Teile der Innenböden und die gesamte, an ein flaches Wasserbecken anschließende Fläche der offenen Dachterrasse. Die Gestaltung aller Inneneinrichtungen für die grundlegenden Wohnfunktionen wie Waschen, Schlafen, Essen, Arbeiten und Unterhaltung basieren symbolisch auf Objekten, die mit dem Strandleben zu tun haben. So bezieht sich das Modul zur Essenszubereitung auf Imbisskarren, wie es sie am Strand gibt. Die Einheiten für Bad, Toilette, Abstell- und Schrankraum lassen an die mobilen Toiletten am Strand denken. Das fertige Haus soll seine eigene Website im Internet haben, die man in Echtzeit besuchen kann, um beispielsweise an den Bildern und Geräuschen des Ozeans teilzuhaben."

C'est Michael Jantzen qui décrit le mieux son projet, association d'une présence concrète sur la plage et de la sublimation virtuelle de celle-ci : « Il s'agit d'une proposition conceptuelle pour maison de plage de week-end à construire sur une parcelle vide entre deux maisons existantes le long de la Pacific Coast Highway à Malibu. La façade donnant sur la route très animée est plaquée sur toute sa hauteur de minces écrans de télévision au plasma qui créent une interface vidéo avec le monde réel. Ces écrans peuvent afficher des images et des sons de la plage réelle masquée par la maison. Un passage en planches conduit les hôtes vers le mur vidéo qu'ils peuvent franchir par une porte en miroir. L'intérieur de ce mur est en partie recouvert d'une trame de miroirs qui reflète la plage réelle derrière la maison. Certains miroirs sont en fait des écrans de plasma qui peuvent afficher en temps réel des images à taille réelle ou des détails visuel et des sons de l'extérieur. Trois murs de la maison sont en béton structurel. Leur surface est enduite de sable de plage projeté. Cette texture est sableuse, dedans comme dehors, suggère que la maison a pu être formée par la plage, à la manière d'un château de sable d'enfant. Le vrai sable de la plage recouvre également une grande partie des sols et toute la terrasse située au sommet de la maison, autour d'un bassin. La conception de tous les équipements de l'intérieur de la maison qui assurent les fonctions basiques – se baigner, dormir, manger, travailler et se distraire – repose symboliquement sur des images liées à l'environnement balnéaire. Les modules de préparation de la nourriture renvoient aux chariots des vendeurs de plage. Les modules de bain, de toilette, de rangement et de placards suggèrent les cabines de toilettes utilisées sur une plage. La maison dispose de son propre site sur Internet et l'on peut y accéder en temps réel pour, entre autres, partager les vues et les sons de l'océan. »

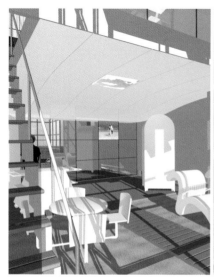  

*Bringing light, water, or even sand into the house, Jantzen conceives of elements such as plasma screens as a part of a dialogue between the "real" environment and its artificial counterpart.*

*Indem er Licht, Wasser und sogar Sand in das Haus integriert, macht Jantzen auch Elemente wie Plasmabildschirme zu einem Teil eines Dialogs zwischen der „realen" Umwelt und ihrem künstlichen Gegenstück.*

*À travers la lumière, l'eau, le sable qu'il introduit dans la maison et des éléments comme les écrans plasma, Jantzen établit un dialogue entre l'environnement « réel » et sa contrepartie artificielle.*

# WES JONES

*Jones, Partners: Architecture*
*141 Nevada Street*
*El Segundo, CA 90245*
*USA*

*Tel: +1 310 414 0761*
*Fax: +1 310 414 0765*
*e-mail: info@jonespartners.com*
*web: www.jonespartners.com*

*Rob Brill Residence* ▶

Wes Jones, born in 1958 in Santa Monica, attended the United States Military Academy at West Point, the University of California at Berkeley (BA) and the Harvard Graduate School of Design where he received a Masters of Architecture degree. A recipient of the Rome Prize in Architecture, he has served as a visiting Professor at Harvard, Rice, Tulane and Columbia Universities. He worked with Eisenman/Robertson, Architects, in New York before becoming Director of Design at Holt Hinshaw Pfau Jones in San Francisco. As partner in charge of design at Holt Hinshaw Pfau Jones, he completed the Astronauts' Memorial at Kennedy Space Center in Florida and the South Campus Chiller Plant for UCLA. Recent projects include the Brill, Stieglitz, Arias-Tsang, and San Clemente residences, Union Square, Golden Plate, San Francisco, and Offices for Andersen Consulting in Kuala Lumpur. Current work includes: Redondo Beach Duplex, private residence, Hollywood; private residence, Mulholland; townhouse, Channel District, Tampa; private compound, Yucca Valley; Editing suites, Venice CA.

Wes Jones, 1958 in Santa Monica geboren, studierte an der United States Military Academy in West Point, der University of California in Berkeley (BA-Abschluss) und an der Harvard Graduate School of Design, wo er den Master of Architecture erwarb. Er erhielt den Prix de Rome in Architektur und war als Gastprofessor an den Universitäten Harvard, Rice, Tulane and Columbia tätig. Wes Jones arbeitete im New Yorker Büro Eisenman/Robertson, Architects, bevor er Director of Design bei Holt Hinshaw Pfau Jones in San Francisco wurde. Als Planungspartner führte er dort das Astronauts' Memorial am Kennedy Space Center in Florida und die Anlage South Campus Chiller Plant für die University of California in Los Angeles (UCLA) aus. Zu seinen jüngsten Projekten gehören die Wohnhäuser Brill, Stieglitz, Arias-Tsang und San Clemente, Union Square, Golden Plate in San Francisco sowie Büros für Andersen Consulting in Kuala Lumpur. Derzeit arbeitet er am Redondo Beach Doppelhaus, Villen in Hollywood und Mulholland sowie Wohnungen und Häusern im Channel District von Tampa, im Yucca Valley und in Venice, Kalifornien.

Wes Jones, né en 1958 à Santa Monica, étudie à l'École militaire de West Point, à l'Université de Californie à Berkeley (B. A.) et à l'Harvard Graduate School of Design dont il est Master of Architecture. Titulaire du prix de Rome d'architecture, il a été professeur invité à Harvard, Rice, Tulane et Columbia. Il a travaillé avec Eisenman/Robertson, architectes à New York, avant de devenir directeur de la conception chez Holt Hinshaw Pfau Jones à San Francisco. Associé en charge de la conception pour eux, il réalise le Mémorial des astronautes au Kennedy Space Center de Floride et l'unité de réfrigération du campus sud de UCLA. Parmi ses récents projets : les maisons Brill, Stieglitz, Arias-Tsang et San Clemente, Union Square/Golden Plate à San, Francisco et des bureaux pour Andersen Consulting à Kuala Lumpur. Il travaille actuellement au projet de Redondo Beach Duplex, une résidence privée à Hollywood, une autre à Mulholland, une maison de ville à Tampa (Channel District) ; un domaine privé dans la Yucca Valley ; les Editing suites à Venice, le tout en Californie.

# ROB BRILL RESIDENCE AND STUDIO

*Silverlake, California, USA, 1998–2000*

*Client: Eric and Nanette Brill. Floor area: 241 m². Costs: $ 300 000.*

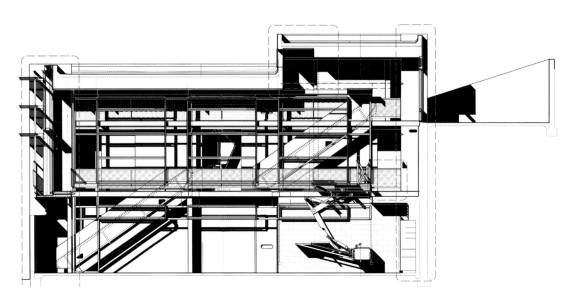

This 241-square-meter residence for a musician is a remodeled martial arts studio located in a fashionable Los Angeles neighborhood. The house was commissioned by Eric and Nanette Brill for Eric's brother Rob Brill. The architect views this as a case study in the efficient use of technology. As he writes, "the difference between using technology as a symbol, and more visibly being technology itself, as an expression arising from within technology rather than one that merely borrows technological form to illustrate some other non-technological interest, is the distinction between the work of Jones, Partners and others who might be considered technologically oriented. Since technology does not admit an author other than nature, the signature architect must make non-or anti-technological adjustments in order to assert authorship." Features he cites to justify this position are the moving gantry, which also serves as a stage for musical performances, and sliding wall panels that serve as acoustic mediators between private and public space. The multiple opaque and translucent wall panels also serve as a flexible division between private and public space. The remodeling was actually more of a reconstruction, because the original structure was "leveled down to the retaining walls," and the "floor separating the studio's workout area from the garage level was removed, creating a three-story living space in one half of the resulting volume, and a stacked tier of private spaces in the other half, above a new garage."

Das 241 m² umfassende Haus für einen Musiker liegt in einer vornehmen Wohngegend von Los Angeles und war vor dem Umbau ein Studio für Kampfsportarten. Es wurde von Eric und Nanette Brill für Eric's Bruder Rob Brill in Auftrag gegeben. Der Architekt betrachtet seinen Entwurf als Fallstudie für die effiziente Nutzung neuer Technologien. Dazu führt er aus: „Der Unterschied zwischen der *Anwendung* von Technologie als Symbol und dem sichtbareren *Sein* von Technologie, als Ausdruck, der von der Technik selbst hervorgebracht wird, anstatt sich technologische Formen nur auszuleihen, um ein anderes, nicht-technologisches Anliegen zu illustrieren, entspricht dem Unterschied zwischen der Arbeit von Jones, Partners und anderen, die man als technologisch orientiert betrachten könnte. Da *Technologie* keinen anderen Urheber zulässt als die Natur, muss der schöpferische Architekt nicht-technologische oder anti-technologische Anpassungen vornehmen, um seine Urheberschaft geltend zu machen." Bauliche Merkmale dieses Wohnhauses sind der bewegliche Stützblock, der auch als Bühne für Konzerte dient, Schiebewände, welche die Räume akustisch verbinden und etliche opake sowie durchscheinende Wandpaneele, welche die privaten von den öffentlichen Räumen des Hauses abgrenzen. Der Umbau war eigentlich mehr ein Wiederaufbau, denn das ursprüngliche Gebäude wurde bis auf die Stützmauern abgerissen.

Cette résidence de 241 m² construite pour un musicien est un studio d'arts martiaux remodelé dans un quartier à la mode de Los Angeles. Il s'agit d'une commande d'Eric et Nanette Brill pour Rob Brill, le frère d'Eric. L'architecte le considère comme une étude sur la mise en œuvre efficace des technologies : « La différence entre *utiliser* une technologie comme symbole, et de façon plus visible *être* la technologie elle-même, comme une expression venue de la technologie même plutôt qu'empruntant tout au plus la forme technologique pour illustrer une quelconque autre intention non technologique, est ce qui distingue le travail de Jones, Partners de celui d'autres praticiens qui se considèrent sensibles à la technologie. Puisque la technologie n'admet pas d'autre auteur que la nature, l'architecte célèbre doit pratiquer des ajustements non- ou anti-technologiques pour affirmer sa signature. » Pour justifier sa position, il cite le pont mobile qui sert aussi de scène à des spectacles musicaux, ou les panneaux de mur coulissants qui font office de médiateurs acoustiques entre les espaces privatifs et de réception. De multiples panneaux opaques et translucides font également fonction de cloisonnements souples entre ces deux zones. La rénovation a surtout pris l'aspect d'une reconstruction, car la structure originale a été « arasée aux murs de soutènement ».

Jones has long been interested in a mechanistic and rather esthetically "harsh" approach to his buildings. This is visible both in the section above and in the images to the right.

Jones hat seit langem einen mechanistischen und ästhetisch „kantig strengen" Zugang zu seinen Gebäuden, was sowohl im Querschnitt als auch auf den Fotos deutlich wird.

Jones s'est longtemps intéressé à une approche mécaniste, esthétiquement assez « brute ». C'est visible à la fois dans la coupe ci-dessus et les images de droite.

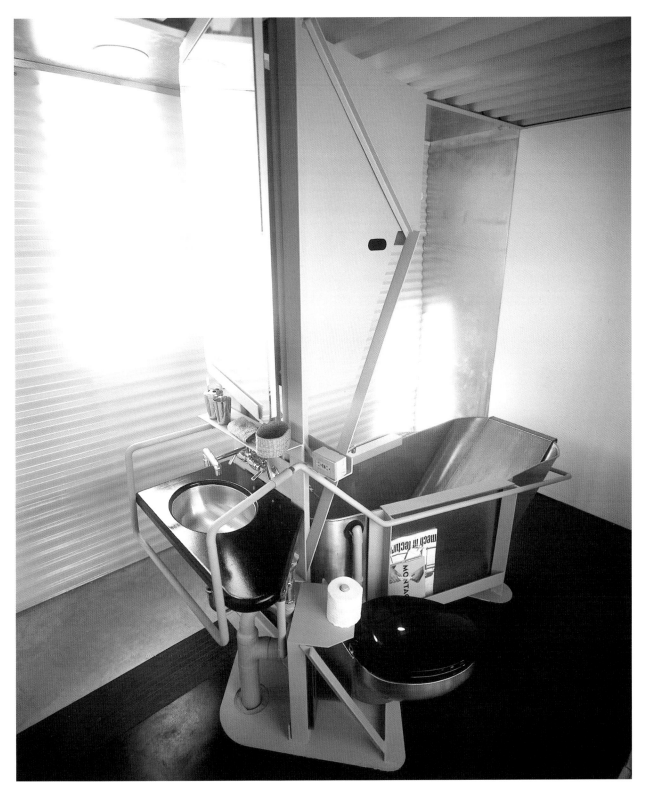

Inspired by industrial space and design, Wes Jones goes so far as to create a bathroom design that looks completely mechanical, almost the opposite of the sleek white lines sought by many architects.

Inspiriert von Industriearchitektur und -design wirkt das Badezimmer nahezu maschinenartig und verkörpert das Gegenteil der eleganten, weißen Linien, nach denen viele Architekten streben.

Inspiré par la conception et les espaces industriels, la salle-de-bains a un aspect entièrement technique, presque à l'opposé de l'approche lisse et des couleurs blanches pratiquées par de nombreux architectes.

# STEPHEN KANNER

*Kanner Architects*
*10924 Le Conte Avenue*
*Los Angeles, CA 90024*
*USA*

*Tel: +1 310 208 0028*
*Fax: +1 310 208 5756*
*e-mail: kanner@kannerarch.com*
*Web: www.kannerarch.com*

Stephen Kanner received his Masters degree in Architecture in 1980 from the University of California at Berkeley. He has been practising architecture since 1980 and has been a licensed architect in the State of California since 1982. Prior to joining Kanner Architects in 1983, he worked for the Cambridge Seven in Boston on the Baltimore Aquarium and the Basketball Hall of Fame projects and subsequently for Skidmore, Owings & Merrill in Los Angeles, where he was one of the project designers on the Texaco Tower in Universal City and the Hughes Headquarters in Marina Del Rey. Kanner, a third-generation Los Angeles architect, worked closely with his father, Charles Kanner, FAIA, (former president of the LA Chapter of the AIA) for 18 years, and they produced more than 150 projects together. He is currently president of Kanner Architects, now in its 56th year of continuous practice. Kanner Architects has worked on numerous projects that encompass commercial and institutional projects, retail, multi-family and single-family homes. Stephen Kanner has been a guest lecturer and critic at several universities. He has also been an organizer and participant in numerous exhibitions such as New Blood 101, 100/100, LA 25 and is the chairman of the new A+D (Architecture + Design) Museum in Los Angeles.

Stephen Kanner erwarb 1980 seinen Master of Architecture an der University of California in Berkeley. Seit diesem Jahr arbeitet er als Architekt und ist seit 1982 im Bundesstaat Kalifornien zugelassen. Bevor er 1983 bei Kanner Architects eintrat, arbeitete er für die Firma Cambridge Seven in Boston am Baltimore Aquarium und an der Basketball Hall of Fame. Anschließend war er für Skidmore, Owings & Merrill in Los Angeles als einer der Projektdesigner beim Bau des Texaco Tower in Universal City und der Hughes Zentrale in Marina Del Rey tätig. Stephen Kanner, Architekt in dritter Generation aus Los Angeles, arbeitete eng mit seinem Vater, Charles Kanner (FAIA), dem ehemaligen Präsidenten des American Institute of Architects, Ortsgruppe LA, zusammen und realisierte in 18 Jahren mehr als 150 Projekte. Stephen Kanner ist Präsident der Firma Kanner Architects, die seit 56 Jahren eine enorme Bandbreite an kommerziellen, institutionellen und privaten Architekturaufträgen ausführt. Daneben ist er Gastdozent und Architekturkritiker an mehreren Universitäten, war Organisator und Teilnehmer an einer Reihe von Ausstellungen wie New Blood 101, 100/100, LA 25. Er ist Vorsitzender des neuen Museums A+D (Architecture + Design) in Los Angeles.

Stephen Kanner est Master of Architecture de l'Université de Californie à Berkeley (1980). Il exerce depuis la même année et reçoit sa licence d'architecte en 1982. Avant de rejoindre Kanner Architects en 1983, il travaille pour The Cambridge Seven (Boston) sur l'aquarium de Baltimore, le projet de Hall of Fame pour le basketball, puis pour Skidmore, Owings & Merrill à Los Angeles. Il est un des concepteurs de la Texaco Tower d'Universal City et du siège de Hughes à Marina del Rey. Il représente la troisième génération d'une famille d'architectes et travaille avec son père, Charles Kanner (FAIA, ancien président du chapitre le Los Angeles de l'AIA) depuis 18 ans. Ils ont réalisé ensemble plus de 150 projets. Il est actuellement président de Kanner Architects, agence qui existe depuis 56 ans et intervient dans les domaines de l'architecture commerciale et institutionnelle, de la distribution et des résidences privées. Stephen Kanner a organisé – ou participé à – de multiples expositions comme New Blood 101, 100/100, LA 25 et préside le nouveau A+D Museum (architecture et design) de Los Angeles.

# SAGAPONAC HOUSE

*Lot N°30, Sagaponac, New York, USA, 2003*

*Client: Coco Brown. Total floor area: 353 m². Costs: $ 950 000.*

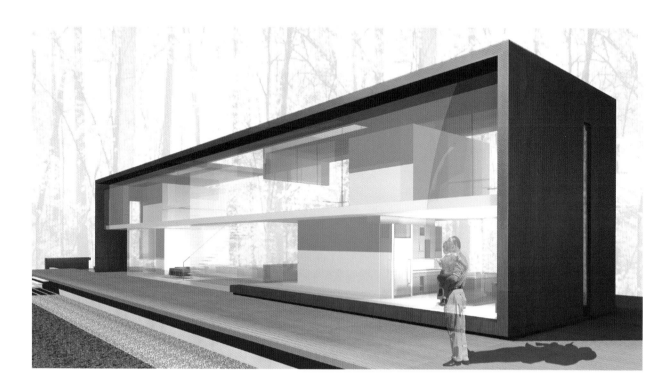

Coco Brown, the president of the Brown Companies, in association with architect Richard Meier, has embarked on a residential development for 34 houses on wooded sites in Southampton. The list of designers retained for the work reads like an international "Who's Who" of contemporary architecture and includes Zaha Hadid, Stephen Holl, MvRdV, Richard Rogers, Shigeru Ban and Jean-Michel Wilmotte. These are single-family residences and are between 200 and 450 square meters in size. Stephen Kanner is building a 353-square-meter 3 bedroom summer house on Lot n° 30 in this development. As he says, "The project's design is intended to be minimalist – almost a mirror of the forest it sits in. If it were to visually disappear, that would be our ultimate goal – a reflection of nature." The architect further explains that a limited budget suggested a simple plan, a 6-meter-wide double rectangle connected by a thin glass hall surrounding a central courtyard. "The narrow width of the rectangular volumes economizes on structural costs due to the repetition of beam and joist sizes," concludes the architect, "while gaining openness and view along both longitudinal elevations." The two-story volume is to be clad in a reddish-orange stained cedar frame, which "pays homage to the spectacular fall colors of New England."

Coco Brown, Präsidentin von Brown Companies, hat in Zusammenarbeit mit dem Architekten Richard Meier ein 34 Häuser umfassendes Wohnsiedlungsprojekt auf einem bewaldeten Grundstück in Southampton initiiert. Die Liste der Gestalter, die für einen Beitrag gewonnen werden konnten, liest sich wie ein „Who's Who" zeitgenössischer Architektur und enthält Namen wie Zaha Hadid, Steven Holl, MvRdV, Richard Rogers, Shigeru Ban oder Jean-Michel Wilmotte. Die Siedlung besteht aus Einfamilienhäusern mit einer Wohnfläche von 200 bis 450 m². Stephen Kanner plant derzeit ein 353 m² großes Sommerhaus mit drei Zimmern, das auf Parzelle Nr. 30 gebaut wird. Er erläutert: „Die Gestaltung des Bauprojekts soll minimalistisch sein – fast wie ein Spiegel des Waldes, in dem es liegt. Wenn es optisch ganz verschwinden würde, hätten wir unser höchstes Ziel erreicht – eine Reflektion der Natur." Der Architekt erklärt weiter, dass das begrenzte Budget einen schlichten Grundriss nahe legte, nämlich zwei gegenüber liegende, jeweils 6 m breite Rechtecke, verbunden durch einen Glaskorridor und einen zentralen Innenhof. Abschließend noch einmal Stephen Kanner: „Durch die geringe Breite der rechteckigen Volumina reduzieren sich zum einen die Baukosten, und zum anderen wird dadurch eine größere Offenheit und Aussichtsqualität entlang der beiden Längsseiten gewonnen. Das zweigeschossige Haus wird durch ein Gestell aus Zedernholz umrahmt, dessen rötlich-orangefarbene Tönung eine Hommage an die spektakulären Herbstfarben von New England sein soll."

Coco Brown, président des Brown Companies, en association avec Richard Meier est à l'origine de ce projet de construction de 34 maisons sur un terrain boisé des environs de Southampton. La liste des architectes appelés fait penser à un *Who's Who* international de l'architecture contemporaine : Zaha Hadid, Steven Holl, MvRdV, Richard Rogers, Shigeru Ban et Jean-Michel Wilmotte. Le projet consiste en résidences de 200 à 450 m² de surface. Stephen Kanner a construit une maison d'été de 353 m² comptant 3 chambres sur la parcelle n° 30 : « La conception de ce projet se veut minimaliste – pratiquement un miroir de la forêt dans laquelle il se trouve. L'objectif ultime serait que la maison disparaisse, comme un reflet de la nature. » L'architecte explique également que les limites du projet poussaient à la simplicité de la solution des doubles rectangles de 6 m de large reliés par un mince mur de verre entourant une cour centrale. « La largeur réduite des volumes rectangulaires permet d'économiser sur les coûts structurels grâce à la répétition des poutres et à la taille des solives », conclut-il, « tout en gagnant en ouverture et en vue sur les deux élévations en longueur. » Le volume sur deux niveaux devrait être habillé de cèdre teinté rouge orange, « en hommage aux spectaculaires couleurs de l'automne en Nouvelle-Angleterre ».

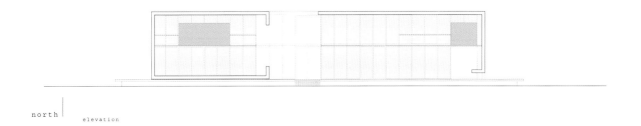

north | elevation

Although actually intended to be built, this design has much of the concept of an "ideal house" a bit like the California Case Study Houses that revealed numerous pioneers of post war Modernism.

Wenngleich zur Realisierung gedacht, hat der Entwurf viel von dem Konzept eines „idealen Hauses", vergleichbar mit den California Case Study Houses, in denen sich zahlreiche Pioniere des Nachkriegsmodernismus offenbarten.

Bien que conçu pour être réalisé, ce projet relève un concept de « maison idéale », un peu comme les Case Study Houses californiennes qui firent connaître de nombreux pionniers du modernisme d'après-guerre.

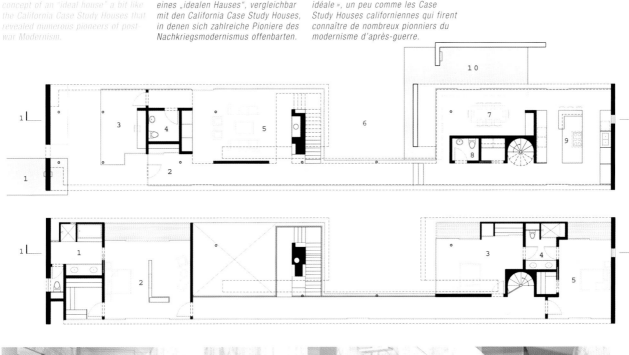

# ANISH KAPOOR

*Marsyas* ▶

Anish Kapoor was born in Bombay in 1954 and has lived and worked in London since the early 1970s. Not an architect, but a sculptor, he studied at the Hornsey College of Art (1973–1977) and the Chelsea School of Art (1977–78), and his first solo exhibition followed in 1980. His early work centered on lightweight materials and bright colors. Subsequent to moving into a ground-floor studio space in the late 1980s, he began to experiment with stone sculpture, but in almost all cases he deals with the ambiguities of perception. As he says, "I don't want to make sculpture about form... I wish to make sculpture about belief, or about passion, about experience that is outside of material concern." His work has been exhibited all over the world and is held in many major international collections. He represented Britain at the XLIV Biennale in Venice and won the Turner Prize in 1991. He has been commissioned to create a large-scale stainless-steel work for Chicago's Millennium Park, scheduled for completion in 2004.

Anish Kapoor, 1954 in Bombay geboren, lebt und arbeitet seit den frühen 1970er Jahren in London. Er ist kein Architekt, sondern Bildhauer, der von 1973 bis 1977 am Hornsey College of Art und von 1977 bis 1978 an der Chelsea School of Art studierte. Seine erste Einzelausstellung hatte er 1980. Seine frühen Arbeiten waren durch die Verwendung leichter Materialien und heller Farben gekennzeichnet. Nachdem er Ende der 1980er Jahre ein geräumiges Erdgeschossatelier bezog, begann er mit Steinskulpturen zu experimentieren. Aber auch hier gilt sein besonderes Interesse der Vieldeutigkeit von Wahrnehmung. Er selbst sagt, dass er keine Skulpturen machen wolle, bei denen es um die Form geht, sondern Skulpturen, die etwas über Glauben oder Leidenschaft, jedenfalls über eine Erfahrung aussagen, die über das Materielle hinaus geht. Seine Arbeiten wurden in der ganzen Welt ausgestellt und sind Teil bedeutender internationaler Sammlungen. 1991 vertrat er Großbritannien auf der Biennale in Venedig und wurde mit dem Turner Prize ausgezeichnet. Derzeit arbeitet er an einer großformatigen Stahlplastik für den Millennium Park in Chicago, die 2004 fertig gestellt sein soll.

Anish Kapoor, né à Bombay en 1954, vit et travaille à Londres depuis le début des années 1970. Sculpteur, et non architecte, il a étudié au Hornsey College of Art (1973–1977) et à la Chelsea School of Art (1977–78). Sa première exposition personnelle s'est tenue en 1980. Ses premières œuvres font appel à des matériaux légers et aux couleurs vives. Après avoir emménagé dans un atelier en rez-de-chaussée, il s'essaye à la sculpture sur pierre, mais continue à s'intéresser aux ambiguités de la perception. « Je ne veux pas faire de la sculpture sur la forme, je veux faire des sculptures sur la croyance, la passion, l'expérience, extérieures à la matérialité. » Ses œuvres ont été exposées dans le monde entier et figurent dans les plus grandes collections. Il a représenté la Grande-Bretagne à la XLIV Biennale de Venise et remporté le Turner Prize en 1991. Il a reçu commande d'une importante pièce en acier inoxydable pour le Millenium Park de Chicago, qui devrait être achevée en 2004.

# MARSYAS

*Turbine Hall, Tate Modern, London, UK, October 9, 2002–April 6, 2003*

*Client: Tate Modern/Unilever. Size: 155 x 23 x 35 m. Costs: not specified.*

After Louise Bourgeois and Juan Muñoz, Anish Kapoor was the third artist to participate in The Unilever Series of commissions for the Turbine Hall at Tate Modern. He was, though, the first to make use of the entire length of Tate Modern's enormous Turbine Hall, which measures 155 meters long, 23 meters wide and 35 meters high. Marsyas was comprised of three steel rings joined by a single span of PVC membrane. The geometry generated by these three rigid steel structures determined the sculpture's overall form, a shift from vertical to horizontal and back to vertical again. As Kapoor stated, "the Turbine Hall at Tate Modern is an enormously difficult space, the great problem is that it demands verticality. This is contrary to every notion about sculpture that I've ever engendered in my work. So I felt that the only way to deal with the vertical is to deal with the full horizontal." The title of the work refers to Marsyas, a satyr in Greek mythology, who was flayed alive by Apollo. Unsurprisingly, Anish Kapoor described the impression he intended with the choice of dark red PVC as being "rather like flayed skin." Because of its large dimensions and positioning, it was impossible to view the entire sculpture from any one vantage point, but the artist succeeded not only in altering the architectural space itself, but in creating a new, almost anti-geometric volume suspended in the void of the Turbine Hall.

Anish Kapoor war nach Louise Bourgeois und Juan Muñoz der dritte Künstler, der an der von Unilever organisierten Serie von Auftragsarbeiten für die Turbinenhalle der Tate Modern teilnahm. Er war jedoch der Erste, der mit seiner Arbeit den gesamten Raum der riesigen Halle in Anspruch nahm. Die Installation mit dem Titel „Marsyas" bestand aus drei Stahlringen, die durch eine durchgehende Haut aus PVC-Folie miteinander verbunden waren. Die Geometrie, die durch die drei feststehenden Stahlringe entstand, bestimmte die Gesamtform der Skulptur, die durch eine Verlagerung vom Vertikalen ins Horizontale und wieder zurück gekennzeichnet war. Dazu Anish Kapoor: „Die Turbinenhalle in der Tate Modern ist ein ungeheuer schwieriger Raum, wobei das größte Problem darin besteht, dass sie Vertikalität verlangt. Und das steht im Widerspruch zu allen Vorstellungen über Skulptur, die ich jemals in meinen Arbeiten zum Ausdruck gebracht habe." Der Titel des Werks bezieht sich auf Marsyas, einen Satyr aus der griechischen Mythologie, der von Apollo bei lebendigem Leib enthäutet wurde. Wenig überraschend sagt Anish Kapoor über die Wirkung, die er mit der Wahl der dunkelroten PVC-Folie erzielen wollte, dass sie einer abgezogenen Haut ähneln sollte. Obwohl die Skulptur wegen ihrer riesigen Dimensionen und ihrer Anordnung im Raum von keinem einzigen Punkt aus zur Gänze überschaubar war, ist es dem Künstler dennoch gelungen, nicht nur den Raum selbst zu verändern, sondern einen neuen, beinahe anti-geometrischen Baukörper durch die Leere der Turbinenhalle schweben zu lassen.

Après Louise Bourgeois et Juan Muñoz, Anish Kapoor a été le troisième artiste à bénéficier d'une commande Unilever pour le Turbine Hall de la Tate Modern. Cependant, il a été le premier à utiliser intégralement cet énorme volume. *Marsyas* était constitué de trois anneaux d'acier entre lesquels était tendue une membrane de PVC. La géométrie issue des rapports de ces éléments rigides déterminait la forme d'ensemble de la sculpture, qui passait de la verticale à l'horizontale pour revenir à la verticale. Comme Kapoor l'explique : « Le Turbine Hall est un espace extrêmement difficile, le grand problème étant qu'il demande une verticalité, ce qui était contraire à toute notion de sculpture rencontrée dans mes travaux jusqu'à présent. » Le titre de l'œuvre renvoie à Marsyas, satyre de la mythologie grecque, qui fut écorché vif par Apollon. Kapoor décrit l'impression recherchée par le choix de PVC rouge sombre comme un effet de « peau d'écorché ». Du fait de ses grandes dimensions et du positionnement de l'œuvre, il était impossible de la voir en totalité d'un seul point de vue. L'artiste a réussi non seulement à modifier le volume architectural, mais à créer un volume presque anti-géométrique suspendu dans le vide de ce hall gigantesque.

Filling the vast space of the Tate Modern Turbine Hall has been a challenge that artists have risen to with varying success. Anish Kapoor managed to reconfigure the space in the image of his own new geometry.

Den riesigen Raum der Turbinenhalle in der Tate Modern haben die beauftragten Künstler mit unterschiedlichem Erfolg ausgefüllt. Anish Kapoor gestaltete den Raum nach dem Bild seiner eigenen, neuen Geometrie um.

Occuper l'énorme espace du hall de la turbine de la Tate Modern est un défi que quelques artistes ont relevé avec un succès varié. Anish Kapoor a réussi à reconfigurer l'espace par une géométrie originale.

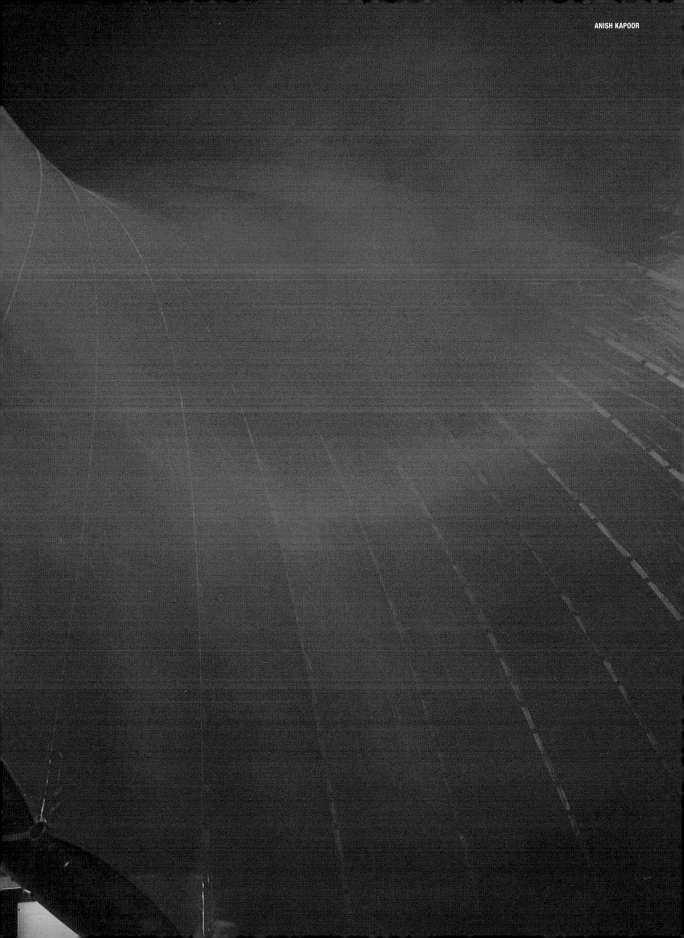

# REM KOOLHAAS/OMA

*Office for Metropolitan Architecture*
*Heer Bokelweg 149*
*3032 AD Rotterdam*
*The Netherlands*

*Tel: +31 10 243 8200*
*Fax: +31 10 243 8202*
*e-mail: office@oma.nl*
*Web: http://www.oma.nl*

Rem Koolhaas was born in Rotterdam in 1944. Before studying at the Architectural Association in London, he tried his hand as a journalist for the Haagse Post and as a screenwriter. He founded the Office for Metropolitan Architecture in London in 1975, and became well known after the 1978 publication of his book *Delirious New York*. OMA is led by four partners: Rem Koolhaas, Ole Scheeren, Ellen van Loon and Joshua Ramus. Their built work includes a group of apartments at Nexus World, Fukuoka (1991), and the Villa dall'Ava, Saint-Cloud (1985–1991). Koolhaas was named head architect of the Euralille project in Lille in 1988, and has worked on a design for the new Jussieu University Library in Paris. His 1400 page book *S,M,L,XL* (Monacelli Press, 1995) has more than fulfilled his promise as an influential writer. He won the 2000 Pritzker Prize and the 2003 Praemium Imperiale Award for architecture. Recent work of OMA includes a house, Bordeaux, France, 1998; the campus center at the Illinois Institute of Technology, published here; the new Dutch Embassy in Berlin; the Guggenheim Las Vegas; and the recent Prada boutique in the Soho area of New York. Current work has included the design of OMA's largest project ever: the 575 000-square-meter Headquarters and Cultural Center for China Central Television (CCTV) in Beijing; the 1 850-seat Porto Concert Hall; and the New City Center for Almere, The Netherlands.

Rem Koolhaas, 1944 in Rotterdam geboren, arbeitete vor seinem Studium an der Architectural Association in London als Journalist für die Haagse Post und als Drehbuchautor. 1975 gründete er in London das Office for Metropolitan Architecture (OMA) und wurde mit seinem 1978 erschienenen Buch *Delirious New York* weithin bekannt. OMA wird von vier Partnern geführt: Rem Koolhaas, Ole Scheeren, Ellen van Loon und Joshua Ramus. Zu ihren Bauten gehören die Villa dall'Ava im französischen Saint-Cloud (1985–1991) und Wohnungen in Nexus World im japanischen Fukuoka (1991). 1988 wurde Rem Koolhaas die Leitung des Euralille-Projekts in Lille übertragen; außerdem erarbeitete er einen Entwurf für die neue Bibliothek der Universität Jussieu in Paris. Mit seinem 1 400 Seiten starken Buch *S,M,L,XL* (Monacelli Press, 1995) hat er seinen Status als einflussreicher Theoretiker und Autor bestätigt. Im Jahr 2000 erhielt Koolhaas den Pritzker Prize und 2003 den Architekturpreis Praemium Imperiale. Zu den neueren Projekten gehören ein Wohnhaus in Bordeaux (1998), das hier vorgestellte Campus-Zentrum des Illinois Institute of Technology, das neue Gebäude für die Niederländische Botschaft in Berlin, das Guggenheim Museum in Las Vegas und die neue Prada Boutique im New Yorker Stadtteil Soho. Zu den derzeitigen Projekten zählen der bislang größte Auftrag für OMA, das 575 000 m² umfassende Verwaltungs- und Kulturgebäude für China Central Television (CCTV) in Peking, der Porto Konzertsaal mit 1 850 Plätzen sowie das neue Citycenter für Almere, Niederlande.

Rem Koolhaas naît à Rotterdam en 1944. Avant d'étudier à l'Architectural Association de Londres, il s'essaye au journalisme pour le *Haagse Post* et à l'écriture de scénarii. Il fonde l'Office for Metropolitan Architecture à Londres en 1975 et devient célèbre par la publication en 1978 de son ouvrage *Delirious New York*. OMA est dirigé par quatre partenaires, Rem Koolhaas, Ole Scheeren, Ellen van Loon et Joshua Ramus. Parmi leurs réalisations : un ensemble d'appartements à Nexus Next World (Fukuoka, Japon, 1991) ; la villa dall'Ava (Saint-Cloud, France, 1985–1991). Koolhaas est nommé architecte en chef du projet Euralille à Lille en 1988 et propose un projet de bibliothèque pour la Faculté de Jussieu à Paris. Son livre de 1400 pages *S,M,L,XL* (Monacelli Press, 1995) confirme son influence et son impact de théoricien. Il a remporté le Pritzker Prize en 2000 et le Praemium Imperiale en 2003. Parmi les réalisations récentes : une maison à Bordeaux (1998), le Campus Center de l'Illinois Institute of Technology, publiée ici, la nouvelle ambassade des Pays-Bas à Berlin, le Guggenheim Las Vegas, et tout récemment, la boutique Prada à Soho, New York. Actuellement son agence travaille sur son plus important projet à ce jour, le siège et centre culturel de la télévision centrale chinoise (CCTV) à Pékin (575 000 m²) ; une salle de concert de 1850 places à Porto et le Nouveau centre-ville d'Almere (Pays-Bas).

# McCORMICK TRIBUNE CAMPUS CENTER

*Illinois Institute of Technology, Chicago, Illinois, USA, 2000–2003*

*Client: Illinois Institute of Technology. Floor area: 10 690 m². Total costs: $ 48 200 000.*

*True to his own concept of urban density, OMA took on this project, which runs a train tube right through a campus building, with an obvious relish.*

*Seinem eigenen Konzept urbaner Dichte treu bleibend, übernahm OMA dieses Projekt, bei dem ein Eisenbahntunnel geradewegs durch ein Campusgebäude verläuft.*

*Fidèle à ses idées sur la densité urbaine, OMA a entrepris avec une satisfaction évidente ce projet qui fait passer les trains dans un tube en plein milieu d'un campus.*

In 1938, the Armour Institute of Technology, a modest technical training school located on the south side of Chicago, hired Ludwig Mies van der Rohe (1886–1969) to take over its architectural program. Two years later, Armour and the Lewis Institute merged to form the Illinois Institute of Technology. Armour's original two-hectare campus could not accommodate the combined schools' requirements and Mies was encouraged to press ahead with plans for a new 50-hectare campus. Following the war, the IIT campus developed at the rate of two buildings a year until 1968. Rem Koolhaas and the Office for Metropolitan Architecture were chosen over Zaha Hadid, Peter Eisenman, the team of Werner Sobek and Helmut Jahn and Kazuyo Sejima to design a new campus center in 1998. One extremely unusual element of the Koolhaas design is a reinforced concrete-supported acoustical tube, encased in corrugated stainless steel and enveloping 160 meters of existing Chicago Transit Authority elevated commuter train track. This tube sits directly above the building's concrete roof, and is designed to significantly reduce train noise and vibration (to about 70 decibels when a train passes through the tube). The other element of the design is the 10 690-square-meter, one-story Campus Center building, housing the IIT Welcome Center, dining facilities, the campus radio station, auditorium and meeting rooms, university bookstore, coffee bar, convenience store, post office and student activity offices. Construction began in July 2000 at a total cost of $48.2 million: $34.6 million for the building and $13.6 million for the tube. The new Campus Center is located between 32nd and 33rd Streets, east of State Street and the Mies van der Rohe Campus, unifying the residential (east) side of the Main Campus with the educational (west) side and integrating key student services and facilities in one structure. Its interior circulation patterns are based on OMA's observation of student movements through the site before construction. As the *Chicago Tribune* pointed out in a very critical article ("Details mar the extraordinary in Koolhaas' IIT campus center," by Blair Kamin, Tribune architecture critic, September 28, 2003) budgetary constraints and difficulties building the overhanging tube delayed completion and made the finished result somewhat less convincing than advertised.

Im Jahr 1938 stellte das Armour Institute of Technology, eine bescheidene technische Lehranstalt im Süden Chicagos, Ludwig Mies van der Rohe (1886–1969) als Leiter der Architekturabteilung ein. Zwei Jahre später fusionierten Armour und Lewis Institute und bildeten gemeinsam das Illinois Institute of Technology. Da der ursprüngliche, 2 ha große Armour Campus den Anforderungen nicht mehr entsprach, wurde van der Rohe mit der Planung eines neuen, 50 ha umfassenden Campus beauftragt. Zwischen 1945 und 1968 wuchs der IIT-Campus um jährlich zwei neue Gebäude. Den 1998 veranstalteten Wettbewerb zur Gestaltung eines neuen Campuskomplexes, an dem unter anderen Zaha Hadid, Peter Eisenman, das Team von Werner Sobek und Helmut Jahn sowie Kazuyo Sejima teilnahmen, gewann Rem Koolhaas mit seinem Office for Metropolitan Architecture. Außergewöhnlichstes Element seines Entwurfs ist eine Röhre aus Stahlbeton mit einer Haut aus geriffeltem Edelstahl, die einen 160 m langen Abschnitt der Chicago Transit Hochbahngleise umgibt. Diese Röhre verläuft direkt über dem Betondach des Campusgebäudes und ist so konzipiert, dass sie den bis zu 70 Dezibel starken Lärm und die Vibrationen der durchfahrenden Züge beträchtlich reduziert. Der andere Teil des Entwurfs besteht aus dem eingeschossigen Gebäude des Campus Centers, das auf einer Nutzfläche von 10 690 m² das IIT Welcome Center, Mensa und Cafeteria, die universitätseigene Radiostation, ein Auditorium, Sitzungsräume, eine Universitätsbuchhandlung, Geschäfte, ein Postamt und Studentenbüros beherbergt. Die Bauarbeiten begannen im Juli 2000, die Kosten betrugen 48,2 Millionen Dollar, wobei 34,6 Millionen auf das Gebäude und 13,6 Millionen auf die Schallschutzröhre entfielen. Das neue Campus Center liegt zwischen der 32nd und 33rd Street, östlich der State Street und dem von Mies van der Rohe angelegten Campus. Es verbindet den östlichen Teil des Hauptcampus, auf dem sich Wohnbauten befinden, mit dem von Unterrichtsgebäuden eingenommenen westlichen Teil sowie wichtige Serviceeinrichtungen für Studenten zu einem Gesamtkomplex. Die Wege und Gänge basieren auf Studien, die OMA vor dem Bau im Hinblick darauf erstellt hatte, wie sich die Studenten auf dem Areal bewegen. Der Architekturkritiker Blair Kamin hat in seinem äußerst kritischen Artikel, der am 28. September 2003 in der *Chicago Tribune* erschien, darauf hingewiesen, dass budgetäre Zwänge und technische Schwierigkeiten bei der Konstruktion der Röhre zu Verzögerungen bei der Fertigstellung führten und das Endresultat dadurch weniger überzeugend ausfiel als erwartet wurde.

En 1938, l'Armour Institute of Technology, modeste école de formation au sud de Chicago, chargea Ludwig Mies van der Rohe (1886–1969) de son programme d'architecture. Deux ans plus tard, l'Armour et le Lewis Institute fusionnèrent pour former l'Illinois Institute of Technology. Les deux hectares de l'Armour ne pouvant accueillir les deux écoles, Mies fut pressé de dessiner les plans d'un nouveau campus de 50 hectares. Après la guerre, celui-ci se développa au rythme de deux bâtiments par an jusqu'en 1968. Rem Koolhaas et son agence, l'Office for Metropolitan Architecture, ont été choisis devant Zaha Hadid, Peter Eisenman, l'équipe de Werner Sobek et Helmut Jahn et Kazuyo Sejima pour créer le nouveau centre du campus en 1998. Un élément extrêmement curieux du projet de Koolhaas est un tube acoustique sur piliers en béton armé, gainé de tôle d'acier inoxydable nervurée et enveloppant sur 160 mètres la voie ferrée surélevée, de la Chicago Transit Authority. Il est directement posé sur le toit de béton du bâtiment et doit réduire de façon importante le bruit et les vibrations des trains (environ 70 décibels). L'autre élément du projet est le bâtiment du Campus Center de 10 690 m², qui abrite le Centre d'accueil de l'IIT, un restaurant, la station de radio du campus, un auditorium, des salles de réunion, la librairie de l'université, un café, une boutique, une poste et des bureaux pour les activités étudiantes. La construction qui a débuté en juillet 2000 a coûté 48,2 millions de dollars : 34,6 millions pour le bâtiment et 13,6 pour le tube. Le nouveau Campus Center est situé entre 32nd et 33rd Streets, à l'est de State Street et du Mies van der Rohe Campus. Il réunit la partie résidentielle (est) du campus principal à la partie d'enseignement (ouest) et intègre les principaux services destinés aux étudiants en une seule structure. Les circulations intérieures ont tenu compte d'une étude sur les déplacements des étudiants réalisée avant la construction. Comme le *Chicago Tribune* l'a fait remarquer dans un article très critique du 28 septembre 2003 (« Des détails gâchent ce qu'il y a d'extraordinaire dans l'IIT Campus Center de Koolhaas », selon Blair Kamin, critique d'architecture du *Chicago Tribune*), les contraintes budgétaires et les difficultés à construire le tube en porte-à-faux ont retardé le chantier et donné un résultat final un peu moins convaincant que ce qui avait été annoncé.

*Much of the IIT building carries the distant echo of Miesian modernism, even if the fact that a train runs through it does create quite a detour from the Modernist legacy of the master of this campus.*

*Ein Großteil des IIT-Gebäudes erinnert von Ferne an den Modernismus eines Mies van Rohe, selbst wenn die Röhre eine beträchtliche Abweichung vom modernistischen Vermächtnis des Baumeisters dieses Campus darstellt.*

*Les bâtiments de l'IIT renvoient encore l'écho distant du modernisme miésien, même si l'irruption du train bouscule le legs du grand maître allemand.*

Die Zusammenstellung von teils har-
ten Materialien und unerwarteten
Blickwinkeln trennt OMA von der
Tradition, die van der Rohe während
seiner Amtsdauer am IIT etabliert hat.

Les assemblages de matériaux parfois bruts et les compositions inattendues différencient OMA de la tradition établie par Mies aux États-Unis
au cours de sa présence au IIT.

The presence of the train tube is marked inside the building as well as outside, recalling the layered complexity that OMA has long espoused, sometimes at the expense of a certain simplicity and directness.

Die Präsenz des Bahntunnels kennzeichnet sowohl das Innere als auch das Äußere des Gebäudes und erinnert an die schichtweise aufgebaute Komplexität, die OMA seit langem präferiert.

La présence du tube est aussi forte vue de l'extérieur que de l'intérieur. Elle rappelle la complexité des strates que OMA a longtemps pratiquées, parfois aux dépens d'une certaine simplicité et franchise.

# KENGO KUMA

*Kengo Kuma & Associates*
*2-24-8 Minami Aoyama*
*Minato-ku*
*Tokyo 107-0062*
*Japan*

*Tel: +81 3 3401 7721*
*Fax: +81 3 3401 7778*
*e-mail: kuma@ba2.so-net.ne.jp*
*Web: www02.so-net.ne.jp/~kuma/*

*Great Bamboo Wall* ▶

Born in 1954 in Kanagawa, Japan, Kengo Kuma graduated in 1979 from the University of Tokyo with a Masters in Architecture. In 1985–86, he received an Asian Cultural Council Fellowship Grant and was a visiting scholar at Columbia University. In 1987 he established the Spatial Design Studio, and in 1991 he created Kengo Kuma & Associates. His work includes: the Gunma Toyota Car Show Room (Maebashi, 1989); Maiton Resort Complex (Phuket, Thailand); Rustic, Office Building, Doric, Office Building; M2, Headquarters for Mazda New Design Team (all in Tokyo 1991); Kinjo Golf Club, Club House (Okayama, 1992); Kiro-san Observatory (Ehime, 1994); Atami Guest House, Guest House for Bandai Corp (Atami, 1992–1995); Karuizawa Resort Hotel (Karuizawa, 1993); Tomioka Lakewood Golf Club House (Tomioka, 1993–1996); Toyoma Noh Theater, (Miyagi, 1995–96); and the Japanese Pavilion for the Venice Biennale (Venice, Italy, 1995). He has recently completed the Stone Museum (Nasu, Tochigi) and a Museum of Ando Hiroshige (Batou, Nasu-gun, Tochigi).

Kengo Kuma, geboren 1954 in Kanagawa, Japan, schloss 1979 sein Studium an der Universität Tokio mit dem Master of Architecture ab. Von 1985 bis 1986 arbeitete er mit einem Stipendium des Asian Cultural Council als Gastwissenschaftler an der Columbia University in New York. 1987 gründete Kuma das Spatial Design Studio und 1991 das Büro Kengo Kuma & Associates in Tokio. Zu seinen Bauten gehören: der Gunma Toyota Car Showroom in Maebashi, Japan (1989), die Ferienanlage Maiton in Phuket, Thailand, die Bürogebäude Rustic und Doric sowie M2, der Hauptsitz für die Designabteilung von Mazda, alle 1991 in Tokio ausgeführt; ferner das Klubhaus des Kinjo Golf Club in Okayama (1992), das Gästehaus für die Firma Bandai Corporation in Atami (1992–1995), ein Hotel in Karuizawa (1993), das Klubhaus des Lakewood Golf Club in Tomioka (1993–1996), das Observatorium Kiro-san in Ehime (1994), der Japanische Pavillon auf der Biennale in Venedig (1995) und das Noh-Theater in Toyama, Miyagi (1995–96). Seine neuesten Projekte sind das Steinmuseum in Nasu, Tochigi, sowie ein Museum für die Werke von Ando Hiroshige in Batou, Nasu-gun, Tochigi.

Né en 1954 à Kanagawa, Japon, Kengo Kuma est Master of Architecture de l'Université de Tokyo (1979). En 1985–86, il bénéficie d'une bourse de l'Asian Cultural Council et est chercheur invité à la Columbia University. En 1987, il crée le Spatial Design Studio, et en 1991 Kengo Kuma & Associates. Parmi ses réalisations : le Car Show Room Toyota de Gunma (Maebashi, 1989) ; le Maiton Resort Complex (Phuket, Thaïlande, 1991) ; le Rustic Office Building (Tokyo, 1991) ; l'immeuble de bureaux Doric (Tokyo, 1991) ; le siège du département de design de Mazda (Tokyo, 1991) ; le Kinjo Golf Club, Club House (Okayama, 1992) ; l'Observatoire Kiro-san (Ehime, Japon, 1994) ; l'Atami Guest House pour Bandaï Corp (Atami, 1992–1995) ; le Karuizawa Resort Hotel (Karuizawa, 1993) ; le Club House du Tomioka Lakewood Golf (Tomioka, 1993–1996) ; le Théâtre Nô Toyoma (Miyagi, 1995–96) et le pavillon japonais de la Biennale de Venise en 1995. Il vient d'achever le Musée de la pierre (Nasu, Tochigi) et le Musée Ando Hiroshige (Batou, Nasu-gun, Tochigi).

# GREAT BAMBOO WALL

*Badaling, China, 2000–2002*

*Client: SOHO China Ltd. Floor area: 528 m². Costs: not specified.*

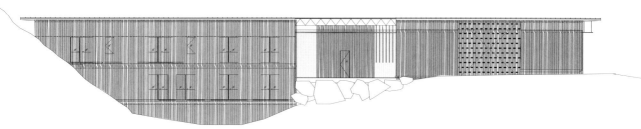

In October 2002, the SOHO (Small Office, Home Office) China group inaugurated the first 11 of 59 planned guest houses located near the Great Wall of China. Created by the young couple Pan Shiyi and his wife Zhang Xin, respectively 39 and 36 years old, SOHO China has called on a number of well-known architects for this project, including Shigeru Ban. Their intention is to make a weekend community mainly for wealthy Chinese clients, and aside from the first 11 villas they have created a 4 000-square-meter club with pools, restaurants, cinemas and art galleries. The cost of the houses ranges from 500 000 to one million euros and they are between 330 and 700 square meters in size. Each house has its own style, or rather that of its architect, though the complex does not give the impression of being a kind of architectural "zoo." The structure designed by Kengo Kuma, called the Great Bamboo Wall, is set on a 1 930-square-meter site and has a total floor area of 528 square meters. Intended as a small hotel unit, it is a reinforced concrete one-story structure (and basement) with a partly steel frame. The partial basement takes advantage of a natural dip in the site under part of the structure. An extensive use of glass and bamboo walls with fairly large openings between each pole and bamboo cladding on pillars gives an impression of lightness and a relationship to the traditional architecture of Asia. Kuma attains a simplicity and a modernity that have more to do with the most recent trends in architecture than with the ancient past, however. As he says about bamboo, "skin and outer surface are different. Concrete has an outer surface, but not skin. On top of that, I don't find concrete to be particularly attractive. That's because without skin, the soul within never appears. Bamboo has particularly beautiful skin. And, bamboo has a soul residing within. In Japan there is a famous children's tale about how 'Princess Kakuyahime,' the Moon Goddess, was born inside a stalk of bamboo. People believed the story that she was born inside a stalk of bamboo because bamboo has a peculiar type of skin and possesses a soul." After this structure, Kuma has undertaken the realization of seven houses in the same project area.

Im Oktober 2002 eröffnete die Firmengruppe SOHO (Small Office, Home Office) China in einem Gebiet nahe der Chinesischen Mauer die ersten elf von insgesamt 59 geplanten Gästehäusern. Das von dem 39-jährigen Pan Shiyi und seiner 36-jährigen Frau Zhang Xin gegründete Unternehmen SOHO China beauftragte eine Reihe bekannter Architekten mit der Planung, darunter auch Shigeru Ban. Die Zielgruppe sind Wochenendgäste, hauptsächlich wohlhabende Chinesen, für die neben den Villen ein 4 000 m² großes Clubareal mit Schwimmbädern, Restaurants und Kunstgalerien angelegt wurde. Die zwischen 330 und 700 m² großen Häuser kosten 500 000 bis eine Million Euro. Zwar hat jedes von ihnen seinen eigenen Stil, oder besser gesagt, den seines Architekten, trotzdem macht die Anlage nicht den Eindruck, als würde hier eine Art „Architektur-Zoo" entstehen. Das von Kengo Kuma entworfene Great-Bamboo-Wall-Gebäude steht auf einem 1 930 m² großen Grundstück und hat eine Nutzfläche von 528 m². Es ist als kleines Hotel gedacht und besteht aus einem eingeschossigen Bauteil aus Stahlbeton mit einem Stahlrahmenteilstück. Der zusätzliche Untergeschossraum ergab sich durch Ausnutzung einer natürlichen Senke, die sich unter einem Teil des Gebäudes befindet. Das Haus selbst vermittelt durch die großzügige Ausstattung mit Glas und Bambus den Eindruck von Leichtigkeit und Nähe zur traditionellen Architektur Asiens. Kuma überzeugt hier jedoch mit einer Schlichtheit und Modernität, die mehr mit den neuesten Architekturtrends als mit der Vergangenheit zu tun haben. Zum Thema Bambus erläutert er: „Es gibt einen Unterschied zwischen Haut und Außenfläche. Beton hat eine Außenfläche, aber keine Haut. Außerdem finde ich Beton nicht besonders attraktiv. Und zwar deshalb, weil ohne Haut die Seele nicht zum Vorschein kommt. Bambus dagegen hat eine besonders schöne Haut. Und Bambus besitzt eine Seele. In Japan gibt es ein berühmtes Kindermärchen, in dem erzählt wird, wie Prinzessin Kakuyahime, die Mondgöttin, aus einem Bambusrohr geboren wurde. Die Menschen glaubten diese Geschichte, eben weil Bambus so eine charakteristische Haut hat und eine Seele besitzt." Nach der Fertigstellung dieses Gebäudes hat Kuma die Planung von weiteren sieben Häusern für dasselbe Projekt übernommen.

En octobre 2002, le SOHO (Small Office, Home Office) China group a inauguré les onze premières maisons d'hôtes sur les 59 qu'il compte édifier près de la Grande muraille de Chine. Créé par un jeune couple, Pan Shiyi et son épouse Zhang Xin, respectivement âgés de 39 et 36 ans, SOHO China a fait appel pour ce projet à un certain nombre d'architectes connus, dont Shigeru Ban. Leur programme est de réaliser des résidences de week-end, principalement destinées à de riches clients chinois. En dehors des onze villas, ils ont déjà créé un club de 4 000 m² comprenant des piscines, des restaurants, des cinémas et des galeries d'art. Le coût des maisons s'élève de 500 000 à 1 million d'euros pour des surfaces de 330 à 700 m². Chacune possède son style propre, ou plutôt celui de son architecte, mais l'ensemble ne donne pas pour autant l'impression de zoo architectural. Le projet de Kengo Kuma, appelé « La grande muraille de bambou » est érigé sur un terrain de 1 930 m² pour 528 m² utiles. Ce petit ensemble hôtelier est une construction en béton armé d'un seul niveau (+ sous-sol) et ossature partiellement en acier. Le sous-sol profite d'un creux naturel du sol. Le recours extensif au verre et aux murs de bambou avec d'assez grandes ouvertures entre chaque pilier de bambou et des espacements marqués entre les lattes du même bois donne une impression de légèreté et rappelle l'architecture traditionnelle de l'Asie. Kuma atteint à une simplicité et une modernité néanmoins plus en rapport avec les tendances récentes de l'architecture qu'avec un passé lointain. Il explique à propos du bambou : « Peau et surface extérieure sont différentes. Le béton possède une surface, pas une peau. De plus, je ne trouve pas le béton particulièrement séduisant. Quand il n'y a pas de peau, l'âme est absente. Le bambou possède précisément une peau magnifique. Et il a une âme en lui. Un célèbre conte japonais pour enfants parle de la Princesse Kakuyahime, déesse de la lune, née dans une âme de bambou. Les gens croient qu'elle est née dans une âme de bambou parce que celui-ci possède une peau particulière et une âme. » Après ce projet, Kuma a entrepris la construction de sept résidences dans la même région.

The Great Bamboo Wall building fits naturally into its site, as can be seen in the elevation on the left and in the photos.

*Das Great-Bamboo-Wall-Gebäude fügt sich harmonisch in seine Umgebung ein, wie im Querschnitt links und in den Fotos zu sehen ist.*

*La maison d'hôtes s'intègre naturellement dans son site, comme le montre l'élévation à gauche, et les photos.*

A light, open structure permits views to the hilly setting and a basin brings an unexpected freshness into the building itself. Though far less durable than the stones of the Great Wall, bamboo is of course a very popular Asian building material.

Eine helle, offene Raumaufteilung ermöglicht Ausblicke auf die umliegende Berglandschaft und bringt eine überraschende Frische in das Gebäude. Wenn auch weit weniger dauerhaft als die Steine der chinesischen Mauer, ist Bambus in Asien ein sehr beliebtes Baumaterial.

La structure légère et ouverte favorise les vues sur le cadre montagneux environnant, tandis qu'un bassin apporte une fraîcheur inattendue dans le bâtiment lui-même. Moins résistant que les pierres de la Grande muraille, le bambou n'en reste pas moins un matériau de construction très populaire en Asie.

The simplicity and directness of the design might reveal the architect's effort to mediate the divide that exists between the architecture of his own country and that of China.

Mit der Einfachheit und Geradlinigkeit des Designs stellte der Architekt eine Verbindung zwischen der Architektur seines eigenen Landes und der Chinas her.

La simplicité et la franchise de conception révèlent cependant un effort pour trouver une voie entre l'architecture de son propre pays et celle de la Chine.

# DANIEL LIBESKIND

*Studio Daniel Libeskind*
*2 Rector Street, 19th Floor*
*New York, NY 10006*
*USA*

*Tel: +1 212 497 9110*
*Fax: +1 646 452 6198*
*e-mail: info@daniel-libeskind.com*
*Web: www.daniel-libeskind.com*

*World Trade Center* ▶

Born in Poland in 1946 and now a US citizen, Daniel Libeskind studied music in Israel and New York before taking up architecture at the Cooper Union in New York. He has taught at Harvard, Yale, Hanover, Graz, Hamburg, and UCLA. His work includes the Jewish Museum in Berlin, which is an extension to the Berlin Museum, 1992–1999; numerous proposals such as his 1997 plan to build an extension to the Victoria & Albert Museum in London; and his prize-winning scheme for the Bremen Philharmonic Hall, 1995. Like Zaha Hadid, Libeskind has had a considerable influence through his theory and his proposals, rather than his limited built work. The Felix Nussbaum Museum in Osnabrück, Germany is in fact one of his first built, completed works. His recent work includes the Imperial War Museum, published here; the Shoah Center in Manchester, England; the Jewish Museum, San Francisco, California; and the JVG University Colleges of Public Administration, Guadalajara, Mexico. Libeskind's victory in the complex competition for the World Trade Center site in Manhattan places him at the forefront of contemporary architecture.

Der amerikanische Architekt Daniel Libeskind wurde 1946 in Polen geboren. Er studierte zunächst Musik in Israel und New York, bevor er an der Cooper Union in New York mit Architektur begann. Er hat in Harvard, Yale, Hannover, Graz, Hamburg und an der UCLA gelehrt. Zu seinen Arbeiten gehören das Jüdische Museum in Berlin, eine Erweiterung des Berlin Museums (1992–1999), zahlreiche Entwürfe wie der zur Erweiterung des Victoria & Albert Museums in London (1997) und der preisgekrönte Wettbewerbsbeitrag für die Philharmonie in Bremen (1995). Wie Zaha Hadid ist Libeskind einflussreicher durch seine Theorien und Entwürfe als durch seine wenigen realisierten Bauten, von denen das Felix Nussbaum Museum in Osnabrück zu den ersten gehört. Zu seinen neuesten Projekten zählen das hier präsentierte Imperial War Museum, das Shoah Center in Manchester, England, das Jewish Museum in San Francisco und die JVG University-Colleges of Public Administration in Guadalajara, Mexiko. Libeskinds Sieg im diffizilen Wettbewerb für die Neugestaltung des World-Trade-Center-Geländes in Manhattan gibt ihm einen Platz in der ersten Reihe der Architekten unserer Zeit.

Né en Pologne en 1946 et aujourd'hui citoyen américain, Daniel Libeskind étudie la musique en Israël et à New York avant de suivre des cours d'architecture à la Cooper Union, à New York. Il a enseigné à Harvard, Yale, Hanovre, Graz, Hambourg et UCLA. Ses réalisations comprennent, entre autres, le musée juif de Berlin, extension du Berlin Museum (1992–1999), et de nombreux projets comme celui de l'extension du Victoria & Albert Museum à Londres et la Philharmonie de Brême qui lui valut un prix en 1995. Comme Zaha Hadid, son influence considérable s'exerce plus à travers son enseignement et ses propositions théoriques que par son œuvre construite relativement limitée. Le Felix Nussbaum Museum à Osnabrück (Allemagne) est en fait l'une de ses premières réalisations. Il a récemment achevé l'Imperial War Museum à Manchester, publié ici, et le Shoah Center, dans la même ville, le Jewish Museum (San Francisco, Californie, USA) et le Collège d'administration publique de l'Université JVG (Guadalajara, Mexique). Sa victoire au concours du World Trade Center à Manhattan l'a placé au premier plan de la scène architecturale contemporaine.

# WORLD TRADE CENTER

*New York, New York, USA, 2003–*

*Client: Lower Manhattan Development Corporation. Office floor area: 900 000 m², retail floor area: 81 750 m². Costs: not specified.*

In the emotionally and politically charged environment of the "Ground Zero" site, Daniel Libeskind has succeeded in creating a consensus around a fragmented design that recalls the violence of the events that marked New York in September 2001.

*In dem emotional und politisch aufgeladenen Umfeld von „Ground Zero" ist es Daniel Libeskind gelungen, die allgemeine Zustimmung zu einem fragmentarischen Design zu erhalten, das an die zerstörerische Gewalt der Ereignisse erinnert, die New York im September 2001 zeichneten.*

*Dans l'environnement politiquement et émotionnellement chargé de Ground Zero, Daniel Libeskind a réussi à créer un consensus autour d'un projet fragmenté qui rappelle la violence des événements dont New York a été victime en septembre 2001.*

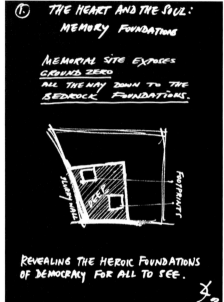

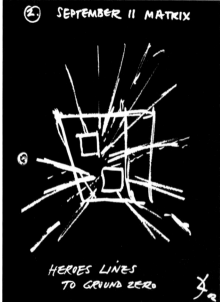

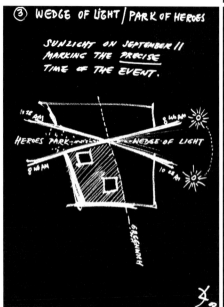

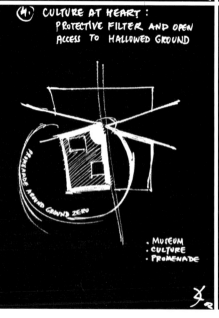

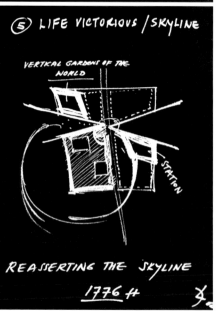

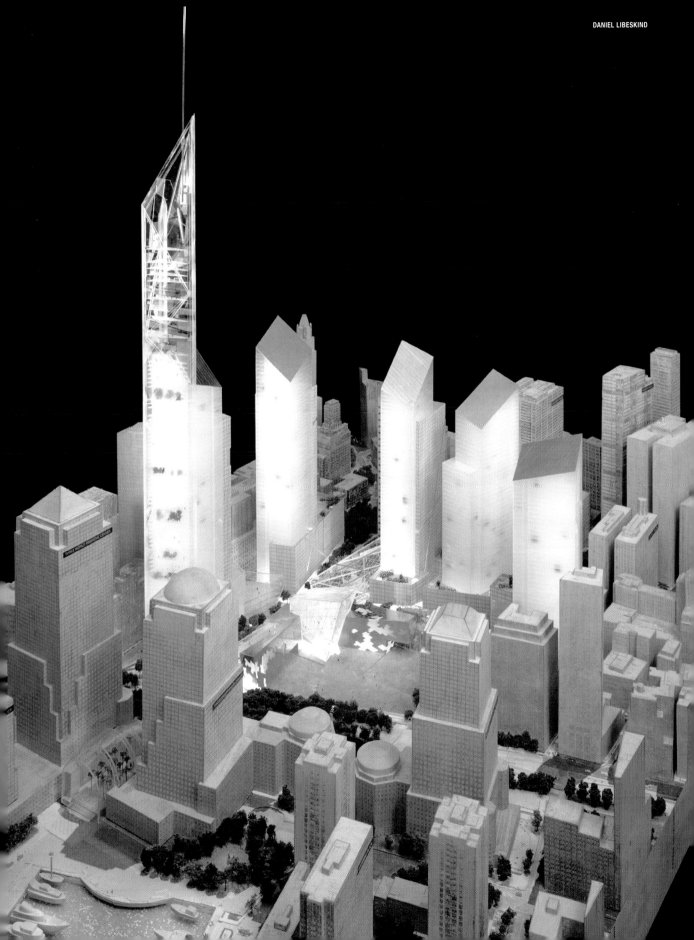

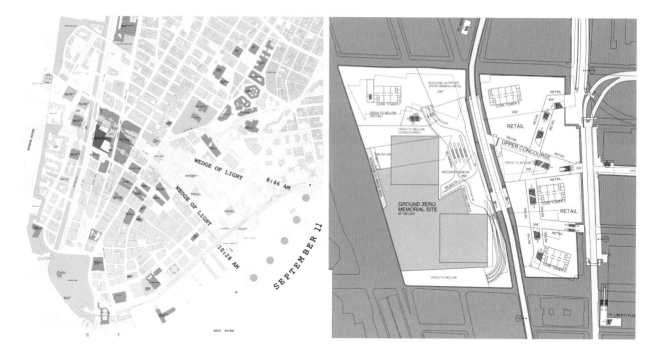

Daniel Libeskind was one of six architectural firms to be invited in December 2002 by the Lower Manhattan Development Corporation (LMDC) to participate in a design study for the World Trade Center site. The seven teams were chosen from 407 submissions by a panel of experts. He won the very highly publicized competition in February 2003 with an unusual combination of features including a 541-meter-high spire and a part of the original World Trade Center foundations left exposed as a memorial to the events of September 11, 2001. The architect stated that, having calculated the arc of the sun, a wedge of natural light would funnel visitors to the memorial site, and that every September 11 between 8:46 a. m., when the first tower was struck by a plane, and 10:28 a. m., when the second tower collapsed, no shadows will be cast by his buildings. The seven-hectare site, which is to be the location for approximately 900 000 square meters of new office space, is the subject of extremely complex negotiations and pressures and comes under the authority of several different organizations. In these circumstances it might be surprising if the original Libeskind plan were to be built as designed; indeed changes began to occur almost immediately after the announcement of the winner. And yet, even Libeskind's competition victory represents a significant step forward for quality architecture in a city that has not always excelled in that area. Then, too, as *The New York Times* wrote in its Editorial on February 28, 2003: "From the moment Daniel Libeskind began to lay out his plan for the World Trade Center site last December, it was clear that the architect had an intuitive feel for the emotional currents swirling around ground zero."

Das Büro von Daniel Libeskind war eine von sechs Architekturfirmen, die im Dezember 2002 von der Lower Manhattan Development Corporation (LMDC) zur Teilnahme an einer Entwurfsstudie für das Areal des ehemaligen World Trade Center eingeladen wurden. Ein Expertengremium hatte diese sieben Architekturteams aus insgesamt 407 Entwürfen ausgewählt. Der anschließende, in den Medien viel beachtete Wettbewerb wurde im Februar 2003 zugunsten von Daniel Libeskind entschieden. Sein Entwurf besteht aus einer ungewöhnlichen Kombination von Elementen, die neben einer 541 m hohen Spirale auch einen Teil des ursprünglichen Fundaments des World Trade Centers einschließt, das als Mahnmal für die Ereignisse vom 11. September 2001 sichtbar bleiben soll. Der Architekt erklärte, seinen Berechnungen nach wandere die Sonne so, dass ein natürlicher Lichtkeil die Besucher wie ein Wegweiser zu der Erinnerungsstätte geleiten würde. Außerdem würden an jedem 11. September zwischen 8:46 Uhr, als der erste Turm durch ein Flugzeug getroffen wurde, und 10:28 Uhr, als der zweite Turm einstürzte, keine Schatten von den umliegenden Gebäuden auf diese Stelle fallen. Das 7 ha große Areal, auf dem neue Bürogebäude mit einer Nutzfläche von circa 900 000 m² errichtet werden sollen, ist Gegenstand äußerst komplizierter Verhandlungen, da es von mehreren Behörden und Organisationen verwaltet wird. Unter diesen Umständen wäre es fast eine Überraschung, wenn der Entwurf von Libeskind so realisiert würde wie ursprünglich geplant. Tatsächlich sind praktisch unmittelbar nach Bekanntgabe des Wettbewerbssiegers erste Veränderungen an seinem Konzept vorgenommen worden. Dennoch ist bereits die Auswahl von Libeskind ein wichtiger Fortschritt für die Sache einer qualitätsbewussten Architektur, besonders in einer Stadt, die auf diesem Gebiet nicht immer mit hervorragenden Leistungen geglänzt hat. Oder, wie es im Leitartikel der *New York Times* vom 28. Februar 2003 hieß: „Ab dem Moment, an dem Daniel Libeskind im Dezember letzten Jahres erstmals seine Pläne für das World Trade Center Areal präsentierte, war klar, dass dieser Architekt ein intuitives Gespür für die emotionalen Strömungen hat, die sich um Ground Zero drehen."

Daniel Libeskind faisait partie des six agences invitées en décembre 2002 par la Lower Manhattan Development Corporation (LMDC) à participer à l'étude de conception pour le site du World Trade Center. Les sept équipes avaient été choisies parmi 407 candidatures par un jury d'experts. L'architecte a remporté ce concours hautement médiatisé en février 2003, grâce à un projet combinant des éléments très divers comme une flèche de 541 m de haut ou la mise à découvert des fondations des anciennes tours en souvenir des événements de 2001. Libeskind a expliqué qu'il avait calculé le mouvement du soleil pour qu'un faisceau de lumière naturelle guide les visiteurs vers le mémorial. Chaque 11 septembre entre 8 h 46, heure du premier attentat, et 10 h 28, l'heure d'effondrement de la seconde tour, aucune ombre ne sera projetée par les nouveaux bâtiments. Le site de 7 hectares, sur lequel devraient s'élever environ 900 000 m² de bureaux, objet de négociations complexes et de fortes pressions, est placé sous l'autorité de plusieurs organismes. Dans ces circonstances, il serait surprenant que le plan de Libeskind soit exécuté comme prévu et des changements ont d'ailleurs été apportés presque immédiatement après l'annonce des résultats du concours. La victoire de l'architecte représente néanmoins une avancée significative pour la qualité de l'architecture dans une ville qui n'a pas toujours excellé dans ce domaine. Comme l'a également noté le *New York Times* dans son éditorial du 28 février 2003 : « Dès ses premiers plans pour le site du World Trade Center en décembre dernier, il était clair que Daniel Libeskind ressentait intuitivement les flux d'émotions qui enveloppent *Ground Zero*. »

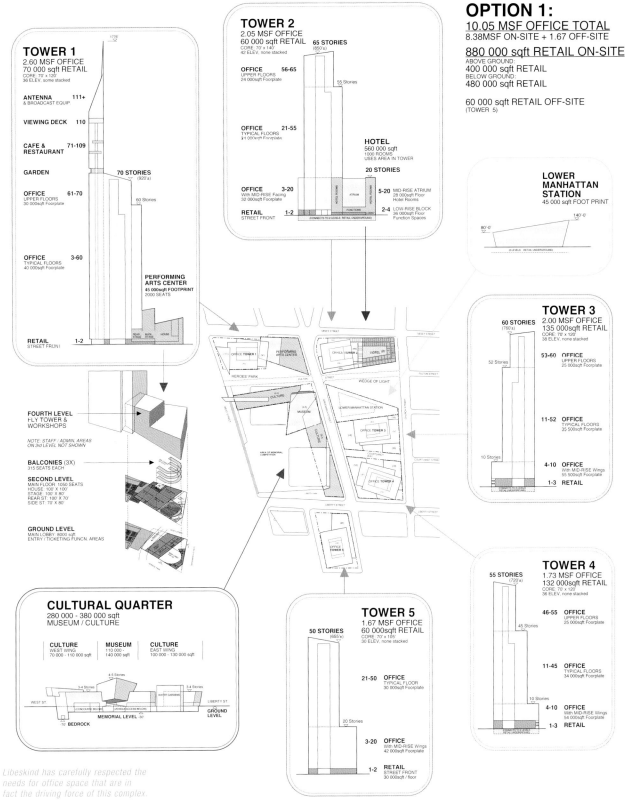

## OPTION 1:
### 10.05 MSF OFFICE TOTAL
8.38MSF ON-SITE + 1.67 OFF-SITE

### 880 000 sqft RETAIL ON-SITE
ABOVE GROUND:
400 000 sqft RETAIL
BELOW GROUND:
480 000 sqft RETAIL

60 000 sqft RETAIL OFF-SITE
(TOWER 5)

## TOWER 1
2.60 MSF OFFICE
70 000 sqft RETAIL
CORE: 70' x 120'
36 ELEV, some stacked

1776'

ANTENNA    111+
& BROADCAST EQUIP.

VIEWING DECK    110

CAFE &    71-109
RESTAURANT

GARDEN

70 STORIES
(920'±)

OFFICE    61-70
UPPER FLOORS
30 000sqft Floorplate

60 Stories

OFFICE    3-60
TYPICAL FLOORS
40 000sqft Floorplate

PERFORMING
ARTS CENTER
45 000sqft FOOTPRINT
2000 SEATS

REAR / MAIN / HOUSE
STAGE

RETAIL    1-2
STREET FRONT

FOURTH LEVEL
FLY TOWER &
WORKSHOPS

NOTE: STAFF / ADMIN. AREAS
ON 3rd LEVEL NOT SHOWN

BALCONIES (3X)
315 SEATS EACH

SECOND LEVEL
MAIN FLOOR: 1050 SEATS
HOUSE: 100' X 100'
STAGE: 100' X 80'
REAR ST: 100' X 70'
SIDE ST: 70' X 80'

GROUND LEVEL
MAIN LOBBY: 8000 sqft
ENTRY / TICKETING FUNCN. AREAS

## TOWER 2
2.05 MSF OFFICE
60 000 sqft RETAIL
CORE: 70' x 140'
42 ELEV, none stacked

65 STORIES
(850'±)

55 Stories

OFFICE
UPPER FLOORS    56-65
24 000sqft Floorplate

OFFICE    21-55
TYPICAL FLOORS
24 000sqft Floorplate

HOTEL
560 000 sqft
1000 ROOMS
USES AREA IN TOWER

20 STORIES

OFFICE    3-20
With MID-RISE Facing
32 000sqft Floorplate

5-20    MID-RISE ATRIUM
28 000sqft Floor
Hotel Rooms

HOTEL ROOMS   ATRIUM   HOTEL ROOMS

RETAIL    1-2
STREET FRONT

2-4    LOW-RISE BLOCK
36 000sqft Floor
Function Spaces

FUNCTIONS
(CONNECTS TO 2 LEVELS RETAIL UNDERGROUND)

## LOWER MANHATTAN STATION
45 000 sqft FOOT PRINT

80'-0"
140'-0"

(2 LEVELS RETAIL UNDERGROUND)

## TOWER 3
2.00 MSF OFFICE
135 000sqft RETAIL
CORE: 70' x 120'
38 ELEV, none stacked

60 STORIES
(760'±)

52 Stories

OFFICE    53-60
UPPER FLOORS
25 000sqft Floorplate

OFFICE    11-52
TYPICAL FLOORS
35 500sqft Floorplate

10 Stories

OFFICE    4-10
With MID-RISE Wings
55 500sqft Floorplate

RETAIL    1-3
(CONNECTS TO 2 LEVELS RETAIL UNDERGROUND)

## TOWER 4
1.73 MSF OFFICE
132 000sqft RETAIL
CORE: 70' x 120'
36 ELEV, none stacked

55 STORIES
(720'±)

OFFICE    46-55
UPPER FLOORS
25 000sqft Floorplate

45 Stories

OFFICE    11-45
TYPICAL FLOORS
34 000sqft Floorplate

10 Stories

OFFICE    4-10
With MID-RISE Wings
54 000sqft Floorplate

RETAIL    1-3
(CONNECTS TO 2 LEVELS RETAIL UNDERGROUND)

## CULTURAL QUARTER
280 000 - 380 000 sqft
MUSEUM / CULTURE

CULTURE
WEST WING
70 000 - 110 000 sqft

MUSEUM
110 000 -
140 000 sqft

CULTURE
EAST WING
100 000 - 130 000 sqft

4-5 Stories
3-4 Stories
3-4 Stories

WEST ST
WATER GARDENS
LIBERTY ST

(CONCOURSE BELOW) (VEHICLE ACCESS BELOW)
GROUND LEVEL

MEMORIAL LEVEL -30'

-70' BEDROCK

## TOWER 5
1.67 MSF OFFICE
60 000sqft RETAIL
CORE: 70' x 105'
30 ELEV, none stacked

50 STORIES
(655'±)

OFFICE    21-50
TYPICAL FLOOR
30 000sqft Floorplate

20 Stories

OFFICE    3-20
With MID-RISE Wings
42 000sqft Floorplate

RETAIL    1-2
STREET FRONT
30 000sqft / floor

*Libeskind has carefully respected the
needs for office space that are in
fact the driving force of this complex.*

*Libeskind hat sorgfältig den Bedarf
nach Büroraum berücksichtigt, in der
Tat die treibende Kraft für diesen
Komplex.*

*Libeskind a tenu compte des besoins
en surfaces de bureaux, qui constituent en fait la source de finance-
ment de ce projet.*

*Although the plans have evolved even since these drawings were made, a central garden marks the location of the original World Trade Center towers, and serves as a place for remembering the victims.*

*Auch wenn sich die Grundrisse seit Entstehung dieser Zeichnung weiterentwickelt haben, markiert ein zentraler Garten den Standort der ursprünglichen Twin Towers und dient als ein Ort zum Gedenken an die Opfer.*

*Bien que les plans aient évolué depuis ces premiers dessins, un jardin central marquera le site des premières tours du World Trade Center, et fera fonction de lieu de souvenir.*

The original World Trade Center made little if any space for parks. In Libeskind's, the heart of the complex has become green, even though he did originally propose a more mineral or brutal solution for this space.

Das ehemalige World Trade Center ließ nur wenig Raum für Parkanlagen. In Libeskinds Version hat die Anlage ein grünes Herz bekommen, obwohl er selbst ursprünglich eine anorganischere oder schroffere Raumlösung vorgeschlagen hatte.

L'ancien World Trade Center ne laissait pas beaucoup de place aux espaces verts. Dans le projet Libeskind, le cœur du complexe est végétal, même si l'architecte avait utilisé au départ une solution plus minérale, ou brutale.

The architect has imagined a convivial and active space for commerce and movement of vast numbers of people.

Der Architekt hat einen Raum für den Geschäfts- und Besucher-verkehr einer riesigen Anzahl von Menschen ersonnen.

Pour le commerce, l'architecte a imaginé un espace actif et convivial qui tient compte des déplacements d'un très grand nombre d'usagers.

Despite the acceptance of his overall project, Libeskind will not be responsible for every building in the complex and some of the fragmented appearance of his designs will surely give way to more pedestrian architecture.

Trotz der Akzeptanz für sein Gesamtprojekt wird Libeskind nicht für jedes Gebäude der Anlage verantwortlich sein, und der bruchstückhafte Charakter seines Designs wird sicher teilweise einer prosaischeren Architektur Platz machen.

Si son projet d'ensemble a été accepté, Libeskind n'est pas responsable de la totalité des immeubles que comptera le complexe, et certains aspects fragmentés de ses plans laisseront sans doute place à une architecture mieux adaptée aux piétons.

# IMPERIAL WAR MUSEUM NORTH

### Manchester, UK, 2000–2002

Client: The Trustees of the Imperial War Museum, London. Total floor area: 6 500 m². Costs: £ 15 600 000.

The Imperial War Museum was established by an Act of Parliament in 1920. Its purpose is to collect, preserve and display material and information connected with military operations in which Britain or the Commonwealth have been involved since August 1914. With four branches in the South-East, the Imperial War Museum had wanted for some time to offer the population in the north access to its exceptionally rich collections of films, photographs, art, documents, objects, and services. The aluminum-clad building, Daniel Libeskind's first structure in the UK, is based on the concept of a world shattered by conflict, a fragmented globe reassembled in three interlocking shards. These shards represent conflict on land, in the air and on water. Visitors enter through the Air Shard, which is 55 meters high and open to the elements. It houses a viewing platform at 29 meters with views across the Manchester Ship Canal toward the city center. The Earth Shard is curved and houses the main public areas of the Museum, exhibition space and the special exhibitions gallery. The Water Shard, overlooking the Manchester Ship Canal, accommodates a 160-seat restaurant. In his project text, the architect writes, "Paul Valéry pointed out the world is permanently threatened by two dangers: order and disorder. This project develops the realm of the in between, the inter-est, the realm of democratic openness, plurality and potential. By navigating the course between rigid totalities on one hand, and the chaos of events on the other, this building reflects an evolving identity open to profound public participation, access and education. The Museum is therefore a catalyst for focussing energies, both entrepreneurial and spiritual, and moulding them into a creative expression."

Das Imperial War Museum wurde 1920 gegründet. Seine Aufgabe ist es, Material und Informationen über Militäroperationen, in die Großbritannien oder das Commonwealth seit August 1914 involviert waren, zu sammeln, zu konservieren und auszustellen. Die Verantwortlichen des Museums, das mit vier Außenstellen im Südosten von England vertreten war, wollten schon seit längerem, dass auch die Bevölkerung im Norden des Landes Zugang zu seinen äußerst umfangreichen Sammlungen von Filmen, Fotos, Kunstwerken, Dokumenten, Objekten und Dienstleistungen erhält, und beauftragte Daniel Libeskind mit diesem Projekt. Libeskind hat sein erstes in Großbritannien realisiertes Gebäude mit Aluminium verkleidet. Es basiert auf dem bildhaften Gestaltungskonzept einer durch Konflikte in Trümmer gegangenen Welt, einer fragmentierten Erdkugel, die in drei Bruchstücken, die sich gegenseitig durchdringen, wieder zusammenfindet. Diese Bruchstücke repräsentieren den bewaffneten Konflikt zu Land, in der Luft und auf See. Der Eintritt ins Museum erfolgt durch den 55 m hohen, offenen Luft-Teil, der in 29 m Höhe mit einer Aussichtsplattform ausgestattet ist. Im gewölbten Baukörper, der die Erde symbolisiert, sind die öffentlichen Bereiche des Museums mit den Räumen für die permanente und die Sonderausstellungen untergebracht, während der wiederum den Kanal überblickende Wasser-Teil ein Restaurant mit 160 Plätzen beherbergt. In seiner Projektbeschreibung erklärt Libeskind: „Paul Valéry hat einmal bemerkt, dass die Welt ständig von zwei Gefahren bedroht sei: Ordnung und Unordnung. Dieses Projekt entwickelt das Reich, das dazwischen liegt, das inter-est, das Reich der demokratischen Offenheit, der Pluralität und des Potentials. Indem es den Kurs hält zwischen starrer Totalität auf der einen Seite und dem Chaos der Ereignisse auf der anderen Seite, entfaltet dieses Gebäude eine Identität, die offen ist für die Beteiligung der Öffentlichkeit."

L'Imperial War Museum a été créé par un acte du Parlement de 1920. Son objectif est de réunir, préserver et exposer les matériaux et informations liés aux opérations militaires auxquelles ont participé la Grande-Bretagne et le Commonwealth depuis août 1914. Disposant de quatre installations dans le Sud-Est de l'Angleterre, le musée voulait depuis un certain temps offrir aux populations du nord un accès à ses collections exceptionnellement riches en films, photographies, œuvres d'art, documents, objets et à ses services. Première réalisation de Daniel Libeskind au Royaume-Uni, le bâtiment habillé d'aluminium repose sur un concept de monde bouleversé par les conflits, que traduit la forme d'un globe éclaté en trois fragments imbriqués. Ils représentent les conflits sur terre, dans l'air et sur mer. Les visiteurs pénètrent dans l'« Air Shard », de 55 m de haut, ouvert sur le ciel, qui abrite un belvédère à 29 m de haut donnant sur le Ship Canal de Manchester et le centre-ville. Le « Earth Shard » incurvé accueille les principales zones ouvertes au public, un espace d'exposition et la galerie des expositions spéciales. Le « Water Shard », au-dessus du canal, contient un restaurant de 160 couverts. Dans sa présentation du projet, l'architecte écrivait : « Paul Valéry a fait remarquer que le monde est en permanence menacé par deux dangers : l'ordre et le désordre. Ce projet développe le domaine de l'entre-deux, le inter est, celui de l'ouverture démocratique, la pluralité et le potentiel. En navigant entre des entités rigides d'un côté et le chaos des événements de l'autre, ce bâtiment reflète une identité en évolution, ouverte à la participation, à l'accès et à l'éducation approfondie du public. Le musée est ainsi un catalyseur qui concentre les énergies à la fois spirituelles et d'esprit d'entreprise pour en faire une expression créative. »

Though less abruptly fragmented than
many of Libeskind's other designs,
the Imperial War Museum nonetheless does evoke the ferocity of war.

Wenn auch auf weniger schroffe
Weise fragmentarisch als viele
andere Entwürfe von Libeskind,
evoziert das Imperial War Museum
dennoch die Grausamkeit von Krieg.

Bien que moins abruptement fragmenté que beaucoup d'autres projets
de Libeskind, le Imperial War
Museum évoque à sa façon la
férocité de la guerre.

The metal-sheathed forms of the
Museum appear sculptural, in a
sometimes ominous way. This is certainly not a tribute to war as some
military people might imagine it.

Die mit Metall ummantelten, skulpturalen Formen des Museums wirken
manchmal bedrohlich. Das ist keines-
falls als Tribut an den Krieg zu verstehen, wie einige Militärbegeisterte
vielleicht meinen könnten.

Les formes gainées de métal du
Musée sont d'un caractère sculptural
parfois inquiétant. Il ne s'agit certainement pas d'une ode à la guerre
telle que certains militaires auraient
pu l'imaginer.

Overhanging forms and sweeping
curves characterize the design in
a flux of movement, where cutting
edges are more common than
soothing esthetics.

Überhängende Formen und Bogenlinien sind kennzeichnend für die
Dynamik der Gestaltung, die sich
mehr durch Kanten als eine glättende
Ästhetik auszeichnet.

Les formes suspendues et les courbes
généreuses créent des flux de mouvements, d'une esthétique plus abrupte
et agressive qu'apaisante.

As he did in the Jewish Museum in Berlin, Libeskind shows a mastery here of the evocative power of color and lighting.

Wie in seinem Jüdischen Museum in Berlin demonstriert Libeskind auch hier seine Meisterschaft im Umgang mit Farbe und Licht.

Comme pour le Musée juif de Berlin, Libeskind témoigne ici d'une maîtrise de la puissance évocatrice de la couleur et de l'éclairage.

Angled walls and interrupted lines of light seem to imply that there is no clear way forward in conflict.

Schräge Wände und unterbrochene Lichtstreifen deuten auf Konflikte ohne klaren Ausweg.

Les murs inclinés et les traits de lumière interrompus semblent impliquer qu'il n'existe pas d'issue claire aux conflits.

À somber atmosphere assures that that the architect does not participate here in a glorification of war, but in an explanation.

Die düstere Atmosphäre macht deutlich, dass es dem Architekten hier nicht um eine Glorifizierung von Krieg, sondern um eine Erklärung geht.

L'atmosphère sombre montre que l'architecte ne participe pas à une quelconque glorification de la guerre mais à son explication.

Streaks of light and vehicles and aircraft hanging at odd angles have more to do with the effects of explosion than of any ordered march to victory.

Die Zickzacklinien der Lichtstreifen und die aufgehängten Luft- und anderen Fahrzeuge implizieren eher Auswirkungen einer Explosion als einen geordneten Marsch zum Sieg.

Des éclairs lumineux, des véhicules et des avions suspendus selon des angles étranges évoquent davantage les effets d'une explosion qu'une marche victorieuse.

# GREG LYNN FORM

*Greg Lynn FORM*
*1817 Lincoln Boulevard*
*Venice, CA 90291*
*USA*

*Tel: +1 310 821 2629*
*Fax: +1 310 821 9729*
*e-mail: node@glform.com*
*Web: www.glform.com*

Greg Lynn was born in 1964. He received his Bachelor of Philosophy and Bachelor of Environmental Design from Miami University of Ohio, (1986), and his Master of Architecture from Princeton University (1988). He worked in the offices of Antoine Predock (1987) and Peter Eisenman (1987–1991) before creating his present firm, FORM, in 1994. He has worked on the Ark of the World Museum and Interpretive Center (Costa Rica, 1999) and the New York Korean Presbyterian Church (Long Island City, New York, 1997–1999) with Garofalo Architects and Michael McInturf. Recent work includes: Expanding the Gap, Rendel + Spitz Gallery (Cologne, Germany, January 2002); Predator: Exhibition with Fabian Marcaccio (Wexner Center for the Arts, Columbus, OH); Imaginary Forces Exhibition Design (Wexner Center for the Arts, Columbus, OH, January 2001); Visionaire Case Design (6 250 custom cases for Visionaire magazine, 2000); PGLife.com Showroom, Stockholm, Sweden, designed in collaboration with Dynamo Sthlm (Stockholm, 2000); and the Cincinnati Country Day School (Cincinnati, OH, designed in collaboration with Michael McInturf Architects, Cincinnati, and GBBN Architects, Cincinnati (1998–2000). Ongoing projects include: Transformation of Kleiburg (Bijlmermeer, Amsterdam, The Netherlands, 500 units of housing, urban planning and design, commenced November 2000, expected completion in 2005); Uniserve Corporation Headquarters (Los Angeles, CA, designed in collaboration with House and Robertson Architects, Inc.); and Imaginary Forces New York Offices (designed in collaboration with Open Office Architects).

Greg Lynn, 1964 geboren, erwarb 1986 den Bachelor of Philosophy und den Bachelor of Environmental Design an der Miami University of Ohio und 1988 den Master of Architecture an der Princeton University. 1987 arbeitete er im Büro von Antoine Predock und von 1987 bis 1991 bei Peter Eisenman, bevor er 1994 seine eigene Firma namens FORM gründete. Zu seinen Projekten gehören die in Zusammenarbeit mit Garofalo Architects und Michael McInturf entstandene New York Korean Pres-byterian Church in Long Island City, New York (1997–1999) sowie das Ark of the World Museum und Interpretive Center in Costa Rica (1999). Zu seinen neuesten Arbei-ten zählen: die mit Michael McInturf Architects und GBBN Architects (beide in Cincinnati) geplante Cincinnati Country Day School in Cincinnati, Ohio (1998–2000), das Design für „Visionaire Case", 6 250 Etuis für Kunden von Visionaire magazine (2000), der in Zusammenarbeit mit Dynamo Sthlm (Dynamo Stockholm) gestaltete Sho-wroom für PGLife.com in Stockholm (2000), die mit Fabian Marcaccio gestaltete Ausstellung „Predator" und die Ausstellung „Imaginary Forces" (Januar 2001), beide am Wexner Center for the Arts in Columbus, Ohio, sowie Expanding the Gap, Galerie Rendel + Spitz in Köln (Januar 2002). Zu den aktuellen Projekten von Greg Lynn gehören: „Transformation of Kleiburg" in Bijlmermeer, Amsterdam, ein Projekt, das 500 Wohnungen sowie städtebauliche Planungen umfasst (2000–2005); ferner die Zentrale der Uniserve Corporation in Los Angeles (in Zusammenarbeit mit House and Robertson Architects, Inc.) sowie die New Yorker Büros Imaginary Forces (in Zusammenarbeit mit Open Office Architects).

Greg Lynn, né en 1964, est Bachelor de philosophie et de design environnemental de l'University of Ohio (1986) et Master of Architecture de la Princeton University (1988). Il travaille dans les agences d'Antoine Predock (1987) et Peter Eisenman (1987–1991) avant de créer FORM en 1994. Il est intervenu sur l'Ark of the World Museum and Interpretive Center (Costa Rica, 1999) ; la New York Korean Presbyterian Church (Long Island City, New York, 1997–1999) avec Garofalo Architects et Michael McInturf. Parmi ses interventions récentes : Expanding the Gap, Rendel + Spitz Gallery (Cologne, Allemagne, janvier 2002) ; Predator : une exposition avec Fabian Marcaccio (Wexner Center for the Arts, Columbus, Ohio, USA) ; Imaginary Forces, conception d'exposition Exhibition Design (Wexner Center for the Arts, Columbus, Ohio, janvier 2001) ; Visionaire Case Design (6 250 cas d'étude pour le magazine Visionaire, 2000) ; showroom de PGLife.com, en collaboration avec Dynamo Sthlm (Stockholm, Suède, 2000) et la Cincinnati Country Day School (Cincinnati, Ohio, USA, conçue en collaboration avec Michael McInturf Architects (Cincinnati) et GBBN Architects (Cincinnati), (1998–2000). Projets en cours : transformation de Kleiburg (Bijlmermeer, Amsterdam, Pays-Bas, projet de 500 logements, urbanisme et concep-tion, lancé en novembre 2000, et qui devrait être achevé en 2005) ; siège de Uniserve Corporation (Los Angeles, Californie, USA, conçu en collaboration avec House et Robertson Architects, Inc. ; bureaux de Imaginary Forces à New York Offices (conçus en collaboration avec Open Office Architects).

# ARK OF THE WORLD MUSEUM

*San Jose, Costa Rica, 2002–*

*Client: The President of Costa Rica/Minister of Agriculture and Livestock. Project area: 7200 m². Costs: not specified.*

*Intended as a tribute to ecological diversity, the Ark of the World has an obviously biological inspiration in its forms and even its colors.*

*Als Tribut an die ökologische Vielfalt ist das Gebäude Ark of the World sowohl in seinen Formen als auch Farben offensichtlich von der Natur inspiriert.*

*Hommage à la diversité écologique, l'Ark of the World est d'inspiration biologique évidente, dans ses formes comme dans ses couleurs.*

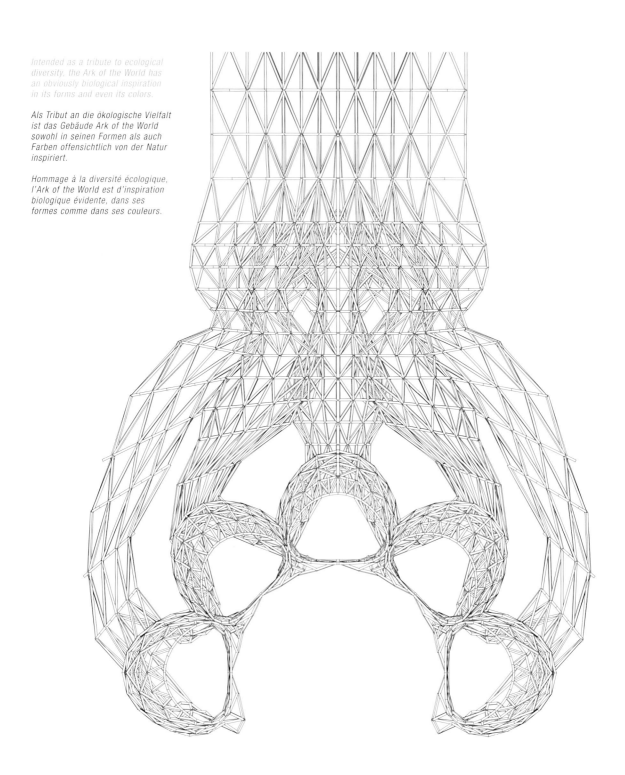

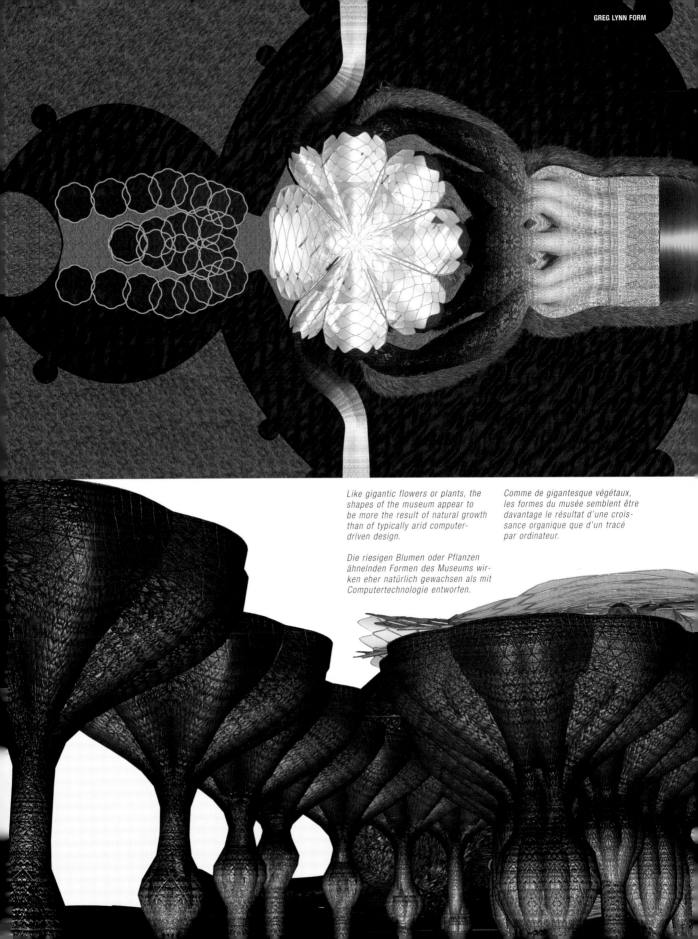

*Like gigantic flowers or plants, the
shapes of the museum appear to
be more the result of natural growth
than of typically arid computer-
driven design.*

*Die riesigen Blumen oder Pflanzen
ähnelnden Formen des Museums wirken eher natürlich gewachsen als mit
Computertechnologie entworfen.*

*Comme de gigantesque végétaux,
les formes du musée semblent être
davantage le résultat d'une crois-
sance organique que d'un tracé
par ordinateur.*

This project was conceived for the government of Costa Rica as "an institution that celebrates the ecological diversity, environmental preservation, eco-tourism and cultural heritage" of the country. Located in the rain forests of Costa Rica's interior, it is intended as "a mixture of natural history museum, ecology center and contemporary art museum." The design proposal is inspired by local flora and fauna both in terms of color and of symbolism. A central vertical space includes a three-story helicoidal stairway leading to a glass fiber reinforced fabric canopy for viewing the forest. Around the central area where representations of the Costa Rican natural environment are displayed, there are galleries for contemporary art, also to be inspired by the forests. On the ground floor, a natural history exhibition called the Consilience Museum is designed on the basis of E.O. Wilson's concepts. The ground floor blends into an outdoor amphitheater and stage. The creation of the museum is to coincide with the launch of the Ark of the World Awards in ecology.

Das Architekturprojekt wurde für die Regierung von Costa Rica entworfen als „eine Institution, welche die ökologische Vielfalt, den Schutz der Umwelt, den Öko-Tourismus und das kulturelle Erbe des Landes würdigt und bewahrt." Das in einem der Regenwälder im Landesinnern von Costa Rica angesiedelte Projekt soll eine Mischung aus naturhistorischem Museum, ökologischem Zentrum und Museum für zeitgenössische Kunst werden. Dabei sind sowohl Farbgebung als auch Symbolik des Entwurfs von der lokalen Flora und Fauna inspiriert. Ein zentral gelegener, vertikaler Raum umschließt eine spiralförmige Treppe, die über drei Geschosse bis zu einem Vordach aus glasfaserverstärktem Gewebe mit Blick über den umliegenden Regenwald hinaufführt. Um den Hauptbereich, der sich mit ökologischen Themen befasst, gruppieren sich Ausstellungsräume für zeitgenössische Kunst, während das im Erdgeschoss befindliche, nach den Konzepten des amerikanischen Zoologen Edward Osborne Wilson gestaltete Consilience Museum naturhistorischen Themen gewidmet ist. Das Erdgeschoss geht anschließend in ein Freilichttheater über. Das Museum soll zeitgleich mit der erstmaligen Verleihung des Ark of the World Award für Ökologie fertig gestellt werden.

« Institution qui célèbre la diversité écologique, la protection de l'environnement, l'écotourisme et le patrimoine culturel », ce projet a été conçu à la demande du Costa Rica. Édifié dans la forêt tropicale de l'intérieur du pays, il se veut « un mélange de muséum d'histoire naturelle, de centre d'écologie et de musée d'art contemporain ». La proposition est inspirée par la flore et la faune locales, toutes deux traitées en termes de couleurs et de symbolisme. Un volume vertical central comprend un escalier hélicoïdal sur trois niveaux conduisant à un auvent en toile renforcée de fibre de verre d'où on peut observer la forêt. Autour de la zone centrale où se trouvent des représentations de l'environnement naturel costaricain, sont implantées des galeries d'art contemporain, également inspirées par les forêts. Au rez-de-chaussée, une exposition d'histoire naturelle intitulée le Consilience Museum a été conçue d'après les concepts de E. O. Wilson. Le rez-de-chaussée se transforme ensuite en amphithéâtre et scène de plein air. La création du musée devrait coïncider avec le lancement des « Ark of the World Awards » d'écologie.

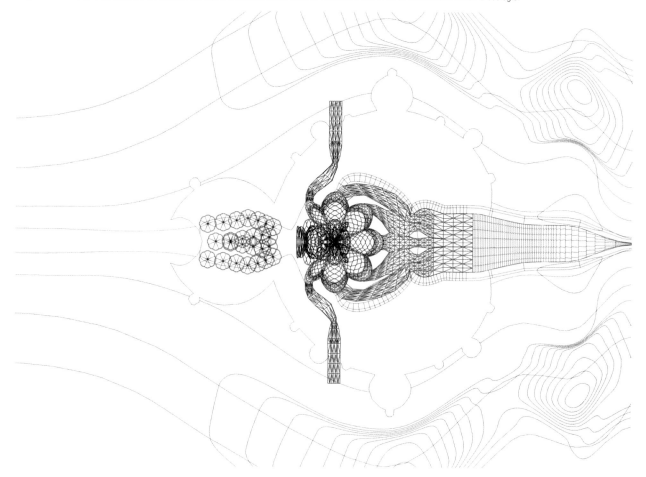

*Esthetically, the Ark of the World is a surprising mixture of nature-inspired colors and shapes, assuming an almost monstrous proportion.*

*Ästhetisch überrascht Ark of the World mit einer Mixtur aus biologisch inspirierten Formen und Farben, die fast monströse Proportionen annehmen.*

*L'Ark of the World est un mélange de couleurs et de formes inspirées par la nature, qui prennent des proportions presque monstrueuses.*

# FUMIHIKO MAKI

*Maki and Associates*
*Hillside West Building C*
*13-4 Hachiyama-cho, Shibuya-ku*
*Tokyo 150-0035*
*Japan*

*Tel: +81 3 3780 3880*
*Fax: +81 3 3780 3881*
*e-mail: contact@maki-and-associates.co.jp*
*web: www.maki-and-associates.co.jp*

Born in Tokyo in 1928, Fumihiko Maki received his BArch degree from the University of Tokyo in 1952, and Master of Architecture degrees from the Cranbrook Academy of Art (1953) and the Harvard Graduate School of Design (1954). He worked for Skidmore Owings & Merrill in New York (1954–55) and Sert Jackson and Associates in Cambridge, Massachusetts (1955–1958) before creating his own firm, Maki and Associates, in Tokyo in 1965. Notable buildings include: Fujisawa Municipal Gymnasium (Fujisawa, Kanagawa, 1984); Spiral (Minato-ku, Tokyo, 1985); National Museum of Modern Art (Sakyo-ku, Kyoto, 1986); Tepia (Minato-ku, Tokyo, 1989); Nippon Convention Center Makuhari Messe (Chiba, Chiba, 1989); Tokyo Metropolitan Gymnasium (Shibuya, Tokyo, 1990); Center for the Arts Yerba Buena Gardens (San Francisco, California, 1993). Recent projects have included: Nippon Convention Center Makuhari Messe Phase II (Chiba, Chiba, completed in 1997), and the Hillside West buildings (completed in 1998), part of his ongoing Hillside Terrace project. More recent and current work includes the Yokohama Bayside Tower (Yokohama, Kanagawa, 2003); TV Asahi Broadcast Center (Minato-ku, Tokyo, 2003); Niigata International Convention Center (Niigata, Niigata, 2003); MIT Media Laboratory Expansion (Cambridge, MA, USA, 2004); National Language Research Institute (Tachikawa, Tokyo, 2004); Washington University Visual Arts and Design Center (St. Louis, MI, USA, 2004); and the Nakatsu City Museum (Nakatsu, Oita, 2005).

Fumihiko Maki, geboren 1928 in Tokio, erwarb 1952 den Bachelor of Architecture an der Universität Tokio, den Master of Architecture 1953 an der Cranbrook Academy of Art und 1954 an der Harvard Graduate School of Design. Er arbeitete in den Büros Skidmore Owings & Merrill in New York (1954–55) und Sert Jackson and Associates in Cambridge, Massachusetts (1955–1958), bevor er 1965 seine eigene Firma in Tokio gründete. Zu seinen herausragenden Bauten gehören die städtische Sporthalle in Fujisawa, Kanagawa (1984), das Medienzentrum Spiral, Minato-ku in Tokio (1985), das Nationalmuseum für moderne Kunst in Sakyo-ku, Kyoto (1986), das Tepia-Gebäude in Minato-ku, Tokio (1989), das Nippon Convention Center Makuhari Messe in Chiba (1989), die städtische Sporthalle in Shibuya, Tokio (1990) und das Center for the Arts Yerba Buena Gardens in San Francisco (1993). Zu seinen neueren Projekten zählen: das Nippon Convention Center Makuhari Messe Phase II in Chiba (1997) und die Hillside West Gebäude (1998), letztere sind Teil seines fortlaufenden Hillside Terrace Projekts. Makis aktuellste Arbeiten sind: der Yokohama Bayside Tower in Yokohama, Kanagawa (2003), das TV Asahi Broadcast Center in Minato-ku, Tokio (2003), das International Convention Center in Niigata (2003), die Erweiterung des MIT-Medienlabors in Cambridge, Massachusetts (2004), das National Language Research Institute in Tachikawa, Tokio (2004), das Visual Arts and Design Center der Washington University in St. Louis, Missouri (2004) sowie das städtische Museum in Nakatsu, Oita, das 2005 fertig gestellt werden soll.

Né à Tokyo en 1928, Fumihiko Maki est B. Arch de l'Université de Tokyo en 1952, et Master of Architecture de la Cranbrook Academy of Art (1953) et de l'Harvard Graduate School of Design (1954). Il travaille pour Skidmore Owings & Merrill à New York (1954–55), et Sert Jackson and Associates à Cambridge, Massachusetts (1955–1958), avant de créer sa propre agence, Maki and Associates, à Tokyo (1965). Parmi ses réalisations les plus notables : le gymnase municipal de Fujisawa (Fujisawa, Kanagawa, Japon,1984) ; Spiral (Minato-ku, Tokyo, 1985) ; le Musée national d'art moderne (Sakyo-ku, Kyoto, 1986) ; Tepia (Minato-ku, Tokyo, 1989) ; le Centre de Congrès Nippon de Makuhari, (Chiba, Japon, 1989) ; le gymnase métropolitain de Tokyo (Shibuya, Tokyo, 1990) ; le Center for the Arts Yerba Buena Gardens (San Francisco, Californie, 1993). Il a achevé en 1998 la Phase II (extension) du Centre de Congrès Nippon de Makuhari (Chiba) et les immeubles de Hillside West qui font partie de son projet en cours pour Hillside Terrace. Parmi ses réalisations et projets les plus récents : la Yokohama Bayside Tower (Yokohama, Kanagawa, 2003) ; le centre d'émission de TV Asahi (Minato-ku, Tokyo, 2003) ; le centre international de congrès de Niigata (Niigata, Niigata, 2003) ; l'extension du laboratoire des médias du MIT (Cambridge, MA, USA, 2004) ; l'Institut national de recherches sur le langage (Tachikawa, Tokyo, 2004) ; le Washington University Visual Arts and Design Center (St. Louis, MI, USA, 2004) et le musée de Nakatsu (Nakatsu, Oita, Japon, 2005).

# TRIAD

*Harmonic Drive Co., Hodaka, Japan, 2000–2002*

*Client: Harmonic Drive Systems Inc. Total floor area: 712 m² (laboratory), 354 m² (gallery), 33 m² (guardhouse). Costs: not specified.*

As its name implies, Triad consists of three independent buildings – a guardhouse, gallery and research center. Though of different natures, the small structures (total floor area 1 099 square meters) make up a coherent composition set against a mountain backdrop. The Harmonic Drive company, which set up its main factory on this site early in the 1990s, is known for specialized instruments used in spacecraft and telescopes. The gallery in the new complex is intended for the display of the owner's collection of works by the Japanese artist Yohikuni Iida. The guardhouse measures 3.6 x 10 x 3.6 meters and is cantilevered over a gentle slope. This hanging volume is intended to give an impression of forward movement. The landscaping, made up of several elliptical mounds and plates with different surface finishes, also embodies the concept of movement. The gallery is divided into three exhibition spaces, the largest of which is intended for the best-known work of Iida, "Screen Canyon." The research center is clad in welded stainless steel, but its form and structure were directly influenced by the precision work to be done within its walls. As the architect has stated, "utmost attention was given to the delineation of roof edges, as this complex is always seen against the natural landscape background of sky, mountains, and vegetation. The thin protruded edge of the Research Center and Gallery terrace canopy are comprised of honeycomb cores sandwiched by 6 mm steel plates. These were prefabricated in pieces, and then joined together to form a whole."

Wie der Name schon andeutet, besteht Triad aus drei einzelnen Gebäuden – einem Haus für die Wachleute, einer Galerie und einem Forschungszentrum. Obwohl von unterschiedlicher Art und Funktion bilden die mit einer Gesamtnutzfläche von 1 099 m² eher kleinformatigen Bauten eine ausgewogene Komposition, die sich vor einer Bergkulisse abhebt. Die Firma Harmonic Drive, deren Hauptfabrik vor gut zehn Jahren auf demselben Grundstück errichtet wurde, ist bekannt für die Herstellung von Spezialinstrumenten, die in Raumfahrzeugen und Teleskopen eingesetzt werden. Die neue Galerie ist als Ausstellungsfläche für die dem Eigentümer der Firma gehörende Sammlung von Arbeiten des japanischen Künstlers Yohikuni Iida gedacht. Das Gebäude für den Sicherheitsdienst misst 3,6 x 10 x 3,6 m und kragt über einen sanft gewölbten Abhang aus, was den Eindruck einer Vorwärtsbewegung vermitteln soll. Auch die Landschaftsgestaltung mit ihren ellipsenförmigen Erdwällen sowie den Wegplatten mit unterschiedlicher Oberflächenbeschaffenheit folgt diesem dynamischen Gestaltungskonzept. Das Innere der Galerie ist in drei Ausstellungsräume aufgeteilt, deren größter die wohl bekannteste Arbeit von Iida enthält – „Screen Canyon". Das Forschungszentrum ist mit einer geschweißten Ummantelung aus rostfreiem Stahl verkleidet, während es in Form und Konstruktionsweise direkt durch die Präzisionstechniken, mit denen in seinem Inneren gearbeitet wird, beeinflusst ist. Der Architekt über seinen Entwurf: „Größte Sorgfalt wurde auf die Ausführung der Dachkonturen verwendet, da diese Anlage immer gegen den Hintergrund der natürlichen Landschaft von Himmel, Bergen und Vegetation wahrgenommen wird. Der dünne, hervorstehende Außenrand des Forschungszentrums und das Terrassendach des Ausstellungsgebäudes bestehen aus einem Wabenkern zwischen 6 mm starken Stahlplatten. Diese wurden in Teilen vorgefertigt und dann als Ganzes zusammengefügt."

Comme son nom le sous-entend, Triad consiste en trois bâtiments indépendants : un poste de garde, une galerie et un centre de recherches. Bien que de nature différente, ces petites structures (surface totale au sol de 1 099 m²) forment une composition cohérente face au panorama de montagnes. La société Harmonic Drive qui a construit son usine principale sur ce site dans les années 1990 est spécialisée dans les instruments pour télescopes et l'exploration de l'espace. La galerie présente la collection du propriétaire d'œuvres de l'artiste japonais Yohikuni Iida. Le poste de garde (3,6 x 10 x 3,6 m) se détache en porte-à-faux sur une pente légère. Volume en suspension, il veut donner une impression de mouvement dynamique vers l'avant. L'aménagement paysager, constitué de plusieurs monticules elliptiques et de plateaux différents, incarne également cette notion de mouvement. La galerie est divisée en trois espaces d'exposition, le plus grand étant réservé à l'œuvre la plus célèbre de Iida, « Screen Canyon ». Le centre de recherches est habillé d'acier inoxydable soudé mais sa forme et sa structure sont directement influencées par les travaux de précision accomplis entre ses murs. Comme l'architecte le fait remarquer : « La plus grande attention a été portée à la délinéation des bordures du toit, car ce complexe est toujours vu sur le fond d'un paysage naturel de ciel, de montagnes et de végétation. La finesse de l'épaisseur du toit en avancée du Centre et de l'auvent de la terrasse de la galerie sont en structure en nid d'abeille prise en sandwich entre des plaques d'acier de 6 mm d'épaisseur. Ils ont été fabriqués en pièces séparées remontées ensemble. »

As he has in some earlier projects,
Fumihiko Maki here fully assumes
the sculptural aspect of his work,
as these angled, strong blocks show.

Wie bei einigen früheren Projekten
lässt Fumihiko Maki auch hier den
skulpturalen Aspekt seiner Gestaltung
voll zur Geltung kommen, so bei
den winkelförmigen, kraftvollen
Baukörpern.

Comme dans certains projets
antérieurs, Fumihiko Maki assume
ici entièrement l'aspect sculptural
de son travail, comme le montrent
les formes puissantes de ces blocs
inclinés.

*The smooth wrap-around welded steel skin of the research center contrasts with the more rectilinear volumes of the rest of the complex.*

*Die Haut aus geschweißtem Stahl, die sich in sanften Rundungen um das Forschungszentrum legt, kontrastiert mit den eher eckigen Formen der restlichen Gebäude.*

*La peau d'acier soudé qui enveloppe délicatement le centre de recherche contraste avec les volumes plus rectilignes du reste des installations.*

# MICHAEL MALTZAN

*Michael Maltzan Architecture Inc.*
*2801 Hyperion Avenue Suite 107*
*Los Angeles, CA 90027*
*USA*

*Tel: +1 323 913 3098*
*Fax: +1 323 913 5932*
*e-mail: info@mmaltzan.com*
*web: www.mmaltzan.com*

*MoMAQNS* ▶

Michael Maltzan was born in 1959 on Long Island, New York. He holds both a Bachelor of Fine Arts and a Bachelor of Architecture from Rhode Island School of Design (1984, 1985) and a Master of Architecture degree from Harvard (1987). Since establishing his own firm in 1995, Michael Maltzan has been responsible for the design of a wide range of arts, educational, commercial, institutional and residential projects including the Mark Taper Center/Inner-City Arts campus, Harvard/Westlake School's Feldman/Horn Center for the Arts, the Getty Information Institute Digital Laboratory, and MoMAQNS in Long Island City which opened in June 2002. He is currently working on the design of the Kidspace Children's Museum in Pasadena, California and the UCLA Hammer Museum in Los Angeles, and was recently awarded commissions for both the new Sonoma County Museum in Santa Rosa and the Fresno Metropolitan Museum. Maltzan held the Jerde Chair at USC in 2002 and was the Elliot Noyes Visiting Professor at Harvard in 2004. He has lectured widely in the US and abroad. His work has won numerous design awards and has recently been exhibited at the Harvard Design School and the Venice Biennale.

Michael Maltzan, geboren 1959 in Long Island, New York, erwarb 1984 den Bachelor of Fine Arts und 1985 den Bachelor of Architecture an der Rhode Island School of Design sowie 1987 den Master of Architecture in Harvard. Seit er 1995 seine eigene Firma gründete, hat Michael Maltzan eine große Bandbreite an Architekturprojekten in den Bereichen Kunst, Bildung, Wirtschaft, öffentliche Einrichtungen und Wohnungsbau realisiert. Zu diesen gehören das Mark Taper Center/Inner-City Arts Campus, das Feldman/Horn Center for the Arts der Westlake School in Harvard, das Getty Information Institute Digital Laboratory sowie das im Juni 2002 eröffnete Museum of Modern Art Queens in Long Island City. Derzeit arbeitet er an der Gestaltung des Kindermuseums Kidspace im kalifornischen Pasadena und am UCLA Hammer Museum in Los Angeles. Außerdem wurde er als Planer für das neue Sonoma County Museum in Santa Rosa und das Fresno Metropolitan Museum ausgewählt. Maltzan hatte 2002 den Jerde Lehrstuhl an der University of Southern California und 2004 die Elliot Noyes Gastprofessur in Harvard inne. Er hat eine Vielzahl von Vorträgen sowohl in den USA wie auch im Ausland gehalten. Seine Arbeit wurde zudem mit zahlreichen Designpreisen ausgezeichnet und vor kurzem an der Harvard Design School sowie der Biennale in Venedig präsentiert.

Michael Maltzan est né en 1959 à Long Island (New York, USA). Il est Bachelor en beaux-arts et architecture de la Rhode Island School of Design (1984–85) et Master of Architecture de Harvard (1987). Depuis la création de son agence en 1995, il a réalisé un grand nombre de projets dans le domaine des arts, de l'éducation, du commerce, des institutions publiques et du logement, dont le Mark Taper Center/Inner-City Arts campus, la Harvard/Westlake School's Feldman/Horn Center for the Arts, le Getty Information Institute Digital Laboratory et le MoMAQNS à Long Island City qui a ouvert ses portes en juin 2002. Il travaille actuellement à la conception du Kidspace Childrens' Museum à Pasadena (Californie) et au UCLA Hammer Museum à Los Angeles. Il a récemment reçu commande du nouveau musée du comté de Sonoma à Santa Rosa et du Metropolitan, Museum de Fresno. Maltzan a occupé la chaire Jerde à USC en 2002 et a été professeur invité Elliot Noyes à Harvard en 2004. Il a donné de nombreuses conférences aux États-Unis et dans le monde et a remporté de multiples distinctions. Il a récemment été l'objet d'expositions à la Harvard Design School et à la Biennale de Venise.

# MoMAQNS

*Museum of Modern Art, Long Island City, Queens, New York, USA, 2000–2002*

*Client: Museum of Modern Art, New York. Building area: 14 287 m². Costs: $ 35 000 000.*

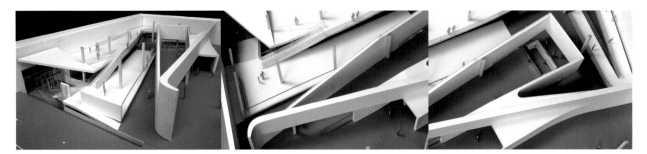

*The architect innovated inside of the basic rectangular volume of this former factory to create angles and varying floor levels.*

*Der Architekt erneuerte das rechteckige Innere der ehemaligen Fabrik, indem er unterschiedliche Winkel und Ebenen einsetzte.*

*À l'intérieur du volume parallélépipédique d'une ancienne usine que l'architecte a innové par des variations de niveaux ou des formes angulaires.*

This former factory for the Swingline Staples company was conceived as the temporary Long Island City home for New York's Museum of Modern Art during expansion and renovation work being carried out in Manhattan by the Japanese architect Yoshio Taniguchi. As Michael Maltzan has said of the $35 million project, "of critical significance was re-imagining an established institution 'moving' to a satellite site, the former Swingline Staples factory building. Believing that the temporary facility should not forecast the soon-to-be-remade Manhattan MoMA, we looked, instead, to the complex context of the project, as well as to the experience of movement in creating an identity for MoMAQNS. This is manifest as the visitor experiences a progressive sequence of elements beginning with fleetingly legible roofscape signage and extending, through a series of expanding and contracting spaces, the processional trajectory culminating in the galleries." Other members of the MoMAQNS project were Cooper Robertson and Partners, New York, architects for the conversion of the former factory into a permanent MoMA facility, and the New York office of Base Design, a Belgian "image development company." The project brings to mind the Temporary Contemporary (now the Geffen Contemporary) designed by Frank Gehry (1983) in downtown Los Angeles. That former bus garage was used for exhibitions while the Museum of Contemporary Art, designed by Arata Isozaki, was under construction. It became so popular that the Museum decided to retain it as an alternative exhibition space. Once the new Manhattan MoMA opens, MoMAQNS will house study centers, workshops and permanent art storage.

Die ehemalige Fabrik der Firma Swingline Staples in Long Island City ist als vorübergehendes Zuhause für das New Yorker Museum of Modern Art konzipiert, während dessen Gebäude in Manhattan von dem japanischen Architekten Yoshio Taniguchi renoviert und erweitert wird. Michael Maltzan über das 35 Millionen Dollar teure Projekt: „Von entscheidender Bedeutung war, dass wir ein neues Image für eine etablierte Institution kreieren, die an einen Nebenschauplatz, das ehemalige Swingline Staples Fabrikgebäude, ‚umzieht'. In der Überzeugung, dass die vorübergehende Einrichtung nicht das bald fertig gestellte MoMA in Manhattan vorwegnehmen sollte, setzten wir uns in der Schaffung einer Identität für das MoMAQNS (Museum of Modern Art Queens) mit der komplexen Umgebung des Projekts und der Erfahrung von Bewegung auseinander. Dieser Zugang manifestiert sich darin, dass die Museumsbesucher eine progressive Folge von gestalterischen Elementen wahrnehmen, angefangen von den angedeuteten Schriftzeichen auf dem Dach über eine Reihe sich abwechselnd ausdehnender und zusammenziehender Räume, bis der prozessionsartige Weg seinen Gipfelpunkt in den Ausstellungsräumen findet." Zusammen mit Michael Maltzan arbeiteten außerdem am MoMAQNS-Projekt: die Architekten von Cooper Robertson and Partners aus New York sowie die New Yorker Niederlassung von Base Design, eine belgischen Imageberatungsfirma. Das Projekt erinnert an das 1983 von Frank O. Gehry realisierte Temporary Contemporary – das heutige Geffen Contemporary – in Downtown Los Angeles. Diese ehemalige Busgarage wurde so populär, dass die Museumsverantwortlichen beschlossen, es als zusätzliche Ausstellungsfläche zu behalten. Nach der Wiedereröffnung des Manhattener Domizils von MoMA wird das neue Gebäude von MoMAQNS Studienräume, Werkstätten und ein Depot beherbergen.

Cette ancienne usine de la société Swingline Staples a été retenue pour accueillir temporairement le Museum of Modern Art de New York à Long Island pendant la rénovation de son siège de Manhattan par l'architecte japonais Yoshio Taniguchi. Michael Maltzan a présenté ainsi ce projet de 35 millions de dollars : « Re-imaginer une installation établie ‹ déménageant › vers un site satellite, l'ancienne usine d'agrafes Swingline, revêtait une signification critique. Convaincu que cette installation temporaire ne devait pas faire ombrage au MoMA de Manhattan en cours de réfection, nous avons plutôt regardé du côté du contexte compliqué du projet ainsi que de l'expérience du mouvement dans la création d'une identité pour ce MoMAQNS. C'est manifeste lorsque le visiteur découvre la séquence progressive d'éléments qui commence par la signalétique du toit qu'il lit en passant et se poursuit par une série d'espace se dilatant ou se contractant, dans un parcours d'ordre processionnel qui culmine dans les galeries. » Les autres acteurs de ce projet ont été Cooper Robertson and Partners, New York, architectes et l'agence de New York de Base Design, une « société de développement d'image » belge. Le projet fait penser au Temporary Contemporary (aujourd'hui Geffen Contemporary) conçu par Frank Gehry (1983) dans le centre de Los Angeles, ancien garage de bus, qui fut si populaire que le musée décida de le conserver et d'en faire un espace d'expositions alternatif. Une fois le MoMA de Manhattan rouvert, le MoMAQNS accueillera des centres d'étude, des ateliers et des réserves permanentes du musée.

Signaled by the very large scale letters "MoMA" on the exterior, the old Swingline Factory immediately takes on a very "current" appearance in the semi-industrial setting of Long Island City (Queens).

Wie die riesigen Buchstaben "MoMA" auf der Fassade signalisieren, hat die alte Swingline Fabrik einen sehr „aktuellen Look" in ihrer fast industriellen Umgebung von Long Island City (Queens) kreiert.

Signalée en façade par les énormes lettres constituant le mot MoMA, l'ancienne usine Swingline retrouve une nouvelle modernité dans le contexte semi-industriel de Long Island City (Queens).

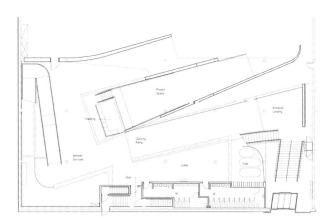

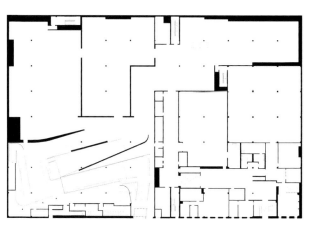

The logo of the museum is repeated
in the entrance areas above.

Das Logo wiederholt sich im Eingangsbereich des Museums (oben).

Le logo MoMAQNS est répété dans
la zone d'entrée (ci-dessus).

*Working within the generous darkened volumes of the factory, the architect has inserted elevated passageways and cantilevered volumes that differ from the strict rectilinear layout that the Museum of Modern Art long preferred for its exhibition spaces in New York.*

*In das Innere der großzügigen, dunklen Baukörper der Fabrik setzte der Architekt erhöhte Durchgänge und freitragende Volumen, die sich von der streng linearen Raumanordnung des Museum of Modern Art in Manhattan unterscheiden.*

*Intervenant dans les volumes généreux et sombres de l'usine, l'architecte a inséré des passages surélevés et des volumes en porte-à-faux très différents de la stricte orthogonalité longtemps préférée par le Museum of Modern Art pour son établissement de New York.*

Kraftvolle weiße Körper, stellenweise auf dicke Pfeiler gesetzt, strukturieren den Innenraum, dessen Decke im Kontrast dazu schwarz gestrichen wurde.

De puissants volumes blancs, parfois montés sur d'épais pilotis ordonnent les volumes, dont les plafonds ont été peints en noir pour accentuer le contraste.

# RICHARD MEIER

*Richard Meier & Partners, Architects LLP*
*475 Tenth Avenue, 6th Floor*
*New York, NY 10018*
*USA*

*Tel: +1 212 967 6060*
*Fax: +1 212 967 3207*
*e-mail: mail@richardmeier.com*
*Web: www.richardmeier.com*

*Restaurant 66* ▶

Born in Newark, New Jersey in 1934, Richard Meier received his architectural training at Cornell University, and worked in the office of Marcel Breuer (1960–1963) before establishing his own practice in 1963. He won the 1984 Pritzker Prize and the 1988 Royal Gold Medal. His notable buildings include The Atheneum, (New Harmony, Indiana, 1975–1979); Museum of Decorative Arts (Frankfurt, Germany, 1979–1984); High Museum of Art (Atlanta, Georgia, 1980–1983); Canal Plus Headquarters (Paris, France, 1988–1991); City Hall and Library (The Hague, The Netherlands, 1990–1995); Barcelona Museum of Contemporary Art (Barcelona, Spain, 1988–1995); and the Getty Center (Los Angeles, California, 1984–1997). Recent work includes the US Courthouse and Federal Building (Phoenix, Arizona, 1995–2000); 173–176 Perry Street Condominium Towers (New York, NY, 2001–02); Jubilee Church (Rome, 2003); Crystal Cathedral International Center for Possibility Thinking (Garden Grove, CA, 2003); and the Arp Museum (Rolandseck, Germany).

Richard Meier, geboren 1934 in Newark, New Jersey, studierte Architektur an der Cornell University und arbeitete in der Firma von Marcel Breuer (1960–1963), bevor er 1963 sein eigenes Büro eröffnete. Er wurde 1984 mit dem Pritzker Prize und 1988 mit der Royal Gold Medal ausgezeichnet. Zu seinen bedeutendsten Bauten gehören: The Atheneum in New Harmony, Indiana (1975–1979), das Museum für Kunsthandwerk in Frankfurt am Main (1979–1984), das High Museum of Art in Atlanta, Georgia (1980–1983), das Getty Center in Los Angeles (1984–1997), die Zentrale von Canal Plus in Paris (1988–1991), das Museum für zeitgenössische Kunst in Barcelona (1988–1995) und Rathaus und Bibliothek in Den Haag (1990–1995). Zu seinen jüngsten Projekten zählen das US Courthouse and Federal Building in Phoenix, Arizona (1995–2000), Condominium Towers in 173–176 Street, New York (2001-02), die Kirche des Heiligen Jahres in Rom (2003), das Crystal Cathedral International Center for Possibility Thinking im kalifornischen Garden Grove (2003) sowie das Arp Museum im deutschen Rolandseck.

Né à Newark (New Jersey), en 1934, Richard Meier étudie à la Cornell University et travaille dans l'agence de Marcel Breuer (1960–1963), avant de s'installer à son compte en 1963. Il obtient le Prix Pritzker en 1984 et la Royal Gold Medal en 1988. Principales réalisations : The Atheneum, New Harmony (Indiana, USA, 1975–1979) ; Musée des Arts Décoratifs de Francfort-sur-le-Main (1979–1984) ; High Museum of Art (Atlanta, Géorgie, 1980–1983) ; siège de Canal + (Paris, 1988–1991) ; hôtel de ville et bibliothèque (La Haye, 1990–1995) ; Musée d'Art Contemporain de Barcelone (1988–1995) ; Getty Center (Los Angeles, Californie, 1984–1996). Travaux récents : Tribunal fédéral et immeuble de l'administration fédérale à Phoenix (Arizona, USA, 1995–2000) ; les tours Condominium, 173-176 Perry Street (New York, NY, 2001–02); l'église du Jubilée (Rome, 2003) ; le Crystal Cathedral International Center for Possibility Thinking (Garden Grove, Californie, USA, 2003) et le Arp Museum (Rolandseck, Allemagne).

# RESTAURANT 66

*New York, New York, USA, 2003*

*Client: Phil Suarez and Jean-Georges Vongerichten. Floor area: 808 m². Costs: not specified.*

Located at 241 Church Street in the Tribeca area of Manhattan, 66 is an open-space restaurant with large frosted glass panes subdividing the dining areas. A 3.5 meter-high curved glass wall marks the entrance and fish tanks separate the dining area for 150 guests from the kitchen. A frosted glass wall marks the bar area. Red silk banners with Chinese ideograms hang above a 13.4-meter epoxy resin communal table. The dining tables also designed by the architect are made of ice blue poured epoxy resin with stainless steel bases. Other furniture is by Eames (Herman Miller), Bertoia (Knoll), and Eero Saarinen (Knoll). Housed in the Textile Building, designed in 1901 by Henry Hardenbergh, the architect of the Plaza Hotel and Dakota apartment building, this restaurant is the sixth opened in New York by the Strasbourg-born chef Jean-Georges Vongerichten. Vongerichten, who worked here as he has elsewhere with Phil Suarez, is also responsible for the Paris restaurant Market. The floor area of the facility is about 808 square meters. Its turn-of-the-century origin is made apparent by leaving visible the original iron columns, painted in Richard Meier's trademark white.

Das Restaurant 66 befindet sich in der Church Street 241 im Manhattaner Stadtteil Tribeca. Sein loftartiger Innenraum wird durch große Mattglasscheiben untergliedert. Eine gewölbte, 3,5 m hohe Glaswand markiert den Eingangsbereich, während Aquarien die Trennlinie zwischen der Küche und dem Speisesaal mit 150 Plätzen bilden. Auch die Bar wird durch eine Wand aus Mattglas abgegrenzt. Rotseidene Banner mit chinesischen Schriftzeichen hängen über einem 13,4 m langen, durchgehenden Tisch aus Epoxydharz. Auch die vom Architekten entworfenen Einzeltische sind aus eisblauem, gegossenem Epoxydharz, haben aber einen Sockel aus Edelstahl. Die anderen Einrichtungsgegenstände sind Entwürfe von Eames (Herman Miller), Bertoia (Knoll) und Eero Saarinen (Knoll). Das 808 m² große Restaurant befindet sich in dem 1901 von dem Architekten des Hotel Plaza und des Apartmenthauses Dakota, Henry Hardenbergh, entworfenen Textile Building. Es ist das neueste von insgesamt sechs ebenfalls in New York ansässigen Lokalen des in Straßburg geborenen Chefkochs Jean-Georges Vongerichten, dem auch das Pariser Restaurant Market gehört. Der historische Ursprung des Hauses wurde beim Umbau kenntlich gemacht, indem man die Eisensäulen in ihrer ursprünglichen Form beließ, nur angestrichen in Richard Meiers Markenzeichen, der Farbe Weiß.

Installé au 241 Church Street dans le quartier de Tribeca à Manhattan, le 66 est un restaurant de plan ouvert de 808 m² au sol subdivisés par de grands panneaux de verre givré. Un mur de verre incurvé de 3,5 m de haut marque l'entrée, et des aquariums séparent la salle à manger de 150 couverts de la cuisine. Un autre mur de verre givré met en valeur le bar. Des bannières de soie rouge à idéogrammes chinois sont suspendues au-dessus d'une table d'hôte en résine époxy de 13,4 m de long. Les tables du restaurant, également conçues par l'architecte, sont en résine époxy bleu glacier moulée à piétement en acier inoxydable. D'autres meubles sont signés Eames (Herman Miller), Bertoia (Knoll) et Eero Saarinen (Knoll). Installé dans le Textile Building, conçu en 1901 par Henry Hardenbergh, l'architecte du Plaza Hotel et de l'immeuble Dakota, ce restaurant est le sixième ouvert à New York par le chef strasbourgeois Jean-Georges Vongerichten, qui a travaillé sur ce projet comme pour les autres avec Phil Suarez. Il est également à l'origine du restaurant parisien le Market. L'origine historique de l'immeuble retrouve ses droits dans les colonnes métalliques apparentes, peintes dans le blanc qui est la signature de Richard Meier.

Richard Meier's trademark white design is here applied to a pre-existing iron column while red flags set off the purity of the architect's lines.

Richard Meiers Markenzeichen, das weiße Design, zeigt sich hier an einer originalen Eisensäule, während rote Banner die puristischen Linien des Architekten hervorheben.

Le blanc caractéristique de Richard Meier s'applique ici aux anciennes colonnes métalliques. L'alignement de bannières rouges fait ressortir la pureté des lignes de l'architecte.

Though a wooden floor and the iron column again visible here may not seem very typical of Richard Meier, his crisp delimitation of space and surfaces is everywhere in evidence.

Wenngleich Holzboden und Eisensäulen nicht sehr typisch für Richard Meier sein mögen, ist seine klare Definition von Raum und Oberfläche überall evident.

Si le sol en bois et les colonnes métalliques ne sont pas vraiment typiques du style de Meier, son sens de la délimitation tendue de l'espace et des surfaces est omniprésent.

Black and silver furniture as well as screens and glass surfaces stand out against the white walls of the restaurant.

Möbel in Schwarz und Silber sowie Raumteiler und Glaswände heben sich gut gegen die weißen Wänden des Restaurants ab.

Les meubles en noir et blanc ainsi que les écrans et les plans de verre ressortent sur le fond des murs blancs du restaurant.

Rigorous and rectilinear the 66 Restaurant may show Richard Meier under a less strict angle than some of his new buildings, but the spirit of the architect has surely marked this location.

Im Restaurant 66 zeigt sich Richard Meier vielleicht von einer weniger strengen Seite als in anderen von ihm gestalteten Gebäuden, doch ist auch diese Arbeit stark von seinem Stil und seiner Haltung geprägt.

Rigoureux et d'une stricte géométrie rectiligne, le 66 Restaurant montre Richard Meier sous un angle moins strict que certaines de ses récentes réalisations, même si l'esprit de son architecture marque définitivement ce lieu.

# JUBILEE CHURCH

*(Dio Padre Misericordioso), Tor Tre Teste, Rome, Italy, 1996–2003*

*Client: Vicariato of Rome. Floor area: 830 m² (church), 1 450 m² (community center), 10 000 m² (site). Costs: not specified.*

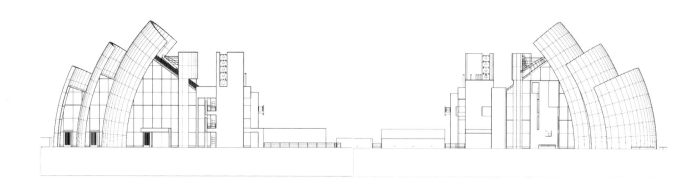

| | | |
|---|---|---|
| *A succession of shells like sails billowing in the wind marks this church, set up on its platform in Rome to mark the Jubilee year.* | *Eine Abfolge von Schalensegmenten, die wie Segel wirken, kennzeichnet die Kirche, die zum katholischen Jubiläumsjahr in Rom errichtet wurde.* | *Une succession de coques, telles des voiles gonflés par le vent, signalent cette église, édifiée à Rome pour marquer l'année du Jubilée.* |

Sitting on its glistening plaza, the Jublilee church at sunset takes on an even more ship-like appearance. Meier has often used nautical metaphors in his work, but in this context the successive sails are surprising.

Die auf einem schimmernden Platz ruhende Jubiläumskirche sieht bei Sonnenuntergang sogar noch schiffs-ähnlicher aus. Meier hat zwar bereits in früheren Arbeiten nautische Meta-phern eingesetzt, aber in diesem Kontext sind die segelartigen Formen neu und ungewöhnlich.

Posée sur une plazza de travertin poli, l'église du Jubilée fait encore plus penser à un bateau au coucher du soleil. Si Meier a souvent utilisé des métaphores nautiques dans son œuvre, l'utilisation de cette succes-sion de voiles n'en est pas moins surprenante.

Commissioned by the Vicariato of Rome, this church is set on a triangular site on the boundary of a public park surrounded by 10-story apartment buildings in a community of approximately 30 000 residents. The project features the use of concrete, stucco, travertine and glass and three dramatic shells or arcs that evoke billowing white sails. Unprecedented in Meier's work, the concrete arcs are graduated in height from 17 to 27 meters. The invited competition to design the structure included Tadao Ando, Günter Behnisch, Santiago Calatrava, Peter Eisenman, and Frank Gehry, as well as Meier, who won in the spring of 1996. Construction began in 1998, and although the architect has designed the Hartford Seminary in Connecticut (1981) and the International Center for Possibility Thinking at the Crystal Cathedral in Southern California (2003), this was his first church. As always, Richard Meier places an emphasis on light. "Light is the protagonist of our understanding and reading of space. Light is the means by which we are able to experience what we call sacred. Light is at the origins of this building," he says. Commenting on the fact that he may be the first Jewish architect asked to design a Catholic church, Meier says, "I feel extremely proud that I was the one chosen to design this church. It is very clear that the Catholic Church chose my design based on its merits, not because of a need to make a statement in regard to their relationship to Jews throughout history. Three of the architects in the competition were Jewish. They were chosen to compete because they were among the top architects of our time." His sources of inspiration, he says, were "the churches in which the presence of the sacred could be felt: Alvar Aalto's churches in Finland, Frank Lloyd Wright's Wayfairer's Chapel in the United States along with the Chapel at Ronchamp and La Tourette by Le Corbusier." The Jubilee Church was inaugurated on October 26, 2003 to mark the 25th anniversary of the Pontificate of John Paul II.

Die Jubiläumskirche gehört zu einer Gemeinde mit circa 30 000 Einwohnern. Sie steht auf einem dreiseitigen Grundstück am Rand eines öffentlichen Parks und ist von zehnstöckigen Wohnblocks umgeben. Ein besonderes Gestaltungsmerkmal des mit Beton, Gipsputz, Travertin und Glas ausgestatteten Bauwerks sind drei dramatisch geformte Bögen, die an Segel denken lassen, die sich im Wind blähen. Diese in Meiers Werk noch nie da gewesenen Betonformen sind der Höhe nach von 17 bis 27 m gestaffelt. Neben Meier wurden auch Tadao Ando, Günter Behnisch, Santiago Calatrava, Peter Eisenman and Frank O. Gehry zu dem Wettbewerb für die Gestaltung dieses Projekts eingeladen, den Meier im Frühjahr 1996 für sich entschied. Mit den Bauarbeiten wurde 1998 begonnen und obwohl der Architekt zuvor das Hartford Priesterseminar in Connecticut (1981) und das International Center for Possibility Thinking der Crystal Cathedral in Südkalifornien (2003) geplant hatte, ist dies sein erster Sakralbau. Wie immer hebt Richard Meier in seinem Entwurf speziell das Licht hervor: „Licht ist der Protagonist unseres Verständnisses und unserer Auffassung von Raum. Das Licht ist das Medium, durch welches wir das erleben können, was wir heilig nennen. Licht liegt am Ursprung dieses Gebäudes." Als Antwort auf die Tatsache, dass er vermutlich der erste jüdische Architekt ist, der mit der Gestaltung einer katholischen Kirche betraut wurde, sagt Meier: „Ich bin ungeheuer stolz darauf, dass ich ausgewählt wurde, um diese Kirche zu entwerfen. Dabei ist ganz klar, dass die Katholische Kirche meinen Entwurf aufgrund seiner Vorzüge wählte, und nicht weil es ihr darum ging, eine Aussage über ihr Verhältnis zu Juden zu machen. Drei der Architekten, die am Wettbewerb teilgenommen haben, sind jüdisch. Und sie wurden zu dem Wettbewerb eingeladen, weil sie zu den besten Architekten unserer Zeit gehören." Seine Quelle der Inspiration, erläutert Meier, waren „Kirchen, in denen man die Präsenz des Heiligen fühlen kann: Alvar Aaltos Kirchen in Finnland, Frank Lloyd Wrights Wayfairer Kapelle in den Vereinigten Staaten und die Wallfahrtskirche zu Ronchamp sowie das Kloster La Tourette von Le Corbusier." Die Jubilee Church wurde zur Feier des 25-jährigen Pontifikats von Johannes Paul II. am 26. Oktober 2003 eingeweiht.

L'église est implantée sur un terrain triangulaire en bordure d'un parc public entouré d'immeubles de logements de 10 étages dans un ensemble qui compte environ 30 000 résidents. Le projet qui fait appel au béton, au stuc, au travertin et au verre se caractérise par trois coques ou arcs spectaculaires qui évoquent des voiles blanches et gonflées. Motif sans précédent dans l'œuvre de Meier, ces arcs de béton s'étagent de 17 à 27 mètres. Le concours sur invitation comprenait Tadao Ando, Günther Behnisch, Santiago Calatrava, Peter Eisenman et Frank Gehry ainsi que Meier qui le remporta en 1996. C'était son premier projet d'église même s'il a déjà conçu le Séminaire de Hartford (Connecticut, 1981), l'International Center for Possibility Thinking de la Crystal Cathedral (Californie du sud, 2003). Le chantier débuta en 1998. Comme toujours, Meier a mis l'accent sur la lumière : « La lumière est le protagoniste qui nous fait comprendre et lire l'espace. La lumière est le moyen par lequel nous sommes en mesure de faire l'expérience de ce que nous appelons le sacré. La lumière est à l'origine de ce projet. » Commentant le fait qu'il est peut-être le premier architecte juif à concevoir une église, il ajoute : « Je me sens extrêmement fier d'avoir été choisi… il est clair que l'Église catholique a retenu mon projet pour ses mérites, et non pas pour marquer une position par rapport à sa relation avec les Juifs au cours de l'histoire. Trois des architectes invités étaient juifs. Ils avaient été sélectionnés parce qu'ils faisaient partie des tout premiers architectes de notre temps. » Ses sources d'inspiration ont été « des églises dans lesquelles ont peut sentir la présence du sacré : celles de Alvar Aalto en Finlande, la Wayfairer's Chapel de Frank Lloyd Wright aux États-Unis, la chapelle de Ronchamp et le couvent de la Tourette par Le Corbusier ». L'église du Jubilée a été inaugurée le 26 octobre 2003, pour marquer le 25ème anniversaire du pontificat de Jean-Paul II.

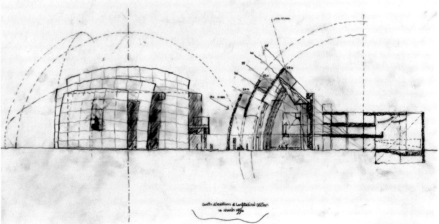

As always attentive to the effects of light in his architecture, Richard Meier has created a light-filled church with a markedly asymmetrical interior design.

Wie immer sorgfältig auf die Wirkung des Lichts in seiner Architektur bedacht, hat Richard Meier eine lichter-tullte Kirche mit einem ausgesprochen asymmetrischen Innenraum entworfen.

Toujours attentif aux effets de la lumière dans son architecture, Meier a créé une église extrêmement lumineuse sur un plan intérieur fortement asymétrique.

# MEYER EN VAN SCHOOTEN

*Meyer en Van Schooten Architecten B. V.*
*P. O. Box 2737*
*1000 CS Amsterdam*
*The Netherlands*

*Tel: +31 20 5319 800*
*Fax: +31 20 53 19 801*
*e-mail: office@meyer-vanschooten.nl*
*Web: www.meyer-vanschooten.nl*

Roberto Meyer was born in 1959 in Bogotá, Colombia, while Jeroen van Schooten was born in Nieuwer Amstel, The Netherlands in 1960. They created their firm Meyer en Van Schooten Architecten B. V. in Amsterdam in 1984. Their work includes housing in Enschede, Apeldoorn, Amsterdam, Rotterdam, Zaandam and Arnhem. They have also built a number of bridges (IJburg, Amsterdam, 1998). Their recent work includes: 60 apartments (Geuzenbaan, Amsterdam); central library/30 apartments/offices/shops (Almere-Stad); 150 apartments + parking (Verolme terrain, Alblasserdam); 52 apartments in block 11 and 78 apartments in block 14b Gershwin (south axis, Amsterdam); and the 160-apartment Veranda complex in Rotterdam. Their ING building published here won several awards, including the 2002 Netherlands Steel Prize (Nationale Staalprijs 2002) and the 2003 Aluminum Architecture Award 2003 (Nederlandse Aluminium Award Architectuur 2003). Upcoming work includes a Science Center for the University of Amsterdam, to be completed in 2007.

Roberto Meyer wurde 1959 in Bogotá, Kolumbien, und Jeroen van Schooten 1960 im niederländischen Nieuwer Amstel geboren. Zusammen gründeten sie 1984 ihre Firma Meyer en Van Schooten Architecten B.V. in Amsterdam. Zu ihren Arbeiten gehören Wohnbauten in Enschede, Apeldoorn, Amsterdam, Rotterdam, Zaandam und Arnheim. Außerdem planten sie eine Reihe von Brücken, wie die von IJburg, Amsterdam (1998). Zu ihren jüngsten Projekten zählen: 60 Wohnungen in Geuzenbaan, Amsterdam, eine Anlage aus Bücherei, 30 Wohnungen, Büros und Geschäften in Almere-Stad, 150 Wohnungen mit Parkplatz auf dem Verolme Gelände in Alblasserdam, 52 Wohnungen in Block 11 und 78 Wohnungen in Block 14b der Gershwin Südachse in Amsterdam sowie die Anlage Veranda mit 160 Wohnungen in Rotterdam. Ihr hier vorgestelltes ING-Gebäude erhielt zahlreiche Auszeichnungen, wie 2002 den Nationale Staalprijs (Niederländische Stahlpreis) und 2003 den Nederlandse Aluminium Award Architectuur. Zu ihren nächsten Aufgaben gehört ein Wissenschaftszentrum für die Universität Amsterdam, das 2007 fertig gestellt sein soll.

Roberto Meyer est né en 1959 à Bogotá (Colombie) et Jeroen van Schooten à Nieuwer Amstel (Pays-Bas) en 1960. Ils ont créé leur agence Meyer en Van Schooten Architecten B.V. à Amsterdam en 1984. Leurs réalisations comprennent des logements à Enschede, Apeldoorn, Amsterdam, Rotterdam, Zaandam et Arnhem. Ils ont également construit plusieurs ponts (IJburg, Amsterdam, 1998). Parmi leurs travaux récents : 60 appartements (Geuzenbaan, Amsterdam) ; Bibliothèque centrale/30 appartements/bureaux/ commerces (Almere-Stad) ; 150 appartements et parkings (Verolme Terrain, Alblasserdam) ; 52 appartements (bloc 11) et 78 appartements (bloc 14 b Gershwin (Axe sud, Amsterdam), et l'ensemble Veranda de 160 appartements à Rotterdam. L'immeuble ING, publié ici, a remporté plusieurs prix dont le Nationale Staalprijs 2002 (Prix de l'acier) et le Prix néerlandais de l'aluminium 2003. Ils travaillent actuellement au Centre des sciences de l'Université d'Amsterdam, prévu pour 2007.

# ING GROUP HEADQUARTERS

*Amsterdam, The Netherlands, 1998–2002*

*Client: ING Group N.V. Building area: 3 500 m², office floor area: 7 500 m². Costs: not specified.*

Built on a long, narrow site near Amsterdam's Ring Road, the ING headquarters lies between the Zuidas area of high-rise buildings and a green zone called De Nieuwe Meer. The architects intentionally kept the structure low on the "green" side and made it rise in the direction of the city. In order to allow motorists a view toward the green zone and at the same time to give the offices a view over the highway, the building is set up on pilotis ranging in height from 9 to 12.5 meters. A great deal of attention was paid to the energy efficiency of the structure, for example with a double-skin façade that facilitates natural ventilation while providing a sound barrier against traffic noise. A pumping system makes use of an aquifer located 120 meters under the building to provide cold/warm thermal storage. Successive stories within the building "intermingle and offer glimpses from one to another. Atriums, loggias and gardens vary the interior space as well. As the architects have written, "the new headquarters symbolizes the banking and insurance conglomerate as a dynamic, fast-moving international network. Transparency, innovation, eco-friendliness and openness were the main starting points for the design." Another interesting element in the design process is the request of the client that the building last between 50 and 100 years. Set up on V-shaped stilts, the structure looks as though it might just move on before that.

Die ING-Zentrale wurde auf einem lang gestreckten, schmalen Grundstück errichtet, das nahe der Amsterdamer Ringautobahn zwischen der Hochhausgegend Zuidas und dem Naherholungsgebiet De Nieuwe Meer liegt. Bewusst hielten die Architekten das Gebäude zur „grünen Seite" hin niedrig und ließen es zur Stadtseite hin ansteigen. Um den Autofahrern nicht den Blick ins Grüne zu verstellen und den Büros gleichzeitig einen Ausblick über die Schnellstraße hinweg zu gewähren, wurde das Gebäude auf 9 bis 12,5 m hohe Stützpfeiler gesetzt. Große Sorgfalt wurde auch auf ein effizientes Energiesystem verwendet, beispielsweise mit einer doppelwandigen Fassade, die für natürliche Belüftung sorgt und einen Schutz gegen den Verkehrslärm bietet. Außerdem wird durch eine Pumpanlage eine 120 m unterhalb des Gebäudes liegende, wasserführende Schicht als Thermospeicher genutzt. Im Inneren sind die Stockwerke nicht klar abgegrenzt, sondern gehen ineinander über, so dass sich immer wieder Durchblicke von einem Geschoss zum anderen öffnen. Auch Atrien, Loggien und Wintergärten bringen Abwechslung in den Innenraum. Die Architekten über ihr Projekt: „Mit der neuen Zentrale stellt sich der Bank- und Versicherungskonzern als ein dynamisches, internationales Netzwerk dar. Dabei waren die Aspekte Transparenz, Innovation, Umweltfreundlichkeit und Offenheit für uns entwurfsbestimmend." Wichtig war zudem die Anforderung des Auftraggebers, das Gebäude solle eine Lebensdauer von 50 bis 100 Jahren haben. Mit seinen V-förmigen Stelzen sieht es jedoch aus, als könnte es schon vor dieser Zeit einfach weiterziehen.

Édifié sur un long terrain étroit en bordure de l'autoroute périphérique d'Amsterdam, le siège d'ING est situé entre le quartier de tours de Zuidas et une zone verte, De Nieuwe Meer. Sur le côté «vert», les architectes ont volontairement maintenu une faible hauteur qui s'accroît rapidement vers le côté ville. Pour permettre aux automobilistes de conserver une vision de la zone verte et offrir aux bureaux une vue qui passe par-dessus l'autoroute, l'immeuble est posé sur des pilotis dont la hauteur varie de 9 à 12,5 m. Une grande attention a été portée à l'autonomie énergétique du bâtiment, par exemple grâce à une façade à double-peau qui permet une ventilation naturelle et protège du bruit de la circulation. Un système de pompage utilise la nappe phréatique à 120 m de profondeur pour le stockage thermique. Les différents étages «s'imbriquent et offrent des vues l'un sur l'autre». Atriums, loggia et jardins diversifient l'intérieur de l'espace. Comme le précisent les architectes : «La nouvelle approche internationale, de transparence, d'innovation, de sensibilité écologique et d'ouverture a constitué le principal point de départ du projet. » Un autre élément intéressant, à la demande du client, est que l'immeuble dure de 50 à 100 ans. Posé sur ses pilotis en V, on a l'impression qu'il pourrait bien avoir envie de se transporter ailleurs avant cette date.

Like an apparition out of a "Star Wars" movie, the ING Headquarters building looks almost as though it is ready to move forward on its legs.

Die an ein Wesen aus „Star Wars" erinnernde ING-Zentrale sieht fast so aus, als könne sie sich auf ihren Stelzenbeinen vorwärtsbewegen.

Comme sorti d'un film de la série Star Wars, le siège d'ING donne l'impression d'être prêt à déambuler sur ses grandes jambes inclinées.

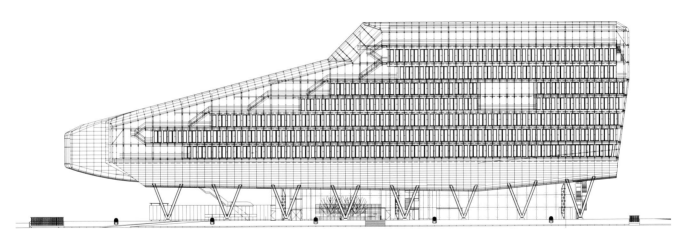

Massive as seen from almost any angle, the weight of the structure seems all the more imposing since it is lifted off the ground.

Das Gewicht des von fast jedem Blickwinkel massiv aussehenden Gebäudes wirkt umso eindrucksvoller, wenn man bedenkt, dass es auf Stützpfeilern ruht.

Massif sous presque tous ses angles, l'immeuble semble d'un poids d'autant plus imposant qu'il est surélevé par rapport au sol.

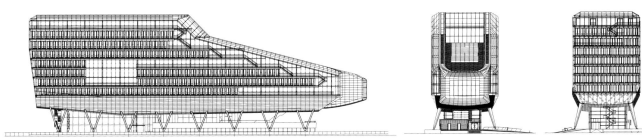

Though the image above gives the impression that the structure spreads wider as it rises, sections show that this is not the case.

Obwohl das Bild oben den Eindruck erweckt, dass das Gebäude nach oben breiter wird, beweist der Querschnitt das Gegenteil.

Contrairement à l'impression donnée par l'image ci-dessus, la structure n'est pas évasée vers le haut comme le montrent les coupes ci-dessous.

Ground level images give an impression of lightness since the weight of the structure is carried on the external tilted "legs."

Die Bilder vom Innenraum im Erdgeschoss vermitteln einen Eindruck von Leichtigkeit, während das Gewicht des Gebäudes von den schräggestellten „Beinen" getragen wird.

Les photos prises au niveau du sol donnent une impression de légèreté du fait de la surélévation sur pilotis.

The glazed airiness of the ground floor is repeated in this space, where a zig-zagging stairway goes up the glass façade.

Die luftige Atmosphäre im Erdgeschoss wiederholt sich in diesem Raum, wo eine Treppe im Zickzack die Glasfassade entlang nach oben führt.

La transparence aérienne du rez-de-chaussée se retrouve à l'intérieur du volume, marqué par un escalier en zigzag qui semble escalader la façade de verre.

Though the density of the metallic
structure gives a technical or mechanical appearance to the whole,
the space is filled with light.

Obwohl die dichte Metallkonstruk-
tion dem Ganzen eine technische
Note verleiht, ist der Innenraum
von Licht erfüllt.

Si la densité de la présence du
métal donne un aspect technique
ou mécanique, les volumes sont
très lumineux.

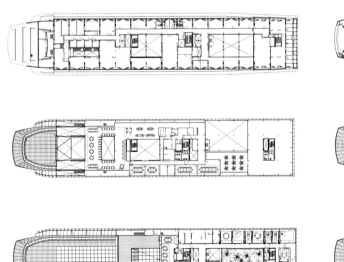

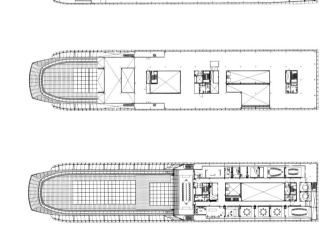

Floor plans show the fundamental regularity of the design and the effect of the progressively increasing area of the glazed roof. Above, a board room in the upper level.

Die Grundrisse zeigen die Regelmäßigkeit der Gestaltung und die mit jedem Stockwerk größer werdende Fläche der Dachverglasung. Oben: ein Sitzungsraum im Obergeschoss.

Les plans des niveaux montrent le parti pris de régularité de la conception et l'effet du toit de verre dont la taille croît peu à peu. Ci-dessus, une salle du conseil au niveau supérieur.

# OSCAR NIEMEYER

Oscar Niemeyer
Avenida Atlantica 3940
Rio de Janeiro
Brazil

Tel: +55 21 5234 890
Fax: +55 21 2676 388
Web: www.niemeyer.org.br

*Serpentine Gallery Pavilion 2003* ▶

Born in Rio de Janeiro in 1907, Oscar Niemeyer studied at the Escola Nacional de Belas Artes. He graduated in 1934 and joined a team of Brazilian architects collaborating with Le Corbusier on a new Ministry of Education and Health in Rio de Janeiro. It was Lucio Costa, for whom he worked as an assistant, who introduced Niemeyer to Le Corbusier. Between 1940 and 1954, his work was based in three cities: Rio de Janeiro, Sao Paulo and Belo Horizonte. In 1956 Niemeyer was appointed architectural adviser to Nova Cap – an organization responsible for implementing Lucio Costa's plans for Brazil's new capital. The following year, he became its chief architect, designing most of the city's important buildings. In 1964 he sought exile in France for political reasons. There, amongst other structures, he designed the building for the French Communist Party in Paris. With the end of the dictatorship he returned to Brazil, immediately resuming his professional activities. He was awarded the Gold Medal of the American Institute of Architecture in 1970 and the 1988 Pritzker Prize.

Oscar Niemeyer, geboren 1907 in Rio de Janeiro, schloss sich unmittelbar nach seinem Studienabschluss 1934 an der Escola Nacional de Belas Artes einer Gruppe brasilianischer Architekten an, die zusammen mit Le Corbusier das neue Ministerium für Bildung und Gesundheit in Rio de Janeiro planten. Lucio Costa, für den Niemeyer als Assistent arbeitete, stellte ihn Le Corbusier vor. Zwischen 1940 und 1954 war Niemeyer an drei Orten tätig: Rio de Janeiro, Sao Paulo und Belo Horizonte. 1956 wurde er zum architektonischen Berater von Nova Cap ernannt – einer Organisation, die gegründet worden war, um Lucio Costas Pläne für Brasiliens neue Hauptstadt zu realisieren. Im folgenden Jahr wurde er zum leitenden Architekten berufen, der die meisten wichtigen Gebäude der Stadt entwarf. 1964 ging er aus politischen Gründen nach Frankreich ins Exil und plante dort unter anderem das Gebäude der Kommunistischen Partei Frankreichs in Paris. Mit dem Ende der Diktatur kehrte er nach Brasilien zurück und nahm sofort seine Aktivitäten als Architekturprofessor wieder auf. 1970 erhielt er die Gold Medal des American Institute of Architects und 1988 den Pritzker Prize.

Né à Rio de Janeiro en 1907, Oscar Niemeyer étudie à la Escola Nacional de Belas Artes. Diplômé en 1934, il fait partie de l'équipe d'architectes brésiliens qui collabore avec Le Corbusier pour le nouveau ministère de l'éducation et de la santé à Rio. C'est Lucio Costa, dont il est assistant, qui l'introduit auprès de Le Corbusier. De 1940 à 1954, il intervient essentiellement dans trois villes : Rio de Janeiro, Sao Paulo et Belo Horizonte. En 1956, il est nommé conseiller pour l'architecure de Nova Cap, organisme chargé du développement des plans de Costa pour la nouvelle capitale. L'année suivante, il devient son architecte en chef, dessinant la plupart des bâtiments importants de Brasilia. En 1964, il s'exile en France pour des raisons politiques. Là, entre autres, il construit le siège du parti communiste à Paris. À la fin de la dictature, il retourne au Brésil, reprenant immédiatement ses responsabilités professionnelles. Il reçoit la médaille d'or de l'American Institute of Architecture en 1970 et le Pritzker Prize en 1988.

# SERPENTINE GALLERY PAVILION 2003

*Kensington Gardens, London, UK, 2003*

*Client: Serpentine Gallery, Kensington Gardens. Floor area: 250 m². Costs: not specified.*

"I am delighted to be designing the Serpentine Gallery Pavilion, my first structure in the United Kingdom," wrote Oscar Niemeyer. "My idea was to keep this project different, free and audacious. That is what I prefer. I like to draw, I like to see from the blank sheet of paper a palace, a cathedral, the figure of a woman appearing. But life for me is much more important than architecture." In these times of computer-generated architecture, it is a rare privilege to see the recent work of an architect who worked with Le Corbusier in the mid-1930s. The Pavilion he created for the Serpentine Gallery does have very much the spirit of one of his own sketches brought to life. After first refusing to design this small structure, Niemeyer accepted when the director of the Serpentine, Julia Peyton-Jones, went to Rio to meet him. One of his long-time collaborators, the engineer Jose Carlos Sussekind, and Arups in London actually made certain that the Pavilion was built. Made of concrete and steel, the structure looks more like a permanent addition to the Kensington Gardens than it is. "My architecture followed the old examples," said Niemeyer when he received the 1988 Pritzker Prize. "The beauty prevailing over the limitations of the constructive logic. My work proceeded, indifferent to the unavoidable criticism set forth by those who take the trouble to examine the minimum details, so very true of what mediocrity is capable of." It appears that in these circumstances, Niemeyer wanted to create nothing else than a resumé of his own work. "I wanted to give a flavor of everything that characterizes my work," he said to *The Financial Times*. The first thing was to create something floating above the ground. In a small building occupying a small space, using concrete, and few supports and girders, we can give an idea of what my architecture is all about."

„Ich bin hocherfreut, den Serpentine Gallery Pavilion zu entwerfen, mein erstes Bauwerk in Großbritannien", schrieb Oscar Niemeyer. „Meine Idee war, dieses Projekt anders wirken zu lassen – frei und verwegen. Das ist es, was ich bevorzuge. Ich zeichne gern und ich mag es, auf einem weißen Blatt Papier einen Palast, eine Kathedrale, die Gestalt einer näher kommenden Frau entstehen zu sehen. Aber das Leben ist für mich viel wichtiger als die Architektur." In diesen Zeiten computerergenerierten Gestaltens ist es ein seltenes Privileg, die neueste Arbeit eines Architekten zu sehen, der schon Mitte der 1930er Jahre mit Le Corbusier zusammengearbeitet hat. Der von Niemeyer entworfene Pavillon hat in der Tat eine spirituelle Energie – er wirkt, als sei seine Zeichnung zum Leben erwacht. Die aus Beton und Stahl bestehende Konstruktion sieht allerdings dauerhafter aus, als sie wirklich ist. Der Architekt sagte 1988 in seiner Dankesrede zur Verleihung des Pritzker Prize: „Meine Architektur folgte den alten Vorbildern. Das heißt, die Ästhetik hat immer die Begrenzungen der konstruktiven Logik überwogen. Meine Arbeit entwickelte sich unabhängig von der unvermeidlichen Kritik derer, die sich die Mühe machen, jedes kleinste Detail zu untersuchen – was so treffend charakterisiert, wozu Mittelmäßigkeit fähig ist." Es scheint, als habe Niemeyer mit dem Serpentine Gallery Pavilion ein Resümee seiner architektonischen Arbeit präsentieren wollen. In einem Interview mit der *Financial Times* fasste er zusammen: „Ich wollte einen Eindruck von all dem vermitteln, was für mein Werk charakteristisch ist. Dabei ging es mir vornehmlich darum, etwas zu gestalten, das über dem Erdboden schwebt. Indem wir in einem kleinen Gebäude, das wenig Raum einnimmt, Beton, ein paar Stützen und Träger verwenden, können wir eine Vorstellung davon vermitteln, worum es in meiner Architektur geht."

« Je suis ravi de concevoir le pavillon de la Serpentine Gallery, ma première réalisation au Royaume-Uni », a écrit Oscar Niemeyer. « Mon idée a été de trouver une approche différente, libre et audacieuse. C'est ce que je préfère. J'aime dessiner, j'aime voir apparaître sur la feuille blanche un palais, une cathédrale, la figure d'une femme. Mais pour moi la vie est beaucoup plus importante que l'architecture. » En ces temps d'architecture générée par ordinateur, c'est un privilège rare de voir naître une œuvre récente d'un architecte qui a travaillé avec Le Corbusier au milieu des années 1930. Son pavillon pour la Serpentine Gallery fait penser à l'animation de l'un de ses croquis. En béton et en acier, la structure pourrait être une addition permanente aux Kensington Gardens, ce qu'elle n'est pas. « Mon architecture a suivi des exemples anciens », a déclaré Niemeyer en recevant le Pritzker Prize 1988. « La beauté prend le pas sur les limites de la logique de construction. Mon œuvre a progressé, indifférente aux critiques inévitables avancées par ceux qui perdent leur temps à examiner des détails sans importance, bon exemple de ce dont la médiocrité est capable. » Niemeyer souhaitait créer un résumé de son œuvre. « Je voulais donner le goût de tout ce qui caractérise mon œuvre », a-t-il déclaré au *Financial Times*. « La première étape a été de créer quelque chose qui flotte au-dessus du sol. À travers une petite construction qui occupe une petite parcelle, à partir du béton, de quelques poutres et supports, on peut donner une idée de ce qu'est l'architecture. »

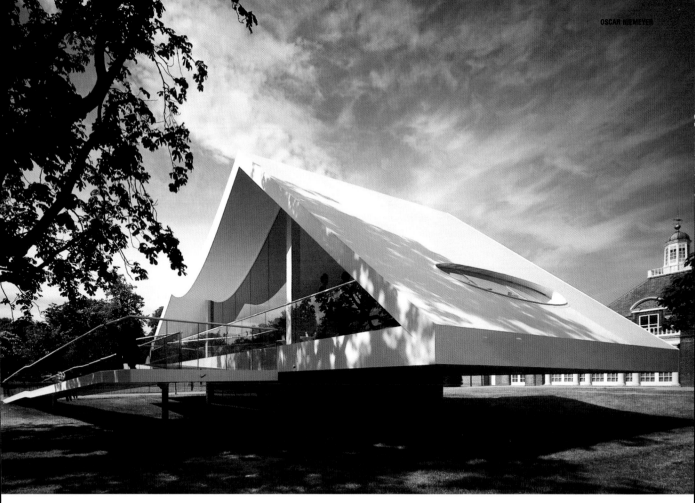

Succeeding Toyo Ito in Kensington Gardens as the architect of the Serpentine's temporary summer pavilion Oscar Niemeyer calls on a typically daring use of wide expanses of white concrete.

Der auf Toyo Ito als Architekt des Sommerpavillons der Serpentine Gallery in Kensington Gardens folgende Oscar Niemeyer präsentiert einen typisch wagemutigen Einsatz großer, weißer Betonflächen.

Succédant à Toyo Ito pour construire le pavillon d'été temporaire de la Serpentine dans les Kensington Gardens, Oscar Niemeyer utilise les grands plans de béton blanc qui lui sont familiers.

Using as few supports and girders as possible, the structure offers light, open spaces that appear more tent-like than solid.

À partir d'un nombre aussi réduit que possible de poutres et de poteaux, la structure offre des espaces ouverts et lumineux qui font davantage penser à une tente qu'à une construction lourde.

Unter Verwendung so weniger Stützen und Träger wie möglich bietet der Bau helle, offene Räume, die ihn mehr wie ein Zelt als ein massives Gebäude wirken lassen.

Oscar Niemeyer clearly still masters the dramatic design that made him famous in Brasilia and elsewhere.

Oscar Niemeyer ist nach wie vor ein Meister der dramatischen Form-gebung, die ihn in Brasilia und anderswo berühmt gemacht hat.

Oscar Niemeyer maîtrise toujours le style spectaculaire qui l'a rendu célèbre à Brasilia et dans le monde.

# JEAN NOUVEL

*Architectures Jean Nouvel*
*10, Cité d'Angoulème*
*75011 Paris*
*France*

*Tel: +33 1 49 23 83 83*
*Fax: +33 1 43 14 81 10*

*Monolith, Expo.02* ▶

Born in 1945 in Sarlat, France, Jean Nouvel was admitted to the École des Beaux-Arts in Bordeaux in 1964. In 1970, he created his first office with François Seigneur. His first widely noticed project was the Institut du Monde Arabe in Paris (1981–1987, with Architecture Studio). Other works include his Nemausus housing (Nîmes, 1985–1987); offices for the CLM/BBDO advertising firm (Issy-les-Moulineaux, 1988–1992); Lyon Opera House (Lyon, 1986–1993); Vinci Conference Center (Tours, 1989–1993); Euralille Shopping Center (Lille, 1991–1994); Fondation Cartier (Paris, 1991–1995); Galeries Lafayette (Berlin, 1992–1996); and his unbuilt projects for the 400-meter-tall "Tour sans fin," La Défense (Paris, 1989); Grand Stade for the 1998 World Cup (Paris, 1994); and Tenaga Nasional Tower (Kuala Lumpur, 1995). His largest recently completed project is the Music and Conference Center in Lucerne, Switzerland (1998–2000). He won both the competition for the Museum of Arts and Civilizations, Paris, and the competition for the refurbishment of the Reina Sofia Center, Madrid in 1999. Recent work includes the Dentsu advertising agency tower in Tokyo and plans for the Standard Hotel in Soho (New York). In 2003, Jean Nouvel won a competition sponsored by the Aga Khan Trust for Culture for the design of the waterfront Corniche in Doha, Qatar, and was called on to design the new Guggenheim Museum in Rio de Janeiro.

Jean Nouvel, geboren 1945 im französischen Sarlat, studierte ab 1964 an der École des Beaux-Arts in Bordeaux. 1970 gründete er zusammen mit François Seigneur sein erstes Architekturbüro. Weithin bekannt wurde Nouvel mit seinem Institut du Monde Arabe in Paris (1981–1987), bei dem er mit Architecture Studio zusammenarbeitete. Zu seinen weiteren Arbeiten zählen: die Wohnanlage Nemausus in Nîmes (1985–1987), das Opernhaus in Lyon (1986–1993), die Büros der Werbeagentur CLM/BBDO in Issy-les-Moulineaux (1988–1992), das Kongresszentrum Vinci in Tours (1989–1993), das Einkaufszentrum Euralille in Lille (1991–1994), die Fondation Cartier in Paris (1991–1995) und die Galeries Lafayette in Berlin (1992–1996). Außerdem plante Jean Nouvel den 400 m hohen Turm „Tour sans fin" in La Défense, Paris (1989), das Grand Stade für die Fußball-Weltmeisterschaft von 1998 in Paris (1994) und den Tenaga Nasional Tower in Kuala Lumpur (1995), die aber alle nicht realisiert wurden. Sein umfangreichstes, in neuerer Zeit fertig gestelltes Projekt ist das Musik- und Kongresszentrum in Luzern (1998–2000). Im Jahr 1999 gewann er sowohl den Wettbewerb für das Musée des Arts et Civilisations in Paris sowie für die Modernisierung des Reina Sofia Zentrums in Madrid (1999). Zu seinen jüngsten Arbeiten zählen der Turm für die Werbeagentur Dentsu in Tokio und Entwürfe für das Standard Hotel in Soho, New York. 2003 gewann Jean Nouvel den vom Aga Khan Trust for Culture gesponserten Wettbewerb für die Gestaltung der Uferpromenade in Doha auf der arabischen Halbinsel Qatar und wurde mit der Planung des neuen Guggenheim Museums in Rio de Janeiro beauftragt.

Né en 1945 à Sarlat, Jean Nouvel est admis à l'École des Beaux-Arts de Bordeaux en 1964. En 1970, il crée une première agence avec François Seigneur. Son premier projet vraiment remarqué est l'Institut du Monde Arabe, à Paris, (1981–1987, avec Architecture Studio). Parmi ses autres réalisations : les immeubles d'appartements Nemausus, à Nîmes (1985–1987), les bureaux de l'agence de publicité CLM/BBDO (Issy-les-Moulineaux, 1988–1992), l'Opéra de Lyon (1986–1993), le palais des congrès Vinci (Tours, 1989–1993), le centre commercial Euralille (Lille, 1991–1994), la Fondation Cartier (Paris, 1991–1995), les galeries Lafayette (Berlin, 1992–1996). Parmi ses projets non réalisés : une tour de 400 m « La tour sans fin » (La Défense, Paris, 1989), le Grand Stade de la Coupe du monde de football 1998 (Paris, 1994), la Tour nationale Tenaga (Kuala Lumpur, Malaisie, 1995). En 1999, il a remporté les concours du Musée des Arts et Civilisations (Paris) et de la restructuration-extension du Centro Reina Sofia (Madrid). Parmi ses réalisations récentes : la tour du goupe publicitaire Dentsu à Tokyo et le Standard Hotel à Soho (New York). En 2003, il a remporté un concours organisé par l'Aga Khan Trust for Culture pour la nouvelle corniche de Doha au Qatar, et a été choisi pour le nouveau Guggenheim Museum de Rio de Janeiro.

# MONOLITH, EXPO.02

*Morat, Switzerland, 2000–01*

*Client: Swiss Expo.02. Dimensions: 34 x 34 x 34 m. Costs: € 36 000 000 (all interventions).*

For the Swiss National Exhibition, in principle organized every 25 years, it was decided in 2002 to situate the pavilions in four different cities near Neuchâtel. In each case, the buildings had to be temporary and situated whenever possible on the lakes of Neuchâtel and Morat. Jean Nouvel was chosen as the main architect involved in the attractive historic city of Morat. He conceived a series of interventions, the most visible of which was a monolithic block of rusting steel sitting off the shore in the lake. Another unexpected structure was an exhibition area occupied by the Fondation Cartier and made of stacks of logs. Actually, with its reference to logging, this structure may have had more to do with Switzerland than some of the other elements of the exhibitions. Using tents, containers and military camouflage, Nouvel occupied Morat with his temporary designs in a manner and style that in some cases approached installation art more than architecture. Unlike the other cities involved in Expo.02, Morat, at Nouvel's instigation, did not create a closed-off area for the pavilions – rather the different elements were dispersed in proximity to the lake, with a simple ticketing system allowing entry to each area in whatever order the visitor preferred. This spreading of the Expo throughout the city was in part due to the relatively dense town configuration but it also permitted a real discovery of the city. For those interested in Nouvel, seeking out and recognizing his interventions became a part of the adventure of visiting the Expo. Nouvel's Expo.02 became part of Morat rather than being an incoherent addition. Although Expo.02 in Morat has not been as widely published as many other recent works by Jean Nouvel, it is amongst his most inventive and surprising efforts. He showed in particular that he was sensitive to changing circumstances, where astonishing new buildings may not be as much in the spirit of the times as an ability to use simple materials and designs to redefine space and serve a specific purpose.

Die Organisatoren der Schweizer Landesausstellung, die in der Regel alle 25 Jahre stattfindet, beschlossen für das Jahr 2002, die Ausstellungspavillons auf vier verschiedene Standorte nahe der Kantonshauptstadt Neuchâtel zu verteilen. Die Bauten sollten temporär sein und, wenn möglich, direkt auf dem Neuenburger oder Murtensee liegen. Jean Nouvel, der als leitender Architekt für die historische Gemeinde Murten ausgewählt worden war, entwarf eine Reihe von Arbeiten, deren hervorstechendste ein monolithischer Block aus rostigem Stahl war, der in einiger Entfernung vom Ufer aus dem Wasser ragte. Ebenfalls sehr ungewöhnlich war eine andere Arbeit, eine Ausstellungsfläche für die Fondation Cartier, die aus übereinander gestapelten Holzstämmen bestand. Mit ihrem Bezug auf die Holzindustrie hatte diese Konstruktion mehr mit der Schweiz zu tun als viele andere Beiträge. Einige von Nouvels Konstruktionen waren mit Bestandteilen wie Zelten, Containern und Tarnnetzen der Installationskunst näher als der Architektur. Im Gegensatz zu anderen Standorten der Expo.02 verzichtete Murten – auf Nouvels Betreiben – auf einen abgegrenzten Bereich für die Pavillons. Stattdessen wurden die einzelnen Objekte in Seenähe verteilt. Ein unkompliziertes Kartensystem erlaubte den Besuchern, alle Ausstellungsbereiche in beliebiger Reihenfolge zu besichtigen. Dass sich die Expo so über die ganze Stadt ausbreiten konnte, ergab sich aus Murtens relativ dichtem Stadtgefüge, das den Ausstellungsbesuchern die Gelegenheit bot, die Stadt wirklich zu entdecken. Für die Fans von Nouvel trug das Aufspüren und Identifizieren seiner Arbeiten zu der besonderen Qualität dieser Expo bei. Nouvel ließ seine Expo-Beiträge mehr zu einem Teil der Stadt werden als sie nur zusammenhanglos hinzu zu fügen. Obwohl die Ausstellung nicht so große Beachtung in den Medien fand wie andere seiner Projekte, gehört sie zu seinen einfallsreichsten und überraschendsten Arbeiten. Er bewies hier eine besondere Sensibilität gegenüber sich verändernden Verhältnissen, in denen spektakuläre neue Gebäude möglicherweise weniger zeitgemäß sind als die Fähigkeit, mit einfachen Materialien und Gestaltungsformen einen Raum zu definieren und einem bestimmten Zweck zu dienen.

L'Exposition nationale suisse, qui se tient en principe tous les 25 ans, avait décidé de s'implanter dans la région de Neuchâtel. Les bâtiments devaient être temporaires et situés dans une large mesure sur les lacs de Neuchâtel et de Morat. Jean Nouvel a été choisi pour le projet de la charmante petite cité historique de Morat. Il a conçu une série d'interventions dont la plus visible était un bloc monolithique en acier rouillé posé à quelques encablures de la rive. Une autre création étonnante était l'espace d'exposition occupé par la Fondation Cartier, construite à partir d'empilements de grumes. Par sa référence aux rondins, elle était sans doute plus en rapport avec la Suisse que certains autres éléments des expositions. À l'aide de tentes, de conteneurs et de camouflage militaire, les projets temporaires de Nouvel ont occupé Morat d'une façon et dans un style plus proches de l'installation que de l'architecture. À la différence d'autres villes participant à Expo.02, Morat, à l'instigation de l'architecte, n'avait pas créé de zone fermée mais préféré disperser les divers lieux à proximité du lac, un système de billetterie permettant à chacun de visiter ce qu'il voulait dans l'ordre de ses préférences. Cette dilution de l'Expo, due en partie à la configuration relativement dense de la ville, en permettait cependant une authentique découverte. Pour ceux qui s'intéressent au travail de Nouvel, la recherche et la reconnaissance de ses interventions participaient au plaisir de la visite. Son intervention faisait partie de la ville, plutôt que de se contenter de n'être qu'un simple ajout sans cohérence. Bien que ce travail n'ait pas reçu une couverture médiatique aussi abondante que celle d'autres réalisations récentes de l'architecte, elle fait partie de ses réalisations les plus inventives et les plus étonnantes. Il a montré en particulier qu'il était sensible à des circonstances particulières, que créer une construction qui surprenne était peut-être moins dans l'esprit du moment que la capacité à faire appel à des plans et des matériaux simples pour redéfinir l'espace et répondre à un objectif bien défini.

*Nouvel's contribution to Expo.02 in Morat was not limited to the rusting metal Monolith. He also conceived a number of the lakeside installations.*

*Nouvels Beitrag zur Expo.02 beschränkte sich nicht auf den Monolith aus rostigem Metall. Er entwarf auch etliche der um den Murtensee herum installierten Arbeiten.*

*La contribution de Nouvel à Expo.02 à Morat ne se limitait pas à ce monolithe d'aspect rouillé. Il y a également conçu un certain nombre d'autres installations en bordure du lac.*

# NOX

NOX/Lars Spuybroek
Heer Bokelweg 163, 3032 AD Rotterdam, The Netherlands
Tel/Fax: +31 10 477 2853, e-mail: nox@luna.nl

Lars Spuybroek
Professor of Digital Design Techniques
University of Kassel, Germany
Tel.: +49 561 804 2352, e-mail: lars@architektur.uni-kassel.de

Lars Spuybroek is the principal of NOX. Since the early 1990s he has been involved in research on the relationship between architecture and media, and often more specifically between architecture and computing. He was the editor-publisher of one of the first magazines on the subject (*NOX*, and later also *Forum*), and has made videos (Soft City) and interactive electronic artworks (Soft Site, edit Spline, deep Surface). More recently, he has focused more on architecture (HtwoOexpo, Blow Out, V2_lab, wetGRID, D-tower, Son-O-house, Maison Folie). His work has won several prizes and was represented at the Venice Biennale in 2000 and 2002. In 2003 NOX participated in the important international exhibitions "Zoomorphic" at the Victoria & Albert in London and "Non Standard Architectures" at the Centre Pompidou in Paris. NOX is currently finishing the interactive tower for the Dutch city of Doetinchem (D-Tower), "a house where sounds live" (Son-O-house), and a complex of cultural buildings in Lille, France (Maison Folies), as well as working on competitions for the European Central Bank in Frankfurt and the New Centre Pompidou in Metz, France (competition won by Shigeru Ban). Lars Spuybroek has lectured widely. He has taught at several universities in Holland and is a regular visiting professor at Columbia University in New York. Since 2002 he has held a tenured professorship at the University of Kassel in Germany, where he chairs the CAD/digital design techniques department. He is also working on a book, *Machining Architecture*, which is to be published by Thames & Hudson in 2004.

Lars Spuybroek, der Leiter von NOX, beschäftigt sich seit Anfang der 1990er Jahre mit dem Verhältnis zwischen Architektur und Medien, insbesondere zwischen Architektur und Computerwesen. Er war Herausgeber und Verleger einer der ersten Zeitschriften zu diesem Thema, *NOX* (später auch *Forum*), und hat Videos (Soft City) wie auch interaktive elektronische Kunstwerke (Soft Site, edit Spline, deep Surface) produziert. In jüngster Zeit hat er sich mehr auf die Architektur konzentriert, mit Projekten wie HtwoOexpo, Blow Out, V2_lab, wetGRID, D-tower, Son-O-house und Maison Folie. Er wurde mit mehreren Preisen ausgezeichnet und war in den Jahren 2000 und 2002 auf der Biennale in Venedig vertreten. 2003 nahm NOX an den bedeutenden internationalen Ausstellungen „Zoomorphic" am Victoria & Albert Museum in London und „Non Standard Architectures" am Pariser Centre Pompidou teil. Zu den aktuellen Projekten von NOX gehören der interaktive Turm D-Tower für die niederländische Stadt Doetinchem, das Son-O-house, „ein Haus, in dem Geräusche leben", das Kulturzentrum Maison Folies im französischen Lille sowie die Wettbewerbsbeiträge für die Europäische Zentralbank in Frankfurt und das neue Centre Pompidou in Metz (Wettbewerbssieger: Shigeru Ban). Lars Spuybroek hat an mehreren niederländischen Universitäten gelehrt und ist regelmäßig als Gastprofessor an der Columbia University in New York. Seit 2002 hat er eine Professur an der Abteilung CAD/digitale Designtechniken der Universität Kassel inne. Außerdem arbeitet er an einem Buch mit dem Titel *Machining Architecture*, das 2004 bei Thames & Hudson erscheinen soll.

Lars Spuybroek, qui dirige NOX, s'intéresse depuis le début des années 1990 aux relations entre l'architecture et les médias, et plus spécifiquement l'architecture et l'informatique. Il a été rédacteur-en-chef de l'un des premiers magazines consacrés à ce sujet (*NOX*, puis plus tard *FORUM*) et a réalisé des vidéos (Soft City) et des œuvres artistiques interactives (SoftSite, edit Spline, deep Surface). Plus récemment, il s'est davantage impliqué dans l'architecture (HtwoOexpo, BlowOut, V2_lab, wetGRID, D-tower, Son-O-House, Maison Folie). Son travail a remporté plusieurs distinctions et a été présenté aux Biennales de Venise de 2000 et 2002. En 2003, NOX a participé à l'importante exposition « Zoomorphic » au Victoria & Albert Museum à Londres, et à « Architectures non standard » au Centre Pompidou à Paris. NOX termine actuellement une tour interactive pour la ville néerlandaise de Doetinchem (D-Tower), « une maison du son » (Son-O-house) et un complexe d'installations culturelles à Lille, en France (Maison Folie). L'agence a participé à des concours pour la Banque centrale européenne et le nouveau Centre Pompidou à Metz, en France (remporté par Shigeru Ban). Lars Spuybroek donne de nombreuses conférences, a enseigné dans plusieurs universités aux Pays-Bas et est régulièrement professeur invité à la Columbia University à New York. Depuis 2002, il est professeur titulaire à l'Université de Kassel (Allemagne), où il dirige le département des techniques de CAO. Il a rédigé un livre *Machining Architecture*, publié par Thames & Hudson en 2004.

# SON-O-HOUSE

*Son en Breugel, The Netherlands, 2000–2003*

*Client: Enterprise Group. Floor area: 300 m². Costs: € 410 000.*

These images demonstrate that the apparently complex design of the Son-O-House evolves from the idea of the assembly of simple strips of paper.

Diese Bilder demonstrieren, dass sich die komplexe Gestaltung des Son-O-House aus der Idee einfacher, miteinander verflochtener Papierstreifen entwickelt hat.

Ces images montrent la conception apparemment complexe de la Son-O-House qui évolue à partir de l'idée d'un assemblage de simples bandes de papier.

As NOX prinicipal Lars Spuybroek explains, "the Son-O-House is one of our typical 'art' projects which allows us to proceed more carefully and slowly (over a period of three to four years) while generating a lot of knowledge that we apply to larger and speedier projects. Son-O-House is what we call 'a house where sounds live,' not being a 'real' house, but a structure that refers to living and the bodily movements that accompany habit and habitation. In the Son-O-House a sound work is continuously generating new sound patterns activated by sensors picking up actual movements of visitors." More specifically, the structure is derived from a set of movements of bodies, limbs and hands (on three scales) that are inscribed on paper bands as cuts. These paper bands are then stapled together, creating an arabesque of complex intertwining lines that is then made into a three-dimensional "porous structure." An analog computing model is then "digitized and remodeled on the basis of combing and curling rules which results in the very complex model of interlacing vaults which sometimes lean on each other or sometimes cut into each other." Spuybroek goes on to explain that "in this house-that-is-not-a-house we position eight sensors at strategic spots to indirectly influence the music. This system of sounds, composed and programmed by sound artist Edwin van der Heide, is based on moiré effects of interference of closely related frequencies. As a visitor one does not influence the sound directly, which is so often the case with interactive art. One influences the landscape itself that generates the sounds. The score is an evolutionary memoryscape that develops with the traced behavior of the actual bodies in the space."

Lars Spuybroek erklärt: „Das Son-O-House ist eins von unseren typischen ‚Kunst'-Projekten … Es ist kein ‚reales' Haus, sondern eine Konstruktion, die sich an den Lebensäußerungen und Bewegungen der Menschen orientiert, die sich darin bewegen oder wohnen. Im Son-O-House erzeugt eine Soundanlage ständig neue Geräuschmuster, die von den durch Sensoren übertragenen Bewegungen der Bewohner ausgelöst werden." Anders gesagt: Die Form entstand aus einer Serie von Bewegungen von Körpern, Gliedmaßen und Händen, die als Schnitte auf Papierstreifen fixiert wurden. Diese Papierstreifen wurden zusammengeheftet, woraus eine Arabeske aus komplexen, miteinander verflochtenen Linien entstand. Diese wurde dann zu einem dreidimensionalen „durchlässigen Gebilde" geformt. Anschließend wurde ein analoges Computermodell „nach demselben Prinzip wie Haare geflochten werden, digitalisiert und umgeformt, was zu unserem komplexen Modell verschlungener Gewölbe führt, die sich aneinander anlehnen oder überschneiden." Spuybroek abschließend: „In diesem Haus-das-kein-Haus-ist haben wir an strategischen Punkten acht Sensoren installiert, um die Musik indirekt zu beeinflussen. Dieses Soundsystem, das von Edwin van der Heide komponiert und programmiert wurde, basiert auf dem Moiré-Effekt, der durch die Überlagerung eng beieinander liegender Frequenzen entsteht. Anders als bei vielen anderen interaktiven Kunstprojekten kann man hier als Besucher die Musik nicht direkt beeinflussen. Man beeinflusst vielmehr die Umgebung selbst, die den Sound hervorbringt. Dabei stellt die Partitur eine evolutionäre Erinnerungslandschaft dar, die sich mit dem aufgezeichneten Verhalten realer Körper im Raum entfaltet."

Comme l'explique Lars Spuybroek : « La Son-O-House est l'un de ces projets ‹ artistiques › typiques qui nous permettent d'avancer plus soigneusement et plus lentement (sur trois ou quatre ans) tout en générant une masse de connaissances dont bénéficieront des projets plus importants et plus pressés … Ce n'est pas une ‹ vraie › maison, mais une structure qui se réfère à la vie et aux mouvements corporels qui accompagnent les habitudes et le fait d'habiter. Dans cette maison une centrale sonore génère en continu de nouveaux motifs sonores activés par des capteurs qui enregistrent les mouvements réels des visiteurs. » Plus précisément, cette structure est issue de l'ensemble des mouvements des corps, des membres et des mains (sur trois échelles) qui s'inscrivent sur des bandes de papiers. Celles-ci sont ensuite agrafées ensemble, pour créer une arabesque de lignes entrelacées complexes qui se transforme en « structure poreuse » en trois dimensions. Un modèle de calcul analogique est ensuite « numérisé et remodelé sur la base de lignes qui donnent un modèle très complexe de voûtes entrelacées qui tantôt s'inclinent l'une sur l'autre, tantôt s'entrecoupent ». Spuybroek explique également que « dans cette maison-qui-n'est-pas-une-maison, nous positionnons huit capteurs à des endroits stratégiques qui influencent indirectement la musique. Ce système de sons, composés et programmés par l'artiste sonore Edwin van der Heide, repose sur des effets de moirages d'interférences de fréquences proches. Le visiteur n'influence pas directement le son, ce qui est si souvent le cas dans l'art interactif, mais influence le paysage lui-même qui génère les sons. Le résultat est un paysage mémorisé évolutif qui se développe concurremment au traçage du comportement des corps dans l'espace. »

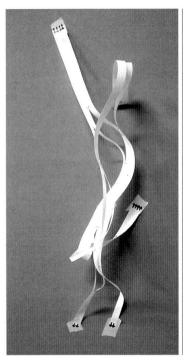

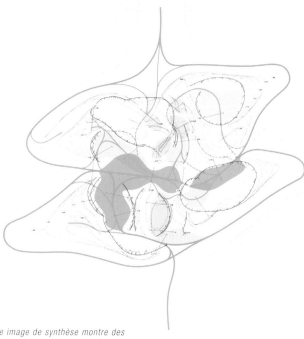

The more finished computer images of the house show its curious shapes that might approach biological forms.

Die Computerdarstellungen des Hauses zeigen die Nähe der merkwürdigen Formen zu Naturgebilden.

Une image de synthèse montre des formes curieuses qui ne sont pas très éloignées de formes biologiques.

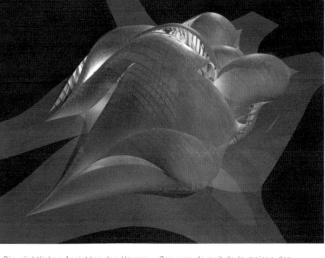

These night views of the Son-O-House give the impression of a living entity, glowing and possibly even moving as its sounds are influenced by visitors' movements.

Die nächtlichen Ansichten des Hauses lassen an ein lebendiges, im Dunkeln leuchtendes Wesen denken, das sich im Rhythmus seiner Besucher bewegt.

Ces vues de nuit de la maison donnent l'impression d'un organisme vivant, irradiant et même mobile puisque les formes sont influencées par les mouvements des visiteurs.

# OFFICE OF MOBILE DESIGN

*Office of Mobile Design*
*1725 Abbot Kinney Boulevard*
*Venice, CA 90291*
*USA*

*Tel: +1 310 439 1129*
*Fax: +1 310 439 2495*
*e-mail: Jennifer@designmobile.com*
*Web: www.designmobile.com*

Born in 1965 in New York, Jennifer Siegal obtained her Master of Architecture degree from the Southern California Institute of Architecture (SCI-Arc) in 1994. She has been the Principal of the Office of Mobile Design in Venice, California since 1998. Previously she worked in the offices of Hodgetts+Fung (1994–95), Mark Mack (1992), and Skidmore, Owings & Merrill in San Francisco (1988). She was also an apprentice and resident at Arcosanti (Codes Junction, Arizona, 1987). Recent work includes: Swellhouse (Los Angeles, CA, 2003, mass-customized/pre-fabricated eco-friendly house); Portable House (San Diego, CA, 2003, pre-fabricated eco-friendly mobile house); Seatrain Residence, Los Angeles, CA, custom residence on 1 hectare in industrial/downtown Los Angeles, composed of 2 pairs of stacked ISO shipping containers sheltered under a 15-meter steel and glass roof membrane), and the Museum of History and Perception (Marfa, TX, 1998, temporary Museum for Donald Judd's Chinati Foundation and community while support for a permanent structure is raised).

Jennifer Siegal, 1965 in New York geboren, erwarb 1994 den Master of Architecture am Southern California Institute of Architecture (SCI-Arc). Seit 1998 ist sie Direktorin der Firma Office of Mobile Design im kalifornischen Venice. Zuvor hat sie in den Büros von Hodgetts+Fung (1994–95), Mark Mack (1992) und Skidmore, Owings & Merrill in San Francisco (1988) gearbeitet und war außerdem Volontärin bei Arcosanti in Codes Junction, Arizona (1987). Jennifer Siegal gestaltete das Museum of History and Perception in Marfa, Texas (1998), ein Bauwerk, in dem Donald Judds Chinati Foundation für die Dauer der Arbeiten am endgültigen Gebäude untergebracht ist. Zu ihren neuesten Arbeiten zählen: das umweltfreundliche Fertigteilhaus Swellhouse in Los Angeles (2003), das umweltfreundliche und mobile Haus Portable House in San Diego (2003) und die Villa Seatrain in Los Angeles. Letzteres ist ein auf einem 1 ha großen Grundstück im innerstädtischen Gewerbegebiet von Los Angeles realisiertes Wohnhaus, das aus zwei Paar übereinander gestapelten ISO-Schiffscontainern besteht, die von einer 15 m messenden Konstruktion aus Stahl und Glas überdacht sind.

Née en 1965 à New York, Jennifer Siegal est Master of Architecture du Southern California Institute of Architeture (SCI-Arc, 1994). Elle dirige l'agence Office of Mobile Design à Venice, Californie, depuis 1998. Elle avait auparavant travaillé pour Hodgetts+Fung (1994–95), Mark Mack (1992) et Skidmore, Owings & Merrill à San Francisco (1988). Elle a également été apprentie-stagiaire à Arcosanti (Codes Junction, Arizona, 1987). Parmi ses réalisations récentes : Swellhouse (maison mobile préfabriquée écologique prévue pour une production en série, Los Angeles, Californie, 2003,) ; Portable House (maison mobile préfabriquée écologique (San Diego, Californie, 2003) ; Seatrain Residence (résidence privée sur un terrain de 1ha, au centre de Los Angeles, composée de deux paires de conteneurs d'expédition sous une membrane de 15 mètres de long en acier et verre) et le Museum of History and Perception (musée temporaire pour la Fondation Chinati de Donald Judd en attendant la construction d'une structure permanente, Marfa, Texas, 1998).

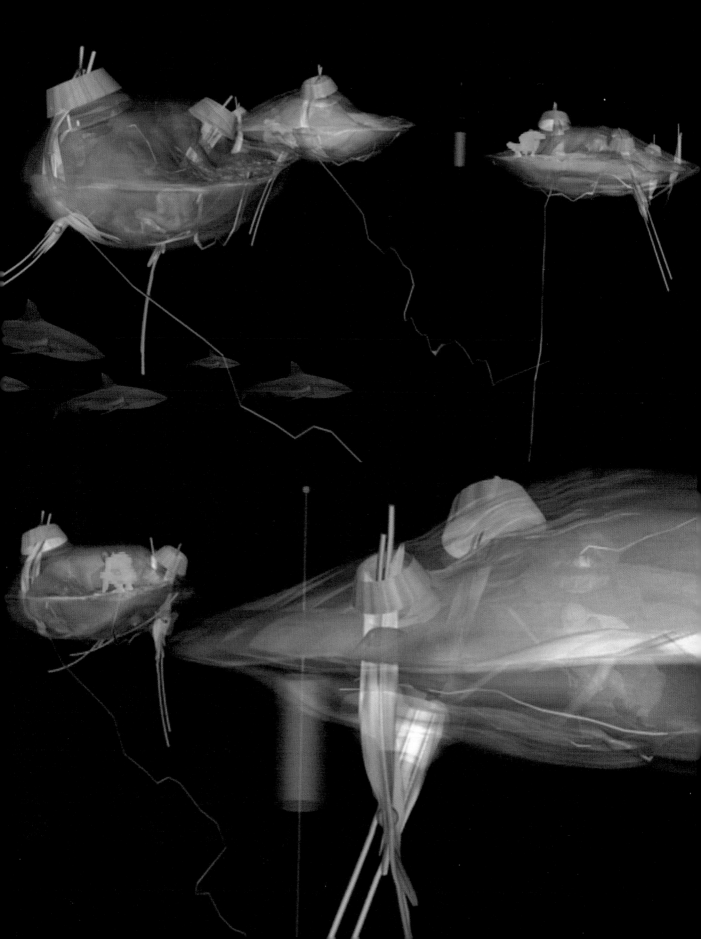

# HYDRA HOUSE

## *2003*

*Client: Wallpaper Magazine Inventional Competition. Floor area: not specified. Costs: not specified.*

The architects of the Hydra House begin their description of their project with dictionary definitions: "hy.dra: n. Any of several small freshwater polyps of the genus Hydra and the related genera, having naked cylindrical body and an oral opening surrounded by tentacles. Hy.dra: n. The many-headed serpent that was slain by Hercules. hy.dranth: n. A feeding zooid in a hydroid colony, having an oral opening surrounded by tentacles *(hydr(a)* + Gk. *anthos* flower). In fact, they have imagined an underwater structure with a pneumatic exterior skin made up of two layers of inflated neoprene. Structural stalks provide internal power, communication, mechanical requirements, and a self-sufficient energy collecting system. This is what they call a "mass-customized mobile modular structure" that is responsive to environmental issues of global warming and water desalination and recycling. Groups of these houses could be connected together by "suction-like tentacles attached to each independent housing unit, forming colonies and allowing for external passage." Water supply is dealt with in an innovative manner: "Water: rainwater with stretched bladder and desalination (97% of the planet's water is salt water in the seas and oceans) and treated waste water. Each tube either pulls sea water upward (see bottom skin punctures drawing directly from the ocean) or distributes desalinized water downward to provide potable and washing water." Power is provided by "photovoltaics, salt crystallization and thermocouple energy conductors," resulting in total energy self-sufficiency, according to the architects.

Die Architekten des Hydra House beginnen ihre Projektbeschreibung mit einer terminologischen Definition: „hy.dra: n. Ein Süßwasserpolyp von der Gattung Hydra oder verwandter Gattungen, mit einem nackten, zylindrischen Körper und einer Mundöffnung, die von Tentakeln gesäumt ist. Hy.dra: n. Die neunköpfige, riesige Schlange, die von Herkules getötet wurde. Hy.dranth: n. Ein nährendes, tierartiges Lebewesen in einer Hydrakolonie, das wie die Polypen eine Mundöffnung mit Tentakeln besitzt. *(hydr(a)* + Gr. *anthos*, Blume)." Tatsächlich hat das Team von Office of Mobile Design einen Unterwasserbau mit einer pneumatischen Außenhaut entworfen, die aus zwei luftgefüllten Neopren-Schichten besteht. Senkrechte, pflanzenstielartige Tragwerke enthalten die notwendigen mechanischen Vorrichtungen und sorgen für die interne Strom- und Energieversorgung. Laut Beschreibung der Planer handelt es sich bei ihrem Projekt um „eine in Massen produzierbare, individuell gestaltbare mobile Modulkonstruktion, die auf allgemeine Umweltprobleme wie Erderwärmung, Meerwasserentsalzung und Abfallrecycling reagiert. Die einzelnen Wohneinheiten können sich durch ihre Tentakel, die wie Ansaugrohre funktionieren, zu Gruppen verbinden. Dadurch entstehen Kolonien und eine Fortbewegung im Außenraum wird möglich." Auch die Wasserversorgung funktioniert nach innovativen Methoden: „Regenwasser mit Auffangbecken und Speicher, Meerwasserentsalzung (97% der Wassermenge unseres Planeten besteht aus dem Salzwasser der Meere und Ozeane) und Abwasseraufbereitung. Die beiden für die Wasserversorgung zuständigen Röhren ziehen das Meerwasser entweder nach oben oder verteilen das entsalzte Wasser nach unten, wo es zum Trinken oder Waschen verwendet werden kann." Der Strom wird durch Photovoltaik, Salzkristallisation und Thermoelemente gewonnen, was nach Aussage der Architekten in einer vollkommen autarken Energieversorgung resultiert.

OMD débute sa description de la Hydra House par des définitions du dictionnaire : « Hydre : polype d'eau douce du gène Hydra et espèces voisines, possédant un corps cylindrique nu et une ouverture buccale surmontée de tentacules. Serpent à plusieurs têtes tué par Hercule. Hydrante : zooïde nourricier dans une colonie d'hydroïdes, dont l'ouverture buccale est entourée de tentacules. Étymologie : du grec *hydr(a)*, eau, et *anthos*, fleur. » Concrètement, l'agence a imaginé une structure sous-marine à peau extérieure pneumatique composée de deux couches de néoprène gonflable. Une structure colonnaire produit l'électricité nécessaire, assure la communication, diverses fonctions mécaniques et un système autonome de production d'énergie. Il s'agit d'une structure modulaire mobile adaptée à une production en masse qui répond aux enjeux environnementaux de réchauffement de la planète et de désalinisation et recyclage de l'eau. Des groupes de ces maisons peuvent se connecter par « des tentacules à succion attachées à chaque unité de logement indépendante, formant des colonies et permettant des passages par l'extérieur ». L'approvisionnement en eau bénéficie d'une technique nouvelle : « Eau : eau de pluie dans une vessie extensible et désalinisation (97% de l'eau de la planète se trouve dans les mers et les océans) et eaux usées recyclées. Chaque tube soit pompe l'eau de mer vers le haut, soit la distribue une fois désalée vers le bas, sous forme d'eau pour la boisson ou la toilette. » L'énergie est apportée par « des conducteurs photovoltaïques à cristallisation saline et thermocouple » qui assurent, selon les architectes, une autosuffisance énergétique totale.

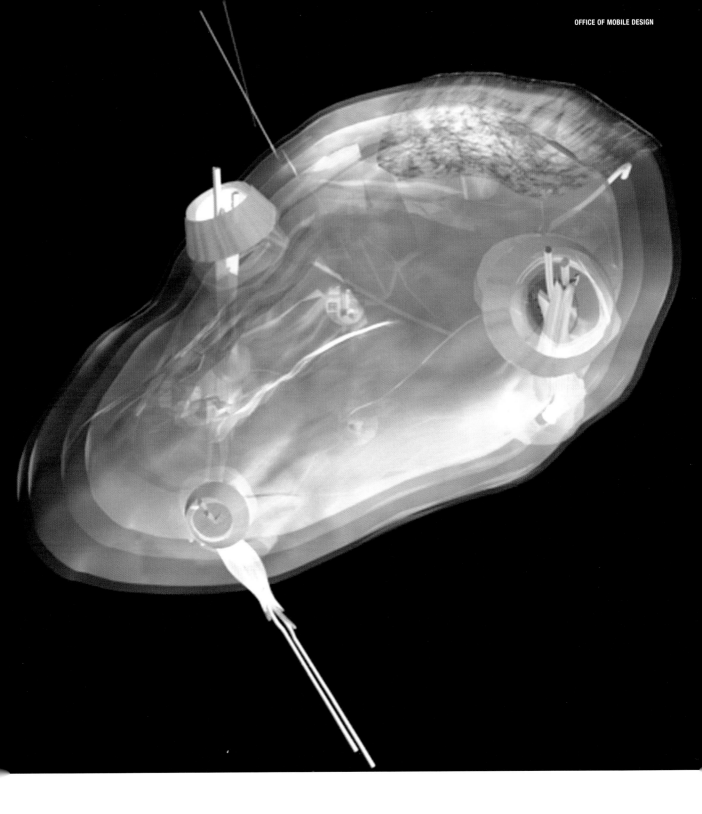

Jennifer Siegal and the Office of Mobile Design have taken the idea of living under the sea a step closer to reality with this self-sufficient undersea house.

Jennifer Siegal und das Office of Mobile Design brachten die Idee vom Leben auf dem Meeresboden mit ihrem autarken Unterwasser-Haus der Realität ein Stück näher.

Jennifer Siegal et l'Office of Mobile Design se sont rapprochés de la réalité d'une vie sous les eaux dans cette maison sous-marine autonome.

# PORTABLE HOUSE + ECOVILLE

*Los Angeles, California, USA, 2003*

*Client: Dr. Lance Stone/Tom Ellison. Floor area: not specified. Costs: not specified.*

Office of Mobile Design principal Jennifer Siegal writes, "harkening back to original prehistoric models of shelter and dwelling, the Portable House adapts, relocates and reorients itself to accommodate an ever-changing environment. It offers an eco-sensitive and economical alternative to the increasingly expensive permanent structures that constitute most of today's housing options. At the same time, the Portable House calls into question preconceived notions of the trailer home and trailer park, creating an entirely new option for those with disposable income but insufficient resources for entering the conventional housing market." More clearly put, the architects have tried to create a flexible living environment that can be moved, relating back to some of the earliest forms of nomadic existence. The central kitchen and bath element separates the sleeping areas from the living spaces. It is imagined that numerous units could be placed together, creating a temporary community. The units could also be stacked, providing a roof garden and ground floor workspace, for example. As the architects say, "whether momentarily located in the open landscape, briefly situated in an urban space, or positioned for a more lengthy stay, the Portable House accommodates a wide range of economic needs and simple functions." The idea of Eco-Ville would be to create a "sustainable Artist-in-Residence live/work community." A series of Portable House units would be put together in stacked configurations, with workspace below and living space above.

Die Leiterin von Office of Mobile Design, Jennifer Siegal, schreibt: „Auf die ersten, prähistorischen Modelle für Schutz und Behausung zurückgehend, positioniert und strukturiert sich das Portable House immer wieder neu, um sich an seine stetig wandelnde Umwelt anzupassen. Es bietet damit eine ökologisch sensible und ökonomisch vernünftige Alternative zu den immer teurer werdenden Massivbauten, die den Großteil der heutigen Wohnangebote ausmachen. Gleichzeitig stellt das Portable House vorgefertigte Meinungen über Wohnwagenkolonien in Frage. Es bietet vollkommen neue Wohnmöglichkeiten für Menschen, die zwar ein eigenes Einkommen haben, deren Geldmittel für den konventionellen Immobilienmarkt jedoch nicht ausreichen." Mit anderen Worten: Indem sie sich auf einige der frühesten Formen nomadischer Existenz besannen, haben die Architekten versucht, eine flexible und mobile Wohnarchitektur zu entwickeln. In ihrem Entwurf werden die Schlaf- und Wohnräume durch ein zentrales Element getrennt, in dem sich Küche und Bad befinden. Die Planer haben die Vorstellung, dass man mehrere solcher Wohneinheiten zusammen aufstellen könnte, um vorübergehend eine Gemeinschaft zu bilden. Man könnte auch einzelne Module übereinander stapeln, um das obere als Dachgarten und das untere als Arbeitsbereich zu nutzen. „Ob vorübergehend in einer Landschaft oder kurzfristig im städtischen Raum aufgebaut, um sich für längere Zeit an einem Ort niederzulassen, das Portable House bietet eine Vielfalt an ökonomischen Vorteilen und unkomplizierten Funktionen." Dem Projekt liegt die Idee eines „Eco-Ville" zugrunde, einer ökologisch nachhaltigen Lebens- und Arbeitsgemeinschaft für Künstler. Hierbei könnte eine Serie übereinander gestellter Portable House-Einheiten Ateliers und Werkstätten im unteren und Wohnräume im oberen Bereich ergeben.

Jennifer Siegal, qui dirige l'Office of Mobile Design, décrit ainsi ce projet : « Retour aux modèles originaux préhistoriques d'abri et d'habitat, la Portable House s'adapte, se réimplante, se réoriente d'elle-même en fonction d'un environnement en changement permanent. Elle offre une alternative sensible à l'écologie, et économique aux constructions permanentes de plus en plus coûteuses qui constituent aujourd'hui l'essentiel des options de logement. En même temps, elle remet en question les notions préconçues sur les mobil homes et les parcs pour mobil homes, offrant un choix entièrement nouveau à ceux qui disposent d'un certain revenu non suffisant cependant pour accéder au marché du logement conventionnel. » Plus clairement, les architectes ont essayé de créer un environnement de vie flexible et mobile qui renvoie à certaines formes antérieures de nomadisme. L'élément central cuisine/bains sépare la zone de nuit de celle de séjour. On imagine que plusieurs unités pourraient être regroupées pour constituer une communauté temporaire, ou être empilées, avec toit-terrasse, jardin et espace de travail en rez-de-chaussée par exemple. Comme le précisent les architectes : « Qu'elle soit momentanément installée dans un paysage dégagé, ou brièvement implantée dans l'espace urbain, ou positionnée pour un séjour plus long, la Portable House répond à une large gamme de besoins économiques et de fonctions simples. » Le concept d'Eco-Ville consisterait à créer « une communauté autonome de vie et de travail pour artistes en résidence ». Des unités seraient réunies selon une configuration empilée, avec des ateliers en bas et les espaces de vie au-dessus.

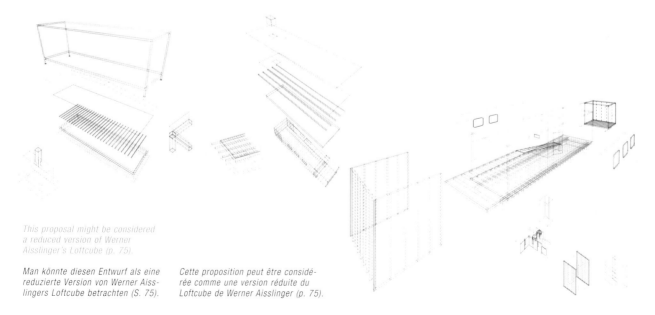

*This proposal might be considered a reduced version of Werner Aisslinger's Loftcube (p. 75).*

*Man könnte diesen Entwurf als eine reduzierte Version von Werner Aisslingers Loftcube betrachten (S. 75).*

*Cette proposition peut être considérée comme une version réduite du Loftcube de Werner Aisslinger (p. 75).*

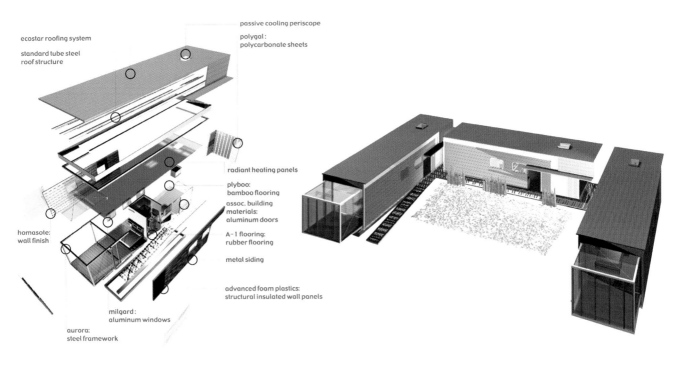

ecostar roofing system

standard tube steel
roof structure

passive cooling periscope

polygal:
polycarbonate sheets

radiant heating panels

plyboo:
bamboo flooring

assoc. building
materials:
aluminum doors

A-1 flooring:
rubber flooring

metal siding

advanced foam plastics:
structural insulated wall panels

homasote:
wall finish

milgard:
aluminum windows

aurora:
steel framework

Like elements from mobile homes
that can easily be assembled and
taken apart, the Portable House is a
practical proposal that might be used
to solve housing problems in many
parts of the world.

Mobilheimen ähnelnd, die leicht auf-
und wieder abgebaut werden können,
stellt das Portable House einen praktischen Entwurf dar, um die in vielen
Teilen der Welt herrschenden Wohnungsprobleme zu lösen.

Comme des éléments de maisons
mobiles facilement assemblées ou
démontés, la Portable House est une
proposition pratique à résoudre des
problèmes de logement dans de nombreux pays du monde.

The Office of Mobile Design imagi
nes entire communities formed of
Portable Houses, perhaps at the
periphery of large cities as the
image below right suggests.

Die Architekten vom Office of Mobile
Design denken an ganze Gemeinden,
die sich aus Portable Houses bilden
könnten, oder an die Peripherie
großer Städte.

L'Office of Mobile Design a imaginé
des communautés entières compo-
sées de Portable Houses, qui pourraient être installées en périphérie de
grandes villes.

# DOMINIQUE PERRAULT

*DPA – Dominique Perrault Architecte*
*26, Rue Bruneseau*
*75629 Paris cedex 13*
*France*

*Tel: +33 1 44 06 00 00*
*Fax: +33 1 44 06 00 01*
*e-mail: contact.presse@perraultarchitecte.com*
*Web: www.perraultarchitecte.com*

Dominique Perrault was born in 1953 in Clermont-Ferrand, France. He received his diploma as an architect from the Beaux-Arts UP 6 in Paris in 1978. He received a further degree in urbanism at the École Nationale des Ponts et Chaussées, Paris in 1979. He created his own firm in 1981 in Paris. Recent and current work includes the Engineering School (ESIEE) (Marne-la-Vallée, 1984–1987); the Hôtel industriel Jean-Baptiste Berlier (Paris, 1986–1990); Hôtel du département de la Meuse (Bar-le-Duc, France, 1988–1994); Bibliotheque Nationale de France (Paris, France, 1989–1997); Olympic Velodrome, Swimming and Diving Pool (Berlin, Germany, 1992–1998); and a large-scale study of the urbanism of Bordeaux (1992–2000). He is of course best known for his French National Library, Paris (1989–1997). Current work includes: an extension of the Court of Justice of the European Community (Luxembourg); construction of the Montigalà Stadium near to Barcelona; the design of several supermarkets for the MPreis chain in Austria; redesign of the urban waterfront "Las Teresitas" and the construction of a 5 star hotel in Tenerife, Canary Islands; and the refurbishment of the Piazza Gramsci (Cinisello Balsamo, Milan, Italy). He recently won the competition to design the new Mariinsky Theater in St. Petersburg.

Dominique Perrault, 1953 in Clermont-Ferrand geboren, erwarb 1978 sein Architekturdiplom an der École des Beaux-Arts (UP 6) in Paris und 1979 ein weiteres Diplom in Stadtplanung an der École Nationale des Ponts et Chaussées in Paris. 1981 gründete er in Paris seine eigene Firma. Zu seinen jüngeren Arbeiten gehören die Ingenieurschule (ESIEE) in Marne-la-Vallée (1984–1987), das Hôtel industriel Jean-Baptiste Berlier in Paris (1986–1990), das Hôtel du département de la Meuse in Bar-le-Duc (1988–1994), sein bekanntestes Bauwerk, die Bibliothèque Nationale de France in Paris (1989–1997), die Olympische Radsporthalle und die Schwimm- und Tauchsporthalle in Berlin (1992–1998) sowie eine groß angelegte Studie zur Stadtentwicklung von Bordeaux (1992–2000). Zu seinen aktuellen Projekten zählen: ein Erweiterungsbau für den Gerichtshof der Europäischen Gemeinschaft in Luxemburg, der Bau des Montigalà Stadiums bei Barcelona, das Design mehrerer Filialen für die Supermarktkette M-Preis in Österreich, die Umgestaltung des Uferbezirks Las Teresitas und die Realisierung eines Fünf-Sterne-Hotels auf Teneriffa sowie die Modernisierung der Piazza Gramsci in Cinisello Balsamo, Mailand. Vor kurzem gewann er den Wettbewerb zur Gestaltung des neuen Mariinsky Theaters in St. Petersburg.

Dominique Perrault naît en 1953 à Clermont-Ferrand. Il est diplômé d'architecture de l'École des Beaux-Arts de Paris (UP 6) en 1978, et diplômé en urbanisme de l'École Nationale des Ponts et Chaussées, Paris (1979). Il crée son agence en 1981 à Paris. Parmi ses réalisations : l'École d'ingénieurs ESIEE (Marne-la-Vallée, 1984–1987), l'hôtel industriel Jean-Baptiste Berlier (Paris, 1986–1990), l'hôtel du département de la Meuse (Bar-le-Duc, France, 1988–1994), la Bibliothèque de France (Paris, 1989–1997), le vélodrome et la piscine olympiques (Berlin, 1992–1998) et une étude urbanistique de fond sur la ville de Bordeaux (1992–2000). Parmi ses réalisations récentes : une extension de la Cour de justice de la Communauté européenne (Luxembourg) ; le stade de Montigalà, près de Barcelone ; la conception de plusieurs supermarchés pour la chaîne M-Preis en Autriche ; le réaménagement du front de mer « Las Teresitas » et la construction d'un hôtel de luxe à Ténériffe (Îles Canaries). Il a récemment remporté le concours pour le nouveau théâtre Mariinsky à Saint-Pétersbourg.

# TOWN HALL / HYBRID HOTEL

*Innsbruck, Austria, 1996–2002*

*Client: Rathauspassage GmbH, Town of Innsbruck. Gross floor area: 48 000 m². Costs: € 50 000 000.*
*Associated architect: Rolf Reichert, RPM Architekten (Munich, Germany).*

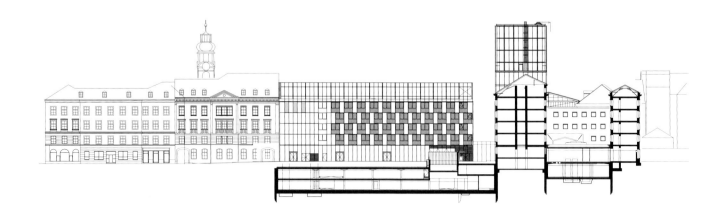

The architect clearly plays on the different types of cladding of this building to animate it and to give varying effects according to the parts of the structure concerned.

Der Architekt spielt mit unterschiedlichen Arten von Verkleidung, um Abwechslung in die Fassaden zu bringen und um jeweils entsprechende Effekte zu erzielen.

L'architecte a joué sur les différents types d'habillages de façades pour les animer et créer des effets variées en fonctions des parties de la structure concernée.

P 462.463

In the historical center of Innsbruck, a hybrid client – the city of Innsbruck (public) and a group of local entrepreneurs/property owners (private) – proposed a complex, symbolic brief which included the construction of a new Town Hall while preserving the existing building, to remodel a public square, build a hotel opening onto the square, to link the unit to the public circulation network and covered galleries, and to create a lower shopping floor. The floor area of the complex is 35 200 square meters. Covering a city block, the project was envisaged by the architect as the creation of "an urban landscape, a new skyline in the city." The Town Hall stands out because of its glass bell tower, but also because of the rooftop placement of the City Council Chambers. A roof garden above the hotel offers spectacular views of the surrounding mountains. A glass-covered passageway was designed to be the "backbone" of the project. As Dominique Perrault says, "the identity resides in the choice of materials and the architectural language used. Glass, transparent or white, translucent or colored, becomes the reference material. The window carpentry is black, thick or thin depending on whether it is fixed or hinged. The language uses Mondrian as a reference point – the geometry of the absolute. However, we find ourselves in the field of architecture, where the notion of "pure" does not exist in the same way as in painting. The buildings are clad in metal cloth, sun shading or visual protection. This material provides different sheens, different types of light, in other words, a different complexity which creates a modern, hybrid architecture, like the client, like the history of the site, like our European culture, a mixture of the abstract and the figurative, trade and politics, culture and leisure."

Im historischen Stadtkern von Innsbruck entstand im Auftrag der Stadt sowie einer Gemeinschaft lokaler Unternehmer und Grundbesitzer ein komplexes und symbolträchtiges Projekt. Es umfasst den Bau eines neuen Rathauses unter Einbeziehung des bestehenden Gebäudes, die Umgestaltung eines öffentlichen Platzes, den Bau eines Hotels, die Anbindung der Anlage an das öffentliche Verkehrsnetz sowie eine überdachte Einkaufsstraße und Ausstellungsräume. Der Komplex, der eine Gesamtnutzfläche von 35 200 m² hat und einen ganzen Häuserblock einnimmt, wurde vom Architekten als „eine urbane Landschaft, eine neue Skyline für die Stadt", konzipiert. Das Rathaus hebt sich vom Rest der Anlage ab, was nicht nur an seinem gläsernen Glockenturm liegt, sondern auch am auf das Dach gesetzten Sitzungssaal des Gemeinderats. Von einem anderen Dachausbau, der auf dem Hotel gelegenen Gartenterrasse, hat man einen fantastischen Ausblick auf die umliegenden Berge. Ein verglaster Durchgang ist das „Rückgrat" des Gebäudes. Dominique Perrault über seine Gestaltung: „Die Identität liegt in der Wahl der Materialien und der Formensprache. Glas, transparent oder weiß, durchscheinend oder farbig, spielt hierbei eine wichtige Rolle. Die Fensterumrahmungen sind aus schwarzem Holz, ob breit oder schmal hängt davon ab, ob die Fenster feststehend oder aufklappbar sind. Die Formensprache nimmt auf Mondrian und seine Geometrie des Absoluten Bezug. Nur dass wir uns hier im Bereich der Architektur befinden, wo die Vorstellung von ‚Reinheit' eine andere ist als in der Malerei. Die Gebäudeteile sind mit Metalltuch ummantelt, das als Sonnen- oder Sichtschutz fungiert. Dieses Material sorgt für unterschiedliche Glanz- und Lichteffekte und schafft damit eine Komplexität, aus der eine moderne, hybride Architektur entsteht. Hybrid wie die aus öffentlichem und privatem Sektor zusammengekommenen Auftraggeber, wie die Geschichte des Standorts, wie unsere gesamte europäische Kultur, eine Mischung aus abstrakten und figurativen Elementen, aus Handel und Politik, Kultur und Freizeit."

C'est un groupe hybride de commanditaires composé de la municipalité, de promoteurs et de propriétaires privés qui avait lancé un appel d'offre pour la construction d'un nouvel hôtel de ville – l'ancien étant sauvegardé – le remodelage d'une place et la construction d'un hôtel en bordure, la liaison entre le réseau de circulation public et des galeries couvertes et la création d'un niveau de commerces. La surface au sol de ce complexe, qui occupe un pâté entier du centre historique d'Innsbruck, est de 35 200 m². Pour l'architecte, il était l'opportunité de créer « un paysage urbain, un nouveau panorama dans la ville ». L'hôtel de ville se détache de l'ensemble par son clocher de verre, et l'implantation en toiture de la salle du conseil municipal. Un toit-terrasse en jardin au sommet de l'hôtel offre des vues spectaculaires sur les montagnes environnantes. Un passage couvert en verre sert de « colonne vertébrale » à l'ensemble. Comme l'explique Dominique Perrault : « L'identité réside dans le choix des matériaux et le langage architectural. Le verre, transparent ou blanc, translucide ou coloré, est le matériau de référence. La menuiserie métallique des fenêtres est noire, fine ou épaisse selon le système d'ouverture. Le langage a pris Mondrian comme pointe de référence, la géométrie de l'absolu. Cependant, nous nous trouvons dans le champ de l'architecture, où la notion de ‹ pur › n'existe pas de la même façon qu'en peinture. Les bâtiments sont habillés d'une toile métallique, de protections solaires et visuelles. Ce matériau offre différentes brillances, différents types de lumière, en d'autres termes, une complexité différente qui crée une architecture moderne et hybride – comme le groupe de ses commanditaires, comme l'histoire de ce site, comme notre culture européenne, mélange d'abstrait et de figuratif, de commerce et de politique, de culture et de loisirs. »

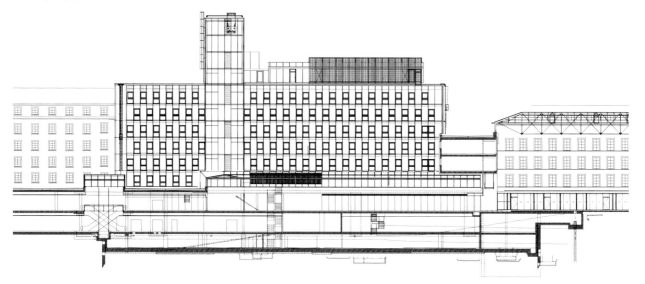

The rather substantial nature of the 35 200-square meter building is visible in the section above. To the right, glass of varying colors enlivens an atrium in the old part of the building.

Die beträchtlichen Ausmaße des Gebäudes werden aus obigem Querschnitt ersichtlich. Rechts: Glastafeln in verschiedenen Farben beleben einen überdachten Innenhof im alten Gebäudeteil.

Les importantes dimensions de ce projet de 35 200 m² apparaissent dans la coupe ci-dessus. À droite, des verres de couleurs différentes animent un atrium dans la partie ancienne du bâtiment.

Dominique Perrault has created a symphony of glass surfaces that bring light into the building while providing a changing backdrop to the activity of the Town Hall.

Dominique Perrault hat eine Symphonie aus Glasflächen geschaffen, die Licht in das Gebäude bringen und Abwechslung für die Aktivitäten im Rathausgebäude bieten.

Dominique Perrault a créé une symphonie de panneaux de verre qui éclaire l'intérieur du bâtiment tout en apportant au fond changeant aux activités de l'hôtel de ville.

# PLEXUS R+D

*plexus r + d, Inc.*
*914 Howell Mill Road, Suite 100*
*Atlanta, GA 30318*
*USA*

*Tel: +1 404 815 6776*
*Fax: +1 404 815 9978*
*e-mail: office@plexus-architecture.com*
*Web: www.plexus-architecture.com*

*Park and Observation Tower* ▶

Jordan Williams received his education at Princeton (1992) and the University of Florida (1988). Erik Lewitt attended Princeton (1992) and the University of Florida (1988) as well. The design staff of their firm includes seven persons. Their completed projects include: La Villa office building (with JSA, Jacksonville, FL, 2002); Southern Polytechnic State University Gateway (Marieta, GA, 2001); Husk Jennings Advertising (with JSA, Jacksonville, 2001); Barcelona Residence (Jacksonville, 2001); and Franklins Printing (with Farrington Design Group, Atlanta, 2000). Current work includes: Southern Polytechnic State University Gateway (Marieta, GA, 2004); Beijing Zhongguanchun Life Science Park (with JSA, Beijing, China, 2004); plexus on Ponce (Atlanta, 2004); Midtown West Master Plan (Atlanta, 2004); Atlanta Train Depot (Atlanta, 2004); Piedmont Center (Atlanta, 2004); and Moreland Live/Work (Atlanta, 2004).

Jordan Williams erwarb 1988 den Bachelor of Science an der University of Florida und 1992 den Master of Architecture in Princeton. Auch Erik Lewitt schloss 1988 sein Studium an der University of Florida mit dem Bachelor of Science und 1992 in Princeton mit dem Master of Arts ab. Das Planungsteam ihrer Firma besteht aus sieben Mitarbeitern. Zu ihren realisierten Projekten zählen: das Gebäude für Franklins Printing in Atlanta (2000) – in Zusammenarbeit mit Farrington Design Group –, die Bürogebäude Husk Jennings Advertising (2001) und La Villa (2002), beide in Zusammenarbeit mit JSA und beide in Jacksonville, Florida, sowie die Villa Barcelo-na in Jacksonville (2001). Zu ihren aktuellen Projekten gehören der Zugang zur Southern Polytechnic State University in Marieta, Georgia (2004), der Wissenschaftspark Beijing Zhongguanchun Life Science Park (mit JSA) in Peking (2004), der Plexus on Ponce (2004), der Masterplan für Midtown West, das Atlanta Train Depot sowie More-land Live/Work, alle in Atlanta und alle für 2004 geplant.

Jordan Williams et Eric Lewitt ont tous deux étudié à Princeton (Master of Architecture 1992) et à l'Université de Floride (B. Sc. 1988). L'équipe de conception de leur agence compte sept collaborateurs. Ils ont réalisé à ce jour : l'immeuble de bureaux La Villa (avec JSA, Jacksonville, Floride, 2002) ; l'agence Husk Jennings Advertising (avec JSA, Jacksonville, Floride, 2001) ; Barcelona Residence (Jacksonville, 2001) ; l'imprimerie Franklins (avec Farrington Design Group, Atlanta, 2000). Parmi leurs chantiers actuels : le portail d'entrée de la Southern Polytechnic State University (Marieta, Géorgie, 2004) ; le parc des sciences Zhongguanchum (avec JSA, Pékin, Chine, 2004) ; plexus on Ponce (Atlanta, 2004) ; le plan directeur centre ouest (Atlanta, 2004) ; le dépôt ferroviaire d'Atlanta (Atlanta, 2004) ; Piedmont Center (Atlanta, 2004) et Moreland Live/Work (Atlanta, 2004).

# PARK AND OBSERVATION TOWER

*Busan, South Korea, 2003–*

*Client: Bexco. Total floor area: 6 850 m². Costs: not specified.*

This project includes a new park, a facility for the Busan International Film Festival (3 716-square-meter Film and Media Center), an observation tower (1 741 square meters) and a 1 393-square-meter Exhibition and Tourism Center. Busan is the second largest city in Korea and has an ambitious plan to develop itself into an international maritime metropolis. The competition brief for this project provides that the "Busan Tower Complex will be a landmark symbolizing the emerging status of this dynamic and growing port city." The Film and Media Center is carved into Yongdu Hill and is covered by the platform of the Observation Tower. In Korean, the word "yongdu" means the "head of the dragon" and the Yongdu Hill Park is one of the oldest of the city's green areas. The spaces carved out of Yongdu Hill for the Film and Media Center would be left natural "similar to the walls of a stone quarry," while the research, housing and theater facilities would be clad either in translucent curtain wall or metal panels and pre-cast concrete. The Tower would be a steel frame structure with a combination of metal panel and curtain wall cladding, offering both a symbol of the city and a vantage point for viewing day and night. The Exhibition and Tourism Center is to be located at the top of Yongdu Hill Park and connect the Park Level with the base of the Observation Tower. The design calls for an "open and flexible steel frame clad in translucent glass curtain wall."

Der Bauplan für das Projekt umfasst einen neu angelegten Park, ein 3 716 m² großes Film- und Medienzentrum, das gleichzeitig als Spielstätte für das Internationale Filmfestival von Busan dient, eine 1 741 m² große Beobachtungswarte sowie ein 1 393 m² großes Ausstellungs- und Tourismuszentrum. In der Projektbeschreibung für den Architekturwettbewerb hieß es: „Der Busan Tower Complex soll Wahrzeichen und Symbol für die wachsende Bedeutung dieser dynamischen Hafenstadt werden." Ein Teil des Komplexes, das Film- und Medienzentrum, wird in den Yongdu Berg eingebettet und von der Plattform der Beobachtungswarte überdeckt. Der Yongdu Hill Park ist eine der ältesten Grünanlagen der Stadt. Während die Stellen, die für das Film- und Medienzentrum aus dem Berg gebrochen wurden, in ihrem natürlichen Zustand belassen werden, so dass sie wie die Wände eines Steinbruchs aussehen, sollen die für Forschung, Wohnen und Theater vorgesehenen Bauteile entweder mit durchscheinenden Vorhangwänden oder Metalltafeln und großflächigen Betonfertigteilen ummantelt werden. Der Turm besteht aus einer Stahlrahmenkonstruktion mit einer Verkleidung aus Metallplatten und Vorhängwänden und wird somit sowohl zu einem markanten Wahrzeichen für die Stadt als auch zu einem Tag und Nacht sichtbaren Orientierungspunkt. Das Ausstellungs- und Tourismuszentrum befindet sich am oberen Ende des Parks und soll diesen mit dem Beobachtungsturm verbinden. Auch dieser Bauteil soll aus einem offenen und flexiblen Stahlrahmen bestehen und mit einer durchsichtigen Vorhangwand aus Glas umhüllt werden.

Busan, seconde ville de Corée du Sud, s'est dotée d'un ambitieux plan pour devenir une métropole maritime de niveau international. Ce projet comprend un parc, le siège du festival international de cinéma de Busan (Centre du cinéma et des médias de 3 716 m²), une tour d'observation (1 741 m²) et un centre d'expositions et de tourisme de 1 393 m². Le sujet du concours précise que « le complexe de la tour de Busan sera un monument symbolisant le statut émergeant de cette ville portuaire dynamique en plein développement. » Le Centre du cinéma et des médias est creusé dans la colline de Yongdu et recouvert par la plate-forme de la tour d'observation. En coréen, le mot Yongdu signifie « tête de dragon » et le parc de cette colline est l'un des plus anciens espaces verts de la ville. Les volumes creusés seront laissés à l'état naturel « comme les parois d'une carrière », tandis que les équipements de recherche, le théâtre et les logements seront habillés d'un mur-rideau translucide ou de panneaux métalliques et de béton préfabriqué. La tour devrait être une construction à ossature d'acier recouverte d'un habillage combinant mur-rideau et panneaux métalliques, et sera à la fois un symbole pour la ville et un point de vue accessible de jour et de nuit. Le Centre d'expositions et de tourisme sera implanté au sommet de la colline et connectée au niveau du parc à la base de la tour d'observation, « une ossature ouverte et souple en acier habillée d'un mur-rideau de verre translucide ».

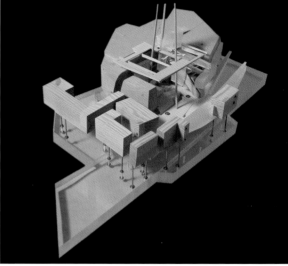

*Taking advantage of the Asian taste for daring new forms in architecture, plexus r+d imagines an astonishing tower and facilities to house a film festival.*

*Sich die asiatische Vorliebe für neue und gewagte Architekturformen zunutze machend, hat plexus r+d einen ungewöhnlichen Turm und Bauten für ein Filmfestival entworfen.*

*Profitant du goût asiatique pour les formes architecturales audacieuses, plexus r+d a imaginé une tour et des équipements étonnants pour abriter un festival du cinéma.*

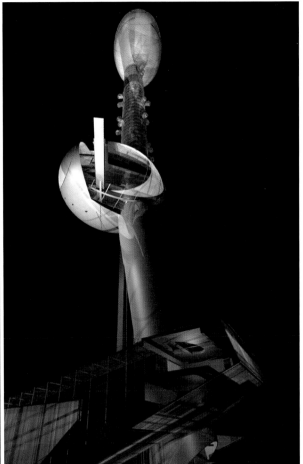

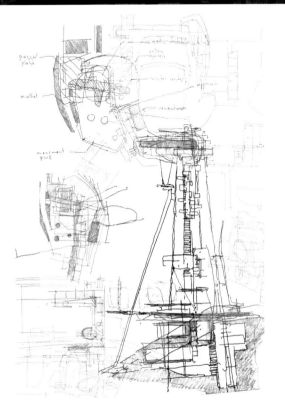

# DIRK JAN POSTEL

*Kraaijvanger.Urbis*
*Watertorenweg 336*
*Postbus 4003*
*3006 Rotterdam*
*The Netherlands*

*Tel: +31 10 498 9292*
*Fax: +31 10 498 9200*
*e-mail: mail@kraaijvanger.urbis.nl*
*Web: www.dirkjanpostel.nl*

Dirk Jan Postel, born in 1957, graduated in architecture from the Technical University of Delft (1986). He has been an associate of the Kraaijvanger.Urbis office for architecture and urban design since 1992. He is a visiting tutor at the Technical University of Delft, and at the Departments of Architecture and Civil Engineering at Queens College, Belfast; Bath School of Architecture; Birmingham School of Architecture; and the University of Central England. He is also the co-founder of GCI, a company for glass consulting and innovation. His work includes: Town Hall (Den Bosch, 1997–2004); Theater (Alphen aan den Rijn, 1999–2005); the Temple de l'Amour II (published here, Burgundy, 2000–01); The British School in The Netherlands (Voorschoten, 1999–2003); Traffic Control Center (Dutch Ministry of Transport, Utrecht, 1998–2000); Bonhoeffer College, Castricum High School (1998–2000); The British School in The Netherlands (The Hague, 1994–1997); 'De Barones' shopping arcade, department store and housing in the center of Breda (with CZWG architects, 1993–1997); The Glass House (Almelo, 1996–97); and the Glass Bridge (Rotterdam 1993–94).

Dirk Jan Postel, 1957 geboren, schloss 1986 sein Architekturstudium an der Technischen Universität von Delft ab. Seit 1992 ist er Teilhaber in dem Büro für Architektur und Stadtplanung Kraaijvanger.Urbis. Außerdem ist er als Gastdozent an der TU Delft und an den Fakultäten für Architektur und Bauwesen der Hochschulen Queens College Belfast, Bath School of Architecture, Birmingham School of Architecture und University of Central England tätig. Dirk Jan Postel gehört zu den Gründern von GCI, einer Beratungsfirma für den Bereich Glas. Zu seinen Bauten zählen: die Glasbrücke in Rotterdam (1993–1994) und – in Zusammenarbeit mit der Architektengruppe CZWG – das Einkaufszentrum mit Wohnungen De Barones in der Innenstadt von Breda (1993–1997), The British School in The Netherlands in Den Haag (1994–1997), ferner The Glass House in Almelo (1996–97), das Rathaus in Den Bosch (1997–2004), das Verkehrskontrollzentrum für das Niederländische Verkehrsministerium in Utrecht (1998–2000), das Bonhoeffer College der Castricum High School (1998–2000), The British School in The Netherlands in Voorschoten (1999–2003), das Theater in Alphen aan den Rijn (1999–2005) und der hier vorgestellte Temple de l'Amour II in Burgund (2000–01).

Dirk Jan Postel, né en 1957, est diplômé en architecture de l'Université technique de Delft en 1986. Depuis 1992, il est associé de l'agence d'architecture et d'urbanisme Kraaijvanger.Urbis. Il est tuteur invité à son université d'origine et aux départements d'architecture et d'ingénierie civile de Queens College à Belfats, à la Bath School of Architecture, à la Birmingham School of Architecture et à l'University of Central England. Il est également cofondateur de GCI, cabinet de consultant et d'innovation dans le domaine du verre. Parmi ses réalisations : un hôtel de ville (Den Bosch, 1997–2004) ; un théâtre (Alphen aan den Rijn, 1999–2005) ; le Temple de l'amour II, publié ici (Bourgogne, France, 2000–01) ; The British School (Voorschoten, 1999–2003) ; un centre de contrôle de la circulation (Ministère néerlandais des transports, Utrecht, 1998–2000) ; le Bohnoeffer College (Castricum High School, 1998–2000) ; The British School (La Haye, 1994–1997) ; le centre commercial, grand magasin et logements « De Barones » au centre de Breda, avec CZWG architectes (1993–1997) : la Maison de verre (Almelo, 1996–97) et le Pont de verre (Rotterdam, 1993–94).

# TEMPLE DE L'AMOUR II

*Talus du Temple, Bourgogne, France, 2000–01*

Client: Mr. and Mrs. Erik Wolters, Amsterdam. Floor area: 44 m². Costs: € 49 000.

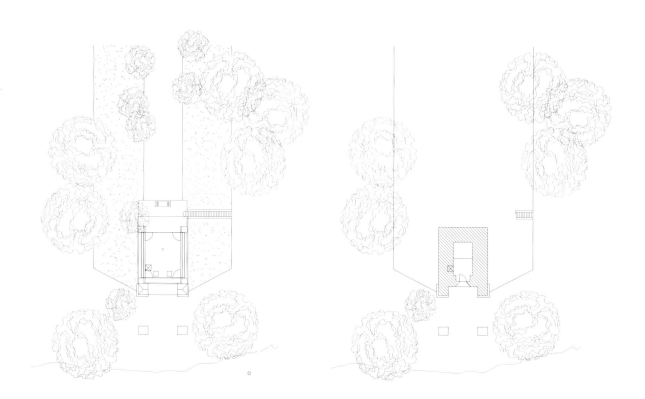

In the mid-1990s, an 18th-century folly called "Le Temple de l'Amour" located near Avalon in the Burgundy area of France was turned into a small summer residence for a Dutch neurologist. Dirk Jan Postel designed a laminated glass skylight for the house. The opposite end of the site is bordered by the abutment of a demolished railway bridge, and Postel convinced the owner to turn a former gunpowder vault into a guest room. As the architect says, "This construction has a classical, almost Ledoux-like expression, with its large blocks of local limestone." Postel devised a cantilevered roof consisting of a timber stressed skin construction. Laminated glass panels on either side carry its 2000-kg load. Lateral stability is provided by full height laminated, hardened glass panels. "The aim of the design," says the architect, "is to express the magic of the roof 'floating on nothing'. The detailing is coherent, non-conspicuous, minimal. As if the glass is cut through the ancient stone." This approach to "minimalist historic preservation" won the 2002 DuPont Benedictus Award given for the use of laminated glass in construction.

Mitte der 1990er Jahre wurde ein nahe Avalon im französischen Burgund gelegener Gartenpavillon für einen holländischen Neurologen zu einem kleinen Sommerhaus umgebaut. Für diesen „Temple de l'Amour" aus dem 18. Jahrhundert entwarf Dirk Jan Postel ein Oberlichtfenster aus Schichtglas. Später überzeugte er den Eigentümer, ein ehemaliges Munitionsdepot, das in einem der verbliebenen Gewölbepfeiler einer abgerissenen Eisenbahnbrücke untergebracht war, in einen Raum für Gäste umzuwandeln. Dazu der Architekt: „Diese Konstruktion hat ein klassisches, ein wenig an die Bauten von Ledoux erinnerndes Gepräge, mit ihren großen Blöcken aus hiesigem Kalkstein." Postel entwarf für diesen Bauteil ein auskragendes, in Schalenbauweise gefertigtes Holzdach. Dessen Gewicht von 2000 kg ruht an den Längsseiten auf Schichtglasplatten, während die Querseitenstabilität durch zwei raumhohe Wände aus gehärtetem Schichtglas gegeben ist. Der Architekt über sein Projekt: „Meinem Entwurf liegt das Ziel zugrunde, die Magie eines Dachs auszudrücken, das ‚auf dem Nichts schwebt'. Die Ausführung ist im Detail kohärent, unauffällig, minimal. Als ob das Glas durch den alten Stein schneiden würde." Dieser Zugang zu einer „minimalistischen Erhaltungsweise historischer Bausubstanz" wurde 2002 mit dem Preis DuPont Benedictus ausgezeichnet.

C'est au milieu des années 1990 qu'une folie du XVIIIᵉ siècle appelée « Le temple de l'amour » située près d'Avalon, en Bourgogne, a été transformée en petite résidence estivale pour un neurologue néerlandais. Non loin, Dirk Jan Postel a conçu ce pavillon en verre feuilleté. Une extrémité du terrain est bordée par la culée d'un pont de chemin de fer détruit, et Postel a transformé l'ancienne chambre d'explosion voûtée en chambre d'amis. Il explique que « avec ses gros blocs de calcaire local, cette construction présente un aspect classique qui fait presque penser à Ledoux ». L'architecte a dessiné un toit en porte-à-faux à charpente à peau contrainte. Les panneaux en verre feuilleté trempé supportent sa charge de 2 tonnes. La stabilité latérale est assurée par des panneaux de verre feuilleté toute hauteur. « L'objectif de ce projet », explique l'architecte, « est d'exprimer la magie d'un toit ‹ flottant sur rien ›. L'exécution est cohérente, discrète, minimale. Comme si le verre reposait sur les blocs de pierre anciens. » Cette approche de « conservation historique minimaliste » a remporté le Prix DuPont Benedictus 2002 pour l'utilisation du verre feuilleté dans la construction.

The architect imagined a guest house set into the abutment of a demolished railway bridge. As he says, its proportions might even recall the proportions and materials of Ledoux.

In dem Gästehaus, das in den Gewölbepfeiler einer ehemaligen Eisenbahnbrücke einfügt ist, finden sich Anklänge an die Proportionen und Materialien von Ledoux.

L'architecte a créé une maison d'amis dans la culée d'un pont de chemin de fer démoli, dont les proportions et les matériaux lui rappellent Claude-Nicolas Ledoux.

A "roof floating on nothing" in fact sits on sheets of laminated glass atop the old railway bridge structure.

Das „schwebende Dach" ruht in Wirklichkeit auf Schichtglasplatten, die auf die alte Bausubstanz der Eisenbahnbrücke gesetzt wurden.

Ce « toit flottant sur rien » repose en fait sur des feuilles de verre feuilleté posées sur la structure de l'ancien pont.

This innovative use of laminated glass won the architect the 2002 DuPont Benedictus Award. Indeed, Postel's project is a demonstration of the great advances that have been made in materials such as glass.

Die innovative Nutzung von Schichtglas brachte dem Architekten den DuPont Benedictus Preis des Jahres 2002 ein. Tatsächlich demonstriert Postels Projekt anschaulich die großen Fortschritte, die in Baumaterialien wie Glas gemacht wurden.

Cette utilisation novatrice du verre feuilleté a valu à l'architecte le Prix DuPont Benedictus 2002. Le projet est une démonstration des avancées réalisées dans des matériaux comme le verre.

# PROPELLER Z

*propeller z*
*Mariahilferstr. 101/3/55, 1060 Vienna, Austria*

*Tel: +43 1 595 2727–0, Fax: +43 1 595 2727-27*
*e-mail: mail@propellerz.at, Web: www.propellerz.at*

Korkut Akkalay was born in Istanbul, Turkey, in 1965. He studied architecture at the Academy of Fine Arts, Istanbul (1984–1990) and became a partner in propeller z in 1994. Kabru was born in Salzburg, Austria in1966. He studied technical physics at the University of Linz and the Graz University of Technology (1986–1988); architecture at the Vienna University of Technology (1988–2002); industrial design at the Academy of applied Arts, Vienna (1990–1995) and also joined propeller z as a partner in 1994. Kriso Leinfellner was born in Graz, Austria, in 1970. He studied architecture at the Graz University of Technology (1988–89) and at the University of Applied Art (1989–1996) and at the Gerrit Rietveld Academie, Amsterdam (1995–96). He has been a partner of propeller z since 1996 and of Lichtwitz Leinfellner Niessner office for visual communication since 1998. Philipp Tschofen was born in Vienna in 1968. He studied at the Vienna University of Economics and Business Administration (1986-1988), architecture at the Vienna University of Technology (1988–1998) and at the University of Michigan at Ann Arbor (1992). He has been a partner in propeller z since 1994. Carmen Wiederin was born in Landeck, Tyrol, Austria, in 1964, studied architecture and interior design at the Academy of Applied Arts, Vienna (1984-90) and has also been a partner in propeller z since 1994. Their completed projects include: Basis Wien (Vienna, 1997); SGL House (Vienna, 2002); Hutchison 3 offices at Gasometer C (Vienna, 2002); DBL House (Vienna, 2002); GIL fashion area 1 and 2 (Vienna, 2000); and Meteorit Exhibition Complex (Essen, Germany, 1998). Current projects include: Weninger Winery, Sopron-Balf, Hungary; Haus VD3, Vienna.

Korkut Akkalay, 1965 in Istanbul geboren, studierte von 1984 bis 1990 Architektur an der Kunstakademie in Istanbul. 1994 wurde er Teilhaber bei dem Wiener Architekturbüro propeller z. Kabru, 1966 in Salzburg geboren, studierte technische Physik an der Universität Linz und der Technischen Universität in Graz (1986–1988), Architektur an der TU Wien (1988–2002), Industriedesign an der Universität für Angewandte Kunst in Wien (1990–1995) und trat ebenfalls 1994 als Teilhaber bei propeller z ein. Kriso Leinfellner, 1970 in Graz geboren, studierte Architektur an der TU Graz (1988–89) sowie Industriedesign an der Universität für Angewandte Kunst (1989–1996) und der Gerrit Rietveld Academie in Amsterdam (1995–96). Leinfellner ist seit 1996 Teilhaber bei propeller z und seit 1998 im Büro für visuelle Kommunikation Lichtwitz Leinfellner Niessner. Philipp Tschofen, geboren 1968 in Wien, studierte zunächst Betriebswirtschaft in Wien (1986–1988), dann Architektur an der TU Wien (1988–1998) und an der University of Michigan in Ann Arbor (1992). Er ist seit 1994 Teilhaber bei propeller z. Carmen Wiederin, geboren 1964 in Landeck, Tirol, studierte Architektur und Innenarchitektur an der Universität für Angewandte Kunst in Wien (1984–1990) und ist ebenfalls seit 1994 als Teilhaberin bei propeller z tätig. Zu ihren gemeinsamen Projekten gehören: Basis Wien (1997), das SGL-Haus (2002), die Büros für Hutchison 3 im Gasometer C (2002), das DBL-Haus (2002) und das Modegeschäft GIL 1 und 2 (2000), alle in Wien, sowie das Kunstprojekt Meteoroid in Essen (1998). Die jüngsten Arbeiten des Teams sind Weingut Weninger, Sopron-Balf in Ungarn sowie Haus VD3 in Wien.

Korkut Akkalay est né à Istanbul en 1965. Il étudie l'architecture à l'Académie des Beaux-Arts de cette ville (1984–1990) et devient associé de propeller z en 1994. Kabru est né à Salzbourg (Autriche) en 1966 et étudie la physique à l'Université de Linz et à l'Université de technologie de Graz (1986–1988), le design industriel à l'Académie des arts appliqués (Vienne 1990–1995), puis l'architecture à l'Université de technologie de Vienne (1998–2002). Il entre chez propeller z comme associé en 1994. Kriso Leinfellner est né à Graz (Autriche) en 1970. Il étudie l'architecture à l'Université de technologie de Graz (1988–89) et le design industriel à l'Université des arts appliqués (1989–1996) et la Gerrit Rietveld Academie (Amsterdam, 1995–96). Il est associé de propeller z depuis 1996 et de Lichtwitz Leinfellner Niessner, agence de communication visuelle, depuis 1998. Philipp Tschofen, né à Vienne en 1968, étudie à l'Université de Sciences économiques et d'Administration des affaires de Vienne (1986–1988), puis s'oriente vers l'architecture à l'Université de technologie de Vienne (1988–1998) et à l'Université du Michigan (Ann Arbor, 1992). Il est associé de propeller z depuis 1994. Carmen Wiederin, née à Landeck (Tyrol, Autriche) en 1964, étudie l'architecture et l'architecture intérieure à l'Académie des arts appliqués de Vienne (1984–1990). Elle s'associe à propeller z en 1994. Parmi leurs réalisations : Basis Wien (Vienne, 1997) ; maison SGL (Vienne, 2002) ; bureaux Hutchinson 3 au Gazomètre C (Vienne, 2002) ; maison DBL (Vienne, 2002) ; bureaux et boutique de mode pour GIL (Vienne, 2000) et le complexe d'expositions Meteorit (Essen, Allemagne, 1998). Actuellement, propeller z travaille sur des projets variés : établissement vinicole Weninger (Sopron-Balf, Hongrie) et maison VD3 (Vienne).

# DBL HOUSE, SGL HOUSE

*Vienna, Austria, 2001–02*

*Client: private. Total floor area: DBL: 94,8 m² (unit 1), 85,7 m² (unit 2); SGL: 240,5 m². Costs: not specified.*

Two houses, located on adjacent sites in the western outskirts of Vienna, deal with different sets of problems. The DBL house is located on a 500-square-meter site and had a maximum permissible "footprint" of 88 square meters. The program called for two units of approximately 100 square meters in floor area belonging to two sisters, and the architects allowed the clients a good deal of choice in differentiating their residences. The first unit is a compact rigid concrete box, raised above the ground, resting only on a concrete staircase and three steel struts. The second unit is located below and profits from the structure of the more solid mass, using glass, and light marine plywood walls. A glass strip separates the two units. The SGL House has a much bigger site (1 100 square meters) and a higher total floor area than the combined units of the DBL House (240,5 square meters). Because of a sloping site, a split-level approach is adopted. The bedrooms were conceived as individual concrete boxes which support the sloping roof. Both houses use a concrete structure clad with boatbuilding plywood and fibre-cement shingles or primed and painted. Inside, there are hardwood parquet and epoxy resin floors and integrated furniture. HPL is used, as is wax-finished boatbuilding plywood.

Bei der Gestaltung zweier Häuser, die auf benachbarten Grundstücken in einem westlichen Randbezirk von Wien stehen, ging es um jeweils unterschiedliche Probleme. Das DBL-Haus steht auf einem 500 m² großen Grundstück und hat eine zulässige Grundfläche von max. 88 m². Das Haus, das einem Schwesternpaar gehört, sollte zwei Wohneinheiten mit einer Nutzfläche von je 100 m² umfassen. Innerhalb dieses Rahmens gaben die Architekten den beiden Bauherrinnen eine Vielfalt an gestalterischen Möglichkeiten, um ihre Wohnbereiche voneinander zu unterscheiden. Die erste Einheit besteht aus einer kompakten, erhöht angelegten Betonbox, die auf einer Betontreppe und drei Stahlverstrebungen ruht. Der zweite Teil profitiert von der Konstruktion des massiveren ersten Teils in seiner Verwendung von Glas und Wänden aus hellblauem Sperrholz. Beide Teile sind durch einen Glasstreifen voneinander abgegrenzt. Das SGL-Haus liegt auf einem wesentlich großzügigeren, 1 100 m² messenden Grundstück und ist mit einer Nutzfläche von 240,5 m² auch größer als beide Wohneinheiten des DBL-Hauses zusammen. Aufgrund der Hanglage wurde ein Splitlevel-Grundriss gewählt, wobei die Schlafzimmer als individuelle Betonboxen gestaltet wurden, die das abgeschrägte Dach tragen. Beide Häuser bestehen aus einer Betonkonstruktion mit einer Verkleidung aus Sperrholz, wie es beim Schiffsbau verwendet wird, und Faserzementschindeln.

Ces deux maisons édifiées sur des terrains adjacents dans la banlieue ouest de Vienne abordent différents types de problèmes. La DBL House occupe l'emprise au sol maximum autorisée de 88 m² sur un terrain de 500 m². Le programme prévoyait deux appartements de 100m² de surface environ, prévus pour deux sœurs qui ont bénéficié d'une grande liberté pour différencier leur logement. Le premier appartement est une boîte de béton rigide et compacte, surélevée du sol, sur lequel elle s'appuie par un escalier de béton et trois piliers d'acier. Le second, au rez-de-chaussée, profite de la structure massive et fait appel pour ses murs au verre et au contreplaqué marine léger. Un bandeau de verre horizontal sépare les deux appartements. La SGL House, construite sur un terrain plus vaste de 1 100 m², est plus grande que les deux appartements de la SGL réunis (240,5 m²). La pente du terrain a permis d'imbriquer les niveaux. Les chambres sont des boîtes en béton qui soutiennent le toit incliné. Ces deux maisons utilisent une structure en béton habillé de contreplaqué marine et de shingle en fibrociment ou peints. Les matériaux intérieurs sont des parquets en bois, des sols en résine époxy, du contreplaqué marine ciré et des meubles intégrés.

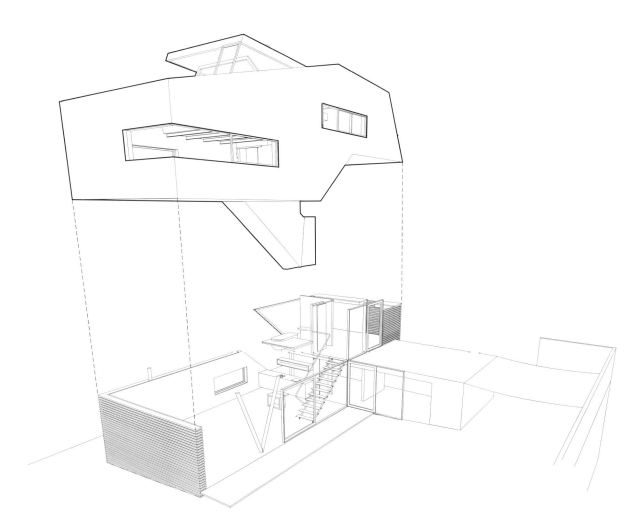

The DBL House resembles a modular assemblage of elements as the drawing above and the photo to the left show. The upper volume is a rigid concrete box.

Das DBL-Haus gleicht einer bausteinartigen Ansammlung von Elementen, wie obige Zeichnung und das Foto links zeigen. Der obere Baukörper besteht aus einer festen Betonbox.

La DBL House évoque un assemblage d'éléments modulaires comme le montrent le dessin ci-dessus et la photo à gauche. Le volume supérieur est une boîte en béton.

These interiors of the DBL House
show an accomplished variation of
closed opaque elements with glazed
openings that emphasize lightness.

In den Innenräumen des DBL-Haus
stehen geschlossene, opake Elemente
im Wechselspiel mit verglasten Öffnungen, die Helligkeit hereinholen.

Ces vues intérieures de la maison
montrent des variations habiles obte-
nues à partir d'éléments opaques fermés et d'ouvertures vitrées qui mettent en valeur une grande légèreté.

More interiors of the DBL house with an open interior design that permits a high degree of flexibility for the owner. A red and white color scheme characterizes the residence.

Weitere Innenansichten des DBL-Hauses lassen eine Offenheit der Innenraumgestaltung erkennen, die den Bewohnerinnen ein hohes Maß an Flexibilität bietet. Die rote und weiße Farbgebung ist charakteristisch für die Wohnräume.

Autres vues intérieures de la DBL House dont le plan ouvert permet une grande souplesse d'utilisation. Une palette chromatique rouge et blanche a été retenue pour l'ensemble de la résidence.

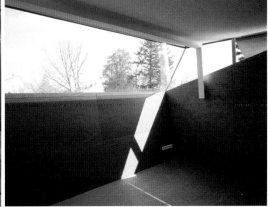

The SGL House is lower and quite different in appearance, even if its design is obviously related to that of the neighboring DBL House. The relative positions of the houses are shown on the plan below.

Das SGL-Haus ist niedriger als das benachbarte DBL-Haus, auch wenn es vom Design offensichtlich mit diesem verwandt ist. Die Lage der beiden Häuser geht aus untenstehendem Grundriss hervor.

La SGL House, plus basse, est assez différente d'aspect de sa voisine la DBL, même si leur conception est proche. Sur le plan ci-dessous : les implantations respectives des deux maisons.

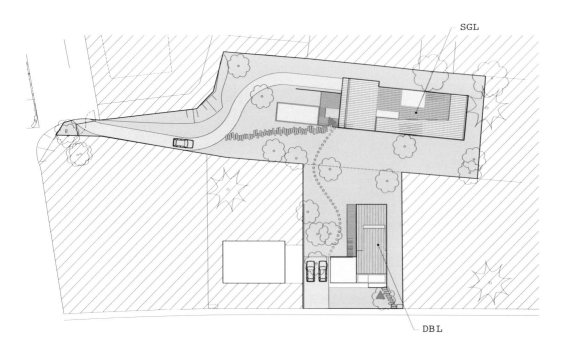

SGL

DBL

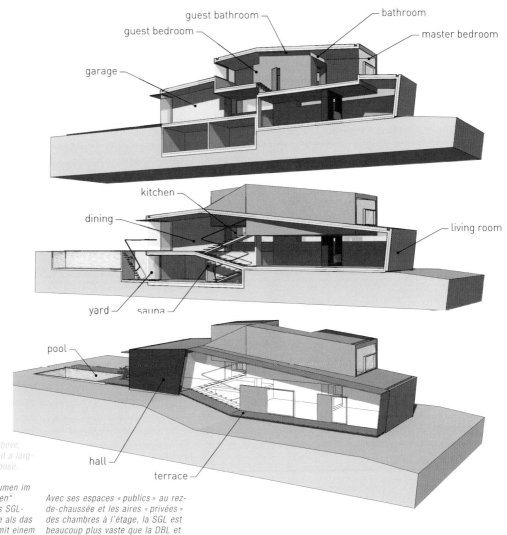

guest bathroom

bathroom

guest bedroom

master bedroom

garage

kitchen

dining

living room

yard

sauna

pool

hall

terrace

With its "public" spaces on the ground level and the "private" or bedroom areas above, the SGL House has a pool and a larger floor area than the DBL House.

Mit seinen „öffentlichen" Räumen im Erdgeschoss und den „privaten" Wohnräumen darüber hat das SGL-Haus eine größere Nutzfläche als das DBL-Haus. Außerdem ist es mit einem Pool ausgestattet.

Avec ses espaces « publics » au rez-de-chaussée et les aires « privées » des chambres à l'étage, la SGL est beaucoup plus vaste que la DBL et possède une piscine.

Interiors of the SGL House immediately express its more spacious
design, but the basic types of
volumetric contrasts seen in the
small house are visible here, too.
Unexpected window placements and
an orchestration of interior volumes
enliven the space.

Die Innenansichten des SGL-Hauses
lassen dessen geräumigere Anlage
erkennen. Die im kleineren Haus ein-
gesetzten, volumetrischen Kontraste
sind jedoch auch hier vorhanden.
Unerwartet platzierte Fenster und
eine Orchestrierung der Bauteile
beleben den Innenraum.

Les intérieurs de la SGL House expri-
ment d'emblée une plus grande gé-
nérosité d'espace, mais on y retrouve
les même types de contrastes volu-
métriques que dans la petite DBL.
Le positionnement inattendu des
fenêtres et l'orchestration des volumes intérieurs animent l'espace.

# MARC ROLINET

*Rolinet et Associés*
*9, rue Pierre Villey*
*75007 Paris*
*France*

*Tel: +33 1 44 42 0110*
*Fax: +33 1 44 42 0120*
*e-mail: rolinet@wanadoo.fr*

*L'Arbresle* ▶

Born in Montbéliard, France, in 1956, Marc Rolinet earned a Masters degree in Urbanism from the prestigious Ecole des Ponts et Chaussées in 1980 and created his own architectural office the following year. Rolinet has built a large number of housing projects in Paris, Marseille and Cergy-Pontoise, including the prestigious Gros Caillou complex on the rue de l'Université in Paris (2001). He also has considerable experience in the area of office buildings, and, more unexpectedly, religious structures. He has completed several projects for the Protestant Diaconesses de Reuilly, as well as churches in Paris, Villeneuve-le-Roi, and Montreuil in the Paris area. Despite the ease with which he works on a large scale, Marc Rolinet has also designed a number of individual homes. He is currently working on housing and office projects in Montpellier, Lisbon, Saint-Malo and Paris.

Marc Rolinet, geboren 1956 im französischen Montbéliard, erwarb 1980 den Master in Stadtplanung an der renommierten École des Ponts et Chaussées und gründete im darauf folgenden Jahr sein eigenes Architekturbüro in Paris. Rolinet hat eine große Zahl an Wohnungsbauprojekten in Paris, Marseille und Cergy-Pontoise realisiert, einschließlich der bekannten Anlage Gros Caillou in der Rue de l'Université in Paris (2001). Er hat auch etliche Sakralbauten für die protestantische Diakonie von Reuilly gebaut und Kirchen in Paris, Villeneuve-le-Roi und Montreuil bei Paris geplant. Neben seiner souveränen Gestaltung von Großbauten hat er ebenfalls eine Reihe von Privathäusern entworfen. Derzeit arbeitet er an mehreren Wohnungsbau- und Büroprojekten in Montpellier, Lissabon, Saint-Malo und Paris.

Né à Montbéliard en 1956, Marc Rolinet est diplômé d'urbanisme de la prestigieuse École des Ponts et Chaussées en 1980 et crée son agence l'année suivante. Il a réalisé un grand nombre de logements à Paris, Marseille et Cergy-Pontoise, dont l'ensemble du Gros Caillou, rue de l'Université à Paris (2001). Son expérience dans le domaine du bureau et même des églises est considérable. Il a réalisé plusieurs projets pour les Diaconesses protestantes de Reuilly, ainsi que des églises à Paris, Villeneuve-le-Roi et Montreuil, en région parisienne. Très à l'aise sur les projets de grande échelle, il a également construit un certain nombre de résidences privées. Il travaille actuellement sur des projets de logements et de bureaux à Paris, Montpellier, Saint-Malo et Lisbonne.

# L'ARBRESLE

*Versailles, France, 2001–02*

*Client: Œuvres et Institutions des Diaconesses de Reuilly. Gross floor area: 620 m². Costs: € 626 000.*

A small activities building set in a park near a Versailles hospital was destroyed by a storm in 1999. Mark Rolinet was called on to replace the structure on a tight budget. For a total cost of 626 000 euros, this 450-square-meter facility was built for an order of Protestant sisters (Communauté des Diaconesses de Reuilly). Aside from the original activities, the new building was to contain rooms for the sisters. The architect divided the project into four zones: on a square base, the activities area; on an oval base a woodworking shop; beneath the residential area, a large storage area, and finally the 37-meter-long living section, set up on pilotis and clad partially in polycarbonate. This cantilevered volume takes advantage of strong metallic supports and a relatively lightweight wood and plastic upper structure. On the whole, this facility has a rather Japanese feeling to it, because of the use of lightweight materials, and because of the four-part angular geometric composition.

Im Jahr 1999 zerstörte ein Sturm ein kleines, zu einem Krankenhaus bei Versailles gehörendes Mehrzweckgebäude. In der Folge beauftragte die protestantische Communauté des Diaconesses de Reuilly Mark Rolinet mit der Planung eines Neubaus. Das knappe Budget hielt er mit Baukosten von insgesamt 626 000 Euro für das fertige 450 m² große Gebäude ein. Zusätzlich zu den ursprünglichen Funktionen sollte das neue Haus auch Wohnräume für die Schwestern enthalten. Der Architekt teilte das Projekt in vier Zonen auf: einen quadratischen Bereich mit Räumen für verschiedene Aktivitäten, einen ovalen Bereich für die Holzwerkstatt, den großen Lagerraum im Untergeschoss und einen Wohnbereich, der mit einer Gesamtlänge von 37 m auf Stützpfeiler aus Metall gesetzt und teilweise mit Polycarbonat verkleidet wurde. Dieser auskragende Baukörper besteht aus einer relativ leichtgewichtigen Konstruktion aus Holz und Kunststoff. Insgesamt wirkt diese Anlage in ihrer Gestaltung ziemlich japanisch, was auf die Verwendung leichter Baumaterialien und die besondere geometrische Komposition der vier Bauteile zurückzuführen ist.

Ce petit bâtiment utilitaire situé dans un parc près d'un hôpital de Versailles avait été détruit au cours d'une tempête en 1999. Marc Rolinet fut appelé par la Communauté des Diaconesses de Reuilly pour le reconstruire, ce qu'il a fait dans le cadre d'un modeste budget de 626 000 euros. En plus de sa fonction d'origine, la nouvelle construction devait également compter des chambres pour les soeurs. Rolinet a divisé le projet en quatre zones, les activités dans une forme carrée, l'atelier de bois dans un ovale, un vaste espace de stockage niché sous la partie résidentielle, qui est un long tube de 37 m posé sur pilotis et partiellement habillé de polycarbonate. Ce volume en porte-à-faux et sa structure relativement légère en bois et plastique repose sur de solides piliers métalliques. La réalisation présente un certain caractère japonais par l'utilisation de matériaux légers et une composition en quatre parties.

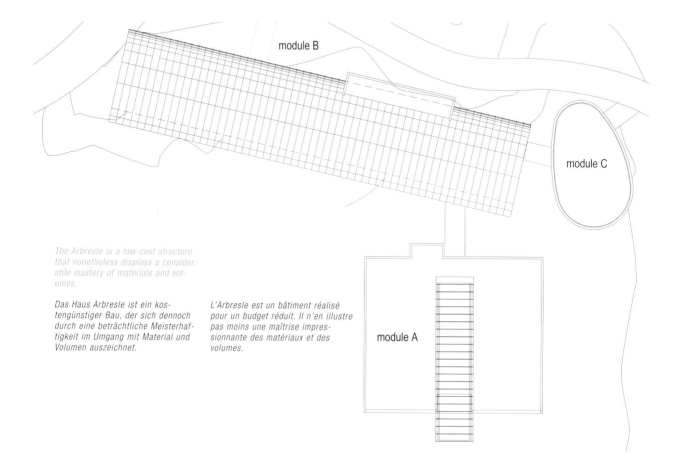

*The Arbresle is a low-cost structure that nonetheless displays a considerable mastery of materials and volumes.*

*Das Haus Arbresle ist ein kostengünstiger Bau, der sich dennoch durch eine beträchtliche Meisterhaftigkeit im Umgang mit Material und Volumen auszeichnet.*

*L'Arbresle est un bâtiment réalisé pour un budget réduit. Il n'en illustre pas moins une maîtrise impressionnante des matériaux et des volumes.*

Interior spaces of the residential area include the hallway which is faced on one side with curved polycarbonate. This surface lets a diffused light in during the day and glows from within at night.

Zu den Räumen im Wohntrakt gehört ein Flur, der an einer Seite mit gewölbtem Polycarbonat verkleidet ist. Diese Oberfläche lässt tagsüber ein diffuses Licht ein und leuchtet nachts von innen.

Les espaces intérieurs de la partie résidentielle comprennent un hall qui court le long de la partie incurvée en polycarbonate. Cette surface diffuse une lumière douce pendant la journée et irradie pendant la nuit.

*The residential volume is seen above and below, set up on pilotis. To the right, below, the oval workshop space identified as "Module C" on the plans.*

*Die beiden Fotos oben und unten links zeigen den auf Stützpfeilern ruhenden, auskragenden Wohntrakt. Unten rechts: Der ovale Werkstatt-raum ist auf dem Grundriss mit „Module C" ausgewiesen.*

*Le volume résidentiel, ci-dessus, et ci-dessous, est posé sur des pilotis. À droite, en bas, l'atelier ovale dési-gné comme « Module C » sur les plans.*

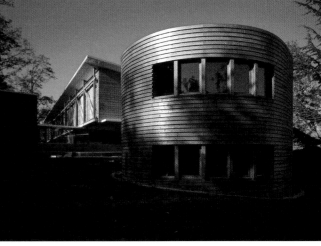

# SAUNDERS & WILHELMSEN

*Saunders Arkitektur*
*Nygårdsgaten 2a, 5015 Bergen, Norway*
*Tel: +47 55 36 8506*
*e-mail: todd@saunders-wilhelmsen.no*

*Wilhelmsen Arkitektur*
*Pedersens Gaten 32, 4013 Stavanger, Norway*
*Tel: +47 917 444 76*
*e-mail: tommie@online.no*

*Web: www.saunders-wilhelmsen.no*

*Summer House* ▶

Todd Saunders was born in 1969 in Gander, Newfoundland. He obtained his Master in Architecture from McGill University (Montreal, Canada, 1993–1995), and a Bachelor of Environmental Planning from the Nova Scotia College of Art and Design (1988–1992). Has worked in Austria, Germany, Russia, Latvia, and Norway. He teaches part-time at the Bergen School of Architecture. Tommie Wilhelmsen, born in 1973, is Norwegian, and was educated as an architect at the Bergen Architecture School. He has worked in Norway and Germany (with Behnisch, Behnisch & Partner in 1998), and teaches part-time at the Bergen School of Architecture. They created Saunders & Wilhelmsen in 2002 and obviously do not as yet have a large body of work, but their spirit and freshness of point of view is visible in the projects published here. For practical reasons, the two young architects were recently obliged to separate their office in Bergen into two different locations, and Tommie Wilhelmsen is now in Stavanger.

Todd Saunders, geboren 1969 in Gander, Neufundland, erwarb 1992 den Bachelor of Environmental Planning am Nova Scotia College of Art and Design und 1995 seinen Master of Architecture an der McGill University in Montreal. Er hat Projekte in Österreich, Deutschland, Russland, Lettland und Norwegen durchgeführt. Derzeit lehrt er an der Hochschule für Architektur im norwegischen Bergen. Tommie Wilhelmsen, 1973 in Norwegen geboren, studierte an der Hochschule für Architektur in Bergen und war in Norwegen und in Deutschland 1998 bei Behnisch, Behnisch & Partner tätig. Auch er lehrt an der Hochschule für Architektur in Bergen. Zusammen gründeten sie 2002 das Büro Saunders & Wilhelmsen. Zwar haben sie erst wenige Projekte realisiert, aber ihr frischer Geist und origineller Zugang wird in den hier vorgestellten Arbeiten offenkundig. Aus Gründen der Zweckmäßigkeit haben die beiden jungen Architekten ihr Büro in Bergen vor kurzem auf zwei Standorte aufgeteilt und Tommie Wilhelmsen ist nun in Stavanger tätig.

Todd Saunders, né à Gander (Terre-Neuve, Canada) en 1969, est Master of Architecture de la McGill University (Montréal, Canada, 1993–1995) et Bachelor en programmation environnementale du Nova Scotia College of Art and Design (1988–1992). Il a travaillé en Autriche, Allemagne, Russie, Lettonie et Norvège. Il enseigne à temps partiel à l'École d'architecture de Bergen (Norvège). Tommie Wilhelmsen, né en 1973, est Norvégien et a étudié l'architecture à l'École d'architecture de Bergen. Il a travaillé en Norvège et en Allemagne (chez Behnisch, Behnisch & Partner, 1998) et enseigne à temps partiel à Bergen. Ils ont créé l'agence Saunders & Wilhelmsen en 2002 et s'ils ne sont pas encore très actifs, la nouveauté de leurs idées et de leur esprit est évidente dans les projets publiés ici. Pour des raisons pratiques, ils ont du récemment séparer leurs bureaux, et Tommie Wilhelmsen est maintenant installé à Stavanger.

# SUMMER HOUSE

*Hardanger Fjord, Norway, 2003*

*Client: private. Floor area: 20 m² + 30 m². Costs: € 30 000 (site included).*

On a site they bought to create experimental architecture in order to convince potential clients of their abilities, Saunders and Wilhelmsen imagined a two-part structure. The first is a 20-square-meter "anything goes room" or bedroom, atelier, writer's studio etc. The second, 30-square-meter section includes the kitchen and living area, plus a bedroom, shower and toilet. It is possible to walk up onto the roof via an integrated stairway. The deck is made of local spruce and the building is unexpectedly insulated with recycled newspapers. The folding structure is made of birch plywood that has been treated with cold-pressed linseed oil. The site is on the west coast of Norway, about 70 km from Bergen on one of the largest and most beautiful fjords of the country. As the architects describe this adventure, "we made a structure that would be a part of the natural surroundings, yet in a sensitive contrast to the dramatic landscape. A long thin floating outdoor floor connects the two parts of the structure. This outdoor floor made the space twice as large in the summer, and connected the two buildings… The front of this arrangement faces the fjords, but the inner space towards the mountain creates an evening space that can be complemented by a small fire."

Auf einem Grundstück, das sie kauften, um dort mit neuen, experimentellen Architekturformen potentielle Auftraggeber von ihrem Können zu überzeugen, realisierten Saunders und Wilhelmsen einen zweiteiligen Entwurf. Der erste Bauteil besteht aus einem 20 m² großen Raum, der als „anything goes" oder Schlafzimmer, Künstleratelier, Arbeitsraum eines Schriftstellers u. ä. genutzt werden kann. Der zweite, 30 m² große Teil enthält die Küche und den Wohnraum, dazu ein Schlafzimmer, eine Dusche und Toilette. In seinem Innern führt eine Treppe auf das Dach. Die Plattform ist aus lokalem Fichtenholz gefertigt, während eines der Gebäude, das originellerweise mit recyceltem Zeitungspapier isoliert wurde, aus Birkensperrholz besteht, das mit kaltgepresstem Leinsamenöl behandelt wurde. Das Grundstück liegt an der Westküste von Norwegen, etwa 70 km von Bergen entfernt, an einem der größten und schönsten Fjorde des Landes. Saunders und Wilhelmsen beschreiben ihr Abenteuer so: „Wir entwarfen ein Gebäude, das Teil der natürlichen Umgebung ist und dennoch einen sensiblen Kontrast zur dramatischen Landschaft bildet. Die Vorderseite der beiden Baukörper, die durch eine lang gestreckte Bodenfläche miteinander verbunden sind, wendet sich dem Fjord zu. Der zum Berg ausgerichtete Innenraum bietet dagegen einen Bereich für den Abend, der durch ein kleines Kaminfeuer vervollständigt werden kann."

Sur un terrain spécialement acquis pour expérimenter leurs idées architecturales et convaincre leurs clients potentiels de leur capacité, Saunders et Wilhelmsen ont imaginé une construction en deux parties. La première est une « pièce à tout faire », ou chambre, atelier, bureau d'écrivain, etc., de 20 m². La seconde, de 30 m², comprend une cuisine, un séjour, une chambre, une douche et des toilettes. On peut monter sur le toit via un escalier intégré. La terrasse est en lattes d'épicéa local et l'isolation du bâtiment est assurée par des journaux recyclés. La structure pliable est en contreplaqué de bouleau traité à l'huile de lin pressée à froid. Le site se trouve sur la côte ouest de la Norvège, à 70 km environ de Bergen, au bord de l'un des plus vastes et plus magnifiques fjords du pays. Les architectes décrivent ainsi leur aventure : « Nous avons réalisé une construction qui est un élément de l'environnement naturel tout en contrastant avec le paysage spectaculaire. Une mince plate-forme flottante extérieur réunit les deux parties. Elle double l'espace disponible en été… Son avancée donne sur le fjord, mais sa partie intérieure, orientée vers les montagnes, offre le soir un séjour extérieur réchauffé par une petite cheminée. »

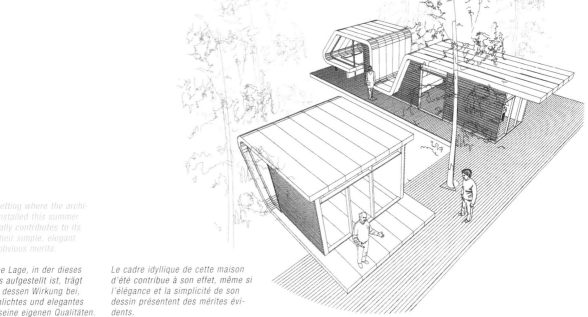

The idyllic setting where the architects have installed this summer house naturally contributes to its effect, but their simple, elegant design has obvious merits.

Die idyllische Lage, in der dieses Sommerhaus aufgestellt ist, trägt natürlich zu dessen Wirkung bei, doch ihr schlichtes und elegantes Design hat seine eigenen Qualitäten.

Le cadre idyllique de cette maison d'été contribue à son effet, même si l'élégance et la simplicité de son dessin présentent des mérites évidents.

The wooden platform extends the usable surface of the house and allows its inhabitants to enjoy the surroundings, just as the ample glazing of the house opens the view out and allows light in.

Die Holzplattform vergrößert die Nutzfläche des Hauses und erlaubt seinen Bewohnern, die Umgebung zu genießen. Hierzu tragen auch die großzügigen Verglasungen bei, die den Blick nach draußen freigeben und das Licht hereinholen.

La plate-forme en bois agrandit la surface utile de la maison et permet à ses habitants de profiter de l'environnement, de même que les vastes baies vitrées qui laissent entrer la lumière naturelle.

Original in its simplicity and in the way it is perched on the water, this small house is a model for modest vacation residences.

Originell in seiner Schlichtheit und Platzierung am Uferrand, könnte das kleine Haus als Vorbild für erschwingliche Ferienhäuser dienen.

Originale dans sa simplicité et dans son positionnement au-dessus de l'eau, cette petite maison pourrait servir de modèle de résidence de vacances.

# LOOK-OUT POINT

*Aurland, Sogn Og Fjord, Norway, 2002–2005*

*Client: Norwegian Public Roads Administration and Tourist Board. Height: 9 m, length: 23 m, width: 4 m. Costs: € 600 000 (including traffic planning).*

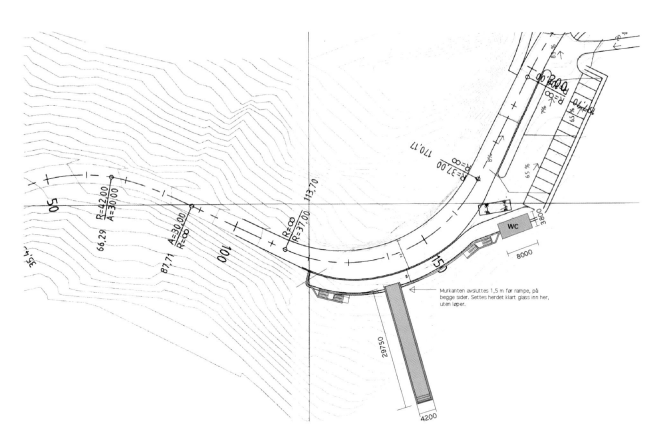

Murkanten avsluttes 1,5 m før rampe, på begge sider. Settes herdet klart glass inn her, uten løper.

Located in the fjords of western Norway, this inherently modest project nonetheless shows the inventiveness of the young architects. Visitors are invited to walk to the end of the platform, set some 640 meters above the Aurlandsfjorden. Being built for the Norwegian Highways Department (Statens Vegvesen), the structure will be 4 meters wide, 23 meters long, and 9 meters above the hillside at the end point. As the architects describe it, "nature first and architecture second was the guiding principal when we sat down to design this project. It was immediately obvious to us that in such beautiful surroundings one must make the least possible encroachment in the existing landscape and terrain. The landscape is so fantastic that it is difficult to improve the place, but at the same time it is very easy to destroy the atmosphere by inserting too many elements into the site. Even though we have chosen an expressive form, the concept is a form of minimalism, in an attempt to conserve and complement the existing site." The architects are quite proud of the fact that their design will require that no trees be cut during construction.

Das in der westnorwegischen Fjordregion realisierte Projekt ist äußerst bescheiden. Dennoch bezeugt es den Einfallsreichtum der beiden jungen Architekten. Die Besucher der 4 m breiten und 23 m langen, für die norwegische Autobahnbehörde gebaute Aussichtsplattform werden eingeladen, zu dem 9 m über dem Bergabhang aufragenden Ende zu gehen, von wo sie den etwa 640 m darunter liegenden Aurlandsfjord überblicken können. Die beiden Architekten über ihre Arbeit: „Erstens die Natur und zweitens die Architektur, lautete unser oberstes Prinzip, als wir mit der Planung dieses Projekts begannen. Es war uns sofort klar, dass wir in einer derart schönen Umgebung so wenig wie möglich in die Landschaft und das Terrain eingreifen durften. Diese Landschaft ist so fantastisch, dass es schwer ist, den Standort zu verbessern. Aber wir hätten die Atmosphäre sehr leicht zerstören können, wenn wir zu viele Elemente hinzufügt hätten. Trotzdem haben wir uns für eine expressive Form entschieden, deren Gestaltungskonzept eher minimalistisch ist, weil wir bestrebt waren, den bestehenden Standort zu erhalten und zu vervollständigen."

Même si ce projet qui domine un fjord norvégien semble modeste, il illustre l'inventivité de ses jeunes architectes. Construit par le département des routes de Norvège (Statens Vegvesen) ce belvédère de 4 m de large, 23 de long et de 9 m au-dessus du sol. Les visiteurs sont invités à avancer jusqu'à l'extrémité de la plateforme qui domine de quelque 640 m l'Aurlandsfjorden. Selon les architectes : « La nature d'abord, l'architecture ensuite, a été le principe de base qui nous a guidé dans la conception de ce projet. Il nous a semblé immédiatement évident que dans un cadre aussi magnifique on se devait d'intervenir le moins possible, que ce soit sur le paysage ou le sol. Le panorama est si fantastique qu'il était difficile d'imaginer améliorer le lieu, mais en même temps il était très facile de détruire son atmosphère en insérant trop d'éléments. Même si nous avons choisi une forme expressive, son concept est une forme de minimalisme, une tentative de conserver et de venir en complément du site existant. » Les deux architectes sont fiers que le chantier n'ait entraîné la suppression d'aucun arbre.

*Dependent for its effect on the spectacular natural setting, the Lookout Point is simple and elegant in its solution for this steeply sloped site*

*Die in ihrer Wirkung von der spektakulären Landschaft abhängige Aussichtsplattform bietet eine ebenso einfache wie elegante Lösung.*

*Implanté dans un cadre spectaculaire, ce belvédère est une solution élégante et simple au problème de l'escarpement du terrain.*

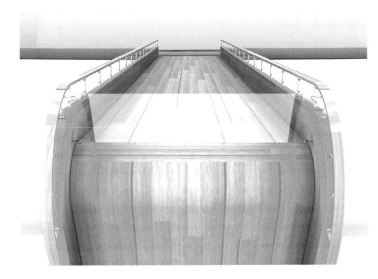

# WERNER SOBEK

Werner Sobek Ingenieure
Albstrasse 14
70597 Stuttgart
Germany

Tel: +49 711 76 7500
Fax: +49 711 76 75044
e-mail: mail@wsi-stuttgart.com
Web: www.wsi-stuttgart.com

*House R 128* ▶

Werner Sobek was born in 1953 in Aalen, Germany. He studied architecture and civil engineering at the University of Stuttgart (1974–1980) and did post-graduate research in "Wide-Span Lightweight Structures" at the University of Stuttgart (1980–1986). He received his PhD in civil engineering at the same University in 1987. He worked as a structural engineer in the office of Schlaich, Bergermann & Partner (Stuttgart, 1987–1991) before creating his own office in 1991. Since 1995 he has been a Professor at the University of Stuttgart where he succeeded Frei Otto as Director of the Institute for Lightweight Structures. His projects include: École Nationale d'Art Décoratif (Limoges, France, 1991–1994); Dome service hall Deutsche Bank (Hanover, 1992–1995); Art and Media Science Center (Karlsruhe, 1992–1997); Facade Interbank (with Hans Hollein, Lima, Peru, 1996–1999); New Bangkok International Airport (Thailand, with Murphy/Jahn, 1995–2004); Private residence R 128 (published here, Stuttgart, 1998–2000), and fair pavilions for Audi and BMW.

Werner Sobek, 1953 in Aalen geboren, studierte von 1974 bis 1980 Architektur und Bauwesen an der Universität Stuttgart und führte dort von 1980 bis 1986 Forschungsarbeiten zum Thema „weitgespannte Leichtbauten" durch. 1987 erwarb er an derselben Universität seinen Doktortitel in Bauwesen. Von 1987 bis 1991 arbeitete er als Bauingenieur bei Schlaich, Bergermann & Partner in Stuttgart, bevor er 1991 sein eigenes Büro in Stuttgart gründete. Seit 1995 ist er als Professor an der Universität Stuttgart tätig, wo er als Nachfolger von Frei Otto Direktor des Instituts für Leichtbauten wurde. Zu seinen Projekten zählen: die École Nationale d'Art Décoratif in Limoges (1991–1994), die Kuppel in der Schalterhalle der Deutschen Bank in Hannover (1992–1995), das ZKM in Karlsruhe (1992–1997), der neue internationale Flughafen in Bangkok (mit Murphy/Jahn, 1995–2004), die Fassade der Interbank (mit Hans Hollein) in Lima, Peru (1996–1999), das hier vorgestellte Wohnhaus R 128 in Stuttgart (1998–2000) sowie Messestände für Audi und BMW.

Werner Sobek, né en 1953 à Aalen, en Allemagne, étudie l'architecture et l'ingénierie civile à l'Université de Stuttgart (1974–1980) et mène une recherche de post-diplôme sur les structures légères de longue portée également à Stuttgart (1980–1986). Il est Ph. D. en ingénierie civile en 1987. Ingénieur structurel à l'agence Schlaich, Bergermann & Partner (Stuttgart, 1987–1991), il fonde la sienne en 1991. Depuis 1995, il est professeur à l'Université de Stuttgart où il a succédé à Frei Otto à la direction de l'Institut des structures légères. Parmi ses projets : École national d'arts décoratifs (Limoges, France, 1991–1994) ; dôme du hall de la Deutsche Bank (Hanovre, 1992–1995) ; Centre des arts et des médias (Karlsruhe, 1992–1997) ; façade d'Interbank (avec Hans Hollein, Lima, Pérou, 1996–1999) ; nouvel aéroport international de Bangkok (Thaïlande, avec Murphy/Jahn, 1995–2004) ; résidence privée, R 128, publiée ici (Stuttgart, 1998–2000) et pavillons de salons pour Audi et BMW.

# HOUSE R 128

*Stuttgart, Germany, 1999–2000*

*Client: Ursula und Werner Sobek. Total floor area: 250 m². Costs: not specified.*

The steep hillside of this 250-square-meter house made construction difficult. An existing 1923 structure was first demolished, and work such as that on the foundation had to be carried out by hand. A great deal of attention was paid to the ease of construction and finishing. The floors, for example, consist of prefabricated plastic-covered wood panels measuring 3.75 x 2.8 meters that are just placed between the floor beams without the use of screws. Aluminum ceiling panels are also clipped in place. The electrical or water lines are placed in aluminum ducts in the walls, never under plaster, to facilitate maintenance. The 11.2-meter, four-story building is made of a bolted steel skeleton with twelve columns arranged on a 3.85 x 2.9 meter grid. The façade is made of triple-glazed panels filled with inert gas and measuring 2.8 meters high by 1.36 meters wide on the north and south – 1.42 meters wide on the west and east. A mechanical ventilation system controls airflow and allows heat to be recovered from exhaust air. Air is blown through a heat exchanger situated below the foundation, taking advantage of the more constant temperature of the earth. Solar panels in the roof run the mechanical ventilation system and heat pump. Werner Sobek has announced that he intended to design only three houses in his life, each one requiring ten years of research. This one, made from twelve tons of steel and twenty tons of glass, was erected in an amazing eleven weeks. A second, teardrop-shaped carbon fiber structure so light it would not need foundations is already in the works.

Die Konstruktion des 250 m² großen Wohnhauses wurde durch seine Lage an einem stark abschüssigen Berghang erschwert. Insgesamt wurde große Sorgfalt auf den glatten Ablauf der Endfertigung verwandt. So bestehen beispielsweise die Böden aus vorgefertigten, 3,75 x 2,80 m großen Holzpaneelen mit Kunststoffüberzug, die ohne Einsatz von Schrauben einfach zwischen die Fußbodenbalken eingesetzt wurden. Auch die Deckenplatten aus Aluminium wurden lediglich mit einer Halterung befestigt. Sowohl elektrische Leitungen wie auch Wasserrohre verlaufen durch Aluminiumröhren in den Wänden, liegen aber nicht unter Gipsputz, was die Instandhaltung erleichtert. Die Konstruktion des 11,20 m hohen, viergeschossigen Hauses besteht aus einem verschraubten Stahlskelett mit zwölf Säulen, die innerhalb eines Grundrasters von 3,85 x 2,9 m angeordnet sind. Die Fassade setzt sich aus dreifach verglasten und mit Schutzgas gefüllten Tafeln zusammen, die an der Nord- und Südseite jeweils 2,80 m hoch und 1,36 m beziehungsweise an der West- und Ostseite 1,42 m breit sind. Ein mechanisches Belüftungssystem steuert den Luftstrom und ermöglicht eine Wärmerückgewinnung aus Abluft. Die Luft wird durch einen Wärmeaustauscher geblasen, der unter dem Fundament liegt und die konstante Temperatur des Erdbodens nutzt. Das Belüftungssystem und die Wärmepumpe werden durch Solartafeln angetrieben, die im Dach montiert sind. Werner Sobek hat angekündigt, er wolle in seinem ganzen Leben nur drei Häuser entwerfen, da jedes davon zehn Jahre Forschungsarbeit in Anspruch nimmt. Das hier vorgestellte Haus, das aus zwölf Tonnen Stahl und 20 Tonnen Glas gefertigt ist, wurde in der unglaublich kurzen Zeit von nur elf Wochen errichtet. Ein zweiter Entwurf, eine tropfenförmige Konstruktion aus Kohlenstoff-Faser, die so leicht ist, dass sie keinerlei Unterbau benötigt, ist bereits in Arbeit.

L'escarpement de la pente sur laquelle s'élève cette maison de 250 m² a rendu le chantier difficile. Une grande attention a été portée à la facilité de construction et d'aménagement. Par exemple, les sols consistent en panneaux de bois enduits de plastique de 3,75 x 2,8 m posés entre les solives, sans boulonnage. Les panneaux d'aluminium de la toiture sont simplement clipsés. Les conduites électriques ou d'eau passent par des tuyaux d'aluminium dans les murs, mais jamais sous enduit de plâtre pour faciliter leur maintenance. La maison de 11,2 m de haut et de quatre niveaux fait appel à un squelette d'acier riveté à 12 colonnes disposées selon une trame de 3,85 x 2,9 m. La façade est en panneaux de verre triple épaisseur séparés par une couche de gaz inerte, qui mesurent 2,8 x 1,36 m de haut au nord et au sud, et 2,8 x 1,42 m à l'est et à l'ouest. Un système de ventilation mécanique contrôle l'aération et permet de récupérer la chaleur de l'air usé. L'air est traité par une pompe à chaleur située sous les fondations, pour bénéficier de la température plus constante du sol. Des panneaux solaires en toiture alimentent le système de ventilation mécanique et la pompe à chaleur. Werner Sobek a annoncé sa volonté de ne construire que trois maisons au cours de sa carrière, chacune nécessitant dix années de recherches. Celle-ci, qui a demandé 12 tonnes d'acier et 20 de verre, a été montée très rapidement en 11 semaines. Une seconde construction en forme de goutte et en fibre de carbone, si légère qu'elle ne nécessite même pas de fondations, est déjà en chantier.

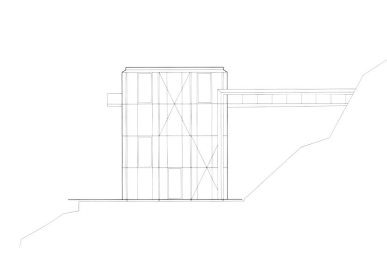

Making an ecologically sensitive house out of glass is already a considerable challenge. Succeeding in making it esthetically attractive and in harmony with its setting is a triumph.

Ein ökologisch sensibles Haus aus Glas zu bauen, ist eine große Herausforderung. Es ästhetisch attraktiv und in Harmonie mit seiner Umgebung zu gestalten, ist ein Triumph.

Réaliser une maison d'esprit écologique est un défi considérable, réussir à la rendre esthétiquement séduisante et en harmonie avec son cadre est une performance rare.

The extreme simplicity of the layout and the entirely glazed walls make the house astonishing to look at from the exterior and allow full views out toward Stuttgart.

*Die äußerste Schlichtheit der Anordnung und die zur Gänze verglasten Wände machen das Haus zu einer auffallenden Erscheinung und erlauben einen freien Rundblick.*

*L'extrême simplicité du plan et les parois entièrement vitrées donnent un aspect étonnant à la maison vue de l'extérieur et permettent une vision panoramique de Stuttgart.*

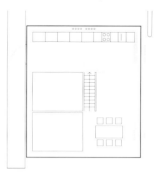

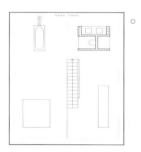

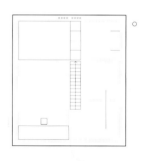

*The reduction of this house to its bare minimum does not make it less interesting, quite the contrary. Its highly engineered nature is not at all apparent and that is its success.*

*Die Reduzierung dieses Gebäudes auf ein absolutes Minimum macht es nicht weniger interessant, ganz im Gegenteil. Dass sein stark ingenieurtechnischer Charakter in keiner Weise spürbar wird, ist ein weiterer Grund für seinen Erfolg.*

*La réduction de la maison au minimum possible ne la rend pas moins intéressante, bien au contraire. Avoir su faire oublier sa haute technicité est une de ses réussites.*

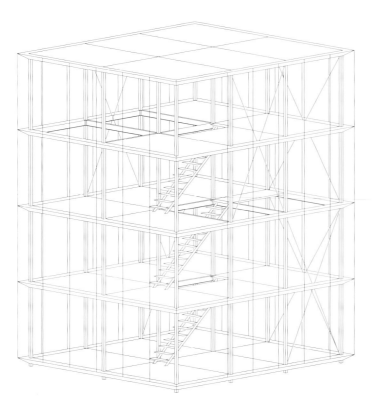

The extreme lightness of the structural elements of the house almost seems to make the floors hover in space with no visible means of support.

*Die extreme Leichtigkeit der Konstruktionsteile lassen die Geschossböden fast ohne sichtbare Stützvorrichtungen im Raum schweben.*

*La légèreté extrême des éléments structurels donne l'impression que les niveaux flottent dans l'espace, sans support visible.*

Conceived on a strict grid system, the house is sparely furnished with couches and chairs designed by Le Corbusier and Breuer.

Das innerhalb eines exakten Grundrasters entworfene Haus ist spärlich möbliert mit Sofas und Stühlen, entworfen von Le Corbusier und Breuer.

Conçu sur une trame rigoureuse, la maison est parcimonieusement meublée de sièges et de canapés modernistes de le Corbusier et Breuer.

# EDUARDO SOUTO DE MOURA

*Souto Moura Arquitectos Lda.*
*R. do Aleixo, 531° A*
*4150-043 Porto*
*Portugal*

*Tel: +351 22 618 7547*
*Fax: +351 22 610 8092*
*e-mail: souto.moura@mail.telepac.pt*

*Manoel de Oliveira Movie Theater* ▶

Eduardo Souto de Moura was born in Porto, Portugal, in 1952. He graduated from the School of Architecture of Porto (ESBAP) in 1980. He was an Assistant Professor at the Faculty of Architecture in Porto (FAUP) from 1981 to 1991. He worked in the office of Alvaro Siza from 1974 to 1979 and created his own office the following year. Recent work includes Row houses in the Rua Lugarinho, Porto, Portugal (1996); Renovation of the Municipal Market in Braga (1997); the Silo Norte Shopping building; a house and wine cellar, Valladolid, Spain (1999); and the project for the Portuguese Pavilion, Expo 2000 Hanover (with Alvaro Siza, 1999). Current work includes the conversion of the building of the Carvoeira da Foz, Porto and a project for the Braga Stadium.

Eduardo Souto de Moura, geboren 1952 im portugiesischen Porto, schloss 1980 sein Studium an der Architekturschule von Porto (ESBAP) ab. Von 1981 bis 1991 lehrte er am Fachbereich Architektur der Universität Porto (FAUP). Bevor er sich 1980 mit einem eigenen Büro selbstständig machte, arbeitete er von 1974 bis 1979 im Büro von Alvaro Siza. Zu seinen neueren Projekten gehören eine Reihenhausanlage in der Rua Lugarinho in Porto (1996), die Renovierung des städtischen Marktes in Braga (1997), das Einkaufszentrum Silo Norte, ein Wohnhaus und Weinkeller im spanischen Valladolid (1999) und der in Zusammenarbeit mit Alvaro Siza entstandene Portugiesische Pavillon für die Expo 2000 in Hannover (1999). Gegenwärtig arbeitet Souto de Moura unter anderem am Umbau des Gebäudes der Carvoeira da Foz in Porto und an einem Projekt für das Stadium in Braga.

Né en 1952 à Porto, au Portugal, Eduardo Souto de Moura est diplômé de l'École d'architecture de Porto (ESBAP, 1980). Il a été Professeur assistant à la faculté d'architecture de Porto (FAUP) de 1981 à 1991. Après avoir travaillé auprès d'Alvaro Siza de 1974 à 1979, il a fondé sa propre agence en 1980. Parmi ses réalisations récentes : des maisons alignées Rua Lugarinho (Porto, 1996), la rénovation du marché municipal de Braga (1997), le centre commercial de Silo Norte, une maison et un chais (Valladolid, Espagne, 1999) et le pavillon portugais d'Expo 2000 (Hanovre, Allemagne, avec Alvaro Siza, 1999). Il travaille actuellement à la reconversion de l'immeuble de la Carvoeira da Foz (Porto) et à un projet de stade à Braga.

# MANOEL DE OLIVEIRA MOVIE THEATER

*Porto, Portugal, 2001–2003*

*Client: City of Porto. Total floor area: 1 476 m². Costs: not specified.*

Built on a 1020-square-meter lot located about 35 meters from the two planned fifteen-story towers, this is an essentially cubic structure which nonetheless has an inclined roof. Clad largely in zinc, the structure makes use of unpolished inox foil on the ground floor and dark gray monopaste on the upper level. Dark wood floors and grey marble stairways mark the interior. An access toward a new street south of the site has been provided for. A trapezoidal auditorium and a library facing both the river and the sea are part of the 1 476-square-meter scheme.

Das Gebäude wurde auf einem 1 020 m² großen Grundstück gebaut, das ca. 35 m von zwei geplanten 15-geschossigen Wohntürmen entfernt liegt. Es ist eine im Wesentlichen kubische Konstruktion, hat aber dennoch ein Schrägdach. Der größtenteils mit Zink verkleidete Bau ist im Erdgeschoss mit unpolierter, nichtoxidierbarer Folie und im Obergeschoss mit dunkelgrauer Monopaste ausgestattet. Außerdem ist der Innenraum durch dunkle Holzböden und Treppen aus grauem Marmor gekennzeichnet. Ein trapezförmiges Auditorium und eine Bibliothek, die sich sowohl dem Fluss als auch dem Meer zuwenden, vervollständigen das 1 476 m² umfassende Gebäude.

Construite sur une parcelle de 1 020 m² à 35 m environ de deux tours de quinze étages qui devraient être bientôt réalisées, cette structure essentiellement cubique n'en possède pas moins un toit incliné. Pour l'essentiel habillée de zinc, elle fait appel à de l'acier inox non poli pour son rez-de-chaussée et à un monopaste gris foncé au niveau supérieur. L'intérieur se distingue par des sols en bois foncé et un escalier de marbre gris. Un accès par une rue nouvelle qui devrait passer au sud du terrain a été prévu. Ce projet de 1 476 m² comprend une salle de cinéma trapézoïdale et une bibliothèque qui font face au fleuve et à la mer.

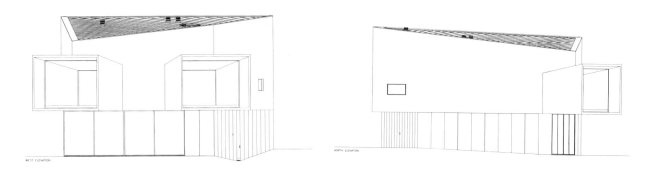

WEST ELEVATION                    NORTH ELEVATION

As is typically the case with his work, Souto de Moura uses a reduced modern vocabulary, but articulates this structure in an unexpected way, with its alternation of almost blank surfaces and broad high openings.

Wie es für seine Arbeiten typisch ist, setzt Souto de Moura auch hier eine reduzierte, moderne Formensprache ein, überrascht bei diesem Gebäude jedoch mit dem Wechsel von nahezu undurchbrochenen Oberflächen und weiten, hohen Fensteröffnungen.

À sa manière typique, Souto de Moura utilise un vocabulaire moderne minimal, mais articule son projet de façon inattendue par l'alternance de surfaces presque aveugles et de vastes ouvertures.

In elevation (left) or even in some photographs, the structure does bring to mind the shape of a movie camera, an appropriate metaphor for this structure.

Im Aufriss (links) und in einigen Ansichten erinnert die Form des Gebäudes an eine Filmkamera, eine passende Metapher für ein Kino.

En élévation (à gauche) et même dans certaines photographies, le bâtiment fait penser à une caméra, métaphore appropriée pour un cinéma.

Simple surfaces that are disposed in unexpected ways animate the interior. Light too is filtered in where it is not usually found, from below or from the sides.

Einfache Oberflächen, auf unerwartete Weise angeordnet, beleben den Innenraum. Auch das Licht fällt auf unübliche Weise ein, nämlich von unten oder von der Seite.

Des plans simples, mais disposés de manière inattendue, animent l'intérieur. La lumière filtrée arrive selon des angles d'orientation rarement utilisées, comme le bas ou les côtés.

The alternation of dark and light, as well as the asymmetrical placement of stairways, is reminiscent here of the work of the mentor of Souto de Moura, Alvaro Siza.

Im Wechsel zwischen Dunkel und Hell oder in der asymmetrischen Ausrichtung der Treppen finden sich Anklänge an die Arbeit des Mentors von Souto de Moura, Alvaro Siza.

L'alternance de plans sombre ou lumineux, et l'implantation asymétrique de l'escalier rappellent l'œuvre du mentor de Souto de Moura, Alvaro Siza.

# PHILIPPE STARCK

*Philippe Starck*
*18/20, rue du Faubourg du Temple*
*75011 Paris*
*France*

*Tel: +33 1 48 07 54 54*
*Fax: +33 1 48 07 54 64*
*e-mail: info@philippe-starck.com*
*Web: www.philippe-starck.com*

*TASCHEN Store ▶*

Philippe Starck was born in 1949 and attended the École Nissim de Camondo in Paris. Though he is of course best known as a furniture and object designer, his projects as an architect include the Café Costes (Paris, 1984); Royalton Hotel (New York, 1988); Laguiole Knife Factory (Laguiole, 1988); Paramount Hotel (New York, 1990); Nani Nani Building (Tokyo, 1989); Asahi Beer Building (Tokyo, 1989); the Teatriz Restaurant (Madrid, 1990); and his Baron Vert building in Osaka (1990). He has also designed a number of private houses and apartment blocks, for example Lemoult in Paris (1987), The Angle in Antwerp (1991), apartment buildings in Los Angeles (1991), and a private house in Madrid (1991). More recently, he completed the interior design of the Saint Martin's Lane and Sanderson Hotels in London. In 2000, he completed the TASCHEN Store in Paris, and the following year the Clift Hotel in San Franciso.

Philippe Starck, 1949 in Paris geboren, studierte an der dortigen École Nissim de Camondo. Obwohl er vor allem als Designer von Möbeln und Gebrauchsobjekten bekannt wurde, hat er auch Architekturprojekte ausgeführt. Zu diesen gehören das Café Costes in Paris (1984), das Royalton Hotel (1988) und das Paramount Hotel (1990), beide in New York, die Laguiole Messerfabrik in Laguiole, Frankreich (1988), das Nani Nani-Gebäude (1989) und das Gebäude der Asahi-Brauerei (1989), beide in Tokio, das Restaurant Teatriz in Madrid (1990) sowie das Baron Vert Building in Osaka (1990). Darüber hinaus hat Starck auch eine Reihe von Privathäusern und Apartmentgebäuden entworfen, so das Haus Lemoult in Paris (1987), das Haus The Angle in Antwerpen (1991), Wohnbauten in Los Angeles (1991) und ein Haus in Madrid (1991). In jüngerer Zeit führte er die Innenraumgestaltung der Londoner Hotels Saint Martin's Lane und Sanderson durch. Im Jahr 2000 realisierte er die Buchhandlung TASCHEN in Paris und im folgenden Jahr das Clift Hotel in San Francisco.

Philippe Starck, né en 1949, a suivi les cours de l'École Nissim de Camondo à Paris. S'il est surtout connu comme designer de produits et de mobilier, il est aussi l'auteur d'interventions architecturales comme le Café Costes (Paris, 1984), le Royalton Hotel (New York, 1988), l'usine de coutellerie de Laguiole (Laguiole, 1988), le Paramount Hotel (New York, 1990), le Nani Nani Building (Tokyo, 1989), l'Asahi Beer Building (Tokyo, 1989), le Teatriz Restaurant (Madrid, 1990) et le Baron Vert Building (Osaka, 1990). Il a également conçu un certain nombre de résidences privées et d'immeubles d'appartements comme la maison Le Moult (Paris, 1987), The Angle (Anvers, 1991), un immeuble à Los Angeles (1991) et une maison à Madrid (1991). Plus récemment, il a achevé l'aménagement intérieur des hôtels Saint Martin's Lane et Sanderson à Londres. En 2002, il a conçu la librairie TASCHEN à Paris et en 2003 le Clift Hotel à San Francisco.

# TASCHEN STORE

*Los Angeles, California, USA, 2002–03*

Design: Philippe Starck. Art: Albert Oehlen.

The TASCHEN Store is located at 354 N. Beverly Drive, in Beverly Hills. It occupies one-third of an existing art-deco building in the middle of Beverly Hills' commercial district, one block away from Rodeo Drive, and near Frank Lloyd Wright's Anderton Court Shops (1952), Richard Meier's Gagosian Gallery, the Museum of Television & Radio, and a Prada boutique yet to be completed by Rem Koolhaas. The store is one-story with a mezzanine and terrace to the rear. The space is tall and narrow. The main room is four meters wide (including bookshelves) and 30.5 meters long. The coffered wood ceiling is five meters high. There are two long display tables centered in the main room. They were laser-scanned with CAD-CAM software on the basis of a small-scale model made by Starck's office. They are metalized with bronze finish. There is also a similarly made bar table that is located underneath a glass ceiling (the glass floor of the mezzanine). To each side of the bar table are lavender colored upholstered niches with built-in banquettes. At the rear of the main room is an all-glass mezzanine room. Glass wall panels are art glass made of layers of sand-blasted, laminated glass with a drip-motif design. They were made by Pictet in Paris. There is a glass "coffee bar alcove" located at the rear of the main sales room. Walls, ceilings, bar counter and shelves, are all finished in lavender-hued mirrored glass that is engraved with a pattern designed by Starck. Kanner Architects were the local office in charge of the project (Executive architect) and TASCHEN called on German artist Albert Oehlen to produce twenty works for the bookshop. These computer generated images constitute a sequence of collages inspired by the publisher's titles.

Die Buchhandlung TASCHEN findet sich unter der Adresse 354 N. Beverly Drive in Beverly Hills. Sie nimmt ein Drittel eines Art déco Gebäudes ein, das im Zentrum des Geschäftsviertels von Beverly Hills liegt, einen Häuserblock vom Rodeo Drive entfernt und in der Nähe von Frank Lloyd Wrights Anderton Court Shops (1952), Richard Meiers Gagosian Gallery, dem Museum of Television & Radio sowie einer derzeit von Rem Koolhaas gestalteten Prada Boutique. Das eingeschossige Geschäft hat einen Mezzaninraum mit kassettierter Holzdecke und an der Hinterseite eine Terrasse. Der hohe und schmale Hauptraum ist 4 m breit (einschließlich der Bücherregale), 30,5 m lang und 5 m hoch. Die beiden langen, in der Mitte des Raums aufgestellten Büchertische wurden mit einer CAD-CAM Software und Laserscanner nach einem kleinformatigen Modell angefertigt. Sie sind mit einer Metallschicht bedeckt und bronziert. Ein als Coffee-Bar dienender Tisch ähnlicher Machart steht am hinteren Ende des Verkaufsraums unter einer Glasdecke, die gleichzeitig den Glasboden des Mezzanins bildet. Zu beiden Seiten dieses Tisches befinden sich lilafarben ausgepolsterte Nischen mit eingebauten Sitzbänken. Die Wände des vollständig aus Glas konstruierten Mezzaninraums bestehen aus sandgestrahltem Schichtglas mit Tropfmotiv-Design. Sie wurden von der Pariser Firma Pictet angefertigt. Die Oberflächen sämtlicher Wände, der Decke, Bar-Theke und Regale sind aus lavendelfarbenem Spiegelglas, das mit einem von Starck entworfenen Gravurmuster verziert wurde. Die architektonische Leitung des Projekts lag bei dem in Los Angeles ansässigen Büro von Kanner Architects. TASCHEN gab speziell für die Buchhandlung 20 Arbeiten bei dem deutschen Künstler Albert Oehlen in Auftrag. Seine computergenerierten Darstellungen bilden eine Serie von Collagen, zu denen sich der Künstler von den Buchtiteln des Verlags inspirieren ließ.

Au 354 N. Beverly Drive, la Librairie TASCHEN occupe le tiers d'un bâtiment de style Art-déco du quartier commercial de Beverly Hills, à un bloc de Rodeo Drive et non loin des Anderton Court Shops de Frank Lloyd Wright (1952), de la Gagosian Gallery de Richard Meier, du Musée de la télévision et de la radio et d'une boutique Prada en cours d'achèvement par Rem Koolhaas. Le volume haut et étroit se déploie sur un seul niveau, mais avec une mezzanine et une terrasse à l'arrière. La salle principale mesure 4 m de large (y compris les rayonnages) et 30,5 m de long. Le plafond de bois à caissons est à 5 m de haut. Le centre de l'espace est occupé par deux longues tables de présentation métallisées de finition bronze, réalisées par commande numérique à partir d'une maquette à petite échelle fournie par l'agence de Starck. On trouve un bar de traitement similaire sous un plafond de verre qui est le sol de la mezzanine. De chaque côté de ce bar ont été installées des banquettes dans des niches rembourrées de couleur lavande. La pièce en mezzanine, à l'arrière, est entièrement en verre. Les panneaux qui recouvrent les murs sont en couches de verre feuilleté sablé avec un motif de couture. Elles ont été réalisées par les ateliers Pictet à Paris. Au fond de l'espace de vente est installé un « bar à café en alcôve ». Les murs, les plafonds, le bar et les rayonnages sont tous en verre miroir de nuance lavande gravé d'un motif dessiné par P. Starck. Kannen Architects ont été les architectes exécutifs et TASCHEN a fait appel à l'artiste allemand Albert Oehlen pour une suite de vingt œuvres réalisées par ordinateur, collages inspirés des titres publiés par l'éditeur.

*Inspired by titles in the TASCHEN catalogue, works by Albert Oehlen animate the space that Philippe Starck has created.*

*Die von Büchern aus dem Programm des TASCHEN Verlags inspirierten Arbeiten von Albert Oehlen beleben den Innenraum.*

*Inspirées de titres du catalogue TASCHEN, des œuvres d'Albert Oehlen animent l'espace créé par Philippe Starck.*

Furniture by Starck blends with unusual surfaces, creating a surprising
backdrop for books that have in
themselves often attained the status
of cult objects.

Einrichtungsgegenstände von Starck
verschmelzen mit ausgefallenen
Oberflächen zu einem ungewöhnlichen Hintergrund für Bücher, von
denen einige bereits selbst den Status von Kultobjekten erlangt haben.

Le mobilier de Starck se mélange
à des effets de surface inhabituels,
créant un fond surprenant pour des
livres qui sont eux-mêmes souvent
devenus des objets-cultes.

Philippe Starck's own monograph published by TASCHEN forms a décor (lower left) while other books take their place in an environment where design and publications accompany each other like equivalent forms of expression. Starck's décor borders on the kitsch, which in the environment of Los Angeles is hardly an accident. The designer amuses himself even as he accomplishes the essential commercial task he set out to deal with.

Die von TASCHEN veröffentlichte Monografie von Philippe Starck bildet ein eigenes Dekor (unten links), während die anderen Bücher in einem Umfeld präsentiert werden, in dem sich Design und Druckwerke wie gleichwertige Ausdrucksformen ergänzen. Starcks Innenraumgestaltung grenzt an Kitsch, was im Kontext von Los Angeles kaum ein Zufall sein dürfte. Der Designer löst seine im Grunde rein kommerzielle Aufgabe mit Amüsement und Ironie.

La monographie de Philippe Starck publiée par TASCHEN forme un décor (en bas à gauche) tandis que d'autres livres trouvent leur place dans un environnement ou le design intérieur et les livres s'accompagnent mutuellement, comme des formes d'expression équivalente. Le décor imaginé par Starck frise le kitsch, ce qui n'est pas un hasard dans le contexte de Los Angeles. Le designer s'amuse, même lorsqu'il répond aux exigences de tâches commerciales.

# JYRKI TASA

*Jyrki Tasa*
*Architectural Office*
*Nurmela-Raimoranta-Tasa Ltd.*
*Kalevankatu 31*
*00100 Helsinki*
*Finland*

*Tel: +358 9686 6780*
*Fax: +358 9685 7588*
*e-mail: tasa@n-r-t.fi*

*House Moby Dick* ▶

Born in Turku, Finland, in 1944, Jyrki Tasa graduated from the Helsinki University of Technology in 1973. He set up an architectural office with Matti Nurmela and Kari Raimoranta in Helsinki the same year. He has been a professor at the University of Oulu since 1988. He has won 20 first prizes in architectural competitions. He won the Finnish State Prize in Architecture and Planning in 1987. His most significant work includes the Malmi Post Office, the Kuhmo Library, the Paavo Nurmi Stadium in Turku, the Into House in Espoo, the BE Pop Shopping Center in Pori, and the Moby Dick house published here. All of these projects are located in Finland.

Jyrki Tasa, 1944 im finnischen Turku geboren, schloss 1973 sein Studium an der Technischen Universität Helsinki ab. Im selben Jahr gründete er zusammen mit Matti Nurmela und Kari Raimoranta ein Architekturbüro in Helsinki. Seit 1988 lehrt er außerdem an der Universität von Oulu. Jyrki Tasa ist im Laufe seiner Karriere aus 20 Architekturwettbewerben als Sieger hervorgegangen und 1987 wurde ihm der Finnische Staatspreis für Architektur und Bauplanung verliehen. Zu seinen wichtigsten, alle in Finnland realisierten Bauten, gehören das Postamt in Malmi, die Bibliothek in Kuhmo, das Paavo Nurmi Stadium in Turku, das Haus Into in Espoo, das Einkaufszentrum BE Pop in Pori sowie das hier vorgestellte Haus Moby Dick.

Né en 1944 à Tuku, en Finlande, Jyrki Tasa est diplômé de l'Université de Technologie d'Helsinki en 1973. Il crée son agence d'architecture avec Matti Nurmela et Kari Raimoranta à Helsinki la même année. Il enseigne à l'Université d'Oulu depuis 1988 et a remporté 20 premiers prix de concours architecturaux. Il a reçu le Prix d'architecture et d'urbanisme de l'État finlandais en 1987. Parmi ses réalisations les plus marquantes, toutes en Finlande : la poste de Malmi, la bibliothèque de Kuhmo, le stade Paavo Nurmi à Turku, la maison Into à Espoo, le centre commercial BE Pop à Pori et la maison Moby Dick publiée ici.

# HOUSE MOBY DICK

*Espoo, Finland, 2002–03*

*Client: a four person family (private). Total floor area: 570 m². Costs: not specified.*

Few houses appear as different as this one when seen from one side (below) or the other (right). Elevations show better how this surprising transition is accomplished.

Wenige Häuser wirken so unterschiedlich, wenn man sie von verschiedenen Seiten (unten und rechts) betrachtet. Die Aufrisse machen die Ausführung der Übergänge deutlich.

Peu de maisons présentent autant de différences d'une façade (ci-dessous) à l'autre (à droite). Les élévations expliquent cette surprenante transition.

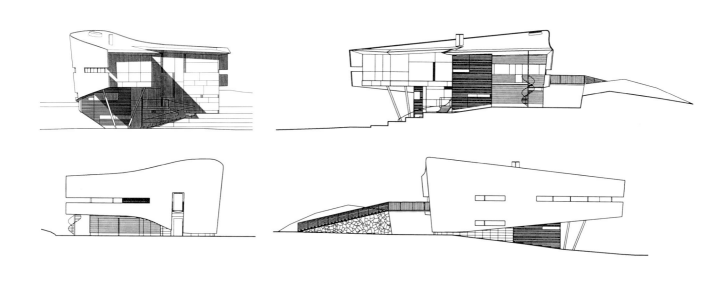

Built for a four-person family, this 570-square-meter "biomorphic" house is approached via a stone stairway and a steel bridge leading to the first floor above ground level. At the entrance level, there are a living room, library, master bedroom, and two balconies. The ground floor contains the children's spaces, a guestroom, and a garage, while a sauna, fireplace, and gym are in the basement of the house. A two-story-high winter garden, three translucent glass and steel bridges and a staircase forming the spatial core of the house all participate in the open movement of the residence. The stairway offers views into every area of the house. The curving exterior of the structure, evoked by its name "Moby Dick," contrasts with the rectangular interior walls. Made with concrete-filled steel pillars, concrete-steel composite slabs and a steel and wood roof, the house is mostly clad with plywood or pine. The house is equipped with a heat pump and floor heating system.

Der Zugang zu dem für eine vierköpfige Familie gebauten „biomorphen" Haus erfolgt über eine Steintreppe und eine Stahlbrücke, die zum ersten Stock führen. Auf dieser Ebene liegen ein Wohnraum, die Bibliothek, das Elternschlafzimmer und zwei Balkone. Das Erdgeschoss enthält die Räume der Kinder, ein Gästezimmer und eine Garage, während Sauna, Kamin und Fitnessraum im Souterrain untergebracht sind. Ein Wintergarten mit doppelter Raumhöhe, drei durchscheinende Brücken aus Glas und Stahl und ein Treppenaufgang bilden den räumlichen Kern des Gebäudes und tragen in ihrer Gesamtheit zu seiner offenen, rhythmischen Gestaltung bei. Die geschwungenen Fassaden, von denen das Haus den Namen Moby Dick hat, kontrastieren mit den rechtwinkligen Innenwänden. Die Konstruktion besteht aus Stahlsäulen mit Betonfüllung, Betonstahlplatten und einem Dach aus Stahl und Holz. Die Außenverkleidung ist hauptsächlich aus Sperrholz oder Kiefernholz gefertigt.

On accède à cette maison biomorphique de 570 m², construite pour une famille de quatre personnes, par une allée pavée et une passerelle d'acier menant directement au premier niveau au-dessus du rez-de-chaussée. Il contient le séjour, une bibliothèque, la chambre principale et deux balcons. Le rez-de-chaussée regroupe les espaces pour les enfants, une chambre d'amis et un garage, tandis que le sous-sol comprend un sauna, une cheminée et une salle de gymnastique. Le jardin intérieur sur deux niveaux, trois murs de verre translucide, des passerelles et un escalier en acier constituent le noyau de cette maison et assurent une circulation ouverte. La façade incurvée, qui justifie le nom de « Moby Dick » contraste avec les murs intérieurs orthogonaux. L'ensemble a fait appel à des piliers d'acier remplis de béton, des dalles de béton armé, un toit en bois et acier. La façade est habillée pour l'essentiel de contreplaqué ou de pin.

Contrary to what the closed entrance façade might imply, the house is bright, open and light its in articulation.

Im Gegensatz zu dem, was man von der geschlossenen Eingangsfassade erwarten könnte, ist das Haus hell, offen und von lockerer Eleganz.

Contrairement à ce que la façade d'entrée fermée laisse entendre, la maison est très ouverte et d'articulation légère.

Daylight floods the interior space where wood and glazing form the major surfaces. Plans below show the rather unusual disposition of the structure.

Das Tageslicht durchflutet den Innenraum, in dem Holz und Glas vorherrschen. Die Grundrisse unten zeigen die ungewöhnliche Anordnung des Gebäudes.

La lumière naturelle inonde l'intérieur, traité essentiellement en bois et en verre. Les plans ci-dessous montrent le plan assez curieux de la maison.

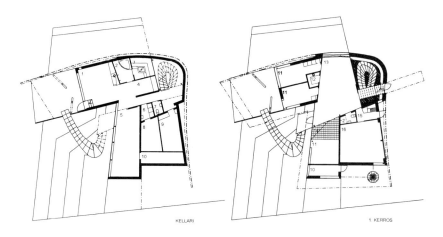

KELLARI

1. KERROS

An unusual irregular spiral staircase connects the interior levels of the house, and the architect uses a full palette of materials to surprise and delight the inhabitant or visitor.

Eine auffallend unregelmäßige Wendeltreppe verbindet die Geschossebenen des Hauses. Die volle Palette von Materialien überrascht Bewohner wie Besucher.

Un curieux escalier irrégulier relie les niveaux intérieurs. L'architecte a fait appel à une palette variée de matériaux pour surprendre et ravir l'occupant ou le visiteur.

# JEAN-MICHEL WILMOTTE

*Wilmotte & Associés SA*
*68, rue du Faubourg Saint-Antoine*
*75012 Paris*
*France*

*Tel: +33 1 53 02 22 22, Fax: +33 1 43 44 17 11*
*e-mail: wilmotte@wanadoo.fr*

Born in 1948, a graduate of the Camondo school in Paris, Jean-Michel Wilmotte created his own firm in 1975. Although he is best known for his work in interior design Wilmotte joined the Order of Architects in France in 1993. With approximately 80 employees, his office works on industrial and furniture design, such as the new lighting fixtures and benches installed on the Champs-Elysées, but he also participated in the competition for the British Museum, making use of the experience he gathered as architect of the Decorative Arts Department of the Louvre for the Richelieu wing, completed in 1993. As an architect, Jean-Michel Wilmotte completed two buildings in Tokyo, the International Executive Office building in the Shinjuku area, and the New N°3 Arai building, while he also carried out the furniture design for the Bank of Luxembourg building, completed by Arquitectonica in 1994. He completed the Gana Art Center, Seoul (South Korea, 1996-1998) and a museum for objects given to French President Jacques Chirac in Sarran (France, 2000). Current projects include new showrooms for Chaumet, John Galliano and Montblanc International; interior design of the new LVMH Headquarters in Paris as well as numerous housing, cultural or rehabilitation projects in France, Italy and Korea. He is also working on the interior design of the Museum of Islamic Arts (I. M. Pei architect, Doha, Qatar). His reputation for cultural facilities has also led him to work on the Centre National du Costume de Scène (National Center for Theater Costumes) located in Moulins, France – a refurbishment of military barracks to house exhibition spaces for costumes, training centre and a research department (5 720 m²); and the Museum of Jewish Art in Bruxelles, a 4 500 m² renovation and construction project.

Jean-Michel Wilmotte, 1948 geboren, graduierte an der École Camondo in Paris und gründete 1975 seine eigene Firma. Obwohl er vor allem als Innenarchitekt bekannt wurde, trat er 1993 dem französischen Architektenverband bei. Mit seinen ca. 80 Mitarbeitern ist das Büro hauptsächlich in den Bereichen Industrie- und Möbeldesign tätig; es hat etwa die neuen Beleuchtungskörper und Sitzbänke auf den Champs-Elysées entworfen. Jean-Michel Wilmotte beteiligte sich auch an dem Wettbewerb für die Ausstattung des British Museum, wobei er seine Erfahrungen mit der 1993 fertig gestellten Abteilung für angewandte Kunst im Richelieu-Flügel des Louvre nutzen konnte. Zu seinen Bauprojekten gehören zwei Bürogebäude in Tokio, das International Executive Office im Shinjuku-Viertel und das New N°3 Arai-Gebäude. Ferner das Gana Art Center in Seoul, Südkorea (1996–1998) sowie ein Museum für die Geschenke, die der französische Präsident Jacques Chirac auf seinen Staatsbesuchen erhalten hat, im französischen Sarran (2000). Außerdem entwarf er die Möbel für das 1994 von der Gruppe Arquitectonica realisierte Gebäude der Bank von Luxemburg. Zur Zeit arbeitet Wilmotte an neuen Showrooms für Chaumet, John Galliano und Montblanc International, an der Innenraumgestaltung der neuen LVMH Zentrale in Paris und an einer Reihe von Projekten in den Bereichen Wohnungsbau, Kultur und Rehabilitation in Frankreich, Italien und Korea. Außerdem entwirft er die Ausstattung des von I. M. Pei geplanten Museum für Islamische Kunst in Doha, Qatar. Sein guter Ruf für die Gestaltung von Kultureinrichtungen führte auch zu seiner Arbeit am Centre National du Costume de Scène (nationales Zentrum für Theaterkostüme) im französischen Moulins – einer 5 720 m² umfassenden Adaptierung ehemaliger Militärbaracken zu Ausstellungsräumen für Kostüme, einem Ausbildungszentrum und einer Forschungsabteilung – und am Museum für Jüdische Kunst in Brüssel, einem 4 500 m² umfassenden Renovierungs- und Bauprojekt.

Né en 1948, diplômé de l'École Camondo à Paris, il crée sa propre agence en 1975. Surtout connu pour ses travaux d'architecture intérieure, il s'inscrit à l'ordre des architectes en 1993. Comptant environ 80 collaborateurs, son agence qui intervient également sur le design de mobilier public comme les nouveaux bancs et lampadaires des Champs-Élysées, a également participé au concours du British Museum, mettant à profit son expérience de l'architecture du département des arts décoratifs du Louvre (1993). Jean-Michel Wilmotte a réalisé deux immeubles à Tokyo, l'International Executive Office Building dans le quartier de Shinjuku et le New N°3 Arai Building. Il a conçu le mobilier de la Banque du Luxembourg, réalisée par Arquitectonica en 1994. Il vient de terminer le Gana Art Center (Séoul, Corée du Sud, 1996–1998) et le musée des cadeaux reçus par le président Chirac (Sarran, France, 2000). Il travaille à de nouveaux showrooms pour Chaumet, John Galliano et Montblanc International, les aménagements intérieurs du nouveau siège LVMH à Paris ainsi que de nombreux projets de logements, d'équipements culturels et de réhabilitaion de bâtiments en France, Italie et Corée, et l'aménagement intérieur du Musée des arts islamiques de Doha (architecte I. M. Pei, Doha, Qatar). Sa réputation dans le domaine des équipements culturels l'a amené à intervenir sur le Centre national du costume de scène (Moulins, France), rénovation d'une caserne pour accueillir des expositions de costumes, un centre de formation et de recherche (5 720 m²), et le Musée de l'art juif à Bruxelles, projet de rénovation et de construction de 4 500 m².

# BORDEAUX LAC CONVENTION CENTER

*Bordeaux, France, 2001–2003*

*Client: City of Bordeaux. Total floor area: 11 890 m². Costs: € 19 000 000.*
*Associated architect: Jean-Marie Mazière*

*Wilmotte's simple light canopy gives this large structure a modernity and freshness that it might have lacked otherwise.*

*Wilmottes schlichtes und leichtes Vordach verleiht diesem großen Gebäude eine Modernität und Frische, die ihm sonst fehlen würde.*

*Le simple auvent dessiné par Wilmotte confère au bâtiment une modernité et une fraîcheur dont il aurait pu manquer.*

Jean-Michel Wilmotte won the competition to renovate and expand an existing facility in Bordeaux in 1999. The project involves a total of 11 890 square meters of usable space and includes three amphitheaters, respectively for 1 360, 355 and 195 spectators. The largest of these amphitheaters has a 400-square-meter stage. A 3 000-square-meter exhibition area that can be divided into three sections is also part of the plan. Each space, including the amphitheaters, can function independently or as a coherent whole. The Convention Center is set between a lake, a casino and hotels. The casino entrance facing away from the lake has been made the main entrance to the complex. A large glazed arch faces the lake and recuperates one of the main elements of the existing architecture. Visitors are encouraged to follow a north-south axis from the entrance toward the lakeside. Here as in many of his past projects, Wilmotte places an emphasis on clarity in every sense of the word, from organizational simplicity to the omnipresence of light heightened by the use of white surfaces and marble flooring. Whether in renovation and expansion work, as was the case here, or in entirely new construction, Jean-Michel Wilmotte has proven to be one of the most flexible and efficient quality architects on the French scene.

Im Jahr 1999 gewann Jean-Michel Wilmotte den Wettbewerb für die Renovierung und Erweiterung eines bestehenden Gebäudes in Bordeaux. Das Projekt enthält drei Amphitheater mit 1 360, 355 und 195 Sitzen. Das größte der drei Theater hat eine 400 m² große Bühne. Außerdem ist in dem Gebäude eine 3 000 m² große Ausstellungsfläche untergebracht, die in drei Bereiche unterteilt werden kann. Jeder einzelne Bereich, einschließlich der Theaterräume, kann unabhängig oder als Teil eines zusammenhängenden Ganzen genutzt werden. Das Kongresszentrum liegt in unmittelbarer Nachbarschaft zu einem See, einem Spielkasino und Hotels, wobei der Zugang zu dem neuen Komplex über den vom See abgewandten Kasinoeingang erfolgt. Eine ausladend gewölbte Glasfassade ist zum See ausgerichtet. Die Besucher werden eingeladen, einer vom Eingang bis zum Seeufer verlaufenden Nord-Süd-Achse zu folgen. Ebenso wie in vielen seiner früheren Bauten legt Wilmotte auch hier den Schwerpunkt auf Klarheit. Dies zieht sich durch jedes Gestaltungselement – von der Schlichtheit der räumlichen Anordnung bis zur Allgegenwart des Lichts. Letzteres wird durch die weißen Wandoberflächen und Marmorböden noch gesteigert. Sei es bei Renovierungs- und Erweiterungsarbeiten wie in diesem Fall oder bei völlig neuen Bauten, Jean-Michel Wilmotte ist einer der flexibelsten und effizientesten Vertreter der französischen Qualitätsarchitektur.

Jean-Michel Wilmotte a remporté le concours pour la rénovation et l'extension du Palais des congrès de Bordeaux en 1999. Ce projet de 11 890 m² utiles comprend trois amphithéâtres de 1360, 355 et 196 places. Le plus grand est équipé d'une scène de 400 m². Un espace d'exposition de 3 000 m², divisible en trois sections, complète le programme. Chaque espace, y compris les amphithéâtres, peut fonctionner indépendamment ou avec l'ensemble. Le Palais des congrès est implanté entre un lac, un casino et des hôtels et l'entrée du casino, regardant de l'autre côté du lac, sert d'entrée principale au complexe. Face au lac, un grand arc vitré récupère l'un des principaux éléments des bâtiments existants. Ici, comme dans beaucoup de ses projets antérieurs, Wilmotte met l'accent sur la clarté dans tous les sens du terme, la simplicité d'organisation, l'omniprésence de la lumière soulignée par les surfaces blanches et les sols en marbre. Que ce soit dans ses chantiers de rénovation ou d'extension, comme ici, ou dans ses constructions entièrement nouvelles, l'architecte se révèle l'un des praticiens les plus efficaces de la scène française.

The large glazed surface continues in the notched stone side element seen above. At night, the transparency and lightness of the design are even more visible than during the day.

Gläserne Einkerbungen gestalten auch die seitliche Steinfassade (oben). Nachts kommen Transparenz und Leichtigkeit der Gestaltung noch deutlicher zur Geltung als bei Tag.

Les vastes surfaces vitrées se poursuivent dans les blocs latéraux en pierre à échancrures. La nuit, la transparence et la légèreté du projet sont encore plus évidentes.

*Die Innenraumgestaltung erinnert an die Art von Raumgliederung und Materialauswahl japanischer Architekten wie etwa Fumihiko Maki.*

*Le traitement des volumes intérieurs rappelle le type d'articulation et de matériaux de certains architectes japonais, comme Fumihiko Maki.*

# KEN YEANG

*T. R. Hamzah & Yeang Sdn. Bhd.*
*8 Jalan 1, Taman Sri Ukay*
*Off Jalan Ulu Kelang*
*68000 Ampang, Selangor*
*Malaysia*

*Tel: +603 4257 -1948 / -1966*
*Fax: +603 4256 -1005 / -9330*
*e-mail: trhy@tm.net.my*
*Web: www.trhamzahyeang.com*

*Mewah Oils Headquarters* ▶

Born in 1948 in Penang, Malaysia, Ken Yeang attended the Architectural Association in London, 1966–1971, and Cambridge University (Wolfson College) 1971–1975. Much of his subsequent work was based on his PhD dissertation in Cambridge on ecological design. His work (with Tengku Robert Hamzah as TR Hamzah & Yeang created in 1976 in Kuala Lumpur) includes the MBF Tower (Penang, 1990–1993); the Menara Mesiniaga Tower (1989–1992), a recipient of the 1995 Aga Khan Award; a tower in Ho Chi Minh City (Vietnam, 1992–1994); the Tokyo-Nara Tower (Japan, 1997); and the Menara UMNO (Penang, 1998). His published books include *The Architecture of Malaysia* (Pepin Press, 1992, Kuala Lumpur, 1992), and *The Skyscraper, Bioclimatically Considered: A Design Primer* (AD, London, 1997). Ken Yeang was President of the Malaysian Institute of Architects from 1983 to 1986.

Ken Yeang, geboren 1948 in Penang, Malaysia, studierte von 1966 bis 1971 an der Architectural Association (AA) in London und von 1971 bis 1975 am Wolfson College der Cambridge University. Ein Großteil seiner späteren Projekte basiert auf seiner Dissertation über ökologisches Baudesign. 1976 gründete er zusammen mit Tengku Robert Hamzah das Büro TR Hamzah & Yeang in Kuala Lumpur. Zu ihren Bauten gehören: Menara Mesiniaga (1989–1992) – 1995 mit dem Aga Khan Award ausgezeichnet –, die Hochhaustürme MBF in Penang (1990–1993), ein Hochhaus in Ho Chi Minh Stadt, Vietnam (1992–1994), der Tokyo-Nara Tower in Tokio (1997) sowie das Gebäude Menara UMNO in Penang (1998). Er veröffentliche unter anderem *The Architecture of Malaysia* (Pepin Press, Kuala Lumpur, 1992) und *The Skyscraper, Bioclimatically Considered: A Design Primer* (AD, 1997, London). Von 1983 bis 1986 war Ken Yeang Präsident des malaysischen Architektenverbands.

Né en 1948 à Penang (Malaisie), Ken Yeang a étudié à l'Architectural Association de Londres (1966–1971) et à la Cambridge University (Wolfson College, 1971–1975). Une grande partie de son travail est issu de sa thèse de Ph. D. à Cambridge sur la conception écologique. Ses réalisations (avec Tengku Robert Hamzah pour TR Hamzah & Yeang créé en 1976 à Kuala Lumpur) comprend la tour MBF (Penang, 1990–1993) ; la tour Menara Mesiniaga, Prix Aga Khan 1995 (1989–1992) ; une tour à Ho Chi Minh Ville (Vietnam, 1992–1994) ; la tour Tokyo-Nara (Tokyo, Japon, 1997) et le Menara UMNO (Penang, 1998). Il a publié : *The Architecture of Malaysia* (Pepin Press, Kuala Lumpur, 1992) et *The Skyscraper, Bioclimatically Considered : A Design Primer* (AD, Londres, 1997). Ken Yeang a été président de l'Institut malais d'architecture de 1983 à 1986.

# MEWAH OILS HEADQUARTERS
# PULAU INDAH PARK

*Port Klang, Selangor, Malaysia, 2001–2003*

Client: Mewah-Oils Sdn. Bhd. Gross floor area: 19 250 m². Costs: not specified.

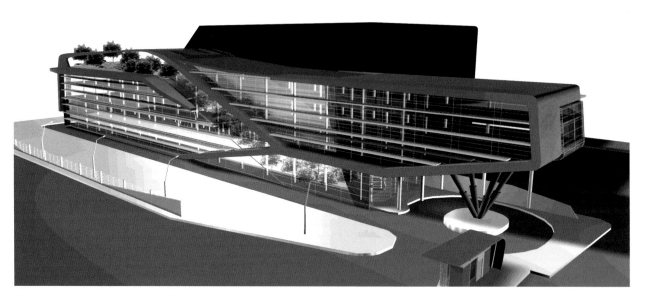

The continuous red wrapping that Ken Yeang places around this structure as well as its cantilevered end recall a number of other contemporary designs seen in this volume, ranging from those of Neil Denari to those of Meyer en Van Schooten.

Die durchgehende rote Ummantelung, die Ken Yeang um dieses Gebäude einschließlich des auskragenden Seitenteils legt, lässt an eine Reihe anderer Bauten denken, die in diesem Band vorgestellt werden, von Neil Denari bis Meyer en Van Schooten.

Ce ruban rouge continu dont Ken Yean enveloppe le bâtiment, et son extrémité en porte-à-faux, rappelle un certain nombre de projets contemporains, comme ceux de Neil Denari ou de Meyer en Van Schooten, par exemple.

The project is the headquarters building for a Singapore-based company that produces palm oil products and specialty fats. The program is for a four-story office (overall height 34 meters) with a four-story packing plant, and a 32-meter-high single-volume space to house an automated warehouse. The gross area of the complex is 19 250 square meters. As the architects explain, "the warehouse forms a towering backdrop to the north. The office block forms a thin southern frontage in an extruded form that penetrates along its entire long section by a landscaped ramp that connects the ground floor vegetation to the roof garden and terrace. This inner public space is given full expression in the form of the building. The atrium volume is naturally ventilated by clerestories, which open onto the roof gardens at the upper western end." A linear, cascading watercourse lines the ramp hall. Ken Yeang has always been very concerned with ecological issues and in this instance, as he says, "what could have been a regular industrial plant and office is transformed into an ecological 'green-lung' that enhances the well-being of the building's users and the biomass of the site."

Die Firmenzentrale eines in Singapur ansässigen Herstellers von Palmölprodukten und Spezialfetten umfasst ein vierstöckiges Bürogebäude mit einer Höhe von 34 m, eine ebenfalls vierstöckige Verpackungshalle und einen 32 m hohen Bauteil für das Warenlager. Die Gesamtnutzfläche der Anlage beträgt 19 250 m². Die beteiligten Architekten erläutern: „Das Lagerhaus ragt an der Nordseite auf, während das Bürogebäude eine lang gestreckte Vorderfront bildet. Über deren gesamte Länge zieht sich eine Rampe, die eine Verbindung zwischen der Vegetation auf dem Erdboden und dem Dachgarten herstellt. Das Atrium wird durch Oberlichtaufbauten belüftet, die sich zu den Dachgärten an der westlichen Dachseite öffnen lassen." Im Inneren wird die Rampe von einem kaskadenartigen Wasserlauf gesäumt. Ken Yeang, der sich bereits in sämtlichen vorangegangen Arbeiten intensiv mit ökologischen Fragen beschäftigt hat, sagt über dieses Projekt: „Anstelle eines normalen Fabrikgebäudes haben wir eine umweltfreundliche ‚grüne Lunge' gestaltet, die sich positiv auf das Wohlbefinden der Nutzer und die Biomasse des Standorts auswirkt."

Cet immeuble est le siège social d'une société de Singapour spécialisée dans les sous-produits de l'huile de palme. De 34 m de haut, il comprend sur quatre niveaux des bureaux, un atelier de conditionnement et un volume de 32 m de haut pour un entrepôt automatisé. Sa surface utile totale est de 19 250 m². Selon les termes de l'architecte : « L'entrepôt forme une masse qui se relève au nord, la partie des bureaux décrivant une fine avancée vers le sud à travers une forme extrudée qui pénètre le bâtiment sur toute sa longueur sous la forme d'une rampe paysagée reliant la végétation du rez-de-chaussée au jardin sur le toit et à une terrasse. Cette rampe interne s'exprime dans la forme du bâtiment. Le volume de l'atrium est ventilé par des lanterneaux qui ouvrent sur les jardins en toiture à l'extrémité ouest. » Un filet d'eau borde l'espace public intérieur qui entoure la rampe. Ken Yeang, toujours très concerné par les enjeux écologiques, fait remarquer que « ce qui aurait pu n'être qu'un banal immeuble d'activités industrielles est devenu un ‹ poumon vert › écologique qui améliore les conditions de vie de ses utilisateurs et la biomasse du site ».

Seen in a computer elevation above
and in construction, the Mewah Oils
building gives a sense of movement
and continuity.

Wie in obigem Computeraufriss und
im Bau zu sehen, vermittelt das Gebäude von Mewah Oils ein Gefühl
von Bewegung und Kontinuität.

En image de synthèse, ci-dessus,
et en chantier, l'immeuble donne un
sentiment de mouvement et de continuité.

The elevated forward edge of the building almost resembles a vast treaded vehicle ready to move forward.

Der erhöhte, nach vorn weisende Teil des Gebäudes wirkt fast wie ein riesiges Kettenfahrzeug, das sich gerade in Bewegung setzt.

La partie avant surélevée du bâtiment fait presque penser à un énorme véhicule prêt à démarrer.

# SHOEI YOH

*Shoei Yoh + Architects*
*1-12-30 Heiwa*
*Minami-ku, Fukuoka-shi 815-0071*
*Japan*

*Tel: +81 92 521 4782*
*Fax: +81 92 521 6718*
*e-mail: yohshoei@jade.dti.ne.jp*

*Sasebo Harbor Ferry Terminal* ▶

Born in 1940 in Kumamoto City, Shoei Yoh received a degree in economics from Keio Gijuku University, Tokyo (1962) and studied Fine and Applied Arts at Wittenberg University in Springfield, Ohio (1964). Self-trained as an architect, he opened Shoei Yoh + Architects in Fukuoka in 1970, and gained a local reputation in industrial and interior design. His Stainless-Steel House with Light Lattice (Nagasaki, Nagasaki, 1980) was widely published. More recent work such as his Kanada Children Training House (Tagawa, Fukuoka, 1994) and his Uchino Community Center for Seniors & Children (Kaho, Fukuoka, 1995) show his flair for spectacular forms, which draw, in their sense of space or in certain techniques, on Japanese tradition. Shoei Yoh is a Professor of Architecture and Urban Design at the Graduate School of Keio University. Recent work includes: Kyushu Gakuin Lutheran Junior High School (Kumamoto, 2003); Tohno Obstetrics and Gynecology Clinic, Dining Hall (Fukuoka, 2003); Kitano Liquor Shop (Kobe, 2004); Suzuki House (Fukuoka, 2004); Tenjin Minami Subway Station (Fukuoka, 2005); and Ohno City Civic Center and Primary School (Ohno, 2005).

Shoei Yoh, 1940 im japanischen Kumamoto geboren, schloss 1962 sein Studium der Wirtschaftswissenschaften an der Universität Keio Gijuku in Tokio ab. 1964 begann er ein Kunststudium an der Wittenberg University in Springfield, Ohio. Als Architekt Autodidakt, gründete Yoh 1970 das Büro Shoei Yoh + Architects in Fukuoka und machte sich einen Namen in den Bereichen Industriebau und Innenarchitektur. Mit seinem Stainless-Steel House in Nagasaki (1980) wurde er über die regionalen Grenzen hinaus bekannt. Neuere Arbeiten wie sein Kanada Children Training House in Tagawa, Fukuoka (1994) und das Uchino Gemeindezentrum für Senioren und Kinder in Kaho, Fukuoka (1995) zeugen von seiner Vorliebe für spektakuläre Formen, die in ihrem Raumgefühl und in gewissen Techniken von der traditionellen japanischen Architektur beeinflusst sind. Shoei Yoh ist Professor für Architektur und Städtebau am Graduiertenkolleg der Keio-Universität. Zu seinen jüngsten Projekten zählen: die lutherische Schule Kyushu Gakuin in Kumamoto (2003), der Speisesaal der Tohno Klinik für Geburtshilfe und Gynäkologie in Fukuoka (2003), die Spirituosenhandlung Kitano in Kobe (2004), das Haus Suzuki in Fukuoka (2004), die U-Bahnstation Tenjin Minami in Fukuoka (2005) sowie das Behördenzentrum mit Grundschule in Ohno (2005).

Né en 1940 à Kumamoto, Shoei Yoh est diplômé en économie de l'Université Keio Gijuku (Tokyo, 1962) puis étudie les beaux-arts et les arts appliqués à la Wittenberg University (Springfield, Ohio, 1964). Architecte autodidacte, il crée Shoei Yoh + Architects à Fukuoka en 1970 et se fait connaître localement dans les domaines du design industriel et de l'architecture intérieure. Sa Maison en acier inoxydable à treillis léger (Nagasaki, 1980) est largement publiée. Des réalisations plus récentes comme sa Maison de formation des enfants Kanasa (Tagawa, Fukuoka, 1995) et son Centre communautaire Uchino pour enfants et personnes âgées (Kaho, Fukuoka, 1995) montrent son sens des formes spectaculaires inspiré, dans leur sens de l'espace et l'utilisation de certaines techniques de la tradition japonaise. Il est professeur d'architecture et d'urbanisme à l'École supérieure de l'Université Keio. Parmi ses travaux récents : collège luthérien de Kyushu Gakuin (Kumamoto, 2003) ; clinique d'obstétrique et de gynécologie Tohno, salle à manger (Fukuoaka, 2003) ; magasin de spiritueux Kitano (Kobe, 2004) ; maison Suzuki (Fukuoka, 2004), station de métro de Tenjin Minami (Fukuoka, 2005) et Centre municipal et école primaire de Ohno (Ohno, 2005).

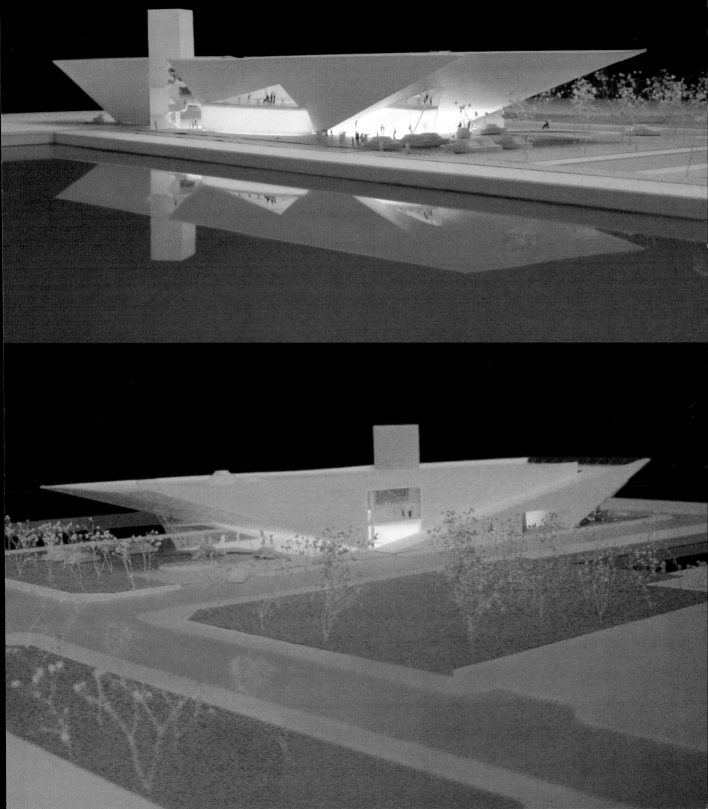

# SASEBO HARBOR FERRY TERMINAL

*Sasebo, Nagasaki, Japan, 2001*

*Client: City of Sasebo. Floor area: 2 000 m². Costs: € 10 000 000.*

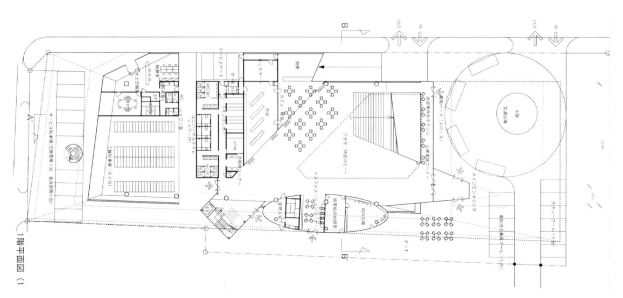

For this open 2001 competition, the city of Sasebo sought "a new ferry terminal imagined as an architecture of the coastal landscape." Sasebo, with a population of 240 000 people, is the second largest city in the Nagasaki Prefecture. The Japanese Maritime Self-Defense Force and the US Navy's Seventh Fleet have shared a base there since June 1946. In the description of his competition entry, Shoei Yoh writes, "as a symbolic landmark of the naval harbor, the ferry terminal building facing the downtown area and Sasebo railroad station is intended for waiting, dating, chatting and relaxing. The visual effect of the building is made by a huge overhanging car park… Roof parking provides a vista both in the direction of the sea and of the town, as does the 2nd floor office and waiting space and the embarkation/disembarkation lobby on the first floor above ground level. The other end of the building with a slanted glass wall faces Akasaki Mountain, reducing solar heat on the west side which houses the Water Police Station." Today, Shoei Yoh looks back at his loss of this competition with a certain nostalgia. "All the walls were to be made of transparent glass," he says, "and the enormous overhanging roof was designed to offer a maximum number of parking spaces, at the same time as it would have given shade to passengers under the eaves waiting to take a taxi or a bus to go into town. The overhang was essential," he concludes, "but the jury might have been concerned about the initial cost, which would in fact have saved a great deal of money in the future."

Im Jahr 2001 organisierte die japanische Stadt Sasebo einen Wettbewerb mit dem Thema: „Ein neuer Terminal für den Fährbetrieb, dessen Architektur als Teil der Küstenlandschaft gestaltet werden soll." Sasebo hat 240 000 Einwohner und ist die zweitgrößte Stadt der Präfektur Nagasaki. Seit 1946 teilen sich dort die japanischen Seeverteidigungskräfte und die Siebte Flotte der US Navy einen Marinestützpunkt. In der Beschreibung seines Wettbewerbsbeitrags erläutert Shoei Yoh: „Als ein Wahrzeichen des Marinehafens wendet sich der Schiffsterminal der Innenstadt und dem Bahnhof von Sasebo zu und ist als Warteraum und Treffpunkt zum Plaudern und Entspannen gedacht. Sein spektakulärstes Merkmal ist ein riesiger, weit über das Gebäude vorspringender Parkplatz auf dem Dach. Von dort, wie auch vom Büro und Warteraum im zweiten sowie der Abfertigungshalle im ersten Stock bieten sich Ausblicke in Richtung Meer und auf die Stadt. Das andere, dem Berg Akasaki zugewandte Ende des Gebäudes ist mit einer schräggestellten Glaswand versehen, die zur Reduktion der Sonnenwärme an der Westseite beiträgt, wo die Räume der Wasserschutzpolizei untergebracht sind." Heute blickt Shoei Yoh mit leiser Wehmut auf seinen Entwurf zurück, mit dem er beim Wettbewerb keinen Erfolg hatte: „Sämtliche Wände hätten aus Transparentglas bestanden, und das enorme auskragende Dach war so konzipiert, dass es eine möglichst große Zahl an Parkplätzen geboten hätte. Gleichzeitig hätte es den Passagieren, die unter seiner überhängenden Kante auf Taxi oder Bus warteten, optimalen Sonnenschutz geboten. Dieser vorspringende Teil war besonders wichtig," so der Architekt abschließend, „aber möglicherweise schienen der Wettbewerbsjury die Baukosten dafür zu hoch, obwohl diese Investition in der Zukunft eine Menge Geld gespart hätte."

L'objet de ce concours ouvert lancé par la ville de Sasebo consistait en « un nouveau terminal pour ferries pensé comme une architecture du paysage côtier ». Sasebo – 240 000 habitants – est la seconde ville de la préfecture de Nagasaki. Les forces d'autodéfense maritime japonaise et la Septième flotte américaine s'y partagent une base depuis juin 1946. Dans le descriptif, Shoei Yoh écrit : « Monument symbolique du port, le bâtiment du terminal des ferries qui fait face au centre-ville et à la gare de Sasebo a pour objectif de favoriser l'attente, les rendez-vous, les échanges et la détente. Son effet visuel vient de son énorme parking en porte-à-faux… le parking en toiture offre des vues à la fois sur la mer et la ville, de même que les bureaux et les salles d'attente au deuxième étage, et le hall d'embarquement/débarquement au premier étage. L'autre extrémité du bâtiment à mur de verre incliné fait face à la montagne d'Akasaki, ce qui permet de réduire le gain solaire sur la façade ouest qui abrite le poste de la police maritime. » Aujourd'hui, Shoei Yoh, qui n'a pas remporté ce concours, considère son projet avec certains regrets : « Tous les murs devaient être en verre transparent », précise-t-il, « et l'énorme porte-à-faux du toit offrir le maximum de places de parking possibles, tout en protégeant les passagers en attente d'un bus ou d'un taxi. Le porte-à-faux était essentiel, mais le jury a pu s'inquiéter de son coût initial qui aurait en fait économisé beaucoup de dépenses dans le futur. »

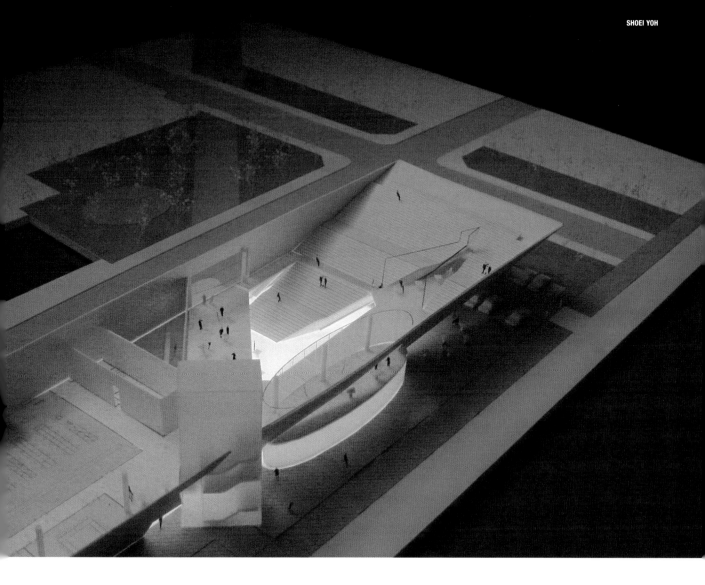

Although it was not to be built, Shoei Yoh's Terminal was clearly thought out to accomplish its projected passenger flow as this model and these drawings show.

Obwohl er nicht realisiert wurde, war der Terminal von Shoei Yoh so konzipiert, dass er den zu erwartenden Passagierverkehr bewältigt hätte, wie Modell und Zeichnungen zeigen.

Non réalisé, le projet de terminal de Shoei Yoh témoigne d'une réflexion approfondie du traitement des flux de passagers, comme le montre maquette, plans et croquis.

# AKIRA YONEDA

*Akira Yoneda Architect/Architecton*
*1-7-16-612 Honcho*
*Shibuya-ku, Tokyo 151-0071*
*Japan*

*Tel: +81 3 337 40 846*
*Fax: +81 3 536 52 216*
*e-mail: a-tecton@pj8.so-net.ne.jp*

*Bloc* ▶

Akira Yoneda was born in Hyogo, Japan in 1959. He received his BE (Bachelor of Engineering) degree from the University of Tokyo in 1982 and Masters of Architecture degrees from both the University of Tokyo (1984) and the Harvard University Graduate School of Design (1991). He worked for the Takenaka Corporation, Design Department, in Tokyo (1984–1989) before creating his own firm, Architecton, in Tokyo (1991). His work includes: Kyokuto Kaihatu Kogyo Miki Plant Office (Miki, Hyogo, 1996); White Echoes/House (Nerima-ku, Tokyo, 1998); ambi-flux/House (Minato-ku, Tokyo, 2000); nkm/House (Arakawa-ku, Tokyo, 2001); Beaver House (Koto-ku, Tokyo, 2002); connoid/House (Meguro-ku, Tokyo, 2002); Bloc/House (Kobe, Hyogo, 2002); and the White Base/House & Studio (Koganei, Tokyo, to be completed in 2004).

Akira Yoneda, geboren 1959 in Hyogo, Japan, erwarb 1982 seinen Bachelor of Engineering an der Universität Tokio und jeweils einen Master of Architecture an der Universität Tokio (1984) und an der Harvard University Graduate School of Design (1991). Von 1984 bis 1989 arbeitete er in der Designabteilung der Firma Takenaka Corporation in Tokio und gründete 1991 sein eigenes Büro, Architecton, in Tokio. Zu seinen Arbeiten zählen: das Bürogebäude der Fabrikanlage Kyokuto Kaihatu Kogyo in Miki, Hyogo (1996), das Haus White Echoes in Nerima-ku (1998), das Haus ambi-flux in Minato-ku (2000), das Haus nkm in Arakawa-ku (2001), das Beaver House in Koto-ku (2002), das Haus connoid in Meguro-ku (2002), alle in Tokio; ferner das Haus Bloc in Kobe, Hyogo (2002) und das Haus mit Atelier White Base in Koganei, Tokio, das 2004 fertig gestellt sein soll.

Akira Yoneda, né à Hyogo, Japon, en 1959 est Bachelor (ingénierie) de l'Université de Tokyo (1982), et Master of Architecture de l'Université de Tokyo (1984) et de la Harvard University Graduate School of Design (1991). Il travaille pour le département de design de la Takenaka Corporation (Tokyo, 1984–1989) avant de créer son agence, Architecton, à Tokyo en 1991. Parmi ses réalisations : Usine et bureaux Kyokuto Kaihatu (Miki, Kogyo, 1996) ; White Echoes House (Nerima-ku, Tokyo, 1998) ; Ambi-flux House (Minato-ku, Tokyo, 2000) ; nkm House (Arakawa-ku, Tokyo, 2001) ; Beaver House (Koto-ku, Tokyo, 2002) ; Connoid House (Meguro-ku, Tokyo, 2002) ; Bloc/House (Kobe, Hyogo, 2002) et la White Base, maison et studio (Koganei, Tokyo ; 2004).

# BLOC

*Kobe, Hyogo, Japan, 2001–02*

*Client: private. Floor area: 242 m². Costs: not specified.*

The unusual volume of the roof or
upper volume of the Bloc House is
emphasized by its green color. The
"bloc" seems to hover above its intentionally less substantial looking base.

Der ungewöhnliche Charakter des
oberen Bauteils, gleichzeitig Dach
des Gebäudes, wird durch seine
grüne Farbe noch verstärkt.

Le volume inhabituel de la partie
supérieure, ou toit, de la Bloc House
est mis en valeur par sa couleur
verte.

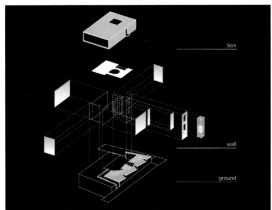
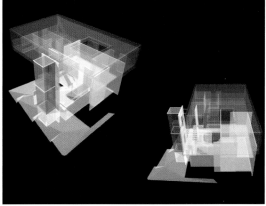

Despite being radically different from its neighbors, the Bloc House somehow does fit in, given Japanese tolerance for unusual or quirky architecture.

Obwohl radikal anders als seine Nachbargebäude, wirkt das Bloc House nicht unpassend, bedenkt man die Toleranz der Japaner für ungewöhnliche Architektur.

Radicalement différente de ses voisines, la Bloc House s'y intègre cependant, et ce d'autant plus que les Japonais acceptent facilement les formes architecturales bizarres.

Built with Masahiro Ikeda, this 242-square-meter house is set on a 276-square-meter site. It is a steel frame structure designed for an elderly client who lost her "European style" house in the 1995 earthquake. It has a spectacular view of the harbor of Kobe and the Inland Sea beyond. The house consists of "white planes" on the first and second levels, with a large green slab floating above. The maximum overhang of this block (10 meters) gives an unusual appearance to the house, which surprisingly enough does not seem "top-heavy." Rather the overhanging volume looks light because the glass and support walls below are unusually thin. Particularly at night, the "Bloc" that the house is named after looks like it is hovering above the port. The residence area of the client is actually contained in this green volume that is symbolically intended to recall the shoreline beyond. The section below is for the occasional visit of her adult children, and also includes a library and entrance hall.

Das 242 m² umfassende Wohnhaus, das Yoneda zusammen mit Masahiro Ikeda realisierte, steht auf einem 276 m² großen Grundstück, und besteht aus einer Stahlrahmenkonstruktion. Das Haus, von dem aus man einen fantastischen Blick auf den Hafen von Kobe und das Binnenmeer dahinter hat, ist auf den ersten beiden Ebenen aus senkrechten, weißen Flächen zusammengesetzt, über die ein ausladender, grüner Riegel gelegt wurde. Dieser bis zu 10 m vorspringende Teil verleiht dem Gebäude ein auffallendes Äußeres, dennoch wirkt es überraschender Weise nicht „kopflastig". Besonders nachts wirkt der „Block", als würde er über dem Hafen schweben. Mit seiner grünen Farbgebung soll außerdem die hinter diesem Wohngebiet liegende Küstenlinie symbolisiert werden. Der darunter liegende Bereich des Hauses ist für die gelegentlichen Besuche der erwachsenen Kinder der Hausherrin gedacht und enthält zudem eine Bibliothek und einen Eingang mit Vorraum.

Construite en collaboration avec Masahiro Ikeda, cette maison de 242 m² à ossature en acier occupe un terrain de 276 m². Elle offre une vue spectaculaire sur le port de Kobe et la mer intérieure du Japon. Elle se compose au premier et au second niveau, de «plans blancs» surmontés par une grande dalle verte. Le porte-à-faux maximum de cet élément (10 m) contribue à l'aspect étonnant de cette maison qui ne semble pas pour autant écrasée. Le volume en porte-à-faux semble même léger grâce à la minceur des murs de soutènement et des parois de verre qui le soutiennent. Ce «Bloc» pour reprendre le nom de la maison semble flotter au-dessus du port, en particulier la nuit. Contenant la partie résidentielle, il veut symboliquement rappeler la ligne de la côte. La partie inférieure est prévue pour le séjour des enfants du propriétaire et comprend également une bibliothèque et le hall d'entrée.

Communication between the upper and lower levels of the house creates opportunities for a hovering lightness that is willfully asymmetric.

Der Dialog zwischen den oberen und unteren Ebenen schafft Momente einer schwebenden und eigenwillig asymmetrischen Leichtigkeit.

La communication entre les niveaux supérieurs et inférieurs accentue les effets de légèreté en suspension et de parti pris asymétrique.

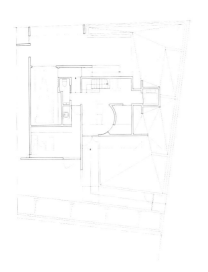

Plans show the lower and then upper level of the house with its dominant upper block.

*Die Grundrisse zeigen die untere (links), mittlere und obere Geschoss-ebene mit ihrem dominanten „Block".*

*Plans des différents niveaux de la maison, dont celui de la « dalle » qui domine la composition.*

A clever use of light and dark as well as the green tone imposed by the coloring of the upper block create a complex orchestration of floating, opaque elements with frequent openings.

Der intelligente Einsatz von Hell und Dunkel sorgt für ein komplexes Zusammenspiel fließender, opaker Elemente und häufig wiederkehrender Öffnungen.

L'utilisation intelligente de la lumière et de l'ombre crée une orchestration complexe d'éléments opaques et flottants entrecoupés de fréquentes ouvertures.

# CARLOS ZAPATA

*Wood + Zapata Inc.*
*444 Broadway*
*New York, NY 10013*
*USA*

*Tel: +1 212 966 9292*
*Fax: +1 212 966 9242*
*Web: www.wood-zapata.com*

*Quito House* ▶

Carlos Zapata obtained his Master of Architecture degree from Columbia University and his Bachelor of Architecture at the Pratt Institute. He was a Vice President of Ellerbe Becket (New York, 1986–1991) before creating the Carlos Zapata Design Studio in Miami in 1991. He has also been a Principal of Wood and Zapata Inc. in Boston since 1996. Current work includes the new 63 000-seat Chicago Bears Stadium at Soldier Field (Chicago); Concourse J., Miami International Airport (Miami, for United Airlines), as well as private houses in Montauk, New York and Golden Beach, Florida. Completed projects include the Hamilton Square Specialty Market and 800-car (10-story) Parking Garage (Philadelphia, PA); Chicago Bears Field House and Indoor Practice Facility (Lake Forest, Illinois); the Quito House in Miravalle, Ecuador, published here; the Landes House (Golden Beach, Florida) and JPBT Advisors Headquarters (Miami, Florida).

Carlos Zapata erwarb seinen Bachelor of Architecture am Pratt Institute in New York und seinen Master of Architecture an der Columbia University. Von 1986 bis 1991 war er Vizepräsident der Firma Ellerbe Becket in New York, bevor er 1991 das Carlos Zapata Design Studio in Miami gründete. Seit 1996 ist er außerdem Direktor von Wood and Zapata Inc. in Boston. Zu seinen aktuellen Projekten gehören das neue, mit 63 000 Sitzen ausgestattete Stadium der Chicago Bears am Soldier Field in Chicago, die Halle J am Miami International Airport für United Airlines sowie Wohnhäuser in Montauk, New York, und Golden Beach, Florida. Zu seinen fertig gestellten Bauten zählen: der Spezialitätenmarkt Hamilton Square und ein zehngeschossiges Parkhaus mit 800 Plätzen in Philadelphia, das Field House und eine Trainingshalle für die Chicago Bears in Lake Forest, Illinois, das hier vorgestellte Quito House in Miravalle, Ecuador, das Haus Landes in Golden Beach, Florida, sowie die Zentrale von JPBT Advisors in Miami.

Carlos Zapata, Bachelor of Architecture du Pratt Institute et Master of Architecture de la Columbia University, a été vice-président de Ellerbe Becket (New York, 1986–1991), avant de fonder le Carlos Zapata Design Studio à Miami en 1991. Il dirige également Wood and Zapata Inc. à Boston, depuis 1996. Parmi ses travaux récents : le nouveau stade des Bears de Chicago, 63 000 places (Soldier Field, Chicago) ; le Hall J de l'aéroport international de Miami pour United Airlines et des résidences privées à Montauk, New York et Golden Beach (Floride). Il est également l'auteur du Marché d'Hamilton Square et de son parking de 800 places (Philadelphie, Pennsylvanie) ; du club des Bears et du stade d'entraînement couvert (Lake Forest, Illinois) ; de la Quito House (Miravalle, Équateur), publiée ici ; de la Landes House (Golden Beach, Floride) et du siège de JPBT Advisros (Miami, Floride).

# QUITO HOUSE

*Miravalle, Quito, Ecuador, 1998–2002*

*Client: private. Total floor area: 743 m². Costs: not specified.*

With its forward leaning façade and surprising terrace, this house would stand out in any environnement.

*Das mit seiner nach vorn geneigten Fassade und stegartigen Terrasse überraschende Haus würde in jeder Umgebung auffallen.*

*La façade inclinée vers l'avant et l'étonnante terrasse de cette maison se feraient remarquer dans n'importe quel environnement.*

With its cantilevered volume and
oblique columns the house appears
to be ready to slide backward, or to
take off.

Mit seinem auskragenden Baukörper
und den schrägen Säulen wirkt das
Haus, als würde es gleich nach
hinten kippen oder auch abheben.

Le volume en porte-à-faux et les
colonnes obliques donnent l'impression que la maison va glisser vers
l'arrière ou s'envoler.

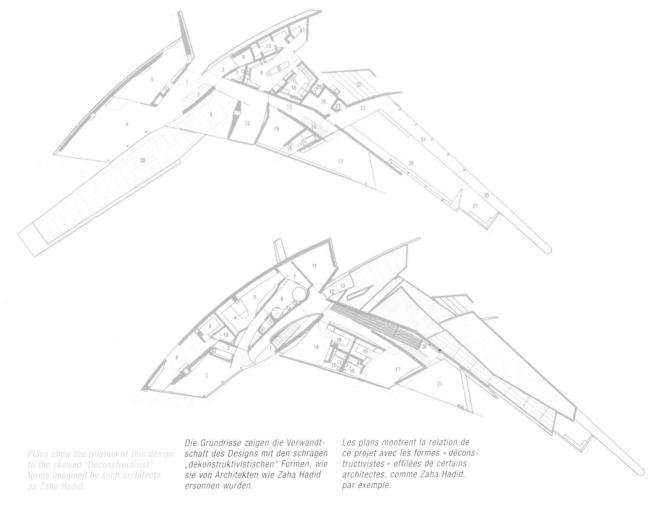

Plans show the relation of this design
to the skewed "Deconstructivist"
forms imagined by such architects
as Zaha Hadid.

Die Grundrisse zeigen die Verwandt-
schaft des Designs mit den schrägen
„dekonstruktivistischen" Formen, wie
sie von Architekten wie Zaha Hadid
ersonnen wurden.

Les plans montrent la relation de
ce projet avec les formes « décons-
tructivistes » effilées de certains
architectes, comme Zaha Hadid,
par exemple.

Built on an inclined, 5 000-square-meter site very close to Quito with a 180° view of the valley of Miravalle and the Andes Mountains, this 743-square-meter house is part of a development with 80 other parcels of land. The main materials are poured-in-place concrete, stucco, glass, granite, zinc, stainless steel, and local wood. The architects write, "the house is an assembly of fluid, energetic, puzzle-like fragments which together fuse with the terrain and accentuate its natural contours. The resulting composition is therefore brought together with a powerful gesture inherent in the terrain itself." Two V-shaped floors are split apart by the main staircase opposite the entrance. The first wing of the first floor contains a living room adjacent to a family room and separated from it by a movable translucent wall. The second wing of the first floor contains a formal dining room, with an informal dining room adjacent to it. A movable wall allows the two dining rooms to become one for special functions. An interior garden next to the main entrance, the guest bathroom, the kitchen area, the laundry with exterior patio, a guest room with bathroom shared by a playroom and storage space are also located here. The children's wing contains two bedrooms with their respective bathrooms. The second wing of the second floor contains the master bedroom, a painter's studio adjacent to it, and the master bathroom adjacent to an open private garden.

Das Wohnhaus hat eine Gesamtnutzfläche von 743 m² und steht auf einem 5 000 m² großen, leicht abschüssigen Grundstück nahe Quito mit Aussicht auf das Tal von Miravalle und die umliegenden Berge der Anden. Es ist zusammen mit 80 weiteren Parzellen Teil eines Bauprojekts. Die Baumaterialien für dieses Gebäude sind Gussbeton, Gipsputz, Glas, Granit, Zink, rostfreier Stahl und lokales Holz. Die Architekten über ihren Entwurf: „Das Haus ist eine Zusammenstellung fließender, energetischer, puzzleartiger Fragmente, die zusammen mit dem Terrain verschmelzen und dessen natürliche Konturen akzentuieren. Die endgültige Komposition ist folglich aus einer vom Terrain selbst ausgehenden, kraftvollen Geste entstanden." Im Innern bildet die gegenüber dem Eingang liegende Treppe die Trennlinie zwischen den beiden V-förmigen Geschossen. Der vordere Trakt des unteren Stockwerks enthält zwei Wohnbereiche, die sich durch eine durchscheinende Schiebewand voneinander abgrenzen lassen. Im hinteren Trakt befinden sich ein großes und ein kleineres Esszimmer, die sich wiederum durch Öffnen einer Schiebewand für besondere Anlässe zusammenlegen lassen. Ebenfalls in diesem Teil des Hauses liegen ein Wintergarten neben dem Haupteingang, der Küchenbereich, ein Gästezimmer mit Bad, ein Spielzimmer, mehrere Neben- und Versorgungsräume und ein Patio. Der von den Kindern bewohnte Teil enthält zwei Schlafzimmer mit dazugehörigen Badezimmern. Im Obergeschoss sind das Elternschlafzimmer, daran angrenzend ein Maleratelier und ein Badezimmer untergebracht, das sich zu einem kleinen Garten hinaus öffnet.

Construite près de Quito sur un terrain de 5 000 m² bénéficiant d'une vue à 180° sur la vallée de Miravalle et les Andes, cette résidence de 743 m² fait partie d'un lotissement de 80 parcelles. Les principaux matériaux sont le béton coulé sur place, le stuc, le verre, le granit, le zinc, l'acier inoxydable et le bois de la région. Pour l'architecte : « Cette maison est un assemblage de fragments de puzzle, fluides et énergétiques qui fusionnent avec le terrain et font ressortir son profil naturel. La composition qui en résulte est un geste puissant inhérent au site. » Deux niveaux en V séparés par l'escalier principal s'ouvrent de chaque côté de l'entrée. La première aile du premier niveau contient un séjour adjacent à un salon familial dont il est séparé par un mur translucide. La seconde aile de ce niveau contient une salle à manger de réception et une salle à manger familiale, qu'un cloisonnement mobile permet de réunir en certaines occasions. La même zone comprend également un jardin intérieur près de l'entrée principale, une chambre d'invités, la cuisine, la lingerie et son patio extérieur, une salle de jeux, une salle de bains et un espace de rangement. L'aile des enfants contient deux chambres et leurs salles de bains respectives. La seconde aile du second niveau est occupée par la chambre principale, un atelier de peinture adjacent et la salle de bains principale ouvrant sur un jardin privatif.

*The forward tilting glazed façade of the house allows unusual interior spaces to be created with a combination of ample light and a certain amount of protection from the bright sky.*

*Die vornüber geneigte Glasfassade des Hauses erlaubt eine ungewöhnliche Innenraumgestaltung und bietet sowohl reichlich Tageslicht als auch Schutz vor direkter Sonneneinstrahlung.*

*La façade vitrée inclinée de la maison permet de créer des volumes intérieurs inhabituels qui combinent un généreux éclairage naturel à un certain degré de protection solaire.*

Skewed walls or stairways animate interior spaces and a warm color scheme gives the whole a friendly, open appearance.

Die abgeschrägten Wände und Treppen beleben die Innenräume, während die warme Farbgebung dem Ganzen eine freundliche, offene Note verleiht.

Les murs penchés et les escaliers animent les volumes intérieurs. La coloration chaleureuse confère à l'ensemble un aspect amical et ouvert.

One might imagine a rectilinear
modernist design as seen through the
deforming effect of a wide-angle lens
in the picture above, but it is the
architecture itself that leans forward.

Bei der Abbildung könnte es sich um
ein durch ein Weitwinkelobjektiv ver-
zerrtes, modernistisches Design han-
deln, doch es ist die Architektur
selbst, die sich vornüber neigt.

On pourrait presque imaginer un
projet moderniste déformé par un
objectif grand angle : en réalité,
c'est la maison elle-même qui
a décidé de se pencher en avant.

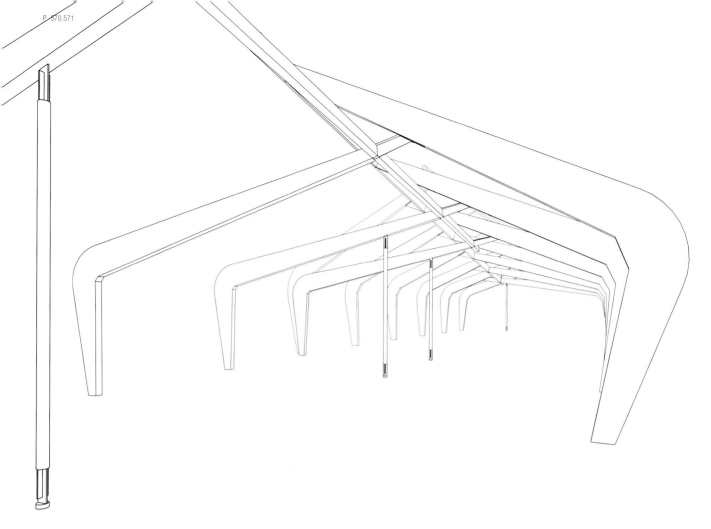

Located on a small peninsula in a moat, the shape of this house was influenced by a neighboring work by the American sculptor Richard Serra. His concrete wall called "Sea Level" was at the origin of the long form of Zuuk's structure. Meaning "the imagination," the De Verbeelding Pavilion makes use of structural elements that are frequently found in local barns, but since there are exhibition spaces in the structure, it had to meet usual requirements than other rural buildings. A glass strip in the roof provides interior lighting and the "light and pleasant space" wanted for this international center for landscape art. A glass plinth also brings light reflected off the water into the building. A glass wall also offers a view over the water to toward Richard Serra's sculpture.

Der Pavillon liegt auf einer kleinen Landzunge, die sich in eine Dammgrube erstreckt. Seine Form wurde von einer Arbeit des amerikanischen Bildhauers Richard Serra inspiriert. Auf dessen in unmittelbarer Nachbarschaft errichtete Betonwand mit dem Titel „Sea Level" geht die lang gestreckte Gestalt von Zuuks Arbeit zurück. Der Pavillon wird „de Verbeelding" genannt, was „die Imagination" bedeutet. Bei dieser Konstruktion wurden Baumaterialien verwendet, wie man sie auch in den für diese Region typischen Scheunen findet. Da Zuuks Bauwerk jedoch für Ausstellungen konzipiert ist, musste es gleichzeitig sehr speziellen Erfordernissen entsprechen. So sorgt beispielsweise ein in das Dach integriertes Glasband für die Beleuchtung der Innenräume und für das „leichte und angenehme" Raumgefühl, das für dieses internationale Zentrum der Land-Art gewünscht wurde. Auch ein Glassockel bringt Licht, das vom umliegenden Wasser in das Innere reflektiert wird, während man durch eine Glaswand einen Ausblick über das Wasser auf die Skulptur von Richard Serra hat.

La forme de cette maison posée sur une petite avancée de terre sur un plan d'eau, a été influencée par une œuvre voisine du sculpteur américain Richard Serra, « Sea Level », qui est en fait un mur de béton. Ce pavillon qui porte le nom d'« Imagination » fait appel à certains éléments structurels que l'on trouve fréquemment dans les granges de la région. Cependant, l'organisation d'expositions a imposé des contraintes techniques autres que celles de simples bâtiments agricoles. Un bandeau de verre dans le toit capte l'éclairage naturel et participe à ce concept « d'espace léger et plaisant » que voulait le Centre d'art du paysage dans lequel il se trouve. Une plinthe de verre apporte à l'intérieur la lumière réfléchie par la surface de l'eau. Un mur de verre ouvre une perspective par-dessus l'eau vers la sculpture de Richard Serra.

*Like interlocking fingers the roof elements close over what becomes the interior space, almost as though the architecture itself were created by its covering.*

*Die sich wie Finger verschränkenden Dachteile definieren den Innenraum, so als würde die Architektur selbst von ihrer Ummantelung hervorgebracht.*

*Comme des doigts croisés, les éléments de la toiture se referment sur ce qui devient alors le volume intérieur. L'architecture est créée par sa couverture.*

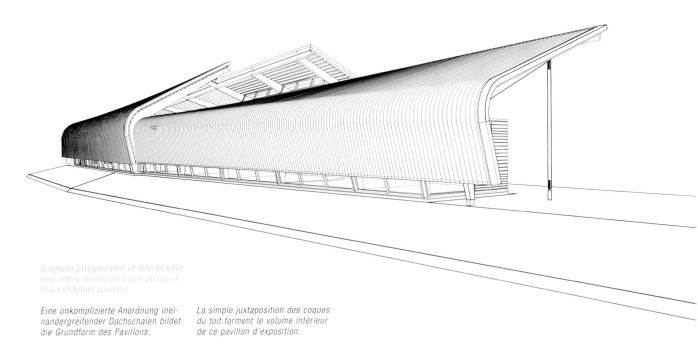

*A simple juxtaposition of interlocking roof shells forms the basic space of this exhibition pavilion.*

Eine unkomplizierte Anordnung ineinandergreifender Dachschalen bildet die Grundform des Pavillons.

La simple juxtaposition des coques du toit forment le volume intérieur de ce pavillon d'exposition.

# DE VERBEELDING PAVILION

*Zeewolde, The Netherlands, 2001*

Client: Stichting de Kunstbaan. Floor area: 375 m². Costs: € 425 000.

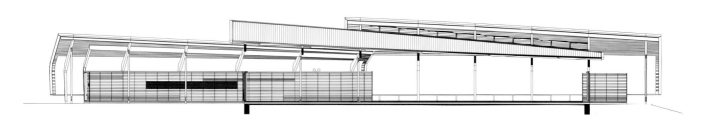

# RENÉ VAN ZUUK

*Rene van Zuuk Architekten BV*
*De Fantasie 9*
*1324 HZ Almere*
*The Netherlands*

*Tel: +31 36 537 9139*
*Fax: +31 36 537 9259*
*e-mail: mail@renevanzuuk.com*
*Web: www.renevanzuuk.com*

*De Verbeelding Pavilion ▶*

René van Zuuk received a Master of Sciences degree from the Technical University of Eindhoven (1988) and created his own firm in 1993. He has a design staff of five persons. Prior to that date, he worked for Skidmore, Owings Merrill in London and Chicago (1988–89) and at Facilitair Bureau voor Bouwkunde Rotterdam, Hoogstad, van Tilburg Architecten (1989–1992). His notable completed projects include: ARCAM Architectural Center (Amsterdam, 2003); Art Pavilion "De Verbeelding," (Zeewolde, 2001); Center for Plastic Arts "CBK" (Alphen aan de Rijn, The Netherlands, 2000); Educational Farm "Griftsteede" (Utrecht, 1999); 4 Canal Houses (Java Island, Amsterdam, 1997); Lock House "Oostersluis" (Groningen, 1995); Villa van Diepen (Almere, 1995); and 8 Bridges (Nieuwsloten, The Netherlands, 1993). Current work includes: Blok 16 housing and fitness complex (Almere, 2003); bridge for bicycles and pedestrians (Almere, 2003); bridge keeper's house (Middelburg, The Netherlands, unbuilt); and office building "Zilverparkkade" (Lelystad, The Netherlands, 2004).

René van Zuuk erwarb 1988 den Master of Sciences an der Technischen Universität Eindhoven und gründete 1993 seine eigene Firma, wo er heute mit fünf Mitarbeitern tätig ist. Davor hat er für Skidmore, Owings & Merrill in London und Chicago (1988–89) und im Facilitair Bureau voor Bouwkunde Rotterdam, Hoogstad, van Tilburg Architecten (1989–1992) gearbeitet. Zu seinen wichtigsten, alle in den Niederlanden realisierten Bauten zählen: acht Brücken in Nieuwsloten (1993), die Villa van Diepen in Almere (1995), das Haus Oostersluis in Groningen (1995), vier Kanalhäuser auf der Java-Insel in Amsterdam (1997), das Schulbauernhaus Griftsteede in Utrecht (1999), das Center for Plastic Arts CBK in Alphen aan de Rijn (2000), der Kunstpavillon de Verbeelding in Zeewolde (2001) und das ARCAM Architectural Center in Amsterdam (2003). Zu den aktuellen Projekten von Zuuks gehören die Wohnanlage mit Fitnesscenter Blok 16 (2003), eine Fußgänger- und Fahrradbrücke, beide 2003 in Almere entstanden, das bislang unrealisierte Haus des Brückenwärters in Middelburg sowie das Bürogebäude „Zilverparkkade" in Lelystad (2004).

René van Zuuk, Master of Sciences de l'Université technique d'Eindhoven (1988), crée son agence en 1993. Son équipe de conception compte cinq collaborateurs. Auparavant, il avait travaillé pour Skidmore, Owins Merrill à Londres et Chicago (1988–89) et chez Facilitair Bureau voor Bouwkunde Rotterdam, Hoogstad, van Tilburg Architecten (1989–1992). Parmi ses réalisations les plus remarquées, toutes aux Pays-Bas : Centre d'architecture ARCAM (Amsterdam, 2003) ; Art Pavilion « De Verbeelding » (Zeewolde, 2001) ; Center for Plastic Arts CBK (Alphen aan de Rijn, 2000) ; ferme d'enseignement Grifsteede (Utrecht, 1999) ; 4 maisons de canal (Java Island, Amsterdam, 1997) ; Lock House Oousterluis (Groningue, 1995) ; villa van Diepen (Almere, 1995) et 8 ponts (Nieuwsloten, 1993). Plus récemment, il a achevé : le Blok 16, logements et salle de remise en forme (Almere, 2003) ; un pont piétonnier (Almere, 2003) ; une maison de pontonnier (Middlebourg, non construit) et l'immeuble de bureaux Zilverparkkade (Lelystad, 2004).

A swimming pool is largely sheltered by the house and participates in its unusual combination of materials and skewed angles.

Der Swimmingpool ist größtenteils vom Haus geschützt und trägt zu der ungewöhnlichen Kombination von Materialien und schrägen Winkeln bei.

Une piscine participe à l'esprit d'ensemble par un mariage inhabituel de matériaux et les profils des murs et du plafond.

Opening in a simple unadorned manner onto its watery environment, the pavilion is at once innovative and quite simple in its conception.

Der Pavillon, der sich auf schmucklose Weise zu seiner sumpfigen Umgebung hin öffnet, ist ebenso innovativ wie einfach in seiner Konzeption.

S'ouvrant en toute simplicité sur son environnement lacustre, le pavillon est à la fois novateur et assez simple de conception.

# INDEX OF PLACES

# CREDITS

## PHOTO CREDITS

**CREDITS PLANS / DRAWINGS / CAD VISUALIZATIONS**

# Architecture

**Peter Gössel** / goessel@aol.com
**Philip Jodidio** / pj002@dial.oleane.com

New!

New!

**TADAO ANDO. COMPLETE WORKS**
Philip Jodidio / Hardcover, **XXL-format**: 30.8 x 39 cm
(12.1 x 15.3 in.), 504 pp. / English/German/French edition
3–8228–2164–0
€ 99.99 / $ 125 / £ 69.99 / ¥ 15.000

**RENZO PIANO. WORKS 1966–2004**
Philip Jodidio / Hardcover, **XXL-format**: 30.8 x 39 cm
(12.1 x 15.3 in.), 496 pp. / English/German/French edition
3–8228–5768–8
€ 99.99 / $ 125 / £ 69.99 / ¥ 15.000

 New!

 New!

 New!

**ALVAR AALTO**
Louna Lahti, Ed. Peter Gössel / Softcover with
flaps, format: 18.5 x 23 cm (7.3 x 9.1 in.),
96 pp. / 3–8228–3527–7
€ 6.99 / $ 9.99 / £ 4.99 / ¥ 1.500

**ANTONI GAUDÍ**
Maria Antonietta Crippa / Ed. Peter Gössel /
Softcover with flaps, format: 18.5 x 23 cm
(7.3 x 9.1 in.), 96 pp. / 3–8228–2518–2
€ 6.99 / $ 9.99 / £ 4.99 / ¥ 1.500

**WALTER GROPIUS**
Gilbert Lupfer, Paul Sigel, Ed. Peter Gössel /
Softcover with flaps, format: 18.5 x 23 cm
(7.3 x 9.1 in.), 96 pp. / 3–8228–3531–5
€ 6.99 / $ 9.99 / £ 4.99 / ¥ 1.500

**LE CORBUSIER**
Jean-Louis Cohen, Ed. Peter Gössel /
Softcover with flaps, format: 18.5 x 23 cm
(7.3 x 9.1 in.), 96 pp. / 3–8228–3535–8
€ 6.99 / $ 9.99 / £ 4.99 / ¥ 1.500

**ADOLF LOOS**
August Sarnitz / Ed. Peter Gössel / Softcover
with flaps, format: 18.5 x 23 cm (7.3 x 9.1 in.),
96 pp. / 3–8228–2772–X
€ 6.99 / $ 9.99 / £ 4.99 / ¥ 1.500

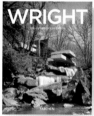

**RICHARD NEUTRA**
Barbara Lamprecht / Ed. Peter Gössel /
Softcover with flaps, format: 18.5 x 23 cm
(7.3 x 9.1 in.), 96 pp. / 3–8228–2773–8
€ 6.99 / $ 9.99 / £ 4.99 / ¥ 1.500

**HANS SCHAROUN**
Eberhard Syring, Jörg Kirschenmann /
Ed. Peter Gössel / Softcover with flaps,
format: 18.5 x 23 cm (7.3 x 9.1 in.),
96 pp. / 3–8228–2778–9
€ 6.99 / $ 9.99 / £ 4.99 / ¥ 1.500

**KARL FRIEDRICH SCHINKEL**
Martin Steffens / Ed. Peter Gössel /
Softcover with flaps, format: 18.5 x 23 cm
(7.3 x 9.1 in.), 96 pp. / 3–8228–2760–6
€ 6.99 / $ 9.99 / £ 4.99 / ¥ 1.500

**FRANK LLOYD WRIGHT**
Bruce Brooks Pfeiffer / Ed. Peter Gössel /
Softcover with flaps, format: 18.5 x 23 cm
(7.3 x 9.1 in.), 96 pp. / 3–8228–2757–6
€ 6.99 / $ 9.99 / £ 4.99 / ¥ 1.500

**CASE STUDY HOUSES**
Elizabeth A.T. Smith / Ed. Peter Gössel / Hardcover,
**XXL-format**: 40 x 31 cm (15.7 x 12.2 in.), 440 pp. /
English/German/French edition / 3–8228–6412–9
€ 150 / $ 200 / £ 100 / ¥ 25.000

**NEUTRA. COMPLETE WORKS**
Barbara Lamprecht / Ed. Peter Gössel / Hardcover,
**XXL-format**: 40 x 31 cm (15.7 x 12.2 in.), 464 pp. /
English/German/French edition / 3–8228–6622–9
€ 150 / $ 200 / £ 100 / ¥ 25.000

**ARCHITECTURE NOW!**
Philip Jodidio / Flexi-cover, format:
19.6 x 24.9 cm (7.7 x 9.8 in.), 576 pp. /
English/German/French edition
3–8228–6065–4
€ 29.99 / $ 39.99 / £ 19.99 / ¥ 5.900

**ARCHITECTURE NOW! VOL. II**
Philip Jodidio / Flexi-cover, format:
19.6 x 24.9 cm (7.7 x 9.8 in.), 576 pp. /
English/German/French edition
3–8228–1594–2
€ 29.99 / $ 39.99 / £ 19.99 / ¥ 5.900